T0255427

Lecture Notes in Computer Science 10760

Commenced Publication in 1973
Founding and Former Series Editors:
Gerhard Goos, Juris Hartmanis, and Jan van Leeuwen

Editorial Board

More information about this series at http://www.springer.com/series/7408

Marten Lohstroh · Patricia Derler
Marjan Sirjani (Eds.)

Principles of Modeling

Essays Dedicated to Edward A. Lee
on the Occasion of His 60th Birthday

 Springer

Editors
Marten Lohstroh
University of California, Berkeley
Berkeley, CA
USA

Patricia Derler
National Instruments
Berkeley, CA
USA

Marjan Sirjani
Mälardalen University, Västerås, Sweden
Reykjavík University
Reykjavik
Iceland

ISSN 0302-9743   ISSN 1611-3349   (electronic)
Lecture Notes in Computer Science
ISBN 978-3-319-95245-1   ISBN 978-3-319-95246-8   (eBook)
https://doi.org/10.1007/978-3-319-95246-8

Library of Congress Control Number: 2018947456

LNCS Sublibrary: SL2 – Programming and Software Engineering

Cover illustration: Confusing the Map with the Territory (By Rusi Mchedlishvili and Marten Lohstroh)

This Springer imprint is published by the registered company Springer Nature Switzerland AG
The registered company address is: Gewerbestrasse 11, 6330 Cham, Switzerland

Fig. 1. *Self Portrait* (acrylic on canvas, 2007, 24″ × 24″) by Edward A. Lee

Preface

It is our great pleasure to dedicate this Festschrift volume to the scholarship and teaching of Edward A. Lee, Robert S. Pepper Distinguished Professor Emeritus and Professor in the Graduate School in the Department of Electrical Engineering and Computer Sciences at the University of California, Berkeley.

Fig. 2. "You will never strike oil by drilling through the map." A phrase coined by Solomon Golomb [2]. (Artwork by R. Mchedlishvili and M. Lohstroh)

The title of this Festschrift is *Principles of Modeling* because Edward has long been devoted to research that centers on the role of models in science and engineering. Edward has been examining the use and limitations of models, their formal properties, their role in cognition and interplay with creativity, and their ability to represent reality and physics. He admonishes not to "confuse the map with the territory"[1] (this also inspired Fig. 2, the cover art for this book) and he is keen to quote George Box's famous phrase: "All models are wrong, but some are useful" [1], notwithstanding that models and their ability to provide layered abstractions have been a key enabler of the Digital Revolution.

At the same time, Edward points out that the layers of abstraction that work so well for information technology fail to expose details that are necessary for the realization of other classes of systems, such as cyber-physical systems or time-sensitive systems (Fig. 3). He also emphasizes that, for engineers, modeling is a "two-way street" since, unlike scientists, engineers can manipulate both the model and the thing being modeled. As such, we have the ability to improve our designs by giving expression to useful properties such as concurrency, determinism, and time representation, both in our models and the realizations thereof. As an educator and engineer (and self-proclaimed nerd), Edward is very cognizant of the origin of ideas and design artifacts, and he is

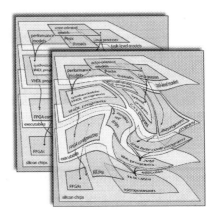

Fig. 3. Layers of abstraction that work so well for information technology break down for time-sensitive systems. (By Edward A. Lee)

---

[1] It was Polish-American scientist and philosopher Alfred Korzybski who first remarked that "the map is not the territory" [3].

consistent and thorough at crediting the people who formed them. In other words, he acknowledges not only the giants on whose shoulders we stand, but also our contemporaries from whose ideas we can gain impetus. Edward genuinely enjoys engaging other minds and exchanging ideas—preferably via code—and has contributed greatly to the fields of embedded systems, real-time computing, computer architecture, modeling and simulation, and systems design.

It was heartwarming that so many fellow leaders in these fields were excited to contribute articles to this special publication and were willing to travel from afar to attend the Edward A. Lee Festschrift Symposium, held at the Berkeley City Club on Friday October 13, 2017. Among the attendees of this day-long symposium we welcomed many of Edward's collaborators, colleagues, industrial fellows, current and former graduate students, friends and family, his wife, Rhonda, and, of course, Edward himself. It was an unforgettable event that featured an array of phenomenal talks keynoting technical contributions—punctuated with personal anecdotes and references to Edward's work—a highly engaging panel discussion on the topic of determinism, and an opportunity to relax and socialize during the reception that followed in the evening.

Fig. 4. Attendees of the Edward A. Lee Festschrift Symposium (Photo by Rusi Mchedlishvili)

We, as organizers, are grateful to all authors for accepting our invitation and submitting first-rate contributions, to the reviewers who provided invaluable feedback on the submissions, to all presenters, panelists, and session chairs, for sharing their unique perspectives, as well as to everyone who helped make the symposium such a memorable event. We are grateful to Berkeley faculty members Prabal Dutta, Jan Rabaey, Alberto Sangiovanni-Vincentelli, and Sanjit Seshia for their generous financial support, and we would like to thank Springer for granting us the opportunity to publish this Festschrift in their *Lecture Notes in Computer Science* series.

In his three decades of teaching at one of the most prestigious universities in the world, Edward has influenced many students, scholars, and members of industry with his contagious drive for hands-on experimentation and his inquisitive mind that is always in pursuit of grounding observations in a sound framework of theory. These traits, together with a wealth of experience, steadfast commitment, and proverbial efficiency, serve as an impetus and inspiration—to his students and collaborators alike—for rising above one's self and achieving insightful research results.

Despite being a professor emeritus, Edward still considers himself a student, and is ever so eager to learn. Edward has a real passion for programming and has kept honing his programming skills throughout his career. He has an extraordinary capacity and willingness to experience paradigm shifts in technology, not least by learning and mastering new programming languages—a feat that not many professionals are able to pull off as gracefully as he can. Edward also has a passion for art—as an

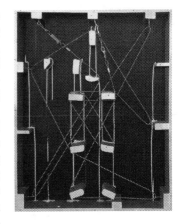

Fig. 5. *All Tied Up* (Construction, 1998, $3' \times 4'$) by Edward A. Lee

undergraduate in college, he took more art classes than engineering classes. He has always continued to create artwork, among which are paintings (Fig. 1), mashups (Fig. 6), and photographs. Over the years, some of his works have become permanent fixtures on the walls of the Donald O. Pederson Center in Cory Hall, one of which is shown in Fig. 5.

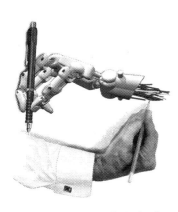

Fig. 6. *Human and Technology Forming Each Other* (By Edward A. Lee, Plato and the Nerd: The Creative Partnership of Humans and Technology)

More recently, Edward has focused on the philosophy of engineering, which he discusses in his first book for a general audience: *Plato and the Nerd: The Creative Partnership of Humans and Technology*. This book, written for literate technologists and numerate humanists, examines the role of digital technology in our lives and explains why it has been so transformative and liberating, while it tempers runaway enthusiasm that may lead one to believe that anything physical is computational. Living in a time where we witness the tremendous impact of technology, but cannot always seem to agree on whether to fear or to embrace it, we need more torchbearers like Edward. We hope that he will continue to inspire and illuminate us with his brilliance for many, many years to come.

Fiat Lux!

May 2018

Marten Lohstroh
Patricia Derler
Marjan Sirjani

References

1. George EP Box. Science and statistics. *Journal of the American Statistical Association*, 71(356):791–799, 1976.
2. Solomon W Golomb. Mathematical models: Uses and limitations. *IEEE Transactions on Reliability*, 20(3):130–131, 1971.
3. Alfred Korzybski. A non-aristotelian system and its necessity for rigour in mathematics and physics. *American Association for the Advancement of Science in New Orleans, Louisiana*, December 1931.

Photos from the Symposium

Fig. 7. Edward A. Lee (Photo by Rusi Mchedlishvili)

Fig. 8. A view from the audience (Photo by Rusi Mchedlishvili)

Fig. 9. Panel discussion with Stephen A. Edwards, Gul Agha, Ruzena Bajcsy, Thomas Henzinger, and Hermann Kopetz (Photo by Ben Zhang)

Fig. 10. Edward Lee engaging in the panel discussion on determinism (Photo by Ben Zhang)

Fig. 11. Marten Lohstroh, Patricia Derler, Marjan Sirjani, and Edward Lee during the closing remarks (Photo by Chamberlain Fong)

Fig. 12. Stephen Neuendorffer, Xiaojun Liu, Elaine Cheong, Edward Lee, Thomas Feng, and Jie Liu (Photo by Rusi Mchedlishvili)

Fig. 13. Christian Buckl, Edward Lee, Janette Cardoso, Marjan Sirjani, and John Eidson (Photo by Rusi Mchedlishvili)

Fig. 14. Hermann Kopetz, Thomas Henzinger, and Radu Grosu (Photo by Rusi Mchedlishvili)

Fig. 15. Edward Lee, Chadlia Jerad, and Christopher Brooks (Photo by Rusi Mchedlishvili)

Fig. 16. Edward Lee and his wife, Rhonda Righter (Photo by Rusi Mchedlishvili)

Fig. 17. Christopher Brooks, Janette Cardoso, and Patricia Derler (Photo by Rusi Mchedlishvili)

Fig. 18. Edward Lee and his PhD advisor David Messerschmitt (Photo by Rusi Mchedlishvili)

Fig. 19. Edward Lee's mother, Kitty Fassett; Rhonda Righter and Edward Lee in the background (Photo by Rusi Mchedlishvili)

Personal Notes for Edward

From Rajeev Alur Dear Edward, you have been an inspiration and a role model to me all these years. Your breadth of knowledge, ability to connect insights from diverse fields into coherent research themes, a natural gift for communicating, and leadership in defining cyber-physical systems as a scientific discipline are all exemplary. Wishing you the best at this mode-change in your life!

From Sanjoy Baruah Thanks very much for all that you have done to keep the "science" strong in our small corner of computer science... Thanks, too, for your endeavors in education and outreach in real-time computing–I feel fortunate to belong to a community in which one of our foremost research contributors is also such a gifted and willing communicator. You have strengthened our discipline tremendously!

From Shuvra S. Bhattacharyya It has truly been a privilege to be your PhD student and collaborator. I am deeply grateful for your great positive influence on my career. Happy birthday and my very best wishes!

From David Broman I would like to thank you for the really great time we have had together. The years that I worked in your group have really shaped me as a researcher, and I will always be extremely grateful for all the support and encouragement that you have given me. Besides all the interesting research we have done together, I am even more grateful for our friendship. It has been a pleasure to meet your family, and you are always welcome to come and visit my family in Stockholm again. Happy birthday!

From Janette Cardoso I was a very privileged guest in your lab during my sabbatical during 2010–2011. Ever since, I refer to you as an admirable scientist. In addition to your technical contributions, you have two human qualities that I highly appreciate: you always value collaborations and give credit to people you work with; and you are not afraid to express doubts, or recognize possible errors. These rare qualities are the foundation of human respect and esteem. Working with you is richly rewarding!

From Marco Di Natale It is always a pleasure to work with you. I am always looking at you as a role model for how to work in research in the purest sense, with strong ethics and without compromises; pursuing what you believe is important and worthy, regardless of trends, outside interests, metrics and money, with continuing enthusiasm and passion.

From Stephen A. Edwards Thanks for everything: direction, structure, freedom, inspiration, and a level to aspire to. I'm not sure who I would be or what I would be doing were it not for your help, but I'm sure it wouldn't be as good. I'm still annoyed at you, however, for making it look so easy. I still haven't figured out how to do half of what you've done.

From Alain Girault Cher Edward, many thanks for all the fun, inspiration, guidance, kindness. I enjoyed each day of my postdoc at UCB in your group. One part of my current research is still based on Ptolemy and SDF, and another part is based on PRET, so, as you see, your inspiration has been invaluable. I know how much I owe you. Thanks for everything and happy birthday!

From Soonhoi Ha I am always thankful that I was privileged to be involved in the development of Ptolemy Classic from its birth as your second PhD student. Naturally, I became an advocate of formal models of computation and their mixture for system behavior specification in the design of embedded systems. In retrospect, I enjoyed my graduate years very much with good memories of having parties at your house, going for a picnic in the park, having any-time any-where discussions on research topics, and so on. After graduation, whenever I meet an alumnus of your laboratory in any place, we feel closely related. Thank you for being the center of such a community. You are my role model, showing students the pleasure and passion for research and still actively writing code, which I find very difficult as a professor with various duties. I'd like to bless you abundantly in Jesus's name. Congratulations on your 60th birthday!

From Reinhard von Hanxleden Dear Edward, I'm not sure I ever mentioned this to you, but a while before our first "official" meeting in the early 2000s, I sat in on a class you taught at UCB in the fall of 1995. When a student presented the result of a computation that would have been a bit tedious to check and not all that enlightening right then, you incorporated this nicely with an "I trust you on this" and moved on from there—which I assume not only made that student a bit proud at that moment, but also motivated most of us to check for ourselves later. Ever since then, "how would Edward handle this" has been a standard tool for me, and probably also for pretty much all the members of my group fortunate enough to have spent time with you. Thank you—and happy birthday!

From Tom Henzinger Happy birthday, Edward, and thank you for being such an inspiring and thought-provoking colleague over the years!

From Christoph Kirsch I wish you all the best for your 60th birthday! The first time we met was in late 1999 when I joined Tom Henzinger's group as a postdoc. I still remember your group lunches to which I was soon invited and that I enjoyed very much. The friendly atmosphere and the inspiring conversations with you felt like a liberation of the mind from which I still benefit to this day. Thank you, Edward!

From Hermann Kopetz Dear Edward, you have achieved a tremendously important paradigm shift: bringing the issues around real-time into the minds of many computer scientists. This is a most important contribution, since it helps to build a new foundation for systems that leave the confines of cyber-space and act in the physical world of things. Happy birthday and many more years of great contributions!

From Eugenio Moggi I had the privilege to meet Edward only once, at a workshop in Uppsala in 2017. His invited talked was very thought provoking. In particular, he gave a very simple example of a non-deterministic system: three balls with different masses hitting each other at the "same" time. His point was that determinism is very desirable for system analysis, but it should not be taken for granted. Also, chatting with him over a beer was "thought provoking." At some point we discussed Donald Rumsfeld's "known unknowns" and "unknown unknowns," and I was wondering what could possibly be an "unknown known." Edward said: "A prejudice!" I was baffled by his answer, but in retrospect it was a very good example. Also, in academia, we make a lot of implicit assumptions and take things for granted. What can save us from our prejudices is the ability to change our views when the evidence is against them, or simply accept that there are alternative views and no clear evidence to prefer one to the other.

From Pierluigi Nuzzo Happy birthday, Edward! Thank you for constantly being a role model, and such an inspiring professor, educator, researcher, and collaborator. Thank you for your leadership and guidance in the many research centers and efforts I was part of during my journey at Berkeley. Thank you for your support during key stages of my path. Thank you for all the interactions we have had, both technical and philosophical, the great discussions during "formal" meetings as well as the uplifting, impromptu conversations over coffee in Cory Hall. My very best wishes for the journey ahead!

From Alberto Sangiovanni-Vincentelli It has been 35 years since I saw you the first time in Cory Hall while you were studying for your PhD! What a long trip! It has been a super great pleasure to work with you, to enjoy wines and food, and exchange stories about our families. There have been difficult times for both of us due to the health of our kids, and I believe sharing our preoccupations helped considerably (at least me). Your generosity in helping the Berkeley community cannot be overemphasized. You went way above the lines of duty in all endeavors and we all should be grateful to you. And yes, I am a big fan of Plato! You are indeed like a good bottle of wine: you grow better with age! All the very best for your "retired" (what a joke!) life. You have been a wonderful friend and colleague.

From Sanjit Seshia Dear Edward, long before I started on the Berkeley faculty, I was inspired by your research and writings on embedded software and systems. Arriving at Cal and working closely with you on a range of amazing projects, spanning research and teaching, has truly been a dream come true. Thank you for your leadership and wisdom, and for being a fountain of inspiration! Wishing you a happy birthday and all the very best!

From Bruno Sinopoli Thank you for being true and pure to science. You have inspired and keep inspiring many of us. I will always be indebted to you for our discussions and for your continued support.

From Marjan Sirjani Edward is a "one of a kind" person who has a broad and yet deep understanding and knowledge of electrical engineering, control engineering, hardware and computer architecture, embedded and real-time systems, programming, computer network, and physics… and that's why he has no choice but to become a philosopher! In his first book for a general audience, *Plato and the Nerd: The Creative Partnership of*

Humans and Technology, he speaks with his philosopher's hat on. Edward calls himself a citizen of the world, he does not classify people, he says there are only two types of people, those who classify people and those who do not. He is also a warrior, he fights his battles by writing books.

From Walid Taha Since our first meeting, you have been a constant source of inspiration, starting from the way you summarized the outcomes of a complex meeting with exceptional precision when we first met in 1999, to asking the most insightful questions during a talk I gave about why functional programming matters for real-time systems, to explaining in so many ways—sometimes on a dime—why CPS matters, to your genuine modesty and kindness. Thank you for everything. Happy birthday, and here is to many more happy years!

From Martin Törngren In 2007 I had the opportunity to meet Edward Lee for the first time at a Dagstuhl seminar on Model-Based Engineering of Embedded Real-Time Systems. We had a useful exchange that included not only research but also rather advanced cyber-physical systems exercise in the form of table-tennis! This combined mode of interactions was probably decisive for my initiative to reach out to Edward, asking for the possibility to visit UC Berkeley. As a result, I did a sabbatical during 2011–2012 with Edward's group. The stay at Berkeley was a great success in many ways for me professionally and for my family. The inspiration and the collaborative work has been important for my career since. It led me in the direction of research in cyber-physical systems, in turn, among other things, leading to road-mapping efforts on CPS with the European Commission. Like at Dagstuhl, while at UC Berkeley, I insisted on interactions that also involved applied motion control (advanced CPS)—in this case in terms of juggling. I believe this is something that was appreciated at UC Berkeley. Edward continues to be an important inspiration and role model for me and he is always welcome to Stockholm for further exchanges of both scientific and applied CPS nature; like juggling!

From Stavros Tripakis I'd like to thank Edward for finding the time and energy to support my research at UC Berkeley at a difficult moment in his life. Thank you Edward and happy birthday!

From Reinhard Wilhelm Dear Edward, it is really impossible to repeat one's professional life or most of the research attempts one has tried. It is, at least theoretically, possible to predict one's professional success and personal happiness. Beyond this predictability, I wish you even more professional success and personal happiness for the time to come.

Organization

This Festschrift was organized by Edward's doctoral student Marten Lohstroh, his former postdoc Patricia Derler, and his friend and colleague Marjan Sirjani.

Acknowledgments. We are grateful to Prabal Dutta, Jan Rabaey, Alberto Sangiovanni-Vincentelli, and Sanjit Seshia, and Edward A. Lee for sponsoring the symposium. We thank Christopher Brooks and Mary Stewart for their invaluable advice and support. We thank Tommasso Dreossi, Jessica Gamble, Antonio Iannopollo, Gil Lederman, Mehrdad Niknami, Matt Weber, and Ben Zhang for their assistance during the event. Last but not least, we would like to acknowledge the reviewers for their constructive feedback.

Reviewers

Agha, Gul
Alur, Rajeev
Baruah, Sanjoy
Berry, Gerard
Bhattacharyya, Shuvra
Broman, David
Caulfield, Benjamin
Cardoso, Janette
Costanzo, John
Cremona, Fabio
Damm, Werner
Derler, Patricia
Dreossi, Tommaso
Edwards, Stephen A.
Eidson, John
Fremont, Daniel J.
Geilen, Mark
Ghosh, Shromona
Girault, Alain
Grazioli, Filippo
Grosu, Radu
Ha, Soonhoi
Hanxleden von, Reinhard
Iannopollo, Antonio

Incer, Inigo
Jin, Baihong
Khamespanah, Ehsan
Kim, Edward
Kirsch, Christoph
Kopetz, Hermann
Lederman, Gil
Liu, Jie
Lohstroh, Marten
Niknami, Mehrdad
Nuzzo, Pierluigi
Sinopoli, Bruno
Stergiou, Christos
Sztipanovits, Janos
Taha, Walid
Törngren, Martin
Tripakis, Stavros
Raco, Deni
Rabe, Markus N.
Vazquez-Chanlatte, Marcell
Weber, Matthew
Wetter, Michael
Wilhelm, Reinhard

Contents

You Can Program What You Want but You Cannot Compute What You Want

Alireza S. Abyaneh and Christoph M. Kirsch$^{(\boxtimes)}$

Department of Computer Sciences, University of Salzburg, Salzburg, Austria
{alireza.abyaneh,christoph.kirsch}@cs.uni-salzburg.at

Abstract. Computers are the most fascinating machines ever invented. Virtually everyone uses them in one form or another every day. However, most people only have a vague understanding of how computers work, let alone how to program them. Yet computing has become a commodity almost like energy, food, or water. The question is if the general public, for modern society to work properly, needs to understand computing better than what people generally know about, say, producing electricity or clean water. We argue that the intractability and even undecidability of so many important problems in computer science are the reason that computing is indeed different. It is the limits of computability, not just the capabilities of computers, that is the source of unbounded potential in the automation of everything. The challenge is to teach people not just programming but also how programming is the neverending process of overcoming those limits. We have developed a system called selfie that implements a self-referential compiler, emulator, and hypervisor that can compile, execute, and virtualize itself. We use selfie to teach undergraduate and graduate students computer science from first principles. In particular, we show them how self-referentiality in selfie is capability and limitation of computing at the same time. Here, we discuss ongoing early work on integrating verification technology into selfie as yet another way of exploring what computing is.

1 Introduction

How many people know how to read and write and understand at least some elementary arithmetic? What about elementary set theory, in particular, Cantor's diagonal argument then? And, if some people know and understand that, do they also know how diagonalization beautifully explains the limits of computability [13] as the source of unbounded potential in computing? Teaching and understanding Cantor is actually not that hard and should be part of any school curriculum. Connecting Cantor to computing, however, that is, teaching and understanding Gödel, Turing, and others, is a lot more difficult. But there ought to be a way to reach out to larger audiences. The trend towards teaching how to code already in school is an important step forward. However, we believe that

© Springer International Publishing AG, part of Springer Nature 2018
M. Lohstroh et al. (Eds.): Lee Festschrift, LNCS 10760, pp. 1–15, 2018.
https://doi.org/10.1007/978-3-319-95246-8_1

understanding the limits of computability is at least as important as learning how to code, if not more important, especially for broader audiences.

We have developed a software system called selfie[1] in a tiny subset of C called C* that implements a self-compiling compiler, a self-executing emulator of a tiny MIPS subset called MIPSter targeted by the compiler, and a self-hosting hypervisor that virtualizes a MIPSter machine [8]. Selfie is written in a single, self-contained file of around 7k lines of C* code. Selfie compiles itself, executes the code it generates including the emulator itself, and can even virtualize the execution of that code.

Through compilation, emulation, and virtualization, selfie provides three different perspectives on how to create the semantics of formalisms such as C* and MIPSter code using these very formalisms. Selfie, just like Cantor's diagonal argument, employs self-referentiality. Learning about self-referentiality is difficult for many students but nevertheless seen by us as key to understanding basic principles of computer science including the limits of computability. Selfie is a sandbox for teaching undergraduate and graduate students computer science from first principles. However, we also use selfie in classes targeting broader audiences by identifying and exemplifying in selfie basic principles of computer science everyone should know about [8].

In order to provide another perspective on computing and in particular its limitations and how to overcome them, we have recently begun a new project integrating verification technology into selfie. We have already started implementing a state-of-the-art SAT solver in selfie and are working on an SMT solver and a symbolic execution engine for MIPSter. We report on the effort here which is still in an early stage but has already lead to some interesting insights.

We first introduce the programming language C* and the MIPSter instruction set by example and point out that we removed undefined behavior in all signed integer operations of C* through wrap-around semantics. However, as part of an ongoing effort, we are also exploring alternatives such as using unsigned integers only. Establishing a well-defined semantics of C* and MIPSter before trying to verify anything is in fact the first positive outcome of the effort.

We then provide an overview of selfie and argue that the simplicity and realism of system and language may lead to something beyond a purely educational effort. In particular, we show performance data comparing execution time and code size of programs written in C and ported to C* when compiled with state-of-the-art C compilers. The programs are mostly microbenchmarks written for this purpose but also one macrobenchmark which is a state-of-the-art SAT solver. It turns out that modern C compilers produce code for both versions with essentially the same performance characteristics. In short, C* is simple but still fast, motivating us to see it as a promising target for verification from within the system. We conclude with an outlook on how the project may evolve.

---

[1] http://selfie.cs.uni-salzburg.at.

2 Programming

C* is a tiny subset of the programming language C [7]. C* features global variable declarations with optional initialization as well as procedures with parameters and local variables. C* has five statements (assignment, while loop, if-then-else, procedure call, and return) as well as five built-in functions that are sufficient to bootstrap selfie (exit, malloc, open, read, write). In particular, there is no free and no close. C* features standard arithmetic (+, -, *, /, %) and comparison (==, !=, <, <=, >, >=) operators as well as integer, character, and string literals. C* includes the unary * operator for dereferencing pointers hence the name but excludes data types other than int and int* [12], bitwise and Boolean operators, and many other features.

Listing 1.1. Simplified atoi procedure in selfie

```
1   int atoi(int* s) {
2     int i;
3     int n;
4     int c;
5
6     // the conversion of the ASCII string in s to its
7     // numerical value n begins with the leftmost digit in s
8     i = 0;
9
10    // and the numerical value 0 for n
11    n = 0;
12
13    // load character (one byte) at index i in s from memory
14    // requires bit shifting since memory access is in words
15    c = loadCharacter(s, i);
16
17    // loop until s is terminated
18    while (c != 0) {
19      // the numerical value of ASCII-encoded decimal digits
20      // is offset by the ASCII code of '0' (which is 48)
21      c = c - '0';
22
23      // assert: 0 <= c <= 9 and 0 <= n * 10 + c <= INT_MAX
24
25      // use base 10 to compute numerical value
26      n = n * 10 + c;
27
28      // go to the next digit
29      i = i + 1;
30
31      c = loadCharacter(s, i);
32    }
33
34    return n;
35  }
```

The C* grammar is LL(1) with six keywords (int, while, if, else, return, void) and 22 symbols (=, +, -, *, /, %, ==, !=, <, <=, >, >=, ,, (,), {, }, ;, integer, character, string, identifier). Whitespace is ignored including one-line comments (//).

For an example of C* code, consider Listing 1.1 which shows a simplified C* implementation of the standard atoi procedure for converting a (decimal) number represented as an ASCII string into its numerical integer value.

An ASCII string in C is a null-terminated sequence of bytes, one byte per character, contiguously stored in memory. Here, the only non-standard part of the implementation are the calls to loadCharacter in Lines 15 and 31 to retrieve the individual characters of the string s. Because of the lack of a byte-size data type such as char we can only access memory at the granularity of signed integers (or pointers to signed integers). Signed integers contain four bytes, that is, up to four characters which are then retrieved individually through bit shifting, see Listing 1.2 for details, in particular Lines 13 through 15.

Listing 1.2. loadCharacter procedure in selfie

```
1   int loadCharacter(int* s, int i) {
2     // assert: i >= 0
3     int a;
4
5     // a is the index of the word where the
6     // to-be-loaded i-th character in s is
7     a = i / SIZEOFINT;
8
9     // shift to-be-loaded character to the left
10    // resetting all bits to the left of it then
11    // shift to-be-loaded character all the way
12    // to the right and return
13    return rightShift(leftShift(*(s + a),
14      ((SIZEOFINT - 1) - (i % SIZEOFINT)) * 8),
15        (SIZEOFINT - 1) * 8);
16  }
```

The C* semantics in selfie is, to the best of our knowledge, standard C semantics except for undefined behavior through arithmetic overflow. In particular, C* programs compiled and executed by selfie implement standard C semantics with 32-bit wrap-around semantics for all arithmetic operators on signed integers and pointers. This is true even if the bootstrapping compiler does not implement wrap-around semantics (except for multiplication). The system nevertheless prints a console warning for any overflow (and division by zero) that occurs during runtime. However, because of efficiency concerns, the actual result of a multiplication operation depends on the semantics implemented by the bootstrapping compiler.

The MIPSter instruction set generated by selfie is a tiny subset of MIPS32 [5]. It consists of 16 instructions (nop, addu, subu, multu, divu, mfhi, mflo, slt, jr, syscall, addiu, lw, sw, beq, jal, j). MIPSter allows straightforward compilation of C* programs into MIPSter code. Bitwise and sub-word data transfer instructions are not needed.

Listing 1.3. MIPS assembly for the `atoi` procedure in selfie

```
0x168(~18): lw $t0,-12($fp) // while (c != 0)
0x16C(~18): addiu $t1,$zero,0
0x170(~18): beq $t0,$t1,4[0x184]
0x178(~18): addiu $t0,$zero,1
0x17C(~18): beq $zero,$zero,2[0x188]
0x184(~18): addiu $t0,$zero,0
0x188(~18): beq $zero,$t0,31[0x208]
0x190(~21): lw $t0,-12($fp) // c = c - '0'
0x194(~21): addiu $t1,$zero,48
0x198(~21): subu $t0,$t0,$t1
0x19C(~21): sw $t0,-12($fp)
0x1A0(~26): lw $t0,-8($fp) // n = n * 10 + c
0x1A4(~26): addiu $t1,$zero,10
0x1A8(~26): multu $t0,$t1
0x1AC(~26): mflo $t0
0x1B8(~26): lw $t1,-12($fp)
0x1BC(~26): addu $t0,$t0,$t1
0x1C0(~26): sw $t0,-8($fp)
0x1C4(~29): lw $t0,-4($fp) // i = i + 1
0x1C8(~29): addiu $t1,$zero,1
0x1CC(~29): addu $t0,$t0,$t1
0x1D0(~29): sw $t0,-4($fp)
0x1D4(~31): lw $t0,8($fp) // push s onto call stack
0x1D8(~31): addiu $sp,$sp,-4
0x1DC(~31): sw $t0,0($sp)
0x1E0(~31): lw $t0,-4($fp) // push i onto call stack
0x1E4(~31): addiu $sp,$sp,-4
0x1E8(~31): sw $t0,0($sp)
0x1EC(~31): jal 0xE1D[0x3874] // call loadCharacter(s, i)
0x1F4(~31): addiu $t0,$v0,0 // c = loadCharacter(s, i)
0x1F8(~31): addiu $v0,$zero,0
0x1FC(~31): sw $t0,-12($fp)
0x200(~34): beq $zero,$zero,-39[0x168] // go back to while
```

Listing 1.3 shows the MIPSter code generated by selfie for the `while` loop in the `atoi` code in Listing 1.1. The first line reads as follows. The instruction `lw $t0,-12($fp)` is stored in memory at address `0x168` and has been generated for source code at approximately Line 18. In fact, the instruction loads the current value of the local variable c occurring in the loop condition c != 0 into the temporary CPU register `$t0`. The value is stored in memory on the call stack, 12 bytes below the address to which the frame pointer `$fp` refers. The next instruction loads the value 0 into another temporary register `$t1` to prepare for the comparison with `$t0` in the following branch instruction. The code that follows is inefficient but straightforward to generate keeping the compiler simple. It loads 1 or 0 into `$t0` depending on whether the loop condition evaluates to true or false, respectively. Only then the branch instruction at `0x188` either enters the loop body or terminates the loop by branching to the first instruction past the code implementing the loop body at `0x208`.

Listing 1.4. C* code preventing integer overflows in the `atoi` procedure in selfie

```
...
while (c != 0) {
  c = c - '0';

  if (c < 0)
    // c was not a decimal digit
    return -1;
  else if (c > 9)
    // c was not a decimal digit
    return -1;

  // use base 10 but avoid integer overflow
  if (n < INT_MAX / 10)
    n = n * 10 + c;
  else if (n == INT_MAX / 10) {
    if (c <= INT_MAX % 10)
      n = n * 10 + c;
    else if (c == (INT_MAX % 10) + 1)
      // s must be terminated next, check below
      n = INT_MIN;
    else
      // s contains a decimal number larger than INT_MAX
      return -1;
  } else
    // s contains a decimal number larger than INT_MAX
    return -1;

  i = i + 1;
  c = loadCharacter(s, i);

  if (n == INT_MIN)
    if (c != 0)
      // n is INT_MIN but s is not terminated yet
      return -1;
}
...
```

The rest of the code is hopefully self-explanatory leaving us more space to show in Listing 1.4 the actual implementation of `atoi` in selfie that prevents the occurrence of any integer overflows during scanning of integer literals. The code is considerably more complex than the simplified code in Listing 1.1 but nevertheless an important part of the educational experience with selfie. In fact, the whole implementation of selfie is designed to avoid integer overflows and there are indeed none in our experiments which include self-compilation, self-execution, and self-hosting of selfie. A proof of absence is of course another story which is ongoing work as discussed next.

3 Computing

Selfie is a self-contained system of a C* compiler, a MIPSter emulator, and a MIPSter hypervisor implemented in a single 7k-line file of C* code.[2] Selfie can compile, execute, and virtualize itself. In particular, the C* compiler targets the MIPSter emulator which can execute any MIPSter code including its own implementation any number of times until time and space run out. The MIPSter

[2] https://github.com/cksystemsteaching/selfie/releases/tag/Festschrift17.

hypervisor virtualizes the machine emulated by the emulator and can therefore host any MIPSter code execution, again including its own implementation any number of times. The difference between emulator and hypervisor is that the emulator interprets MIPSter code while the hypervisor asks the machine on which it runs to interpret MIPSter code on its behalf in temporal and spatial isolation through context switching and virtual memory. Thus the hypervisor requires at least one emulator instance to run on.

Self-compilation, self-execution, and self-hosting with selfie enable three distinguished features of the system:

1. Selfie not only compiles itself, it can even execute the compiled code in the same invocation of the system, to compile itself again and enable checking if the code it then generates is the same as the code it executes (fixed-point of self-compilation). The backend of the compiler is even implemented next to the frontend of the emulator. In particular, encoding and decoding of machine instructions is literally done next to each other in the source code. Also, system call wrappers are generated by the compiler next to the actual system call implementations in the emulator.

2. Selfie can execute any MIPSter code including itself [11]. Interestingly, executing an emulator such as mipster on itself is arguably the simplest form of an operating system kernel (top emulator) running on a given processor (bottom emulator), just very inefficiently as interpreter of code rather than through context switching and virtual memory. However, the top emulator does provide a machine instance perfectly isolated from the machine instance on which it runs as provided by the bottom emulator. In fact, enhancing the top emulator to emulate multiple isolated machine instances is easy using a dedicated interpreter per instance. With selfie this can be done by students in a one-week homework assignment. It is only the speed of code execution that gets exponentially slower in the number of emulators running on top of each other, but for that there is virtualization.

3. Selfie can virtualize a MIPSter machine for hosting the execution of any MIPSter code including itself. In contrast to code interpretation, however, machine virtualization maintains the speed of code execution modulo the overhead of context switching and virtual memory. Nevertheless, emulator and hypervisor in selfie share most of their code and are supposed to provide functionally indistinguishable machine instances, just through very different means. Selfie can even alternate between emulation and virtualization of the same machine instance at runtime.

Selfie has originally been developed exclusively for educational purposes. By now, we use the system in introductory architecture, compiler, and operating systems classes. There is also an advanced operating systems class based on selfie as well as an introductory computer science class for students not majoring in computer science. In that class selfie helps exemplifying basic principles of computer science. A textbook in early draft form is available online.[3]

---

[3] http://leanpub.com/selfie.

3.1   Software Verification in Selfie

We recently noticed that selfie has also potential in making more advanced topics such as software verification accessible to broader and younger audiences. We have therefore started a project integrating verification technology into selfie. Surprisingly, this effort appears to have potential in research as well. Selfie is simple yet realistic. In fact, programming language and software system are so simple that selfie may be amenable to formal reasoning from within the system itself. Moreover, C* is still sufficiently realistic to serve as input to state-of-the-art compiler optimizations. In short, C* is simple but may still be fast.

While there is considerable amount of literature on software verification and related topics there is little hands-on information on how to do what we are interested in. Ideally, we would like to have selfie perform self-verification of non-trivial correctness properties [9] and self-optimization of its own implementation. This may or may not be feasible but at least verifier and optimizer "only" need to work on selfie code and not "any" code. We are even free to trade-off complexity between subject and object. In other words, we can make the system smarter or the code, that is, its proof obligations simpler.

Because of selfie's dual role in education and research, we are interested in the absolute simplest yet sufficiently efficient design. There are essentially two key challenges that we are facing in this project. The first challenge is to figure out what the simplest way of doing things actually is. For example, it is difficult to choose the right data structures sufficient for our purpose. The second challenge is to figure out which optimizations dominate others in their effect on performance and scalability and are actually needed for our purpose.

So far, we have considered SAT and SMT solvers [2], (bounded) model checkers [1,2,14], symbolic execution engines [3,4], and even inductive theorem provers [6]. The very first step we have already taken is to implement a naïve SAT solver in selfie which we call babysat. We also implemented a parser for SAT instances encoded in the DIMACS CNF file format. The babysat algorithm simply enumerates all possible variable assignments of a given SAT instance and takes 58 lines of C* code. In contrast, even the most naïve implementations we found online feature some form of optimization such as a watchlist, for example. However, at least for SAT, instead of introducing optimizations one by one, we decided to take microsat,[4] an existing state-of-the-art SAT solver implemented in C, port it to C*, and integrate it into selfie.

We are now working on implementations of a naïve SMT solver with babysat and microsat in the backend as well as a naïve symbolic execution engine for MIPSter code. The idea is to stay away from any optimizations unless we have evidence that they are really needed to make the system scale up to selfie. Also, naïve implementations often turn out to have significant pedagogical value helping students and us understand the problem better.

---

[4] https://github.com/marijnheule/microsat.

3.2   C* Performance

To our initial surprise, we noticed that the C* port of microsat is not slower than the original C version in our experiments. The port of microsat to C* essentially requires three potentially performance-relevant modifications:

1. structs and arrays are eliminated by removing their declarations and replacing their access operators with adequate pointer arithmetic and casting,
2. control-flow statements such as break, continue, and goto are eliminated by introducing new variables that enable modifying the truth value of loop conditions without changing the rest of the program state, and
3. logical operators such as &&, | |, and ! are eliminated by replacing them with adequately nested if statements.

All other modifications are minor. In particular, macros are easily expanded, for loops are turned into while loops, and, more surprisingly, all bitwise operators in the microsat implementation can be replaced by simple integer arithmetic.

We report on a macrobenchmark with microsat and on eight microbenchmarks each focusing on a particular aspect of the three modifications. Our experiments ran on a 512 GB NUMA machine with four 16-core 2.3 GHz AMD Opteron 6376 processors (16 KB L1 data cache, 64KB L1 instruction cache, 16MB L2 cache, 16 MB L3 cache) and Linux kernel version 3.13.0. We used gcc 6.4 and 7.2 as well as clang 4.0.1 to generate 32-bit binaries with −O0 and −O3 optimization levels. For simplicity, selfie only supports 32-bit binaries.

Tables 1, 2, and 3 show the data obtained with x86 binaries generated by gcc 6.4, gcc 7.2, and clang 4.0.1, respectively. The microsat performance data shows the total execution time of running microsat on the industrial benchmark of the SAT 2004 competition[5] with a timeout of 120 s. Instances that took less than 5 s to solve were excluded. We repeated the experiment to obtain a ±5% margin of

Table 1. Performance and binary size of C* over C using gcc 6.4

Benchmark	−O0				−O3			
	C [sec.]	C* [sec.]	Perf. [%]	Size [%]	C [sec.]	C* [sec.]	Perf. [%]	Size [%]
microsat	4036.26	6912.24	58.3	64.1	2671.34	2678.82	99.6	88.9
struct	97.41	327.48	29.7	91.8	0.23	0.25	92	92.8
array	160.63	308.83	52	91.6	7.09	39.05	18.2	101.1
array pointer	-	270.85	59.3	91.3	-	7.13	99.4	93.6
struct with int*	-	326.9	29.8	91.5	-	0.23	100	93
array of int*	-	306.61	52.4	91.3	-	7.12	99.6	93.6
break	65.12	65.51	99.4	99.6	26.71	17.17	155.6	100.5
logical and	90.63	90.6	100	100	41.49	41.49	100	100
logical or	118.85	100.15	118.7	100	68.02	68.06	99.9	100

---

[5] http://www.satcompetition.org.

Table 2. Performance and binary size of C* over C using gcc 7.2

Benchmark	−O0				−O3			
	C [sec.]	C* [sec.]	Perf. [%]	Size [%]	C [sec.]	C* [sec.]	Perf. [%]	Size [%]
microsat	4037.47	6907.40	58.4	64	2866.97	2817.88	101.9	77.8
struct	110.77	327.92	33.8	91.6	0.31	0.31	100	92.9
array	160.03	312.1	51.3	91.4	4.69	37.67	12.5	98.3
array pointer	-	264.67	60.5	91.1	-	4.7	99.8	93.3
struct with int⋆	-	325.67	34	91.6	-	0.31	100	92.9
array of int⋆	-	307.86	52	91.3	-	4.69	100	93.3
break	64.81	65.51	98.9	99.6	26.71	26.71	100	99.9
logical and	90.06	90.14	99.9	100	24.13	24.1	100.1	100
logical or	120.55	101.89	118.3	100	44.92	44.91	100	100

Table 3. Performance and binary size of C* over C using clang 4.0.1

Benchmark	−O0				−O3			
	C [sec.]	C* [sec.]	Perf. [%]	Size [%]	C [sec.]	C* [sec.]	Perf. [%]	Size [%]
microsat	4011.74	7787.89	51.5	73.3	2630.39	2514.90	104.2	90.1
struct	89.26	418.07	21.4	98.2	33.8	22.7	148.9	98.2
array	106.02	416.14	25.5	98.3	34.42	32.66	105.4	98.3
array pointer	-	329.07	32.2	98.2	-	6	573.7	98.2
struct with int⋆	-	418.85	21.3	98.2	-	33.86	99.8	98.2
array of int⋆	-	420.94	25.2	98.2	-	6.01	572.7	98.2
break	72.05	72.41	99.5	99.9	27.63	27.63	100	99.9
logical and	99.4	98.93	100.5	100	48.27	48.27	100	100
logical or	131.77	137.98	95.5	100	65.97	65.97	100	100

error with a probability of 90%. For the microbenchmark performance data the margin of error is ±2% with a probability of 99%.

In nearly all cases, the size of x86 binaries generated from C* versions of the code is either the same or less than the size of the binaries generated from the corresponding C versions. Without any compiler optimizations (option −O0), code generated from C* versions is generally slower by up to around 79%. There is one notable exception which is the microbenchmark replacing the logical operator || with adequate if statements. Code generated from the C* version with both versions of gcc runs around 18% faster in this case.

With compiler optimizations (option −O3), the picture is quite different. Performance is generally the same for both the C and C* versions in nearly all benchmarks, in particular the macrobenchmark with microsat. However, there are some notable exceptions as well. For example, struct access mimicked in C* and compiled with clang is faster than the original in C. However, with array access and gcc it is the opposite.

Structs and Arrays. In order to measure the impact of porting C structs and arrays to C* pointer arithmetics and casting, we designed five microbenchmarks that share the code in Listing 1.5 for exercising struct and array accesses in two nested while loops. The input1 and input2 parameters were set to 200,000,000 and 100, respectively.

Listing 1.5. Code for microbenchmarking struct and array access performance

```
1  int* ptr; // used in inlined code
2  ...;
3  while (i < input1) {
4    j = input2;
5    while (j > 0) {
6      // inline code here for microbenchmarking
7      // struct and array access performance
8      ...;
9      j = j - 1;
10   }
11   i = i + 1;
12 }
```

Listing 1.6 shows the C code for measuring struct and array access performance. For example, for measuring struct access performance we inlined the body of the struct-access procedure into the body of the inner while loop in Listing 1.5.

Listing 1.6. Struct and array microbenchmarks in C

```
1  struct strc_t {
2    int* f1;
3    int f2;
4    int f3;
5  };
6  struct strc_t* strc;
7
8  void struct_access() {
9    strc->f1 = ptr + j;
10   strc->f2 = j;
11   strc->f3 = strc->f2 + j;
12 }
13
14 void array_access() {
15   strc->f1[j] = 1;
16   strc->f2 = j;
17   strc->f3 = strc->f2 + j;
18 }
```

Listing 1.7 shows the C* version of the C code in Listing 1.6 using getters and setters for struct and array access through pointer arithmetics and casting. This method is used in our C* port of microsat as well as in the implementation of selfie. The array access performance with C* is poor using both versions of gcc with −O3 since they fail to move the loop-invariant base address of the array outside the loops.

Listing 1.7. Struct and array microbenchmarks in C*

```
1   int* getF1(int* strc) { return (int*) *strc; }
2   int  getF2(int* strc) { return *(strc + 1);  }
3   int  getF3(int* strc) { return *(strc + 2);  }
4   void setF1(int* strc, int* f1) { *strc = (int) f1; }
5   void setF2(int* strc, int  f2) { *(strc + 1) = f2; }
6   void setF3(int* strc, int  f3) { *(strc + 2) = f3; }
7
8   int* strc;
9
10  void struct_access() {
11    setF1(strc, ptr + j);
12    setF2(strc, j);
13    setF3(strc, getF2(strc) + j);
14  }
15
16  void array_access() {
17    *(getF1(strc) + j) = 1;
18    setF2(strc, j);
19    setF3(strc, getF2(strc) + j);
20  }
21
22  int* array;
23
24  void array_pointer_access() {
25    *(array + j) = 1; // with array set to getF1(strc)
26    setF2(strc, j);
27    setF3(strc, getF2(strc) + j);
28  }
```

We therefore designed another microbenchmark in C* for measuring array access performance when using a variable called `array` that caches the pointer to the beginning of the accessed array. The data shows that this modification restores the array access performance of the optimized C* code compiled with both versions of gcc. With clang performance even multiplies by a factor of five. However, the code generated for the array access microbenchmark in C as well as in C* is inefficient.

Listing 1.8. Struct and array microbenchmark with content typed as `int*`

```
1   int* getF1(int** strc) {return *strc; }
2   int  getF2(int** strc) {return (int) *(strc + 1);}
3   int  getF3(int** strc) {return (int) *(strc + 2);}
4   void setF1(int** strc, int* f1) {*strc = f1;}
5   void setF2(int** strc, int  f2) {*(strc + 1) = (int*) f2;}
6   void setF3(int** strc, int  f3) {*(strc + 2) = (int*) f3;}
7
8   int** strc;
9
10  void struct_with_intstar_access() {
11    setF1(strc, ptr + j);
12    setF2(strc, j);
13    setF3(strc, getF2(strc) + j);
14  }
15
16  void array_of_intstar_access() {
17    *(getF1(strc) + j) = 1;
18    setF2(strc, j);
19    setF3(strc, getF2(strc) + j);
20  }
```

The fact that array access performance with C* is so poor with both versions of gcc made us look even closer and design two more microbenchmarks as shown in Listing 1.8. The code is not proper C* which we acknowledge by underlining the obtained data. However, the code still reveals that gcc is able to optimize struct and array access through pointer arithmetics and casting if the struct is declared as int** rather than just int* and casting in the getters and setters is adapted accordingly.

Control Flow. Listing 1.9 shows on the left C code using a break statement and on the right its equivalent C* version. The C* code avoids the break statement by using a variable tmp for saving and restoring the loop variable j which we modify temporarily in order to mimic the behavior of the original C code. We used this technique in the C* port of microsat to eliminate break, continue, and goto statements.

Listing 1.9. C code and its equivalent C* version replacing break

```
1                                    int tmp;
2    while (i < input1) {            while (i < input1) {
3      j = input2;                     j = input2;
4      while (j > 0) {                 while (j > 0) {
5        if (j < input3) {               if (j < input3) {
6          ...;                            ...;
7                                          tmp = j;
8          break;                          j = 0;
9        }                             } else
10       j = j - 1;                      j = j - 1;
11     }                             }
12                                   j = tmp;
13     i = i + 1;                    i = i + 1;
14   }                             }
```

The data shows that performance is generally unaffected except when using gcc 6.4 with -O3. In this case, surprisingly, performance increases significantly with the C* version.

Boolean Operators. Listing 1.10 shows the microbenchmark for eliminating the logical operator && using adequately nested if statements. The microbenchmark for || works similarly. We used this technique in the C* port of microsat.

Listing 1.10. C code and its equivalent C* version replacing &&

```
1    while (i < input1) {            while (i < input1) {
2      j = input2;                     j = input2;
3      while (j > 0) {                 while (j > 0) {
4        if (j < input3 && j % 12) {     if (j < input3)
5                                          if (j % 12) {
6          ...;                              ...;
7        }                               }
8        j = j - 1;                      j = j - 1;
9      }                             }
10     i = i + 1;                    i = i + 1;
11   }                             }
```

The data shows that performance is generally maintained. In fact, the generated code is almost the same for the C and C* versions using any of the compilers with -O3. As mentioned before, performance even improves for | | when using both versions of gcc with -O0.

4   Conclusions

Software verification is difficult. Many important problems in that field are intractable or even undecidable. However, that challenge and the fact that verification provides another way of constructing the semantics of formalisms is our motivation to try integrating verification technology into selfie. We see verification integrated with compilation, emulation, and virtualization as key to advancing both the rigorous and efficient design of software systems as well as the computer science education of broader audiences. What is the meaning of code and how is it constructed by a machine? What happens during execution? How does that become a utility? Why can I not compute everything and how is this a good thing? The simplicity and realism of selfie has already helped us give increasingly better answers to some of these questions. We conclude that with the verification technology already available there is a good chance that we are able to continue that development with selfie even in a largely intractable and undecidable problem domain.

Acknowledgements. Selfie is the result of more than ten years of studying and teaching systems engineering. Many colleagues and students have been involved in its development through inspiring conversations as well as numerous coding sessions. In particular, we thank Martin Aigner, Sebastian Arming, Christian Barthel, Armin Biere, Heidi Graf, Andreas Haas, Marijn Heule, Thomas Hütter, Michael Lippautz, Cornelia Mayer, James Noble, Simone Oblasser, Peter Palfrader, Sarah Sallinger, Raja Sengupta, and Ana Sokolova as well as all the students who have taken our compiler and operating systems classes over the years. The design of the C* compiler is inspired by the Oberon compiler of Professor Niklaus Wirth from ETH Zurich [15]. The design of the microkernel in selfie is inspired by microkernels of Professor Jochen Liedtke from University of Karlsruhe [10].

Work on selfie has been supported by the National Research Network RiSE on Rigorous Systems Engineering (Austrian Science Fund (FWF) Grant S11404-N23 and S11411-N23), a Google PhD Fellowship, and a Google Research Grant.

References

1. Biere, A., Cimatti, A., Clarke, E., Zhu, Y.: Symbolic model checking without BDDs. In: Cleaveland, W.R. (ed.) TACAS 1999. LNCS, vol. 1579, pp. 193–207. Springer, Heidelberg (1999). https://doi.org/10.1007/3-540-49059-0_14
2. Biere, A., Heule, M., van Maaren, H., Walsh, T. (eds.): Handbook of Satisfiability, Frontiers in Artificial Intelligence and Applications, vol. 185. IOS Press, Amsterdam (2009)
3. Cadar, C., Dunbar, D., Engler, D.: KLEE: unassisted and automatic generation of high-coverage tests for complex systems programs. In: Proceedings of USENIX Conference on Operating Systems Design and Implementation (OSDI), pp. 209–224. USENIX Association (2008)

4. Godefroid, P., Levin, M.Y., Molnar, D.: Automated whitebox fuzz testing. In: Proceedings of Symposium on Network and Distributed Systems Security (NDSS), pp. 151–166 (2008)
5. Hennessy, J.L., Patterson, D.A.: Computer Architecture: A Quantitative Approach. Morgan Kaufmann, Burlington (2011)
6. Kaufmann, M., Manolios, P., Moore, J.S.: Computer-Aided Reasoning: An Approach. Kluwer, Alphen aan den Rijn (2000)
7. Kernighan, B.W., Ritchie, D.M.: The C Programming Language. Prentice Hall, Upper Saddle River (2000)
8. Kirsch, C.: Selfie and the basics. In: Proceedings of ACM SIGPLAN International Symposium on New Ideas, New Paradigms, and Reflections on Programming and Software (Onward!). ACM (2017)
9. Kumar, R.: Self-compilation and self-verification. Ph.D. thesis, University of Cambridge (2015)
10. Liedtke, J.: Toward real microkernels. Commun. ACM **39**(9), 70–77 (1996)
11. Reynolds, J.C.: Definitional interpreters for higher-order programming languages. In: Proceedings of ACM Annual Conference, pp. 717–740 (1972)
12. Richards, M., Whitby-Strevens, C.: BCPL: The Language and its Compiler. Cambridge University Press, Cambridge (2009)
13. Sipser, M.: Introduction to the Theory of Computation. International Thomson Publishing, Stamford (1996)
14. Vizel, Y., Weissenbacher, G., Malik, S.: Boolean satisfiability solvers and their applications in model checking. Proc. IEEE **103**(11), 2021–2035 (2015)
15. Wirth, N.: Compiler Construction. Addison Wesley, Boston (1996)

Transforming Threads into Actors: Learning Concurrency Structure from Execution Traces

Gul Agha[⊠] and Karl Palmskog

University of Illinois at Urbana-Champaign, Urbana, IL 61801, USA
{agha,palmskog}@illinois.edu

Abstract. The threads and shared memory model is still the most commonly used programming model. However, programs written using threads interacting with shared memory model are notoriously bug-prone and hard to comprehend. An important reason for this lack of comprehensibility is thread based programs obscure the natural structure of concurrency in a distributed world: *actors* executing autonomously with their own internal logic and interacting at arms length with each other. While actors encapsulate their internal state, enabling consistency invariants of the data structures to be maintained locally, thread-based programs use control-centric synchronization primitives (such as locks) that are divorced from the concurrency structure of a program. Making the concurrency structure explicit provides useful documentation for developers. Moreover, it may be useful for refactoring thread-based object-oriented programs into an actor-oriented programs based on message-passing and isolated state. We present a novel algorithm based on Bayesian inference that automatically infers the concurrency structure of programs from their traces. The concurrency structure is inferred as consistency invariants of program data, and expressed in terms of annotations on data fields and method parameters. We illustrate our algorithm on Java programs using type annotations in Java classes and suggest how such annotations may be useful.

Keywords: Concurrency · Actors · Shared memory · Threads · Java
Dynamic analysis · Bayesian inference

1 Introduction

A natural way to model the world is as a collection of actors that are autonomous and concurrent [25]. The notion of actors has been developed as a programming model [1,3] and given a formal semantics [2]. An actor encapsulates (isolates) its local state; other actors may access an actor's data only through an interface defined by the latter. Such encapsulation, or isolation of data, enables us to guarantee the consistency of the data that is owned by an actor.

An alternative for concurrency is independent threads of control manipulating shared memory. As Lee points out, a fundamental problem with threads is

© Springer International Publishing AG, part of Springer Nature 2018
M. Lohstroh et al. (Eds.): Lee Festschrift, LNCS 10760, pp. 16–37, 2018.
https://doi.org/10.1007/978-3-319-95246-8_2

the unrestricted nondeterminism of thread interleavings in the absence of synchronization primitives [30]. In addition to being difficult to understand and maintain, this makes thread-based programs notoriously prone to bugs such as data races, deadlocks, and atomicity violations [36].

In practical terms, an important reason for concurrency-related bugs in thread-based programs is that control-centric synchronization primitives that enable atomic actions with respect to other threads, e.g., *locks*, are divorced from *consistency invariants* relating data structures in programs.

Consider an object representing a concurrently accessed *list*. This list object may have an array field and an integer field, where the integer field indicates how much of the array field is in use. In other words, there is an *invariant* which relates the array and integer fields. *Locks* must prevent the two fields from being modified concurrently by different threads. Otherwise, the program could exhibit a *"high-level race"* [4,9], where the list object reaches an inconsistent state. Observe that in a thread-based program, there is no explicit connection between the invariant and the code that uses locks to preserve the invariant against concurrent modification.

In order to make the *concurrency structure* in a program perspicuous, we need to make its consistency invariants explicit. Making the concurrency structure of programs with threads and shared memory explicit is desirable for several reasons. For example, if a certain consistency invariant is documented, a programmer can use this knowledge to avoid unintended atomicity violations when calling methods in existing classes and when adding new methods; both may require adding synchronization for accessing fields. Moreover, as we argue in this paper, knowledge of the concurrency structure of a multi-threaded object-oriented program can be used to *transform* this program to use the actor model, i.e., to introduce message-passing interfaces between active program components to isolate their state [1,29,31].

One way to express consistency invariants is to provide annotations on data fields and method parameters. Since we are mainly interested in the *existence* of invariants between fields, and not their exact formulation in some program logic such as JML [13], only basic annotation facilities are required. An example of such annotations are those provided by Java 8 [43]. In earlier work, Vaziri et al. provided the syntax and semantics for a set of annotations which represent consistency invariants, and proved their soundness in a minimal calculus for a Java-like language [17].

Unfortunately, manually adding consistency invariant annotations is time-consuming and error-prone. Annotating a legacy program requires understanding the program through its use of control-centric primitives. Even for relatively small and simple programs of a few hundred lines, the conversion process can take several hours. The manually produced annotations can also be problematic in two ways: first, unrelated fields may be connected by annotations; and second, related fields may not be connected. The first type of erroneous annotations underestimate the permitted degree of concurrency; the second type is consistent with unintended executions due to high-level data races. Several techniques based on either *static* or *dynamic* program analysis to infer annotations related to consistency invariants have been proposed [15,27,34,37]. However, these techniques have serious limitations–both in the kind of data-centric primitives they can infer, and in the precision and stability of their results.

In this paper, we present a novel machine learning algorithm that automatically infers consistency invariant annotations for concurrent programs using the threads and shared memory model from program execution traces. The algorithm, called Bayesian Annotation Inference Technique (BAIT), is based on *Bayesian inference* [44]. BAIT achieves robustness against intermittent deviations from normal behavior in a trace by weighing such occurrences against a preponderance of contrary evidence and correspondingly devaluing their impact. BAIT performs its analysis *on-the-fly* and scales to large programs and long executions. BAIT improves the accuracy of its results as the number of observations grows by taking into account the *distance* (in terms of basic operations) between two related observations, thus distinguishing between unrelated computation phases. Finally, we discuss how such annotations may be facilitate transformation of threaded programs analyzed into actor-based programs.

2   Concurrency Structure Annotations and Actors

To concretize our discussion of concurrency structure, annotation inference, and actors, we consider Java programs. We describe our concurrency structure annotations for these programs, and how they related to program behavior using a running example. We then outline how annotations can be used to transform the example program to use actors.

2.1   Syntax and Semantics of Annotations

To capture consistency invariants, we adapt core constructs from the calculus of Dolby et al. [17] to the syntax of Java 8 type annotations. We consider three kinds of annotations: *atomic sets*, *aliases*, and *unitfors*. An atomic set is a group of fields inside an object that are connected by a consistency invariant; objects can contain multiple, but disjoint atomic sets. An alias extends atomic sets beyond object boundaries–an alias merges the atomic set containing a field with an atomic set in the object that is the field's value. A unitfor intuitively merges atomic sets of objects passed as parameters to a method with atomic sets in the callee object, but only for the duration of the method call.

Figure 1 shows Java code with our annotations. The `@AtomicSets` annotation on line 1 declares an atomic set L, and the `@Atomic`(`"L"`) annotations of the field declarations for `size` and `elements` and these fields to L. The class List corresponds to the example mentioned in Sect. 1: the value of a list's `size` integer field must equal the number of elements in the `elements` array actually used to store list entries, so the fields `size` and `elements` form an atomic set. Each List object has its own atomic set L. Recall that atomic sets express the *existence* of

```
@AtomicSets({"L"})                          @AtomicSets({"U"})
class List {                                class DownloadManager {
  @Atomic("L") int size;                      @Atomic("U") @Alias("L") List urls;
  @Atomic("L") Object[] elements;

  public int size() {                         public boolean hasNextURL() {
    return size;                                return urls.size() > 0;
  }                                           }
  public Object get(int index) {              public URL getNextURL() {
    if (0 <= index && index < size)             if (urls.size() == 0)
      return elements[index];                     return null;
    else
      return null;                              URL url = (URL) urls.get(0);
  }                                             urls.remove(0);
  public void                                   announceStartInGUI(url);
    addAll(@UnitFor("L") List o) {              return url;
    this.size = this.size + o.size;           }
    /* ... */                                 /* ... */
  }                                         }
  /* ... */
}
```

Fig. 1. Example annotated Java classes.

consistency invariants, without requiring an explicit expression such invariant, e.g., `size < elements.length`, for the class `List`.

Semantically, an atomic set is associated with one or more *units of work*. A unit of work is a method that preserves the consistency of its associated atomic sets when executed sequentially. Thus, atomic sets can ensure the application's consistency by inserting synchronization operations that guarantee the sequential execution of all units of work. By default, all non-private methods of a class are units of work for all atomic sets declared in the class or any of its subclasses. Like field declarations, atomic sets use classes as scopes, but are instance specific at runtime. Consider the methods `get(int)` and `addAll(List)` from Fig. 1. Each method is (implicitly) a unit of work for the atomic set L of its receiver `List` object. Hence, two threads, t_1 and t_2, that concurrently invoke `get(int)` and `addAll(List)` on a `List` l cannot interleave when accessing l's field: either t_1 executes `get(int)` first, or t_2 executes `addAll(List)` first. The interleaved case where t_2 has updated l.`size` but not l.`elements`, which causes t_1 to violate the array bounds cannot occur.

For aliases, consider the `DownloadManager` class from Fig. 1. The alias annotation `@Alias("L")` of the `urls` field declaration combines the atomic set L in `List` with the atomic set U. Hence, the method `getNextURL()` is a unit of work for this combined atomic set; its access to the `urls` list cannot be interleaved, which guarantees that no other thread can empty the list between the invocations of `urls.get(0)` and `urls.remove(0)`.

The `unitfor` annotation allows methods to be declared as units of work for atomic sets in the method's parameters. For example, the method `addAll(List)` is not only a unit of work for the atomic set L of its receiver `List` object but also for the atomic set L of its argument. Hence, if two threads, t_1 and t_2, concurrently invoke `get(int)` on a `List` l and pass the same l as the argument to `addAll(List)`, they still cannot interleave when accessing l's field.

The program in Fig. 2 illustrates how the classes in Fig. 1 can be used to implement concurrent downloading of a collection of files given as URLs. Note that the program uses control-centric synchronization in the form of Java monitors. While this particular use of monitors gives rise to program behavior consistent with the meaning of the concurrency structure annotations in the `List` and `DownloadManager` classes, other uses can easily cause atomicity violations. We suggest that another option is to refactor the program to use actors and message-passing rather than explicit threads and synchronization, as described below.

```java
class DownloadThread extends Thread {
  DownloadManager manager;

  public void run() {
    while (true) {
      URL url;
      synchronized(manager) { // atomic access to manager
        if (!manager.hasNextURL()) break;
        url = manager.getNextURL();
      }
      download(url); // blocks while waiting for data
    }
  }
  /* ... */
}

public class Download {
  public static void main(String[] args) {
    // create manager and thread objects
    DownloadManager manager = new DownloadManager();
    for (int i = 0; i < 31; i++) {
      manager.addURL(new URL("http://www.example.com/f" + i));
    }
    DownloadThread t1 = new DownloadThread(manager);
    DownloadThread t2 = new DownloadThread(manager);
    t1.start();
    t2.start();
  }
}
```

Fig. 2. Example download program that uses threads to manage multiple network connections. Threads share a single manager that maintains the list of URLs to download. The program uses control-centric synchronization (Java monitors).

2.2 From Annotations and Threads to Actors

The aliased atomic sets in `List` and `DownloadManager` in Fig. 1 suggest that we can encapsulate as a single actor one instance of the latter containing an instance of the former. Then, instead of synchronizing on a `DownloadManager` instance, which would require assuming shared memory, we can simply use message passing to retrieve URLs and rely on actors having a single locus of control.

To enable wrapping objects into actors and passing (immutable) actor names instead of in-memory object references, we also have to change the program to rely on interfaces rather than classes directly in the code. Figure 3 shows two classes in the resulting program. We use the syntax **new actor** to indicate actor-wrapped objects.

```
class DownloadThread extends Thread implements IDownloadThread {
  IDownloadManager manager;

  public void run() {
    URL url;
    // message-passing semantics
    while((url = this.manager.getNextURL()) != null) {
      download(url); // blocks while waiting for data
    }
  }
  /* ... */
}

public class Download {
  public static void main(String[] args) {
    // actor initializations
    IDownloadManager manager = new actor DownloadManager();
    for (int i = 0; i < 31; i++) { // message-passing semantics
      manager.addURL(new URL("http://www.example.com/f" + i));
    }
    IDownloadThread t1 = new actor DownloadThread(manager);
    IDownloadThread t2 = new actor DownloadThread(manager);
    t1.start();
    t2.start();
  }
}
```

Fig. 3. Actor program involving classes from Figs. 1 and 2.

Note that in order to execute the program in Fig. 3, the runtime system must perform actor initialization on **new actor** assignments and convert method invocations on actor names to message passing. However, not all programs can be straightforwardly converted in this way. In particular, to preserve program semantics, data passed through a message passing interface must have the same meaning to the sender and the receiver.

Consider the example where the receiver resides in a different runtime environment, memory references from the sender will not be valid: a message m sent from actor A to actor B at runtime may contain references to objects at A's location which do not exist at B's location. What is required is that the data passed in messages be immutable, e.g., consist of only actor names and constants. In the example actor program, only actor references (manager) and immutable URL objects are passed in messages. In the case of a Java Virtual Machine (JVM) based actor framework such as Akka [32], A may live in a different JVM than B, so that some object references in m do not refer to meaningful memory locations in the JVM of B. Even when actors live in the same JVM, Akka developers recommend messages be made *immutable* [33], i.e., that their contents are passed as (unchangeable) values. This was the case in the actor program in Fig. 3: the only objects passed in messages have class URL, and all its instances are by nature completely immutable.

Nevertheless, passing whole mutable objects (rather than references) in actor messages can be consistent with the behavior of the original object-oriented program in some situations. For example, if actors other than the receiver do not interact with the object at all after the message with the object has been sent, different actors will never have an inconsistent view of the object. More generally, if actors pass *ownership* of objects in messages [8], behavior is preserved in a distributed environment. Weaker guarantees than ownership passing may sometimes be acceptable, such as when actors promise not to call methods that mutate a received object's state [39]. For example, the *Pony* object-oriented actor language has a *type system* which can account for many of these situations and guarantee expected behavior in distributed program runtime settings [12]; however, the programmer must add such type annotations manually.

We believe that both static and dynamic inference can assist in inferring properties such as immutability and ownership passing to establish preservation of behavior of actorized programs with their original purely object-oriented behavior [5,39,40,45]. If safe message-passing behavior cannot be established for some methods automatically by inference, one option is to make the actor decomposition more *coarse-grained*, i.e., let fewer objects be wrapped by actors in the program translation. This results in less concurrency, and less flexibility in distributing actors at runtime to different locations, but does not require complex refactoring of the program to ensure the actor message-passing semantics preserves the original behavior.

3   Annotation Inference Example

In this section, we use an example based on the code in Sect. 2 to explain the key concepts in BAIT. Suppose that we are given the classes List and DownloadManager from Fig. 1 but without the annotations. Moreover, we use the code from Fig. 2 that downloads files in parallel, and manages its network connections via threads. (Note that the synchronization in the DownloadThread method run() makes calls to the DownloadManager instance atomic.) We show how our algorithm infers the annotations during an execution of the program.

BAIT observes program execution as a sequence of concurrency-related events. One such sequence is partially displayed in Fig. 4. BAIT infers data-centric synchronization annotations based on the two following intuitions:

1. the fields of an object that a thread accesses together, without interleaving, likely belong to the same atomic set; and
2. groups of objects that a thread accesses together are likely to be connected by aliases.

In the partial execution shown in Fig. 4, one of the downloading threads invokes getNextURL() to request a new URL to download from the shared manager. After ensuring that the list of pending URLs contains an entry, the manager picks and removes the first entry. The manager then announces the start of the download in the program's user interface and finally returns the value to the thread.

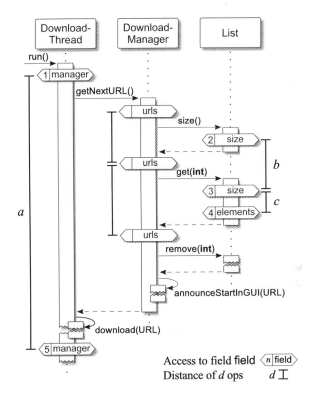

Fig. 4. Sample execution of the program from Fig. 2 used to demonstrate the basic ideas of the algorithm.

3.1   Inference of Atomic Sets

BAIT assumes that the methods of a program perform semantically meaningful operations and that the trace during an execution (mostly) represents the intended behavior of the program—for example, such a trace may be generated by running an existing integration test.

Given these assumptions, the fields of an object accessed atomically by a method in close succession are likely connected by some invariant. The set of fields that a method accesses atomically is consequently a *candidate atomic set*; the method itself is a *candidate unit of work* for this atomic set. For example, the get(**int**) method reads the fields size and elements in the same list object. In the sample execution of Fig. 4, the reads (accesses 3 and 4) happen close together and without interleaving. Thus, we have evidence that the class List should contain an atomic set with these two fields. Method get(**int**) is the *context* of the field accesses and thus a unit of work for this potential atomic set.

However, field accesses within a method may be far apart. For example, the two accesses to the thread object's manager field in the run() method of DownloadThread (1 and 5) are separated by a method call with many operations. Observing a large *distance* like a between two field accesses diminishes the likeliness of an invariant between the fields. Such an observation hence counts as evidence *against* an atomic set containing the fields. The same is true for interleaved accesses to fields by multiple threads.

The central idea of the algorithm is to use this evidence for and against atomic sets in Bayesian inference. Collecting evidence, BAIT updates its *belief* that fields belong to the same atomic set. If the belief is high enough at the end of the execution—intuitively, there was stronger evidence for an atomic set than against it—BAIT outputs corresponding **@Atomic** annotations.

3.2 Inference of Aliases

Since high-level semantic operations often employ low-level operations, field accesses may belong to different contexts. In Fig. 4, access 2 happens within the size() method, while access 3 happens within the get(**int**) method of List. Increasing the distance between the accesses ($b > c$) suffices to adjust the atomic set evidence in this case. However, the context that contains both accesses is no longer obvious.

The algorithm uses the lowest common ancestor in the call tree as the context for field accesses belonging to different methods. For accesses 2 and 3, e.g., this is the getNextURL() method. Intuitively, we observe a pair of nearby atomic accesses to urls.size within that context. Besides being evidence for an atomic set containing field size, this suggests that getNextURL() is a unit of work for this atomic set. Because the method accesses size via the field urls, there should be an alias from the atomic set containing urls to the one containing size.

However, aliases can remove all concurrency from the program when they include objects shared between threads. In Fig. 5, two download threads share a manager. Each thread's run() method is context for two nearby atomic accesses to the field urls in the manager object (accesses 6, 7 and 8, 9). Performing inference as above, this suggests an alias that merges the atomic set in class DownloadThread containing the manager field with the atomic set in DownloadManager containing the urls field. The alias would make the run() method a unit of work for the manager's atomic set that contains the urls field. As a consequence, the execution of the run() methods must be sequentialized, which would mean that only one of the two threads can be active at all, reducing performance.

BAIT mitigates the sequentialization problem by tracking which objects threads access together and weakening the belief in aliases across the boundaries of such object clusters. In our example, both threads access themselves, the manager, and the list object. Thus, the heuristic detects three clusters of objects: two that are accessed by a single thread (the thread objects themselves), and one that is accessed by both threads (the manager and the list object). Maintaining the boundaries between these clusters, the heuristic prevents aliases from manager to manager.urls, but it allows an alias from urls to urls.size.

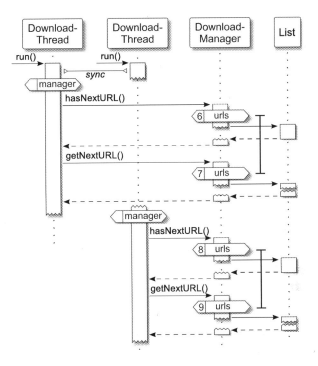

Fig. 5. Sample execution of the program in Fig. 2 that highlights a challenge in alias inference.

4   Algorithm

In this section, we describe BAIT in detail, building upon the ideas introduced in Sect. 3.

4.1   Field Access Observations

During the execution of a workload, the algorithm records *get* and *put* operations on the fields of each object. These observations are captured in the scope of a method call for a thread. From two consecutive observations for the *same* object, BAIT generates a *field access event* e, which is a tuple

$$(f, g, d, a) \in \mathrm{Fd} \times \mathrm{Fd} \times \mathbb{N} \times \mathrm{At}.$$

Here, Fd denotes the set of all fields in the program; f is the first field accessed, g is the second field. The distance d between the two accesses is the number of basic operations executed by the thread, such as Java byte code instructions. The entry $a \in \mathrm{At} = \{\text{atomic, interleaved}\}$ signals whether access to both f and g was atomic or access to g was interleaved with some other thread. To detect such interleaved accesses, BAIT relies on a separate race detection algorithm such as FastTrack [21], which is used in the implementation described in Sect. 5.

4.2 Bayesian Detection of Semantic Invariants

Using the generated field access events, the algorithm aims to determine whether there are invariants that hold between pairs of fields. Consider two fields f and g accessed in method m of a thread when executing a program on some workload. Suppose the workload generates the events $e_1, \ldots, e_n$, all related to f and g. Write H for the hypothesis that there exists a semantic invariant connecting f and g in the method, and $\neg H$ for the negated hypothesis that there is no such invariant.

Our goal is to find out to what degree the *evidence*, in the form of $e_1, \ldots, e_n$, supports the conclusion that H holds. In the Bayesian probabilistic reasoning framework [44], this degree of support is formalized as the conditional probability of H given $e_1, \ldots, e_n$, which through Bayes's formula can be written as

$$P(H|e_1, \ldots, e_n) = \frac{P(e_1, \ldots, e_n|H) \cdot P(H)}{P(e_1, \ldots, e_n)}. \tag{1}$$

Unfortunately, the right-hand side is difficult to estimate because it would require guessing the absolute probability that the events $e_1, \ldots, e_n$ occur in a program. For estimation, it is more convenient to use relative values such as the so-called odds and likelihood ratios. Intuitively, the likelihood ratio expresses how many times more likely an event is when the hypothesis is true versus when the hypothesis is false. Thus, we divide the left-hand side of Eq. 1 with its complementary form, yielding

$$\frac{P(H|e_1, \ldots, e_n)}{P(\neg H|e_1, \ldots, e_n)} = \frac{P(e_1, \ldots, e_n|H)}{P(e_1, \ldots, e_n|\neg H)} \cdot \frac{P(H)}{P(\neg H)}.$$

What the equation says is that our revised belief in H, when presented with $e_1, \ldots, e_n$, is equal to the ratio of the chances of observing $e_1, \ldots, e_n$ under H and $\neg H$, times our initial belief in H. We call the revised belief *posterior odds*, the ratio of the chances of making observations the *likelihood ratio*, and our initial belief the *prior odds*. More compactly, then, we write the equation as

$$O(H|e_1, \ldots, e_n) = L(e_1, \ldots, e_n|H) \cdot O(H). \tag{2}$$

These quantities are easier to estimate than probabilities, yet must be recomputed from scratch every time new evidence is added. However, if $e_1, \ldots, e_n$ are *conditionally independent* given H, an assumption discussed in Sect. 4.3, we have

$$P(e_1, \ldots, e_n|H) = \prod_{k=1}^{n} P(e_k|H),$$

and similarly for $\neg H$, which together with Eq. 2 gives

$$O(H|e_1, \ldots, e_n) = O(H) \cdot \prod_{k=1}^{n} L(e_k|H).$$

This equation suggests that recursive, on-the-fly computation of odds is possible, as becomes clear when adding one more piece of evidence e_{n+1}, yielding

$$O(H|e_1,\ldots,e_n,e_{n+1}) = L(e_{n+1}|H) \cdot O(H|e_1,\ldots,e_n).$$

We set $O(H) = 1$, that is, we assume that H and $\neg H$ are initially equally likely. We have thus reduced the problem of obtaining the degree of support for H to computing $L(e|H)$, given the data from e.

4.3   Conditional Independence of Events

Conditional independence means that knowledge of H, or $\neg H$, makes evidence up to that point irrelevant with respect to future evidence. Equivalently, under conditional independence, the hypothesis influences the evidence directly, without systematic interference from external factors. However, in a run of the algorithm directly on the JVM, the evidence produced can clearly be skewed through systematic influence from the chosen workload and the scheduler. While a workload is simple to revise, controlling thread schedules is difficult for programs running on the JVM. JPF provides a virtual machine implemented on top of the regular JVM that enables full control over nondeterminism such as scheduling points. Hence, running the algorithm on JPF with random scheduling can rule out influence by the scheduler.

Another way to address this problem is to refine the (coarse-grained) hypothesis space that either H or $\neg H$ holds into multi-valued variables [44]. This leads to a considerably more complicated mapping of evidence to likelihoods ratios. Instead of taking this route, we argue that the influence of external factors can be minimized by running BAIT on workloads with sufficient code coverage for long enough to exhibit all critical interleavings, using JPF where feasible.

Although BAIT can falsely conclude that two fields are related by an invariant (and thus include them in an atomic set or add an alias) when they are not, the resulting behavior is still safe. However, performance may suffer because of such an error, due to increased overhead from synchronization and reduction of concurrency.

4.4   Estimation of Likelihood Ratios

Suppose the field access event e reports we have a distance d between atomic accesses of f and g. Intuitively, the likelihood ratio $L(e|H)$ we assign based on e should have the following properties:

1. As d decreases, $L(e|H)$ must increase, but only up to some point, after which it becomes a flat maximum value; even if atomic accesses of f and g happen in close proximity, it is not conclusive that H holds.
2. As d increases, $L(e|H)$ must decrease, but only to some minimum value greater than zero; one observation should not make it impossible to conclude that H holds.

BAIT therefore uses a *logistic function* $\ell(d)$, as shown in Fig. 6, to map field access events to likelihood ratios. For example, accesses 2, 3, and 4 in Fig. 4 occur in close succession. We interpret this as evidence that it is more likely than not that an invariant connects the fields size and elements. Hence, we assign the distances b and c, with $b > c$, likelihood ratios $\ell(c) > \ell(b) > 1$. In contrast, the large distance a diminishes our belief that an invariant connects the two accesses to the manager field. Thus, we set $1 > \ell(a) > 0$. We leave the exact parameters of the logistic curve—its steepness and minimum and maximum likelihood ratios— to be determined during an implementation of the algorithm.

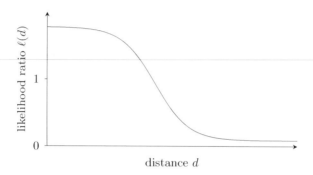

Fig. 6. Logistic curve for mapping atomic-access distances to likelihood ratios.

However, distance is not the only criterion for estimating the likelihood ratio. Suppose that e reports interleaved access. We then disregard the distance and set $L(e|H)$ to a real number p ("penalty") close to zero. This reflects that, intuitively, our belief in an invariant goes down significantly after witnessing interleaving, while not making it impossible to infer the invariant's existence later on, through overwhelming atomic access. BAIT is thus robust against sporadic errors like very rare data races. We again leave the precise value of p to an implementation.

In summary, given a field access event $e = (f, g, d, a)$, we define the estimated likelihood ratio for e as

$$\ell(d, a) = \begin{cases} \ell(d) & \text{if } a = \text{atomic;} \\ p & \text{if } a = \text{interleaved.} \end{cases}$$

4.5   Belief Configurations

We can now define how BAIT stores odds of invariants and uses likelihood ratios to update these odds in the course of workload execution.

Odds are stored in *affinity matrices*. An affinity matrix A is a symmetric map from pairs of fields (f, g) to real numbers. Symmetric means that the value assigned to (f, g) equals the one assigned to (g, f). Setting x as the value of (f, g), written $A[(f, g) \mapsto x]$, maintains the symmetry: after the update, it is $A(g, f) = x$.

Belief configurations describe the algorithm's state. A belief configuration B contains an affinity matrix A_m for every method m. Recall that an access event for a thread t in method m is a tuple consisting of two fields $f, g \in \text{Fd}$, a distance $d \in \mathbb{N}$, and an atomicity indicator $a \in \text{At}$. The transition function for belief configurations

$$\delta_{t,m} : \text{Config} \times \text{Fd} \times \text{Fd} \times \mathbb{N} \times \text{At} \rightarrow \text{Config}$$

is now defined as $\delta_{t,m}\big(B, (f, g, d, a)\big) = B[m \mapsto A'_m]$ with

$$A'_m = A_m\big[(f, g) \mapsto \ell(d, a) \cdot A_m(f, g)\big]. \tag{3}$$

For all methods m, define an initial affinity matrix A_m^{init} such that $A_m^{\text{init}}(f, g) = 1$ for all $(f, g) \in \text{Fd} \times \text{Fd}$ and an initial belief configuration B^{init} with $B^{\text{init}}(m) = A_m^{\text{init}}$. Then, if the events $e_1, \ldots, e_n$ are generated in t for m, the algorithm computes the final belief configuration

$$\delta_{t,m}(\cdots \delta_{t,m}(B^{\text{init}}, e_1) \cdots, e_n).$$

4.6   Inference of Aliases and Unitfors

Inference of aliases and unitfors is done at the same time as inference of atomic sets, and in a similar way, but with several important differences.

Suppose we observe an atomic access of the field g after an access of f in the method m. Within m, the object that contains f and g may be known by a source code identifier, that is, by a field or parameter name n. For example, in Fig. 4, the field access event generated for the accesses 2 and 3 occurs in method getNextURL(). Within that method, the list object that contains the accessed size field is known by the field name url. Hence the method observes the accesses in the context of this name, as urls.size; and more generally, m observes the accesses of f and g as $n.f$ and $n.g$.

Such an observation indicates that m performs multiple operations on another object (the list in our example). As before, if the distance d between the accesses $n.f$ and $n.g$ is small, then these operations likely maintain an invariant. Therefore, they should be atomic, which means that an atomic set containing n should be extended—by an alias—to also contain $n.f$ and $n.g$. Translated to our example, the close accesses to urls.size count as evidence for an alias that merges the manager object's atomic set containing urls with the list object's atomic set containing size.

In summary, to infer aliases and units of work, we associate with each identifier n an affinity matrix A_n, and update this matrix with the likelihood ratio $\ell(d)$, penalizing interleaved accesses as for atomic sets above. Then, most straightforwardly, if $A_n(f, g) > 1$ for A_n in the final configuration, this suggests an alias from the inferred atomic set of n—should n be a field name—to the inferred atomic set of f and g. Should n be a parameter of m, then this suggests declaring m a unit of work for the atomic set of f and g in n.

Preventing Global Locks. Without further adjustments, inferring aliases this way can lead to undesirable global locks, as shown in Fig. 5: if an alias merges an atomic set in a thread object with an atomic set S in an object shared between threads, then the thread's methods become units of work for S. Consequently, only one thread object can execute at a time, making (this part of) the program sequential.

We apply the following heuristic to detect this situation and lower the respective alias beliefs. Whenever a thread t accesses a field in object o, we record t as the owner of o. Using this data, we maintain an *alias factor* α for objects. Consider the situation in Fig. 5, just after the left thread t_l's call to `getNextURL()` has returned. At this point, t_l owns itself, the manager object, and the list object. When the right thread t_r accesses its local `manager` field just after that, BAIT detects that t_r owns the object that contains the accessed `manager` field (itself), but another thread owns the object that is the field's *value* (t_l owns the manager object). Therefore, the thread object t_r and the manager object appear to belong to two different clusters in the object graph upon which different threads operate concurrently. Merging these clusters with an alias would remove the concurrency. Therefore, we set a fixed alias factor α in the range $(0, 1)$ for the manager object (the field's value). Otherwise, if t_r was the owner of itself *and* the manager object, we set α based on the recorded (same-thread) distance between the accesses, which can result both in lowering or raising belief in an alias.

Given an atomic field access event, we use the computed alias factor α for the field-containing object as weight when updating an alias affinity matrix. Adapting Eq. 3, the updated affinity matrix A'_n for the name n of o is thus computed as

$$A'_n = A_n\big[(f, g) \mapsto \alpha \cdot \ell(d, a) \cdot A_n(f, g)\big].$$

In the example shown in Fig. 5, the alias factor $\alpha < 1$ for the manager object prevents the small distance between the observed accesses of `manager.urls` ($6, 7$ and $8, 9$) in the `run()` methods from increasing the odds of the problematic alias from `DownloadThread.manager` to `DownloadManager.urls`.

A slight modification of the heuristic is necessary to account for clusters consisting of more than two objects. In its current form, the heuristic detects a different owner thread for the first accessed object o of a cluster, and the same owner for the second object v, say, accessed via field f in o. However, the access of f establishes the current thread as the owner of o. Thus, when accessing a third object w via the field g in o, the heuristic would detect different owners again, discouraging an alias even though the previous thread operated on o, v, and w. BAIT solves this problem by not only recording the current owning thread t_o for each object, but also the previous (distinct) owning thread t'_o. Different clusters are detected only if $t_o \neq t_v$ and $t'_o \neq t_v$. Thus, for the access of w we have $t'_o = t_w$ and correctly associate w with o and v.

4.7   Atomic Set, Alias and Unitfor Formation

After the workload of the program has finished executing, all atomic set field affinity matrices are merged into a single matrix. From this combined matrix, the atomic sets are extracted by using the matrix values as edge-weights on the fully-connected graph of all fields (node set Fd), removing the edges with weight less than a threshold (e.g., 1), and grouping the fields in the remaining connected components by their declaring class (accounting for inheritance). The atomic sets are added as annotations to the class hierarchy, which forms the basis for computing aliases using the alias affinity matrices. Finally, unitfors are inferred using the class hierarchy and the alias affinity matrices.

5   Implementation Concerns

Most directly, BAIT can be implemented for Java programs using instrumentation at the byte code level. In an initial phase, the instrumented byte code is executed, allowing the BAIT implementation to record field accesses and build and update the affinity matrices. In the next phase, the BAIT implementation can use the final affinity matrices to infer and output the annotations, or even fully annotated code.

While the algorithm mandates logistic functions for mapping distances to likelihood ratios for atomic sets and aliases, an implementation may settle for an approximation of such a function, e.g., a coarse-grained piecewise approximation. Minor extensions of the algorithm may be necessary to handle realistic Java programs, which may contain arrays, synchronized blocks, and wait–notify synchronization. Earlier work may be prove pertinent for such extensions [16]. Additional optimizations are possible, such as removal of non-aliased `final` fields from atomic sets. While the algorithm requires tracking all names that a field-owning object can have, an implementation may choose to only track the last known name at runtime. We believe this would give a reasonable tradeoff between overhead and correctness. Another implementation option besides instrumentation is to implement the dynamic analysis inside a special-purpose JVM such as Java PathFinder [42].

Finally, any implementation will have to make choices regarding several parameters that can affect the inferred annotations, most prominently the parameters that define (piecewise approximations of)) logistic functions for atomic set and alias likelihoods. Such parameters may be calibrated, e.g., on simple test cases.

6   Related Work

The automatic inference of a program's concurrency semantics has been treated in the context of data race detection. There, the concurrency semantics is used to warn about violations of the likely *intended* atomicity semantics of variables.

A dynamic approach that learns the atomicity intentions for shared variables from execution traces is the *AVIO* system of Lu et al. [37,38]. In contrast, Artho et al. [4] introduce the notion of high-level data races and explicitly design their dynamic algorithm to consider races on sets of semantically related variables. The *AssetFuzzer* algorithm of Lai et al. [28] uses partial order relaxation to detect potential, but unmanifested, violations in the execution trace. All of these methods are similar to our algorithm in that they work without user annotations. The *Atomizer* system of Flanagan and Freund [20] additionally considers *windows of vulnerability*, but requires a few source code annotations and potentially raises false alarms. The *MUVI* tool of Lu et al. [35] follows a static approach to inferring atomicity intentions at the variable level.

The static heuristic [24,46] of defining one atomic set per class that contains all non-static fields has also been proposed in the context of race detection. Targeting race detection, none of the aforementioned approaches considers aliasing information, which is essential for our use case. Huang and Milanova's static inference system for the AJ types defined by Dolby et al. [17] significantly reduces the number of annotations that a developer has to write [27]. While simplifying the use of AJ, it needs a set of foundational annotations. Hence, their and our methods complement each other: the static inference rules propagate the base annotations inferred by our analysis, yielding a complete set of annotations. Liu et al. [34] present a technique for statically inferring atomic sets based on program dependence analysis. The inferred sets are then used for finding atomic composition bugs dynamically in programs. This is a different focus compared to our algorithm, whose main aim is to provide annotations for documentation and safe execution. In addition, our algorithm also infers aliases, which are arguably harder to infer than atomic sets, least of all statically.

Dinges et al. [15,16] present a dynamic inference algorithm of data-centric concurrency annotations as described by Vaziri et al. [17]. The algorithm is based on classification of fields into atomic sets using simple set membership criteria rather than careful weighing of evidence as in BAIT. Additionally, unlike BAIT, the algorithm does not scale to long executions with many field accesses, and does not improve results as more evidence becomes available; in some cases, results may even become significantly worse after observing more field accesses, since previous conclusions are replaced.

Flanagan et al. [22] present a sound and complete dynamic atomicity checker for Java programs. The tool, Velodrome, takes a workload and list of methods that are assumed to be atomic as input, and outputs a list of atomicity violations. Biswas et al. [7] improve on the significant overhead introduced by Velodrome in their DoubleChecker tool, while maintaining soundness and completeness. A tentative list of atomic methods can be derived from the annotations produced by an implementation of BAIT by enumerating all methods that are units of work for some atomic set.

Atomic sets take a declarative approach to synchronization. *Synchronizers* [14,23] provide a similar notion in the context of actor systems, where they constrain the message dispatch in a group of actors. The available constraints differ from atomic sets in that synchronizers can provide *temporal* atomicity— messages arrive at the same time—not the *spatial* atomicity offered by atomic sets. Synchronizers do not support transitive extensions similar to aliases in atomic sets. Moreover, expressing the non-interleaving of message sequences, which is the actor equivalent of non-interleaved access to shared data, is more complicated. In its simplest form, such non-interleaving in messages to a single actor is expressed in terms of *local synchronization constraints* which force an ordering on messages to a given actor [26,47]. Local synchronization constraints may be used to force FIFO ordering of messages between pairs of senders or recipients, or to ensure that a two actors follow a more complex communication protocol. Synchronizers generalize this to multiple actors: by disabling a specific type of message until another has been received, synchronizers can force an ordering between messages sent to different actors. Another declarative approach to ensuring synchronization at the actor level is that of multiparty session types [10,41].

By boosting belief in the existence of an invariant after atomic access and maintaining or possibly even strengthening that belief unless witnessing interleaved access, BAIT follows the approach of *accentuating the positive* [37,48] by suppressing rarely observed Heisenbugs that violate atomicity. Non-deadlock bugs: 74 (Atomicity: 51, Order: 24, Other: 2), Deadlock bugs: 31 A study of real-world concurrency bugs [36] finds that nearly half of all errors are related to atomicity; with deadlocks ruled out, that fraction rises to nearly 70 %. While this kind of safety comes at the cost of a coarser concurrency semantics, the experiments of Weeratunge et al. [48] suggest that a low runtime overhead of 15 % can be achieved.

The problems inherent in threads and their usual synchronization primitives, such as locks and monitors, have been examined previously, e.g., by Lee [30]. Lee argues against letting programmers start with maximally nondeterministic interleaving of threads and adding just enough determinism to avoid concurrency errors. Instead, he proposes that programmers start from a deterministic model and selectively add operations for nondeterministic composition where appropriate. While the resulting executions have more coarse-grained concurrency and thus potentially worse performance, they are inherently easier to reason about due to many thread interleavings being ruled out. Lee suggests to focus on development of coordination languages rather than thread-based primitives and libraries. We believe the concurrency structure annotations we showed in this paper can be viewed as a kind of data-driven coordination language.

7   Discussion

Although the use of actor languages (e.g., through Akka [32] and Erlang [19]) has grown dramatically in recent years, threads with shared memory and control-centric primitives continue to dominate concurrent programming. Thread-based programming often obscures key properties in programs and leads programmers to introduce concurrency bugs such as atomicity violations [36]. Moreover, it is hard to scale the thread-based model–one reason actors have been used to implement large-scale applications such as Facebook chat servers and Twitter.

In this paper, we highlight consistency invariants involving class fields and method parameters which may help reduce bugs in thread-based object-oriented programs. Unfortunately, we expect that programmers in general will not manually write, document, and check such invariants when writing thread-based programs. Our algorithm improves on the state of the art for inferring invariant annotations automatically, freeing programmers of some of the burden.

Consistency invariant annotations are useful in several ways besides giving programmers an understanding of atomicity requirements of data structures. For example, if a class contains several atomic sets of fields, and each method accesses fields from only one atomic set, this suggests decomposing the class into several classes with methods that access only the fields in the decomposed class. While such lower-level concerns are important, we can also ask high-level questions, such as whether concurrent programs can avoid dealing with threads (partially or entirely).

As discussed earlier, the actor model avoids explicit locks by introducing a unit of computation, an *actor*, that has its own state, an independent single locus of control, and communicates with others via asynchronous message passing [3]. The actor-oriented programming approach of Lee [29,31] drops the requirement for independent control and asynchrony in message passing. In particular, Lee emphasizes the difference between object-orientation and actors as one that pertains to whether communication implies *transfer of control* from the sender to the receiver. In semantic terms, Lee's notion of actor-oriented programming incorporates programming abstractions that may be built using meta-actors which can used to customize naming and scheduling [6,18]. Clavel et al. [11] give a formal semantics to reason about such systems.

According to the hierarchy of platforms presented by Lee [29], actor-oriented models are above object-oriented programs, with the latter being closer to low-level concepts such as executables and silicon chips. From this perspective, an implementation of the algorithm we presented and our suggested actor program transformations can assist in raising the abstraction level of programs, making them amenable to conversion to concurrent programs following actor-oriented design techniques. Further exploration of such techniques will be needed to improve legacy concurrent codes, facilitating their dependability and maintainability.

Acknowledgements. The authors thank Peter Dinges, Farah Hariri, and Darko Marinov. This work is supported in part by the National Science Foundation under grants NSF CCF 14-38982 and NSF CCF 16-17401, and by AFOSR/AFRL Air Force Research Laboratory and the Air Force Office of Scientific Research under agreement FA8750-11-2-0084 for the Assured Cloud Computing at the University of Illinois at Urbana-Champaign.

References

1. Agha, G.: Concurrent object-oriented programming. Commun. ACM **33**(9), 125–141 (1990)
2. Agha, G., Mason, I.A., Smith, S.F., Talcott, C.L.: A foundation for actor computation. J. Funct. Program. **7**(1), 1–72 (1997)
3. Agha, G.A.: ACTORS - A Model of Concurrent Computation in Distributed Systems. MIT Press Series in Artificial Intelligence. MIT Press, Cambridge (1986)

4. Artho, C., Havelund, K., Biere, A.: High-level data races. In: NDDL 2003, pp. 82–93. ICEIS Press (2003)
5. Artzi, S., Quinonez, J., Kieżun, A., Ernst, M.D.: Parameter reference immutability: formal definition, inference tool, and comparison. Autom. Softw. Eng. **16**(1), 145–192 (2009)
6. Astley, M., Sturman, D.C., Agha, G.: Customizable middleware for modular distributed software. Commun. ACM **44**(5), 99–107 (2001)
7. Biswas, S., Huang, J., Sengupta, A., Bond, M.D.: Doublechecker: efficient sound and precise atomicity checking. In: PLDI 2014. ACM (2014)
8. Boyapati, C., Lee, R., Rinard, M.C.: Ownership types for safe programming: preventing data races and deadlocks. In: OOPSLA 2002, pp. 211–230. ACM (2002)
9. Burrows, M., Leino, K.R.M.: Finding stale-value errors in concurrent programs. Concurr. Pract. Exp. **16**(12), 1161–1172 (2004)
10. Charalambides, M., Dinges, P., Agha, G.A.: Parameterized, concurrent session types for asynchronous multi-actor interactions. Sci. Comput. Program. **115–116**, 100–126 (2016)
11. Clavel, M., et al.: Reflection, metalevel computation, and strategies. In: Clavel, M., et al. (eds.) All About Maude - A High-Performance Logical Framework. LNCS, vol. 4350, pp. 419–458. Springer, Heidelberg (2007). https://doi.org/10.1007/978-3-540-71999-1_14
12. Clebsch, S., Drossopoulou, S., Blessing, S., McNeil, A.: Deny capabilities for safe, fast actors. In: Proceedings of the 5th International Workshop on Programming Based on Actors, Agents, and Decentralized Control, AGERE! 2015, pp. 1–12. ACM, New York (2015)
13. Cok, D.R.: OpenJML: JML for Java 7 by extending OpenJDK. In: Bobaru, M., Havelund, K., Holzmann, G.J., Joshi, R. (eds.) NFM 2011. LNCS, vol. 6617, pp. 472–479. Springer, Heidelberg (2011). https://doi.org/10.1007/978-3-642-20398-5_35
14. Dinges, P., Agha, G.: Scoped synchronization constraints for large scale actor systems. In: Sirjani, M. (ed.) COORDINATION 2012. LNCS, vol. 7274, pp. 89–103. Springer, Heidelberg (2012). https://doi.org/10.1007/978-3-642-30829-1_7
15. Dinges, P., Charalambides, M., Agha, G.: Automated inference of atomic sets for safe concurrent execution. In: Proceedings of the 11th ACM SIGPLAN-SIGSOFT Workshop on Program Analysis for Software Tools and Engineering, PASTE 2013, pp. 1–8. ACM, New York (2013)
16. Dinges, P., Charalambides, M., Agha, G.: Automated inference of atomic sets for safe concurrent execution. Technical report, UIUC, April 2013. http://hdl.handle.net/2142/43357
17. Dolby, J., Hammer, C., Marino, D., Tip, F., Vaziri, M., Vitek, J.: A data-centric approach to synchronization. ACM TOPLAS **34**(1), 4 (2012)
18. Donkervoet, B., Agha, G.: Reflecting on aspect-oriented programming, metaprogramming, and adaptive distributed monitoring. In: de Boer, F.S., Bonsangue, M.M., Graf, S., de Roever, W.-P. (eds.) FMCO 2006. LNCS, vol. 4709, pp. 246–265. Springer, Heidelberg (2007). https://doi.org/10.1007/978-3-540-74792-5_11
19. Erlang programming language. https://www.erlang.org
20. Flanagan, C., Freund, S.N.: Atomizer: a dynamic atomicity checker for multithreaded programs. Sci. Comput. Program. **71**(2), 89–109 (2008)
21. Flanagan, C., Freund, S.N.: FastTrack: efficient and precise dynamic race detection. In: Proceedings of the 2009 ACM SIGPLAN Conference on Programming Language Design and Implementation, PLDI 2009, pp. 121–133. ACM, New York (2009)

22. Flanagan, C., Freund, S.N., Yi, J.: Velodrome: a sound and complete dynamic atomicity checker for multithreaded programs. In: Proceedings of the 2008 ACM SIGPLAN Conference on Programming Language Design and Implementation, PLDI 2008, pp. 293–303. ACM, New York (2008)

23. Frølund, S., Agha, G.: A language framework for multi-object coordination. In: Nierstrasz, O.M. (ed.) ECOOP 1993. LNCS, vol. 707, pp. 346–360. Springer, Heidelberg (1993). https://doi.org/10.1007/3-540-47910-4_18

24. Hammer, C., Dolby, J., Vaziri, M., Tip, F.: Dynamic detection of atomic-set-serializability violations. In: ICSE 2008, pp. 231–240. ACM (2008)

25. Hewitt, C., Bishop, P.B., Steiger, R.: A universal modular ACTOR formalism for artificial intelligence. In: Nilsson, N.J. (ed.) Proceedings of the 3rd International Joint Conference on Artificial Intelligence, Standford, CA, USA, 20–23 August 1973, pp. 235–245. William Kaufmann (1973)

26. Houck, C.R., Agha, G.: HAL: a high-level actor language and its distributed implementation. In: Shin, K.G. (ed.) Proceedings of the 1992 International Conference on Parallel Processing, University of Michigan, An Arbor, Michigan, USA, 17–21 August 1992, Volume II: Software, pp. 158–165. CRC Press (1992)

27. Huang, W., Milanova, A.: Inferring AJ types for concurrent libraries. In: FOOL 2012, pp. 82–88 (2012)

28. Lai, Z., Cheung, S.C., Chan, W.K.: Detecting atomic-set serializability violations in multithreaded programs through active randomized testing. In: ICSE 2010, pp. 235–244. ACM (2010)

29. Lee, E.A.: Model-driven development-from object-oriented design to actor-oriented design. In: Workshop on Software Engineering for Embedded Systems: From Requirements to Implementation (a.k.a. The Monterey Workshop) (2003)

30. Lee, E.A.: The problem with threads. Computer 39(5), 33–42 (2006)

31. Lee, E.A., Liu, X., Neuendorffer, S.: Classes and inheritance in actor-oriented design. ACM Trans. Embed. Comput. Syst. 8(4), 29:1–29:26 (2009)

32. Lightbend: Akka. https://akka.io

33. Lightbend: Akka and the Java memory model. https://doc.akka.io/docs/akka/current/general/jmm.html

34. Liu, P., Dolby, J., Zhang, C.: Finding incorrect compositions of atomicity. In: Proceedings of the 2013 9th Joint Meeting on Foundations of Software Engineering, ESEC/FSE 2013, pp. 158–168. ACM, New York (2013)

35. Lu, S., Park, S., Hu, C., Ma, X., Jiang, W., Li, Z., Popa, R.A., Zhou, Y.: MUVI: automatically inferring multi-variable access correlations and detecting related semantic and concurrency bugs. In: SOSP 2007, pp. 103–116. ACM (2007)

36. Lu, S., Park, S., Seo, E., Zhou, Y.: Learning from mistakes: a comprehensive study on real world concurrency bug characteristics. In: ASPLOS 2008, pp. 329–339. ACM (2008)

37. Lu, S., Park, S., Zhou, Y.: Detecting concurrency bugs from the perspectives of synchronization intentions. IEEE Trans. Parallel Distrib. Syst. 23(6), 1060–1072 (2012)

38. Lu, S., Tucek, J., Qin, F., Zhou, Y.: AVIO: detecting atomicity violations via access-interleaving invariants. IEEE Micro 27(1), 26–35 (2007)

39. Milanova, A., Dong, Y.: Inference and checking of object immutability. In: Proceedings of the 13th International Conference on Principles and Practices of Programming on the Java Platform: Virtual Machines, Languages, and Tools, PPPJ 2016, pp. 6:1–6:12. ACM, New York (2016)

40. Negara, S., Karmani, R.K., Agha, G.A.: Inferring ownership transfer for efficient message passing. In: Cascaval, C., Yew, P. (eds.) Proceedings of the 16th ACM SIG-PLAN Symposium on Principles and Practice of Parallel Programming, PPOPP 2011, San Antonio, TX, USA, 12–16 February 2011, pp. 81–90. ACM (2011)
41. Neykova, R., Yoshida, N.: Multiparty session actors. In: Kühn, E., Pugliese, R. (eds.) COORDINATION 2014. LNCS, vol. 8459, pp. 131–146. Springer, Heidelberg (2014). https://doi.org/10.1007/978-3-662-43376-8_9
42. Palmskog, K., Hariri, F., Marinov, D.: A case study on executing instrumented code in Java PathFinder. In: Proceedings of JPF Workshop, JPF 2015 (2015)
43. Papi, M.M., Ernst, M.D.: Compile-time type-checking for custom type qualifiers in Java. In: Companion to the 22nd ACM SIGPLAN Conference on Object-Oriented Programming Systems and Applications Companion, OOPSLA 2007, pp. 809–810. ACM, New York (2007)
44. Pearl, J.: Probabilistic Reasoning in Intelligent Systems: Networks of Plausible Inference. Morgan Kaufmann Publishers Inc., San Francisco (1988)
45. Srinivasan, S., Mycroft, A.: Kilim: isolation-typed actors for Java. In: Vitek, J. (ed.) ECOOP 2008. LNCS, vol. 5142, pp. 104–128. Springer, Heidelberg (2008). https://doi.org/10.1007/978-3-540-70592-5_6
46. Sumner, W.N., Hammer, C., Dolby, J.: Marathon: detecting atomic-set serializability violations with conflict graphs. In: Khurshid, S., Sen, K. (eds.) RV 2011. LNCS, vol. 7186, pp. 161–176. Springer, Heidelberg (2012). https://doi.org/10.1007/978-3-642-29860-8_13
47. Tomlinson, C., Kim, W., Scheevel, M., Singh, V., Will, B., Agha, G.: Rosette: an object-oriented concurrent systems architecture. SIGPLAN Not. **24**(4), 91–93 (1989)
48. Weeratunge, D., Zhang, X., Jagannathan, S.: Accentuating the positive: atomicity inference and enforcement using correct executions. In: OOPSLA 2011, pp. 19–34. ACM (2011)

Interfaces for Stream Processing Systems

Rajeev Alur$^{(\boxtimes)}$, Konstantinos Mamouras, Caleb Stanford, and Val Tannen

University of Pennsylvania, Philadelphia, PA, USA
{alur,mamouras,castan,val}@cis.upenn.edu

Abstract. Efficient processing of input data streams is central to IoT systems, and the goal of this paper is to develop a logical foundation for specifying the computation of such stream processing. In the proposed model, both the input and output of a stream processing system consists of tagged data items with a dependency relation over tags that captures the logical ordering constraints over data items. While a system processes the input data one item at a time, incrementally producing output data items, its semantics is a function from input data traces to output data traces, where a data trace is an equivalence class of sequences of data items induced by the dependency relation. This data-trace transduction model generalizes both acyclic Kahn process networks and relational query processors, and can specify computations over data streams with a rich variety of ordering and synchronization characteristics. To form complex systems from simpler ones, we define sequential composition and parallel composition operations over data-trace transductions, and show how to define commonly used idioms in stream processing such as sliding windows, key-based partitioning, and map-reduce.

1 Introduction

The last few years have witnessed an explosion of IoT systems in a diverse range of applications such as smart buildings, wearable devices, and healthcare. A key component of an effective IoT system is the ability to continuously process incoming data streams and make decisions in response in a timely manner. Systems such as Apache Storm (see `storm.apache.org`) and Twitter Heron [12] provide the necessary infrastructure to implement distributed stream processing systems with the focus mainly on high performance and fault tolerance. What's less developed though is the support for high-level programming abstractions for such systems so that *correctness with respect to formal requirements* and *predictable performance* can be assured at design time. The goal of this paper is to provide a logical foundation for modeling distributed stream processing systems.

An essential step towards developing the desired formal computational model for stream processing systems is to understand the *interface*, that is, the types of input, the types of output, and the logical computations such systems perform. (See [3] for the role of interfaces in system design.) As a starting point, we can view the input to be a sequence of data items that the system consumes one item at a time in a streaming fashion. Assuming a strict linear order over input

© Springer International Publishing AG, part of Springer Nature 2018
M. Lohstroh et al. (Eds.): Lee Festschrift, LNCS 10760, pp. 38–60, 2018.
https://doi.org/10.1007/978-3-319-95246-8_3

items is however not the ideal abstraction for two reasons. First, in an actual implementation, the input data items may arrive at multiple physical locations and there may be no meaningful logical way to impose an ordering among items arriving at different locations. Second, for the computation to be performed on the input data items, it may suffice to view the data as a *relation*, that is, a *bag* of items without any ordering. Such lack of ordering also has computational benefits since it can be exploited for parallelization of the implementation. *Partially ordered multisets* (pomsets), a structure studied extensively in concurrency theory [20], generalize both sequences and bags, and thus, assuming the input of a stream processing system to be a pomset seems general enough.

While the input logically consists of partially ordered data items, a stream processing system consumes it one item at a time, and we need a representation that is suitable for such a streaming model of computation. Inspired by the definition of *Mazurkiewicz traces* in concurrency theory [18], we model the input as a *data trace*. We assume that each data item consists of a *tag* and a value of a basic data type associated with this tag. The ordering of items is specified by a (symmetric) *dependency relation* over the set of tags. Two sequences of data items are considered equivalent if one can be obtained from the other by repeatedly commuting two adjacent items with independent tags, and a data trace is an equivalence class of such sequences. For instance, when all the tags are mutually dependent, a sequence of items represents only itself, and when all the tags are mutually independent, a sequence of items represents the bag of items it contains. A suitable choice of tags along with the associated dependency relation, allows us to model input streams with a rich variety of ordering and synchronization characteristics.

As the system processes each input item in a streaming manner, it responds by producing output data items. Even though the cumulative output items produced in a response to an input sequence is linearly ordered based on the order in which the input gets processed, we need the flexibility to view output items as only partially ordered. For instance, consider a system that implements *key-based partitioning* by mapping a linearly ordered input sequence to a *set* of linearly ordered sub-streams, one per key. To model such a system the output items corresponding to distinct keys should be unordered. For this purpose, we allow the output items to have their own tags along with a dependency relation over these tags, and a sequence of outputs produced by the system is interpreted as the corresponding data trace.

While a system processes the input in a specific order by consuming items one by one in a streaming manner, it is required to interpret the input sequence as a data trace, that is, outputs produced while processing two equivalent input sequences should be equivalent. Formally, this means that a stream processor defines a *function from input data traces to output data traces*. Such a *data-trace transduction* is the proposed interface model for distributed stream processing systems. We define this model in Sect. 2, and illustrate it using a variety of examples and relating it to existing models in literature such as Kahn process networks [11,14] and streaming extensions of database query languages [6,15].

In Sect. 3, we define two basic operations on data-trace transductions that can be used to construct complex systems from simpler ones. Given two data-trace transductions f and g, the *sequential composition* $f \gg g$ feeds the output data trace produced by f as input to g, and is defined when the output type of f coincides with the input type of g, while the *parallel composition* $f \parallel g$ executes the two in parallel, and is defined when there are no common tags in the outputs of f and g (that is, the output data items produced by the two components are independent). We illustrate how these two operations can be used to define common computing idioms in stream processing systems such as sliding windows and map reduce.

2   Data-Trace Transductions

In order to describe the behavior of a distributed stream processing system we must specify its *interface*, that is: the type of the input stream, the type of the output stream, and the input/output transformation that the system performs. This section contains formal descriptions of three key concepts: (1) *data traces* for describing finite collections of partially ordered data items, (2) *data-trace transductions* for modeling the input/output behavior of a stream processing system, and (3) *data-string transductions* for specifying the behavior of sequential implementations of such systems.

2.1   Data Traces

We use data traces to model streams in which the data items are partially ordered. Data traces generalize sequences (data items are linearly ordered), relations (data items are unordered), and independent stream channels (data items are organized as a collection of linearly ordered subsets). The concatenation operation, the prefix order, and the residuation operation on sequences can be generalized naturally to the setting of data traces.

Definition 1 (Data Type). A *data type* $A = (\Sigma, (T_\sigma)_{\sigma \in \Sigma})$ consists of a potentially infinite *tag alphabet* Σ and a value type T_σ for every tag $\sigma \in \Sigma$. The set of *elements* of type A is equal to $\{(\sigma, d) \mid \sigma \in \Sigma \text{ and } d \in T_\sigma\}$, which we will also denote by A. The set of *sequences* over A is denoted as A^*.   □

Example 2. Suppose we want to process a stream that consists of sensor measurements and special symbols that indicate the end of a one-second interval. The data type for this input stream involves the tags $\Sigma = \{M, \#\}$, where M is meant to indicate a sensor measurement and $\#$ is an end-of-second marker. The value sets for these tags are $T_M = \mathbb{N}$ (natural numbers), and $T_\# = \mathbb{U}$ is the unit type (singleton). So, the data type $A = (\Sigma, T_M, T_\#)$ contains measurements (M, d), where d is a natural number, and the end-of-second symbol $\#$.   □

Definition 3 (Dependence Relation and Induced Congruence). A *dependence relation* on a tag alphabet Σ is a symmetric binary relation on Σ. We say that the tags σ, τ are *independent* (w.r.t. a dependence relation D) if $(\sigma, \tau) \notin D$. For a data type $A = (\Sigma, (T_\sigma)_{\sigma \in \Sigma})$ and a dependence relation D on Σ, we define the dependence relation that is induced on A by D as $\{((\sigma, d), (\sigma', d')) \in A \times A \mid (\sigma, \sigma') \in D\}$, which we will also denote by D. Define $\equiv_D$ to be the smallest congruence (w.r.t. sequence concatenation) on A^* containing $\{(ab, ba) \in A^* \times A^* \mid (a, b) \notin D\}$. □

According to the definition of the relation $\equiv_D$ above, two sequences are equivalent if one can be obtained from the other by performing commutations of adjacent items with independent tags.

Example 4 (Dependence Relation). For the data type of Example 2, we consider the dependence relation $D = \{(\texttt{M}, \texttt{\#}), (\texttt{\#}, \texttt{M}), (\texttt{\#}, \texttt{\#})\}$. The dependence relation can be visualized as an undirected graph:

This means that the tag $\texttt{M}$ is independent of itself, and therefore consecutive $\texttt{M}$-tagged items are considered unordered. For example, the sequences

$$(\texttt{M}, 5)\,(\texttt{M}, 8)\,(\texttt{M}, 5)\,\texttt{\#}\,(\texttt{M}, 9) \quad (\texttt{M}, 5)\,(\texttt{M}, 5)\,(\texttt{M}, 8)\,\texttt{\#}\,(\texttt{M}, 9) \quad (\texttt{M}, 8)\,(\texttt{M}, 5)\,(\texttt{M}, 5)\,\texttt{\#}\,(\texttt{M}, 9)$$

are all equivalent w.r.t. $\equiv_D$. □

Definition 5 (Data Traces, Concatenation, Prefix Relation). A *data-trace type* is a pair $X = (A, D)$, where $A = (\Sigma, (T_\sigma)_{\sigma \in \Sigma})$ is a data type and D is a dependence relation on the tag alphabet Σ. A *data trace* of type X is a congruence class of the relation $\equiv_D$. We also write X to denote the set of data traces of type X. Since the equivalence $\equiv_D$ is a congruence w.r.t. sequence concatenation, the operation of concatenation is also well-defined on data traces: $[u] \cdot [v] = [uv]$ for sequences u and v, where $[u]$ is the congruence class of u. We define the relation $\leq$ on the data traces of X as a generalization of the prefix partial order on sequences: for data traces $\mathbf{u}$ and $\mathbf{v}$ of type X, $\mathbf{u} \leq \mathbf{v}$ iff there are sequences $u \in \mathbf{u}$ and $v \in \mathbf{v}$ such that $u \leq v$ (i.e., u is a prefix of v). □

The relation $\leq$ on data traces of a fixed type is easily checked to be a partial order. Since it generalizes the prefix order on sequences (when the congruence classes of $\equiv_D$ are singleton sets), we will call $\leq$ the *prefix order* on data traces.

Example 6 (Data Traces). Consider the data-trace type $X = (A, D)$, where A is the data type of Example 2 and D is the dependence relation of Example 4. A data trace of X can be represented as a sequence of multisets (bags) of natural numbers and visualized as a pomset. For example, the data trace that corresponds to the sequence $(\texttt{M}, 5)\,(\texttt{M}, 7)\,\texttt{\#}\,(\texttt{M}, 9)\,(\texttt{M}, 8)\,(\texttt{M}, 9)\,\texttt{\#}\,(\texttt{M}, 6)$ can be visualized as the following labeled partial order (pomset)

$$\begin{array}{c} (\mathtt{M},5) \\ (\mathtt{M},7) \end{array} \gtrless \# \lessgtr \begin{array}{c} (\mathtt{M},9) \\ (\mathtt{M},8) \\ (\mathtt{M},9) \end{array} \gtrless \# \,\text{---}\, (\mathtt{M},6)$$

where a line from left to right indicates that the item on the right must occur after the item on the left. The end-of-second markers # separate multisets of natural numbers. So, the set of data traces of X has an isomorphic representation as the set $\mathsf{Bag}(\mathbb{N})^+$ of nonempty sequences of multisets of natural numbers. In particular, the empty sequence ε is represented as $\emptyset$ and the single-element sequence # is represented as $\emptyset\,\emptyset$. □

Let us observe that a singleton tag alphabet can be used to model sequences or multisets over a basic type of values. For the data type given by $\Sigma = \{\sigma\}$ and $T_\sigma = T$ there are two possible dependence relations for Σ, namely $\emptyset$ and $\{(\sigma,\sigma)\}$. The data traces of $(\Sigma, T, \emptyset)$ are multisets over T, which we denote as $\mathsf{Bag}(T)$, and the data traces of $(\Sigma, T, \{(\sigma,\sigma)\})$ are sequences over T.

Let us consider the slightly more complicated case of a tag alphabet $\Sigma = \{\sigma,\tau\}$ consisting of two elements (together with data values sets T_σ and T_τ). The two tags can be used to describe more complex sets of data traces:

1. Dependence relation $D = \{(\sigma,\sigma),(\sigma,\tau),(\tau,\sigma),(\tau,\tau)\}$: The set of data traces is (up to a bijection) $(T_\sigma \oplus T_\tau)^*$, where $\oplus$ is the disjoint union operation.
2. $D = \{(\sigma,\sigma),(\tau,\tau)\}$: The set of data traces is $T_\sigma^* \times T_\tau^*$.
3. $D = \{(\sigma,\sigma),(\sigma,\tau),(\tau,\sigma)\}$: In a data trace the items tagged with σ separate (possibly empty) multisets of items tagged with τ. For example:

$$\sigma \,\text{---}\, \sigma \lessgtr \begin{array}{c} \tau \\ \tau \end{array} \gtrless \sigma \,\text{---}\, \sigma \lessgtr \begin{array}{c} \tau \\ \tau \\ \tau \end{array} \gtrless \sigma \,\text{---}\, \tau$$

So, the set of data traces is $\mathsf{Bag}(T_\tau) \cdot (T_\sigma \cdot \mathsf{Bag}(T_\tau))^*$, where $\cdot$ is the concatenation operation for sequences.

4. $D = \{(\sigma,\sigma)\}$: The set of data traces is $T_\sigma^* \times \mathsf{Bag}(T_\tau)$.
5. $D = \{(\sigma,\tau),(\tau,\sigma)\}$: A data trace is an alternating sequence of σ-multisets (multisets with data items tagged with σ) and τ-multisets. More formally, the set of data traces is

$$\{\varepsilon\} \cup \mathsf{Bag}_1(T_\sigma) \cdot (\mathsf{Bag}_1(T_\tau) \cdot \mathsf{Bag}_1(T_\sigma))^* \cdot \mathsf{Bag}(T_\tau)$$
$$\cup \mathsf{Bag}_1(T_\tau) \cdot (\mathsf{Bag}_1(T_\sigma) \cdot \mathsf{Bag}_1(T_\tau))^* \cdot \mathsf{Bag}(T_\sigma),$$

where $\mathsf{Bag}_1(T)$ is the set of nonempty multisets over T.
6. $D = \emptyset$: The set of data traces is $\mathsf{Bag}(T_\sigma \oplus T_\tau)$, which is isomorphic to $\mathsf{Bag}(T_\sigma) \times \mathsf{Bag}(T_\tau)$.

The cases that have been omitted are symmetric to the ones presented above.

Example 7 (Multiple Input and Output Channels). Suppose we want to model a streaming system with multiple independent input and output channels, where the items within each channel are linearly ordered but the

Fig. 1. Multiple channels I_1 and I_2, displayed on the left graphically, and on the right as the single trace type which actually defines them.

channels are completely independent. These assumptions are appropriate for distributed streaming systems, where the channels are implemented as network connections. This is the setting of (acyclic) *Kahn Process Networks* [11] and the more restricted synchronous dataflow models [14]. We introduce tags $\Sigma_I = \{I_1, \ldots, I_m\}$ for m input channels, and tags $\Sigma_O = \{O_1, \ldots, O_n\}$ for n output channels. The dependence relation for the input consists of all pairs (I_i, I_i) with $i = 1, \ldots, m$. This means that for all indexes $i \neq j$ the tags I_i and I_j are independent (Fig. 1). Similarly, the dependence relation for the output consists of all pairs (O_i, O_i) with $i = 1, \ldots, n$. Assume that the value types associated with the input tags are $T_1, \ldots, T_m$, and the value types associated with the output tags are $U_1, \ldots, U_n$. As we will show later in Proposition 10, the sets of input and output data traces are (up to a bijection) $T_1^* \times \cdots \times T_m^*$ and $U_1^* \times \cdots \times U_m^*$ respectively. □

Definition 8 (Residuals). Let u and v be sequences over a set A. If u is a prefix of v, then we define the *residual* of v by u, denoted $u^{-1}v$, to be the unique sequence w such that $v = uw$.

Let X be a data-trace type. Suppose $\mathbf{u}$ and $\mathbf{v}$ are of type X with $\mathbf{u} \leq \mathbf{v}$. Choose any representatives u and v of the traces $\mathbf{u}$ and $\mathbf{v}$ respectively such that $u \leq v$. Then, define the *residual* of $\mathbf{v}$ by $\mathbf{u}$ to be $\mathbf{u}^{-1}\mathbf{v} = [u^{-1}v]$. □

The left cancellation property of Lemma 9 below is needed for establishing that the residuation operation of Definition 8 is well-defined on traces, i.e. the trace $[u^{-1}v]$ does not depend on the choice of representatives u and v. It follows for traces $\mathbf{u}, \mathbf{v}$ with $\mathbf{u} \leq \mathbf{v}$ that $\mathbf{u}^{-1}\mathbf{v}$ is the unique trace $\mathbf{w}$ s.t. $\mathbf{v} = \mathbf{u} \cdot \mathbf{w}$.

Lemma 9 (Left and Right Cancellation). *Let $X = (A, D)$ be a data-trace type. The following properties hold for all sequences $u, u', v, v' \in A^*$:*

1. *Left cancellation: If $u \equiv_D u'$ and $uv \equiv_D u'v'$ then $v \equiv_D v'$.*
2. *Right cancellation: If $v \equiv_D v'$ and $uv \equiv_D u'v'$ then $u \equiv_D u'$.* □

Proposition 10 (Independent Ordered Channels). *Let A be the data type with tag alphabet consisting of $C_1, \ldots, C_n$, and with respective value types $T_1, \ldots, T_n$. Define the data-trace type $X = (A, D)$, where $D = \{(C_i, C_i) \mid i = 1, \ldots, n\}$ is the dependence relation. The set of data traces X is isomorphic to $Y = T_1^* \times \cdots \times T_n^*$, where the concatenation operation on the elements of Y is defined componentwise.*

Proposition 10 establishes a bijection between $Y = T_1^* \times \cdots \times T_n^*$ and a set of appropriately defined data traces X. The bijection involves the concatenation operation. This implies that the prefix order and the residuation operation can be defined on Y so that they agree with the corresponding structure on the data traces. Since $\cdot$ on Y is componentwise concatenation, the order $\leq$ on Y is the componentwise prefix order. Finally, residuals are also defined componentwise on Y. So, the expanded structures $(Y, \cdot, \leq, ^{-1})$ and $(X, \cdot, \leq, ^{-1})$ are isomorphic.

Proposition 11 (Independent Unordered Channels). *Let A be the data-trace type with tag alphabet consisting of $C_1, \ldots, C_n$, and with respective value types $T_1, \ldots, T_n$. Define the data-trace type $X = (A, D)$, where $D = \emptyset$ is the dependence relation. The set of data traces X is isomorphic to $Y = \mathsf{Bag}(T_1) \times \cdots \times \mathsf{Bag}(T_n)$, where the concatenation operation on the elements of Y is componentwise multiset union.*   □

Given the isomorphism between $Y = \mathsf{Bag}(T_1) \times \cdots \times \mathsf{Bag}(T_n)$ and the set of data traces described in Proposition 11, we define the prefix relation and residuation on Y that are induced by $\cdot$ on Y as follows: $\leq$ is defined as componentwise multiset containment, and $(P_1, \ldots, P_n)^{-1}(Q_1, \ldots, Q_n) = (Q_1 \setminus P_1, \ldots, Q_n \setminus P_n)$ where $\setminus$ is the multiset difference operation. It follows that this additional structure on Y agrees with the corresponding structure on the traces.

2.2   Data-Trace Transductions

Data-trace transductions formalize the notion of an *interface* for stream processing systems. Consider the analogy with a functional model of computation: the interface of a program consists of the input type, the output type, and a mapping that describes the input/output behavior of the program. Correspondingly, the interface for a stream processing systems consists of: (1) the type X of input data traces, (2) the type Y of output data traces, and (3) a monotone mapping $\beta : X \to Y$ that specifies the cumulative output after having consumed a prefix of the input stream. The monotonicity requirement captures the idea that output items cannot be retracted after they have been emitted. Since a transduction is a function from trace histories, it allows the modeling of systems that maintain state, where the output that is emitted at every step depends potentially on the entire input history.

Definition 12 (Data-Trace Transductions). Let $X = (A, D)$ and $Y = (B, E)$ be data-trace types. A *data-trace transduction* with input type X and output type Y is a function $\beta : X \to Y$ that is monotone w.r.t. the prefix order on data traces: $\mathbf{u} \leq \mathbf{v}$ implies that $\beta(\mathbf{u}) \leq \beta(\mathbf{v})$ for all traces $\mathbf{u}, \mathbf{v} \in X$. We write $\mathcal{T}(X, Y)$ to denote the set of all data-trace transductions from X to Y.   □

Figure 2 visualizes a data-trace transduction $\beta : X \to Y$ as a block diagram element, where the input wire is annotated with the input type X and the output wire is annotated with the output type Y.

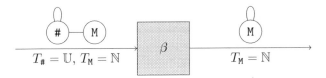

Fig. 2. A stream processing interface (data-trace transduction), consisting of (1) the input trace type, (2) the output trace type, and (3) the monotone map β.

Example 13. Suppose the input is a sequence of natural numbers, and we want to define the data-trace transduction that outputs the current data item if it is strictly larger than all data items seen so far. This is described by the trace transduction $\beta : \mathbb{N}^* \to \mathbb{N}^*$, given by $\beta(\varepsilon) = \varepsilon$ and

$$\beta(a_1 \ldots a_{n-1}a_n) = \begin{cases} \beta(a_1 \ldots a_{n-1}) \, a_n, & \text{if } a_n > a_i \text{ for all } i = 1, \ldots, n-1; \\ \beta(a_1 \ldots a_{n-1}), & \text{otherwise.} \end{cases}$$

In particular, the definition implies that $\beta(a_1) = a_1$. The table

Current item	Input history	β output
	ε	ε
3	3	3
1	3 1	3
5	3 1 5	3 5
2	3 1 5 2	3 5

gives the values of the transduction β for all prefixes of the stream 3 1 5 2.   □

2.3   Data-String Transductions

In the previous section we defined the notion of a data-trace transduction, which describes abstractly the behavior of a distributed stream processing system using a monotone function from input data traces to output data traces. In a *sequential implementation* of a stream processor the input is consumed in a sequential fashion, i.e. one item at a time, and the output items are produced in a specific linear order. Such sequential implementations are formally represented as *data-string transductions*. We establish in this section a precise correspondence between string transductions and trace transductions. We identify a consistency property that characterizes when a string transduction implements a trace transduction of a given input/output type. Moreover, we show how to obtain from a given trace transduction the set of all its possible sequential implementations.

Definition 14 (Data-String Transductions). Let A and B be data types. A *data-string transduction* with input type A and output type B is a function $f : A^* \to B^*$. Let $\mathcal{S}(A, B)$ be the set of string transductions from A to B.   □

A data-string transduction $f : A^* \to B^*$ describes a streaming computation where the input items arrive in a linear order. For an input sequence $u \in A^*$

the value $f(u)$ gives the output items that are emitted right after consuming the sequence u. In other words, $f(u)$ is the output that is triggered by the arrival of the last data item of u. We say that f is a *one-step* description of the computation because it gives the *output increment* that is emitted at every step.

Let A be an arbitrary set, Y be a data-trace type, and $f : A^* \to Y$. We define the *lifting* of f to be the function $\overline{f} : A^* \to Y$ that maps a sequence $a_1 a_2 \ldots a_n \in A^*$ to $\overline{f}(a_1 a_2 \ldots a_n) = f(\varepsilon) \cdot f(a_1) \cdot f(a_1 a_2) \cdots f(a_1 a_2 \ldots a_n)$. In particular, the definition implies that $\overline{f}(\varepsilon) = f(\varepsilon)$. That is, $\overline{f}$ accumulates the outputs of f for all prefixes of the input. Notice that $\overline{f}$ is *monotone* w.r.t. the prefix order: $u \leq v$ implies that $\overline{f}(u) \leq \overline{f}(v)$ for all $u, v \in A^*$. Suppose now that $\varphi : A^* \to Y$ is a monotone function. The *derivative* $\partial \varphi : A^* \to Y$ of φ is defined as follows: $(\partial \varphi)(\varepsilon) = \varphi(\varepsilon)$ and $(\partial \varphi)(ua) = \varphi(u)^{-1} \varphi(ua)$ for all $u \in A^*$ and $a \in A$. Notice that in the definition of ∂ we use the residuation operation of Definition 8. The lifting and derivative operators witness a bijection between the class of functions from A^* to Y and the monotone subset of this class. That is, $\partial \overline{f} = f$ for every $f : A^* \to Y$ and $\overline{\partial \varphi} = \varphi$ for every monotone $\varphi : A^* \to Y$.

Definition 15 (The Implementation Relation). Let $X = (A, D)$ and $Y = (B, E)$ be data-trace types. We say that a string transduction $f : A^* \to B^*$ *implements* a trace transduction $\beta : X \to Y$ (or that f is a *sequential implementation* of β) if $\beta([u]) = [\overline{f}(u)]$ for all $u \in A^*$. □

An implementation f of a trace transduction β is meant to give the *output increment* that is emitted at every step of the streaming computation, assuming the input is presented as a totally ordered sequence. That is, for input u the value $f(u)$ gives some arbitrarily chosen linearization of the output items that are emitted after consuming u. The lifting $\overline{f}$ gives the *cumulative output* that has been emitted after consuming a prefix of the input stream.

Example 16. The trace transduction β of Example 13 can be implemented as a string transduction $f : \mathbb{N}^* \to \mathbb{N}^*$, given by $f(\varepsilon) = \varepsilon$ and

$$f(a_1 \ldots a_{n-1} a_n) = \begin{cases} a_n, & \text{if } a_n > a_i \text{ for all } i = 1, \ldots, n-1; \\ \varepsilon, & \text{otherwise.} \end{cases}$$

The following table gives the values of the implementation f on input prefixes:

Current item	Input history	f output	β output
	ε	ε	ε
3	3	3	3
1	3 1	ε	3
5	3 1 5	5	3 5
2	3 1 5 2	ε	3 5

Notice in the table that $\beta(3\,1\,5\,2) = f(\varepsilon) \cdot f(3) \cdot f(3\,1) \cdot f(3\,1\,5) \cdot f(3\,1\,5\,2)$. □

Definition 17 (Consistency). Let $X = (A, D)$ and $Y = (B, E)$ be data-trace types. A data-string transduction $f \in \mathcal{S}(A, B)$ is (X, Y)-*consistent* if $u \equiv_D v$ implies $\overline{f}(u) \equiv_E \overline{f}(v)$ for all $u, v \in A^*$. □

Definition 17 essentially says that a string transduction f is consistent when it gives equivalent cumulative outputs for equivalent input sequences. The definition of the consistency property is given in terms of the lifting $\bar{f}$ of f. An equivalent formulation of this property, which is expressed directly in terms of f, is given in Theorem 18 below.

Theorem 18 (Characterization of Consistency). *Let $X = (A, D)$ and $Y = (B, E)$ be data-trace types, and $f \in \mathcal{S}(A, B)$. The function f is (X, Y)-consistent if and only if the following two conditions hold:*

(1) For all $u \in A^*$ and $a, b \in A$, $(a, b) \notin D$ implies $f(ua)f(uab) \equiv_E f(ub)f(uba)$.

(2) For all $u, v \in A^*$ and $a \in A$, $u \equiv_D v$ implies that $f(ua) \equiv_E f(va)$. $\qquad \square$

The following theorem establishes a correspondence between string and trace transductions. The consistent string transductions are exactly the ones that implement trace transductions. Moreover, the set of all implementations of a trace transduction can be given as a dependent function space by ranging over all possible linearizations of output increments. In other words, an implementation results from a trace transduction by choosing output increment linearizations.

Theorem 19 (Trace Transductions & Implementations). *Let $X = (A, D)$ and $Y = (B, E)$ be data-trace types. The following hold:*

(1) A data-string transduction f of $\mathcal{S}(A, B)$ implements some trace transduction of $\mathcal{T}(X, Y)$ iff f is (X, Y)-consistent.

(2) The set of all implementations of a data-trace transduction $\beta \in \mathcal{T}(X, Y)$ is the dependent function space $\prod_{u \in A^*} (\partial \gamma)(u)$, where the function $\gamma : A^* \to Y$ is given by $\gamma(u) = \beta([u])$ for all $u \in A^*$. $\qquad \square$

Part (2) of Theorem 19 defines the monotone function $\gamma : A^* \to Y$ in terms of the trace transduction β. Intuitively, γ gives the cumulative output trace for every possible linearization of the input trace. It follows that $\partial \gamma : A^* \to Y$ gives the output increment, which is a trace, for every possible input sequence. So, the lifting of $\partial \gamma$ is equal to γ. Finally, an implementation of β can be obtained by choosing for every input sequence $u \in A^*$ some linearization of the output increment $(\partial \gamma)(u) \in Y$. In other words, any implementation of a data-trace transduction is specified uniquely by a linearization choice function for all possible output increments. For the special case where the function $[\cdot] : B^* \to Y$ is injective, i.e. every trace of Y has one linearization, there is exactly one implementation for a given trace transduction. We will describe later in Example 21 a trace transduction that has several different sequential implementations.

2.4   Examples of Data-Trace Transductions

In this section we present examples that illustrate the concept of a *data-trace transduction* and its *implementations* for several streaming computations on streams of partially ordered elements. We start by considering examples that fit into the model of process networks [11, 14], where the inputs and outputs are organized in collections of independent linearly ordered channels.

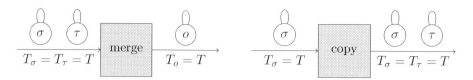

Fig. 3. Stream processing interfaces for merge (Example 20) and copy (Example 21).

Example 20 (Deterministic Merge). Consider the streaming computation where two linearly ordered input channels are merged into one. More specifically, this transformation reads cyclically items from the two input channels and passes them unchanged to the output channel. As described in Example 7, the input type is specified by the tag alphabet $\Sigma = \{\sigma, \tau\}$ with data values T for each tag, and the dependence relation $D = \{(\sigma, \sigma), (\tau, \tau)\}$. So, an input data trace is essentially an element of $T^* \times T^*$. The output type is specified by the tag alphabet $\{o\}$, the value type $T_o = T$, and the dependence relation $\{(o, o)\}$. So, the set of output data traces is essentially T^*. See the left diagram in Fig. 3. The trace transduction merge : $T^* \times T^* \to T^*$ is given as follows:

$$\mathrm{merge}(x_1 \ldots x_m, y_1 \ldots y_n) = \begin{cases} x_1 \, y_1 \, \ldots \, x_m \, y_m, & \text{if } m \leq n; \\ x_1 \, y_1 \, \ldots \, x_n \, y_n, & \text{if } m > n. \end{cases}$$

The sequential implementation of merge can be represented as a function $f : A^* \to T^*$ with $A = (\{\sigma\} \times T) \cup (\{\tau\} \times T)$, where $f(\varepsilon) = \varepsilon$ and

$$f(w(\sigma, x)) = \begin{cases} x \, y_{m+1}, & \text{if } \mathrm{length}(w|_\sigma) = m, w|_\tau = y_1 \ldots y_n \text{ and } m < n \\ \varepsilon, & \text{otherwise} \end{cases}$$

$$f(w\,(\tau, y)) = \begin{cases} x_{n+1} \, y, & \text{if } w|_\sigma = x_1 \ldots x_m, \mathrm{length}(w|_\tau) = n \text{ and } n < m \\ \varepsilon, & \text{otherwise} \end{cases}$$

for all $w \in A^*$. For an input tag, $\sigma \, w|_\sigma$ is the subsequence obtained from w by keeping only the values of the σ-tagged items. □

Example 21 (Copy). The copy transformation creates two copies of the input stream by reading each item from the input channel and copying it to two output channels. An input data trace is an element of T^*, and an output data trace is an element of $T^* \times T^*$. See the right diagram in Fig. 3. The trace transduction for this computation is given by copy$(u) = (u, u)$ for all $u \in T^*$. A possible implementation of copy can be given as $f : T^* \to B^*$, where $B = (\{\sigma\} \times T) \cup (\{\tau\} \times T)$. We put $f(\varepsilon) = \varepsilon$ and $f(ua) = (\sigma, a)\,(\tau, a)$ for all $u \in A^*$. Notice that the implementation makes the arbitrary choice to emit (σ, a) before (τ, a), but it is also possible to emit the items in reverse order. □

Example 22 (Key-based Partitioning). Consider the computation that maps a linearly ordered input sequence of data items of type T (each of which contains a key), to a set of linearly ordered sub-streams, one per key. The function key $: T \rightarrow K$ extracts the key from each input value. The input type is specified by a singleton tag alphabet $\{\sigma\}$, the data value set T, and the dependence relation $\{(\sigma, \sigma)\}$. The output type is specified by the tag alphabet K, value types $T_k = T$ for every key $k \in K$, and the dependence relation $\{(k, k) \mid k \in K\}$. So, an input trace is represented as an element of T^*, and an output trace can is represented as a K-indexed tuple, that is, a function $K \rightarrow T^*$. The trace transduction partition$_{\mathrm{key}} : T^* \rightarrow (K \rightarrow T^*)$ describes the partitioning of the input stream into sub-streams according to the key extraction map key: partition$_{\mathrm{key}}(u)(k) = u|_k$ for all $u \in T^*$ and $k \in K$, where $u|_k$ denotes the subsequence of u that consists of all items whose key is equal to k. The unique implementation of this transduction can be represented as a function $f : T^* \rightarrow (K \times T)^*$ given by $f(\varepsilon) = \varepsilon$ and $f(wx) = (\mathrm{key}(x), x)$ for all $w \in T^*$ and $x \in T$. $\quad\square$

Proposition 10 states that a set $T_1^* \times \cdots \times T_m^*$ can be isomorphically represented as a set of data traces, and also that the prefix relation on the traces corresponds via the isomorphism to the componentwise prefix order on $T_1^* \times \cdots \times T_m^*$. Theorem 23 then follows immediately.

Theorem 23. *Every monotone function $F : T_1^* \times \cdots \times T_m^* \rightarrow U_1^* \times \cdots \times U_n^*$ can be represented as a data-trace transduction.*

Another important case is when the input stream is considered to be unordered, therefore any finite prefix should be viewed as a multiset (relation) of data items. In this case, any reasonable definition of a streaming transduction should encompass the *monotone operations* on relations. Monotonicity implies that as the input relations get gradually extended with more tuples, the output relations can also be incrementally extended with more tuples. This computation is consistent with the streaming model, and it fits naturally in our framework.

Example 24 (Operations of Relational Algebra). First, we consider the relation-to-relation operations *map* and *filter* that are generalizations of the operations *project* and *select* from relational algebra. Suppose that the sets of input and output data traces are (up to a bijection) $\mathsf{Bag}(T)$. Given a function $op : T \rightarrow T$ and a predicate $\phi \subseteq T$, the trace transductions $map_{op} : \mathsf{Bag}(T) \rightarrow \mathsf{Bag}(T)$ and $filter_\phi : \mathsf{Bag}(T) \rightarrow \mathsf{Bag}(T)$ are defined by:

$$map_{op}(M) = \{op(a) \mid a \in M\} \qquad filter_\phi(M) = \{a \in M \mid a \in \phi\}$$

for every multiset M over T. The respective sequential implementations map$_{op} : T^* \rightarrow T^*$ and filter$_\phi : T^* \rightarrow T^*$ are defined as follows:

$$\mathrm{map}_{op}(\varepsilon) = \varepsilon \qquad \mathrm{filter}_\phi(\varepsilon) = \varepsilon$$
$$\mathrm{map}_{op}(wa) = op(a) \quad \mathrm{filter}_\phi(wa) = a, \text{ if } a \in \phi \quad \mathrm{filter}_\phi(wa) = \varepsilon, \text{ if } a \notin \phi$$

for all $w \in T^*$ and $a \in T$.

Consider now the *relational join* operation for relations over T w.r.t. the binary predicate $\theta \subseteq T \times T$. An input data trace can be viewed as an element of

$\mathsf{Bag}(T) \times \mathsf{Bag}(T)$, and an output trace as an element of $\mathsf{Bag}(T \times T)$. The trace transduction $join_\theta : \mathsf{Bag}(T) \times \mathsf{Bag}(T) \to \mathsf{Bag}(T \times T)$ is given by

$$join_\theta(M, N) = \{(a, b) \in M \times N \mid (a, b) \in \theta\} \text{ for multisets } M, N \text{ over } T.$$

Suppose the names of the input relations are Q and R respectively. An implementation of θ-join can be represented as a function $join_\theta : \{(\mathsf{Q}, d), (\mathsf{R}, d) \mid d \in T\}^* \to (T \times T)^*$, given by $join_\theta(\varepsilon) = \varepsilon$ and

$$join_\theta(w(\mathsf{Q}, d)) = \mathsf{filter}_\theta((d, d_1)\,(d, d_2)\,\ldots\,(d, d_n)),$$

where $(\mathsf{R}, d_1), (\mathsf{R}, d_2), \ldots, (\mathsf{R}, d_n)$ are the R-tagged elements that appear in the sequence w (from left to right). The function $join_\theta$ is defined symmetrically when the input ends with a R-tagged element.

The relational operation that removes duplicates from a relation has a sequential implementation that can be represented as a function $\mathsf{distinct} : T^* \to T^*$, given by $\mathsf{distinct}(\varepsilon) = \varepsilon$ and

$$\mathsf{distinct}(wa) = \begin{cases} a, & \text{if } a \text{ does not appear in } w \\ \varepsilon, & \text{if } a \text{ appears in } w \end{cases}$$

for all $w \in T^*$ and $a \in T$.   □

Example 24 lists several commonly used relational operations that can be represented as data-trace transductions. In fact, every monotone relational operation is representable, as stated in Theorem 25 below. The result follows immediately from Proposition 11.

Theorem 25. *Every monotone operator $F : \mathsf{Bag}(T_1) \times \cdots \times \mathsf{Bag}(T_n) \to \mathsf{Bag}(T)$ can be represented as a data-trace transduction.*

Consider now the important case of computing an *aggregate* (such as sum, max, and min) on an unordered input. This computation is meaningful for a static input relation, but becomes meaningless in the streaming setting. Any partial results depend on a particular linear order for the input tuples, which is inconsistent with the notion of an unordered input. So, for a computation of relational aggregates in the streaming setting we must assume that the input contains linearly ordered *punctuation markers* that trigger the emission of output (see [15] for a generalization of this idea). The input can then be viewed as an ordered sequence of relations (each relation is delineated by markers), and it is meaningful to compute at every marker occurrence an aggregate over all tuples seen so far. Our formal definition of data-trace transductions captures these subtle aspects of streaming computation with relational data.

Example 26 (Streaming Maximum). Suppose the input stream consists of unordered natural numbers and special symbols # that are linearly ordered. We will specify the computation that emits at every # occurrence the maximum of all numbers seen so far. More specifically, the input type is given by $\Sigma = \{\sigma, \tau\}$,

$T_\sigma = \mathbb{N}$, $T_\tau = \mathbb{U}$ (unit type), and $D = \{(\sigma, \tau), (\tau, \sigma), (\tau, \tau)\}$. So, an input data trace is essentially a nonempty sequence of multisets of numbers, i.e. an element of $\mathsf{Bag}(\mathbb{N})^+$. The correspondence between traces and elements of $\mathsf{Bag}(\mathbb{N})^+$ is illustrated by the following examples:

$$\varepsilon \mapsto \emptyset \qquad 1\ 2 \mapsto \{1,2\} \qquad 1\ 2\ \#\ 3 \mapsto \{1,2\}\ \{3\}$$
$$1 \mapsto \{1\} \qquad 1\ 2\ \# \mapsto \{1,2\}\ \emptyset \qquad 1\ 2\ \#\ 3\ \# \mapsto \{1,2\}\ \{3\}\ \emptyset$$

The streaming maximum computation is described (Fig. 4) by the trace transduction $\mathrm{smax} : \mathsf{Bag}(\mathbb{N})^+ \to \mathbb{N}^*$, given as: $\mathrm{smax}(R) = \varepsilon$, $\mathrm{smax}(R_1 R_2) = \max(R_1)$, and

$$\mathrm{smax}(R_1 \ldots R_n) = \max(R_1)\ \max(R_1 \cup R_2)\ \cdots\ \max(R_1 \cup R_2 \cup \cdots \cup R_{n-1}).$$

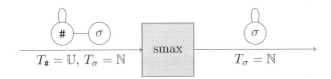

Fig. 4. Stream processing interface for streaming maximum (Example 26).

Notice that the last relation R_n of the input sequence is the collection of elements after the last occurrence of a # symbol, and therefore they are not included in any maximum calculation above. The sequential implementation of smax can be represented as a function $f : (\mathbb{N} \cup \{\#\})^* \to \mathbb{N}^*$, which outputs at every # occurrence the maximum number seen so far. That is, $f(\varepsilon) = \varepsilon$ and

$$f(a_1 a_2 \ldots a_n) = \begin{cases} \varepsilon, & \text{if } a_n \in \mathbb{N}; \\ \max \text{ of } \{a_1, a_2, \ldots, a_n\} \setminus \{\#\}, & \text{if } a_n = \#. \end{cases}$$

for all sequences $a_1 a_2 \ldots a_n \in (\mathbb{N} \cup \{\#\})^*$.   □

3 Operations on Data-Trace Transductions

In many distributed stream processing algorithms, the desired computation is passed through nodes which are composed *in parallel* and *in sequence*. Both *composition operations* can be implemented concurrently with potential time savings, and the decomposition makes this concurrency visible and exploitable. Crucial to the usefulness of an interface model, therefore, is that these composition operations correspond to semantic composition operations on the interfaces. In turn, given an interface for the overall computation, we may reason that only some distributed decompositions are possible.

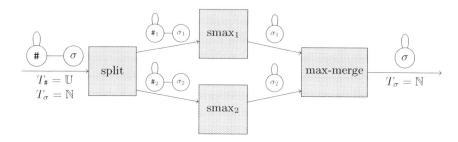

Fig. 5. Distributed evaluation of smax (Example 27).

In this section we define the sequential composition of two data-trace transductions, and the parallel composition of a (possibly infinite) family of data-trace transductions. We then define the implementation of both of these operations as operations on string transductions. A general block diagram, without feedback, can be obtained by the combination of (string or trace) transductions in sequence and in parallel.

Example 27 (Distributed evaluation of smax**).** For example, consider the problem of computing the maximum (smax), as in Example 26. We notice that the σ-tagged natural numbers are independent, forming a multiset, so the multiset could be split into multiple smaller sets and handled by separate components. To do so, we first have a component which copies the synchronization tags # into $\#_1$ and $\#_2$, and alternates sending σ tags to σ_1 and σ_2. This split component breaks the input stream into two independent streams. Next, components $smax_1$ and $smax_2$, which are instances of smax, handle each of the two input streams $\{\sigma_1, \#_1\}$ and $\{\sigma_2, \#_2\}$ separately, producing output tagged σ_1 and σ_2. Finally, a variant of Example 20, max-merge, can be constructed which takes one σ_1 and one σ_2 output and, rather than just producing both, maximizes the two arguments to produce a single σ tag. Altogether, the resulting block diagram of Fig. 5 computes smax. We write:

$$\text{smax} = \text{split} \gg (\text{smax}_1 \| \text{smax}_2) \gg \text{max-merge},$$

which is an important sense in which computations like *Streaming Maximum* can be parallelized.   □

Definition 28 (Sequential Composition). Let X, Y, and Z be data-trace types, and let $\alpha \in \mathcal{T}(X, Y)$ and $\beta \in \mathcal{T}(Y, Z)$ be data-trace transductions. The *sequential composition* of α and β, denoted $\gamma = \alpha \gg \beta$, is the data-trace transduction in $\mathcal{T}(X, Z)$ defined by $\gamma(\mathbf{u}) = \beta(\alpha(\mathbf{u}))$ for all $\mathbf{u} \in X$.   □

Definition 29 (Parallel Composition). Let I be any index set. For each $i \in I$, let $X_i = (A_i, D_i)$ and $Y_i = (B_i, E_i)$ be trace types, and let $\alpha_i \in \mathcal{T}(X_i, Y_i)$. We require that for all $i \neq j$, A_i is disjoint from A_j and B_i is disjoint from B_j. Additionally, we require that $\alpha_i(\varepsilon) = \varepsilon$ for all but finitely many i.

Let $A = \bigcup_{i \in I} A_i$, $B = \bigcup_{i \in I} B_i$, $D = \bigcup_{i \in I} D_i$, and $E = \bigcup_{i \in I} E_i$. Let $X = (A, D)$ and $Y = (B, E)$. The *parallel composition* of all α_i, denoted $\alpha = \big\|_{i \in I} \alpha_i$, is the data-trace transduction in $\mathcal{T}(X, Y)$ defined by $\alpha(\mathbf{u})|_{Y_i} = \alpha_i(\mathbf{u}|_{X_i})$, for all $\mathbf{u} \in X$ and for all $i \in I$. Here $|_{Y_i}$ means the projection of a trace to Y_i.   □

Definition 28 gives a well-defined trace transduction because the composition of monotone functions is monotone. In Definition 29, we have defined the value of $\alpha(\mathbf{u})$ by specifying the component of the output in each of the independent output streams Y_i. Specifically, a trace in Y is given uniquely by a trace in Y_i for each i, and the only restriction is that finitely many of the traces Y_i must be non-empty. Since each character in $\mathbf{u}$ only projects to one X_i and since $\alpha_i(\varepsilon) = \varepsilon$ for all but finitely many i, we satisfy this restriction, and parallel composition is well-defined. For only two (or a finite number) of channels, we can use the notation $f_1 \| f_2$ instead of $\big\|_{i \in I} f_i$.

Proposition 30 (Basic Properties). *Whenever binary operations $\gg$ and $\|$ are defined, $\gg$ is associative and $\|$ is associative and commutative.*

Definition 31 (Implementation of Sequential Composition). Let A, B, and C be data types. Let $f \in \mathcal{S}(A, B)$ and $g \in \mathcal{S}(B, C)$ be data-string transductions. The *sequential composition* of f and g, written $h = f \gg g$, is the unique data-string transduction in $\mathcal{S}(A, C)$ satisfying $\overline{h} = \overline{g} \circ \overline{f}$. I.e., $h(u) = \partial(\overline{g} \circ \overline{f})$. □

On input an item $a \in A$, we pass it to f, collect any result, and pass the result of that to g (if any). Because there may be multiple intermediate outputs from f, or none at all, this is most succinctly expressed by $\partial(\overline{g} \circ \overline{f})$.

Lemma 32. *Let $X = (A, D)$, $Y = (B, E)$, $Z = (C, F)$ be data-trace types, $\alpha \in \mathcal{T}(X, Y)$, and $\beta \in \mathcal{T}(Y, Z)$. If $f \in \mathcal{S}(A, B)$ implements α and $g \in \mathcal{S}(B, C)$ implements β, then $f \gg g$ implements $\alpha \gg \beta$.*

Definition 33 (Implementation of Parallel Composition). Let $(I, <)$ be an *ordered* index set. For each i, let A_i, B_i be data types and let $f_i \in \mathcal{S}(A_i, B_i)$ be a data-string transduction. As in Definition 29, we require that for all $i \neq j$, A_i is disjoint from A_j and B_i is disjoint from B_j; Also as in Definition 29, assume that $f_i(\varepsilon) = \varepsilon$ for all but finitely many i, say $i_1 < i_2 < \cdots < i_m$. Define $A = \bigcup_i A_i$ and $B = \bigcup_i B_i$. The *parallel composition* of all f_i, written $f = \big\|_{i \in (I, <)} f_i$, is the data-string transduction in $\mathcal{S}(A, B)$ defined as follows. First, $f(\varepsilon) = f_{i_1}(\varepsilon) f_{i_2}(\varepsilon) \cdots f_{i_m}(\varepsilon)$. Second, for all i, for all $a_i \in A_i$, and for all $u \in A^*$, $f(ua_i) = f_i(u|_{A_i} a_i)$, where $u|_{A_i}$ is the projection of u to A_i.   □

We initially output $f_i(\varepsilon)$ for any i for which that is nonempty. Then, on input an item $a_i \in A_i$, we pass it to f_i, collect any result, and output that result (if any). Thus, while the definition allows an infinite family of string transductions, on a finite input stream only a finite number will need to be used.

The index set must be ordered for the reason that, on input ε, we need to produce the outputs $f_i(\varepsilon)$ in some order. By Theorem 19, any data-trace transduction can be implemented by some data-string transduction, and this construction picks just one possible implementation. Other than on input ε, the order does not matter. Regardless of the order, the following lemma states that we implement the desired data-trace transduction.

Lemma 34. *Let I be an (unordered) index set. Let $X_i = (A_i, D_i)$, $Y_i = (B_i, E_i)$, and $\alpha_i \in \mathcal{T}(X_i, Y_i)$, such that the parallel composition $\alpha = \|_{i \in I} \alpha_i$ is defined. If $f_i \in \mathcal{S}(A_i, B_i)$ implements α_i for all i, then for any ordering $(I, <)$ of I, $f = \|_{i \in (I, <)} f_i$ implements α.*

We now illustrate various examples of how these composition operations on trace transductions, which can be implemented as string transductions, can be used.

Example 35 (Partition by key, Reduce & Collect). Consider an input data stream of credit card transactions. For simplicity, we assume that each data item is simply a key-value pair (k, v), where k is a *key* that identifies uniquely a credit card account and v is the monetary value of a purchase. We write K to denote the set of keys, and V for the set of values. Suppose that the input stream contains additionally end-of-minute markers **#**, which indicate the end of each one-minute interval and are used to trigger output. We want to perform the following computation: "find at the end of each minute the maximum total purchases associated with a credit card account". This computation can be structured into a pipeline of three stages:

1. *Stage* partition: Split the input stream into a set of sub-streams, one for each key. The marker items **#** are propagated to every sub-stream.

$$\text{input type}: \text{tags } K \cup \{\#\},$$
$$\text{values } T_k = V \text{ for every } k \in K \text{ and } T_\# = \mathbb{U},$$
$$\text{full dependence relation } (K \cup \{\#\}) \times (K \cup \{\#\})$$
$$\text{output type}: \text{tags } K \cup \{\#_k \mid k \in K\},$$
$$\text{values } T'_k = V \text{ and } T'_{\#_k} = \mathbb{U} \text{ for every } k \in K,$$
$$\text{dependencies } \bigcup_{k \in K} (\{k, \#_k\} \times \{k, \#_k\})$$

The definition of the data-trace transduction is similar to the one in Example 22, with the difference that **#** markers have to be propagated to every output channel.

2. For each key $k \in K$ perform a *reduce* operation, denoted reduce_k, that outputs at every occurrence of a **#** symbol the total of the values over the entire history of the k-th sub-stream. For reduce_k we have:

$$\text{input}: \text{tags } \{k, \#_k\}, \text{ values } V \text{ and } \mathbb{U}, \text{ dependencies } \{k, \#_k\} \times \{k, \#_k\}$$
$$\text{output}: \text{tags } \{k\}, \text{ values } V, \text{ dependencies } \{k\} \times \{k\}$$

The overall reduce stage is the parallel composition $\|_{k \in K} \text{reduce}_k$.

3. The outputs of all the reduce operations (one for each key, triggered by the same occurrence of #) are aggregated using a collect operation, which outputs the maximum of the intermediate results.

input : tags K, values V for each $k \in K$, dependencies $\{(k,k) \mid k \in K\}$

output : tags $\{o\}$, values V, dependencies $\{(o,o)\}$

The overall streaming map-reduce computation is given by a sequential composition with three stages: partition $\gg (\|_{k \in K} \text{reduce}_k) \gg$ collect (Fig. 6).

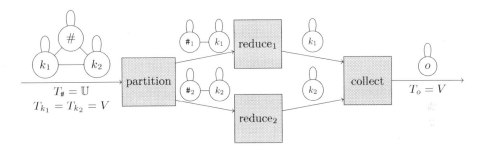

Fig. 6. Partition by key, reduce, and collect with two keys (Example 35).

Example 36 (Streaming Variant of Map-Reduce [9]). Suppose the input data stream contains key-value pairs, where the *input keys* K are partition identifiers and the values V are fragments of text files. The *intermediate keys* K' are words, and the corresponding values V' are natural numbers. The input stream contains additionally special markers # that are used to trigger output. The overall computation is the following: "output at every # occurrence the word frequency count for every word that appeared since the previous # occurrence". So, this is a *tumbling window* version of a map-reduce operation on a static data set [9]. The computation can be expressed as a pipeline of five stages:

1. *Stage* partition: Split the stream into a set of sub-streams, one for each input key. The marker items # are propagated to every sub-stream. This stage is similar to the one described in Example 35.
2. *Stage* map: Apply a function map : $K \times V \rightarrow (K' \times V')^*$ function to each key-value pair of the input stream. This function scans the text fragment and outputs a pair $(w, 1)$ for every word w that it encounters. The marker items # are propagated to every sub-stream. This stage is expressed as the parallel composition of transductions $\{\text{map}_k \mid k \in K\}$ with input/output types:

input type : tags $\{k, \#_k\}$,

values V for the tag k, and $\mathbb{U}$ for the tag $\#_k$,

dependence relation $\{k, \#_k\} \times \{k, \#_k\}$

output type : tags $\{k, \#_k\}$,

values $K' \times V'$ for the tag k, and $\mathbb{U}$ for the tag $\#_k$,

dependence relation $\{k, \#_k\} \times \{k, \#_k\}$

3. *Stage* reshuffle: The outputs from all map_k, $k \in K$, transductions between consecutive # occurrences are collected and reorganized on the basis of the intermediate keys.

> input type : tags $K \cup \{\#_k \mid k \in K\}$,
>> values $K' \times V'$ for the every tag $k \in K$, and $\mathbb{U}$ for every tag $\#_k$,
>> dependence relation $\bigcup_{k \in K}(\{k, \#_k\} \times \{k, \#_k\})$
>
> output type : tags $K' \cup \{\#_{k'} \mid k' \in K'\}$,
>> values V' for the every tag $k' \in K'$, and $\mathbb{U}$ for every tag $\#_{k'}$,
>> dependencies $\bigcup_{k' \in K'}\{(k', \#_{k'}), (\#_{k'}, k'), (\#_{k'}, \#_{k'})\}$

4. *Stage* reduce: For each intermediate key $k' \in K'$ perform a *reduce* operation, denoted $\text{reduce}_{k'}$, that outputs at every occurrence of a # the total frequency count for the word k' since the previous occurrence of a # symbol. The data-trace types for reduce_k we have:

> input type : tags $\{k', \#_{k'}\}$,
>> values V' for the tag k', and $\mathbb{U}$ for the tag $\#_{k'}$,
>> dependencies $\{(k', \#_{k'}), (\#_{k'}, k'), (\#_{k'}, \#_{k'})\}$
>
> output type : tags $\{k', \#_{k'}\}$,
>> values V' for the tag k', and $\mathbb{U}$ for the tag $\#_{k'}$,
>> dependencies $\{(k', \#_{k'}), (\#_{k'}, k'), (\#_{k'}, \#_{k'})\}$

The overall reduce stage is the parallel composition $\text{reduce}_{k'_1} \parallel \cdots \parallel \text{reduce}_{k'_n}$, where $k'_1, \ldots, k'_n$ is an enumeration of the intermediate keys.

5. *Stage* collect: The outputs of all the reduce operations (one for each key, triggered by the same occurrence of #) are collected into a single multiset.

> input type : tags $K' \cup \{\#_{k'} \mid k' \in K'\}$,
>> values V' for the every tag $k' \in K'$, and $\mathbb{U}$ for every tag $\#_{k'}$,
>> dependencies $\bigcup_{k' \in K'}\{(k', \#_{k'}), (\#_{k'}, k'), (\#_{k'}, \#_{k'})\}$
>
> output type : tags $\{o, \#\}$,
>> values $K' \times V'$ for the tag o, and $\mathbb{U}$ for every tag #,
>> dependencies $\{(o, \#), (\#, o), (\#, \#)\}$

The overall streaming map-reduce computation is given by a sequential composition with five stages:

$$\text{partition} \gg (\|_{k \in K} \text{map}_k) \gg \text{reshuffle} \gg (\|_{k' \in K'} \text{reduce}_{k'}) \gg \text{collect}.$$

Example 37 (Time-Based Sliding Window). Suppose that the input is a sequence of items of the form (v, t), where v is a value and t is a timestamp. We assume additionally that the items arrive in increasing order of timestamps, that is, in an input sequence $(v_1, t_1) \cdots (v_n, t_n)$ it holds that $t_1 \leq \cdots \leq t_n$.

We want to compute a so-called *moving aggregate*: "compute every second the sum of the values over the last 10 s". This sliding-window computation can be set up as a pipeline of three stages:

1. *Stage* mark: Insert at the end of every second an end-of-second marker #.
2. *Stage* unit: Compute at every occurrence of a # marker the sum of the values over the last second. The output of this state is a sequence of partial sums, i.e. one value for each one-second interval.
3. *Stage* window: Compute with every new item the sum of the last 10 items.

The overall sliding window computation is expressed as: mark ≫ unit ≫ window (Fig. 7).

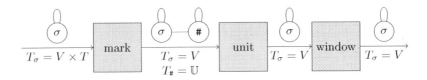

Fig. 7. Sliding window computation (Example 37).

4   Related Work

Synchronous Computation Models: The data-trace transduction model is a synchronous model of computation as it implicitly relies on the *synchrony hypothesis*: the time needed to process a single input item by the system is sufficiently small so that it can respond by producing outputs before the next input item arrives [7]. Data-trace transductions are a generalization of what is considered by acyclic *Kahn process networks* [11], where the interface consists of a finite number of input and output channels. A process network consists of a collection of processes, where each process is a sequential program that can read from the input channels and write to the output channels. The input/output channels are modeled as first-in first-out queues. A specialization of process networks is the model of *Synchronous Dataflow* [14], where each process reads a fixed finite number of items from the input queues and also emits a fixed finite number of items as output. We accommodate a finite number of independent input or output streams, but also allow more complicated independence relations on the input and output, and in particular, viewing the input or output stream as a bag of events is not possible in Kahn process networks. We do not consider any particular implementation for data-trace transductions in this paper, but dataflow networks could be considered as a particular implementation for a subclass of our interfaces.

Merging of Multiple Input and Output Channels: In our model, even stream processing components with multiple input channels receive the items *merged* into a linear order. Traditionally, this merging of two streams into one linearly ordered stream has been considered a nondeterministic operation, and there is a body of work investigating the semantics and properties of dataflow systems built from such nondeterministic nodes. Brock and Ackerman [8] show that the relation from inputs to possible outputs is not compositional, i.e. it is not an adequate semantics for these systems. Panangaden and Shanbhogue [19] consider variants of nondeterministic merge and their expressive power. Because we disallow these inherently nondeterministic merge operations, our semantics is simple and compositional. In particular the function from input histories to output histories is deterministic, and the nondeterminism of merge is hidden by expressing it only in the types, in the independence relation. We also have not considered feedback in a network defined by operations.

Partial Order Semantics for Concurrency: The traditional model for asynchronous systems is based on *interleaving* the steps of concurrent processes, and the observational semantics of an asynchronous system consists of a set of behaviors, where a behavior is a (linear) sequence of interspersed input and output events (see, for instance, the model of I/O automata [16]). Such a semantics does not capture the distinction between coincidental ordering of observed events versus *causality* between them (see [13] for a discussion of causality in concurrent systems). This motivated the development of a variety of models with partial order semantics such as pomsets [20] and Mazurkiewicz traces [18]. We build upon the ideas in this line of research though our context, namely, synchronous, deterministic, streaming processors, is quite different.

Streaming Extensions of Database Query Languages: There is a large body of work on streaming query languages and database systems such as Aurora [2], Borealis [1], STREAM [6], and StreamInsight [4]. The query language supported by these systems (for example, CQL [6]) is typically a version of SQL with additional constructs for sliding windows over data streams. This allows for rich relational queries, including set-aggregations (e.g. sum, maximum, minimum, average, count) and joins over multiple data streams. A precise semantics for how to merge events from different streams has been defined using the notion of *synchronization markers* [15]. The pomset view central to the formalism of data-trace transductions is strictly more general, and gives the ability to view the stream in many different ways, for example: as a linearly ordered sequence, as a relation, or even as a sequence of relations. This is useful for describing streaming computations that combine relational operations with sequence-aware operations. Extending relational query languages to pomsets has been studied in [10], though not in the context of streaming.

5   Conclusion

We have proposed data-trace transductions as a mathematical model for specifying the observable behavior of a stream processing system. This allows consumption of inputs and production of outputs in an incremental manner that is suitable for streaming computation, while retaining the ability to view input and output streams as partially ordered multisets. The basic operations of sequential composition and parallel composition can be defined naturally on data-trace transductions. The examples illustrate that the flexibility of our model is useful to specify the desired behavior of a wide variety of commonly used components in stream processing systems.

Defining the interface model is only the first step towards a programming system and supporting analysis tools that can help designers build stream processing systems with formal guarantees of correctness and performance. An immediate next step is to formalize a *transducer* model to define the computations of data-trace transductions with a type system that enforces the consistency requirement of Definition 17. Future directions include defining a declarative query language to specify data-trace transductions (see [10] for operations over pomsets and [5,17] for specifying quantitative properties of linearly ordered streams), efficient implementation of data-trace transductions on existing high-performance architectures for stream processing (such as Apache Storm), and techniques for verifying correctness and performance properties of data-trace transductions.

References

1. Abadi, D., Ahmad, Y., Balazinska, M., Cetintemel, U., Cherniack, M., Hwang, J.H., Lindner, W., Maskey, A., Rasin, A., Ryvkina, E., Tatbul, N., Xing, Y., Zdonik, S.: The design of the Borealis stream processing engine. In: Proceedings of the 2nd Biennial Conference on Innovative Data Systems Research (CIDR), pp. 277–289 (2005)
2. Abadi, D., Carney, D., Cetintemel, U., Cherniack, M., Convey, C., Lee, S., Stonebraker, M., Tatbul, N., Zdonik, S.: Aurora: a new model and architecture for data stream management. VLDB J. **12**(2), 120–139 (2003)
3. de Alfaro, L., Henzinger, T.: Interface automata. In: Proceedings of the Ninth Annual ACM Symposium on Foundations of Software Engineering (FSE), pp. 109–120 (2001)
4. Ali, M., Chandramouli, B., Goldstein, J., Schindlauer, R.: The extensibility framework in Microsoft StreamInsight. In: Proceedings of the 27th IEEE International Conference on Data Engineering (ICDE), pp. 1242–1253 (2011)
5. Alur, R., Fisman, D., Raghothaman, M.: Regular programming for quantitative properties of data streams. In: Thiemann, P. (ed.) ESOP 2016. LNCS, vol. 9632, pp. 15–40. Springer, Heidelberg (2016). https://doi.org/10.1007/978-3-662-49498-1_2
6. Arasu, A., Babu, S., Widom, J.: The CQL continuous query language: semantic foundations and query execution. VLDB J. **15**(2), 121–142 (2006)

7. Benveniste, A., Caspi, P., Edwards, S., Halbwachs, N., Guernic, P.L., de Simone, R.: The synchronous languages 12 years later. Proc. IEEE **91**(1), 64–83 (2003)
8. Brock, J.D., Ackerman, W.B.: Scenarios: a model of non-determinate computation. In: Díaz, J., Ramos, I. (eds.) ICFPC 1981. LNCS, vol. 107, pp. 252–259. Springer, Heidelberg (1981). https://doi.org/10.1007/3-540-10699-5_102
9. Dean, J., Ghemawat, S.: MapReduce: simplified data processing on large clusters. In: Proceedings of the 6th Conference on Symposium on Operating Systems Design and Implementation, OSDI 2004, pp. 137–149. USENIX Association (2004). https://www.usenix.org/legacy/publications/library/proceedings/osdi04/tech/dean.html
10. Grumbach, S., Milo, T.: An algebra of pomsets. Inf. Comput. **150**, 268–306 (1999)
11. Kahn, G.: The semantics of a simple language for parallel programming. Inf. Process. **74**, 471–475 (1974)
12. Kulkarni, S., Bhagat, N., Fu, M., Kedigehalli, V., Kellogg, C., Mittal, S., Patel, J., Ramasamy, K., Taneja, S.: Twitter heron: stream processing at scale. In: Proceedings of the ACM SIGMOD International Conference on Management of Data, pp. 239–250 (2015)
13. Lamport, L.: Time, clocks, and the ordering of events in a distributed system. Commun. ACM **21**, 558–565 (1978)
14. Lee, E.A., Messerschmitt, D.G.: Synchronous data flow. Proc. IEEE **75**(9), 1235–1245 (1987)
15. Li, J., Maier, D., Tufte, K., Papamidos, V., Tucker, P.: Semantics and evaluation techniques for window aggregates in data streams. In: Proceedings of the ACM SIGMOD International Conference on Management of Data, pp. 311–322 (2015)
16. Lynch, N.: Distributed Algorithms. Morgan Kaufmann, Burlington (1996)
17. Mamouras, K., Raghothaman, M., Alur, R., Ives, Z., Khanna, S.: StreamQRE: modular specification and efficient evaluation of quantitative queries over streaming data. In: Proceedings of 38th ACM SIGPLAN Conference on Programming Language Design and Implementation, pp. 693–708 (2017)
18. Mazurkiewicz, A.: Trace theory. In: Brauer, W., Reisig, W., Rozenberg, G. (eds.) ACPN 1986. LNCS, vol. 255, pp. 278–324. Springer, Heidelberg (1987). https://doi.org/10.1007/3-540-17906-2_30
19. Panangaden, P., Shanbhogue, V.: The expressive power of indeterminate dataflow primitives. Inf. Comput. **98**(1), 99–131 (1992)
20. Pratt, V.: Modeling concurrency with partial orders. Int. J. Parallel Program. **15**(1), 33–71 (1986)

Simulation-Based Reachability Analysis for Nonlinear Systems Using Componentwise Contraction Properties

Murat Arcak$^{(\boxtimes)}$ and John Maidens

University of California, Berkeley, Berkeley, USA
{arcak,maidens}@berkeley.edu

Abstract. A shortcoming of existing reachability approaches for nonlinear systems is the poor scalability with the number of continuous state variables. To mitigate this problem we present a simulation-based approach where we first sample a number of trajectories of the system and next establish bounds on the convergence or divergence between the samples and neighboring trajectories that are not explicitly simulated. We compute these bounds using contraction theory and reduce the conservatism by partitioning the state vector into several components and analyzing contraction properties separately in each direction. Among other benefits this allows us to analyze the effect of constant but uncertain parameters by treating them as state variables and partitioning them into a separate direction. We next present a numerical procedure to search for weighted norms that yield a prescribed contraction rate, which can be incorporated in the reachability algorithm to adjust the weights to minimize the growth of the reachable set. The proposed reachability method is illustrated with examples, including a magnetic resonance imaging application.

1 Introduction

Reachability analysis is critical for testing and verification of control systems [1], and for formal methods-based control synthesis where reachability dictates the transitions in a discrete-state abstraction of a system with continuous dynamics [2]. Existing reachability approaches for nonlinear systems include level set methods [3], linear or piecewise linear approximations of nonlinear models followed by linear reachability techniques [4,5], interval Taylor series methods [6,7], and differential inequality methods [8,9]. However, these results typically scale poorly with the number of continuous state variables, limiting their applicability in practice.

On the other hand trajectory-based approaches [10–12] scale well with the state dimension, as they take advantage of inexpensive numerical simulations and are naturally parallelizable. In [13] we leveraged concepts from *contraction theory* [14,15] to develop a new trajectory-based approach where we first sample a number of trajectories of the system and next establish bounds on the divergence

© Springer International Publishing AG, part of Springer Nature 2018
M. Lohstroh et al. (Eds.): Lee Festschrift, LNCS 10760, pp. 61–76, 2018.
https://doi.org/10.1007/978-3-319-95246-8_4

between the samples and neighboring trajectories. We then use these bounds to provide a guaranteed over-approximation of the reachable set. Unlike [11] that uses Lipschitz constants to bound the divergence between trajectories we use matrix measures that can take negative values, thus allowing for convergence of trajectories and reducing the conservatism in the over-approximation. Another related reference, [10], uses sensitivity equations to track the convergence or divergence properties along simulated trajectories; however, this approach does not guarantee that the computed approximation contains the true reachable set.

In this note we generalize [13] by partitioning the state vector into several components and analyzing the growth or contraction properties in the direction defined by each component. Unlike [13] which searches for a single growth or contraction rate to cover every direction of the state space, the new approach takes advantage of directions that offer more favorable rates. With this generalization we can now analyze the effect of constant but uncertain parameters by treating them as state variables and partitioning them into a separate direction along which no growth occurs. A related approach is employed in [16] where every state variable defines a separate direction; however, this may lead to overly conservative results since the dynamics associated with multiple state variables may possess a more favorable rate than the individual state variables in isolation.

In Sect. 2 we present the main contraction result and a corollary that serves as the starting point for the reachability algorithm. In Sect. 3 we detail the algorithm and demonstrate with an example that it can significantly reduce the conservatism in [13, 16]. In Sect. 4 we present an application to magnetic resonance imaging. Next, in Sect. 5 we derive a numerical procedure to search for weighted norms that yield a prescribed contraction rate, which can be incorporated in the reachability algorithm to adjust the weights to minimize the growth of the reachable set as it propagates through time. Finally, in Sect. 6 we prove the componentwise contraction result presented in Sect. 2.

In the sequel we make use of matrix measures, as defined in [17]. Let $|\cdot|$ be a norm on $\mathbb{R}^n$ and let $\|\cdot\|$ denote the induced matrix norm. The measure $\mu(A)$ of a matrix $A \in \mathbb{R}^{n \times n}$ is the upper right-hand derivative of $\|\cdot\|$ at $I \in \mathbb{R}^{n \times n}$ in the direction of A:

$$\mu(A) \triangleq \lim_{h \to 0^+} \frac{\|I + hA\| - 1}{h}. \tag{1}$$

Unlike a norm the matrix measure can take negative values, as evident in the table below.

2   Componentwise Contraction

Consider the nonlinear dynamical system

$$\dot{x}(t) = f(t, x(t)), \quad x(t) \in \mathbb{R}^n, \tag{2}$$

where $f : [0, \infty) \times \mathbb{R}^n \mapsto \mathbb{R}^n$ is continuous in t and continuously differentiable in x. We partition the state vector x into k components, $x = [x_1^T \cdots x_k^T]^T$, where

Table 1. Commonly used vector norms and their corresponding matrix norms and measures.

Vector norm	Induced matrix norm	Induced matrix measure
$\|x\|_1 = \sum_j \|x_j\|$	$\|A\|_1 = \max_j \sum_i \|a_{ij}\|$	$\mu_1(A) = \max_j \left(a_{jj} + \sum_{i \neq j} \|a_{ij}\|\right)$
$\|x\|_2 = \sqrt{\sum_j x_j^2}$	$\|A\|_2 = \sqrt{\max_j \lambda_j(A^T A)}$	$\mu_2(A) = \max_j \frac{1}{2}\left(\lambda_j(A + A^T)\right)$
$\|x\|_\infty = \max_j \|x_j\|$	$\|A\|_\infty = \max_i \sum_j \|a_{ij}\|$	$\mu_\infty(A) = \max_i \left(a_{ii} + \sum_{j \neq i} \|a_{ij}\|\right)$

$x_i \in \mathbb{R}^{n_i}$, $i = 1, \ldots, k$, and $n_1 + \cdots + n_k = n$. Likewise we decompose the $n \times n$ Jacobian matrix $J(t, x) = (\partial f / \partial x)(t, x)$ into conformal blocks

$$J_{ij}(t, x) \in \mathbb{R}^{n_i \times n_j}, \quad i, j = 1, \ldots, k.$$

The following proposition gives a growth bound between two trajectories of the system (2). Variants of this proposition appear in [18–20]; we provide an independent proof in Sect. 6.

Proposition 1. *Let $C \in \mathbb{R}^{k \times k}$ be a constant matrix such that*

$$C_{ij} \geq \begin{cases} \mu(J_{ii}(t, x)) & i = j \\ \|J_{ij}(t, x)\| & i \neq j \end{cases} \tag{3}$$

for all $(t, x) \in [0, T] \times \mathcal{D}$ on some domain $\mathcal{D} \subset \mathbb{R}^n$. If $x(\cdot)$ and $z(\cdot)$ are two trajectories of (2) such that every trajectory starting on the line segment $\{sx(0) + (1 - s)z(0) : s \in [0, 1]\}$ remains in $\mathcal{D}$ until time T, then

$$\begin{bmatrix} \|x_1(t) - z_1(t)\| \\ \vdots \\ \|x_k(t) - z_k(t)\| \end{bmatrix} \leq \exp(Ct) \begin{bmatrix} \|x_1(0) - z_1(0)\| \\ \vdots \\ \|x_k(0) - z_k(0)\| \end{bmatrix} \quad \forall t \in [0, T], \tag{4}$$

where $\leq$ denotes element-wise inequality. $\square$

We can use a different vector norm for each component in (4), say $\|\cdot\|_{p_i}$ for $x_i(t) - z_i(t)$, provided that we interpret (3) as

$$C_{ij} \geq \begin{cases} \mu_{p_i}(J_{ii}(t, x)) & i = j \\ \|J_{ij}(t, x)\|_{p_i, p_j} & i \neq j, \end{cases} \tag{5}$$

where $\mu_{p_i}(\cdot)$ is the matrix measure for $\|\cdot\|_{p_i}$, and $\|\cdot\|_{p_i, p_j}$ is the mixed norm defined as

$$\|A\|_{p_i, p_j} = \max_{\|x\|_{p_j} = 1} \|Ax\|_{p_i}.$$

We next derive a corollary to Proposition 1 that is useful for reachability analysis. Let $\xi(t, x_0)$ denote the solution of (2) starting from x_0 at $t = 0$, and define the reachable set at time t from initial set Z as

$$Reach_t(Z) \triangleq \{\xi(t, z) : z \in Z\}.$$

Likewise define the reachable set over the time interval $[0, T]$ as

$$Reach_{[0,T]}(Z) \triangleq \cup_{t \in [0,T]} Reach_t(Z).$$

Corollary 1. *Let $x(\cdot)$ be a trajectory of (2) and define the norm ball of initial conditions*

$$\mathcal{B}_{(\epsilon_1, \cdots, \epsilon_k)}(x(0)) \triangleq \{z : |x_1(0) - z_1| \leq \epsilon_1, \cdots, |x_k(0) - z_k| \leq \epsilon_k\},$$

centered at $x(0)$. Suppose a coarse over-approximating set $\mathcal{D} \subset \mathbb{R}^n$ is available such that

$$Reach_{[0,T]}(\mathcal{B}_{(\epsilon_1, \cdots, \epsilon_k)}(x(0))) \subset \mathcal{D} \tag{6}$$

and $C \in \mathbb{R}^{k \times k}$ satisfies (3) for all $(t, x) \in [0, T] \times \mathcal{D}$. Then,

$$Reach_T(\mathcal{B}_{(\epsilon_1, \cdots, \epsilon_k)}(x(0))) \subset \mathcal{B}_{(\delta_1, \cdots, \delta_k)}(x(T)) \tag{7}$$

where

$$\begin{bmatrix} \delta_1 \\ \vdots \\ \delta_k \end{bmatrix} = \exp(CT) \begin{bmatrix} \epsilon_1 \\ \vdots \\ \epsilon_k \end{bmatrix}. \tag{8}$$

□

Corollary 1 relies on a coarse over-approximation $\mathcal{D}$ of the reachable set in (6) to find a constant matrix C satisfying (3). It then uses this C in (7)–(8) to find a more accurate over-approximation of the reachable set at the end of the time interval. One can choose $\mathcal{D}$ to be a bounded invariant set for the system (2), or the entire state space if a global upper bound exists on the right-hand side of (3). For a less conservative estimate one can find a bound on each component of the vector field f on an invariant set of interest,

$$|f_i(t, x)| \leq M_i, \quad i = 1, \ldots, k, \tag{9}$$

and let

$$\mathcal{D} = \mathcal{B}_{(\epsilon_1 + M_1 T, \cdots, \epsilon_k + M_k T)}(x(0)), \tag{10}$$

which gives a tighter bound when the interval length T is smaller.

3   Simulation-Based Reachability Algorithm

Given a sequence of simulation points $x[l] \triangleq x(t_l)$, $l = 0, 1, \ldots, L$, Algorithm 1 below tracks the evolution of the initial norm ball along this trajectory by applying Corollary 1 along with the bound (10) to each interval $[t_l, t_{l+1}]$, $l = 0, 1, \ldots, L - 1$.

A similar approach to reachability was pursued in [13], using the special case of Proposition 1 for $k = 1$. The choice $k = 1$ amounts to looking for a single growth or contraction rate to cover every direction of the state space, which is conservative when some directions offer more favorable rates than others. The

---

Algorithm 1. Algorithm for bounding reachable tube along a sample trajectory

---

Require: Vector $\epsilon = [\epsilon_1, \cdots, \epsilon_k]^T$ for the initial ball size, sequence of simulation points
$x[l] \triangleq x(t_l)$, $l = 0, 1, \ldots, L$, and bounds $M_1, \cdots, M_k$ as in (9)

1: Set $\delta[0] = \epsilon$
2: **for** l from 0 to $L - 1$ **do**
3:     Compute matrix C_l that satisfies (3) for
4:         $t_l \leq t \leq t_{l+1}$ and $x \in \mathcal{B}_{(\delta_1[l]+M_1(t_{l+1}-t_l),\cdots,\delta_k[l]+M_k(t_{l+1}-t_l))}(x[l])$.
5:     Set $\delta[l+1] = \exp(C_l(t_{l+1} - t_l))\delta[l]$
6: **end for**
7: **return** $\mathcal{B}_{\delta_1[l],\cdots,\delta_k[l]}(x[l])$, $l = 1, \ldots, L$

---

other extreme, $k = n$, used in [16] can also lead to overly conservative results, since the dynamics associated with multiple state variables may possess a more favorable rate than the individual state variables in isolation. The following example illustrates that intermediate choices of k may give tighter bounds than the extremes $k = 1$ and $k = n$.

Example 1. We consider the harmonic oscillator

$$\dot{p}(t) = \omega q(t) \tag{11}$$
$$\dot{q}(t) = -\omega p(t) \tag{12}$$

and treat the constant frequency ω as a state variable satisfying

$$\dot{\omega}(t) = 0, \tag{13}$$

so that we can view different values of ω as variations of the initial condition $\omega(0)$. Thus, the state vector is $x = [p\ q\ \omega]^T$ and the Jacobian matrix for (11)–(13) is

$$J(x) = \begin{bmatrix} 0 & \omega & q \\ -\omega & 0 & -p \\ 0 & 0 & 0 \end{bmatrix}. \tag{14}$$

If we partition x into $k = 2$ components as $x_1 = [p\ q]^T$ and $x_2 = \omega$, then

$$J_{11}(x) = \begin{bmatrix} 0 & \omega \\ -\omega & 0 \end{bmatrix} \quad J_{12}(x) = \begin{bmatrix} q \\ -p \end{bmatrix} \quad J_{21}(x) = \begin{bmatrix} 0 & 0 \end{bmatrix} \quad J_{22}(x) = 0, \tag{15}$$

and the matrix measures and norms induced by the Euclidean norm are

$$\mu(J_{11}(x)) = 0, \quad \|J_{12}(x)\| = r \triangleq \sqrt{p^2 + q^2}, \quad \|J_{21}(x)\| = 0, \quad \mu(J_{22}(x)) = 0.$$

Thus,

$$C = \begin{bmatrix} 0 & \bar{r} \\ 0 & 0 \end{bmatrix}$$

satisfies (3) on the invariant set $r \leq \bar{r}$, and it follows from Corollary 1 that the initial norm ball

$$\{(p, q, \omega) : (p - p(0))^2 + (q - q(0))^2 \leq \epsilon_1^2, \ |\omega - \omega(0)| \leq \epsilon_2\} \quad (16)$$

evolves to

$$\{(p, q, \omega) : (p - p(T))^2 + (q - q(T))^2 \leq \delta_1^2, \ |\omega - \omega(T)| \leq \delta_2\}, \quad (17)$$

where $\omega(T) = \omega(0)$ is the nominal frequency with which the sample trajectory is obtained, and

$$\delta_1 = \epsilon_1 + \bar{r}\epsilon_2 T, \quad \delta_2 = \epsilon_2 \quad (18)$$

from (8). Note that (18) correctly predicts the absence of growth in the ω direction, while accounting for the effect of frequency variation on (p, q) by enlarging the radius of the corresponding ball to $\delta_1 = \epsilon_1 + \bar{r}\epsilon_2 T$. Algorithm 1 gives a tighter estimate of δ_1 by applying Corollary 1 along with the bound (10) in every interval $[t_l, t_{l+1}]$, $l = 0, 1, \ldots, L-1$, of the simulated trajectory. A result of this algorithm is shown in Fig. 1 (left) when $w = 1$ and $\epsilon_2 = 0.02$, that is when a $\pm 2\%$ uncertainty is allowed around the nominal frequency. The right panel shows the result with $\epsilon_2 = 0$, in which case there is no uncertainty in frequency and the radius of the norm ball remains constant.

In this example we applied Proposition 1 by partitioning the state into $k = 2$ components. The alternative choice $k = 1$ (no partition) amounts to searching for a single growth rate in each direction and fails to identify the lack of change in the ω direction. Indeed the matrix measure of (14) is positive for any choice of the norm and, thus, the norm ball grows in every direction. The choice $k = 3$ is also overly conservative because it misses the non-expansion property of the combined (p, q) dynamics (11)–(12), instead applying (8) with a matrix of the form

$$C = \begin{bmatrix} 0 & \bar{\omega} & \bar{r} \\ \bar{\omega} & 0 & \bar{r} \\ 0 & 0 & 0 \end{bmatrix},$$

which falsely predicts a rapid growth of the norm ball in the (p, q) direction even when no uncertainty is present in the frequency.

4   Application: Reachable Sets in MRI

In magnetic resonance imaging (MRI) excitation pulse sequences often assume that the magnetization vector describing the system's state begins at the equilibrium [23]. To improve the quality of reconstructed images, such sequences are often used repeatedly and the resulting images averaged to obtain a high-quality image [24]. Achieving this requires a significant amount of time between pulses to ensure that spins in diverse states and with diverse tissue properties all return to the equilibrium before the next excitation pulse can be applied. This can lead

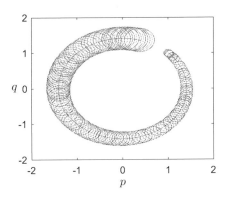 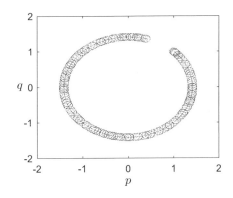

Fig. 1. Algorithm 1 applied to a sample trajectory of (11)–(13) with $\omega = 1$. The initial norm ball is as in (16) with $\epsilon_1 = 0.1$. The plot on the left takes $\epsilon_2 = 0.02$, which means a $\pm 2\%$ uncertainty around the nominal frequency $\omega = 1$. This uncertainty leads to a growth of the radius of the norm ball in the (p, q) direction. The plot on the right takes $\epsilon_2 = 0$ and, since there is no uncertainty in the frequency, the radius of the norm ball in the (p, q) direction remains constant. The bound M_1 used in the algorithm is calculated on the invariant set $\sqrt{p^2 + q^2} \leq 2$.

to long acquisitions that could be expedited if we could prove that all states have reached a neighborhood of the equilibrium after a certain time interval has elapsed.

We consider a model that describes the evolution of the magnetic moment of a collection of spins, evolving according to the Bloch Equation for spins in a constant B_0 field:

$$\frac{d}{dt}\begin{bmatrix} M_x \\ M_y \\ M_z \end{bmatrix} = \begin{bmatrix} -\frac{1}{T_2} & \gamma B_0 & 0 \\ -\gamma B_0 & -\frac{1}{T_2} & 0 \\ 0 & 0 & -\frac{1}{T_1} \end{bmatrix} \begin{bmatrix} M_x \\ M_y \\ M_z \end{bmatrix} + \begin{bmatrix} 0 \\ 0 \\ \frac{M_0}{T_1} \end{bmatrix}$$

Introducing the vector of states $x = [M_x, M_y, M_z, \frac{1}{T_1}, \frac{1}{T_2}]^T$, which include the uncertain relaxation constants $1/T_1$ and $1/T_2$, and defining the known parameters $\theta_1 = \gamma B_0$, $\theta_2 = M_0$, we write these equations as

$$\dot{x} = \begin{bmatrix} -x_1 x_5 + \theta_1 x_2 \\ -\theta_1 x_1 - x_2 x_5 \\ -x_4 x_3 + \theta_2 x_4 \\ 0 \\ 0 \end{bmatrix}, \tag{19}$$

and the Jacobian of this system as

$$J(t, x) = \begin{bmatrix} -x_5 & \theta_1 & 0 & 0 & -x_1 \\ -\theta_1 & -x_5 & 0 & 0 & -x_2 \\ 0 & 0 & -x_4 & (\theta_2 - x_3) & 0 \\ 0 & 0 & 0 & 0 & 0 \\ 0 & 0 & 0 & 0 & 0 \end{bmatrix}.$$

Note that for any $0 < r_1 < R_1$ and $0 < r_2 < R_2$ the set

$$\mathcal{D} = \{x \in \mathbb{R}^5 : x_1^2 + x_2^2 \leq \theta_2^2, x_3^2 \leq \theta_2^2, r_1 \leq x_4 \leq R_1, r_2 \leq x_5 \leq R_2\}$$

is forward invariant and a norm ball of the form described in Corollary 1. Partitioning the state space into blocks as (x_1, x_2), (x_3), (x_4), (x_5), and using the Euclidean norm we see that

$$\mu(J_{11}(t,x)) = \max_j \frac{1}{2}\lambda_j(\begin{bmatrix} -x_5 & \theta_1 \\ -\theta_1 & -x_5 \end{bmatrix}^T + \begin{bmatrix} -x_5 & \theta_1 \\ -\theta_1 & -x_5 \end{bmatrix}) = \max_j \lambda_j \begin{bmatrix} -x_5 & 0 \\ 0 & -x_5 \end{bmatrix}$$

$$= -x_5 \leq -r_2$$

$$\mu(J_{22}(t,x)) = -x_4 \leq -r_1$$
$$\|J_{14}(t,x)\| = \sqrt{(-x_1)^2 + (-x_2)^2} \leq \theta_2$$
$$\|J_{23}(t,x)\| = |\theta_2 - x_3| \leq 2\theta_2$$

and all others are zero. Thus we can set

$$C = \begin{bmatrix} -r_2 & 0 & 0 & \theta_2 \\ 0 & -r_1 & 2\theta_2 & 0 \\ 0 & 0 & 0 & 0 \\ 0 & 0 & 0 & 0 \end{bmatrix}.$$

We simulate ball widths for three groupings of states: a single group ($k = 1$) with all five states, $k = 5$ independent groups of 1 state and the partition of $k = 4$ blocks of states described above. In Fig. 2 we see that while the single group and independent groups both lead to the exponential expansion of the ball radii, by grouping states in an appropriate manner we can achieve stable ball radius dynamics. Additional details on simulation parameters, and source code to reproduce the results in Fig. 2 can be found at https://github.com/maidens/Edward-A-Lee-Festschrift-2017.

5 Automatic Selection of Weighted Norms

In [13] we demonstrated that using *weighted* 1-, 2- or ∞-norms, where the weights are adjusted along the simulated trajectory, can significantly tighten the overapproximation of the reachable tube. In particular we showed that bounding the matrix measure induced by weighted 1-, 2- or ∞-norms can be expressed as constraints that are convex functions of the weights, and used this fact to develop a heuristic for minimizing the growth of the reachable set. The authors of [21] use the linear matrix inequality (LMI) constraint corresponding to the weighted 2-norm together with interval bounds on the Jacobian to argue that optimal bounds on the Jacobian matrix measure can be computed automatically by solving a sequence of semidefinite programs (SDPs).

We now extend this SDP approach to componentwise contraction and present a procedure to search for weighted norms that yield a prescribed contraction

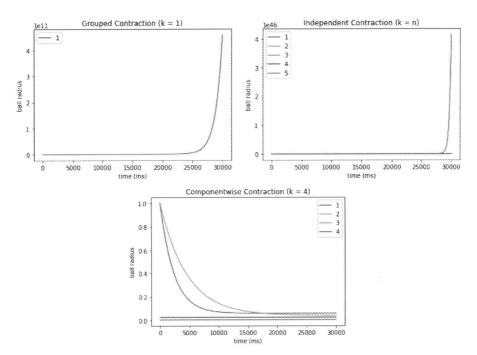

Fig. 2. Simulated ball radii using three state groupings. Top, left: a single group ($k = 1$) with all five states; top, right: $k = 5$ independent groups of 1 state; bottom: the partition of $k = 4$ blocks of states described above.

rate. To this end, in Proposition 2 we show that for a fixed matrix C the set of weight matrices for which a weighted 2-norm version of (3) holds is a convex set that can be expressed as the conjunction of an infinite number of LMIs. Then in Proposition 3 we show how polytopic bounds on the Jacobian can be exploited to compute an inner approximation of the set of feasible weight matrices, enabling weight matrices to be selected automatically using a standard numerical SDP solver.

We begin with two Lemmas that demonstrate how weighted matrix measure and norm bounds can be expressed as LMIs. Here the inequality symbol $A \preceq B$ means that $B - A$ is a positive semidefinite matrix.

Lemma 1 *(Lemma 2 of [22]). If*

$$\Gamma A + A^T \Gamma \preceq 2c\Gamma$$

where Γ is a positive definite matrix then $\mu(A) \leq c$ in the norm $x \to |Px|_2$ where $P = \Gamma^{1/2} \succeq 0$.

Lemma 2. *If*

$$A^T \Gamma_i A \preceq c^2 \Gamma_j$$

where Γ_i and Γ_j are positive definite matrices and $c \geq 0$ then $\|A\| \leq c$ where $\|\cdot\|$ denotes the mixed norm

$$\|A\| = \max_{|P_j x|_2 = 1} |P_i A x|_2$$

where $P_i = \Gamma_i^{1/2}$ and $P_j = \Gamma_j^{1/2}$.

Proof. $A^T \Gamma_i A \preceq c^2 \Gamma_j$ implies that for all x

$$|P_i A x|_2^2 = x^T A^T \Gamma_i A x \leq c^2 x^T \Gamma_j x = c^2 |P_j x|_2^2.$$

Thus

$$\|A\|^2 = \max_{|P_j x|_2 = 1} |P_i A x|_2^2 \leq c^2,$$

or equivalently $\|A\| \leq c$.   □

Combining Lemmas 1 and 2 along with the reasoning used to derive Eq. (5), we arrive at the following result:

Proposition 2. *Given a matrix $C \in \mathbb{R}^{k \times k}$, the search for weighted Euclidean norms $x_i \mapsto |P_i x_i|$ for $i = 1, \ldots, k$ in which (3) is satisfied can be formulated as a semidefinite program:*

find $\Gamma_1, \ldots, \Gamma_k$

subject to $\Gamma_i \succeq 0, \quad \forall i = 1, \ldots, k$

$$\Gamma_i J_{ii}(t,x) + J_{ii}(t,x)^T \Gamma_i \preceq 2 c_{ii} \Gamma_i, \quad \forall (t,x) \in [0,T] \times \mathcal{D}, \quad \forall i = 1, \ldots, k \qquad (20)$$

$$J_{ij}(t,x)^T \Gamma_i J_{ij}(t,x) \preceq c_{ij}^2 \Gamma_j \quad \forall (t,x) \in [0,T] \times \mathcal{D}, \quad \forall j \neq i, i = 1, \ldots, k$$

where $\Gamma_i = P_i^T P_i$.

Note that (20) contains an infinite number of LMI constraints and therefore cannot be solved numerically using a standard SDP solver. To address this we show how a conservative inner approximation of the feasible set can be defined in terms of a finite conjunction of LMIs. Before stating this result, we prove the following lemma which shows how an infinite family of LMIs can be conservatively approximated by a finite family of LMIs by assuming the existence of polytopic bounds on the coefficient matrices.

Lemma 3. *For all $i = 0, \ldots, n$ let $F_i(z)$ be a family of symmetric matrices parameterized by $z \in Z$. Assume that there exist a finite set of matrices $\{F_{ik_i} : k_i = 1, \ldots, N_i; i = 0, \ldots, n\}$ such that for each i the family $F_i(z)$ is bounded by the matrix polytope with vertices F_{ik_i}:*

$$\{F_i(z) : z \in Z\} \subseteq Conv(\{F_{ik_i} : k_i = 1, \ldots, N_i\}) \qquad (21)$$

where Conv denotes the convex hull. Then

$$F_{0k_0} + x_1 F_{1k_1} + \ldots x_n F_{nk_n} \succeq 0 \quad \forall (k_0, \ldots k_n) \in [N_0] \times \cdots \times [N_n],$$

where $[N_i] := \{1, \ldots, N_i\}$, *implies*

$$F_0(z) + x_1 F_1(z) + \cdots + x_n F_n(z) \succeq 0 \quad \forall z \in Z.$$

Proof. Let $z \in Z$. Using the assumption (21) we know that for each i there exist nonnegative weights λ_{ik_i} with $\sum_{k_i} \lambda_{ik_i} = 1$ such that $F_i(z) = \sum_{k_i} \lambda_{ik_i} F_{ik_i}$. Therefore

$$F_0(z) + x_1 F_1(z) + \cdots + x_n F_n(z)$$

$$= \sum_{k_0} \lambda_{0k_0} F_{0k_0} + x_1 \sum_{k_1} \lambda_{1k_1} F_{1k_1} + \cdots + x_n \sum_{k_n} \lambda_{nk_n} F_{nk_n}$$

$$= \prod_{j \neq 0} \left(\sum_{k_j} \lambda_{jk_j} \right) \left(\sum_{k_0} \lambda_{0k_0} F_{0k_0} \right) + \cdots + x_n \prod_{j \neq n} \left(\sum_{k_j} \lambda_{jk_j} \right) \left(\sum_{k_n} \lambda_{nk_n} F_{nk_n} \right)$$

$$= \sum_{k_0} \cdots \sum_{k_n} (\lambda_{0k_0} \ldots \lambda_{nk_n})(F_{0k_0} + x_1 F_{1k_1} + \ldots x_n F_{nk_n})$$

$$\succeq 0. \qquad \qquad \square$$

We now state a result that allows us to find a set of weights satisfying (3) by solving only a finite set of LMIs.

Proposition 3. *For each i let $\{E_{i\ell_i} : \ell_i = 1, \ldots, n_i(n_i + 1)/2\}$ be a basis for the space of $n_i \times n_i$ symmetric matrices. Suppose that there exist matrices such that*

$$\{E_{i\ell_i} J_{ii}(t, x) + J_{ii}(t, x)^T E_{i\ell_i} : (t, x) \in [0, T] \times \mathcal{D}\}$$
$$\subseteq Conv(\{F_{i\ell_i k_{i\ell_i}} : k_{i\ell_i} \in [N_{i\ell_i}]\})$$
$$\{J_{ij}(t, x)^T E_{i\ell_i} J_{ij}(t, x) : (t, x) \in [0, T] \times \mathcal{D}\}$$
$$\subseteq Conv(\{\tilde{F}_{ij\ell_i k_{ij\ell_i}} : k_{ij\ell_i} \in [N_{ij\ell_i}]\}).$$

Then any solution to the SDP

$$\textbf{find} \quad x_{i\ell_i} \quad \forall i \in [k] \quad \forall \ell_i \in [n_i(n_i + 1)/2]$$

$$\textbf{subject to} \quad \sum_{\ell_i} x_{i\ell_i} E_{i\ell_i} \succeq 0, \quad \forall i \in [k]$$

$$\sum_{\ell_i} x_{i\ell_i} F_{i\ell_i k_{i\ell_i}} \preceq 2c_{ii} \sum_{\ell_i} x_{i\ell_i} E_{i\ell_i}, \quad \forall i \in [k]$$

$$\forall (k_{i1}, \ldots, k_{i,n_i(n_i+1)/2}) \in [N_{i1}] \times \cdots \times [N_{i,n_i(n_i+1)/2}]$$

$$\sum_{\ell_i} x_{i\ell_i} \tilde{F}_{ij\ell_i k_{ij\ell_i}} \preceq c_{ij}^2 \sum_{\ell_j} x_{j\ell_j} E_{jk_j} \quad \forall i \in [k] \quad \forall j \in [k] \setminus \{i\}$$

$$\forall (k_{ij1}, \ldots, k_{ij,n_i(n_i+1)/2}) \in [N_{ij1}] \times \cdots \times [N_{ij,n_i(n_i+1)/2}]$$

$$(22)$$

yields a solution $\Gamma_i = \sum_{\ell_i} x_{i\ell_i} E_{i\ell_i}$ to (20).

The proof follows in a straightforward manner from (20) by expanding the decision variables as $\Gamma_i = \sum_{\ell_i} x_{i\ell_i} E_{i\ell_i}$ then applying Lemma 3. Note that if $\mathcal{D}$ is compact and $(t, x) \mapsto J(t, x)$ is continuous, it is always possible to find a collection of such matrices F and $\tilde{F}$.

6   Proof of Proposition 1

Let $\psi(t, s)$ denote the solution of (2) with initial condition $sx(0) + (1 - s)z(0)$; that is,

$$\frac{\partial \psi(t, s)}{\partial t} = f(t, \psi(t, s)) \tag{23}$$

$$\psi(0, s) = sx(0) + (1 - s)z(0). \tag{24}$$

In particular,

$$\psi(t, 1) = x(t) \quad \text{and} \quad \psi(t, 0) = z(t). \tag{25}$$

Taking the derivative of both sides of (23) with respect to s we get

$$\frac{\partial^2 \psi(t, s)}{\partial t \partial s} = \frac{\partial f(t, \psi(t, s))}{\partial s} = J(t, \psi(t, s)) \frac{\partial \psi(t, s)}{\partial s},$$

which means that the variable

$$w(t, s) \triangleq \frac{\partial \psi(t, s)}{\partial s} \tag{26}$$

satisfies

$$\frac{\partial w(t, s)}{\partial t} = J(t, \psi(t, s))w(t, s). \tag{27}$$

We then conclude from Lemma 4 below that

$$D^+|w_i(t, s)| \le \mu(J_{ii}(t, \psi(t, s)))|w_i(t, s)| + \sum_{j \ne i} \|J_{ij}(t, \psi(t, s))\|\|w_j(t, s)\|, \tag{28}$$

where D^+ denotes the upper right-hand derivative with respect to t. Since $\psi(t, s) \in \mathcal{D}$ for $t \in [0, T]$ and (3) holds for all $(t, x) \in [0, T] \times \mathcal{D}$, we conclude

$$D^+|w_i(t, s)| \le C_{ii}|w_i(t, s)| + \sum_{j \ne i} C_{ij}|w_j(t, s)|. \tag{29}$$

This means that

$$D^+ \begin{bmatrix} |w_1(t, s)| \\ \vdots \\ |w_k(t, s)| \end{bmatrix} \le C \begin{bmatrix} |w_1(t, s)| \\ \vdots \\ |w_k(t, s)| \end{bmatrix} \tag{30}$$

and, since the matrix C is Metzler ($C_{ij} \ge 0$ when $i \ne j$), it follows from standard comparison theorems for positive systems that

$$\begin{bmatrix} |w_1(t, s)| \\ \vdots \\ |w_k(t, s)| \end{bmatrix} \le \exp(Ct) \begin{bmatrix} |w_1(0, s)| \\ \vdots \\ |w_k(0, s)| \end{bmatrix}. \tag{31}$$

Note from (26) and (24) that

$$w(0, s) = \frac{\partial \psi(0, s)}{\partial s} = x(0) - z(0) \tag{32}$$

and, thus,

$$\begin{bmatrix} |w_1(0, s)| \\ \vdots \\ |w_k(0, s)| \end{bmatrix} = \begin{bmatrix} |x_1(0) - z_1(0)| \\ \vdots \\ |x_k(0) - z_k(0)| \end{bmatrix}. \tag{33}$$

Substituting (33) in (31) we get

$$\begin{bmatrix} |w_1(t, s)| \\ \vdots \\ |w_k(t, s)| \end{bmatrix} \leq \exp(Ct) \begin{bmatrix} |x_1(0) - z_1(0)| \\ \vdots \\ |x_k(0) - z_k(0)| \end{bmatrix}. \tag{34}$$

Next, note from (25) that

$$x(t) - z(t) = \psi(t, 1) - \psi(t, 0) = \int_0^1 \frac{\partial \psi(t, s)}{\partial s} ds = \int_0^1 w(t, s) ds, \tag{35}$$

which implies

$$\begin{bmatrix} |x_1(t) - z_1(t)| \\ \vdots \\ |x_k(t) - z_k(t)| \end{bmatrix} \leq \begin{bmatrix} \int_0^1 |w_1(t, s)| ds \\ \vdots \\ \int_0^1 |w_k(t, s)| ds \end{bmatrix}. \tag{36}$$

Noting from (34) that

$$\begin{bmatrix} \int_0^1 |w_1(t, s)| ds \\ \vdots \\ \int_0^1 |w_k(t, s)| ds \end{bmatrix} \leq \exp(Ct) \begin{bmatrix} |x_1(0) - z_1(0)| \\ \vdots \\ |x_k(0) - z_k(0)| \end{bmatrix} \tag{37}$$

and combining with (36) we obtain (4).   □

Lemma 4. *Consider the linear time-varying system*

$$\dot{w}(t) = A(t)w(t), \quad w(t) \in \mathbb{R}^n, \tag{38}$$

where $A(\cdot)$ is continuous. Suppose we decompose $A(t) \in \mathbb{R}^{n \times n}$ into blocks $A_{ij}(t) \in \mathbb{R}^{n_i \times n_j}$, $i, j = 1, \ldots, k$ such that $n_1 + \cdots + n_k = n$, and let $w_i(t) \in \mathbb{R}^{n_i}$, $i = 1, \ldots, k$, constitute a conformal partition of $w(t) \in \mathbb{R}^n$. Then

$$D^+|w_i(t)| \triangleq \lim_{h \to 0^+} \frac{|w_i(t+h)| - |w_i(t)|}{h}$$
$$\leq \mu(A_{ii}(t))|w_i(t)| + \sum_{j \neq i} \|A_{ij}(t)\| |w_j(t)|. \tag{39}$$

Proof of Lemma 4. Note that

$$
\lim_{h\to 0^+} \frac{|w_i(t+h)| - |w_i(t)|}{h} = \lim_{h\to 0^+} \frac{|w_i(t) + h\dot{w}_i(t)| - |w_i(t)|}{h}
$$

$$
= \lim_{h\to 0^+} \frac{|w_i(t) + hA_{ii}(t)w_i(t) + h\sum_{j\neq i} A_{ij}(t)w_j(t)| - |w_i(t)|}{h}
$$

$$
\leq \lim_{h\to 0^+} \frac{|w_i(t) + hA_{ii}(t)w_i(t)| - |w_i(t)|}{h} + |\sum_{j\neq i} A_{ij}(t)w_j(t)|
$$

$$
\leq \lim_{h\to 0^+} \frac{\|I + hA_{ii}(t)\| - 1}{h}|w_i(t)| + \sum_{j\neq i} \|A_{ij}(t)\|\,|w_j(t)|.
$$

Then (39) follows from the definition of the matrix norm, (1). □

7   Conclusions

In this note we continued the development of reachable tube estimates around simulated trajectories of a nonlinear dynamical system. We followed the contraction approach of [13], which establishes bounds on the convergence or divergence between the samples and neighboring trajectories that are not explicitly simulated. Unlike [13], however, we pursued a componentwise contraction analysis where we partition the state vector into several components and analyze contraction properties separately in each direction. Such partitioning offers new degrees of flexibility in our algorithms to tighten the reachable tube estimates. For example, we can now analyze the effect of constant but uncertain parameters by treating them as state variables and partitioning them into a separate direction.

An important question that must be further studied is how to select the number of components k and how to partition the state vector into k components. Although the examples gave some intuition about the choice of partitioning, the most favorable choice remains problem-specific and further tools are needed to select from among possible partitions. One possibility is to explore using the sparsity structure of the Jacobian $J(t,x)$ and graph cut criteria to automatically generate partition candidates. Once a pool of candidates are identified the reachability algorithm can be performed in parallel for each partition to select for more favorable estimates.

References

1. Kapinski, J., Deshmukh, J.V., Jin, X., Ito, H., Butts, K.: Simulation-based approaches for verification of embedded control systems: an overview of traditional and advanced modeling, testing, and verification techniques. IEEE Control Syst. **36**(6), 45–64 (2016)
2. Tabuada, P.: Verification and Control of Hybrid Systems: A Symbolic Approach. Springer, Heidelberg (2009). https://doi.org/10.1007/978-1-4419-0224-5

3. Mitchell, I., Bayen, A., Tomlin, C.: A time-dependent Hamilton-Jacobi formulation of reachable sets for continuous dynamic games. IEEE Trans. Autom. Control **50**(7), 947–957 (2005)
4. Althoff, M., Stursberg, O., Buss, M.: Reachability analysis of nonlinear systems with uncertain parameters using conservative linearization. In: IEEE Conference Decision Control, pp. 4042–4048 (2008)
5. Chutinan, A., Krogh, B.: Computational techniques for hybrid system verification. IEEE Trans. Autom. Control **48**(1), 64–75 (2003)
6. Lin, Y., Stadtherr, M.A.: Validated solutions of initial value problems for parametric ODEs. Appl. Numer. Math. **57**(10), 1145–1162 (2007)
7. Neher, M., Jackson, K.R., Nedialkov, N.S.: On Taylor model based integration of ODEs. SIAM J. Numer. Anal. **45**, 236–262 (2007)
8. Lakshmikantham, V., Leela, S.: Differential and Integral Inequalities, vol. 1. Academic Press, New York (1969)
9. Scott, J.K., Barton, P.I.: Bounds on the reachable sets of nonlinear control systems. Automatica **49**(1), 93–100 (2013)
10. Donzé, A., Maler, O.: Systematic simulation using sensitivity analysis. In: Bemporad, A., Bicchi, A., Buttazzo, G. (eds.) HSCC 2007. LNCS, vol. 4416, pp. 174–189. Springer, Heidelberg (2007). https://doi.org/10.1007/978-3-540-71493-4_16
11. Huang, Z., Mitra, S.: Computing bounded reach sets from sampled simulation traces. In: Hybrid Systems: Computation and Control, pp. 291–294 (2012)
12. Julius, A.A., Pappas, G.J.: Trajectory based verification using local finite-time invariance. In: Majumdar, R., Tabuada, P. (eds.) HSCC 2009. LNCS, vol. 5469, pp. 223–236. Springer, Heidelberg (2009). https://doi.org/10.1007/978-3-642-00602-9_16
13. Maidens, J., Arcak, M.: Reachability analysis of nonlinear systems using matrix measures. IEEE Trans. Autom. Control **60**(1), 265–270 (2015)
14. Lohmiller, W., Slotine, J.J.: On contraction analysis for nonlinear systems. Automatica **34**, 683–696 (1998)
15. Sontag, E.D.: Contractive systems with inputs. In: Willems, J.C., Hara, S., Ohta, Y., Fujioka, H. (eds.) Perspectives in Mathematical System Theory, Control, and Signal Processing, pp. 217–228. Springer, Heidelberg (2010). https://doi.org/10.1007/978-3-540-93918-4_20
16. Rungger, M., Zamani, M.: SCOTS: a tool for the synthesis of symbolic controllers. In: Proceedings of the 19th International Conference on Hybrid Systems: Computation and Control HSCC 2016 (2016)
17. Desoer, C., Vidyasagar, M.: Feedback systems: input-output properties. In: Society for Industrial and Applied Mathematics, Philadelphia (2009). Academic Press, New York (1975)
18. Kapela, T., Zgliczyński, P.: A Lohner-type algorithm for control systems and ordinary differential equations. Discret. Continuous Dyn. Syst. Ser. B **11**(2), 365–385 (2009)
19. Russo, G., di Bernardo, M., Sontag, E.D.: A contraction approach to the hierarchical analysis and design of networked systems. IEEE Trans. Autom. Control **58**(5), 1328–1331 (2013)
20. Reissig, G., Weber, A., Rungger, M.: Feedback refinement relations for the synthesis of symbolic controllers. IEEE Trans. Autom. Control **62**(4), 1781–1796 (2017)
21. Fan, C., Kapinski, J., Jin, X., Mitra, S.: Locally optimal reach set over-approximation for nonlinear systems. In: Proceedings of the 13th International Conference on Embedded Software. EMSOFT 2016, pp. 6:1–6:10 (2016)

22. Aminzare, Z., Shafi, Y., Arcak, M., Sontag, E.D.: Guaranteeing spatial uniformity in reaction-diffusion systems using weighted L^2 norm contractions. In: Kulkarni, V.V., Stan, G.-B., Raman, K. (eds.) A Systems Theoretic Approach to Systems and Synthetic Biology I: Models and System Characterizations, pp. 73–101. Springer, Dordrecht (2014). https://doi.org/10.1007/978-94-017-9041-3_3
23. Nishimura, D.G.: Principles of Magnetic Resonance Imaging. Lulu, Morrisville (2010)
24. Edelstein, W.A., Glover, G.H., Hardy, C.J., Redington, R.W.: The intrinsic signal-to-noise ratio in NMR imaging. Magn. Reson. Med. **3**(4), 604–618 (1986)

Predictability Issues in Mixed-Criticality Real-Time Systems

Sanjoy Baruah[✉]

Washington University in St. Louis, St. Louis, MO 63130, USA
baruah@wustl.edu
https://sites.wustl.edu/baruah

Abstract. TIMING PREDICTABILITY is an explicit requirement for many safety-critical real-time systems. In building such systems, this requirement is typically met by establishing, to an appropriate level of assurance, that salient run-time temporal properties of the system being designed can be accurately predicted prior to run-time. But what of real-time systems supporting multiple functionalities that are not all equally critical? In such systems, it may suffice to establish the timing predictability of less critical functionalities to lower levels of assurance than is needed for highly critical functionalities. We examine the implications of this fact on the deterministic modeling of real-time systems, and explore means for exploiting it in order to achieve more resource-efficient implementations of mixed-criticality real-time systems.

1 Introduction

Many cyber-physical systems (CPSs) are responsible for highly safety-critical functionalities. Since incorrect run-time behavior by such systems may have potentially disastrous consequences, it is typically required that these systems have their correctness validated prior to deployment; in some application domains such as avionics, such validation is mandated by statutory certification authorities. A rigorous approach towards performing such validation would have us (i) *construct formal models* of the run-time behavior of the system, and make an authoritative and persuasive argument that these models do indeed represent the actual behavior that the system will exhibit during run-time; and (ii) *prove properties* of these models that establish the correctness of the run-time behavior of the system that is modeled.

Such an approach to validating correctness is applicable only if the run-time behavior of the system can be reliably predicted based upon pre-run-time analysis of the model; indeed, such *predictability* has long been considered one of the cornerstone requirements for safety-critical systems [19]. We illustrate the role of predictability in the validation of safety-critical system correctness by considering a (very small) part of the requirement specifications for airbags installed in cars: it is required that the "airbag deploys [only] upon collisions equivalent to hitting a static barrier at speeds 8 mph or higher, within 70 ms

© Springer International Publishing AG, part of Springer Nature 2018
M. Lohstroh et al. (Eds.): Lee Festschrift, LNCS 10760, pp. 77–87, 2018.
https://doi.org/10.1007/978-3-319-95246-8_5

of impact" [12]. Observe that these specifications impose at least two forms of predictability requirements upon the system:

1. *Functional* predictability requirements: the airbag must predictably be shown to inflate upon the occurrence of specified events.
2. *Timing* predictability requirements: the airbag must predictably be shown to inflate within the specified maximum duration of time after the occurrence of a triggering event.

Both predictability requirements, functional and timing, are equally central to establishing correctness; however, most computing devices (processors, networking elements, etc.) are built to ensure functional correctness rather than timing predictability.[1] This is by design: these computing devices are built to implement formalisms such as Turing machines that abstract away notions of time and other physical factors in axiomatizing, and thereby obtaining a formalization of, the process of computation. Thus, this aspect of focusing on functional, rather than timing, properties, is a feature of these devices and not a bug; however, it is an aspect we must explicitly consider as we seek to achieve both functional *and* timing predictability in our CPSs.

2   Current Approaches to Achieving Timing Predictability

In discussing the behavior of a CPS, it is often convenient to consider the CPS as comprising three constituent components:

1. The *programs* that we write in order to achieve the functionality that we desire of our CPS;
2. The *platform* upon which these programs execute during run-time; and
3. The *environment* with which the implementation (i.e., the programs executing upon the platform) interacts through the use of sensors and actuators.

The run-time behavior is defined by this interaction of the implementation with the environment. As discussed above, such behavior may be required to be predictable with regards to both functional and timing properties. Current approaches to obtaining safety-critical systems that possess predictable properties are often centered on the principle of *correctness by construction*: synthesize the systems using a disciplined approach, based upon following well-established guidelines and methodologies, which ensures that the constructed system possesses the desired predictability properties. But any *uncertainty* in the precise characterization of the run-time timing behavior of one or more of the three components of a CPS makes it difficult to achieve timing predictability in this manner. As we will see, some timing uncertainty tends to be present in all but

---

[1] We point out that there are some exceptions to this general rule, in the form of efforts at developing time-deterministic hardware—a particularly noteworthy example is the Precision Timed Machine project [9,11]. See [4] for a survey of research efforts at building predictable systems using current hardware.

the simplest CPS; most current approaches to building safety-critical systems deal with such uncertainty by (i) enforcing deterministic timing behavior upon the computational components that are used to build the system; and (ii) representing the interaction between the implementation and the environment by deterministic models. Let us now separately review how determinism is used in this manner to facilitate timing predictability from the perspectives of each of the three constituent components of a CPS: the programs, the platforms, and the operating environment.

§1. Programs. There appears to be widespread agreement within the safety-critical systems community that the cause of predictability is best served by requiring that programs exhibit deterministic behavior during run-time. This edict argues against the use of general-purpose programming languages in safety-critical systems implementation, instead favoring the use of special-purpose languages that guarantee deterministic behavior. These include languages such as Lustre [13], Esterel [7], and Signal [17] that are based upon the synchronous-reactive (SR) paradigm of computing [6]. The principles of SR programming also underlie the semantics of the coordination language Ptolemy II [10], and the widely-used modeling frameworks Statecharts [15] and Statemate [14]. The SR paradigm of computing makes the same abstraction for programming as the clock does in digital circuit design, by introducing the notion of a logical clock "tick": time is modeled as advancing in discrete steps, each represented by one such tick. A synchronous program interacts with its environment at the beginning of each tick, and computations are structured as an ordering of actions. Each action is assumed to execute atomically, and execution of all the actions assigned to a clock tick are required to converge to a unique fixed point by the end of the tick. In this manner, the (functional) non-determinism that may result from the interleaving of concurrent behaviors is eliminated, and deterministic functional semantics enforced.

§2. Platforms. Safety-critical real-time systems were initially implemented upon custom-built hardware that was explicitly designed to provide timing as well as functional determinism. As these systems became more computationally demanding, however, it became economically infeasible to continue to custom build powerful enough platforms; today safety-critical systems are increasingly implemented upon platforms comprising commercial off-the-shelf (COTS) computing components. Such COTS components are typically developed with an objective of providing improved average-case performance rather than good guaranteed worst-case bounds with regards to extra-functional properties such as timing behavior. Hence they come equipped with advanced features (such as multiple cores on a single CPU, complex networks on chip, cache memory, etc.) that speed up average-case performance but may exhibit unpredictable timing behavior during run-time. In order to enforce deterministic timing behavior upon platforms comprising such components, current practice is to explicitly or implicitly disable those advanced features that compromise determinism. For instance, it is considered good practice in some safety-critical application domains to statically partition (or in some extreme cases, entirely disable) cache memories prior to implementation, the motivation for doing so being that one is willing to forgo the improved average-case performance offered by caches in order to not have to deal with the inherent unpredictability in run-time timing behavior that typically accompanies such performance improvements. Another more extreme illustration of this performance-predictability tradeoff is to be found in the CAST 32 [2] recommendations of the Certification Authorities Software Team that all computing cores except one be disabled upon multicore processors hosting highly safety-critical software.[2]

§3. The Environment. As we have seen above, it is possible to enforce deterministic run-time behavior upon the implementation of a CPS – the programs, and the platforms upon which these programs execute. Let us now turn our attention to the third constituent component of the CPS – the physical environment within which the CPS implementation operates, and with which it interacts through the use of sensors and actuators. Is a similar strategy applicable here?

Here, it should be observed that since the physical environment is external to the system under development and hence typically not under the control of the system developer, it is not really feasible to *enforce* determinism upon the environment – the environment is part of the physical world (the "P" in "CPS"). So the more germane question to ask is: Is the physical world deterministic? The answer, in brief, is that we do not know: this question lies at the heart of some of the deepest and most fundamental issues in disciplines as diverse as physics, philosophy, and religion. However, we believe that the answer to this question is not very relevant to us in our quest for timing predictability: regardless of whether the physical world is deterministic or not, the fact of the matter is that the interaction of any non-trivial CPS with the physical world is likely to be very complex, and is governed by laws that are tremendously complex and chaotic, and often extremely sensitive to initial conditions. Hence, even if such interaction were in fact completely deterministic, we cannot hope to represent it exactly for the purposes of analysis—doing so would yield analysis problems that are computationally hopelessly intractable. Instead, we represent this interaction using models that highlight the relevant aspects of the interaction while abstracting away the less relevant ones. Such models necessarily *approximate*; for safety-critical CPSs, the approximations must err on the side of caution and incorporate safety margins. In order to facilitate the goal of ensuring timing predictability, current practice is to ensure that over-approximations in these models along the timing dimension are deterministic. As we continue to become more ambitious regarding the functionality we desire of our CPSs, their interaction with the physical world continues to increase in complexity and our simplified models of such interaction necessarily incorporate increasingly larger safety margins.

---

[2] The more recent CAST-32A recommendations are somewhat more liberal and allow for exceptions to this under carefully controlled circumstances.

3   The Cost of Achieving Predictability via Determinism

While enforcing determinism as discussed above has proved an effective approach for achieving predictability (in the sense that several large complex CPSs have been successfully developed and deployed), such an approach comes at considerable cost with regards to the *run-time resource efficiency* of the resulting implementation. We will show below how imposing deterministic timing behavior on hardware components, and modeling the interaction of the implementation and the environment in a deterministic manner, has the potential to yield system implementations that severely under-utilize platform resources during run-time.

Platforms. A series of significant advances in computer architecture and in chip-manufacturing technologies has led to a tremendous increase in the computational capabilities of COTS platforms. However, this has had a significant side-effect—many of the features that have enabled this increase in computational capabilities have also resulted in platforms that exhibit great unpredictability and variation in run-time behavior with regards to extra-functional properties. Of particular relevance to us in our quest to achieve timing predictability is variations and unpredictability in the *execution time* of pieces of code upon COTS platforms. It is widely recognized (see, e.g., [21]) that the true worst-case execution time (WCET) of some pieces of code upon some advanced modern COTS platforms may be several orders of magnitude greater than their average execution times, but are extremely unlikely to occur in practice—their occurrence follows from the concurrent happening (a "perfect storm") of a large number of unlikely events. Two strategies are commonly used to achieve timing predictability in the face of this fact:

1. As stated in Sect. 2 above, one approach is by restricting or disabling advanced platform features such as cache, thereby driving up average-case execution times but reducing WCETs.
2. Another approach is to over-approximate the run-time timing behavior and perform pre-runtime analysis under the assumption that actual run-time will be very close to the pre-determined WCET, even though this is very unlikely to happen in practice. (Under such an approach, care must be taken to ensure that *sustainable* [5] techniques are used to perform the pre-runtime analysis.)

It is evident that either strategy leads to inefficient utilization of platform computing capabilities during run-time.

Modeling of Implementation-Environment Interaction. As safety-critical real-time systems continue their trend towards becoming ubiquitous (think self-driving cars, for example), the likelihood of the occurrence of some failure increases; as these systems come to be networked together, the effect of any such failure may be magnified as it cascades rapidly across multiple systems. It therefore becomes increasingly important that we avoid failures; in order to do so, the conservatism we build into our models—the degree of over-approximation—needs to be very large. Such severe over-approximation, too, will result in inefficient implementations of the systems.

How Much Inefficiency?

Both in enforcing deterministic behavior upon platforms and in modeling implementation-environment interaction deterministically, the system designers' choices are determined, in large part, by the *criticality* of the system being designed and the consequences of its failure: the more critical the system (and the more severe the consequences if it fails), the more conservative its design and analysis, and the greater the degree of inefficiency in the resulting implementation. For instance, the determination as to which features of a hardware platform are to be disabled in order to reduce run-time timing unpredictability is driven by consideration of the criticality of the application system being implemented; indeed, the CAST 32 documentation [2] explicitly states that the recommendations there are only meant to guide the implementation of safety-critical software of the three highest DALs (Design Assurance Levels) A, B, and C. With regards to over-approximating the execution time of code, different WCET-estimation tools for doing this have been developed that typically use very different methodologies to make their WCET estimates, and thereby provide estimated upper bounds that may be trusted to different levels of assurance:

- A very conservative WCET estimation tool may be based upon safe static analysis of the code (by *safe* analysis we mean that whenever there are uncertainties regarding run-time behavior such a tool always makes assumptions that are guaranteed to dominate the actual behavior).
- Less conservative tools may be measurement based, repeatedly executing the code and taking measurements of the actual run-time, and then applying statistical methods upon these observed run-times to estimate upper bounds on the maximum possible run-time. Different tools may use different statistical methods that make different assumptions about the distributions of the run-times, and yield WCET bounds that should be trusted to different levels of assurance.

Which WCET-estimation tool is most appropriate to use for the analysis of a particular application depends, once again, upon the criticality of the application – the more critical the application, the more conservative the tool (and consequently, the larger or more pessimistic the WCET estimate). Particular tools may be pre-approved for use in certifying the correctness of systems at certain criticality levels, or at least provide assistance in achieving such certification.[3]

   The bottom line is that when system developers appeal to determinism during implementation and analysis in order to achieve run-time timing predictability, the resulting implementation is likely to make poor use of platform computing resources during run-time. The degree of such inefficiency that a system developer is willing to tolerate depends upon the criticality of the application system

---

[3] As an example from the avionics certification domain, the RapiTime Aero tool (https://www.rapitasystems.com/products/rapitime/aero) offers documentation and tests to support the qualification of tools and processes that seek to achieve DO-17B qualification.

under consideration: the more critical the system the greater the need for timing predictability and the greater the inefficiency that is considered tolerable. This observation—that more critical systems need timing predictability that is more "trusted"—may be exploited in *mixed-criticality systems* to achieve implementations that make more efficient use of platform resources during run-time; this is discussed in the next section.

4 Mixed-Criticality Systems

A typical CPS application comprises multiple sub-systems. Due to considerations of cost, size, energy-efficiency, thermal dissipation, etc., in implementing such applications there is an increasing trend away from federated architectures, in which each sub-system is implemented upon its own hardware platform; instead, *integrated* architectures are preferred, with multiple sub-systems being implemented upon a single shared platform. Example efforts at formalizing and standardizing such integrated architectures include the Integrated Modular Avionics (IMA) [18] effort in the aerospace industry, and Autosar [1] in the automotive domain. Even in highly safety-critical application domains such as aerospace and automotive, typically only a relatively small fraction of the overall system is actually of very high criticality; the remainder of the system consists of less critical code that enhances the overall performance of the application system, but has a lesser effect (or none) upon safety. Hence in an integrated architecture a single platform is supporting different functionalities that are of different criticalities. Such *mixed criticality* systems are increasingly commonly found in embedded computing.

Achieving time-predictability in mixed-criticality systems offers novel challenges and opportunities. As seen in Sect. 3 above, inefficient implementations are the price we pay for using determinism to achieve time-predictability; the degree of conservatism we choose to incorporate into our deterministic designs and analyses (and hence, the degree of inefficiency that we tolerate) is dictated by the criticality of the system being developed. When applied to mixed-criticality systems, such an approach currently mandates that the criticality of the most critical sub-system determines this choice. Indeed, most safety standards (including the generic IEC 61508 [16] functional safety standard) require that the entire system be designed according to the highest level of criticality involved, *unless* "sufficient independence" can be demonstrated amongst functionalities of different criticalities.

Efficient Implementations of Mixed-Criticality Systems

In the context of implementing mixed-criticality systems upon integrated architectures, "sufficient independence" amongst functionalities of different criticalities is currently achieved via *resource partitioning* along both the spatial and timing dimensions; see, for instance, the ARINC 653 software specification [3] for space and time partitioning in safety-critical avionics real-time operating systems. In such partitioning approaches, both the physical resources (processors, memory, buses, etc.) and the time-line are partitioned, with separations amongst the partitions enforced as part of the platform infrastructure and validated at a level of assurance consistent with the highest criticality level that is to be supported upon the platform. Sub-systems of different criticalities are allocated different partitions for their exclusive use, and the run-time (timing and other) correctness of each application is validated when executing upon its allocated partitions by enforcing a level of determinism that is consistent with the criticality of that particular application. We illustrate by a very simple, contrived, example.

Example. Consider a system comprising two jobs J_1 and J_2, both arriving at time-instant 0 and sharing a common deadline at time-instant 10, that are to execute upon a single shared preemptive processor. Job J_1 is of greater criticality than J_2. Suppose that J_1's WCET, determined using tools and methodologies that are consistent with its criticality, is determined to be equal to 6; J_2's WCET, determined using tools and methodologies that are consistent with its criticality (which is lower than J_1's criticality), is determined to be equal to 5. A time-partitioning scheduler would seek to partition the time-interval $[0, 10]$ into two parts of duration 6 and 5, to be assigned to J_1 and J_2 respectively. But since $6 + 5 = 11 > 10$, such a schedule cannot be constructed.

Now suppose that the WCET of the higher-criticality job J_1 is also determined using the tools and methodologies that are consistent with the lower criticality (i.e., J_2's criticality), and the value so determined is equal to 4. Consider a run-time *priority-based* scheduling algorithm that executes J_1 first with greater priority, and only executes J_2 once J_1 has completed execution. Let us seek to validate the correctness of the run-time behaviors that will be expressed by jobs J_1 and J_2 when scheduled by this priority-based algorithm.

- In validating the correctness of job J_1 at a level of assurance consistent with its own criticality level, it is determined that J_1 starts executing at time-instant 0 and executes for at most 6 time units, thereby completing prior to its deadline at time-instant 10.
- In validating the correctness of job J_2 at a level of assurance consistent with its own criticality level, it is determined that the higher-priority job J_1 starts executing at time-instant 0 and executes for at most **4** time units (rather than 6—this is because we may use the WCET-analysis of J_1 that returns an estimate at a level of assurance consistent with J_2's criticality level). Once J_1 completes execution (at or before time-instant 4), job J_2 executes for at most 5 time units and therefore also completes prior to its deadline at time-instant 10.

We thus see that each job is validated correct at a level of assurance consistent with its own criticality level, despite our earlier observation that no correct time-partitioning schedule can be constructed for this instance. ∎

The example above illustrates the main intuition underlying *mixed-criticality scheduling theory*, an approach to the run-time scheduling and pre-run-time schedulability analysis of mixed-criticality systems—see [8] for a survey. This theory builds upon an approach to the pre-run-time verification of such systems that was proposed in a paper by Vestal [20]. In general terms,

1. The approach recognizes that not all predictability properties of a mixed-criticality system are equally critical: some are of greater criticality than others, and must be validated correct to higher levels of assurance.
2. It therefore advocates against imposing determinism (and thereby paying the price in terms of less efficient implementations) upon the system; instead, the run-time behavior of a mixed-criticality system is not required to be deterministic.
3. Prior to run-time, predictability properties are established by performing multiple analyses of the mixed-criticality system, each such analysis having the objective of establishing the correctness of those sub-systems that are of a particular criticality.
4. In performing these analyses, *assumptions* are made about the behavior that is actually expressed by the non-deterministic system. The severity or conservatism/pessimism of the assumptions that are made is consistent with the criticality level being validated: the greater this criticality level, the more severe the assumptions.

In this manner, each sub-system has its desired predictability properties established at an appropriate level of assurance, rather than at a higher level. The resource over-allocation that results from over-validation is therefore avoided; more resource-efficient implementations are the result.

Let us examine how the example introduced earlier in this section fits in with this general approach.

Example. In our example, the criticality of job J_1 is greater than that of J_2; hence, J_1 should have its correctness validated to a greater level of assurance. Therefore, a more conservative WCET-estimation tool is used to determine WCETs for validating J_1's correctness—this tool estimates that J_1 may execute for up to 6 time units. For validating J_2's correctness, a less conservative WCET-estimation tool is used to estimate the WCETs of *both* J_1 and J_2; according to this tool J_1 will execute for at most 4 time units, and J_2 will execute for at most 5 time units.

We note that the run-time behavior of the system when scheduled using the priority-driven scheduler is less predictable than when scheduled using a time-partitioning scheduler (which is, in our example, effectively a lookup table denoting the intervals when each job is to execute). For instance, consider a time-partitioning scheduler that schedules J_1 during the interval $[0, 6]$ and J_2 during $[6, 11]$; for this scheduler[4], we can predict prior to run-time that J_2 will begin to execute at time-instant 6. With respect to the priority-driven scheduler

---

[4] Which, of course, is unable to guarantee that J_2 completes by its deadline.

that prioritizes J_1 over J_2, however, the start-time of J_2's execution depends upon the actual execution time of J_1, which may not be known prior to run-time (and may vary during different runs of the system). However, this loss of predictability does not compromise correctness, since all that is asked of J_2 is that it complete by time-instant 10.   ■

5   Summary

In order to be able to validate the correctness of safety-critical systems prior to their deployment and use, it is necessary that their run-time behavior be predictable prior to run-time. Stankovic and Ramamritham [19] have articulated this desired attribute in the following manner: "[Predictability] means that it should be possible to show, demonstrate, or prove that requirements are met *subject to any assumptions made*, e.g., concerning failures and workloads" (emphasis added). Such assumptions are generally necessary in the validation of non-trivial CPSs, since there is likely to be considerable uncertainty with regards to their precise run-time behavior.

Most current approaches to achieving predictability enforce and assume deterministic run-time timing behavior, but such determinism may result in implementations that are unable to make full use of platform resources during run-time. The mixed-criticality scheduling theory approach to validating the correctness of mixed-criticality systems is predicated upon the thesis that uncertainty inherent in CPSs can be dealt with, and predictability can be achieved, in real-time safety-critical systems without enforcing deterministic timing behavior upon the hardware and software components from which the system is constructed, and/or modeling the interaction between a system implementation and its operating environment in a time-deterministic manner. Achieving predictability without enforcing determinism allows for more resource-efficient implementations.

References

1. AUTOSAR: AUTomotive Open System ARchitecture. http://www.autosar.org
2. Certification Authorities Software Team (CAST) Position paper CAST-32: Multi-core Processors. www.faa.gov/aircraft/air_cert/design_approvals/air_software/cast/cast_papers/. Accessed 30 Oct 2016
3. ARINC.: ARINC 653–1 Avionics Application Software Standard Interface, October 2003
4. Axer, P., Ernst, R., Falk, H., Girault, A., Grund, D., Guan, N., Jonsson, B., Marwedel, P., Reineke, J., Rochange, C., Sebastian, M., Von Hanxleden, R., Wilhelm, R., Yi, W.: Building timing predictable embedded systems. ACM Trans. Embed. Comput. Syst. **13**(4), 82:1–82:37 (2014)
5. Baruah, S., Burns, A.: Sustainable scheduling analysis. In: Proceedings of the IEEE Real-time Systems Symposium, Rio de Janeiro, pp. 159–168. IEEE Computer Society Press, December 2006

6. Benveniste, A., Berry, G.: The synchronous approach to reactive and real-time systems. Proc. IEEE **79**(9), 1270–1282 (1991)
7. Berry, G., Gonthier, G.: The ESTEREL synchronous programming language: design, semantics, implementation. Sci. Comput. Program. **19**, 87–152 (1992)
8. Burns, A., Davis, R.: Mixed-criticality systems: A review (9th edition) (2017). http://www-users.cs.york.ac.uk/~burns/review.pdf. Accessed 29 Aug 2017
9. Edwards, S.A., Kim, S., Lee, E.A., Liu, I., Patel, H.D., Schoeberl, M.: A disruptive computer design idea: architectures with repeatable timing. In: Proceedings of IEEE International Conference on Computer Design (ICCD). IEEE, October 2009
10. Edwards, S.A., Lee, E.A.: The semantics and execution of a synchronous block-diagram language. Sci. Comput. Program. **48**(1), 21–42 (2003)
11. Edwards, S.A., Lee, E.A..: The case for the precision timed (PRET) machine. In: Proceedings of the 44th Annual Conference on Design Automation, SESSION: Wild and Crazy Ideas (WACI), pp. 264–265, June 2007
12. Gabler, H.C., Hinch, J.: Evaluation of advanced air bag deployment algorithm performance using event data recorders. Ann. Adv. Automot. Med. **52**, 175–184 (2008)
13. Halbwachs, N., Caspi, P., Raymond, P., Pilaud, D.: The synchronous dataflow programming language LUSTRE. Proc. IEEE **79**(9), 1305–1320 (1991)
14. Harel, D., Lachover, H., Naamad, A., Pnueli, A., Politi, M., Sherman, R., Shtul-Trauring, A.: Statemate: a working environment for the development of complex reactive systems. In: Proceedings of the 10th International Conference on Software Engineering, ICSE 1988, Los Alamitos, CA, USA, pp. 396–406. IEEE Computer Society Press (1988)
15. Harel, D.: Statecharts: a visual formalism for complex systems. Sci. Comput. Progr. **8**(3), 231–274 (1987)
16. International Electrotechnical Commission.: Functional safety of electrical/ electronic/ programmable electronic safety-related systems (2010). http://www.iec.ch/functionalsafety
17. LeGuernic, P., Gautier, T., Le Borgne, M., Le Maire, C.: Programming real-time applications with SIGNAL. Proc. IEEE **79**(9), 1321–1336 (1991)
18. Prisaznuk, P.J.: Integrated modular avionics. In: Proceedings of the IEEE 1992 National Aerospace and Electronics Conference (NAECON 1992), vol.1, pp. 39–45, May 1992
19. Stankovic, J.A., Ramamritham, K.: What is predictability for real-time systems? Real-Time Syst. **2**(4), 247–254 (1990)
20. Vestal, S.: Preemptive scheduling of multi-criticality systems with varying degrees of execution time assurance. In: Proceedings of the Real-Time Systems Symposium, Tucson, AZ, pp. 239–243. IEEE Computer Society Press, December 2007
21. Wilhelm, R., Engblom, J., Ermedahl, A., Holsti, N., Thesing, S., Whalley, D., Bernat, G., Ferdinand, C., Heckmann, R., Mitra, T., Mueller, F., Puaut, I., Puschner, P., Staschulat, J., Stenström, P.: The worst-case execution-time problem - overview of methods and survey of tools. ACM Trans. Embed. Comput. Syst. **7**(3), 36:1–36:53 (2008)

Model-Based Representations
for Dataflow Schedules

Shuvra S. Bhattacharyya[1,2(✉)] and Johan Lilius[3]

[1] Department of Electrical and Computer Engineering, University of Maryland,
College Park, MD, USA
`ssb@umd.edu`
[2] Department of Pervasive Computing, Tampere University of Technology,
Tampere, Finland
`shuvra.bhattacharyya@tut.fi`
[3] Department of Information Technologies, Åbo Akademi, Åbo, Finland
`Johan.Lilius@abo.fi`

Abstract. Dataflow is widely used as a model of computation in many
application domains, especially domains within the broad area of signal
and information processing. The most common uses of dataflow techniques in these domains are in the modeling of application behavior and
the design of specialized architectures. In this chapter, we discuss a different use of dataflow that involves its application as a formal model for
scheduling applications onto architectures. Scheduling is a critical aspect
of dataflow-based system design that impacts key metrics, including
latency, throughput, buffer memory requirements, and energy efficiency.
Deriving efficient and reliable schedules is an important and challenging
problem that must be addressed in dataflow-based design flows. The concepts and methods reviewed in this chapter help to address this problem
through model-based representations of schedules. These representations
build on the separation of concerns between functional specification and
scheduling in dataflow, and provide a useful new class of abstractions for
designing dataflow graph schedules, as well as for managing, analyzing,
and manipulating schedules within design tools.

Keywords: Dataflow · Model-based design · Signal processing
Scheduling

1 Introduction

This chapter is concerned with model-based schedule representations for implementation of behavioral dataflow models. Dataflow has been studied extensively
for modeling application functionality, especially in the domain of signal processing, as well as for designing efficient architectures. In this chapter, we discuss use
of dataflow formalisms as an intermediate representation—between application
and architecture—in the system design process. Specifically, we review the use
of dataflow as a model for representing *schedules* of dataflow-based application
models.

© Springer International Publishing AG, part of Springer Nature 2018
M. Lohstroh et al. (Eds.): Lee Festschrift, LNCS 10760, pp. 88–105, 2018.
https://doi.org/10.1007/978-3-319-95246-8_6

The derivation of a schedule for a dataflow graph is an important part in the process of deriving an implementation for the graph. The schedule determines on which processor each firing of the dataflow graph will execute (assignment), the relative ordering among firings that are assigned to the same processor (ordering), and the time at which each firing will begin its execution (timing) [12]. Lee and Ha proposed a taxonomy for scheduling strategies based on which of these tasks—assignment, ordering, and timing—are performed at compile time versus at run time [12].

Scheduling has significant impact on most key implementation metrics, including throughput, latency, memory requirements, and metrics related to energy efficiency. Thus, it plays a central role in dataflow-based design flows, and a wide variety of scheduling techniques have been developed for different types of architectures (e.g., see [2, 11]). Well-designed scheduling techniques for dataflow graphs utilize application structure that is exposed in the graphs to optimize the metrics that are most relevant for the targeted class of implementations.

In contrast to the vast literature on scheduling techniques, there has been relatively little work on systematic methods for representing, analyzing, and manipulating schedules that are derived from these techniques. We argue that such methods are highly desirable to enhance the reliability, retargetability, and interoperability of dataflow-based design tools, and that model-based schedule representations provide a valuable foundation for the development of such methods.

With this motivation, we review in this chapter several state of the art approaches for representing dataflow schedules. We focus specifically in this chapter on model based schedule representations that are based on dataflow principles—that is, on dataflow-based schedule representations.

Figure 1 illustrates some ways in which dataflow-based schedule representations can be used in hardware/software design processes. The dashed edges in the figure illustrate interactions between different phases of the design and implementation process that are enabled or strengthened by such representations. For example, the use of a formal schedule representation provides the potential for schedulers or designers to iteratively optimize scheduling results while working at a higher level of abstraction than the implementation target code. Such representations also enable formal analysis techniques to verify properties of the constructed schedules or to identify minimal parts of the schedules that need run-time logic for error detection. Another use of such representations is in streamlining processes for retargeting design flows to different target platforms and implementation languages.

The remainder of this chapter is organized as follows. Section 2 through Sect. 5 review a number of different model-based representations for dataflow schedules. These sections are arranged chronologically. Section 6 covers programmatic schedule representations that are not model-based in and of themselves, but that introduce structured methods for representing schedules that can be useful as an intermediate layer of abstraction between model-based representations and implementation target code. Section 7 summarizes the discussion of the chapter and points to useful directions for further investigation.

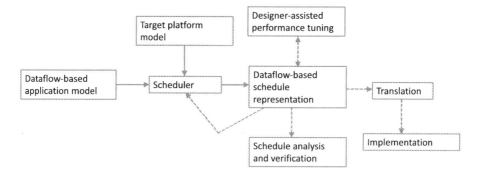

Fig. 1. An illustration of how dataflow-based schedule representations can be used in hardware/software design processes.

2   Synchronization Graphs

The synchronization graph provides a model for analyzing, implementing and optimizing self-timed schedules of homogeneous synchronous dataflow (HSDF) graphs. HSDF is a specialized form of dataflow in which each actor produces and consumes exactly one token on each input/output port on each firing. HSDF is a special case of synchronous dataflow (SDF), where the numbers of tokens produced and consumed on actor ports must be constant (but not necessarily equal to one). Lee and Messerschmitt have developed algorithms for converting SDF graphs to equivalent HSDF graphs [13]. Through the application of these techniques, the synchronization graph model discussed in this section can be applied to general SDF graphs.

Self-timed schedules form one of the four major classes of schedules in Lee and Ha's scheduling taxonomy, which was introduced in Sect. 1. Given a dataflow graph G, a self-timed schedule for G consists of an assignment of the application tasks (graph vertices) in G to a set of processors (such as embedded microprocessors, graphics processing units, or digital signal processors), and an ordering of the subset of tasks that is mapped onto each processor [12]. To enhance predictability and optimization potential, the assignment and ordering of actors is fixed by a self-timed schedule at compile time, while the actual time at which tasks execute is determined at run-time. The run-time dispatching of tasks is performed using synchronization primitives as needed for coordination between processors [12,21].

Given a self-timed schedule for an HSDF-based model of an application, execution of the schedule can be modeled with a form of HSDF graph that is called a *synchronization graph* [3]. The example in Figs. 2 and 3 illustrates the concept of synchronization graphs. In particular, Fig. 3 shows a synchronization graph that corresponds to the application model in Fig. 2 together with the self-timed schedule given by:

$$\alpha_1 = (A1, A2, B1, C1, D1, E1, F1, F2), \alpha_2 = (A3, A4, B2, E2, F3, F4), \quad (1)$$

where the sequences α_1 and α_2 specify the assignment and ordering of tasks on distinct processors in a two-processor multiprocessor system. Figure 2, adapted from [3], shows a dataflow model of a quadrature mirror filter bank application. The "D" markings on selected edges in Figs. 2 and 3 denote nonzero delays associated with the edges.

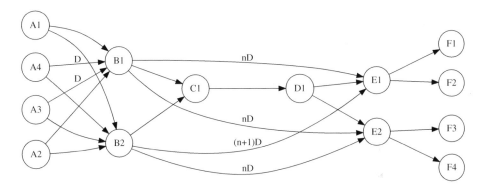

Fig. 2. An HSDF representation of a multiresolution quadrature mirror filter bank.

In general, the edges E in a synchronization graph can be decomposed into disjoint sets E_i, E_c, E_s, where E_i contains edges that model intraprocessor communication between tasks, E_c contains edges that model interprocessor communication, and E_s contains edges that model synchronization [3]. Conventionally, the edges in E_s are placed parallel to the edges in E_i (i.e., connected between the same source and sink vertices). This is the case, for example, in Fig. 3.

When synchronization and interprocessor communication are co-located in this way, the resulting self-timed schedule implementation can be modeled using a data structure called the interprocessor communication graph [22]. The synchronization graph generalizes interprocessor communication graph modeling and analysis techniques by decoupling the roles of synchronization and interprocessor communication.

In particular, the synchronization edges can be decoupled from the interprocessor communication edges subject to certain constraints. Such decoupling can be used, for example, to minimize the amount of synchronization operations that are executed, and control complex trade-offs between latency and throughput during dataflow graph execution [21].

Each synchronization edge $e = (x, y)$ in a synchronization graph represents the following run-time constraint:

$$start(F(y, i)) \geq start(F(x, i - delay(e))) + t(x) \text{ for all } i. \tag{2}$$

Here, $F(z, k)$ represents the kth invocation (*firing*) of task z, $start(f)$ represents the time at which firing f begins execution, $delay(e)$ represents the delay

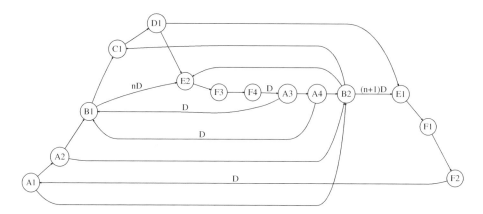

Fig. 3. A synchronization graph that corresponds to the application model in Fig. 2 together with the self-timed schedule shown in Eq. 1.

(number of initial data values) on edge e, and $t(z)$ represents the execution time for a single firing of actor z.

By applying fundamental results from flowgraph analysis [19,20], the throughput of the multiprocessor system that is represented by a synchronization graph Γ can be estimated as

$$\tau(\Gamma) = \min_{\text{cycle } C \text{ in } \Gamma} \frac{Delay(C)}{\sum_{v \in C} t(v)}, \tag{3}$$

where $Delay(C)$ represents the sum of the edge delays over all edges in the cycle C.

The reciprocal of the maximum given in Eq. 3 is called the *maximum cycle mean*, and can be viewed as an estimate of the average time required to execute a single iteration of the given dataflow graph. Equation 3 can be computed using a low complexity algorithm, which makes it very useful as an alternative to conventional simulation-based performance measurement in the analysis, optimization, and design space exploration of signal and information processing systems.

For more details on synchronization graphs and related models and methods for analysis and implementation of self-timed HSDF schedules, we refer the reader to [1,3,21,22].

3   Dataflow Schedule Graphs

Like synchronization graphs and related models for self-timed HSDF schedules, the *dataflow schedule graph* (*DSG*) models schedules in terms of dataflow semantics, and separates the model of a schedule (schedule graph) from that of the application (application graph). However, the DSG goes significantly beyond HSDF-oriented schedule representations in that it can be used to represent dynamic schedules (schedules where the actor assignment or ordering changes at run-time), as well as schedules for application graphs that are based on dynamic dataflow semantics [24].

The DSG model is defined with the assumption that the given application graphs conform to core functional dataflow (CFDF) semantics [16]. CFDF is a highly expressive dataflow model in which each actor A is defined with a set of modes $M(A)$ such each firing of A has a corresponding $m \in M(A)$ associated with it, and also, a side effect of each firing is to determine the mode m' that will correspond to the next firing of A. For a given mode of A, the number of tokens produced and consumed on each port of A must be constant. However, the numbers of tokens produced and consumed can vary across different modes of the same actor. Thus, there is significant flexibility to design actors whose production and consumption vary dynamically.

CFDF subsumes as special cases a number of other well-known dataflow models [17], including cyclo-static dataflow, SDF, and Boolean dataflow (BDF) [5, 7,13]. Thus, DSGs can be used to represent a broad class of static and dynamic schedules for application graphs that are specified in any of these models. For further details on CFDF semantics, we refer the reader to [15,16].

A DSG that is used to represent a schedule for a single processor is called a *sequential DSG* (*SDSG*). Multiple SDSGs can be integrated to represent a multiprocessor schedule by using a *concurrent DSG* (*CDSG*).

An important property of SDSGs, called the *global token population property*, is that the total number of tokens that reside on the non-self-loop (NSL) edges in an SDSG equals at most one throughout execution. By a self-loop edge, we mean an edge whose source and sink vertices are identical. Such edges are used to model state in dataflow graphs.

When an NSL SDSG edge contains a token, the token is referred to as the *DSG token* associated with the current state of the SDSG. Synchronization graphs and interprocessor communication graphs have a similar property that holds for subgraphs that correspond to individual processors in the target architecture [21]. The global token population property is ensured in SDSGs by the design rules for constructing DSG actors. Intuitively, when an SDSG edge contains a single token, the actor at the sink of the edge is the next DSG actor that is to be fired. Technically, since there may be a delay between the time when the single token is consumed by an actor and when the actor produces a new DSG token, there may be times when the SDSG contains no tokens.

In addition to indicating the part of the enclosing schedule that is currently active, SDSG tokens may carry values that are read or written by actors in the SDSG. Such values can be used to achieve various forms of control in the schedule that depend on run-time values of input data or graph parameters.

The actors in an SDSG can be decomposed into two types—*reference actors* (*RAs*) and *schedule control actors* (*SCAs*). An RA is an HSDF actor that has a single input port and a single output port. An RA also has a single application graph actor associated with it as the *referenced actor* of the RA. It is possible for multiple RAs to have the same referenced actor. The referenced actor associated with an RA R is denoted by $ref(R)$.

Intuitively, the firing of an RA R in a DSG corresponds to a guarded or unconditional execution of the application graph actor $ref(R)$. In this way, firings in a DSG result in firings in the corresponding application graph. Here, by a guarded execution of a CFDF actor A, we mean a firing of A, based on its current CFDF mode, that is conditioned on having sufficient data available on the application graph input edges of A along with sufficient empty space available on the output edges of A. The notions of sufficiency here are determined unambiguously by the requirement in CFDF that each mode defines a constant production and consumption rate for the ports of the associated actor.

In addition to being configured as a guarded or unconditional execution, an RA R can also be configured with two optional functions $pre(R)$ and $post(R)$, which can be used, for example, to operate on the DSG token value that is input to R or produce the DSG token value that is output from R. As their names suggest, *pre* and *post* are, respectively, called before and after the guarded or unconditional firing of $ref(R)$ during the associated firing of R.

Whether or not to configure an RA using a guarded or unconditional execution of the referenced actor is a design decision as part of the construction of the overall SDSG. If by static analysis, one can guarantee that the referenced actor will always have sufficient input data and empty space when the RA fires, then the overhead of guarded execution can be avoided, and the referenced actor can be executed unconditionally.

While RAs serve primarily as wrappers for firing application graph actors, SCAs are used to route the SDSG token through the enclosing DSGs. SCAs can therefore be used to achieve dynamic control over the sequences of RAs that are executed. Designers of DSGs or of tools that automatically construct DSGs have significant freedom in formulating SCAs. An SCA can have any number of inputs and any number of inputs. The primary design rule that it must satisfy is referred to as *lumped HSDF semantics* across the inputs and outputs. Specifically, on each firing of an SCA, the total number of tokens consumed across all NSL input edges must equal one, and similarly, exactly one token must be produced across all of the NSL output edges. The actual ports on which the tokens are produced and consumed can vary dynamically as long as there is exactly one consuming port and one producing port on each firing.

Figure 5 illustrates an SDSG representation of one possible schedule for the application graph represented in Fig. 4. In Fig. 4, actors A, B, C, E, F are HSDF actors; actor SW is a BDF switch actor; actor SE is a BDF select actor; and actor D is an SDF actor that consumes one token and produces two tokens on each firing. Actor E produces pairs of identical control token values that are consumed by both the switch and select actors. Recall that BDF actors can be modeled using CFDF semantics so DSG representations can be constructed for BDF schedules.

The SDSG in Fig. 5 includes SCAs of three types—if, fi (endif), and loop. For details on the semantics of these SCAs, we refer the reader to [24]. The loop actor is used in Fig. 5 to iterate actor F two times for each firing of actor D. This iteration is needed because, as described above, D produces two tokens on each

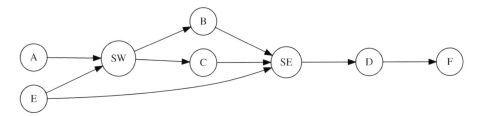

Fig. 4. A BDF application graph that is used to help illustrate SDSGs.

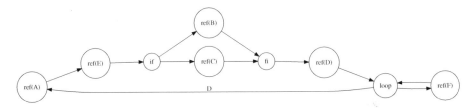

Fig. 5. An SDSG model of a schedule for the BDF application graph of Fig. 4.

firing while F (an HSDF actor) consumes only one token. The delay on the edge (loop, $ref(A)$) indicates that execution of the SDSG begins with $ref(A)$, which in turn triggers a firing of application graph actor A. The edge (loop, $ref(A)$) also models the passage of control from the end of one iteration of the SDSG to the beginning of the next iteration. The *post* function is used by $ref(E)$ to produce a DSG token that encapsulates the value that is produced by the corresponding firing of E in the application graph. This token value is then used by the if actor to determine which port it produces data onto.

While both Figs. 4 and 5 depict dataflow graphs that include actors with dynamically varying dataflow rates, a significant difference between the graphs in the context of our discussion is that only one of them satisfies the global token population property. Also, note that the SDSG in Fig. 5 is not deadlocked even though there is a delay-free cycle (involving actors loop and F). This is due to the lumped HSDF semantics of the loop actor.

For further details on DSGs, including construction rules and applications of concurrent DSGs, we refer the reader to [24].

4 Decision State Modeling

Damavandpeyma et al. introduce a method called *decision state modeling* (*DSM*) for modeling self-timed schedules for SDF graphs [9]. We refer to schedule models that are derived using this method as *DSM graphs*. Unlike the synchronization graph and interprocessor communication graph models discussed in Sect. 2, DSM graphs are formulated directly on SDF graphs, without requiring the conversion to an equivalent HSDF graph as a preprocessing step.

The DSM approach assumes that all firings of an actor are assigned to execute on the same processor, which is not a restriction in the modeling techniques discussed in Sect. 2. For the class of self-times schedules that conform to this restriction, the DSM approach provides the potential for significantly more compact representations (fewer vertices and edges) compared to synchronization graph and interprocessor communication graph modeling.

Furthermore, the technique enables the use of efficient methods for buffer analysis and exploration of trade-offs between buffer sizes and throughput that operate directly on SDF representations (e.g., see [23]). These methods are more effective at deriving buffer sizes (tighter buffer size bounds) because unlike the representations studied in Sect. 2, they preserve the structure of the SDF application graph—in particular, they do not separate individual application graph edges into multiple edges in the schedule graph.

A key concept that is introduced in the DSM graph model is that of *decision states* of the schedule that is being modeled. A decision state of a schedule is a state in which more than one actor can be enabled on a given processor. Such states need special care to adhere to the constraint that each processor can execute at most one actor at a given time.

Associated with each decision state s_d is a set $opp(s_d)$ of actors that are enabled (have sufficient data to fire) in s_d. The elements of $opp(s_d)$ are referred to as the *opponent actors* of the associated decision state. Among the opponent actors, only one actor should be executed in the decision state. This actor is referred to as the *actor of choice* of s_d, which we denote as $choice(s_d)$.

To model the selection of $choice(s_d)$ in the decision state over the other actors in $opp(s_d)$, an actor $\delta(s_d)$ is inserted into the DSM graph. We refer to such an actor as a *decision state actor*. Additionally, an edge directed from $choice(s_d)$ to $\delta(s_d)$ is inserted, as well as edges directed from $\delta(s_d)$ to all opponent actors other than $choice(s_d)$. Production rates, consumption rates, and delays are calculated for all of these inserted edges based on properties of the schedule that is being modeled.

An approach, called *decision state folding*, can be applied to merge decision states that have similar behavior, thereby reducing the number of distinct states that need to be considered. For further details on the construction and application of DSM graphs, we refer the reader to [9].

Figure 6, adapted from an example in [9], shows a DSM graph that is constructed from the SDF application graph shown in Fig. 6 and the two-processor schedule that consists of the schedule (wy^2) on one processor and the schedule $x^5z^3xz^3$ on the other. In this schedule notation, an expression of the form X^n represents n successive firings of the actor X. Thus, for example, the schedule for the first processor corresponds to the firing sequence (w, y, y). This sequence is assumed to be executed repeatedly in a self-timed manner, as with the firing sequence that is assigned to the second processor. Production and consumption rates are annotated in Fig. 6 next to ports on which the rates are not equal to one.

Fig. 6. An application graph example that is used to help illustrate DSM graph modeling.

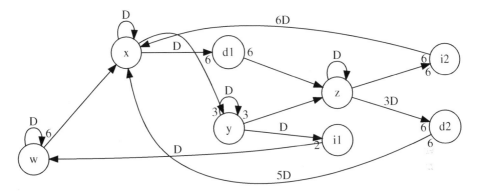

Fig. 7. An illustration of a DSM graph for the application graph shown in Fig. 6.

As in Sect. 2, the "D" markings on selected edges in Fig. 7 denote nonzero delays associated with the edges. For example, the edge $(d2, x)$ has 5 units of delay associated with it. The actors d1 and d2 are decision state actors. The actors i1 and i2 are used in the DSM approach to ensure that each schedule iteration on a given processor completes before firings from the next iteration are allowed to execute. The self-loop edges on actors w, x, y, and z are used to ensure that the firings of a given actor execute sequentially on the processor to which the actor is assigned.

For more details on DSM graphs and SDF-based buffer analysis and throughput optimization techniques that are relevant for this class of graphs, we refer the reader to [9, 23].

5   Partial-Order Transition Schedules

In this section we review a schedule representation proposed by [25] that establishes a partial order (PO) structure on *schedule fragments*. This PO structure guarantees that each of the schedule fragments can be executed atomically, while the scheduling of the fragments is driven by a hierarchical state machine.

In [25], Zebelein et al. introduce the approach in the context of a very powerful and expressive formalism. Here we try to describe the main idea of the approach using a slightly simplified analysis of the running example from Fig. 1 in [25].

In practice, execution of a self-timed schedule implies that actors need to implement an enabledness test, and each processing element needs to run a round-robin scheduler that checks the actors for enabledness. This obviously causes overhead. Being able to atomically execute sequences of actors makes them amenable for optimizations like actor merging [6], or more complex memory optimizations of the buffers [10].

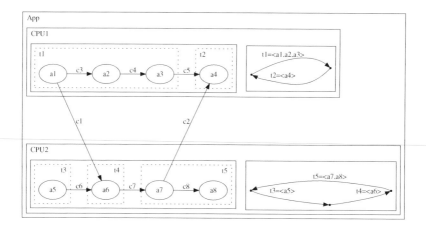

Fig. 8. The partial order schedule from [25].

In Fig. 8 we present the basic structure of the running example from [25]. The approach uses a hierarchy of dataflow networks, where the execution of the transitions is controlled by a state machine.

This example consists of 4 actors $a1, a2, a3, a4$ mapped onto processing element PE1, 4 other actors $a5, a6, a7, a8$ mapped onto processing element PE2, and channels $c1$ and $c2$ that synchronize the behavior between the processing elements. Ignore the dotted boxes $t1, t2, t3$ and $t4$ for the moment. Our goal is to be able to cyclically execute the system. A self-timed execution will obviously work (i.e. each actor is executed when it has enough tokens), and the synchronization over the channels $c1$ and $c2$ will be handled thought the self-timed execution. However if we now require that the sequences $a1 \prec a2 \prec a3 \prec a4$, and $a5 \prec a6 \prec a7 \prec a8$, be executed atomically, the execution will obviously deadlock because of the dependency over the channels $c1$, and $c2$, between $a1 \prec a6$ and $a7 \prec a4$. We thus need to split the partial orders. An initial solution to this through a Quasi-Static Schedule, where the dotted boxes $t1, t2, t3$ and $t4$ in Fig. 8 now represent the static schedules that can be executed as specified by the finite state machines, and the execution time of the transitions is decided at execution time. The problem with this approach is that we still need to do check for token and space availability on the channels prior to the execution. E.g. before executing $t1$ we need to check that $c1$ is empty, e.g. that $t4$ has been executed in the previous cycle. Furthermore this schedule does not allow for all parallelism inherent in the system.

However by further analyzing the dependencies we can construct a more refined partial order where we don not token and space availability checks prior

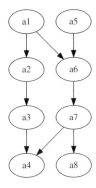

Fig. 9. The basic partial order structure of the example in Fig. 8.

to execution. We give a simple construction that creates a new partition of the partial order, that can be translated into the hierarchical state-machine representation from [25]. Figure 9 shows the dependencies between the actors. The idea is to find paths that start from a processing element, and then traverse other processing elements until they return to the starting processing element.

Such a path above is given by $p_s = \{a1 \prec a6 \prec a7 \prec a4\}$. We can now define a partition of the sequences $a1 \prec a2 \prec a3 \prec a4$ and $a5 \prec a6 \prec a7 \prec a8$ from above such that each of the sequences is split into subsequences so that actors in p_s are in different subsets. E.g., we obtain the following partitions: $p1 = \{a1 \prec \{a2, a3\} \prec a4\}$, and $p2 = \{a5 \prec \{a6, a7\} \prec a8\}$. This new partition is then represented in Fig. 10.

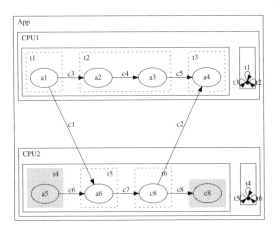

Fig. 10. Dynamic partial order schedule.

The state machines on the right will drive the execution of the partial orders: $t1 : \{a1\}$, $t2 : \{a2 \prec a3\}$, $t3 : \{a4\}$, and $t4 : \{a8 \prec a4\}$, $t5 : \{a6\}$, $t6 : \{a7\}$.

This execution does not need run-time checks for token and space availability on the channels communication channels $c1$ and $c2$.

The construction can be generalized to more complex partial order structures.

6   Programmatic Schedule Representations

The dataflow representations in Sects. 3–5, allow for many different analyses to be applied, however they leave a few steps to the translation and implementation phase, that are still intrinsically part of the dataflow description:

1. resolution of quasi-static schedules, and
2. synchronization of actors with non-deterministic run-times.

The CANALS language [8] is an attempt to provide an approach that fits the middle ground between the high-level models, and raw code, e.g. between the "Dataflow-based schedule representation" and "translation" boxes in Fig. 1. An empirical analysis of a number of dataflow applications that do not fit the SDF paradigm (the MPEG4 decoder being the canonical example) reveals that often the scheduling decisions left to the run-time are dependent on the structure of the tokens, and that if this structure were available in a more high-level representation[1], it would still be amenable to analysis and optimization algorithms. To this end CANALS introduces:

1. A rich data language to model the structure of the tokens and the data stream.
2. Schedules as first-class objects, making synchronization of non-deterministic actors explicit.
3. The ability to describe just-in-time (JIT) scheduling, making design of quasi-static schedules explicit and analyzable.
4. A separate mapping stage that allows mapping to a specific architectures, in particular heterogeneous architectures.

CANALS was originally aimed as a research tool in the theory of models-of-computation, reimplementing some of the insights from the Rialto language [14], and later on as an alternative to RVC-CAL [4], the language used to specify the video codes in the Reconfigurable Video Codec standard. Therefore the best way to describe the features and motivations of CANALS is through the MPEG4 decoder example. Figure 11 gives the definition of the Macroblock decoder stage in CANALS. The structure follows the high-level description of the standard, but makes some features more explicit. A CANALS network has a very particular structure. Each actor (a kernel in CANALS parlance) can only have one input channel[2]. The network is executed left-right, and starts by reading a Macroblock (MB) from the input buffer. To enable parallel and concurrent execution of actors, CANALS introduced a fork-join construction (called Scatter and Gather). The first scatter is actually a choice that checks the macroblock-type and type

---

[1] As compared to being hidden in the C-code of the implementation.
[2] This is done so as to ensure that the scheduling network can be calculated easily.

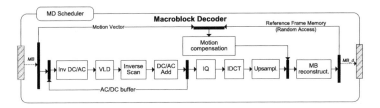

Fig. 11. The macroblock decoder.

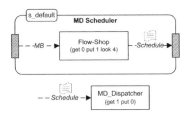

Fig. 12. The macroblock decoder scheduler.

of macroblock and then feeds it to either the motion compensation block, or the full-picture decoding sub-network. At the top level the execution of a CANALS network follows a simple cycle:

1. read the required number of tokes from the input channel
2. decode the tokens
3. calculate the schedule by executing the scheduler
4. send the schedule to the run-time system for execution
5. wait for the execution to terminate
6. goto step 1.

When a token is available it is guaranteed to be of the right type through type-checking and we only need to check for the right number of tokens. Contrary to RVC-CAL this makes the test for enabledness of an actor very simple.

CANALS follows Ptolemy [18] in the hierarchical delineation of scheduling. CANALS allows hierarchical networks, and for each level in the hierarchy a separate scheduler needs to be defined, the default scheduler being a round-robin scheduler. A CANALS scheduler is also a dataflow network, and this feature would in principle allow "schedulers to schedule schedules", but the implications of this were never properly worked out, since all schedules in the examples were represented through a single kernel. Exploiting this feature therefore remains an interesting topic for future work.

The CANALS network for the Macroblock decoding schedule is shown in Fig. 12, and a fragment of the job-shop scheduler is given in Fig. 13. The scheduler is specified as having an input output behavior of get 0 put 1 look 4. This means that it will check for 4 macroblocks in the input buffer, and then calculate 1 schedule as a result, while leaving the input buffer untouched. Notice that there

```
kernel MB -> Schedule Flow-Shop
{
  variable Schedule s;
  variable MB mb1, mb2, mb3, mb4;

  work get 0 put 1 look 4
  {
    // Look at 4 macroblocks and compute a schedule
    // according to the flow-shop algorithm.
     mb1=look(0);  mb2=look(1);  mb3=look(2);  mb4=look(3);
     if (mb1.type == I && mb2.type == I
         && mb3.type == I   && mb3.type == P)
     {
       //schedule 3 MBs of type I and 1 of type P optimally.
     }
     ...
    put(s);
  }
}
```

Fig. 13. A fragment of the jobshop scheduler code.

is a slight discrepancy in the amount of input tokens for the scheduler for the decoder (it requires 4 tokens) and the macro-block decoder itself which only reads one token. This is one of the central features of CANALS, since the scheduler can specify the joint run-time behavior of several instances of a CANALS network.

Thus the scheduler code fragment in Fig. 13 shows how the scheduler will implement a JIT scheduler by constructing a schedule based on the combined macro-block types. This schedule is eventually fed to the dispatcher which will then execute the schedule, and trigger the kernels in the Macroblock Decoder in the calculated order.

The mapping stage follows a similar design, where different concerns are separated into particular sublanguages. In particular CANALS supports: 1. separation of run-time kernel encapsulation mechanisms (e.g., task, thread, openCL kernel etc.) from specific hardware mapping, and 2. abstraction of the communication mechanism between the scheduler and run-time, which enables the scheduler to insert synchronization abstractions that preserve the schedule correctness, while leaving the specific implementation mechanisms to the back-end of the design process.

7   Conclusions

In this chapter we have presented proposals for formalizing the schedule of a dataflow network. The novelty of these approaches lies in how they lift the schedule up to the level of object of study, contrary to previous work where the schedule is seen as part of the implementation task.

Each of the approaches focuses on different aspects, and thus enables different sets of optimizations and analyses, some of which are particularly relevant when mapping to multiprocessor platforms.

1. Synchronization Graphs enable analysis of timing properties from the schedule, which can be used to optimize the throughput and synchronization structure of the implementation.

2. Dataflow Schedule Graphs represent schedules as dataflow graphs that make choices, and iterations in the schedule explicit, and among other things enable the distribution of the schedule, through the use of concurrent dataflow schedule graphs.
3. The Decision State Modeling approach applies to schedules of general SDF graphs, and provides compact graphical representations for this class of schedules. The approach enables the application of efficient buffer analysis and throughput optimization techniques that operate on SDF representations.
4. Partial-Ordered Transition schedules split the schedule fragments that can be executed in a self-timed manner. Although formally very different from Synchronization Graphs and Dataflow Schedule Graphs, the approach enables similar analyses of the schedule, and also a more distributed implementation of the schedule.
5. The final approach that we discuss, CANALS, is not really a model-based approach per-se, since it is a programming language. However it provides an intermediate step in the implementation process, between the dataflow models and the concrete code, and provides an intermediate level of abstraction to design JIT schedulers, and synchronization structures.

The overview of the approaches clearly points to the potential of model-based schedule representation, and also shows that a lot of work remains to be done. Some questions that could be asked are:

1. Is there a meta-modeling framework, that would make it possible to provide a common formalization of schedules that would make each of the presented approaches instances of a generic approach?
2. Since schedules in the various model-based representations discussed in this chapter are also dataflow graphs, one could study the properties of such schedule representations. Then interesting questions that could be explored include the scheduling of such graphs, and optimizing transformations that may be applied to such graphs.

Acknowledgments. This work was supported in part by TEKES—the Finnish Technology Agency for Innovation (FiDiPro project StreamPro 1846/31/2014).

References

1. Bambha, N., Kianzad, V., Khandelia, M., Bhattacharyya, S.S.: Intermediate representations for design automation of multiprocessor DSP systems. J. Des. Autom. Embed. Syst. **7**(4), 307–323 (2002)
2. Bhattacharyya, S.S., Deprettere, E., Leupers, R., Takala, J. (eds.): Handbook of Signal Processing Systems, 2nd edn. Springer, Heidelberg (2013). https://doi.org/10.1007/978-1-4419-6345-1
3. Bhattacharyya, S.S., Sriram, S., Lee, E.A.: Optimizing synchronization in multiprocessor DSP systems. IEEE Trans. Signal Process. **45**(6), 1605–1618 (1997)
4. Bhattacharyya, S.S., Eker, J., Janneck, J.W., Lucarz, C., Mattavelli, M., Raulet, M.: Overview of the MPEG reconfigurable video coding framework. J. Signal Process. Syst. **63**(2), 251–263 (2009)

5. Bilsen, G., Engels, M., Lauwereins, R., Peperstraete, J.A.: Cyclo-static dataflow. IEEE Trans. Signal Process. **44**(2), 397–408 (1996)
6. Boutellier, J., Ersfolk, J., Lilius, J., Mattavelli, M., Roquier, G., Silvén, O.: Actor merging for dataflow process networks. IEEE Trans. Signal Process. **63**(10), 2496–2508 (2015)
7. Buck, J.T., Lee, E.A.: Scheduling dynamic dataflow graphs using the token flow model. In: Proceedings of the International Conference on Acoustics, Speech, and Signal Processing, April 1993
8. Dahlin, A., Ersfolk, J., Yang, G., Habli, H., Lilius, J.: The canals language and its compiler. In: Proceedings of the 12th International Workshop on Software and Compilers for Embedded Systems SCOPES 2009, pp. 43–52. ACM, New York (2009). http://dl.acm.org/citation.cfm?id=1543820.1543829
9. Damavandpeyma, M., Stuijk, S., Basten, T., Geilen, M., Corporaal, H.: Modeling static-order schedules in synchronous dataflow graphs. In: Proceedings of the Design, Automation and Test in Europe Conference and Exhibition, pp. 775–780 (2012)
10. Desnos, K., Pelcat, M., Nezan, J.F., Aridhi, S.: Distributed memory allocation technique for synchronous dataflow graphs. In: 2016 IEEE International Workshop on Signal Processing Systems (SiPS), pp. 45–50. IEEE (2016)
11. Ha, S., Teich, J. (eds.): Handbook of Hardware/Software Codesign. Springer, Heidelberg (2017). https://doi.org/10.1007/978-94-017-7267-9
12. Lee, E.A., Ha, S.: Scheduling strategies for multiprocessor real time DSP. In: Proceedings of the Global Telecommunications Conference, vol. 2, pp. 1279–1283 (1989)
13. Lee, E.A., Messerschmitt, D.G.: Synchronous dataflow. Proc. IEEE **75**(9), 1235–1245 (1987)
14. Lilius, J., Dahlin, A., Morel, L.: Rialto 2.0: a language for heterogeneous computations. In: Hinchey, M., et al. (eds.) BICC/DIPES -2010. IAICT, vol. 329, pp. 7–18. Springer, Heidelberg (2010). https://doi.org/10.1007/978-3-642-15234-4_3
15. Lin, S., et al.: Parameterized sets of dataflow modes and their application to implementation of cognitive radio systems. J. Signal Process. Syst. **80**(1), 3–18 (2015)
16. Plishker, W., Sane, N., Kiemb, M., Anand, K., Bhattacharyya, S.S.: Functional DIF for rapid prototyping. In: Proceedings of the International Symposium on Rapid System Prototyping, pp. 17–23, Monterey, California, June 2008
17. Plishker, W., Sane, N., Kiemb, M., Bhattacharyya, S.S.: Heterogeneous design in functional DIF. In: Bereković, M., Dimopoulos, N., Wong, S. (eds.) SAMOS 2008. LNCS, vol. 5114, pp. 157–166. Springer, Heidelberg (2008). https://doi.org/10.1007/978-3-540-70550-5_18
18. Ptolemaeus, C. (ed.): System Design, Modeling, and Simulation using Ptolemy II. Ptolemy.org (2014). http://ptolemy.org/books/Systems
19. Reiter, R.: Scheduling parallel computations. J. Assoc. Comput. Mach. **15**, 590–599 (1968)
20. Renfors, M., Neuvo, Y.: The maximum sampling rate of digital filters under hardware speed constraints. IEEE Trans. Circ. Syst. **28**, 196–202 (1981)
21. Sriram, S., Bhattacharyya, S.S.: Embedded Multiprocessors: Scheduling and Synchronization, 2nd edn. CRC Press, Boca Raton (2009). ISBN: 1420048015
22. Sriram, S., Lee, E.A.: Determining the order of processor transactions in statically scheduled multiprocessors. J. VLSI Signal Process. Syst. Signal Image Video Technol. **15**(3), 207–220 (1997)

23. Stuijk, S., Geilen, M., Basten, T.: Throughput-buffering trade-off exploration for cyclo-static and synchronous dataflow graphs. IEEE Trans. Comput. **57**(10), 1331–1345 (2008)
24. Wu, H., Shen, C., Sane, N., Plishker, W., Bhattacharyya, S.S.: A model-based schedule representation for heterogeneous mapping of dataflow graphs. In: Proceedings of the International Heterogeneity in Computing Workshop, pp. 66–77, Anchorage, Alaska, May 2011
25. Zebelein, C., Haubelt, C., Falk, J., Schwarzer, T., Teich, J.: Representing mapping and scheduling decisions within dataflow graphs. In: Proceedings of the Forum on Specification and Design Languages (2013)

Hybrid Simulation Safety: Limbos and Zero Crossings

David Broman[✉]

KTH Royal Institute of Technology, Stockholm, Sweden
dbro@kth.se

Abstract. Physical systems can be naturally modeled by combining continuous and discrete models. Such hybrid models may simplify the modeling task of complex system, as well as increase simulation performance. Moreover, modern simulation engines can often efficiently generate simulation traces, but how do we know that the simulation results are correct? If we detect an error, is the error in the model or in the simulation itself? This paper discusses the problem of simulation safety, with the focus on hybrid modeling and simulation. In particular, two key aspects are studied: safe zero-crossing detection and deterministic hybrid event handling. The problems and solutions are discussed and partially implemented in Modelica and Ptolemy II.

Keywords: Modeling · Simulation · Hybrid semantics
Zero-crossing detector

1 Introduction

Modeling is a core activity both within science and engineering. In various domains, there are different kinds of models, such as dynamic models, probabilistic models, software models, and business models. In general, a *model* is an abstraction of something, for instance a process, a system, a behavior, or another model.

Both scientists and engineers make extensive use of models, but for different reasons. As Lee [13] points out, scientists construct models *to understand* the thing being modeled, whereas engineers use models *to construct* what is being modeled. In both cases, the abstraction (the model) contains fewer details than the thing being modeled, which enables the possibility to *analyze* the model. Such analysis can include formal verification, statistical analysis, or simulation.

The latter, *simulation* of models, is the main topic of this paper. Simulation can be seen as a way to perform experiments on a model, instead of experimenting directly on the system or process being modeled [7]. There are many reasons for using modeling and simulation. It can be too dangerous to perform experiments on real systems. It can be cheaper to perform simulations, or the system being modeled might not yet exist.

Regardless of the reason for doing modeling and simulation, it is vital to trust the simulation result to some degree. We say that the *fidelity* of the model is to what extent the model correctly represents the system or processing being modeled. Lee [12,13] often stresses the distinction between the model and what is being modeled, by giving the famous quote by Golomb [10]: "you will never strike oil by drilling through the map". High model fidelity is necessary, but not sufficient to enable trust of simulation results. To trust the map, as an example of a model, we also need to interpret the map safely. For instance, if an English speaking engineer is using a Russian map to find oil, even a map of high fidelity can lead to incorrect conclusions. Misinterpretations of the map (the model) can result in false positives (drilling through an oil pipe instead of an oil field) or true negatives (drilling through a mine field instead of an oil field). As a consequence, to trust the use of models, not only high model fidelity is needed, but also safe interpretation of the model.

If we make the analogy between a model and a computer program, we can distinguish between two kinds of errors [6]: (i) *untrapped errors* that can go unnoticed and then later result in arbitrary incorrect behavior, and (ii) *trapped errors* that are handled directly or before they occur. For a computer program written in the C programming language, an array out-of-bound error can lead to memory corruption, where the actual problem can first go unnoticed, and then crashes the system at a later point in time. This is an example of an untrapped error. By contrast, an array out-of-bound error in Java results in a Java exception, which happens directly when it occurs, and makes it possible for the program itself to handle the error. This latter case is an example of a trapped error. A program language where all errors are trapped errors, either detected at compile time using a type system, or at runtime using runtime checks, is said to be a *safe* language.

This paper introduces the idea of making a distinction between safe and unsafe simulations. A *simulation* is said to be *safe* if no untrapped simulation errors occur. A *simulation environment* is said to be safe if no untrapped simulation errors can occur in any simulation. As a consequence, a natural question is then what we mean by *simulation error*. This paper focuses on two kinds of simulation errors that can occur in hybrid modeling languages [2,5,14–16] and cosimulation environments [4,8]. More specifically, this work concerns both error classification and solution methods. It presents the following main contributions[1]:

- The paper describes two kinds of simulation errors that have traditionally been seen as modeling errors and not as untrapped simulation errors. More specifically, the errors concern (i) *unsafe zero-crossing detection*, and (ii) *unsafe accidental determinism* (Sect. 2).
- It describes an approach to make these untrapped simulation errors trapped, by introducing the concept of a *limbo* state. A simulation enters the limbo state when a simulation error is detected. The modeler has the choice of defining the behavior to leave the limbo state in a safe way and continue the simulation, or to terminate the simulation and report the error as a trapped error (Sect. 3).

---

[1] All examples in the paper are available here: http://www.modelyze.org/limbo.

2   Hybrid Simulation Safety Problems

This section describes two problems with hybrid simulation safety. First, it discusses the infamous bouncing-ball problem, where the numerical accuracies of standard zero-crossing detectors make a bouncing ball tunnel through the ground. Second, the section discusses the relations between *accidental* and *intentional nondeterminism*, and the safety problem resulting from *accidental determinism*. The latter problem is illustrated by simultaneous elastic collisions of frictionless balls.

2.1   Unsafe Zero-Crossing Detection

One classic simple example for demonstrating hybrid modeling and simulation is the bouncing ball model. The model demonstrates how a ball is falling towards the ground, and bounces with an inelastic collision, thus bouncing with decreased height. This model can be expressed in any modeling language that supports (i) a continuous domain for expressing velocity and acceleration, (ii) a construct to numerically detect the collision, and (iii) an action statement that changes the sign and magnitude of the velocity of the ball. The following model is a straight forward implementation in the Modelica language:

```
1   model BouncingBall
2      Real h,v;
3      parameter Real c = 0.7;
4   initial equation
5      h = 3.0;
6   equation
7      der(h) = v;
8      der(v) = -9.81;
9      when h <= 0 then
10        reinit(v, -c*pre(v));
11     end when;
12  end BouncingBall;
```

The model is divided into three sections. The first section (lines 2–3) defines the two state variables (h for the height of the ball and v for the velocity), and one parameter c that states the fraction of the momentum that remains after a collision with the ground. The second section (line 5) states an initial equation. In this case, the height of the ball is initiated to value 3. Note that a Modelica tool will implicitly initialize the other variables to zero, in this case the velocity v. The third section (lines 7–11) declaratively states the equations that holds during the whole simulation. The der operator denotes the derivative of a variable. For instance, der(h) is the derivative of the height. Lines 9–11 lists a when equation, which is activated when the guard h <= 0 becomes true. That is, when the ball touches the ground (h becomes approximately 0) the reinit statement is activated. The reinit statement reinitializes state variable v to the value of expression -c*pre(v), where pre(v) is the left limit value of v, before the guard becomes true. Note how the -c coefficient both changes the magnitude and the direction of the velocity. Although the bouncing ball example is often used as a "hello world" model for hybrid modeling, it also demonstrates two surprising effects.

Figure 1(a) shows the simulation result, plotting the height of the ball. As expected, the ball bounces with decreased height until it visually *appears* to sit still, but then suddenly tunnels through the ground. The model demonstrates two phenomena. First, it shows an example of *Zeno behavior*, where infinite number of events (triggering the when construct in this case) in finite amount of time. The ball continuous to bounce with lower and lower bounces. Second, the simulation trace shows a tunneling effect, where the ball falls through the ground. Figure 1(b) shows the last bounces before the tunneling effect. Note how the height of the last bounce is less than 10^{-9} units.

Note, however, that the tunneling effect is not a consequence of the Zeno condition, but of a numerical effect of how traditional zero-crossing detectors detect and handle zero crossings. As can be seen in Fig. 1(b), a zero-crossing

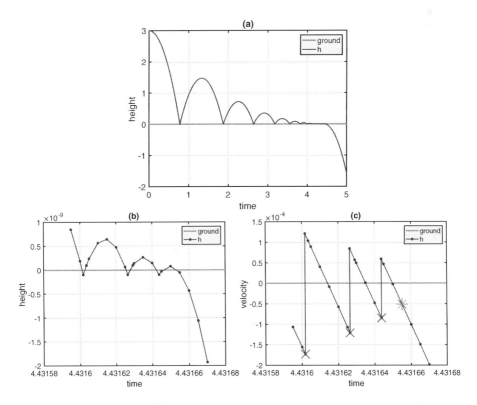

Fig. 1. A bouncing ball that is incorrectly tunneling through the ground. (a) Shows the height of the ball during the whole simulation, whereas the two bottom figures zoom in to the tunneling effect, showing the height (b) and the velocity (c). The simulation was performed using OpenModelica v1.11. (Color figure online)

detector typically overshoots the crossing slightly, before the action is applied. To be able to detect a crossing, the bounce needs to get over a certain tolerance threshold, for the crossing to be detected. Figure 1(c) shows the velocity for the last three bounces. The red crosses mark where zero crossings take place, and where the velocity is changed from positive to negative in the same time instance. At the last instance (marked with a green star) a zero crossing should have been detected, but the bounce has not reached over the tolerance level above zero. Hence, no zero crossing occurs, and the ball tunnels through the ground.

It is important to stress that the Zeno behavior of the model and the numerical tunneling problem are two different things. The former is a property of the model, whereas the latter is a simulation error due to numerical imprecision in a specific simulation tool. The Zeno effect has been extensively studied in the area of hybrid automata, where regularization techniques are used to solve the problem by creating a new model [11]. Traditionally, also the tunneling effect has been seen as a model problem. However, this paper argues the opposite. The tunneling problem is a consequence of an *untrapped simulation error*. A safe simulation environment should handle such problems as *trapped errors*, either by generating an exception state that can be handled within the model, or by terminating the simulation and report an error, before the tunneling effect occurs. A potential solution is discussed in Sect. 3.

2.2   Unsafe Accidental Determinism

The second problem has been extensively discussed in two recent papers by Lee [12,13]. In these papers, Lee discusses the problem of deterministic behavior of simultaneous events, and illustrates the problem using an example with three colliding balls. This section discusses the problem with the same example, but using Modelica instead of Ptolemy II. The key insight in this section is not the difference in modeling environment, but to view the problem as a simulation safety problem, rather than a modeling problem.

Consider the example in Fig. 2 where ball 1 and ball 3 are moving towards ball 2, which is sitting still. In the example, we assume a frictionless surface and perfectly elastic collision, that is, no energy is lost when the balls collide.

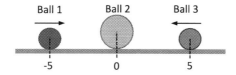

Fig. 2. Illustration of the example with three colliding balls. The balls roll without any friction. Ball 1 and ball 3 move with the same constant speed in opposite directions, where as ball 2 is sitting still before the impact. Note that the problem is a 1-dimensional problem: the balls can only move horizontally, and not in vertical directions.

The following Modelica model defines the dynamics of a frictionless elastic ball, with two state variables: x for the horizontal position, and v for the velocity.

```
1  model Ball
2    Real x;                // Position state
3    Real v;                // Velocity state
4    parameter Real x0;     // Initial position
5    parameter Real v0;     // Initial velocity
6    parameter Real m;      // Mass of the ball
7    parameter Real r;      // Radius
8  initial equation
9    x = x0;
10   v = v0;
11 equation
12   der(x) = v;      // Relation between position and speed
13   der(v) = 0;      // Constant speed, no acceleration
14 end Ball;
```

For an elastic collision, the momentum and the kinetic energy are preserved.

$$m_1 v_1 + m_2 v_2 = m_1 v_1' + m_2 v_2', \qquad \frac{m_1 v_1^2}{2} + \frac{m_2 v_2^2}{2} = \frac{m_1 {v_1'}^2}{2} + \frac{m_2 {v_2'}^2}{2} \qquad (1)$$

Variables v_1 and v_2 represent the velocity before the collision for ball 1 and ball 2, respectively. The velocity after collision is given by v_1' and v_2'. We then have

$$v_1' = \frac{2m_2 v_2 + m_1 v_1 - m_2 v_1}{m_1 + m_2}, \qquad v_2' = \frac{2m_1 v_1 + m_2 v_2 - m_1 v_2}{m_1 + m_2} \qquad (2)$$

in the case where $m_1 \neq 0$ and $m_2 \neq 0$. By instantiating the Ball model into three components b1, b2, and b3, we get the following model:

```
1  model ThreeBalls
2    Ball b1(x0=-5, v0= 1, r=0.5, m=1);
3    Ball b2(x0= 0, v0= 0, r=1.0, m=2);
4    Ball b3(x0= 5, v0=-1, r=0.5, m=1);
5  equation
6    //Detecting collision between ball 1 and ball 2
7    when b2.x - b1.x <= b1.r + b2.r then
8      reinit(b1.v, (2*b2.m*pre(b2.v) + b1.m*pre(b1.v) -
9          b2.m*pre(b1.v))/(b1.m + b2.m));
10     reinit(b2.v, (2*b1.m*pre(b1.v) + b2.m*pre(b2.v) -
11         b1.m*pre(b2.v))/(b1.m + b2.m));
12   end when;
13   //Detecting collision between ball 2 and ball 3
14   when b3.x - b2.x <= b2.r + b3.r then
15     reinit(b2.v, (2*b3.m*pre(b3.v) + b2.m*pre(b2.v) -
16         b3.m*pre(b2.v))/(b2.m + b3.m));
17     reinit(b3.v, (2*b2.m*pre(b2.v) + b3.m*pre(b3.v) -
18         b2.m*pre(b3.v))/(b2.m + b3.m));
19   end when;
20 end ThreeBalls;
```

Note that components b1 (ball 1) and b3 (ball 3) have the same mass m=1 and radius r=0.5, whereas b2 (ball 2) has m=2 and r=1.0. The start positions are −5, 0, and 5, for balls 1, 2, and 3, respectively.

The changes in velocity, according to Eq. (2), are encoded as two when equations, each detecting either the collision between ball 1 and 2, or between ball 2 and 3. What is then the expected simulation trace for this model? One expected output might be the plot in Fig. 3(a). That is, a simultaneous collision occurs, ball 2 does not move, and the other two balls bounce back with the same velocity. This is actually *not* what happens when simulating the model. Let us take a step back and study the behavior of this model in more detail.

Consider Fig. 3(b) and (c). These two simulation traces show the same example as above, with the difference that in Fig. 3(b), ball 1 starts a bit closer to the middle ball, whereas in Fig. 3(c) ball 3 starts a bit closer. As expected, in the first case, ball 1 hits ball 2 first, that makes ball 1 bounce back (it is the lighter of the two) and ball 2 starts to move towards ball 3. Then ball 2 hits ball 3, which bounces back and ball 2 changes direction again. In the first case, ball 3 bounces back at a higher speed because the middle ball's energy from the first hit gives ball 3 the extra speed. As expected, Fig. 3(c) shows the reverse, when ball 3 hits ball 2 first.

Now, imagine that the distances between ball 1 and the middle ball, and ball 3 and the middle ball get closer and closer to equal. As long as one of the balls hits first, this will affect the other ball. Hence, the limit for the two cases are not the same. As Lee [13] points out, the model may be seen as nondeterministic in the case when both the balls collide simultaneously. In that case, either ball 1 or ball 3 hits the middle ball first, but nothing in the model indicates the order. Again, the model is nondeterministic in this specific point.

In the previous two plots, the distances between the balls were not the same. Figure 3(d) shows the actual simulation result when simulating ThreeBalls where the distances between the balls are equal. We get a simulation trace, but is it the correct one? Obviously no. We can notice two things. First, even if ball 1 and ball 3 arrive at the same speed from the same distances to the middle ball, ball 2 moves to the left after impact. Why is the ball moving in that direction and not the opposite direction? Second, note how ball 1 and 2 tunnel through each other, and are at the same position at time 8 (which should be physically impossible). The reason ball 2 moves to the left is that both when equations are activated simultaneously and that the code within the two when blocks (lines 8–11 and lines 15–18) are executed in the order that they are stated in the model. Hence, the velocity for ball 2 is initialized twice (lines 10 and 15), where the last one (line 15) gives the final result.

To make the situation even worse, assume that we switch the order of the two when equations in model ThreeBalls, that is, the when equation for detecting collisions between ball 2 and 3 comes before the when equation for detecting collisions between ball 1 and 2. Modelica is a declarative language, where the order of equations should not matter. Hence, we might expect to get the same incorrect result. Unfortunately, this is not the case. The simulation

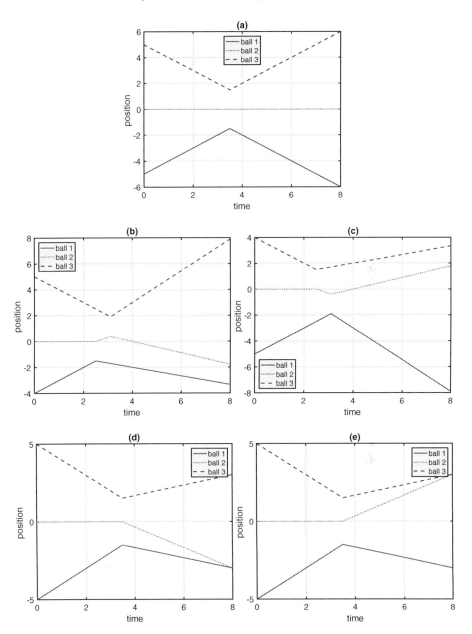

Fig. 3. Simulation cases for the `ThreeBalls` model. (a) Shows an ideal result when the balls have the same initial distances. (b) and (c) Show simulation traces, where initial distances between the balls are not equal. (d) and (e) Show unexpected simulation results, where the initial distances between the balls are the same, but where the when blocks have different order.

result for the new model, where the when equations have switched order, is shown in Fig. 3(e). Note how ball 2 moves in the opposite direction after impact because the order of the impact from ball 1 and 3 has changed.

Lee [13, p. 3:24] argues, based on a similar example, as follows: "It would probably be wise to assume that determinism is incomplete for any modeling framework that is rich enough to help design an understand CPS, where discrete and continuous behaviors inevitably mix". If the order of the evaluation of when equations matter and the order is left unspecified, the model is indeed nondeterministic: there are two possible interpretations. However, this paper argues that it is important to not mix the two separate issues of the determinism of the model, and the determinism of the simulation.

Figure 4 shows a matrix, where we introduce the concepts of intensional determinism/nondeterminism, and accidental determinism/nondeterminism. *Intensional determinism (ID)* for a modeling and simulation environment is typically what is intended in many simulation environments for cyber-physical systems (CPS). ID means that the simulation of deterministic models yields deterministic simulation results. The same model simulated with the same input always results in the same simulation result. *Intensional nondeterminism (IND)* means that the model itself is nondeterministic, and that the simulator may use random samples to generate the simulation result. Monte Carlo methods fall within this category. Many useful formalisms, languages, and environments fall within the categories of ID and IND.

The accidental categories are more problematic. *Accidental nondeterminism (AND)* is when a simulator for a deterministic model generates different simulation traces, even if the same model with the same input is used. If a simulator behaves within the AND-category, it typically means that there is an error in the simulator. For instance, if a simulator is incorrectly using a multithreaded execution environment, where the simulation result depends on the thread interleaving, the simulator might give different results for different executions.

The last category, *accidental determinism (AD)* is the one that is particular interesting in this example. In this case, a nondeterministic model always

	Determinism	Nondeterminism
Intensional	**ID** *"Deterministic model with a deterministic simulation result"*	**IND** *"Nondeterministic model with random choice during simulation"*
Accidental	**AD** *"Nondeterministic model with a deterministic simulation result"*	**AND** *"A deterministic model that results in different simulation results for different executions"*

Fig. 4. A matrix that shows the relationship between intensional determinism/nondeterminism and accidental determinism/nondeterminism.

yields the same simulation result. This is exactly what happens in our simulation example of the `ThreeBalls` model. From Fig. 3(b) and (c) we know that the order in which balls 1 and 3 hit ball 2 has a direct implication on the simulation result. When the distance between the balls is the same, both when equations are activated simultaneously. The Modelica tool then decides on an evaluation order for the equations. If the `reinit` statements were independent of each other, the order would not matter. However, in this case, the order matters. As it turns out, the simulator (OpenModelica v1.11 [9]) executes the constructs in linear order, which is the reason for the different simulation traces for Fig. 3(d) and (e). We have an accidental deterministic behavior, where the original model was nondeterministic, but where the simulation result is deterministic. Recall that the actual activation choice is made on the order the when equations are defined in the file. Accidental determinism is an example of unsafe simulation: the error is untrapped, that is, we get a simulation result without warnings, even though the result itself is not deterministic.

3   Safe Simulations Using the Limbo State

The previous section showed two examples of unsafe simulation behavior. In both cases, the simulation continued and produced a result, without giving any errors or warnings. These are examples of untrapped simulation errors. Although an error occurs at a specific point in time (the tunneling effect or incorrect collision), the simulator still produces a simulation result. The purpose of this section is to illustrate the idea of how to make the untrapped errors trapped, thus enabling safe simulations.

3.1   The Limbo State

The key idea is to introduce three conceptual states in a simulator: (i) the *safe* state, (ii) the *limbo* state, and (iii) the *unsafe* state. During simulation, the simulator is in one of these three states. Note that these are states of *the simulator* itself, and not modes in a specific model. The idea of the limbo state is first described abstractly, followed by a concrete discussion in the context of the previous two problem examples.

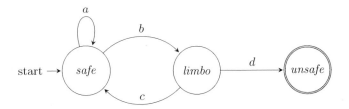

Fig. 5. A finite state machine diagram that includes the limbo state.

Figure 5 depicts a finite state diagram with the three states. A simulation starts in the safe state. If no errors occur, the simulator stays in the safe state. If a potential error occurs, transition b is taken to the limbo state. The limbo state means that the simulator is in between a safe and an unsafe state. The error *can potentially happen*, but has not yet taken place. From the limbo state, either the simulation is safely terminated with an error message (a trapped error), or transition c is taken back to the safe state. It is the modeler's responsibility to augment the model, such that transition c can be taken. If the error occurs in the limbo state, transition d is taken. If the simulator is safe, transition d should happen *when the error occurs*, that is, it should terminate the simulation at the simulation time of the error. Thus, transition d should generate a trapped error, indicating that the simulation reached an unsafe state at a specific point in time.

The reader might now ask why we see the described problems as simulation errors, when the user still can modify the model to avoid the error? Is it not a modeling error then? The point is, again, that the errors which appear during simulation must be trapped. However, the same model can still be valid for different simulation input. For instance, the bouncing ball model in Fig. 1(a) is valid before time 4, since the simulation error happens sometime between time 4 and 5. Let us now consider the two problems in Sect. 2 in turn.

3.2   Safe Zero-Crossing Detector

The tunneling problem described in Sect. 2.1 can easily be detected using multiple levels of zero-crossings [17]. The problem with traditional zero-crossing detectors, such as the when equations in Modelica and level-crossing detector actors in Ptolemy II, is that they can easily be used in an unsafe way. The key idea is instead that a modeling language should *only* provide safe zero-crossing detectors, where the tunneling effect cannot occur.

Figure 6 depicts the structure of a safe zero-crossing detector. A safe zero-crossing detector has a safe region, a limbo region, and an unsafe region. The detector consists of three levels of detection mechanisms: (i) *zero level* that detects the actual zero crossing, (ii) *limbo level* that detects when the limbo region is entered, and (iii) the *unsafe level*, which detects that the model did not leave the limbo state correctly.

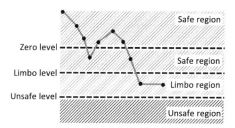

Fig. 6. The three different crossing detection levels and regions.

Returning to the state machine in Fig. 5. Transition a is taken each time the *zero level* is crossed. That is, the simulation is still safe, even if the zero level is crossed. In the bouncing ball example, this happens every time the ball bounces correctly (see the example trajectory line in Fig. 6). Transition b is taken if the variable value crosses the limbo level. In the bouncing ball example, this occurs when the ball is starting to tunnel through the ground. Note that this does not have to be an error. If the modeler detects the tunneling effect, and then changes the mode of the ball to stay still (no acceleration or velocity), the simulation changes state to be safe again (transition c), or stays in the limbo region (see again the example trajectory line in Fig. 6). However, if the model is incorrectly implemented, as in the example in Sect. 2.1, the unsafe level will be crossed. In such a case, the simulation environment should generate a trapped error, by terminating the simulation and by reporting the simulation time of the error. A safe modeling and simulation language should only include safe zero-crossing detectors as primitives, making it impossible to use unsafe zero-crossing detection. Consider now the following Modelica model.

```
1   model SafeBouncingBallFinal
2     Real h,v;
3     discrete Real a(start = -9.81);
4     parameter Real c = 0.7;
5     parameter Real epsilon = 1e-8;
6     Boolean limbo;
7   initial equation
8     h = 3.0;
9     v = 0;
10    limbo = false;
11  equation
12    der(h) = v;
13    der(v) = a;
14    when h <= 0 then
15      reinit(v, -c*pre(v));
16    end when;
17
18    //Limbo state action
19    when limbo then
20      reinit(v,0);
21      a = 0;
22    end when;
23    // Detecting limbo level
24    when h <= -epsilon then
25      limbo = true;
26    end when;
27    // Detecting unsafe level
28    when h <= -2*epsilon then
29      terminate("Unsafe Zero Crossing");
30    end when;
31  end SafeBouncingBallFinal;
```

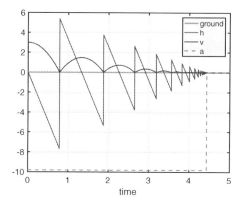

Fig. 7. A safe bouncing ball that stays on the ground. Note how the acceleration a of the ball transitions from −9.81 to 0 when the ball comes to rest.

Figure 7 shows the simulation trace of simulating the model. A few remarks are worth making. We can see that the when equation for detecting the zero crossing is unchanged compared to the previous section. What has been added are two more when equations that detect the limbo level (line 24), and the unsafe level (line 28). If the limbo region is entered (line 24) a boolean variable is updated, which triggers the limbo action (lines 19–22), where the ball is put to rest. Note that if we reach the unsafe region (line 29), the simulation is terminated. In this case, this is done explicitly in the model, but an ideal modeling language should include such detection automatically. It is not obvious how to extend Modelica in this way, but an interesting direction is to be able to specify invariants of safe states, as done with invariants in hybrid automata [1].

A zero-crossing detector can be generalized into a directional level-crossing detector, that can detect arbitrary level in one direction. Figure 8 shows a simple safe level-crossing detector that is implemented as an actor in Ptolemy II. The main model called *Bouncing Ball* is a modified version of the bouncing ball example from [12]. Two changes have been made: (i) the Ball model has been replaced with a ModalBallModel, and (ii) the original level-crossing detector has been replaced with a new safe level-crossing detector. Note that the safe level-crossing detector actor has approximately the same interface as the level-crossing detector in the Ptolemy II standard library, with the main difference that it also has an output port called limbo. The safe level-crossing detector outputs a discrete event on the limbo port if it detects a limbo state. When it is used in the bouncing ball example, it means that the ball is just about to start to tunnel. In the example model, the limbo port is connected to the ModalBallModel actor's stop port. The modal model has two modes, (i) the ball is falling, and (ii) the ball is sitting still. If the modeler forgets to connect the limbo port, the safe level-crossing detector reports a trapped error.

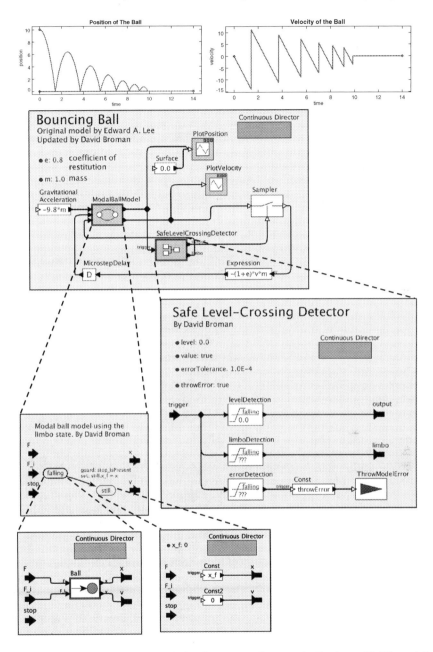

Fig. 8. An implementation of a safe level-crossing detector in Ptolemy II. The original open source model, before extending it with the safe level-crossing detector, is available here: http://ptolemy.org/constructive/models

3.3   Safe Deterministic Event Handling

In the colliding ball example in Sect. 2.2, the root of the accidental deterministic behavior was simultaneous events. It is extremely hard (if not impossible) to guarantee that events cannot happen simultaneously. Numerical imprecision, both due to round-off errors and integration errors, makes it hard to give any guarantees. A naive solution would be to always enforce that no events occur simultaneously by arbitrarily selecting an order. However, this will lead to the problem of accidental determinism. If the order actually matters, such arbitrary deterministic choice would result in an unsafe behavior.

Instead, our proposal is to again make use of the limbo state diagram, as shown in Fig. 5. The transition b should be activated when two events are sufficiently close to each other. The exact meaning of *sufficiently close to each other* can be configured using a numerical tolerance level. This means that a model will transition into the limbo state when simultaneous events occur. This does not have to be an error. If the modeler knows how to handle the specific case, he/she can express this in the model (assuming that the modeling language is expressive enough) and then make a transition back to the safe state. If no such case for simultaneous event is implemented, the simulation tool must report a trapped error. In Modelica, elsewhen constructs can be used to implement such special cases. This is indeed what was done to create the simulation plot in Fig. 3(a). Note that a nondeterministic model with missing cases can be seen as an underspecified model. By adding all missing cases and completely specifying the model, we convert a nondeterministic model into a deterministic model.

4   Conclusions

This paper presents and discusses the idea of safe simulation. In particular, it makes a distinction between trapped and untrapped errors. As part of the solution, the notion of a limbo state is introduced. The preliminary work is illustrated using small examples in Modelica and Ptolemy II. However, to make the approach useful in practice, the safety concepts need to be integrated as explicit parts of a modeling language and a simulation environment. An interesting direction for future work is to investigate if type systems in modeling languages [2,3] can be used to statically detect and eliminate untrapped errors.

Acknowledgments. I would like to thank Edward for the really great collaboration we have had over the years. And, congratulations on your birthday! I would also like to thank Cludio Gomes, Oscar Eriksson, and the anonymous reviewers for many useful comments. Finally, I would like to acknowledge and thank Bernhard Rumpe for pointing out the connection between nondeterminism in models and underspecification.

This project is financially supported by the Swedish Foundation for Strategic Research (FFL15-0032).

References

1. Alur, R., Courcoubetis, C., Henzinger, T.A., Ho, P.-H.: Hybrid automata: an algorithmic approach to the specification and verification of hybrid systems. In: Grossman, R.L., Nerode, A., Ravn, A.P., Rischel, H. (eds.) HS 1991–1992. LNCS, vol. 736, pp. 209–229. Springer, Heidelberg (1993). https://doi.org/10.1007/3-540-57318-6_30
2. Bourke, T., Pouzet, M.: Zélus: a synchronous language with ODEs. In: Proceedings of the 16th International Conference on Hybrid Systems: Computation and Control (HSCC), pp. 113–118. ACM (2013)
3. Broman, D., Fritzson, P., Furic, S.: Types in the Modelica language. In: Proceedings of the Fifth International Modelica Conference, Vienna, Austria, pp. 303–315 (2006)
4. Broman, D., Greenberg, L., Lee, E.A., Masin, M., Tripakis, S., Wetter, M.: Requirements for hybrid cosimulation standards. In: Proceedings of 18th ACM International Conference on Hybrid Systems: Computation and Control (HSCC), pp. 179–188. ACM (2015)
5. Broman, D., Siek, J.G.: Modelyze: a gradually typed host language for embedding equation-based modeling languages. Technical Report UCB/EECS-2012-173, EECS Department, University of California, Berkeley (2012)
6. Cardelli, L.: Type systems. In: The Computer Science and Engineering Handbook, chap. 97. 2 edn. (2004)
7. Cellier, F.E.: Continuous System Modeling. Springer, New York (1991). https://doi.org/10.1007/978-1-4757-3922-0
8. Cremona, F., Lohstroh, M., Broman, D., Lee, E.A., Masin, M., Tripakis, S.: Hybrid co-simulation: it's about time. Softw. Syst. Model. **17**, 1–25 (2017)
9. Fritzson, P., Aronsson, P., Lundvall, H., Nyström, K., Pop, A., Saldamli, L., Broman, D.: The OpenModelica modeling, simulation, and software development environment. Simul. News Europe **15**(44/45), 8–16 (2005)
10. Golomb, S.W.: Mathematical models: uses and limitations. IEEE Trans. Reliab. **20**(3), 130–131 (1971)
11. Johansson, K.H., Egerstedt, M., Lygeros, J., Sastry, S.: On the regularization of Zeno hybrid automata. Syst. Control Lett. **38**(3), 141–150 (1999)
12. Lee, E.A.: Constructive models of discrete and continuous physical phenomena. IEEE Access **2**, 797–821 (2014)
13. Lee, E.A.: Fundamental limits of cyber-physical systems modeling. ACM Trans. Cyber-Phys. Syst. **1**(1), 3 (2016)
14. Modelica Association: Modelica - a unified object-oriented language for physical systems modeling - language specification version 3.4 (2017). http://www.modelica.org
15. Nilsson, H., Peterson, J., Hudak, P.: Functional hybrid modeling. In: Dahl, V., Wadler, P. (eds.) PADL 2003. LNCS, vol. 2562, pp. 376–390. Springer, Heidelberg (2003). https://doi.org/10.1007/3-540-36388-2_25
16. Ptolemaeus, C. (ed.): System Design, Modeling, and Simulation using Ptolemy II. Ptolemy.org, London (2014). http://ptolemy.org/books/Systems
17. Tiller, M.M.: Modelica by Example. Online book (2017). http://book.xogeny.com/. Accessed 9 Sept 2017

Ptolemy-HLA: A Cyber-Physical System Distributed Simulation Framework

Janette Cardoso[⊠] and Pierre Siron

ISAE-SUPAERO, Université de Toulouse, Toulouse, France
{janette.cardoso,pierre.siron}@isae-supaero.fr

Abstract. The Ptolemy-HLA distributed co-simulation framework leverages two open source tools, Ptolemy II and HLA/CERTI, for the simulation of Cyber-Physical Systems (CPS). This framework enables dealing with three important issues: (1) Distribution of a simulation, allowing to scale up models and performance; (2) Interoperability of tools, allowing reusability and interfacing with other simulators or real devices/systems; (3) Heterogeneous simulations (discrete events, continuous time).

The framework extends Ptolemy both, by coordinating the time advance of various Ptolemy instances, and by allowing data communication between them with the help of HLA management services.

These additions enable the creation of HLA federates (i.e., simulators) in a Federation (i.e., a distributed simulation) in an easy way, since the user does not need to be an HLA specialist in order to design a Federate. The paper presents the new components added to Ptolemy, some semantic issues, an application example and performance analysis.

Keywords: Distributed simulation · HLA · Cyber-physical systems

1 Introduction

There are many advantages to a distributed simulation. A first aspect comes from the nature of the systems to be simulated, which are nowadays more and more distributed and complex. It can be more appropriate to build a distributed simulation of a distributed system, as, for example, a fleet of drones, than a monolithic simulation. The distributed simulation is more representative and it mimics the real system without simplifications better. The second aspect is the complexity of the system that is translated in an integration of complex and heterogeneous models. Distributed simulation is often associated with the notion of simulation interoperability offering the possibility of integrating different simulators, such as specific domain simulators. The reuse of a simulator can offer a significant reduction of design and development time as well as improve quality of the simulation. Distributed simulation is also relevant for non-functional requirements. It can reduce the simulation time (parallelization speedup) or enable larger simulations (scalability) [1]. Finally, models can be treated as black-boxes or executed on remote processors, and we can deal with IP issues [2]. For all these reasons,

© Springer International Publishing AG, part of Springer Nature 2018
M. Lohstroh et al. (Eds.): Lee Festschrift, LNCS 10760, pp. 122–142, 2018.
https://doi.org/10.1007/978-3-319-95246-8_8

distributed simulations are adapted for the challenging study of Cyber-Physical Systems, that are complex, heterogeneous and distributed. But performing distributed simulations is difficult, and we propose in this paper a principled and friendly way to build these simulations.

Ptolemy is an open source modeling and simulation tool for heterogeneous systems, developed at the University of California Berkeley. This tool is well suited for modeling CPS [9] by providing different models of computation (MoC), such as continuous time for describing physical systems or discrete event for describing software and control.

The IEEE High-Level Architecture (HLA) standard [15] targets distributed simulation. A CPS can be seen as a federation grouping several federates which communicate via publish/subscribe patterns. This decomposition into federates allows to combine different types of components such as simulation models, executable code (in C++, Java, etc.), and hardware equipment. The key benefits of HLA are interoperability and reuse.

PTIDES [26], a framework implemented in Ptolemy, is used to design event-triggered, distributed, real-time systems. It leverages network time synchronization to provide a coherent global meaning for timestamps in distributed systems. Moreover, it has the nice characteristic that it carefully relates multiple time-lines (physical time, logical time, *oracle* time). However, even if it allows the simulation and execution of a distributed system, the entire system is modeled in only one model.

The Functional Mock-up Interface (FMI) standard for co-simulation allows the exchange and interoperation of model components or subsystems designed with different modeling tools. However, it is up to the user to guarantee a coherent time representation when the simulation is distributed. There are works proposing an integration of HLA and FMI [13,23,24]. An HLA-FMI wrapper that turns a FMU into a full featured HLA federate exists [14], but it seems to deal only with data. FIDE, which stands for FMI Integrated Development Environment [8], is an IDE for building applications using Functional Mock-up Units (FMUs) that implement the FMI standard in the Ptolemy framework. Their work focuses on a master algorithm that deterministically combines discrete and continuous-time dynamics. However, it does not deal with distributed simulation. A detailed analysis of the time representation in the FMI framework is done in [7]. It proposes the superdense model of time using integers (implemented by the class Time in Ptolemy) for solving many problems of time representation. In particular their paper discusses the choice of resolution to be used when the FMUs (components of a co-simulation) have different resolutions. The coordination of different notions of time is an issue that also comes up in cyber-physical systems [29].

FORWARDSIM [10] is a proprietary software toolbox that allows for distributed simulation using the HLA standard. It provides the HLA Blockset for Simulink and the HLA Toolbox for Matlab. The user must know the entire standard well and it is up to the user to call each service by adding the corresponding block to the model.

In this paper, we will present a framework called Ptolemy-HLA: it brings together the heterogeneity provided by Ptolemy (i.e. the possibility to mix continuous, discrete or other MoCs) and interoperability provided by HLA (i.e. the possibility to mix simulation models, pieces of code and physical equipment). We consider that, in relation to ForwardSim, our framework provides a friendly, open-source interface to the user which requires minimal knowledge of the HLA standard. Similar to PTIDES, we carefully tackle time coordination between HLA and Ptolemy timelines. Our approach allows the distributed simulation of models over a network. As of this moment, the Ptolemy-HLA framework does not allow to build applications using FMUs as per the FMI standard.

HLA users can benefit from already existing Ptolemy models that can be easily translated into the Ptolemy-HLA framework. For Ptolemy users, the Ptolemy-HLA framework can be useful if a large model already exists. Splitting the components of such a model into distributed models, running on a same computer or different computers, allows the user to use a good *granularity* of the model. This can improve handling and may be more representative, since each (distributed) model can be more detailed or extended, for example, modeling two aircraft engines separately and/or using a more complex model for the engine. From a single model, e.g., a quad-rotor model, a model of a fleet of quad-rotors can be easily obtained. The interoperability of the HLA standard allows to use models or code, as well as real devices with an interface compliant with this standard.

This paper is organized as follows. An overview of HLA and Ptolemy is presented in Sect. 2. Section 3 describes the co-simulation framework: how time is advanced and how data is exchanged considering the rules of both, Ptolemy and HLA. Section 4 illustrates the results of our approach applied to a concrete case-study: a flight control system of a F14 aircraft. Finally, Sect. 5 presents concluding remarks and our future work.

2   Tools for Distributed Simulation and Heterogenous Simulation

The simulation of Cyber-Physical systems needs to deal with both, heterogeneity and distribution of simulators. We choose two open source tools for taking advantage of each one of these needs: Ptolemy II and HLA/CERTI.

2.1   Ptolemy

Quoting [26] "Ptolemy II is an open-source simulation and modeling tool intended for *experimenting with system design techniques*, particularly those that involve combinations of different types of models". Being interested in cyber-physical system (CPS) modeling and simulation, Ptolemy's ability to represent heterogeneous system, offered by its different Models of Computations (MoC), is a very important feature. A MoC is specified by a component called a Director, represented by a green block as shown in Fig. 1. In this paper, we will deal with two directors: Discrete Event (DE) and Continuous (CT). They will be used for modeling the cyber and physical part of a CPS. For the sake of simplicity, a model with a DE director will be called a DE model. The same is done for the CT director.

Another important feature in Ptolemy is its model time known as superdense time, which allows two distinct ordered events to occur in the same signal without time elapsing between them [7]. A superdense time value can be represented as a pair (t, n), called a timestamp, where t is the model time and n is a microstep (also called an index). The model time represents the time at which an event occurs, and the microstep represents the sequencing of events that occur at the same model time [26]. The initial (default) value for the microstep is 1 when using a DE director in a model and 0 when using a CT director. In this paper, for the sake of simplicity, a timestamp $(t, 1)$ for DE and $(t, 0)$ for CT will be represented only by t. The time t is represented as mr, where m is an integer and time resolution r is a double-precision floating point number. Therefore, the (model) time resolution is the same throughout its execution [26] which is not the case when IEEE-754 double is used. The Ptolemy time representation is implemented by a Java class called `Time`.

Time Advance in Ptolemy [4,26]. Every director in Ptolemy has a local clock. If the director is at the top level of the model, i.e., if there is no enclosing director, then the advance of the clock is entirely controlled by this director. An event in the Ptolemy calendar queue is represented as $e(v, (t, n), A_j)$, where A_j is the jth input port of destination actor A. All events are generated locally, and the director will always advance time to the smallest timestamp of unprocessed events. In a DE model, this timestamp is that of a given event and only the destination actor of this event is executed. In a CT model, the timestamp is computed by a solver, and all actors are executed. If there is more than one event with the same timestamp, the destination actors are fired in the order given by a topological sort of the actors, which is a list of the actors in data-precedence order. This behavior ensures determinism.

Ptolemy also provides a so-called TimeRegulator interface with a `proposeTime` method. This interface is implemented by attributes that wish to be consulted when a director advances time. The director will call the `proposedTime` method, passing it a proposed time to advance to, and the method will return either the same proposed time or a smaller time. This method has a key role in the Ptolemy-HLA framework.

Data Exchange in Ptolemy. Actors in Ptolemy have input and/or output ports. Actors with only input ports are called sink actors (e.g., a `TimeDisplay` as in Fig. 4c) and actors with only output ports are called source actors (e.g., a `DiscreteClock` as in Fig. 4c). A *token* is the unit of data (with a type), such as the numerical value of an *aircraft vertical speed*. It is communicated between two actors via ports: created by one actor A_1, *sent through* an output port i, and *received by* (the input port j) of a destination actor A_2, as represented in Fig. 1. This token can be received by several actors.

Link Between Time Advance and Data in Ptolemy. There is a *production-consumption* phase related to the time advance (if the models are timed). A simplified view is the following: When a token is produced by A_1 (as in Fig. 1) at output port A_{1_i} at current time t, an event $e(v, (t', n'), A_{2_j}), t' \geq t, n' \geq n$, is put in the calendar queue. When this event is the earliest one in the calendar queue, the DE director will advance its (current) time to (t', n'), fire (or execute) A_2 and consume the token in the input port A_{2_j}. Most actors, such as AddSubtract, CurrentTime, Integrator, have $t' = t$ and $n = n'$. Some actors provide mechanisms for delaying events, e.g., TimeDelay $(t' > t, n' = 1)$ or MicrostepDelay $(t' = t, n' = n + 1)$ [26]. A token will be referred to as an event e, $e(t)$, or $e(t, n)$.

2.2   High Level Architecture (HLA) Standard

The High-Level Architecture (HLA) [15,16] is a standard for distributed discrete-event simulations, generally used to support analysis, engineering and training. The approach promotes reusability and interoperability. A simulation entity performing a sequence of computations is called a *federate*, and the set of federates simulating the entire system is called a *federation*. Federates are connected via the Run-Time Infrastructure (RTI), the underlying middleware functioning as the simulation kernel. The lollipop architecture of an HLA federation is depicted in Fig. 2.

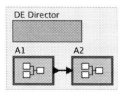

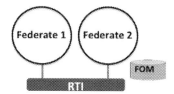

Fig. 1. Ptolemy model.   **Fig. 2.** HLA architecture.

The HLA standard defines a set of rules describing the responsibilities of federations and the federates, e.g., *all data exchange among federates shall occur via the RTI*. Among the rules, an important one concerns the time advance: *A federate delegates its time advance to the RTI*. Another one concerns the sending of data: *A federate cannot send an event earlier than* $t + lah$, where t is its current logical time and *lah* its the lookahead [15].

The standard also defines an interface specification for a set of services required to manage the federates and their interactions. In this paper, we will present the services related to Time Management and Data Management.

Data Exchange in HLA. For each federation, a Federation Object Model (FOM) describes the shared objects, interaction classes and their attributes. The object management services allow message exchange between federates. Let us consider two federates F_1 and F_2: F_1 sends the signal *aircraft vertical speed* to F_2. In HLA terms, F_1 publishes the class Aircraft_speed and F_2 subscribes to attribute v_speed of this class. The HLA services used are, respectively, `publishObjectClass` and `subscribeObjectClassAttributes`. There are two steps concerning the *object management*:

(1) When federate F_1 is launched, it registers an object instance of `Aircraft_speed` class (service `registerObjectInstance`). When federate F_2 is launched, it discovers object instances `Aircraft_speed` related to the attribute `v_speed` it subscribed (callback `discoverObjectInstance`);

(2) During the simulation, F_1 sends through the RTI a new value of `Aircraft_speed.v_speed` using the service `updateAttributeValues` (UAV). The RTI sends this value to F_2 using the callback `reflectAttributeValues` (RAV).

Time Advance in HLA. HLA time management services enable deterministic and reproducible distributed simulations [5]. Each federate manages its own logical time and communicates this time to the RTI that ensures that federates observe events in the same order [12].

The time advance phase in HLA is a two-step process: (1) a federate sends a time advance request service, and (2) waits for the time to be granted, provided by `timeAdvanceGrant` (TAG) service. There are two services for a time advance request: the `timeAdvanceRequest` service (TAR), used to implement time-stepped federates; and the `nextEventRequest` service (NER), used to implement event-based federates. The time step between successive TAR service calls can change during a simulation, but it is frequently chosen as a fixed time step TS. There is a trade-off between the performance and the precision of the simulation according to the time step used. The user needs to carefully make this choice. Such a choice is not required for NER, since the time advance request has the timestamp of the next event. According to the HLA standard, a federate can switch from TAR to NER and NER to TAR during a simulation. However, in our framework, a federate can use one of these services but the user must make the choice before the simulation. The HLA standard does not impose a time representation. In general, the HLA standard proposes IEEE-754 double-precision floating point numbers.

Is There a Link Between Data Exchange and Time Management?
By default, the RAV callbacks are received during the time advance phases and they are delivered in the order messages are received. This is the one and only link between data exchange and time advance for so-called HLA real time simulations. For the sake of repeatability and determinism, the data exchanges are in timestamp order. This order can also reflect causality relations.

When dealing with timed systems as CPS, the messages must be timestamped and the federates are time-constrained and time-regulating[1]. Besides the value

---

[1] A federate can only advance its time if it is granted by the RTI. When this federate is *time-constrained*, this grant is computed by the RTI with knowledge of the time advancements of the *time-regulating* federates, so that the conservative property of the distributed simulation is guaranteed between regulating and constrained federates.

of the attribute of a class instance, the UAV service has a timestamp. When the simulator is at current date t, it computes a new value of the attribute for a date $t*$ in the *future*, $t < t* \leq t+$ lookahead. This lookahead (a value associated with a federate) establishes a lower bound on the timestamps that can be sent. In a distributed simulation, strictly positive lookahead values allow the use of well known, deterministic and efficient distributed algorithms for the time management in the RTI. The lookahead can be equal to zero, and in this case may cause a deadlock. A first alternative is to rely on new algorithms in the RTI, for example the use of the Null Message Prime protocol [6] or the computation of a distributed snapshot [19]. A second alternative is that the user resolves the (possible) deadlock by using the TARA and NERA services[2] instead of sending a message with a zero lookahead [11].

Besides the attribute value of a class instance, the RAV service has a timestamp. The delivery of these callbacks is done in chronological order of the timestamp values. At current time t, during the time advance phase starting by TAR(t') and ending by TAG(t'), all RAV callbacks have a timestamp t'' that respects $t < t'' \leq t'$. These callbacks can concern the same instances of a class or different instances (of the same class or of different classes). For a time advance phase starting with NER(t'), if any callback with timestamp t'' is received, this phase will end with a TAG(t''). If there are any RAV callbacks with timestamps within t'' and t', they will be delivered during the following time advance phase(s). This is the main difference between TAR and NER concerning the way time is advanced. Section 4 shows that the execution time of a federation is also different between TAR and NER. We could have an equality between the timestamps of two RAVs of different object instances. HLA does not allow to specify an order in this case (FIFO order between messages coming from different federates). For the sake of determinism, the user code must produce the same result for the different execution cases. This is not difficult because, generally, the new state computation (and, in general, the sending of a data) in a simulation follows the time advance phase when all the required data is received.

3   Putting Ptolemy and HLA Together

The distributed co-simulation framework must comply with both, HLA and Ptolemy rules, in particular concerning data exchange and time advance ones. As of now, only NER and TAR are implemented in the framework and the lookahead cannot be zero. The way the coupling is designed is discussed next.

---

[2] NERA stands for Next Event Request Available and TARA for Time Advance Request Available. A TARA(t) (respectively, NERA(t)) that ends with a TAG(t) can be followed with the production and the reception of new events timestamped with t. If federates exchange data at the same time in a loop, the loop must be broken by calling TAR(t) (respectively, NER(t)). Then no additional event will be delivered to the federate with timestamp t and time can be advanced.

For the sake of simplicity, a time-stepped federate will be called a TAR federate, and an event-based federate will be called a NER federate. In this work, the RTI compliant with HLA is CERTI, an open source RTI written in C^{++} [25]. However, another RTI could be used.

3.1 How Time Is Advanced in the Ptolemy-HLA Framework

The first thing to point out is the existence of two timelines in a federate: the Ptolemy timeline t and the HLA timeline h. Both timelines use the same global unit (e.g., second or millisecond). Ptolemy (local) logical time t must be compliant with HLA logical time h. It means that the time must be advanced using HLA services NER or TAR, and a new interface called `HlaManager` was designed. Concerning the time, it has a method called `proposeTime` implementing a `TimeRegulator` interface (presented in Sect. 2.1). When Ptolemy wants to advance to the timestamp t' of the earliest event in its calendar queue, the DE director will check if this is possible with the `proposeTime` method. In this section, it is considered that no data exchange exists in the federation, in order to focus on time advance. According to the federate time management NER or TAR, the time will be advanced by calling Algorithms 1 or 2.

As time representation in CERTI and Ptolemy are different, a conversion is needed in both algorithms: f converts `double` to `Time`, and g converts `Time` to `double` [18, 21]. To minimize the comparisons, the time step TS (see Sect. 2.2) in Algorithm 2 is represented as `double` in Ptolemy model.

An important difference can be noticed between Algorithms 1 and 2 when Ptolemy wants to advance to t', the timestamp of the earliest event in its queue:

- at least one $NER(g(t'))$ is called in Algorithm 1, but more $NER(g(t'))$ can be called according to the number of TAG messages received. Each time a $TAG(h'' < g(t'))$ is received, Ptolemy advances to $f(h'')$. When $TAG(h'' = g(t'))$ is received, Ptolemy advances to t';
- k TARs will be called in Algorithm 2, $k \geq 0$, with

$$k = (\lfloor g(t') - h \rfloor / TS \rfloor - 1). \tag{1}$$

When the last TAG is received, Ptolemy advances to t', with the guarantee that $k * TS < g(t') < (k + 1) * TS$.

It is worth mentioning that, after asking to advance to t', Ptolemy time eventually advances to t' and has the same time history, independent of the time management (NER or TAR) used. But HLA time can have a different time history according to the time management, as presented in Fig. 3 and some examples shown next. For the sake of readability, time conversions f and g are not represented in Fig. 3.

Algorithm 1. NER ProposeTime(t')	**Algorithm 2.** TAR ProposeTime(t')
1: NER($g(t')$)	1: **while** $g(t') > h + TS$ **do**
2: **while** not granted **do**	2: TAR($h + TS$)
3: TICK() ▷ Wait $TAG(g(t'))$	3: **while** not granted **do**
4: **end while**	4: TICK() ▷ Wait $TAG(h + TS)$
5: $h \leftarrow g(t')$ ▷ Update HLA time	5: **end while**
6: **return** t' ▷ Update PtII time	6: $h \leftarrow h + TS$ ▷ Update HLA time
	7: **end while**
	8: **return** t' ▷ Update Ptolemy time

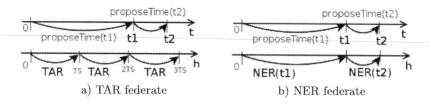

a) TAR federate   b) NER federate

Fig. 3. Time advance using TAR or NER without consider time conversion.

Let us consider federations F_a = {f1}, F_b = {f1,f2} and F_c = {f1,f3}; feder-ates f1, f2 and f3 are depicted in Fig. 4a and b and c. Each federation is used to explain a particular point in the time advance. No federate sends any data through the RTI. To keep track of the time representation in Ptolemy and HLA, an index will be added to the time value v in each timeline: v_T and v_d for Time and double.

Federation F_a: A unique federate advances its time with the RTI.

The f1 model has a (current) Ptolemy start time $t = 0_T$ and HLA start time $h = 0_d$. The unique next event e in the f1 calendar queue is the *stop time* event $e(t' = 4_T)$. Table 1 depicts the services called and its callbacks in this federation, as well the final Ptolemy and HLA time when using NER or TAR (with time step $TS_{f1} = 1_d$) time management. As discussed above in the presentation of proposeTime Algorithms 1 and 2, the Ptolemy final time is the same using NER or TAR as well its time history: {$0, 4_T$}. But the HLA time history is different: {$0, g(4_T)$} when using NER, and {$0_d, 1_d, 2_d, 3_d, 4_d$} when using TAR.

Table 1. Time advance of f1 using NER or TAR.

Type	Service call	Callback	Final h	Final t
NER	NER ($g(4_T)$)	TAG($g(4_T)$)	$g(4_T)$	4_T
TAR	TAR(1_d), TAR(2_d), ... TAR(4_d)	TAG(1_d), TAG(2_d), ... TAG(4_d)	4_d	4_T

(a) Federate f1.   (b) Federate f2.   (c) Federate f3.

Fig. 4. Federates used in $F_a = \{f1\}$, $F_b = \{f1,f2\}$ and $F_c = \{f1,f3\}$.

Federation F_b: Two federates advance their time in coordination with the RTI. Federates f1 and f2 have the same parameters except that f2 has (HLA) time step $TS_{f2} = 2_d$ (needed when TAR is used) and *stop time* is 5_T. Whatever f1 uses NER or TAR, its results (final time and time history) are the same, as depicted in Table 1. For f2, its final Ptolemy time is $t_{f2} = 5_T$ and Ptolemy time history is $\{0, 5_T\}$. The f2 HLA final time 4_d and its time history is $\{0_d, 2_d, 4_d\}$, since $g(5_T) \not\succ 4_d + 2_d$ and so noTAR(6_d) is executed (Algorithm 2, line 1).

Federation F_c: Time coordination with a federate that produces internal events. Federate f3 has two internal events, $e(1_T)$ and $e(3_T)$, produced by DiscreteClock, and has *stop time* $e(4_T)$. Its (HLA) time step is $TS_{f3} = 2$ (needed when TAR is used). Now, besides the event *stop time*, its internal events will be added to the calendar queue. The rule is the same: the Ptolemy model needs to check with HLA if it can advance to the time of the event. The Ptolemy time history of f3 is the same using NER or TAR: $\{0_T, 1_T, 3_T, 4_T\}$. Concerning HLA time history, it is $\{0_d, g(1_T), g(3_T), g(4_T)\}$ when using NER, and $\{0_d, 2_d, 4_d\}$ when using TAR. Ptolemy and HLA time stories of f1 are the same as the ones in federation F_a.

The distribution of a simulation is necessary and/or appropriate, but it comes at a price. Beside the complexity of the implementation, the timestamp of a message can change according to the simulator tool, as presented in [21]. A federate may have two kinds of events: (i) events that are only internal to the model (as f3 participating in Federation F_c above); (ii) events that are sent and received through the RTI. The latter will be discussed in the following.

3.2   How Data Is Exchanged in the Ptolemy-HLA Framework

The unit of data in Ptolemy is a *token*, and in HLA it is the *attribute* of an *object class* described by the FOM. As seen in Sects. 2.1 and 2.2: (i) both are timestamped and have a value with a type; (ii) both have a production-consumtion behavior. The user gives – in a (classical) Ptolemy model or in an HLA federate – the (static) information about who produces and who consumes. In a Ptolemy model, the communication via ports is represented by a link between two actors

A_1 and A_2 (Fig. 1): The A_1 output port sends the data and the A_2 input port receives the data. In an HLA federation, a federate F_1 (as in Fig. 2) must indicate that it publishes an attribute of a class and federate F_2 must indicate it subscribes to this attribute. Besides this static information, let us recall that an HLA federate has two more steps: (a) *After* launching, each object instance is *registered* once by the producer and *discovered* by the consumer; (b) During the simulation, the attribute of an object instance is *updated* by the producer and *reflected* by the consumer; this step occurs each time there is a new sent value. These steps are provided by the Ptolemy-HLA framework – and hidden from the user – making it easier for the user to distribute a simulation.

To establish a relationship between a token and an object class attribute, two new actors, HlaPublisher and HlaSubscriber, are added to the Ptolemy-HLA framework. They are depicted in Fig. 5a and b with parameters Class (Signal) and Attribute (val) according to the FOM (.fed file in Fig. 5c). The type of the ports corresponds to the type of the attribute. As events have a timestamp, time is involved and so the HlaManager interface needs to interact with them. Each actor has two roles: The HlaPublisher registers the object instance and sends the data through the RTI; The HlaSubscriber discovers the object instance and receives the data from the RTI. This is transparent to the user, that must connect the input port of an actor (receiving data from the RTI) to an HlaSubscriber actor, and connect the output port of an actor (sending data through the RTI) to an HlaPublisher actor (see federation F14 in Fig. 8).

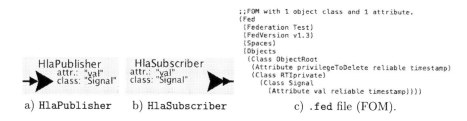

a) HlaPublisher   b) HlaSubscriber   c) .fed file (FOM).

Fig. 5. HlaPublisher and HlaSubscriber icons in accordance with a FOM.

Data Sent by Ptolemy Through the RTI: When the earliest event $e(t)$ in the Ptolemy queue is the input of an HlaPublisher actor, the DE director first advances its time to t (as explained in Sect. 3.1), and then executes the HlaPublisher actor. Its execution consists of sending an update to the federation *at t or as soon as possible*, by calling the HLA service UAV. It means that the HlaPublisher actor provides a mechanism for (possibly) delaying an event (as, e.g., TimeDelay does) when necessary. But when is this necessary? Remember that a federate with lookahead *lah* and current time t cannot send any message before $t+lah$, which delimits a *forbidden* zone (see Sect. 2.2). So, if an HlaPublisher actor is fired at current time t, if $t < f(h + lah)$ (inside the forbidden zone), it will

send a UAV$(g(t) + lah)$; otherwise, it will send a UAV(t). It is worth mentioning the values of the Ptolemy and HLA timelines (t, h) can be different during a simulation, as seen in Sect. 3.1. This can happen in particular at the firing of an HlaPublisher at t, and depends on the time management used:
- TAR: they can be different as represented in Fig. 3a: $(t, h = n * TS \leq g(t))$, $n = 1..k$, k given by Eq. 1, with UAV given by Eq. (3) in Table 2;
- NER: they are the *same*, modulo the time conversion, as represented in Fig. 3b: $(t, h = g(t))$ if no RAV is received or $(t = f(h), h)$ otherwise, with UAV given by Eq. (2) in Table 2.

Table 2. UAV sent by an HlaPublisher.

NER	$UAV(g(t) + lah)$		(2)
TAR	$UAV(g(t) + lah)$ if $g(t) < h + lah$		(3)
	$UAV(g(t))$ otherwise		

Table 3. Event received by an HlaSubscriber.

NER	$e(f(h''))$	(4)
TAR	$e(f(h + TS))$	(5)

Data Received by Ptolemy from the RTI: The data *reception* is started by the arrival of an RAV callback *during* the advance time phase (see Sect. 2.2). Algorithms 1 and 2 are extended to the Algorithms 3 and 4 to take into account the data arrival.

In the Ptolemy-HLA framework, the activation of an HlaSubscriber actor at t follows the reception of a RAV(h'') event received from the RTI (corresponding to a UAV(h'') sent by another federate). The HlaSubscriber activation date depends on the time management used: Eqs. 4 and 5 in Table 3 describe how an HlaSubscriber adds an event from an RAV callback when using NER or TAR respectively.

There is no delay added in the reception in a NER federate (Algorithm 3), but a delay up to an HLA time step can be added in a TAR federate (Algorithm 4), as can be seen in Federation F_d in the sequel. Why is, in a TAR federate, an RAV(h'') callback not translated into an event in the calendar queue at time f(h'') by an HLASubscriber actor, as in a NER federate? The reason is the following: an RAV(h''), $h'' \leq h + TS$, is received, when a TAR federate is waiting for a TAG$(h + TS)$ (after it asked to advance its time with TAR$(h + TS)$). So, at the RAV(h'') reception, the federate is still at h. But if an event $e(f(h'')$, HlaSubs) is put in the queue, and if this actor is directly or indirectly connected to an HLAPublisher, an UAV$(g(f(h'')))$ would be sent through the RTI. This breaks another HLA rule, saying that a federate that did a TAR(h^*) cannot send any UAV message before $h^* + TS$. This is why, in our framework, an RAV(h'') is translated into an event timestamped $e(f(h + TS)$, HlaSubscriber).

Algorithm 3. NER `proposeTime`(t') taking RAVs into account

```
1: if g(t') > h then
2:     NER(g(t'))
3:     while not granted do
4:         TICK()                    ▷ Wait TAG(h'')
5:     end while
6:     h ← h''                       ▷ Update HLA time
7:     if receivedRAV then
8:         t'' ← f(h'')
9:         if t'' > t then           ▷ General case
10:            t' ← t''
11:        else
12:            t' ← t + r
13:        end if
14:        putRAVonHlaSubs(t')
15:    end if
16: end if
17: return t'                        ▷ Update PtII time
```

Algorithm 4. TAR `proposeTime`(t') taking RAVs into account

```
1: while g(t') > h + TS do
2:     TAR(h + TS)
3:     while not granted do
4:         TICK()                    ▷ Wait TAG
5:     end while
6:     h ← h + TS                    ▷ Update HLA time
7:     if receivedRAV then
8:         t'' ← f(h)
9:         if t'' < t' then
10:            t' ← t''
11:        end if
12:        putRAVonHlaSubs(t')
13:        return t' ▷ Update PtII time
14:    end if
15: end while
16: return t' ▷ Update to asked PtII t'
```

Assume there is a Federation F_d with two federates cons1 and prod1, as depicted in Fig. 6a and b respectively. Their HLA time steps are different ($TS_{cons1} = 8$ and $TS_{prod1} = 7$) and so are their end of simulation times (20.0 for cons1 and 13.0 for prod1). Both have $t_0 = 0_T$ and $h_0 = 0_d$ and the same lookahed $lah = 0.1$. Federate prod1 publishes val: the input of HlaPublisher(Signal.val) is connected to the Ramp actor that produces events $e(t)$ with timestamps $3_T, 6_T, 9_T, 12_T$ depicted in Fig. 6b. As seen in Sect. 3.2, the timestamp of the UAV sent to the RTI depends on the time management. Federate cons1 subscribes to attribute val of class Signal using the HlaSubscriber(Signal.val) actor. Figures 6c–f show the plotter in the cons1 federate when the federates use different combinations of time management.

• *Both* prod1 *and* cons1 *use TAR (the result is depicted in* Fig. 6c*)*

The earliest event of cons1 is $e(20_T)$, the end of simulation; from Algorithm 3, a TAR(8) is called, since $g(20_T) > h + 8_d$. The earliest event of prod1 is $e(0; 3_T)$; from Algorithm 3, no TAR is called and its time is advanced to $t = 3_T$, since $g(3_T) < h + 7_d$. The HlaPublisher is executed, and according to Eq. (3) in Table 2, a UAV$(0, g(3_T))$ is sent.

The same behavior appears for the next event in prod1, $e(1; 6_T)$, and UAV$(0, g(6_T))$ is sent. But a TAR(7_d) will be called for event $e(2, 9_T)$ and UAV$(0, g(9_T))$ is sent. When prod1 reaches the end of simulation, cons1 is the only federate and the RTI sends a TAG(8_d). As indicated in Eq. 5 in Table 3, the RAV$(0, g(3_T))$ and RAV$(1, g(6_T))$ are then put in the queue as events $e(0, (f(8_d), 1)$, HlaSubscriber) and $e(1, (f(8_d), 2)$, HlaSubscriber). Notice that they have the same timestamp $f(8_d)$ and different microsteps. After TAR(16_d), prod1 will receive RAV$(2, g(9_T))$ and RAV$(3, g(12_T))$, the events $e(2, (f(16_d), 1)$, HlaSubs) and $e(3, (f(16_d), 2)$, HlaSubsc) are generated. The entire exchange is presented in Fig. 7. This figure can be compared to Fig. 3. Notice that the left

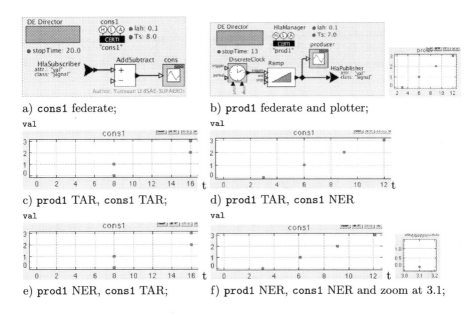

a) cons1 federate;

b) prod1 federate and plotter;

c) prod1 TAR, cons1 TAR;

d) prod1 TAR, cons1 NER

e) prod1 NER, cons1 TAR;

f) prod1 NER, cons1 NER and zoom at 3.1;

Fig. 6. Federation F_d (a,b); plotter at cons1 (c to f).

side of Fig. 7 is similar to Fig. 3a, because prod1 has internal events and Ptolemy wants to advance its time to values others than $k * TS$.

- prod1 = TAR and cons1 = NER (the result is depicted in Fig. 6d)

The behavior of prod1 is the same as above. At cons1, according to Eq. 4 in Table 3, no delay is added to the received RAVs and the translated Ptolemy events are: $e(0, g(3_T))$, $e(1, g(6_T))$, $e(2, g(9_T))$ and $e(3, g(12_T))$.

- prod1 = NER and cons1 = TAR (the result is depicted in Fig. 6e)

When prod1 advances to $t = 3_T$, a $UAV(0, g(3_T) + lah) = UAV(0, g(3.1_T))$ is sent according to Eq. (2) in Table 2 ($lah = 0.1$). As cons1 uses TAR, the corresponding $RAV(0, g(3_T + lah))$ generates an event $e(0, (f(8_d), 1),$ HlaSubscriber$)$, since $g(3_T) + lah < TS = 8_d$. As $g(6_T) + lah < TS = 8_d$, $RAV(1, g(6_T) + lah)$ generates $e(1, (f(8_T), 2),$ HlaSubscriber$)$. Notice that Fig. 6e and c are the same.

- Both prod1 and cons1 use NER (the result is depicted in Fig. 6f)

According to Eq. 4 in Table 3, no delay is added in the received RAV; prod1 sent a $UAV(0, 3.1)$, and cons1 will receive a $RAV(0, 3.1)$ that is translated to $e(0, f(g(3.1)))$ as can be seen in Fig. 6f. The other events are $e(1, f(g(6.1)))$, $e(2, f(g(9.1)))$ and $e(3, f(g(12.1)))$.

These examples point out that the user needs to carefully analyze the semantics of the models. This will be discussed in the following.

3.3 Zooming in on the Boundaries

During the waiting phase of a TAG, many RAVs can be received by a federate (see Algorithms 3 and 4, lines 3–5). These RAVs are memorized in a FIFO.

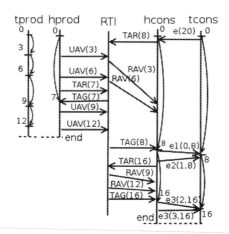

Fig. 7. F_d: cons1/TAR (TS = 8) + prod1/TAR (TS = 7).

After the while loop, a unique Ptolemy time t' is calculated for the firing of the corresponding HLASubscriber actor. The function putRAVonHlaSubscribers(t') empties this FIFO and adds event $e_j(t', \text{HlaSubs})$ to the Ptolemy calendar queue.

How many RAVs can be received? Without lack of generality, let us consider the RAVs from the same instance of a class.

In a TAR federate, k RAVs can be received with different timestamps h'', all $h'' \leq h + TS$, and all will be translated to events $e_j(f(h + TS), n_j), \text{HlaSubs})$, $j = 1..k$, with increasing microsteps. The order in which the RAVs are received is maintained using microsteps. This occurs, for example, in Federation F_d, Fig. 6c and e. This can happen when the federates have different rhythms in the data exchanges: different HLA time steps when using only TAR, or a NER federate sending data to a TAR federate.

Let us consider, for example, the reception of different values from the same sensor. In this case, the freshest value is more useful, and the solution could be to insert only one event $e(f(h + TS, 1), \text{HlaSubs})$ corresponding to the freshest k^{th} RAV. Moreover, the calculation of a new state and, in general, a new output (e.g., the control of an actuator in a CPS) can be meaningful for just one value at a time t.

However, when designing a model, there are always elements where the user should use good software design patterns to ensure the model has the right semantics. One way to tackle the reception of k RAVs(h'') is to add a clock to the federate (subscribing to these attributes) that will dictate the wanted rhythm for the calculation [20]. Another way to tackle the RAV reception is to focus on the sending of the UAV. From the HLA point of view, it is not relevant to send several UAVs for the *same object instance at the same date h*. For example, before sending a UAV of an attribute that is subscribed to by an actuator, a MostRecent actor can be inserted in the input of the HlaPublisher such that only the freshest event will be sent.

Some tests have been added to Algorithms 3 and 4 for taking into account that the time representation of Ptolemy (t) and HLA (h) are different.

The first one is in Algorithm 3 of `proposeTime`, line 12 (NER federates): Because of the needed conversions, it can happen that $f(h'') = t$, e.g., $f(10_d + \epsilon) = 10_T$. In this case, inserting a new event at $e(t,\texttt{HlaSubs})$ can be a problem to the director, since all existing events $e(t,\texttt{HlaSubs})$ have already been executed. Our choice was, in this particular case, to add the time resolution r to t, since it is the shortest value that we can add for advancing the time beyond t. Let us point out that the microstep is used and correctly taken into account in the other cases as depicted in Fig. 6c and e.

The second one is in Algorithm 4 `proposeTime` (TAR federates), and makes the algorithm robust when dealing with a very particular case. This case can happen when t' and $f(h + TS)$ have the *same* (mathematical) values, e.g., $t' = 10_T$ and $h + TS = 10_d$, but $f(h + TS) > t'$. Let us recall two points: (1) The `proposeTime` method in the TimeRegulator interface of a Ptolemy model must return the same proposed time or a smaller time; (2) HLA guarantees that the timestamp of an RAV will never be smaller than the current time h (or larger than $h + TS$). So, if $f(h + TS)$ is bigger than the initial t', caused by the conversion, then the returned time must be t'. Otherwise, the Ptolemy time would advance to a time larger than timestamp t', when there is still an event $e(t')$ in the queue, and this event would be in the past.

Another issue is the following: Is it possible to produce an *internal* event in a Ptolemy federate $\mathbf{f}$ with the same timestamp as an RAV-event received from another federate? Let us consider two federates $\mathbf{f1}$ and $\mathbf{f2}$ sending a data update: except for cases where these federates have exactly the same code (and same time representation), their UAVs rarely have the same timestamp, because $h_{\mathbf{f1}}$ can be different from $h_{\mathbf{f2}}$. In the general case where Ptolemy federates can interoperate with, e.g., C^{++} federates, this can be very difficult or even impossible to achieve, because of the different time representations. But even in a pure Ptolemy federation, because of the RTI time representation, it can still be impossible to have an internal event $t_{\mathbf{f1}} = f(h_{\mathbf{f1}})$.

Ptolemy can be downloaded from website [27]. The Ptolemy-HLA framework can be found at `$PTII/org/hlacerti`. The F14 demo presented in the sequel and others demos are provided, as well as a user guide. Some practical information can be found in the wiki [28].

4   Case Study: F14

Simulation is a very powerful way to perform validation, but one needs confidence in the results. The Ptolemy-HLA framework provides useful information, allowing for performance measures and simulation validation: simulation data (parameters of the federate e.g., name and time management); simulation results (e.g., events in the Ptolemy calendar queue and events coming from the RTI); and simulation statistics (e.g., number of TARs/NERs and number of TAGs,

simulation execution time, execution time between services calls). This information appears in *.csv* text files generated during the simulation (if the user chooses
this option) [3].

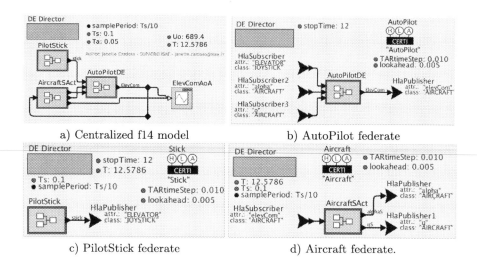

a) Centralized f14 model   b) AutoPilot federate

c) PilotStick federate   d) Aircraft federate.

Fig. 8. The F14 federation of a centralized model.

An aircraft is a very good example of a CPS. Figure 8a depicts a Ptolemy
model of a F14 aircraft derived from a Simulink demo: `PilotStick` and `Aircraft`
have a Continuous director and `AutoPilot` uses a DE MoC [17]. Both continuous
models have a Sampler actor with sampling time 10ms, that provides the input
for `AutoPilot`, and `Aircraft` has a ZeroOrderHold actor in its input. This model
was split up into the three federates represented in Fig. 8b, c and d. Taking
advantage of the interoperability of HLA, the pilot stick simulated in Fig. 8c
was later successfully replaced with a real pilot stick. The results presented in
this section are for the federation with the simulated pilot stick. The first step
is checking the simulation results of the distributed model against those of the
centralized model. Figure 9a shows the simulation results for federate `AutoPilot`
and attribute `elevCom`, comparing the *centralized* and the *distributed* simulation
results of the F14 Federation depicted in Fig. 8. The results were obtained using
NER and TAR (with HLA time step `TS` = 0.010) and two values of the lookahead
(0.005 and 0.010). The error is almost zero in steady state and smaller than 17%
using TAR or NER with the smaller lookahead (0.005).

Concerning the performance related to the time management used by the
federates: Fig. 10 shows the number of time advancement requests in the federate
Aircraft using TAR and NER as a function of the HLA time step `TS`. As expected,
NER is constant, since it does not depend on the HLA time step. Concerning
TAR, the number of time advance requests is the same as NER when the HLA
time step `TS` is equal to the sampling time of Sampler actor (10 ms). For values

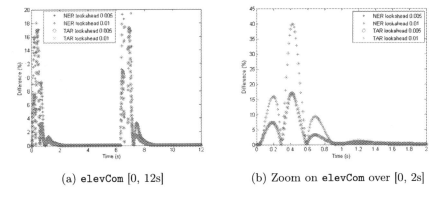

(a) `elevCom` [0, 12s]   (b) Zoom on `elevCom` over [0, 2s]

Fig. 9. Relative difference between *centralized* and *distributed* simulation.

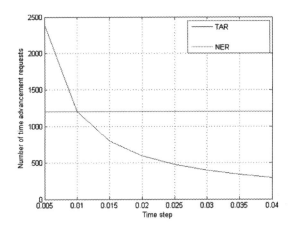

Fig. 10. Time advance requests in the federate Aircraft using TAR and NER.

of TS <10 ms, the performance of the TAR simulation is worse than in the NER case, but the accuracy of the simulation is better. The opposite occurs when TS >10 ms: better performance for TAR as opposed to NER, but worst accuracy, as expected.

5   Conclusion

In this paper, we present Ptolemy-HLA, a distributed simulation framework for complex and heterogeneous systems such as encountered in CPS. We have combined Ptolemy – which allows for heterogeneous systems simulation with a clean time representation – and the use of the HLA standard – which allows for Distributed Discrete Event Simulation (DDES) and interoperability of simulations. We hope this framework gathers the benefits of both. Moreover, Ptolemy and CERTI, an HLA-compliant RTI, are open-source, and so is Ptolemy-HLA.

A key feature in Ptolemy-HLA is that it can be easily installed and experimented with, without requiring in depth knowledge of HLA or the (quite complex) DDES domain. Collaborative contributions by other researches would be welcome.

Topics addressed in this work deal mainly with the existence of different timelines across distributed components and their coordination. The way time is advanced in the framework is carefully discussed and algorithms are presented: first, without data exchange, and then, the more general case that includes data exchange. We also present the way Ptolemy tokens and HLA attributes are translated into one another, taking into account the time advance and the conversion between the two timelines. Other features are implemented in the framework but are not discussed in this paper, such as the use of an initial synchronization point that makes it easier to launch the federation, and the ability to manage several instances of a class (e.g., several f14 aircrafts flying in formation).

The framework presented here allows Ptolemy to be compliant with the HLA standard. Moreover, we think the issues discussed can be re-used for other software needing to be compliant with this standard. We have applied this framework to the study of some CPS. In this paper, we have presented the F14 distributed simulation and some results. We also implemented a federation simulating a fleet of quad-rotors using Ptolemy and MORSE [22], a generic simulator for academic robotics.

Future work include new applications and extensions to this framework. Section 3.3 discusses issues related to data exchange. The last version of HLA provides services for negotiating the rhythm of data exchange between federates. This could be implemented and may simplify the work for the user as well as optimize the performance. Other HLA features not yet used, are the notion of interactions, the ownership management of objects, and the optimized data distributed management (with the introduction of subscribing and publishing regions).

We hope that this research, finalized with a tool, will be useful to tackle the problem of coupling different simulations, and the problem of coupling and distributing real systems. HLA-FMI is a very promising coupling technology. FIDE, a Ptolemy-FMI framework [8] could be combined with the Ptolemy-HLA framework and provide an HLA-FMI coupling.

Since the beginning of this work in 2013, many contributors have been involved, and we want to thank them warmly in this alphabetical and not exhaustive list: Vandita Banka, Christopher Brooks, Tarciana Cabral de Brito Guerra, David Come, Patricia Derler, Maxim Ivanov, Sébastien Jaillant, Gilles Lasnier, Edward Lee, Yanxuan Li, Clément Michel, Claire Pagetti.

Acknowledgements. The authors would like to thank the anonymous reviewers for their valuable comments and suggestions to improve the quality of the paper.

References

1. Adelantado, M., Bussenot, J.L., Rousselot, J.Y., Siron, P., Betoule, M.: HP-CERTI: towards a high performance, high availability open source RTI for composable simulations. In: Fall Simulation Interoperability Workshop, September 2004
2. Bieber, P., Siron, P.: Design and implementation of a distributed interactive simulation security architecture. In: 3rd IEEE International Workshop on Distributed Interactive Simulation and Real-Time Applications, October 1999
3. Cabral De Brito Guerra, T.: Performance analysis of the framework Ptolemy-HLA. Technical report, ISAE/DISC/RT2016/2, September 2016
4. Cardoso, J., Derler, P., Eidson, J.C., Lee, E.A., Matic, S., Yang Zhao, J.Z.: Modeling timed systems. In: Ptolemaeus, C. (ed.) System Design, Modeling, and Simulation using Ptolemy II. Ptolemy.org (2014). http://ptolemy.eecs.berkeley.edu/books/Systems/chapters/ModelingTimedSystems.pdf
5. Chandy, K.M., Misra, J.: Distributed simulation: a case study in design and verification of distributed programs. IEEE Trans. Softw. Eng. **SE-5**(5), 440–452 (1979)
6. Chaudron, J.B., Noulard, E., Siron, P.: Design and model-checking techniques applied to real-time RTI time management. In: Spring Simulation Interoperability Workshop, April 2011
7. Cremona, F., Lohstroh, M., Broman, D., Lee, E.A., Masin, M., Tripakis, S.: Hybrid co-simulation: it's about time. Softw. Syst. Model., 1–25 (2017)
8. Cremona, F., Lohstroh, M., Tripakis, S., Brooks, C., Lee, E.A.: FIDE - an FMI integrated development environment. In: Symposium on Applied Computing, April 2016. http://chess.eecs.berkeley.edu/pubs/1158.html
9. Derler, P., Lee, E.A., Vincentelli, A.S.: Modeling cyber-physical systems. Proc. IEEE **100**(1), 13–28 (2012)
10. Forwardsim (2017). http://www.forwardsim.com/products/hla-toolbox/
11. Fujimoto, R.M.: Zero lookahead and repeatability in the High Level Architecture. In: Spring Simulation Interoperability Workshop, March 1997
12. Fujimoto, R.M.: Time management in the high level architecture. SIMULATION **71**(6), 388–400 (1998)
13. Garro, A., Falcone, A.: On the integration of HLA and FMI for supporting interoperability and reusability in distributed simulation. In: Proceedings of the Symposium on Theory of Modeling and Simulation: DEVS Integrative M&S Symposium, vol. 47, pp. 9–16, 04 2015
14. HLA for FMI. https://www.ds.tools/products/hla-and-dis-for-fmi/
15. IEEE: IEEE standard for modeling and simulation (M&S) High Level Architecture (HLA) - Framework and rules. IEEE Std 1516–2010 (Revision of IEEE Std 1516–2000), pp. 1–38, August 2010
16. Kuhl, F., Dahmann, J., Weatherly, R.: Creating Computer Simulation Systems: An Introduction to the High Level Architecture. Prentice Hall PTR, Upper Saddle River (2000)
17. Lasnier, G., Cardoso, J., Siron, P., Pagetti, C., Derler, P.: Distributed simulation of heterogeneous and real-time systems. In: Proceedings of the 2013 IEEE/ACM 17th International Symposium on Distributed Simulation and Real Time Applications, pp. 55–62. IEEE Computer Society (2013)
18. Li, Y.: A distributed simulation environment for cyber-physical systems. Technical report, ISAE-Supaero, September 2015
19. Mattern, F.: Efficient algorithms for distributed snapshots and global virtual time approximation. J. Parallel Distrib. Comput. **18**(4), 423–434 (1993)

20. Michel, C.: Distributed simulation of cyber-physical systems. Technical report, ISAE-Supaero, April 2017
21. Michel, C., Cardoso, J., Siron, P.: Time management of heterogeneous distributed simulation. In: 31st European Simulation and Modelling Conference, October 2017
22. MORSE. https://www.openrobots.org/morse/doc/latest/morse.html
23. Nägele, T., Hooman, J.: Co-simulation of cyber-physical systems using HLA. In: 2017 IEEE 7th Annual Computing and Communication Workshop and Conference (CCWC), pp. 1–6, January 2017
24. Neema, H., Gohl, J., Lattmann, Z., Sztipanovits, J., Karsai, G., Neema, S., Bapty, T., Batteh, J., Tummescheit, H., Sureshkumar, C.: Model-based integration platform for FMI co-simulation and heterogeneous simulations of cyber-physical systems. In: Proceedings of the 10th International Modelica Conference, pp. 235–245, March 2014. https://modelica.org/events/modelica2014/proceedings/html/ProceedingsOfThe10thModelicaConference.pdf
25. Noulard, E., Rousselot, J.Y., Siron, P.: CERTI: an open source RTI, why and how. In: Spring Simulation Interoperability Workshop, March 2009
26. Cardoso, J., Derler, P., Eidson, J.C., Lee, E.A., Matic, S., Zhao, Y., Zou, J.: Modeling timed systems. In: Ptolemaeus, C. (ed.) System Design, Modeling, and Simulation Using Ptolemy II. Ptolemy.org (2014). http://ptolemy.eecs.berkeley.edu/books/Systems/chapters/Dataflow.pdf
27. Ptolemy source. http://ptolemy.eecs.berkeley.edu/ptolemyII/
28. Ptolemy-HLA. https://www.icyphy.org/hla/wiki/Main/PtII-hlacerti
29. Shrivastava, A., Derler, P., Baboudr, Y.S.L., Stanton, K., Khayatian, M., Andrade, H.A., Weiss, M., Eidson, J., Chandhoke, S.: Time in cyber-physical systems. In: 2016 International Conference on Hardware/Software Codesign and System Synthesis (CODES+ISSS), pp. 1–10, October 2016

Computing Average Response Time

Krishnendu Chatterjee[1], Thomas A. Henzinger[1(✉)], and Jan Otop[2]

[1] IST Austria, Klosterneuburg, Austria
{krishnendu.chatterjee,tah}@ist.ac.at
[2] University of Wrocław, Wrocław, Poland
jotop@cs.uni.wroc.pl

Abstract. Responsiveness—the requirement that every request to a system be eventually handled—is one of the fundamental liveness properties of a reactive system. Average response time is a quantitative measure for the responsiveness requirement used commonly in performance evaluation. We show how average response time can be computed on state-transition graphs, on Markov chains, and on game graphs. In all three cases, we give polynomial-time algorithms.

1 Introduction

Graphs and their generalizations provide the mathematical framework for modeling the behavior of reactive systems. The vertices of the graph represent states of the system, the edges represent transitions, and paths of the graph represent traces of the system. The two classical extensions of the graph model for reactive systems are with (i) probabilities and (ii) interaction with an adversary. In the presence of stochasticity in the system, from every vertex there is a probability distribution of transitions to the next vertex, and this gives rise to a Markov chain. In the presence of an adversary, the vertices of the graph are partitioned into vertices that are controlled by the proponent and vertices that are controlled by the opponent, and the choice of outgoing transition from a vertex is decided, respectively, by the proponent or the opponent. This gives rise to two player games on graphs. While graphs represent closed systems, games on graphs represent systems that interact with an adversarial environment, and Markov chains represent probabilistic systems. Thus, graphs, games on graphs, and Markov chains are fundamental models for the behavior of reactive systems.

One of the fundamental liveness properties in system analysis is the *responsiveness* property, which requires that every request of a system component is eventually granted. The responsiveness property is a qualitative property that

This research was supported in part by the Austrian Science Fund (FWF) under grants S11402-N23, S11407-N23 (RiSE/SHiNE) and Z211-N23 (Wittgenstein Award), ERC Start grant (279307: Graph Games), Vienna Science and Technology Fund (WWTF) through project ICT15-003 and by the National Science Centre (NCN), Poland under grant 2014/15/D/ST6/04543.

M. Lohstroh et al. (Eds.): Lee Festschrift, LNCS 10760, pp. 143–161, 2018.
https://doi.org/10.1007/978-3-319-95246-8_9

classifies every trace of the system as correct or incorrect. In contrast to qualitative properties, the performance evaluation of systems requires quantitative measures on traces. A quantitative property assigns a real number to every trace, in contrast to the Boolean values ("correct" vs. "incorrect") assigned by qualitative properties. A basic quantitative property is the *mean-payoff* property, where every transition of the system is assigned a cost. The mean payoff of a trace is the limit (inferior) of the sequence of average costs c_n (i.e., the "long-run average"), where for every $n > 0$, the average cost c_n is computed over the finite prefix of length n of the trace. Building upon the mean-payoff property, we consider a quantitative version of the responsiveness property, the *average response time* (ART), defined as follows: for every request, the response time for the request is the number of steps to the next grant, and the ART of a trace is the long-run average of all response times of the trace. If there are only finitely many request-grant pairs, than the ART of the trace is a finite average. If there is a request without a subsequent grant, or if an infinite sequence of response times has no upper bound, then the ART is infinite. In this way, the ART property differs from the mean-payoff property, because the mean payoff of a trace is always bounded by the maximum cost of a transition.

The ART of a trace is a natural quantitative measure of the responsiveness, and thus a basic system property for performance evaluation [15]. For graphs, we are interested in the minimal and maximal ART over all traces (i.e., all infinite paths of the graph). For Markov chains, we are interested in the expected value of the ART. For games on graphs, we are interested in the optimal strategy of a system to make the ART as small or as large as possible, no matter how the environment behaves. The ART that is achieved by an optimal strategy of a proponent who tries to make the ART as small as possible (the "minimizer") against an optimal strategy of an opponent who tries to make the ART as large as possible (the "maximizer") is called the ART value of the game.

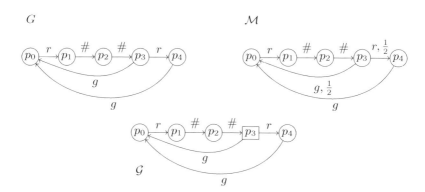

Fig. 1. Three models of a reactive system: the graph G, the Markov chain $\mathcal{M}$, and the game graph $\mathcal{G}$. Transitions in the Markov chain $\mathcal{M}$ are labeled with probabilities; we omit the probability 1 on the unique outgoing transitions from the vertexes p_0, p_1, p_2, and p_4. In the game graph $\mathcal{G}$, circled positions belong to the minimizing proponent, whereas the squared position p_3 belongs to the maximizing opponent.

Example 1. Figure 1 presents the three models G, $\mathcal{M}$, and $\mathcal{G}$ with transitions labeled by the following actions: requests r, grants g, and other instructions $\#$. The graph G has two simple cycles: $C_1 = p_0 p_1 p_2 p_3$ and $C_2 = p_0 p_1 p_2 p_3 p_4$. The cycles C_1, C_2 yield respectively the sequences of actions $r\#\#g$ and $r\#\#rg$. Thus, the ART of C_1 is 3 and the ART of C_2 is $\frac{4+1}{2}$. Any infinite path can be partitioned into cycles C_1 and C_2, and hence the minimal ART of G is $\frac{5}{2}$ and the maximal ART of G is 3.

The Markov chain $\mathcal{M}$ results from the graph G and hence we observe that both cycles C_1 and C_2 occur with equal probability $\frac{1}{2}$. Therefore, the expected ART of $\mathcal{M}$ is $(\frac{1}{2} \cdot \frac{5}{2}) + (\frac{1}{2} \cdot 3) = \frac{11}{4}$.

Finally, the game arena $\mathcal{G}$ results from G by assigning p_3 to the player that attempts to maximize the ART. Thus, the ART value of $\mathcal{G}$ is 3, as the maximizer can always pick the move from p_3 to p_0. Interestingly, to maximize the ART, the opponent does not postpone the grant by moving from p_3 to p_4, but rather issues immediately a grant, which prevents the emission of a promptly satisfied request at (p_3, p_4). Such a promptly satisfied request would decrease the ART and thus the maximizing opponent is better off by issuing the grant quickly.

In summary, the minimal and maximal ART are easily and naturally defined numerical values of a labeled graph, the expected ART is the corresponding value of a labeled Markov chain, and the ART value is the corresponding quantity for a labeled 2-player game graph. In this paper, we present algorithms for computing these four values.

Automata provide a natural framework for specifying qualitative properties. Their extension, weighted automata, provide a framework for expressing quantitative properties [2,9]. While weighted finite automata with mean-payoff measure [2] cannot express the ART property [6], extensions of weighted finite automata with *nesting* have been proposed in [5–8] as a quantitative specification framework that can express the ART property. These works focus on solving the quantitative emptiness and universality questions for entire classes of weighted finite automata [5–7], as well as on the evaluation of such automata classes with respect to probability distributions over words [8]. However, the solution and complexity of computing the specific ART property for graphs (minimal and maximal ART), games on graphs (ART value), and Markov chains (expected ART) has not been studied before.

In this work we consider the specific problem of computing the ART property for graphs, game graphs, and Markov chains. Our main result is that for all three models the ART property can be computed in polynomial time. The precise computational complexities differ for the various models (see Theorems 3, 4, and 5). If we compare our results to previous results for the class of nested weighted finite automata that can express the ART property, we see the following: (a) while solving automaton emptiness is similar in flavor to computing ART on graphs, for general nested weighted automata the resulting complexities are PSPACE and higher, whereas we present polynomial-time algorithms; (b) for Markov chains our results are easily derived from results of [8]; and (c) to the best of our knowledge, the problem of computing ART for games on graphs has not been studied before.

2   Preliminaries

We present notions and notations used throughout the paper. We begin with models of reactive systems: graphs, games and Markov chains (Sect. 2.1). Then, we present basic objectives studied with these models (Sect. 2.2), which lead to computational questions (Sect. 2.3). Finally, we recall previous results on computational questions for mean-payoff objectives (Sect. 2.4).

2.1   Models

Game Arena. A *game arena* $\mathcal{G}$ is a tuple (V, V_1, V_2, E) where (V, E) is a finite graph, (V_1, V_2) is a partition of V into positions of Player 1 and Player 2, respectively. To present results in a uniform way, we consider graphs as arenas with all positions belonging to one player, i.e., we identify $(V, V, \emptyset, E)$ (resp., $(V, V, \emptyset, E)$) with (V, E). We assume (for technical convenience) that for every position $v \in V$ there is at least one outgoing edge.

Game Plays. A game on an arena $\mathcal{G}$ is played as follows: a token is placed at a starting position, and whenever the token is at a Player-1 position, then Player 1 chooses an outgoing edge to move the token, and when the token is at a Player-2 position, then Player 2 does likewise. As a consequence we obtain an infinite sequence of positions, which is called a *play*, and *strategies* are recipes to extend finite prefix of plays (i.e., the recipes to describe how to move tokens). We formally define them below.

Strategies and Plays. Given a game arena $\mathcal{G}$, a function $\sigma_1 : V^* \cdot V_1 \mapsto V$ (resp., $\sigma_2 : V^* \cdot V_2 \mapsto V$) is a *strategy* for Player 1 (resp., Player 2) on $\mathcal{G}$ iff $\sigma_j(v_0 v_1 \ldots v_k) = v$ implies $(v_k, v) \in E$. In other words, given a finite sequence of positions that ends at a Player-1 position (representing the history of interactions), a strategy for Player 1 chooses the next position respecting the edge relationship (to move the token). We denote the set of all strategies for Player 1 (resp., Player 2) on $\mathcal{G}$ by $\mathcal{S}_1[\mathcal{G}]$ (resp., $\mathcal{S}_2[\mathcal{G}]$). A strategy σ_i has *finite memory* if there exist a finite set $\mathcal{M}$, $m_0 \in \mathcal{M}$, and functions $f : \mathcal{M} \times V \to \mathcal{M}$ and $g : \mathcal{M} \times V_i \to V$ such that for all $\boldsymbol{v} = v_0 v_1 \ldots v_k$ with $v_i \in V$, we have $\sigma_i(\boldsymbol{v}) = g(f(\ldots (f(f(m_0, v_0), v_1) \ldots, v_{k-1}), v_k)$. The *memory* of σ_i is said to be $|\mathcal{M}|$, while if $|\mathcal{M}| = 1$, then σ_i is called *memoryless*. Informally, a memoryless strategy does not depend on the history, but only on the current position. A pair of strategies σ_1, σ_2 on $\mathcal{G}$, along with a starting position v, defines a *play* $\pi(\sigma_1, \sigma_2, v)$, which is a word over V. The play $\pi(\sigma_1, \sigma_2, v) = v_0 v_1 \ldots$ is defined inductively as follows: (a) $v_0 = v$; (b) $v_{i+1} = \sigma_1(v_0 \ldots v_i)$ if $v_i \in V_1$; and (c) $v_{i+1} = \sigma_2(v_0 \ldots v_i)$ if $v_i \in V_2$. We define $\Pi(\mathcal{G})$ as the set of all plays on $\mathcal{G}$. Since every position has at least one outgoing edge, every play is indeed infinite.

Labeled Markov Chains. A *(labeled) Markov chain* is a tuple $\langle \Sigma, S, s_0, E \rangle$, where Σ is the alphabet of letters, S is a finite set of states, s_0 is an initial state, $E : S \times \Sigma \times S \mapsto [0, 1]$ is the edge probability function, which for every $s \in S$ satisfies that $\sum_{a \in \Sigma, s' \in S} E(s, a, s') = 1$.

Distributions Given by Markov Chains. Consider a Markov chain $\mathcal{M}$. For every finite word u, the probability of u, denoted $\mathbb{P}_{\mathcal{M}}(u)$, w.r.t. the Markov chain $\mathcal{M}$ is the sum of probabilities of paths labeled by u, where the probability of a path is the product of probabilities of its edges. For basic open sets $u \cdot \Sigma^\omega = \{uw : w \in \Sigma^\omega\}$, we have $\mathbb{P}_{\mathcal{M}}(u \cdot \Sigma^\omega) = \mathbb{P}_{\mathcal{M}}(u)$, and then the probability measure over infinite words defined by $\mathcal{M}$ is the unique extension of the above measure (by Carathéodory's extension theorem [11]). We will denote the unique probability measure defined by $\mathcal{M}$ as $\mathbb{P}_{\mathcal{M}}$.

2.2 Objectives

We consider two types of objectives: quantitative and Boolean. In the following definitions, we consider a game arena $\mathcal{G} = (V, V_1, V_2, E)$.

Quantitative Objectives. A *quantitative objective* in general is a Borel measurable function $f : \Pi(\mathcal{G}) \mapsto \mathbb{R} \cup \{-\infty, \infty\}$. Player 1 (called also Minimizer) plays in a way to construct a play π of a possibly small value $f(\pi)$, whereas Player 2 (called also Maximizer) attempts to maximize $f(\pi)$. The minimal value of the game which Player 1 can ensure (called the lower value) is defined as $\underline{\mathsf{val}}(f, v) = \inf_{\sigma_1 \in \mathcal{S}_1[\mathcal{G}]} \sup_{\sigma_2 \in \mathcal{S}_2[\mathcal{G}]} f(\pi(\sigma_1, \sigma_2, v))$. Player 2 on the other hand can ensure that the value of the game is at least the upper value, denoted as $\overline{\mathsf{val}}(f, v) = \sup_{\sigma_2 \in \mathcal{S}_2[\mathcal{G}]} \inf_{\sigma_1 \in \mathcal{S}_1[\mathcal{G}]} f(\pi(\sigma_1, \sigma_2, v))$. By Borel determinacy [14], the upper and lower values coincide with respect to f, hence we call their value, the value of the game, and denote it by $\mathsf{val}(f, v)$.

Optimal Strategies. Consider a quantitative objective f. A strategy σ for Player 1 (resp., Player 2) is called *optimal* for a position v if and only if we have $\sup_{\sigma_2 \in \mathcal{S}_2[\mathcal{G}]} f(\pi(\sigma, \sigma_2, v)) = \mathsf{val}(f, v)$ (resp., $\inf_{\sigma_1 \in \mathcal{S}_1[\mathcal{G}]} f(\pi(\sigma_1, \sigma, v)) = \mathsf{val}(f, v)$).

Mean-Payoff Objectives. The mean payoff objective is defined by a labeling $\mathsf{wt} : E \mapsto \mathbb{Z}$ of edges E on $\mathcal{G}$ with integers. Given a labeling wt and a play $\pi = v_0 v_1 \ldots$ on $\mathcal{G}$ we define $\mathrm{LIMAVGINF}^{\mathsf{wt}}(\pi) = \liminf_{k \to \infty} \frac{1}{k} \sum_{i=1}^{k} \mathsf{wt}(v_{i-1}, v_i)$. We skip the superscript wt, if it is clear from the context.

Average Response Time Objectives. We define the *average response time* (ART) objective based on an *action labeling* $\mathrm{act} : E \to \{r, g, \#\}$ that assigns actions to moves. Given a play π on $\mathcal{G}$, we define $\mathsf{rt}_i[\pi]$ as the number of positions between the i-th edge labeled with a request and the first following edge labeled with a grant; if there are no grants past the i-th request, we put $\mathsf{rt}_i[\pi] = \infty$. For a play π with infinite number of requests and grants, we define the quantitative objective $\mathrm{ART}(\pi) = \liminf_{k \to \infty} \frac{1}{k} \sum_{i=1}^{k} \mathsf{rt}_i[\pi]$. Finally, we put restrictions on the game arena, discussed below, to avoid plays with finitely many requests.

The G-R Condition. Observe that the value of a play with infinitely many requests and finitely many grants is infinite, i.e., if Player 1 cannot enforce infinitely many grants, he looses. For plays with finitely many requests, there are several ways to define the value of the play: the average over finitely many requests, or Player 1 (resp., Player 2) wins unconditionally. As we are interested in plays with infinitely many requests, we assume the *grant-request* condition (G-R) on games arenas stating that: every grant is followed by a request in the next step. Then, a sequence with infinitely many grants has infinitely many requests, and if there are finitely many requests, then the last request is never granted and the ART is infinite.

The G-R condition eliminates corner cases, and allows us to focus on the core of the problem. Still, our construction can be adapted to work without this condition (Remark 1).

Quantitative Objectives as Random Variables. The quantitative objectives are measurable functions mapping paths to reals, and thus can be interpreted as random variables w.r.t. the probabilistic space we consider. Given a Markov chain $\mathcal{M}$ and a value function f, we consider the following fundamental quantities:

1. **Expected value:** $\mathbb{E}_f(\mathcal{M})$ is the expected value of the random variable defined by the quantitative objective f w.r.t. the probability measure defined by the Markov chain $\mathcal{M}$.
2. **(Cumulative) distribution:** $\mathbb{D}_{\mathcal{M},f}(\lambda) = \mathbb{P}_{\mathcal{M}}(\{\pi : f(\pi) \leq \lambda\})$ is the cumulative distribution function of the random variable defined by f w.r.t. the probability measure defined by the Markov chain $\mathcal{M}$.

Boolean Objectives. A Boolean objective is a function $\Phi : \Pi(\mathcal{G}) \mapsto \{0, 1\}$. We consider two types of Boolean objectives: Büchi and threshold. Büchi objectives Φ_B are defined by a subset F of the positions of the arena. Then, $\Phi_B(\pi) = 1$ iff some position from F occurs infinitely often in π. Threshold objectives are defined by imposing a threshold on a quantitative objective, i.e., given a quantitative objective f and a threshold $\boldsymbol{\theta}$, we consider the set of winning plays to be $\{\pi \in \Pi(\mathcal{G}) : f(\pi) \leq \boldsymbol{\theta}\}$, all plays π whose value does not exceed $\boldsymbol{\theta}$. We define the threshold variants of the quantitative objectives LIMAVGINF, ART as $\mathrm{LIMAVGINF}^{\leq \lambda} = \{\pi \mid \mathrm{LIMAVGINF}(\pi) \leq \lambda\}$, and $\mathrm{ART}^{\leq \lambda} = \{\pi \mid \mathrm{ART}(\pi) \leq \lambda\}$.

Winning Strategies. A strategy σ_1 (resp., σ_2) is *winning* for Player 1 (resp., Player 2) from a position v iff for all strategies σ_2 for Player 2 (resp., all strategies σ_1 for Player 1), the play π defined by σ_1, σ_2 given v satisfies $\Phi(\pi) = 1$ (resp., $\Phi(\pi) = 0$).

2.3   Computational Questions

We present questions, which we study in this paper.

Computational Questions for Games. Given a Boolean objective Φ (resp., quantitative objective f), a game arena $\mathcal{G}$ and a starting position s_0, we consider the following basic computational questions:

– The *game question* asks to determine the player that has the winning strategy for Φ starting from position s_0.
– The *value question* asks to compute $\mathsf{val}(f, s_0)$.

Computational Questions for Markov Chains. Given a quantitative objective f and a Markov chain $\mathcal{M}$, we consider the following basic computational questions:

– The *expected question* asks to compute $\mathbb{E}_f(\mathcal{M})$.
– The *distribution question* asks, given a threshold λ, to compute $\mathbb{D}_{\mathcal{M},f}(\lambda)$.

2.4   Previous Results

We present existing results on the computational questions for two-player games and Markov chains with mean-payoff objectives. The computational questions for ART objectives have not been studied before; we study ART objectives in the following section.

Mean-payoff games admit pseudo-polynomial algorithms for solving games and computing the value of the game [1,16]. The complexity is given w.r.t. the set of positions V, the set of moves E and the maximal absolute value W of the labeling wt.

Theorem 1 ([1,10,16]). *The following assertions hold:*

– *The game question for mean-payoff games can be solved in $O(|V| \cdot |E| \cdot W)$ time. The winner has a memoryless winning strategy.*
– *The value of a mean-payoff game can be computed in $O(|V|^2 \cdot |E| \cdot W \cdot \log(W \cdot V))$ time. Both players admit optimal memoryless strategies.*

For Markov chains with mean-payoff objectives, basic computational questions can be solved in polynomial time. These questions are solved by reductions to linear programming (LP), and hence the exact complexity depends on the exact complexity of LP. To avoid the discussion on the wide-range of methods to solve LP, we only give the size of the LP instance produced by the reductions.

Theorem 2 ([12]). *For $\mathcal{M} = (\Sigma, S, s_0, E)$, the expected question and the distribution question can be computed in polynomial time, by reduction to linear programming with $|S|$ variables and $|S| + |E| + 1$ constraints.*

3 Games and Graphs with ART Objectives

In this section we study one- and two-player games with the average response time (ART) objective. We establish polynomial-time algorithms to determine the winner in these games as well as polynomial time algorithms for computing the value of the game. We begin with examples showing that both players require memory to play optimally. Then, we establish polynomial-time complexity of two-player games with ART objectives (Sect. 3.2). Finally, we discuss one-player games with ART objectives (Sect. 3.3), which inherit a polynomial-time algorithm from the two-player case. We, however, establish better bounds both on the complexity and the memory required to play optimally.

3.1 Memory Requirement for ART Objectives

We begin with an example showing that Player 1 needs memory to win even in a one-player game with an ART objective.

Example 2. Consider a game arena $\mathcal{G}_1$ depicted in Fig. 2. Player 1 has two memoryless strategies. In the first, he stays forever in p_t, which results in the infinite average response time. In the second, in p_t he always moves to p_s. Observe that this case the average response time is $k + 1$.

Consider a finite-memory strategy, in which, each time Player 1 moves from p_k to p_t, he loops n times in position p_t, and then moves to p_s. This strategy gives a play, which repeats infinitely a cycle of length $k + n + 1$, with $n + 1$ requests and response times $k + n + 1$ for the request issued in (p_s, p_1), and $n, n - 1, \ldots, 1$ for requests issued in the loop (p_t, p_t). The ART in this case is $\frac{k+n+1+0.5 \cdot n \cdot (n+1)}{n+1}$, which attains the minimum when $n + 1$ is approximately $\sqrt{2k}$. In such a case, the ART is approximately $\sqrt{2k} + 0.5$, which is smaller than $k + 1$.

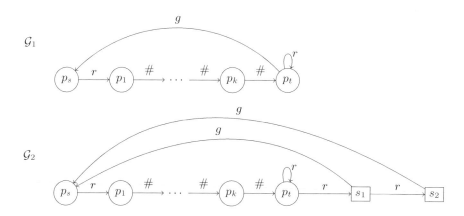

Fig. 2. Examples of games arenas: $\mathcal{G}_1$ where Player 1 requires finite memory to play optimally, and $\mathcal{G}_2$ where Player 2 requires finite memory as well. Circle positions are owned by Player 1 and square ones are owned by Player 2.

Based on Example 2, we can show that Player 2 also requires memory to win against Player 1.

Example 3. Consider a game arena $\mathcal{G}_2$ from Fig. 2, which extends $\mathcal{G}_1$ from Example 2. Recall that Player 1 to play optimally has to loop $\sqrt{2k}+1$ times at position p_t in $\mathcal{G}_1$. Therefore, if Player 1 loops less than $\sqrt{2k}$ times at p_t in $\mathcal{G}_2$, then Player 2 maximizes the average response time by going immediately for a grant, i.e., moving from s_1 to p_s. However, if Player 1 loops more than $\sqrt{2k}$ times at p_t, then Player 2 is better off by delaying a grant even trough issuing a request, i.e., moving from s_1 to s_2 and then to p_s. To play such a strategy, Player 2 requires approximately $\sqrt{2k}$ memory.

3.2   Two-Player Games with ART Objectives

We present the main result of this section.

Theorem 3. *The following assertions hold:*

(1) Let $\lambda = \frac{p}{q}$ with $p, q \in \mathbb{Z}$. The two-player game question with the $\mathrm{ART}^{\leq \lambda}$ objective can be solved in $O(|V|^7 \cdot |E| \cdot \min(|q|, |V|^3))$ time. The winner has a winning strategy with memory bounded by $2|V|^2$.

(2) The value of two-player games with quantitative ART objectives can be computed in $O(|V|^{10} \cdot |E| \cdot \log(|V|))$ time. Both players admit optimal strategies with memory bounded by $2|V|^2$.

In the remaining part of this section, we prove Theorem 3.

Key Ideas. We prove Theorem 3 by reduction to mean-payoff games. We highlight some key ideas of the proof.

1. First, note that for mean-payoff games memoryless strategies are sufficient (see Theorem 1), and, in contrast, memory is required for both players for ART objectives (see Examples 2 and 3). We present a reduction of games with ART objectives to mean-payoff games that involves a polynomial blow-up, and a blow-up is unavoidable due to the memory requirement.
2. As illustrated in Example 3, both players use memory to track the number of *pending* requests, i.e., the number of requests since the last grant. In the reduction, we encode the number of pending requests in the game arena $\mathcal{G}^N$ (Definition 1). We show that it suffices to count up to $2|V|^2$ pending requests (Lemma 4), which yields $2|V|^2$ upper bound on the required memory to play optimally.
3. The general algorithms for mean-payoff games are pseudo-polynomial. In our reduction, the weights in the game arena $\mathcal{G}^N$ correspond to the number of pending requests, and hence they are bounded by $2|V|^2$. Thus for our reduction the weights are polynomial, and the existing algorithms for mean-payoff games [1,16] work in polynomial time when applied to our reduction.

Simple Case: Thresholds $\lambda > |V|$. We proceed with the proof of Theorem 3. First, we observe that games with $\text{ART}^{\leq\lambda}$ objectives can be solved easily if the threshold λ is greater than the number of the positions $|V|$. In such a case Player 1 plays Büchi game to reach grant infinitely often. If Player 1 can win in the Büchi game, he has a memoryless strategy that ensures that ART does not exceed $|V|$. Otherwise, if he fails, Player 2 can force ART to be infinite with a memoryless strategy. Büchi games can be solved in $O(|V|^2)$ time [3,4], and hence:

Lemma 1. *Let* $\mathcal{G} = (V, V_1, V_2, E)$ *be a game arena, act be an action labeling,* $\lambda \in \mathbb{Q}$. *If* $\lambda > |V|$, *then the game with the objective* $\text{ART}^{\leq\lambda}$ *can be solved in* $O(|V|^2)$ *time and the winner has a memoryless winning strategy.*

In the following we consider thresholds λ bounded by $|V|$.

Consider a play π. We define the number of pending requests at position i, denoted by $\text{pr}_i[\pi]$, as the number of edges labeled with a request since the last edge labeled with a grant. Observe that, if j is a position of a grant and there are k requests up to position i, then $\sum_{i=1}^{k} \text{rt}_i[\pi] = \sum_{i=1}^{j} \text{pr}_i[\pi]$. Using this observation, we reduce games with the average response time objective to games with the mean-payoff of pending requests. We encode the number of pending requests in the game. To ensure that the game arena is finite, we compute pending requests up to some bound N. The average of (bounded to N) pending requests underapproximates the average response time (Lemma 2). Later on, we show that for N big enough, both values coincide.

Definition 1 (Arenas $\mathcal{G}^N$). *Consider a game arena* $\mathcal{G} = (V, V_1, V_2, E)$, *an action labeling* $act : E \rightarrow \{r, g, \#\}$, *and* $N > 0$. *We define a game arena* $\mathcal{G}^N$ *and a weight labeling* wt_λ *such that* $\mathcal{G}^N = (V^N, V_1^N, V_2^N, E^N)$ *and*

($\mathbf{V^N, V_1^N, V_2^N}$): $V^N = V \times \{0, \ldots, N\}$, $V_1^N = V_1 \times \{0, \ldots, N\}$, *and* $V_2^N = V_2 \times \{0, \ldots, N\}$,

($\mathbf{E^N}$): *for all* $v_1, v_2 \in V$, $x, y \in \{0, \ldots, N\}$ *we have* $(\langle v_1, x \rangle, \langle v_2, y \rangle) \in E^N$ *iff* $(v_1, v_2) \in E$ *and either*

- $act(v_1, v_2) = r$ *and* $y = \min(x + 1, N)$, *or*
- $act(v_1, v_2) = g$ *and* $y = 0$, *or*
- $act(v_1, v_2) = \#$ *and* $x = y$.

(wt_λ): *for all* $(\langle v_1, x \rangle, \langle v_2, y \rangle) \in E^N$, *we define*

- $wt_\lambda(\langle v_1, x \rangle, \langle v_2, y \rangle) = x$ *if* $act(v_1, v_2) = r$, *and*
- $wt_\lambda(\langle v_1, x \rangle, \langle v_2, y \rangle) = x + \lambda$ *if* $act(v_1, v_2) \in \{g, \#\}$.

Key Ideas. Observe that for every play π on an arena $\mathcal{G}$ there exists a unique corresponding play π' in the arena $\mathcal{G}^N$ and vice versa. Indeed, given a play $\pi = v_0 v_1 v_2$ on $\mathcal{G}$, we transform it into the play π' on $\mathcal{G}^N$ by annotating positions of π' with the number of pending requests bounded to N, i.e., the play $\pi' = (v_0, 0)(v_1, \min(\text{pr}_1[\pi], N))(v_2, \min(\text{pr}_2[\pi], N)) \ldots$. To transform a play π' on $\mathcal{G}^N$ to the corresponding play on $\mathcal{G}$ we project out the second component in each position of π'. Finally, we observe that if a play π' is eventually contained in

$V \times \{0, \ldots, N-1\}$, then it records actual numbers of pending requests, not restricted by N, and hence $\mathrm{ART}(\pi) \leq \lambda$ if and only if $\mathrm{LIMAVGINF}^{\mathrm{wt}_\lambda}(\pi') \leq \lambda$.

Lemma 2. *Let $\mathcal{G}$ be a game arena and act be an action labeling. For every play π on $\mathcal{G}$ and the corresponding play π' on $\mathcal{G}^N$, we have*

1. $\mathrm{ART}(\pi) \leq \lambda$ *implies* $\mathrm{LIMAVGINF}^{\mathrm{wt}_\lambda}(\pi') \leq \lambda$, *and*
2. *if π' eventually stays in $V \times \{0, \ldots, N-1\}$, then $\mathrm{ART}(\pi) \leq \lambda$ if and only if $\mathrm{LIMAVGINF}^{\mathrm{wt}_\lambda}(\pi') \leq \lambda$.*

Proof. Consider $k > 0$ and $\epsilon \geq 0$. Let g_k be the position of the first grant following the k-th request. We show that (*) $\frac{1}{k}\sum_{i=1}^{k} \mathrm{rt}_i[\pi] \leq \lambda + \epsilon$ implies $\frac{1}{g_k}\sum_{i=1}^{g_k} \mathrm{wt}_\lambda(\pi')[i] \leq \lambda + \epsilon$.

Assume that $\frac{1}{k}\sum_{i=1}^{k} \mathrm{rt}_i[\pi] \leq \lambda + \epsilon$, then by simple transformation we get $(\sum_{i=1}^{k} \mathrm{rt}_i[\pi]) + (g_k - k) \cdot (\lambda + \epsilon) \leq g_k(\lambda + \epsilon)$. Now observe that at the position corresponding to a grant the sum of response times is equal to the sum of pending requests over all positions, i.e., $\sum_{i=1}^{k} \mathrm{rt}_i[\pi] = \sum_{i=1}^{g_k} \mathrm{pr}_i[\pi]$. Recall that $\mathrm{wt}_\lambda(\pi')[i] = min(N, \mathrm{pr}_i[\pi]) + \lambda$ if $\mathrm{act}(v_{i-1}, v_i) \neq r$, and $\mathrm{wt}_\lambda(\pi')[i] = min(N, \mathrm{pr}_i[\pi])$ otherwise. Therefore,

$$\sum_{i=1}^{k} \mathrm{rt}_i[\pi] + (g_k - k)(\lambda + \epsilon) \geq \sum_{i=1}^{g_k} \mathrm{wt}_\lambda(\pi')[i] + (g_k - k)\epsilon \geq \sum_{i=1}^{g_k} \mathrm{wt}_\lambda(\pi')[i]$$

Finally, $\frac{1}{g_k}\sum_{i=1}^{g_k} \mathrm{wt}_\lambda(\pi')[i] \leq \lambda + \epsilon$.

If $\mathrm{ART}(\pi) \leq \lambda$, then there exists a sequence $p[1], p[2], \ldots$ such that for every $n > 0$ we have $\frac{1}{p[n]}\sum_{i=1}^{p[n]} \mathrm{rt}_i[\pi] \leq \lambda + \frac{1}{n}$. Observe that due to (*) for all $n > 0$ we have $\frac{1}{g_{p[n]}}\sum_{i=1}^{g_{p[n]}} \mathrm{wt}_\lambda(\pi')[i] \leq \lambda + \frac{1}{n}$, and hence $\mathrm{LIMAVGINF}_\lambda^{\mathrm{wt}}(\pi') \leq \lambda$.

Now, assume that (**) past position K, the play π' is contained in $V \times \{0, \ldots, N-1\}$. We first assume that $K = 1$. Consider k and $\epsilon \geq 0$ such that $\frac{1}{g_k}\sum_{i=1}^{g_k} \mathrm{wt}_\lambda(\pi')[i] \leq \lambda + \epsilon$. Then, $\sum_{i=1}^{g_k} \mathrm{wt}_\lambda(\pi')[i] - g_k(\lambda + \epsilon) \leq 0$. Again, $\sum_{i=1}^{k} \mathrm{rt}_i[\pi] = \sum_{i=1}^{g_k} \mathrm{pr}_i[\pi]$. However, condition (**) implies that for $i \geq K = 1$ we have $\mathrm{wt}_\lambda(\pi')[i] = \mathrm{pr}_i[\pi] + \lambda$ if $\mathrm{act}(v_{i-1}, v_i) \neq r$, and $\mathrm{wt}_\lambda(\pi')[i] = \mathrm{pr}_i[\pi]$ otherwise. Therefore, $\sum_{i=1}^{g_k} \mathrm{wt}_\lambda(\pi')[i] = \sum_{i=1}^{k} \mathrm{rt}_i[\pi] + (g_k - k)\lambda$. Finally, $\frac{1}{k}\sum_{i=1}^{k} \mathrm{rt}_i[\pi] \leq \lambda + \frac{g_k}{k}\epsilon$.

Now, if $\mathrm{LIMAVGINF}_\lambda^{\mathrm{wt}}(\pi') \leq \lambda$, then there exists a sequence $p[1], p[2], \ldots$ such that for all $n > 0$ we have $\frac{1}{g_{p[n]}}\sum_{i=1}^{g_{p[n]}} \mathrm{wt}_\lambda(\pi')[i] \leq \lambda + \frac{1}{n}$. It follows that for all $n > 0$ we have $\frac{1}{p[n]}\sum_{i=1}^{p[n]} \mathrm{rt}_i[\pi] \leq \lambda + \frac{g_{p[n]}}{p[n]}\frac{1}{n}$. We claim that $\frac{g_k}{k}$ is bounded by a constant independent of n, and hence $\mathrm{ART}(\pi) \leq \lambda$. To show that $\frac{g_{p[n]}}{p[n]}$ is bounded by a constant, consider $m_r, m_g, m_\#$ denoting the number of respectively requests, grants and null instructions up to position $g_{p[n]}$. Observe that $g_{p[n]} = m_r + m_g + m_\#$ and $m_r = p[n]$. Condition (G-R), i.e., every grant is immediately followed by a request, implies that $m_g \leq m_r$. Again, by condition (G-R) all moves labeled with $\#$ follow some pending request and hence the weight of such moves is at least $\lambda + 1$. Therefore, to have $\frac{1}{g_{p[n]}}\sum_{i=1}^{g_{p[n]}} \mathrm{wt}_\lambda(\pi')[i] \leq \lambda + 0.5$

(for $n > 2$), the following inequality must hold $m_\# < (4\lambda + 2) \cdot p[n]$. Thus, $\frac{g_{p[n]}}{p[n]} \leq \frac{m_\# + 2p[n]}{p[n]} \leq 4(\lambda + 1)$, i.e., $\frac{g_k}{k}$ is bounded.

Finally, note that even if $K > 0$, a finite prefix does not affect the limit of $\frac{1}{p[n]} \sum_{i=1}^{p[n]} \mathsf{rt}_i[\pi]$. $\qquad \square$

Lemma 2 implies that winning with the $\mathrm{ART}^{\leq \lambda}$ objective on $\mathcal{G}$ implies winning with the objective $\mathrm{LimAvgInf}^{\leq \lambda}$ on $\mathcal{G}^N$ for every N. Next, we prove a cutoff result saying that for $N \geq 2|V|^2$, winning on $\mathcal{G}^N$ with the objective $\mathrm{LimAvgInf}^{\leq \lambda}$ is equivalent to winning with the $\mathrm{ART}^{\leq \lambda}$ objective on $\mathcal{G}$.

Key Ideas. To prove the cutoff result, we consider a winning strategy for Player 1 on $\mathcal{G}^N$ with the objective $\mathrm{LimAvgInf}^{\leq \lambda}$. Without loss of generality, we can assume that this strategy is memoryless [10]. We show that every for $N > 2|\mathcal{G}|^2$, every memoryless winning strategy on $\mathcal{G}^N$ that wins for $\mathrm{LimAvgInf}^{\leq \lambda}$ must ensure that each play eventually stays in $V \times \{0, \ldots, N - 1\}$. Therefore, such a strategy is also winning for $\mathrm{ART}^{\leq \lambda}$ on $\mathcal{G}$ (Lemma 2).

Lemma 3. *Let $\mathcal{G} = (V, V_1, V_2, E)$ be a game arena, act be an action labeling, $\lambda \in \mathbb{Q}$ and let $N \geq 2|V|\lambda$. If Player 1 wins on $\mathcal{G}^N$ with the objective $\mathrm{LimAvgInf}^{\leq \lambda}$, then he has a memoryless winning strategy that ensures that each play eventually stays in $V \times \{0, \ldots, N - 1\}$.*

Proof. If Player 1 wins on $\mathcal{G}^N$ with the objective $\mathrm{LimAvgInf}^{\leq \lambda}$, then he has a memoryless winning strategy σ_1 [10]. Assume towards contradiction that for some play π consistent with σ_1 some position from $G \times \{N\}$ is reachable infinitely often. Consider a graph $\mathcal{G}^N[\sigma_1]$ obtained from arena $\mathcal{G}^N$ by fixing edges of Player 1 according to strategy σ. The nodes of $\mathcal{G}^N[\sigma_1]$ are all positions of $\mathcal{G}^N$. We observe that $\mathcal{G}^N[\sigma_1]$ has a cycle C that contains a position from $G \times \{N\}$ and its length is bounded by the number of nodes of $\mathcal{G}^N[\sigma_1]$, i.e., $|C| \leq |V| \cdot N$.

If cycle C does not contain grants, then C is contained in $G \times \{N\}$, and hence the average weight in C is at least $N > \lambda$. Thus, σ_1 is not winning. Therefore, C contains grants and hence it visits nodes from $G \times \{0\}$. Thus, it contains at least one node from each set $G \times \{i\}$ for $i = 0, 1, \ldots, N$. This gives us that C contains N transitions with weights $0, 1, \ldots, N$. The remaining transitions have the weight at least 0. It follows that the average weight of the cycle C is at least

$$\frac{1}{|C|}\left(\frac{N \cdot (N + 1)}{2}\right) = \frac{N + 1}{2|V|} \geq \frac{2|V|\lambda + 1}{2|V|} > \lambda$$

Thus, σ_1 is not winning. A contradiction. $\qquad \square$

We are ready to prove Theorem 3.

Proof (of Theorem 3). Let $\mathcal{G} = (V, V_1, V_2, E)$. If $\lambda > |V|$, then by Lemma 1, we can decide in $O(|V|^2)$ time whether Player 1 has a winning strategy, and if he does he has a memoryless winning strategy.

Assume that $\lambda \leq |V|$ and let $N = 2|V|^2$. Lemmas 2 and 3 imply the following condition (***):

(***) Player 1 wins on $\mathcal{G}$ with the objective $\mathrm{ART}^{\leq\lambda}$ if and only if Player 1 wins on $\mathcal{G}^N$ with the objective $\mathrm{LIMAVGINF}^{\leq\lambda}$.

For the implication from left to right, consider a winning strategy σ on $\mathcal{G}$ with the objective $\mathrm{ART}^{\leq\lambda}$. Player 1 can use the strategy σ to play on $\mathcal{G}^N$ with the objective $\mathrm{LIMAVGINF}^{\leq\lambda}$. Indeed, consider a play π on $\mathcal{G}$ consistent with σ such that $\mathrm{ART}(\pi) \leq \lambda$. Then, Lemma 2 states that for the corresponding play π' on $\mathcal{G}^N$ we have $\mathrm{LIMAVGINF}^{\mathrm{wt}_\lambda}(\pi') \leq \lambda$. Now, to show the implication from right to left we consider a winning strategy σ on $\mathcal{G}^N$. By Lemma 3, we can assume that σ is memoryless and each play eventually stays in $V \times \{0, \ldots, N-1\}$. Let σ' be a projection of σ on the first component V, i.e., σ' is a strategy on $\mathcal{G}$. Observe that (2) of Lemma 2 implies that each play consistent with σ' is winning for $\mathrm{ART}^{\leq\lambda}$ and hence σ' is a winning strategy on $\mathcal{G}$ with the objective $\mathrm{ART}^{\leq\lambda}$. Since σ is memoryless, the memory of σ' is $N = 2|V|^2$.

Condition (***) implies that, if any player can win with the $\mathrm{ART}^{\leq\lambda}$ objective, then the memory necessary to win is bounded by $2|V|^2$. In particular, for the minimal threshold λ_0, for which Player 1 has a winning strategy, he has a winning strategy with memory bounded by $2|V|^2$. This strategy is the optimal strategy for the quantitative ART objective on $\mathcal{G}$, and hence Player 1 admits optimal strategies with memory bounded by $2|V|^2$. Similarly, for any $n > 0$ and the objective $\mathrm{ART}^{\leq\lambda_0 - \frac{1}{n}}$, Player 2 has a winning strategy with memory bounded by $2|V|^2$. There are finitely many such strategies and some strategy σ_o occurs infinitely often. This strategy σ_o is optimal for Player 2 and it has memory bounded by $2|V|^2$.

We now discuss the value of the minimal threshold, for which Player 1 has a winning strategy, which is the value of the game. Consider a strategy σ for Player 1 with memory bounded by $2|V|^2$. We construct a graph G for Player 2 resulting from fixing in $\mathcal{G}$ all choices of Player 1 according to σ and storing its memory. Such a graph has $2|V|^3$ vertexes and no cycles without a grant, as otherwise Player 2 wins for every $\lambda > 0$. Now, the ART in that graph can be computed as follows. We examine all simple cycles in G that begin with a move labeled with a grant, compute the maximal ART over all such cycles, and denote it by T. Observe that the maximal ART over all paths in G equals T. Indeed, we can construct a path of the ART equal T, and conversely any (finite) path can be split into simple cycles that begin with a move labeled with a grant. Therefore, ART over finite prefixes of any infinite paths does not exceed T. Now, observe that simple cycles in G have length bounded by $2|V|^3$ and hence T is a rational number of the form $\frac{p}{q}$, where $q \leq 2|V|^3$. Now, the value of the ART game on $\mathcal{G}$ is the minimum over values of ART on graphs resulting from fixing a strategy σ with memory $2|V|^2$ for Player 1. Therefore, the value of ART game on $\mathcal{G}$ is a rational number of the form $\frac{p}{q}$, where $q \leq 2|V|^3$ and $p < 2|V|^4$.

The game on $\mathcal{G}^N$ with the objective $\mathrm{LIMAVGINF}^{\leq\lambda}$ can be solved in time $O(nmM)$, where n (resp., m) is the number of positions (resp., moves) of $\mathcal{G}^N$ and M is the bound on the absolute values of weights in $\mathcal{G}^N$ [1]. Recall that $n = |V|N$, $m = |E|N$. Theorem 1 assumes integer weights, and hence for $\lambda = \frac{p}{q}$, we need to multiply all weights by q. However, if $q > 2|V^3|$, the above discussion implies that we can approximate λ by the greatest fraction $\frac{p}{2|V|^3}$ and hence $M = N \cdot \min(q, 2|V|^3|)$. Thus, the game can be solved in $O((|V|N) \cdot (|E|N) \cdot N \cdot \min(q, 2|V|^3|)) = O(|V|^7 \cdot |E| \cdot \min(q, |V|^3|))$. Finally, using the binary search on the possible values of λ and $\mathrm{ART}^{\leq\lambda}$ objective we can find the value of the ART game on $\mathcal{G}$ in $O(|V|^{10}|E| \log(|V|))$. ☐

3.3   Graphs with ART Objectives

In the previous section, we established a polynomial-time algorithm for two-player games with ART objectives. However, if we restrict games to a single player case, we can improve the polynomial bounds.

1. First, the blow-up in the reduction to mean-payoff games is only quadratic in the one-player case.
2. Second, one-player mean-payoff games can be solved in $O(|V||E|)$ time, which is better than pseudo-polynomial bound $O(|V||E|W)$ for two-player mean-payoff games.
3. Third, in one-player case, we establish linear bounds on memory necessary to play optimally (resp., win) with ART objectives (resp., $\mathrm{ART}^{\leq\lambda}$ objectives), which is better than the quadratic bound in the two-player case.

Theorem 4. *The following assertions hold:*

(1) The one-player game question for games $(V, V, \emptyset, E)$ (resp., $(V, \emptyset, V, E)$) with $\mathrm{ART}^{\leq\lambda}$ objective can be solved in $O(|V|^3|E|)$ time. Player 1 (resp., Player 2) has a winning strategy with memory bounded by $2|V|$ (resp., $|V|$).

(2) The value of one-player games (graphs) with quantitative ART objective can be computed in $O(|V|^3|E| \log(|V|))$ time. Player 1 (resp., Player 2) admits optimal strategies with memory bounded by $2|V|$ (resp., $|V|$).

The main improvement is the cutoff result for the one-player case (Lemma 4), which is a counterpart of Lemma 3. We prove this result by a pumping argument. Having Lemma 4, we establish the complexity of one-player games with the $\mathrm{ART}^{\leq\lambda}$ objective.

Lemma 4. *Let $\mathcal{G} = (V, E)$ an a one-player game arena, act be an action labeling, $\lambda \in \mathbb{Q}$ and let $N > |V| + \lambda$. If there exists a play π on $\mathcal{G}^N$ satisfying the objective $\mathrm{LimAvgInf}^{\leq\lambda}$, then there exists a memoryless play satisfying the objective $\mathrm{LimAvgInf}^{\leq\lambda}$ that stays in $V \times \{0, \ldots, N-1\}$.*

Proof. Let π be a play such that $\mathrm{LimAvgInf}(\pi) \leq \lambda$. Observe that when the number of pending requests exceeds λ, then the weight of every move until the following grant exceeds λ. Therefore, shortening the blocks of π in which the number of pending requests exceeds λ decreases all the partial averages. More precisely, let i be a position at which the number of pending requests exceeds λ and $j > i$ be the position of the following grant. Assume that $j - i > |V|$. Then, we can project $\pi[i, j]$ onto its first component (positions of $\mathcal{G}$), remove all the cycles, and lift the resulting path to the path of $\mathcal{G}^N$ starting in $\pi[i]$. We call this final path ρ and we observe that $|\rho| \leq |V|$ and $\pi' = \pi[1, i - i]\rho\pi[j + 1, \infty]$ is a play on $\mathcal{G}^N$ such that all the partial averages are bounded by the partial averages of π. Finally, the number of pending grants between i and $i + |\rho|$ is bounded by $\lambda + |V|$. We list all the positions i, where the number of pending requests exceeds λ, and we iteratively apply the above procedure to all these positions. In the result we obtain a play π^F that satisfies the objective $\text{LIMAVGINF}^{\leq\lambda}$ and the number of pending requests is always bounded by $|V| + \lambda$, i.e., π_F stays in $V \times \{0, \ldots, N - 1\}$. $\qquad\square$

We are ready to prove Theorem 4.

Proof (of Theorem 4). **(1)**: Let $\mathcal{G} = (V, E)$ as all positions belong to one player. If $\lambda > |V|$, then by Lemma 1, we can decide in $O(|V|^2)$ the game question, and if the player has a winning strategy, then he has a memoryless winning strategy.

Assume that $\lambda \leq |V|$ and let $N = 2|V|$. First, we consider the case of all positions belonging to Player 1. Lemmas 2 and 4 imply that, in one-player games, winning on $\mathcal{G}$ with the objective $\text{ART}^{\leq\lambda}$ is equivalent to winning on $\mathcal{G}^N$ with the objective $\text{LIMAVGINF}^{\leq\lambda}$. Moreover, the winning strategy for $\mathcal{G}$ can be obtained from the winning strategy on $\mathcal{G}^N$ by projecting out the second component. Since $\text{LIMAVGINF}^{\leq\lambda}$ admits memoryless winning strategies, to win on $\mathcal{G}$ with the objective $\text{ART}^{\leq\lambda}$ it suffices to consider strategies with memory bounded by $N = 2|V|$. To decide whether Player 1 wins we prune $\mathcal{G}^N$ to positions reachable from the given initial position, which takes $O(|V|N + |E|N)$ time, and we compute the minimal mean cycle [13] in time $O(|V|N \cdot |E|N) = O(|V|^3|E|)$.

Now, consider the case of all positions belonging to Player 2. If there exists a cycle in $\mathcal{G}$ that does not contain grants, then Player 2 can win against $\text{ART}^{\leq\lambda}$ objective for any λ. We can check the existence of such a cycle in $O(|V| + |E|)$ and Player 2 has a memoryless winning strategy in that case. Otherwise, if every cycle contains at least one grant, the number of pending requests is bounded by $|V|$, and hence Player 2 requires $|V|$ memory. Thus, for $N = |V| + 1$, all plays are contained in $V \times \{0, \ldots, N - 1\}$ and Lemma 2 implies that Player 2 wins against $\text{ART}^{\leq\lambda}$ objective if and only if she wins on $\mathcal{G}^N$ against the objective $\text{LIMAVGINF}^{\leq\lambda}$. Now, we prune $\mathcal{G}^N$ to positions reachable from a given initial position, which takes $O(|V|N + |E|N)$ time, and we compute the maximal mean cycle [13] in time $O(|V|N \cdot |E|N) = O(|V|^3|E|)$. This maximal cycle has the average grater than λ if and only if Player 2 wins on $\mathcal{G}^N$ against $\text{LIMAVGINF}^{\leq\lambda}$. The latter is equivalent to Player 2 winning on $\mathcal{G}$ against $\text{ART}^{\leq\lambda}$ objective.

(2): We present the argument for Player 1, as the reasoning for Player 2 is virtually the same. For every $\lambda > 0$, if Player 1 has a winning strategy with $\text{ART}^{\leq\lambda}$, then he has a winning strategy with memory $2|V|$. There are finitely many such strategies and one of them achieves the value of the game. A one-player strategy amounts to a single play, which is a lasso of length bounded by $2|V|^2$. Therefore, the minimal threshold λ_0 such that Player 1 has a winning strategy with $\text{ART}^{\leq\lambda_0}$ belongs to a finite set of rationals $\{\frac{p}{q} \mid p, q \in \mathbb{N}, q \leq 2|V|^2, p \leq 2|V|^3\}$. Therefore, using the binary search and the decision procedure from (1), we can find the minimal λ_0, which is the value of the ART game in $O(|V|^3|E|\log(|V|))$. Finally, observe that the strategy for Player 1 for $\mathrm{ART}^{\leq\lambda_0}$ is the optimal strategy for him. Thus, Player 1 admits optimal strategies with memory bounded by $2|V|$. □

3.4   Discussion

We discuss the applicability and significance of the results on ART objective.

Remark 1 (Discussion on the G-R condition). We have introduced the G-R condition for technical simplicity. We can, however, eliminate it. Observe that the G-R condition has been used only in Lemma 2, which relates plays with ART objectives on $\mathcal{G} = (V, V_1, V_2, E)$ and plays with mean-payoff objectives on $\mathcal{G}^N$.

First, without the G-R condition, there can be plays, in which eventually there are no pending requests. Assume that such plays are winning for Player 1. Then, we proceed as follows:

- We show that (*) if Player 2 has a winning, strategy she has a winning strategy such that length of blocks (of positions) with no pending requests are bounded by $|V|$.
- We redefine $\mathcal{G}^N$ such that after $|\mathcal{G}|$ steps with no pending requests Player 1 wins. The size of such modified arena is $|V| \cdot N + |V|^2$.
- We prove the analogue of Lemma 2 for the modified $\mathcal{G}^N$. Observe that the current proof of Lemma 2 works even if we only assume that blocks (of positions) with no pending requests are bounded by $|\mathcal{G}|$.

The above construction also works if Player 2 wins on plays, in which eventually there are no pending requests.

Remark 2 (Discussion on complexity). In this work, our goal is to establish the first polynomial-time algorithms computing the ART property for game graphs and graphs. The complexities of the polynomial upper bounds we establish are quite high ($\widetilde{O}(|V|^{10} \cdot |E|)$ for game graphs, $\widetilde{O}(|V|^3 \cdot |E|)$ for graphs), and likely to be non-optimal. Our algorithms for games are based on reductions to mean-payoff games, where memoryless strategies are sufficient. We show that quadratic size memory is sufficient for ART objectives. Hence a reduction to mean-payoff games, which encodes memory in the state space, gives rise to a game with $|V|^3$ vertices, $|V|^2 \cdot |E|$ edges, and $W = |V|^2$, and then applying the best-known algorithms for mean-payoff games already gives a high polynomial complexity. Obtaining algorithms with better theoretical bounds as well as practical approaches are interesting directions for future work.

4   Markov Chains

In this section, we discuss Markov chains with ART objectives. We establish polynomial-time algorithms for both the expected value and the distribution questions.

Polynomial-time algorithms for Markov chains with objectives given by nested weighted automata (which can express the ART property) has been established in [8]. Hence, below we present the key ideas to obtain a simple algorithm for ART properties. We omit formal and detailed proofs, which are consequences of the results established in [8].

Key Ideas. We present the key ideas for both cases.

1. *The expected question.* Consider a labeled Markov chain $\mathcal{M} = \langle \Sigma, S, s_0, E \rangle$, where $\Sigma = \{r, g, \#\}$. To compute the expected value $\mathbb{E}_{\mathrm{ART}}(\mathcal{M})$, we first compute the labeling of transitions $\mathtt{wt}$ of $\mathcal{M}$ such that for all $s_1, s_2 \in S$, we put $\mathtt{wt}((s_1, g, s_2)) = \mathtt{wt}((s_1, \#, s_2)) = \bot$, i.e., no weight, and $\mathtt{wt}((s_1, r, s_2))$ is the expected number of steps to reach a grant. This labelling can be computed in polynomial time in $|\mathcal{M}|$, by reduction to linear programming with $|S|$ variables and $|S| + |E| + 1$ constraints [12]. Then, we compute the expected value of the mean-payoff objective $\mathrm{LimAvgInf}^{\mathtt{wt}}$ on $\mathcal{M}$, i.e., $\mathbb{E}_{\mathrm{LimAvgInf}}(\mathcal{M})$. The value $\mathbb{E}_{\mathrm{LimAvgInf}}(\mathcal{M})$ can be computed in polynomial time. Again, it is computed by reduction to linear programming with $|S|$ variables and $|S| + |E| + 1$ constraints [12]. Finally, we return $\mathbb{E}_{\mathrm{LimAvgInf}}(\mathcal{M})$ as $\mathbb{E}_{\mathrm{ART}}(\mathcal{M})$. The key aspect of the correctness proof is that the values $\mathbb{E}_{\mathrm{LimAvgInf}}(\mathcal{M})$ and $\mathbb{E}_{\mathrm{ART}}(\mathcal{M})$ are equal, which follows from [8, Lemma 26].

2. *The distribution question.* To compute the distribution question, we first discuss the case of Markov chains $\mathcal{M}$ consisting of a single recurrent set, i.e., almost all paths visit all states infinitely often. In such a case, the Boolean objective $\mathrm{ART}^{\leq \lambda}$ is a tail event [11] and its probability is either 0 or 1, i.e., for every λ almost all plays satisfy $\mathrm{ART}^{\leq \lambda}$ or almost all plays violate it. Therefore, almost all plays have the same value, which is $\mathbb{E}_{\mathrm{ART}}(\mathcal{M})$. In the general case, we can find in $\mathcal{M}$ subsets $R_1, \ldots, R_k$, which are recurrent sets, i.e., among paths that enter R_i, almost all paths visit all states of R_i infinitely often. We compute all recurrent sets $R_1, \ldots, R_k$ of $\mathcal{M}$ in $O(|S| + |E|)$ time. Then, we compute (in polynomial time) the probabilities $p_1, \ldots, p_k$ of reaching each of these sets from s_0, and expected values $\mathbb{E}_{\mathrm{ART}}(R_1), \ldots, \mathbb{E}_{\mathrm{ART}}(R_k)$, where $\mathbb{E}_{\mathrm{ART}}(R_i)$ is the expected average response time of the Markov chain $(\Sigma, R_i, s_0^i, E \cap R_i \times R_i)$ with some $s_0^i \in R_i$. Probabilities $p_1, \ldots, p_k$ can be computed using linear programming as well. Finally, $\mathbb{D}_{\mathcal{M}, \mathrm{ART}}(\lambda)$, the probability of the set of plays below threshold λ, is the sum of probabilities of reaching the recurrent sets with expected values below λ, i.e., $\mathbb{D}_{\mathcal{M}, \mathrm{ART}}(\lambda) = \sum \{p_i \mid \mathbb{E}_{\mathrm{ART}}(R_i) \leq \lambda\}$. The correctness proof follows from [8, Lemma 27].

Theorem 5. *Consider a Markov chain* $\mathcal{M} = \langle \Sigma, S, s_0, E \rangle$ *and* $\lambda \in \mathbb{Q}$.

- *The expected value* $\mathbb{E}_{\mathrm{ART}}(\mathcal{M})$ *for the ART objective can be computed in polynomial time, by a reduction that takes* $O(|S| + |E|)$ *time and produces two instances of linear programming each with* $|S|$ *variables and* $|S| + |E| + 1$ *constraints.*

– *The cumulative distribution* $\mathbb{D}_{\mathcal{M},\mathrm{ART}}(\lambda)$ *for the* ART *objective can be computed in polynomial time, by a reduction that takes* $O(|S| + |E|)$ *time and produces three instances of linear programming each with* $|S|$ *variables and* $|S| + |E| + 1$ *constraints.*

5   Conclusions

Average response time (ART) is a fundamental quantitative property of reactive systems. We presented the first algorithms that are designed specifically for computing ART values on graphs, game graphs, and Markov chains. All our algorithms are polynomial time. There are several interesting directions for future work. First, while our main objective was to establish polynomial-time upper bounds, algorithms of better complexity may be possible (Remark 2). Second, the problems of computing ART values for more general graph models such as Markov decision processes (i.e., graphs with both probabilistic and nonprobabilistic vertices) and stochastic games (i.e., graphs with probabilistic vertices, Player-1 vertices, and Player-2 vertices) are still open. Finally, the value computation problems remain open for interesting generalizations of the ART property such as the more general ART property which counts the number of tick events between request and grant events, rather than counting the number of all transitions between requests and subsequent grants. While these generalizations of the ART property and of the underlying graph models appear modest, the algorithms presented in this paper cannot be generalized directly to these cases.

References

1. Brim, L., Chaloupka, J., Doyen, L., Gentilini, R., Raskin, J.: Faster algorithms for mean-payoff games. Formal Methods Syst. Des. **38**(2), 97–118 (2011). https://doi.org/10.1007/s10703-010-0105-x
2. Chatterjee, K., Doyen, L., Henzinger, T.A.: Quantitative languages. ACM TOCL **11**(4), 23 (2010)
3. Chatterjee, K., Henzinger, M.: An $O(n^2)$ time algorithm for alternating Büchi games. In: SODA 2012, pp. 1386–1399. ACM-SIAM (2012)
4. Chatterjee, K., Henzinger, M.: Efficient and dynamic algorithms for alternating Büchi games and maximal end-component decomposition. J. ACM **61**(3), 15:1–15:40 (2014)
5. Chatterjee, K., Henzinger, T.A., Otop, J.: Bidirectional nested weighted automata. In: CONCUR 2017 (to appear)
6. Chatterjee, K., Henzinger, T.A., Otop, J.: Nested weighted automata. In: LICS 2015, pp. 725–737 (2015)
7. Chatterjee, K., Henzinger, T.A., Otop, J.: Nested weighted limit-average automata of bounded width. In: MFCS 2016, pp. 24:1–24:14 (2016). https://doi.org/10.4230/LIPIcs.MFCS.2016.24
8. Chatterjee, K., Henzinger, T.A., Otop, J.: Quantitative automata under probabilistic semantics. In: LICS 2016, pp. 76–85 (2016). https://doi.org/10.1145/2933575.2933588

9. Droste, M., Kuich, W., Vogler, H.: Handbook of Weighted Automata, 1st edn. Springer, Heidelberg (2009). https://doi.org/10.1007/978-3-642-01492-5
10. Ehrenfeucht, A., Mycielski, J.: Positional strategies for mean payoff games. Int. J. Game Theory **8**(2), 109–113 (1979)
11. Feller, W.: An Introduction to Probability Theory and its Applications. Wiley, Hoboken (1971)
12. Filar, J., Vrieze, K.: Competitive Markov Decision Processes. Springer, New York (1996). https://doi.org/10.1007/978-1-4612-4054-9
13. Karp, R.M.: A characterization of the minimum cycle mean in a digraph. Discrete Math. **23**(3), 309–311 (1978)
14. Martin, D.A.: Borel determinacy. Ann. Math. **102**(2), 363–371 (1975). Second Series
15. McDermid, J.A.: Software Engineer's Reference Book. Elsevier, Amsterdam (2013)
16. Zwick, U., Paterson, M.: The complexity of mean payoff games on graphs. Theor. Comput. Sci. **158**(1), 343–359 (1996)

Modeling Dynamical Phenomena
in the Era of Big Data

Bruno Sinopoli$^{(\boxtimes)}$ and John A. W. B. Costanzo

Carnegie Mellon University, Pittsburgh, USA
{brunos,costanzo}@ece.cmu.edu

Abstract. As the world around us gets equipped with widespread sensing, computing, communication, and actuation capabilities, opportunities to improve the quality of life arise. Smart infrastructures promise to dramatically increase safety and efficiency. While data abounds, the modeling and understanding of large-scale complex systems, such as energy distribution, transportation, or communication networks, water management systems, and buildings, presents several challenges. Deriving models from first principles via white or gray box modeling is infeasible. Classical black-box modeling is also not practical as model selection is hard, interactions change over time, and evolution can be observed passively without the chance to conduct experiments through data injection or manipulation of the system. Moreover, the causality structure of such systems is largely unknown.

We contend that determining data-driven, minimalistic models, capable of explaining dynamical phenomena and tracking their validity over time, is an essential step toward building dependable systems. In this work we will outline challenges, review existing work, and propose future research directions.

1 Introduction

Many dynamical systems are made up of complex interactions between smaller subsystems. The number of these small subsystems can be staggering, and the advent of IoT and smart infrastructure has given us a magnifying glass with which to observe systems far too complex to model without the volume of data we now have available.

Power systems, for example, are networks of generators and loads; loads are networks of factories and households which in turn are networks of machines controlled by networks of people who are networks of proteins and neurons. There is uncertainty in the decisions of people at the light switch; uncertainty in the availability of green resources; uncertainty in the weather affecting HVAC demand. Some of these interactions are easy to model (e.g., Ohm's Law); some (such as social behavior or weather) are more complicated.

The number of potential interactions is even more problematic. Can we prove faults always remain localized? We know the load will be greater on a hot day, but can the transformer at the street corner handle the extra load when the museum puts on a special exhibit? If not, how much of the city will go dark?

© Springer International Publishing AG, part of Springer Nature 2018
M. Lohstroh et al. (Eds.): Lee Festschrift, LNCS 10760, pp. 162–181, 2018.
https://doi.org/10.1007/978-3-319-95246-8_10

Thousands of people analyze situations like this every day in an attempt to keep the grid up and running. Yet, every few years another power catastrophe makes headlines. When so much data is available—indeed, when the system is so complex as to produce so much data—it is impossible to deduce through first principles what effect every variable has on every other.

What further complicates things is that we do not always have control access to the system. Sometimes access is prohibited by cost or safety standards; injecting billions of dollars into the stock market to see the effect on prices would cost not only the researcher, but the other investors who are unwitting participants in the experiment. Other times we are prohibited by nature from injecting control signals; we cannot, for instance, control the weather to observe its effect on traffic.

The grid is but one example of such a complicated system. In fact, in the era of smart infrastructure, this complicated system is but one *component* of infrastructure as a whole. There are countless systems in which all we have access to is a collection of node processes generating time series data, and no indication of which processes are inputs to which other processes.

1.1   The Era of Big Data

Classical identification techniques rely on large amounts of data to improve the model estimate. The era of big data, in that respect, should be a boon for model identification. Contrary to the days when experiments could take years to yield usable data, today, small and cheap sensors can be deployed and data gathered in a matter of weeks or days.

Yet our knowledge of complex systems has not scaled proportionally to the amount of usable data available. As the number of measurements we can take increases, the number of *things* we are measuring has increased by at least as much—and it is becoming clear that a robust model for a complex system must take *all* of these things into account.

Typical black box modelling fails us here, because the interactions between variables in a complex system grows much faster than the number of variables present, and the weaker the assumptions we make, the more data (and more importantly, processing power) we need to pare down the vast array of candidate models available to us.

1.2   Causal Influence Structure as First Step

It is often assumed that the goal of system identification is to obtain a full model of the entire system. In many applications, however, this lofty goal is unnecessarily high. A good model ought to tell us what processes are interacting in a system, and the exact nature of those interactions. But even just the former piece of information, the structure, is valuable to the engineer.

In a system that is a collection of subsystems, one might want to know, if one of these subsystems goes unstable, which others are immediately at risk?

How do we prevent this instability from infecting the rest of the system? This is the theme of a paper [1] that analyzes the cascading effect of defaults in financial networks. Their analysis focuses on network structure—the links in this case representing interbank liabilities—and relates the magnitude of cascading defaults to the maximum out-degree of the random graph.

In the realm of control engineering, we may be observing a system with dynamics too complex to model. In such cases, a "data-driven" control scheme (even one as simple as Ziegler-Nichols) may be used, which does not require knowledge of the system parameters. Designing a distributed control architecture [23] requires knowledge of which processes in the system are coupled, but if the controller itself is data-driven, this is all that is required.

Structural knowledge may provide sufficient understanding of a complex system to facilitate our engineering objectives. In particular, predicting and possibly preventing the propagation of certain signals through the system, deciding on a decentralized or hierarchical control topology, and even detecting and localizing faults, attacks, or link degradations can be accomplished using only the knowledge of which processes causally influence each other.

We consider the scenario in which we are given a collection of time series, each representing the evolution of some variable over time. The system can be thought of as a "network" of these variables (which we may call "nodes"), each evolving semi-autonomously, but under the "influence" of a few others. Often, these systems, even those with many variables, are "sparse" in the sense that most variables are directly causally influenced by only a few others.

Moreover, even when the full model is desired, knowing the structure can simplify the identification process, as it rules out potentially many possible interactions between the variables considered. Hence, we argue that causal influence modeling is beneficial in a wide variety of situations.

1.3   Challenge: No Control Access

A common technique in identification is to perturb various control inputs in the network and observe the effects of this perturbation and how they propagate through the system. We can sequentially design experiments [4] in order to obtain more information about the system.

In his work on causality, Pearl [18] discusses "interventions," wherein the value of a certain value is fixed, and the effect on the rest of the network is observed. This is why randomized controlled trials are the gold standard in medicine; ideally, the subjects are a representative sample of the population and are split into two groups, where the *only* difference between these groups is whether or not they receive medicine (not even whether they *think* they are.)

However, in many large scale systems, intervention, either through perturbing control signals or through modifying the system itself, may be impractical, unethical, or infeasible. Hence, we need to infer causality based on passive observations.

While we'd like to ask the question: "what would Y become if we changed X'?", we must instead ask: "does knowing X help us better predict Y?". Often, the latter question serves as a decent proxy for the former; however, this comes with a number of caveats. Multiple factors can confuse the connection, such as whether there is enough of a time delay in the system to discern between cause and effect, whether all common causes have been measured and conditioned on, and whether the forces driving the joint evolution of the system are independent.

A collection of observations does not necessarily result from a unique causal structure. One counterexample is presented in the statement of Simpson's Paradox [19], in which two scenarios with the same statistics are presented, but with different conclusions. In both scenarios, the (linear) correlation between A and B is negative, and the partial correlation between A and B given C is positive. However, in one scenario, increasing A results in an increase in B, whereas the opposite is true in the other scenario. In this case, the causal model is *required* to make conclusions about the data (and, consequently, cannot be uniquely obtained from data). However, this is not an exhaustive characterization of all cases in which the causal structure is ambiguous; in particular, examples of Simpson's Paradox typically involve three static variables with a three-variate joint probability distribution, rather than three time series related by dynamic processes.

1.4   Other Challenges and Open Questions

Real systems are vulnerable to failures and attacks, which would render the current model invalid. If the system's dynamics are known, a chi-squared detector [27] can be used to signal that an abnormality has occurred. Other conditions on discernibility of networks are given in [3]. However, as we have argued, there are cases in which knowing the full system model is infeasible and unnecessary to accomplish control objectives. Hence, detecting and localizing these faults without knowing the full system model (or at least requiring as little information about it as possible) is of interest.

Another question of interest is the handling of unobserved variables. These can confound causal inference; when a node is unobserved, all of its children become fully connected, since they will share trends that are only explained by the common parent. We cannot just look at all of the complete subgraphs and infer that they have an unobserved common parent, because that does not cover all cases. It also requires solving an NP-hard problem that is hard to approximate. Dealing with unobserved nodes in trees has been studied [14].

Causal loops, typical of systems with feedback controllers, still can present a problem in causal structure identification. The final result in [12] states (in the linear, time invariant case) that, when every directed cycle contains at least one positive time delay, the skeleton of the graph can be obtained by finding "Wiener-Hopf" separations [11] (a slight variant of Wiener separation, discussed in Sect. 4.1) in the data. Properly identifying directed cycles with no time delay is still an open problem, although it is debatable whether these are physically possible. Granger [8] claims that instantaneous causality is only possible in the first place when the time series represent discrete observations of continuous phenomena, but this presents other problems [6] which hampers our ability to determine the structure (by existing means) altogether.

Organization. In this chapter we address the issues discussed above, as they relate to the modeling of such large-scale, highly-distributed, highly-coupled, dynamical systems. We focus on uncovering the information most relevant to the objectives of the highest-level observers. Section 2 formalizes the characteristics of the problem, and how it differs from modeling classical systems. Section 3 introduces a few relevant notions from the theory of causation. It begins by motivating the acceptance of disturbances as necessary for exciting the system and making sense of causal cycles. Keeping in mind the objectives of inferred causation—namely, the ability to answer certain questions—we present three general causal models, each built off of (and capable of answering a broader class of questions than) the previous one. We review the Inductive Causation algorithm, which reconstructs causal models. Finally, we present a *dynamic* causal influence model and show how the properties of functional causal models translate. Section 4 shows how prior work has applied these notions to specific models, under varied assumptions.

2   Problem Characteristics

Modeling large scale systems presents some unique challenges not present in smaller scale systems.

Unknown Relational Structure. Large numbers of variables result in more complex systems, which require more data to learn. However, such systems are often "sparse" in that most variables depend on few others in the system.

With no *a priori* knowledge of the relational structure, the modeler must assume that each variable takes *all* other variables as an input. This means that more data and computing power are required to learn parameters whose ultimate values are zero. On the other hand, if we could identify the relational structure first, then we can significantly reduce the class of candidate models.

When many variables share similar trends, it is difficult to distinguish cause from effect. Often two variables may have a similar trend although neither one causes the other; when causation does exist, it is not always apparent which is the cause and which is the effect. False findings of causality are problematic because they can lead to poor decision making that results in suboptimal control of the system.

A robust causal structure identification scheme must take into account the difference between *direct* causation and causation by way of an intermediary, and must also distinguish between variables that are causally linked and those which merely have a common cause.

Known and Unknown Forcing Inputs. The variables we observe often interact in a complex way (or else the system could simply be decoupled.) These variables show up as inputs in the dynamics of other variables in the system; such as $\dot{x}_i = f_i(\ldots, x_j, \ldots)$. However, there are also hidden environmental or user factors that drive the evolution of the system.

The inability to observe all of the inputs to a dynamical system makes identification more difficult. Typical workarounds are to assume that the unobserved input is additive and wide-sense stationary [13] (or cyclostationary [25]), in which case the maximum likelihood estimator is the least-squares estimator.

Control Access Limited or Unavailable. The ability to inject a signal into part of the network and observe its effects on other parts of the network is valuable to identification [4]. However, injecting signals into an unknown system can cause undesirable behavior, and is often infeasible.

3   Stochastic Models and Causality

3.1   How Disturbances are Useful

Pearl begins his book on causality [18] with probability theory. He acknowledges the reader's trepidations; causality conveying certainty and probability conveying the lack of certainty. He then justifies this approach by providing a number of reasons why probability theory should be a prerequisite for the study causality. In particular, causal statements in natural language are often applied to the "average" case, or are subject to a multitude of exceptions and conditions too numerous to casually list.

For the control engineer, there is another reason randomness is integral to causal modeling, or at least the brand of causality that is useful to us. Suppose you have a voltage source and a static load. You measure the voltage and current. Is the current caused by the voltage, or the other way around? You cannot change one without altering the other, so one might say there is a paradoxical "bidirectional" causality at play. A better question is what one would do with such information. In particular, if the resistance is known, the voltage and current are essentially two different measurements of the same phenomenon. To ask which causes the other is beyond what many applications care about.

On the other hand, if you have a *varying* voltage source and a *varying* resistor, each with a random actor choosing the voltage or resistance, then now the question of causality makes sense. For instance, if the current drops, but the voltage does not, one can say the current dropped *because* the resistance increased. If we were simply observing three time series with no knowledge of how they were generated, we could still determine that two of them evolve independently, and that the third is causally influenced by both of them.

Notice the second scenario is identical to the first, except that the model incorporates unknown system inputs, which we model as a random disturbance. The implication is two-fold. For starters, randomness allows us to model external intervention, and while we may not have control over that intervention, if we can (even indirectly) observe it, then we can draw conclusions about the system based on its effects. It also describes an arguably more useful system; that varying "resistor" may actually be a factory whose demand for power is a function of resource availability, time of day, product demand, etc. Realistic systems interact with the world, turning one type of energy into other types of energy, and rarely do they do so in a vaccuum.

Often modelers include disturbances begrudgingly, but we argue that a system without disturbances, being deterministic, does not admit any meaningful discussion of causality. If X was predetermined to happen, and Y happened because of X, then we could just as easily say Y was predetermined to happen and skip the intermediary. Hence, from a system-wide perspective, disturbances are absolutely necessary for a proper discussion of how the network interacts with the world.

3.2   Causality

The definition of causality is contentious among philosophers, but engineers care about it primarily for the following reasons:

- When we observe a phenomenon, we'd like to predict what other phenomena will occur (**Prediction**).
- When we want the system to do something, we'd like to know where and how to intervene to affect that outcome (**Intervention**).
- We'd like to explain phenomena that have happened in the past, in particular, infer what might have happened had we done something differently (**Counterfactual**).

Bayesian Networks. Given a set of random variables V with a joint probability distribution $P(v)$ and a directed acyclic graph $\mathcal{G}$ with vertex set V, P is said to be *Markov* relative to $\mathcal{G}$ if

$$P\left(V = (v_1, v_2, \cdots v_n)\right) = \prod_{i=1}^{n} P\left(v_i \mid pa_i\right) \tag{1}$$

where pa_i is the set of parents of vertex v_i in $\mathcal{G}$. If it is also true that no proper subset of pa_i satisfies (1), then $\mathcal{G}$ is called a *Bayesian network* for V.

The problem of inference (of which prediction is a special case) is simply that of calculating, $P(Y \mid X)$, where Y is a set of unobserved variables to be inferred or predicted, and X is a set of observed variables to be used in prediction. In general, this quantity is computed

$$P(y \mid x) = \frac{\sum_s P(y, x, s)}{\sum_{y', s} P(y', x, s)},$$

which can be computed from the graph $\mathcal{G}$ and conditional probabilities $P(x_i \mid pa_i)$.

Causal Bayesian Networks. Purely stochastic models such as Bayesian Networks, although they are quite sufficient in answering the first question, do not allow for a formal study of intervention. The factorization of a joint probability into products of conditional probabilities is not unique, in general; the Pearl-Verma theorem [18, Theorem 1.2.8] only guaranteeing that all directed graphs admitting such a factorization have the same skeleton and open colliders. For example, given the evidence that a patient is receiving chemotherapy, one can more accurately conclude that the patient has cancer; however to decide that we should outlaw chemotherapy to reduce the risk of cancer is absurd.

On the other hand, *causal* Bayesian networks moreover require the specification of *interventional* distributions; that is, all distributions $P_x(\mathbf{v})$ resulting from applying the intervention $do(X = x)$ for all $X \subseteq V$ and all realizations x of X. The power of causal Bayesian networks is that, while it may seem as though specifying a new distribution for each subset of variables is combinatorial in space, a lot of this information is redundant. To wit, for these distributions to be meaningful as "interventional" distributions, they must satisfy certain properties (for instance, if nothing causes X, then its effect on the network should be the same whether we $do(X = x)$ or observe $X = x$.) The properties are as follows [18]:

- $P_x(\mathbf{v})$ is Markov relative to $\mathcal{G}$ (intervening does not destroy any conditional independence relationships);
- $P_x(v_i) = 1$ for any $V_i \in X$ consistent with $X = x$ (applying the intervention $do(X = x)$ guarantees x happens);
- $P_x(v_i \mid pa_i) = P(v_i \mid pa_i)$ for all $V_i \notin X$ whenever pa_i is consistent with $X = x$.

These conditions are sufficiently restrictive that, given a DAG $\mathcal{G}$ and a distribution P which is Markov relative to $\mathcal{G}$, all interventional distributions are uniquely determined and can be found by *truncated factorization*,

$$P_x(\mathbf{v}) = \prod_{i:V_i \notin X} P(v_i \mid pa_i)$$

for all $\mathbf{v}$ consistent with $X = x$ (and 0 for $\mathbf{v}$ not consistent). Note that this differs from the factorization of $P(\mathbf{v})$ in that we have removed all arrows entering those nodes in X and instead fixed their values. We denote the effect of intervention as $P(Y \mid do(X = x)) = P_x(Y)$, and say that X is causing Y if $P(Y \mid do(X = x)) \neq P(Y \mid do(X = x'))$ for some $x \neq x'$.

Note that if $\mathcal{G}$ is a causal Bayesian network for $P(V)$ then it is also a Bayesian network; hence an informal but more intuitive definition of a causal Bayesian network is as follows: among all observationally equivalent Bayesian networks, the *causal* Bayesian network is the one where the arrows point in the direction of causation.

Beyond Causal Bayesian Networks. While causal Bayesian networks are capable of answering interventional questions, they still provide no insight to questions of the third type, called *counterfactuals*. Consider the following scenario with two variables, "treatment" and "recovery." The interventional probabilities are as follows:

- Those treated will recover with 75% probability;
- Those not treated will recover with 25% probability.

One may ask, *given that* a patient *was not* treated and yet still recovered, *would* that patient have *still* recovered if he *had* been treated? One may be tempted to say, since treatment only increases one's probability of recovery, that yes, he would have still recovered. Indeed, that is one possibility. However, there are a number of generative models consistent with these probabilities, and some lead to the opposite conclusion.

Barring quantum effects, it is reasonable to assume that there is some side information which is unobserved, but by which a patient's recovery is entirely determined given whether or not they were treated. Let us call this side information U. For formality's sake we will also denote whether or not the patient was treated as $T \in \{0, 1\}$ and recovery as $R \in \{0, 1\}$. If we know both U and T, then R is entirely determined; however, how nature makes this determination has a profound effect on the correct answer to the counterfactual question.

One possibility is that the treatment only has an effect on those who would not have recovered without the treatment. We can think of U as a proxy for the "severity" of the case; say $U \in \{-1, 0, 1\}$ and $R = \mathbf{1}\{U + T > 0\}$. If the natural distribution of U is such that $U = 0$ in 50% of cases and -1 or 1 respectively in 25% of cases, then the corresponding distributions $P(R \mid do(T))$ do indeed correspond to the interventional distributions defined above. Moreover, the naïve conclusion is correct; since the patient was not treated ($T = 0$) and yet still recovered ($U + T > 0$), we must have $U = 1$. Since $U + 1 > 0$ still holds, the patient would have still recovered if treated.

On the other hand, it may also be the case that, unbeknownst to the medical community, there are two different diseases which are yet indistinguishable. The first disease ($U = 0$) both *requires* treatment T for recovery, but the treatment is 100% effective. The second disease ($U = 1$) is always recoverable without intervention, but is *exacerbated* by treatment T. In this case we have $U \in \{0, 1\}$ and $R = U \oplus T$. With $U \sim Ber(0.25)$ we again obtain the same interventional distributions mentioned earlier; however, the conclusion is different; the patient recovered ($U \oplus T = 1$) without treatment $T = 0$, so he must have had disease $U = 1$ and hence would have been *harmed* by the treatment.

Of course, the likelihood of either scenario is up for debate, but more importantly one cannot distinguish between the two using statistics alone. This is because the variable U does not explicitly appear in stochastic models. These two scenarios are examples of *functional causal models*, in general consisting of a directed graph $\mathcal{G}$ with vertex set V, and a set of equations of the form

$$x_i = f_i(pa_i, u_i) \qquad (2)$$

Table 1. Hierarchy of causal models and the questions they can answer.

	Prediction	Intervention	Counterfactual
BN	YES	NO	NO
CBN	YES	YES	NO
FCM	YES	YES	YES

for each $x_i \in V$, where again pa_i are the parents of x_i in $\mathcal{G}$. The random variables U_i represent disturbances due to unmodeled factors [18], such as those discussed in Sect. 3.1.

The usefulness of these three models has been covered extensively in literature, but recovering them (especially the more powerful ones) from data is still a topic of continuing research. As one might imagine, the more powerful models entail greater difficulty in learning. While it is relatively straightforward to learn a Bayesian network, at least in theory, making the jump to *causal* Bayesian networks without allowing experimentation is difficult. In essence, we desire a model that can answer questions we are not allowed to even *ask* of the real system (Table 1).

In particular, since we cannot intervene on the system, we cannot observe its interventional probabilities. Through observation alone, we can only observe the joint probability $P(V)$ and recover a *class* of observationally equivalent DAG structures $\mathcal{G}'$ consistent with the data.

Hence, additional assumptions need to be made about the *true* causal model, either in the form of fixing the orientations of certain arrows or constraining the class of permissible functions f_i. These are referred to as *causal assumptions*. Among causal assumptions, we further distinguish between two special types:

- *Structural* assumptions; i.e., restrictions on the directions of some of the arrows in $\mathcal{G}$; and
- *Dynamical* assumptions; restrictions on the class of functions a particular f_i may come from.

For instance, if the data has a temporal component, it is clearly appropriate to assume that no arrow between nodes may point backward in time. While this may not be enough information to orient all of the arrows in the causal structure, it is sufficient in many cases, such as when the dynamics are strictly causal (as we define later).

Other structural constraints might include identifying variables that can have no cause, such as solar activity in weather prediction, or race or gender in the social sciences. Such structural assumptions stem from having some semantic information provided with the data, and at least some intuition behind the mechanism being observed.

At the other extreme, consider a causal model with only two variables, a and b. If our aim is to identify the causal structure $\mathcal{G}$, then we clearly are not in a position to make *any* informed structural assumption; such assumption would automatically be so strong as to completely determine the model, even in the absence of data. On the other hand, without any causal assumptions at all, it is impossible to distinguish between $a \rightarrow b$ and $b \rightarrow a$ without interventions; we only observe $P(a, b)$ which can always be factored into both $P(a \mid b)P(b)$ and $P(b \mid a)P(a)$.

In this case, assumptions on the type of functions f_i can be useful. For example, [17] provides two methods of breaking the symmetry, each valid under certain assumptions, and both taking advantage of nonlinearities.

3.3 Inductive Causation

The Inductive Causation algorithm was introduced by Verma and Pearl in 1990 [26] and takes as input a probability distribution $\hat{P}$ (ostensibly learned by, for instance, performing density estimation on a large number of i.i.d samples) and returns a pattern representing the equivalence class of the DAG which generated the data. As noted, two DAGs are equivalent if they have the same skeleton (i.e., undirected version) and same "open colliders"; structures of the form $a \rightarrow c \leftarrow b$ where neither $a \rightarrow b$ nor $b \rightarrow a$ are in the graph.

The first step recovers the skeleton:

For each pair $a, b \in V$, find a set S_{ab} such that a and b are conditionally independent in $\hat{P}$ given S_{ab}. If no such set can be found, add an edge between a and b in $\hat{\mathcal{G}}$.

The second step identifies open colliders:

For each pair of non-adjacent variables a and b with a common neighbor c, check if $c \in S_{ab}$. If not, $a \rightarrow c \leftarrow b$ is in the pattern.

Explanation: Among all structures with skeleton a–c–b, only when $a \rightarrow c \leftarrow b$ does conditioning on c actually *introduce* a dependence between a and b.

In principle, the open collider is the only structure that can be directly determined from the data. However, even after the second step we may be left with undirected edges whose orientations are restricted:

Orient any arrows for which either: (1) an alternative orientation would introduce an open collider, or (2) an alternative orientation would introduce a directed cycle.

3.4 Static versus Dynamic Settings

A typical way one would learn a Bayesian network is by observing multiple independent samples from the network and performing some sort of density estimation to obtain $\hat{P}$, an estimate of the joint probability of V. One can then use the Inductive Causation algorithm to determine the *pattern* of $\mathcal{G}$; a partially directed graph with all open V-structures oriented. We call this the "static" case; while there may be a temporal component to the data, it is characterized by having multiple independent trials, each happening on a relatively short time scale (if any), and where variables are typically measured only once per experiment.

In the smart infrastructure scenario, we do not have multiple independent realizations of the world; instead we have only one realization that evolves in time. While we could envision that we have multiple realizations (each a snapshot in time) of a collection of sensor measurements, these realizations are not independent; they are taken across time, and physical processes typically have a strong dependence on the past evolution of the system.

Hence, the "correct" graphical model is one in which there is a node for each variable and at each time. In this case, we only have one instance of each node. However, in many systems, the dynamics do not change over time; this implies that whenever there is an arrow from $x_i[t - \tau]$ to $x_j[t]$, the associated dynamics are the same regardless of t. Moreover, physics tells us we must have $\tau \geq 0$.

Incorporating these ideas, we find a common theme:

- We have a collection of time series $\{(x_i[t])_{t=0}^\infty \mid i = 1, 2, \ldots, N\}$ which we observe
- A vector-valued stochastic process $e[t] \in \mathbb{R}^N$, pairwise uncorrelated, and unobserved, represents "random actors" in the network
- There is a system of equations governing the evolution of the $\{x_i\}$, such that

$$x_i[t] = f_i (x_i[0 : t - 1], e_i[t], u_i[t], x_1[0 : t], x_2[0 : t], \ldots, x_N[0 : t]) \quad (3)$$

- There is an unknown directed graph $\mathcal{G} = (\mathcal{V}, \mathcal{A})$ such that for all $i, j \in \mathcal{V}$, we have

$$(j, i) \in \mathcal{A} \iff \exists x_j, x_j' : f_i(\cdots, x_j, \cdots) \not\equiv f_i(\cdots, x_j', \cdots). \quad (4)$$

This model is referred to as a *Dynamic Influence Model*. This particular formulation allows the present value of each sequence to depend on the present value of potentially every other sequence. This allows us to model phenomena in which an event instantaneously causes another event, but also requires some notion of "well posedness" (we will later define one in particular, in the linear case) so that the equations are consistent.

Moreover, the e_i are assumed to be uncorrelated. This is because the e_i represent the autonomous behavior of x_i [16]; any correlation of these behaviors would necessarily be the result of some dynamics linking them together (which is what we are trying to model). This is not terribly restrictive, but can result in having to rephrase the problem. For instance, the temperatures at different locations may be statistically dependent if they are spatially close; the e_i could instead represent local, random *fluctuations* in temperature.

Understanding Cyclic Causality. Cyclic causality is often not allowed, particularly in the static case. Bayesian networks are likewise required to be directed acyclic graphs, because a cyclic conditional probability structure is generally ambiguous.

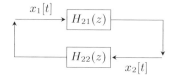

Fig. 1. Feedback model with no external inputs

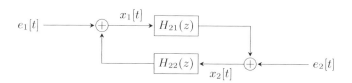

Fig. 2. Feedback model with external inputs

Yet the existence of feedback loops, fundamental to control systems, necessitate the need to consider causal loops. With the addition of a temporal component, causal loops not only make sense, but are often necessary. Models with cyclic causality have been studied, for instance in [9] and [11].

We again stress that disturbances are key to a meaningful discussion of causality. Consider the system with block diagram shown in Fig. 1; a rather familiar looking block diagram, reminiscent of the basic feedback controller studied at the most fundamental levels of control theory, except with no inputs or disturbances.

One might ask, is x_2 causing x_1, or the other way around? Clearly, both are true; a change in one will induce a change in the other, and vice versa. Since this is a physical system, both $G(z)$ and $H(z)$ must be causal. However, if we fit a linear model taking x_1 as input and x_2 as output, we will find that the best linear model is not causal at all. This is because the *future* of x_2 carries some information about the *present* value of x_1, since the present value of x_1 *caused* a change in the future values of x_2. Hence, temporal reasoning tells us that both x_1 and x_2 cause each other.

Statistical independence tells us the opposite. Since the evolution of x_1 and x_2 is deterministic, and the probability of a deterministic event is 1 regardless of what we condition on. Hence, $P(x_1 \mid x_2) = 1 = P(x_1)$ and likewise for x_2. Statistical independence tells us neither x_1 nor x_2 cause each other.

Since temporal reasoning and statistical dependence both fail us, it is difficult to meaningfully discuss causality. But should we? Consider how x_1 and x_2 evolve. If initial conditions are zero, then both x_1 and x_2 are zero. Neither one *caused* that, it's just their equilibrium state. If the initial conditions are nonzero, then what exactly happens depends on the stability of the system, but the response is clearly only caused by the *initial state* of x_1 and x_2. We contend that this, at the very least, makes for a boring system, as an entire infinite-length waveform can be condensed into a few real numbers, and no amount of data collected over time will provide any new information.

On the other hand, consider the same model augmented with a disturbance model, as in Fig. 2. In this case, it is clear that e_1 directly causally influences x_1, and that it causally influences x_2 through x_1. The reverse is true for e_2. As before, the initial state of x_1 and x_2 have an effect on their joint evolution, but this effect is diluted as e_1 and e_2 inject new information into the system. Now, x_1 and x_2 have a non-trivial joint probability structure (provided e_1 and e_2 do), and moreover this model allows intervention (by choosing e_i).

3.5   When Correlation Implies Causation

Even in a sparse network, when one variable is perturbed, the effect is felt far and wide across the entire system. A minimal causal structure should not include direct causal links between two variables when all of their common variance is explained by other paths in the network, or perhaps a common cause.

The assumption that the future cannot cause the past, together with the Pearl-Verma theorem, justifies the use of "predictive causality" to infer true causality; namely, if the *past* values of X can help predict (and are hence not independent of) the present value of Y, conditioned on all common causes of both, then there is a directed path between the past of X and the future of Y. Such a path cannot go backward in time; hence X is causing Y and not the other way around.

Since causal networks are also Bayesian networks, if X causes Y, then it will also be true that X and Y are not independent; i.e., $\Pr(Y \mid X) \neq \Pr(Y)$. This is a symmetric condition, however; the direction of causality cannot be determined from this information alone. In a dynamic setting, however, since the future cannot cause the past, we can discuss a stronger statistical condition, which in this paper we will call **predictive causality**. Given a set of random sequences $S = \{Z_1[0:t], \cdots, Z_k[0:t]\}$, we say that $X[t]$ causally predicts $Y[t]$ given S if

$$
\Pr\left(Y[t] \;\middle|\; Y[0:t-1], \bigcup_{Z \in S} Z[0:t-1], X[0:t-1]\right)
$$

$$
\neq \Pr\left(Y[t] \mid Y[0:t-1], \bigcup_{Z \in S} Z[0:t-1]\right), \tag{5}
$$

where the Z are the time series in S. This test is the general version of Granger causality [8], and the difference in these probabilities' respective entropies is called *transfer entropy* [24].

Just as correlation does not imply causation, however, "predictive causality" still does not imply true causality. Two variables may very well share similar trends but not be causally related. Hence, using predictive causality to infer causation must be handled with care. That said, the conclusion "X is a direct cause of Y" is typically made when it has been determined that *for any* set S with $X \notin S$, X causally predicts Y given S. Equivalently, if *every* predictive model for Y can be *improved* by including X as a predictor, then we conclude that X is a direct cause of Y.

This notion of causality has been controversial in the information sciences, but was later justified by the Causal Markov Condition [18, Theorem 1.4.1]: any distribution consistent with a Markovian causal model must satisfy that every node is independent of its nondescendents, given its parents. Since our observations arrive with known time stamps, we know that nothing of the form $Z[t - k]$ for $k > 0$ can be a descendent of $Y[t]$ in the causal model, as this would imply that the present caused the past.

Linear Models and Granger Causality. Predictive causality has its roots in Granger causality [8], which is equivalent to predictive causality when all variables are Gaussian and linearly related. Rather than learn $P(y[0 : t], x[0 : t])$ (or its various relevant factorizations) over all possible probability distributions, the linear and Gaussian assumption implies that we need only consider the best linear predictor.

With Z a collection of time series, define

$$\sigma^2(y \mid Z) = \min \mathbb{E}_t \left[\left(y[t] - \sum_{q \in Z} \sum_{\tau=1}^{\infty} h_{yq}[\tau] q[t - \tau] \right)^2 \right].$$

Let U be the set containing all time series, including y itself. Then, if $\sigma^2(y \mid U) < \sigma^2(y \mid U \setminus \{x[0 : t]\})$, we say that x is causing y.

Suppose the true model is:

$$x[t + 1] = \sum_{\tau=1}^{\infty} g_\tau x[t - \tau] + \varepsilon_1[t]$$

$$y[t + 1] = \sum_{\tau=1}^{\infty} h_\tau y[t - \tau] + \sum_{\tau=1}^{\infty} f_\tau x[t - \tau] + \varepsilon_2[t].$$

In this case, where the model incorporates a positive time delay (that is, y_t does not depend on x_t), then since $y_{0:t-1}$ are simply noisy functions of $x_{0:t-2}$, it is true that

$$P(x_t \mid x_{0:t-1}, y_{0:t-1}) = P(x_t \mid x_{0:t-1}), \tag{6}$$

and hence we would correctly conclude that y does not cause x.

Recall that Bayesian networks are not unique; provided all inverted forks are preserved, reversing the orientation of an arrow produces an observationally equivalent Bayesian network. When the temporal component is added to consideration this ambiguity disappears.

4   Existing Results

With a general theory of inferred causation outlined above, this section discusses specific applications to particular models. We begin with the simplest models: linear dynamics with wide-sense stationary input, and work up to more general cases.

4.1 Inferring Topology of Linear Systems

A linear dynamic graph (LDG) [11] is a pair $(H(z), \mathbf{e})$, where $\mathbf{e}$ is a vector of n rationally related, wide-sense stationary random processes with $\Phi_{\mathbf{e}}(z)$ diagonal, and $H(z) \in \mathcal{F}^{n \times n}$ with $H_{jj}(z) = 0$ for $j = 1, \ldots, n$.

The output processes $\{x_j\}$ are defined

$$\mathbf{x}[t] = \mathbf{e}[t] + H(z)\mathbf{x}[t]. \tag{7}$$

The *associated directed graph* $\mathcal{G}$ is the directed graph on vertices $\{x_1, \ldots, x_n\}$ with an arc from x_i to x_j if $H_{ji}(z) \neq 0$.

The following results are presented in [11].

1. Let $(H(z), \mathbf{e})$ be a well-posed, topologically identifiable LDG with output $\mathbf{x}$. Then the solution to the *non-causal Wiener filter problem*:

$$\underset{\hat{x}_j \in \text{tf-span}\{x_i\}_{i \neq j}}{\arg \min} \|x_j - \hat{x}_j\|^2 \tag{8}$$

is unique, and satisfies

$$\hat{x}_j = \sum_{i \neq j} W_{ji}(z) x_i, \tag{9}$$

where $W_{ji}(z) \neq 0$ implies $\{i, j\} \in kin(\mathcal{G})$.
2. If $(H(z), \mathbf{e})$ satisfies the above and is additionally *causal*, then the solution to the *causal Wiener filter problem*:

$$\underset{\hat{x}_j \in \text{ctf-span}\{x_i\}_{i \neq j}}{\arg \min} \|x_j - \hat{x}_j\|^2 \tag{10}$$

exists, is unique, and

$$\hat{x}_j = \sum_{i \neq j} W_{ji}^C(z) x_i, \tag{11}$$

where $W_{ji}^C(z) \neq 0$ implies $\{i, j\} \in kin(\mathcal{G})$.
3. If $H(z)$ is additionally *strictly* causal, then the solution to the *Granger filter problem*:

$$\underset{\hat{x}_j \in \text{ctf-span}\{x_1, \ldots, x_n\}}{\arg \min} \|z x_j - \hat{x}_j\|^2 \tag{12}$$

exists, is unique, and

$$\hat{x}_j = \sum_{i \neq j} G_{ji}(z) x_i, \tag{13}$$

where $G_{ji}(z) \neq 0$ implies $i = j$ or i is a parent of j in $\mathcal{G}$.

In the third case, we recover exactly the structure of $\mathcal{G}$, whereas in the first two cases, all that is recovered is the "kin graph," which differs from $\mathcal{G}$ in that it is *undirected*, contains the undirected version of every arc in $\mathcal{G}$, and also contains an edge between every pair of nodes with a common child in $\mathcal{G}$, called "spouses."

Links between spouses are spurious, but remain local in the sense that only nodes separated by two hops can be spuriously linked in the reconstructed graph.

If the associated graph is a directed acyclic graph (DAG), and x_i and x_j do not have an arc between them, we can find a set S that "Wiener separates"[15] x_i and x_j; that is, a set S such that

$$\arg\min_{\hat{x}_j \in \text{tf-span}(S \cup \{x_j\})} \|x_j - \hat{x}_j\|^2$$

does not depend on x_j. Since this is not true if x_i and x_j have an arc between them in the LDG, we can infer that x_i and x_j are not connected by an arc in the LDG. If a spurious link was found in the Wiener projection (11), then we can conclude that they are spouses. Moreover, for any common neighbor x_k of x_i and x_j such that $S \cup \{x_k\}$ does not Wiener separate x_i and x_j, we infer that the inverted fork $x_i \rightarrow x_k \leftarrow x_j$ must be in $\mathcal{G}$, in a process called Inductive Causation [20].

In this general setting, we recover the "pattern" of $\mathcal{G}$; that is, its undirected version along with all open inverted forks. This may leave several links for which we cannot determine the direction of causality. If those links' transfer functions are strictly causal, then we can find the direction using the Granger filter instead.

4.2 Extensions and Nonlinear Models

Cyclostationary Environment. The results of [11] apply to wide-sense stationary processes; for cyclostationary processes, [25] shows similar results by applying a transformation which renders the system multivariate stationary.

Nonlinear Dynamics and Directed Information. In LDGs for which all transfer functions are *strictly causal*, meaning there is a positive time delay in every link, the causal structure can always be uniquely identified by finding the least squares "Granger filter" [11] estimating each node from each other node. *Causally* projecting each node onto the space spanned by all other nodes disregards spurious causality relations such as "cascade" and "common cause" relationships, because it discovers that the most recent ancestor effectively explains all variation attributed to a more distant ancestor or sibling.

Granger causality [8] was developed as a method of deciding, between two processes x and y, whether the data better fit the best strictly causal linear model accepting x as an input and producing y as an output, or the best strictly causal linear model accepting y as an input and producing x as an output. The implicit assumption made is that exactly one of these two models must be valid. This neglects cases in which the correct model is not strictly causal. This may be the case when feedback is present, or when the temporal resolution of measurement is smaller than any physical time delay in the system.

It also neglects the subject of this section, namely, that the process connecting x and y is not linear. James Massey [10] defined a different quality called "directed information":

$$I(X[0:T] \rightarrow Y[0:T]) = \sum_{t=1}^{T} I(X[0:t]; Y[t] \mid Y[0:t-1])$$

$$= \sum_{t=1}^{T} \left(h\left(Y[t] \mid Y[0:t-1]\right) - h\left(Y[t] \mid Y[0:t-1], X[0:t]\right) \right), \tag{14}$$

defined for any pair of time series with a joint probability distribution. It has been shown [2] that, when applied to linear Gaussian models, directed information is equivalent to Granger causality.

Intuitively, directed information is a measure of how much better process Y can be predicted if we use the information in the past of X and Y, rather than the past of Y alone.

Just as directed information is a generalization of Granger causality to non-linear, non-Gaussian systems, Directed Information Graphs (DIG) [7,21] are a generalization of Linear Dynamic Graphs to the same, under the condition that all dynamics are strictly causal.

Link Failures and Time Variant Systems. Many physical systems change over time. The "amount of change" to a system can be quantified in many different ways, and certainly there is a point at which a system's dynamics and structure change so much that the old model no longer provides meaningful information about the system. However, when smaller changes occur (such as when the number of alternative models is finite and small), falsifying the current model in favor of an alternative should be at least as easy as learning a new model from scratch.

A body of work in particular studies the detection and isolation of failures and faults in single links within the network. An eigenspace characterization of network discernibility is presented in [3]. An approach to isolating faulty links, requiring minimal dynamics knowledge, is discussed in the continuous case in [22] by tracking jump discontinuities through the network. In directed acyclic networks, another [5] identifies corrupted links by monitoring for changes in the cross power spectral densities between output nodes in the network.

5 Conclusions

We have motivated the need for causal structure identification in large dynamical systems and argued that the era of big data has made this necessary, as we now have the ability to measure more variables than ever before. We can determine the temperature, pressure, occupancy, traffic density, etc., in any location within the system that we wish; and in complex systems, many variables can have a significant and widespread impact.

We instead look at these complex systems as networks of these variables, similar to how we might look at complex systems as networks of less complex subsystems. By networking at the variable level, we mitigate the need for first principles modeling of any simple subsystems, and avoid overlooking interactions between variables that are not obvious from first principles.

Causal modeling is also simpler than full black box modeling, as we do not necessarily need to fully model the dynamics linking two variables in order to conclude that they interact. If a full model is desired, restricting analysis to those models obeying a particular causal structure reduces the number of parameters to learn, in turn reducing computational complexity and increasing data efficiency.

We have discussed what causality means to the engineer, and how it can be inferred from passive observations. We have explained how spurious interactions can appear in data, and how inferring causality when it does not actually exists can be avoided.

Finally, we have discussed a few generative models and results pertaining to the reconstruction, at least partially, of the causal structure. If the dynamics in the network are strictly causal, then the causal structure can be identified exactly; otherwise, the kin-graph is identified. While this leaves us uncertain of the *direction* of causality, we are typically left with fewer candidate links than when we started.

Many areas of research are ongoing. One such area is tracking the causal structure over time. Many networks change gradually over time, and making slight changes to the causal model as the network evolves should be at least as easy as learning the causal structure from ground zero. Another area is in the proper handling of unobserved nodes, which as we saw can be problematic if these nodes influence multiple child nodes. Moreover, causal modeling opens opportunities for decentralized controller design. Results such as the "revolving door criterion" in [16] allow control engineers to predict the effect of adding closed-loop controllers in interconnected systems.

References

1. Amini, H., Minca, A.: Inhomogeneous financial networks and contagious links. Oper. Res. **64**(5), 1109–1120 (2016)
2. Barnett, L., Barrett, A.B., Seth, A.K.: Granger causality and transfer entropy are equivalent for Gaussian variables. Phys. Rev. Lett. **103**(23), 238701 (2009)
3. Battistelli, G., Tesi, P.: Detecting topology variations in dynamical networks. In: 54th Conference on Decision and Control, pp. 3349–3354. IEEE (2015)
4. Chernoff, H.: Approaches in sequential design of experiments. Technical report, Stanford University, CA, Department of Statistics (1973)
5. Costanzo, J.A., Materassi, D., Sinopoli, B.: Inferring link changes in acyclic networks through power spectral density variations. In: 55th Annual Allerton Conference on Communication, Control, and Computing (2017)
6. Danks, D., Plis, S.: Learning causal structure from undersampled time series. In: NIPS Workshop on Causality (2013)
7. Etesami, J., Kiyavash, N.: Directed information graphs: a generalization of linear dynamical graphs. In: American Control Conference (ACC 2014), pp. 2563–2568. IEEE (2014)
8. Granger, C.: Investigating causal relations by econometric models and cross-spectral methods. Econometrica **37**, 424–438 (1969)

9. Lacerda, G., Spirtes, P.L., Ramsey, J., Hoyer, P.O.: Discovering cyclic causal models by independent components analysis. arXiv preprint arXiv:1206.3273 (2012)
10. Massey, J.: Causality, feedback and directed information. In: Proceedings of International Symposium on Information, Theory and Application, (ISITA-1990), pp. 303–305 (1990)
11. Materassi, D., Salapaka, M.: On the problem of reconstructing an unknown topology via locality properties of the Wiener filter. IEEE Trans. Autom. Control 57(7), 1765–1777 (2012)
12. Materassi, D.: Norbert Wiener's legacy in the study and inference of causation. In: 2014 IEEE Conference on Norbert Wiener in the 21st Century (21CW), pp. 1–6. IEEE (2014)
13. Materassi, D., Innocenti, G.: Topological identification in networks of dynamical systems. IEEE Trans. Autom. Control 55(8), 1860–1871 (2010)
14. Materassi, D., Salapaka, M.V.: Network reconstruction of dynamical polytrees with unobserved nodes. In: 51st Annual Conference on Decision and Control, pp. 4629–4634. IEEE (2012)
15. Materassi, D., Salapaka, M.V.: Reconstruction of directed acyclic networks of dynamical systems. In: American Control Conference (ACC 2013), pp. 4687–4692. IEEE (2013)
16. Materassi, D., Salapaka, M.V.: Graphoid-based methodologies in modeling, analysis, identification and control of networks of dynamic systems. In: American Control Conference (ACC 2016), pp. 4661–4675. IEEE (2016)
17. Mooij, J.M., Peters, J., Janzing, D., Zscheischler, J., Shölkopf, B.: Distinguishing cause from effect using observational data: methods and benchmarks. J. Mach. Learn. Res. 17, 1–102 (2016)
18. Pearl, J.: Causality. Cambridge University Press, Cambridge (2009)
19. Pearl, J.: Simpson's paradox: an anatomy. Department of Statistics, UCLA (2011)
20. Pearl, J., Verma, T.S.: A theory of inferred causation. Stud. Logic Found. Math. 134, 789–811 (1995)
21. Quinn, C.J., Coleman, T.P., Kiyavash, N., Hatsopoulos, N.G.: Estimating the directed information to infer causal relationships in ensemble neural spike train recordings. J. Comput. Neurosci. 30(1), 17–44 (2011)
22. Rahimian, M.A., Preciado, V.M.: Detection and isolation of failures in directed networks of lti systems. IEEE Trans. Control Netw. Syst. 2(2), 183–192 (2015)
23. Sadamoto, T., Ishizaki, T., Imura, J.I.: Hierarchical distributed control for networked linear systems. In: 2014 IEEE 53rd Annual Conference on Decision and Control (CDC), pp. 2447–2452. IEEE (2014)
24. Schreiber, T.: Measuring information transfer. Phys. Rev. Lett. 85(2), 461 (2000)
25. Talukdar, S., Prakash, M., Materassi, D., Salapaka, M.V.: Reconstruction of networks of cyclostationary processes. In: 2015 IEEE 54th Annual Conference on Decision and Control (CDC), pp. 783–788. IEEE (2015)
26. Verma, T.S., Pearl, J.: Equivalence and synthesis of causal models. Technical report R-150, UCLA, Computer Science Department (1990)
27. Weerakkody, S., Sinopoli, B., Kar, S., Datta, A.: Information flow for security in control systems. In: 55th Annual Conference on Decision and Control, pp. 5065–5072. IEEE (2016)

A Formal Semantics for Traffic Sequence Charts

Werner Damm[1,2], Eike Möhlmann[1], Thomas Peikenkamp[1],
and Astrid Rakow[2(✉)]

[1] OFFIS - Institute for Information Technology, Escherweg 2,
26121 Oldenburg, Germany
{damm,e.moehlmann,peikenkamp}@offis.de
[2] Carl von Ossietzky University of Oldenburg, 26111 Oldenburg, Germany
a.rakow@uni-oldenburg.de

Abstract. This paper paves the way for a future scenario catalog-based
approach to acceptance testing for highly autonomous vehicles by providing a rigorous formal semantics for a visual specification language of
traffic sequence charts to be used for building the scenario catalog. It
builds on our previous work on Live Sequence Charts [2] that defines a
semantics sufficiently rich to cover both the requirement analysis phase
and the specification phase for highly autonomous vehicles. This formal
semantics provides the basis for tool support, in particular supporting
the future V&V environment for autonomously driving cars under development by the German automotive industry.

1 Introduction

It is well known that traditional approaches to homologation (i.e., certification
that a product meets a set of regulatory, technical, or safety requirements) fail
for highly autonomous vehicles due to the impossibility of covering sufficiently
many kilometers in field testing to achieve a statistically valid basis for building
safety cases. Extreme variability of environmental contexts results in tremendous complexity in the perception- and trajectory planning systems of highly
autonomous vehicles. The approach taken by the German automotive industry
is to build scenario catalogs that capture, for all conceivable traffic situations,
requirements on such systems to jointly ensure global safety objectives. Test
drives are to be replaced, to a significant extent, by placing the vehicle under
test in test environments, exposing the vehicle to traffic situations that cover
all scenarios in the catalog, and monitoring compliance of the vehicle's reaction
to these scenarios. Such test environments will allow testing separate from one
another the perception components (along all stages, covering preprocessed sensor data, sensor fusion, and object identification algorithms) and the trajectory
planning component (which involves exploring possible future evolutions of the

This research was partly funded by the German Federal Ministry of Education and
Research (BMBF), under grant "CrESt" (01IS16043).

M. Lohstroh et al. (Eds.): Lee Festschrift, LNCS 10760, pp. 182–205, 2018.
https://doi.org/10.1007/978-3-319-95246-8_11

currently perceived traffic situation to decide on the planned maneuver). Projects already running and pushing this approach are the Pegasus project[1] funded by the German Federal Ministry for Economic Affairs and Energy, involving all major German OEMs and Tier 1 companies, and the ENABLE-S3 project[2] funded by the Joint Undertaking ECSEL, including both German and French automotive companies. These projects also cover other domains for building test environments for autonomous systems, such as maritime and rail. OFFIS participates in both these projects and is involved in the planning of follow-up projects pushing a fast implementation of this approach.

There are several challenges which must be addressed to make this approach viable:

(C1) Given the ill-structuredness of the space of real world traffic situations, how can we achieve completeness of scenario catalogs, i.e., demonstrate with high confidence that all relevant real-world situations have been captured?

(C2) Given the remaining likelihood of experiencing failures in perception and interpretation after deployment, how can we establish a process that learns from field incidents and accidents and updates the scenario catalog to avoid such events from reoccuring in the field?

(C3) Given the complexity of real-world traffic situations, how can one at all achieve sufficiently concise specifications to make construction of scenario catalogs feasible?

(C4) How can we assure that the interpretation of scenarios, and thus interpretation of test results, is unambiguous across all test platforms?

All these challenges can only be addressed using a language for capturing scenarios that is intuitively easy to understand, and, most importantly, equipped with a formal (declarative) semantics.

Challenge C1 will be addressed by generalizing from databases of observed traffic flows. A minimal requirement for completeness of a scenario catalog w.r.t. a database of observations is to ensure that a particular observed traffic behavior is already covered by at least one scenario of the catalog. To this end, we define a notion of formal satisfaction, formalizing whether a particular behavior satisfies a scenario specification or not. Although the issue of completeness of the set observations remains, approaches like [1] may guide the design of an ontology to classify observations and index gaps in observed behaviors. Moreover, as experienced in the play-out approach for Live Sequence Charts (LSCs) [11], a formal semantics provides a basis for playing out the current scenario catalog, thus generating traffic flows which in an expert can judge for unrealistic or missing real-life traffic flows.

Challenge C2 requires a formal semantics to identify the gaps between the space of possible worlds described in the scenario catalog, and the concrete in-field incident or accident. Specifically, forthcoming regulations will require autonomously driving cars to record all those perceived environmental artifacts

---

[1] www.pegasusprojekt.de.

[2] www.enable-s3.eu.

relevant to trajectory planning as well as the car's trajectory control for a sufficiently long time period. A formal semantics allows to check the failed scenario(s), offering a basis for refining the scenario specifications to cope with the observed failure in perception or interpretation of the real world.

Challenge C3 demands the use of a declarative specification language, where one single scenario specification stands for a possibly extremely large set of real world traffic situations, defined unambiguously through the satisfaction relation. Also, declarative specification languages allow for separation of concerns, such as focusing on particular kinds of critical situations in isolation, knowing that the car can only pass the test if all scenarios are passed.

Finally, Challenge C4 can be addressed by automatically synthesizing monitors for compliance testing, using the standardized formal semantics.

This paper provides a formal semantics for the declarative visual specification language of traffic sequence charts (henceforth called TSCs), and thus meets a key industrial need. Not surprisingly, this comes with a number of scientific challenges outlined below, which we address by building on a number of previous publications, notably our previous work on introducing LSCs [2], and on automatic synthesis of driving strategies for autonomous vehicles [6].

Much as Message Sequence Charts [15] were lacking expressiveness and formal semantics, motivating the extension to Live Sequence Charts, the ongoing industrial pre-standardization effort for capturing scenarios, called OpenSCE-NARIO [22], falls significantly short in being able to address the above challenges. OpenSCENARIO allows describing what we call existential LSCs, i.e., to give examples of desired behaviors, rather than being able to specify requirements on all possible behaviors, such as in what we call universal LSCs. TSCs "inherit" from LSCs the concepts related to distinguishing between possible and mandatory behaviors, the concepts of pre-charts which is key for characterizing those situations from when on all behaviors must comply to universal charts, and cold and hot conditions for distinguishing case-distinctions from failures. TSCs go beyond LSCs in the sense that they:

- provide a visual specification language for describing first-order predicates on traffic situations;
- introduce a concept we call *oracle* that reflects the need to make current moves dependent on expected future evolutions of traffic flows;
- must cope with a priori unbounded numbers of traffic participants, such as [7];
- must cope with dynamic evolutions of traffic scenarios governed by complex vehicle dynamic models of the car under design, which depend on road surface conditions, and thus generally require the expressivity of non-linear hybrid automata; and
- must include dynamic models of other traffic participants, reflecting observed behaviors in real traffic situations, such as those which can be expressed by probabilistic hybrid automata.

The challenge in providing a formal semantics thus rests in unifying concepts sufficiently expressive to specify requirements on flows of unbounded parallel compositions of (probabilistic) non-linear hybrid automata.

In this paper, we factor out perception failures and assume TSCs with perfect information, thus talking about ground truth in say the position, relative distance, and acceleration of cars. Therefore, we neglect probabilism. Also, we factor out the topic of cooperative driving strategies, and focus on specifying requirements to be achieved by a single car, in the remainder of this paper called *ego*, without further assistance from cooperating vehicles. Neither do we specify communications within TSC for now. Here we represent all traffic participants (including ego) by non-deterministic non-linear hybrid automata and omit means to specify communication. Both these restrictions will be dropped in future work. To deal with perception failures and uncertainties we plan to use probabilistic non-linear hybrid automata. LSCs will be integrated into the TSC formalism to model communication. In this paper we consider only TSCs that consist of so-called snapshot charts. Illustrations of industrial applications of TSCs can be found in [5].

Outline. In the next section we present basic notions. We give an introductory example in Sect. 2. In Sect. 3 we introduce formal notions. An overview of the elements in a single snapshot is given in Sect. 4. Then we show how a snapshot is translated into a multi-sorted first-order formula. Snapshots are combined to build snapshot graphs. Snapshot Charts (SCs) are annotated snapshots graphs. We introduce snapshot graphs and SCs in Sect. 4.4 and then explain how a corresponding real-time formula is derived by composing the snapshot formulas. Before drawing our conclusions, we survey related work in Sect. 5.

2   Example

To give an impression of a TSC specification, we sketch the development of a collision avoidance maneuver as presented in [5]. We consider two adjacent, same-direction freeway lanes, car objects, and obstacle objects (i.e., objects of low or zero velocity, e.g., a construction site or a slow moving vehicle). We examine the scenarios that may arise when a car that drives in the right lane and approaches an obstacle.

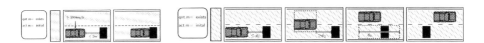

Fig. 1. Car collides with obstacle.   **Fig. 2.** Car avoids collision with obstacle.

We first structure the space of possible scenarios that could unfold in that situation. There are two basic scenarios: either the car stays in the right lane and collides with the obstacle, or it changes lane and avoids the collision. Figure 1 shows a TSC that models a collision scenario. TSCs are to be read from left to right. So, Fig. 1 consists of a header followed by three *snapshots* (*sns*). Sn_1 (black frame with gray hatching) is the empty snapshot and specifies that we allow anything to happen before sn_2. Sn_2 specifies our initial situation: The car is in the right lane, distance $\leq d_1$ away from the obstacle (the black rectangle). The *distance arrow* ⊢⊣ is used to specify bounds on distances between objects. The third snapshot describes a collision between the car and the obstacle. The hatching on the lanes denotes that—for now—we do not constrain whether there are other objects ("don't care"). Figure 2 specifies the collision-avoidance scenario. Again, the sequence of sn_1, sn_2 expresses that *eventually* sn_2 is reached—the car is $\leq d_1$ away from the obstacle. Before the car gets closer to the obstacle than d_2, it starts changing lane (cf. sn_3). The dashed *somewhere-box* surrounding the car indicates that the car may be anywhere within the box. The whole process of changing onto the left lane is hence covered by sn_3. Sn_4 describes that the car has moved into the left lane and drives past the obstacle. Finally, the last snapshot describes that the car has passed the obstacle. Note that we require snapshots (of a sequence) to contiguously hold during a trajectory. Hence, the somewhere-boxes at sn_3 and sn_4 are an important mean to write succinct specifications.

The headers in Figs. 1 and 2 declare that both TSCs are to be understood existentially (quantification mode = exists). That is, we specify that the scenarios of these figures exist. Existential TSCs allow cataloging observations of the real world. In contrast, the TSC of Fig. 3 specifies behavior of ego, the car under design, at a collision avoidance maneuver. It specifies that if ego gets into the situation of sn_1—ego is closer than d_1 to an obstacle—and if the left lane *will be* free for a time duration greater than t (cf. sn_2), then ego changes to the left lane and drives past the obstacle. The TSC of Fig. 3 uses a premise-consequence chart to express "if ego [. . .], then ego changes lane [. . .]." The dashed hexagon contains the premise. Right of it follows the consequence. Our premise consists of two parts: It specifies the initial situation via sn_1 (so the premise expresses "if ego is closer than d_1 to the obstacle") and via sn_2 the future (which adds to the premise: "and if there will be no car at the left lane within a distance of d_4 behind ego up to d_5 in front of ego"). We use the *nowhere-box*, a black frame with diagonal lines, to denote that we rule out the presence of cars within the box. The dimensions of the nowhere-box are specified via the distance arrows anchored at the borders of ego's somewhere-box. The hour glass on top of sn_2 specifies that the left lane will be clear for a time duration greater than or equal to t. The consequence (sn_3 to sn_5) is like sn_3 to sn_5 of Fig. 2, but with the additional annotation of a ☺ bar above it. This annotation specifies how consequence (sn_3 to sn_5) and the future (sn_2 abbreviated by ☺) synchronize; ego has to perform the lane change while the left lane is guaranteed to be clear. Thus, future snapshot sn_2 is concurrent to sn_3 and ends some time during sn_4.

As the activation mode of the TSC of Fig. 3 is always and the quantification mode is all, all trajectories have to satisfy the TSC and if at any time the

Fig. 3. Rule: change lane to avoid collision, if next lane is clear.

premise matches ("ego is close to an obstacle and the left lane will be clear"), the consequence is implied: ("ego changes to the left lane"). The TSC of Fig. 3 specifies a very abstract lane change rule—chosen here for simplicity and ease of the example. A TSC for a concrete implementation will rephrase the future part of the premise of Fig. 3 ("the left lane will be clear") in terms of sensor readings and on-board prediction so that a sufficiently free corridor is guaranteed.

3   Preliminaries

A TSC specification is a set of TSCs together with a world model over which the TSCs are interpreted. In this paper, a TSC consists of an SC only. The formal semantics of TSCs is given by a translation into a multi-sorted temporal formula of a logic $\mathcal{L}$. In the following we introduce the logic $\mathcal{L}$ and the formalism we consider in this paper to specify the world model.

A Multi-sorted Real Time Logic. We consider a multi-sorted first-order real-time logic, which we simply call $\mathcal{L}$ from here on. We consider a *signature* $\Sigma = (Var, \Pi, \Upsilon, \Gamma, \sigma)$ to be given that comprises a set of variable symbols Var and a set of predicate symbols Π, a set of function symbols Υ, a set of type symbols Γ and a function σ that assigns types (sorts) to variable, predicate and function symbols. We denote the set of type respecting ground terms as $\mathcal{I}_\Sigma^T$.

Since TSCs formalize objects and their attributes at a certain time, we introduce the following distinction of variables: $Var = Var_{Obj} \,\dot\cup\, Var_T$, where Var_T is a finite set of so-called *time variables* that take on values in $Time := \mathbb{R}_{\geq 0}$ and Var_{Obj} is a finite or infinite set of so-called *object variables* o_i.

The formulas of $\mathcal{L}$ are inductively defined by the grammar $\varphi := \texttt{True} \mid q(o_1, \ldots, o_n) \mid \exists w\, \varphi(w) \mid \neg\varphi \mid \varphi_1 \wedge \varphi_2 \mid \varphi_1 \mathsf{U}_{[t_1, t_2]}\varphi_2 \mid \tau_1 \bowtie \tau_2$ where $q \in \Pi$ is a predicate of arity greater than or equal to zero, o_i are object variables, w is an object or time variable, t_1, t_2 are time variables, $\tau_1, \tau_2 \in \mathcal{I}_\Sigma^T$, $\sigma(\tau_1) = \sigma(\tau_2)$, and $\bowtie \in \{<, \leq, =, \geq, >\}$.

We assume now a structure $\mathcal{M} = (\mathcal{U}, \mathcal{I})$ of Σ to be given where the *universe* $\mathcal{U}$ is a non-empty set of concrete values and $\mathcal{I}$ is an interpretation of the symbols in Π, Υ, Γ that respect the typing. We consider only valuations μ that respect the variable types. Further, we assume that the local state of each object is made up of its identity and list of attributes $\mathcal{A}(o) = \{a_1, \ldots, a_n\}$ with a fixed but arbitrary order of a_i's. So σ assigns to each object variable $o \in Var_{Obj}$ a type $\mathsf{T} \in \Gamma$, such that a state of on object of type T is a value in $\sigma(id) \times \sigma(a_1) \times \ldots \times \sigma(a_n)$. Given

188 W. Damm et al.

an object variable o, we denote $o.id$ to refer to the object's identity and we use $o.a_i$ to refer to the object's attribute a_i.

The semantics of $\mathcal{L}$ is defined at the end of this section, after the introduction of the semantic model over which we will interpret $\mathcal{L}$'s formulas.

World Model. The TSC semantics is given in terms of formulas of $\mathcal{L}$, that are interpreted on a world model WM. In this paper we assume that WM is given via the parallel composition of (finitely or infinitely many) hybrid automata H_i, that are instances of finitely many automaton classes $\mathcal{C}_j$, where an automata class is defined by the same dynamics laws and list of variables. Intuitively, the automata instances represent objects within the world model. In the next paragraph we present a notion of hybrid automata apt to be used as a formal basis for our world model.

The type, $\sigma(o)$, of an object variable o gets interpreted as an automaton class $\mathcal{C}_i{}^3$. The valuation $\mu(o.a_j)$ at time t of attribute $o.a_j$ is then the value of the variable a_j of H_i at time t. So, for simplicity we do not distinguish between object attributes and variables of H_i.

As minimal requirement on WM we require a global coordinate system in $\mathbb{R} \times \mathbb{R}$ where each object of WM has at least a defined reference position, *pos*.

Although we allow infinitely many objects in the world model, we require that only finitely many are alive at any given time. To this end, we require that a TSC signature has a unary predicate $\texttt{alive}$ and there be an appropriate interpretation of $\texttt{alive}(o)$ to distinguish whether or not o is currently alive in WM. As in [6] the process of becoming alive or non-alive is assumed to be governed by rules that reflect plausibilities of the world model.

The requirements on WM so far are very general in order to impose minimal restrictions. As a WM-instance for traffic scenarios, we have a model in mind, where we distinguish the environment from the objects within the environment. Further, we assume that automata instances of one dedicated class correspond to the type of the car under design, which we call $\texttt{ego}$, so that we can specify requirements on $\texttt{ego}$. Objects of WM have sensors to perceive their surroundings (cf. Fig. 4). A sensor of a car is modeled via an input variable of the hybrid automaton H_{car}. Further, H_{car} controls its acceleration; the acceleration is an output of H_{car} and determines the evolution of the car's position within the environment. To model sensors that observe the object within a sensor orientation (e.g. up to 50 m in front), we postulate that an object has sensor input variables. A topology automaton similar to [3] observes all objects and the environment, and writes as output these sensor variables. It updates these variables so that the front sensor of an object is determined by the position of the object that is currently in front of it. We refer within TSC to objects and the environment, but not to the topology automaton.

---

[3] More generally, a type t is a pair $(\mathcal{U}, Idx)$ where $\mathcal{U}$ is a $|Var_{\sigma(o)}|$ dimensional subspace of WM's state space. Idx specifies the dimensions of WM that belong to objects of t. Given a state $\mathbf{X}$ of WM, $(x_{id_1} \ldots x_{id_n})^T$ gives the state of an object of t, where $(id_1, \ldots, id_n) \in Idx$.

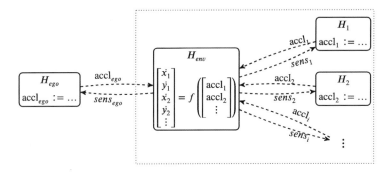

Fig. 4. Sketch of a world model as parallel composition of hybrid automata.

Hybrid Automata and their Runs. In this section we introduce an automata model that is apt to formalize world models. To this end, we consider hybrid I/O automata (HIOA) that distinguish between input, output, and local variables.

An HIOA H is a tuple $(\mathbb{M}, Var^{loc}, Var^{in}, Var^{out}, R^{dscr}, R^{cnt}, \Phi^{init}, \Theta^{inv})^4$ where

- $\mathbb{M}$ is a finite set of *modes*;
- Var^{loc}, Var^{in} and Var^{out} are disjoint sets of *local, input and output variables* over $\mathbb{R}$. We denote $Var^{loc} \cup Var^{in} \cup Var^{out}$ as Var and $Var^{loc} \cup Var^{out}$ as Var^C, the set of controlled variables. $\mathbf{X} \in \mathbb{R}^{|Var|}$ denotes a state of H, where we assume a fixed but arbitrary order of $v \in Var$. Also we denote as x_i the i-th coefficient of $\mathbf{X}$;
- Φ^{init} is a predicate over Var and a mode variable $v_\mathbb{M}$ which describes all combinations of *initial states and modes*;
- Θ^{inv} associates with each mode $m \in \mathbb{M}$ a *local invariant* formula $\Theta^{inv}(m)$;
- R^{dscr} is the *discrete transition relation* with elements $(m, G, \mathcal{A}, m')$ where $m, m' \in \mathbb{M}$, G is a first-order predicate over Var, and $\mathcal{A}$ is a first-order predicate over $Var \cup Var^{C+}$, where Var^{C+} holds decorated variants of variables in Var^C and represents the value after the discrete update. R^{dscr} consists of disjoint sets R^{dscr}_U, the urgent transitions, and R^{dscr}_L, the lazy transitions; and
- R^{cnt} defines the continuous evolutions at each mode m via the function $R^{cnt}(m)$ that maps each $\mathbf{X} \in \mathbb{R}^{|Var|}$ onto a closed subset of $\mathbb{R}^{|Var^C|}$, which is taken as the right-hand side of a differential inclusion.

Let (τ_i) be a *time sequence*, i.e., a sequence of monotonically increasing values of *Time* with $\tau_0 = 0$. A *trajectory* (π_i) with switching times (τ_i) is a sequence of continuously differentiable functions $\pi_i : [\tau_i, \tau_{i+1}) \to \mathbb{R}_{>0}$. $(\pi_i)^t$ denotes the trajectory (π_i) shifted by time t so that $(\pi_i)^t(t') = (\pi_i)(t' + t)$ and $\tau^t(0) = 0$, and with j the smallest index with $\tau_j > t$, $\forall i > 0 : \tau_i^t = \tau_{j+i} - t$. We define

---

[4] HIOAs were introduced by Lynch et al. in [18]. The original definition additionally defines local, input, and output actions. These are omitted here since we do not yet specify communication. However, we plan to integrate LSCs to specify communications.

$\pi(t)$ as the $\pi_i(t)$, such that $\forall j > i : \tau_j > t$, i.e., $\pi(t)$ is the system state after all (possibly super-dense) switches that occur at time t.

A sequence (ρ_i) is a *run* of H with switching times (τ_i), where $\rho_i = [M_i, \mathbf{X}_i^T]^T$, $\mathbf{X}_i = \begin{bmatrix} \mathbf{X}_i^C \\ \mathbf{X}_i^I \end{bmatrix}$, $M_i : [\tau_i, \tau_{i+1}] \to \mathbb{M}$, $\mathbf{X}_i^C : [\tau_i, \tau_{i+1}] \to \mathbb{R}^{|Var^C|}$, and $\mathbf{X}_i^I : [\tau_i, \tau_{i+1}] \to \mathbb{R}^{|Var^m|}$ are continuously differentiable functions, and when it satisfies:

- (ρ_i) starts at an initial state, $\rho_0(0) \models \Phi^{\text{init}}$;
- mode changes at switching times only, $\forall i \in \mathbb{N} \ \forall t \in [\tau_i, \tau_{i+1}) : M_i(t) = M(\tau_i)$;
- the continuous evolution is governed by R^{cnt}, $\forall i \in \mathbb{N}$

$$\forall t \in (\tau_i, \tau_{i+1}) : (d\mathbf{X}_i^C/dt(t), \mathbf{X}_i(t)) \models R^{\text{cnt}}(M_i(\tau_i));$$

- invariants hold, $\forall i \in \mathbb{N} \ \forall t \in [\tau_i, \tau_{i+1}) : \mathbf{X}_i(t) \models \Theta^{\text{inv}}(M_i(t))$;
- urgent discrete transitions are immediately executed, $\forall i \in \mathbb{N}$
  $\forall t \in [\tau_i, \tau_{i+1}) \ \forall (M_i(t), \phi, \mathcal{A}, m') \in R_U^{\text{dscr}}$ we have that $\mathbf{X}_i(t) \not\models \phi$; and
- at switching times either new values are assigned according to R^{dscr} or input changes or the hybrid state is unchanged (stuttering), i.e.

$$\forall i \in \mathbb{N} : (M_i(\tau_{i+1}) = M_{i+1}(\tau_{i+1}) \wedge \mathbf{X}_i^C(\tau_{i+1}) = \mathbf{X}_{i+1}^C(\tau_{i+1}))$$
$$\vee (\exists (m, \phi, \mathcal{A}, m') \in R^{\text{dscr}} : M_i(\tau_{i+1}) = m \wedge M_{i+1}(\tau_{i+1}) = m'$$
$$\wedge \mathbf{X}_{i+1}(\tau_{i+1}) \models \mathcal{A}[Var^C/\mathbf{X}_i^C(\tau_{i+1})] \wedge \mathbf{X}_i^I(\tau_{i+1}) = \mathbf{X}_{i+1}^I(\tau_{i+1})).$$

So the evolution of Var^C is determined by H itself, while values of Var^{in} are assumed to be determined by the environment such that Var^{in} is unconstrained (by H). The projection of a run of H onto $\mathbb{R}^{|Var|}$ is called a trajectory of H.

In case two HIOA $H_i, i \in \{1, 2\}$, share only input variables or read the other's output variables, we define the composition of the two. The parallel composition of H_1 and H_2, $H_1 \| H_2 = H$, is given by

- $\mathbb{M} = \mathbb{M}_1 \times \mathbb{M}_2$;
- $Var^{out} = Var_1^{out} \dot{\cup} Var_2^{out}$, $Var^{in} = (Var_1^{in} \cup Var_2^{in}) - Var^{out}$ and $Var^{loc} = Var_1^{loc} \dot{\cup} Var_2^{loc}$;
- $R^{\text{cnt}}((m_1, m_2)) = R_1^{\text{cnt}}(m_1) \wedge R_2^{\text{cnt}}(m_2)$;
- R_U^{dscr} that consists of transitions:
  (a) $((m_1, m_2), \Phi_1, \mathcal{A}_1, (m_1', m_2))$ for each $(m_1, \Phi_1, \mathcal{A}_1, m_1') \in R_{1,U}^{\text{dscr}}$; and
  (b) transitions of the form (a) with the role of H_1 and H_2 interchanged,
- R_L^{dscr} that is defined analogously to R_U^{dscr}; and
- $\Phi^{\text{init}} = \Phi_1^{\text{init}} \wedge \Phi_2^{\text{init}}$ and $\Theta((m_1, m_2)) = \Theta_1(m_1) \wedge \Theta_2(m_2)$.

Note that input variables of H_i become local variables, if they are driven by outputs of H_j, while output variables stay outputs. We denote the composition of infinitely many hybrid automata H_i, $(\ldots ((H_1 \| H_2) \| H_3) \| \ldots)$, as $\|_\infty H_i$.

Semantics of $\mathcal{L}$. The $\models$ relation is defined inductively over the structure of the formula. To this end, we consider (i) a structure $\mathcal{M}$ of Σ that interprets Σ's symbols on WM; (ii) an infinite trajectory, (π_i), of WM; and (iii) a valuation μ to be given that assigns values to the free variables of a formula φ. We write $\{o \mapsto (\pi_i)|_{Var_{H_i}}\}$ to denote that the value of o at time t is determined by the value of $(\pi_i)(t)|_{Var_{H_i}}$. Since the valuation of object variables is time dependent, the values assigned for object variables need to be time shifted analogously to the trajectory at the definition of the temporal operator U.

For $\varphi = \mathtt{True} \mid q(v_1, \ldots, v_n) \mid t_1 \bowtie t_2 \mid \neg\varphi' \mid \varphi_1 \wedge \varphi_2$ the $\models$ relation is defined as usual.

$(\pi_i), \mu \models \exists t\, \varphi(t)$ iff for some $val \in Time$ it holds that $(\pi_i), \mu' \models \varphi$ with $\mu' := \mu \cup \{t \mapsto val\}$,

$(\pi_i), \mu \models \exists o\, \varphi(o)$ iff for some H_i of automaton class $\mathcal{C}$ holds that $(\pi_i), \mu' \models \varphi$ with $\mu' := \mu \cup \{o \mapsto (\pi_i)|_{Var_{H_i}}\}$ and $\mathcal{I}(\sigma(o)) = \mathcal{C}$.

$(\pi_i), \mu \models \varphi_1 \mathsf{U}_{[t_1, t_2]} \varphi_2$ iff for some $\tau \in [\mu(t_1), \mu(t_2)]$, $(\pi_i)^\tau, \mu^\tau \models \varphi_2$ and $(\pi_i)^u, \mu^u \models \varphi_1$ for all $u \in (0, \tau)$.

The order of precedence is $\{\neg\}, \{\Box, \Diamond\}, \{\wedge\}, \{\vee, \rightarrow, \leftrightarrow\}, \{\mathsf{U}\}$.

Let φ be a closed formula of $\mathcal{L}$ and WM be a HIOA that is interpreted as parallel composition of (possibly infinitely many) hybrid automata. WM $\models \mathsf{A}\varphi$ iff all runs of WM satisfy φ and WM $\models \mathsf{E}\varphi$ iff some run of WM satisfies φ.

4 Compositional Semantics

In this section we present a formal semantics for TSCs that is based on SCs only. The integration of LSCs is future work. Due to lack of space we consider only two headers (A) act.m = initial and qnt.m = exist or (B) act.m = always and qnt.m = all. We start with an overview of snapshots and their semantics, then we introduce snapshot graphs and the more general SCs and their semantics.

4.1 A TSC Specification

A TSC specification is a set of TSCs together with a world model WM about which the TSC formulas are interpreted.

4.2 Snapshots in the Spatial View

In the following we give an overview of snapshots at the spatial view. Their formal semantics will be given in Sect. 4.3 by a translation into a first-order formula. In the spatial view, the placement of symbols specifies the relative positioning of the respective objects. The spatial view certainly represents an important aspect of traffic maneuvers. Properties like collision freedom, distances within a platoon or successful parking maneuvers require reasoning about the spatial dimension. Other views are likely to be helpful as well and nicely combinable within TSCs, but these have not been designed yet.

Fig. 5. Presence: there is a car. Other objects may be there.

Fig. 6. Absence: there is an area of 0.5 km × 1 km where *nowhere* is a car.

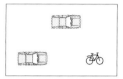

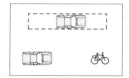

Fig. 7. Relative placement of objects. Constraints on the x- and y- positions of all objects are implied.

Fig. 8. Constraints that relate the positions of the s-box to (i) objects at the bottom and (ii) the upper car are implied. No constraints relate the upper car and the bottom objects.

Firstly, a snapshot collects constraints that hold conjunctively. Hence, the empty snapshot denotes **True**. To fill a snapshot with life, we place visual symbols inside a snapshot frame. The following list gives an overview on the snapshot syntax.

1. Placing a symbol within a snapshot frame means we require such an object to be present. The *nowhere-box* (n-box) allows us to rule out that certain objects are present. At default, we assume that everything is possible, i.e., presence or absence of any object of the world. Figures 5 and 6 illustrate how presence and absence can be expressed.
2. We annotate that objects are in a certain state (have certain attribute values), either by using an appropriately modified object symbol (a car with highlighted indicators) or by labeling it with an appropriate predicate.
3. We specify the placement of objects.
   (a) If we place an object symbol within a snapshot next to another symbol, we specify the relative placement of the respective objects. E.g., we specify in Fig. 7 that, from left to right, first there is the bottom car, then the upper car and then a bike. Any symbol represents at least a distinguished position of its represented object, an *anchor*. A symbol may also represent other anchors, such as its minimal and maximal values along the x- and y-axis, $\underline{x}$, $\overline{x}$, $\underline{y}$ and $\overline{y}$. The relative placement of symbol(anchor)s yields constraints for on the respective objects.
   (b) If we place an object symbol within a *somewhere-box* (s-box), it means that the represented object may be anywhere within the box. Likewise, an n-box means that the object may not be anywhere within the n-box. That way, the spatial order among objects within the snapshot does not need to be total. An illustrating example is given in Fig. 8, where the top

car is within the s-box, allowing it, e.g., to share the same x-position with the other car or with the bike.

(c) We may define distances between objects via distance lines (cf. Fig. 10). These can be considered as special case of predicate arrows (cf. below).

4. We annotate that objects have relations with each other via predicate arrows. Therefore, we connect the related object symbols via an arrow and label it with a predicate of our signature Σ (cf. Fig. 9).

5. We may negate a snapshot by crossing it out (inscribing dashed diagonals).

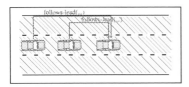

Fig. 9. The leader-follower relation.

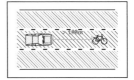

Fig. 10. A car $\geq 100\,$m behind a bike.

4.3   Snapshot Semantics

In the following, we will explain how visual elements in snapshots can be translated into first-order logic formulas referring to the world model. We first sketch the basic translation scheme and give an illustrative example (cf. Fig. 12). We distinguish between symbols $\jmath$ and symbol occurrences s. A symbol like ⬛ can occur in the same snapshot several times (three times in Fig. 9). During the translation process, object symbol occurrences get associated to object variables, and constraints on these variables are derived that encode the visual snapshot. An object symbol $\jmath$ usually encodes constraints on the object type and state of the represented object. An occurrence s of $\jmath$ additionally has a position within a snapshot from which we derive constraints on the relative placement of objects.

For the translation, we assume a so-called *symbol dictionary* (s-dictionary) to be given. The s-dictionary defines the interpretation of visual symbols in terms of the signature Σ and formulas of $\mathcal{L}$. (i) For an object symbol $\jmath$, the s-dictionary specifies $\mathsf{type}_{sdict}(\jmath)$, a type $\mathsf{T} \in \Gamma$. Occurrences s of $\jmath$ get translated to object variables $o_{s.id}$ of type T; (ii) For all modifications $\jmath'$ of an object symbol $\jmath$ (cf. item 2), it specifies a unary predicate $0_{\jmath'}(o_{s.id})$ of $\mathcal{L}$, that encodes the constraints visualized via the modification of $\jmath$; and (iii) The s-dictionary specifies spatial characteristics. For the spatial view we require that each symbol $\jmath$ has an *anchor* position $\jmath.pos$, which is a dedicated position within the symbol or it has to have anchors $\jmath.\underline{x}$, $\jmath.\overline{x}$, $\jmath.\underline{y}$, $\jmath.\overline{y}$. A symbol's anchors are declared at the s-dictionary as, e.g., shown in Fig. 11. By default, $s.\jmath.w$ is translated to $o_{s.id}.w$ where $w \in \{pos, \underline{x}, \overline{x}, \underline{y}, \overline{y}\}$. The anchors $\underline{x}, \overline{x}, \underline{y}, \overline{y}$ represent a bounding box by being interpreted as minimal and maximal positions in two dimensions.

To deal with (s- and n-)boxes in our translation, we introduce the notion of *frames*. Boxes can be nested; if, for instance, we place at a snapshot an s-box

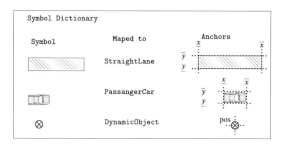

Fig. 11. Excerpt of a symbol dictionary.

and within this s-box a bike symbol and in front of it an n-box symbol within which we place a car symbol, as at the top of Fig. 12 (1), we specify *"somewhere is a bike and in front of it nowhere is a car"*). So the meaning of the symbol occurrences also depends on their container, their frame. A snapshot sn spans a frame, f_{sn}. Also each box symbol occurrence b spans a frame, f_b. Further, we define that a symbol occurrence s belongs to frame f, if s is within the symbol occurrence b spanning f, $f_b = f$, and if there is another symbol b' spanning $f_{b'}$ that contains s then it also contains b, i.e., s is directly placed in f. In our above example, the s-box belongs to the snapshot's frame while the bike and the n-box belong to the s-box's frame. The car belongs to the n-box's frame.

For the translation, we consider the set $\mathcal{S}_f$ of occurrences of object and box symbols that belong to frame f. We assume that each symbol occurrence $s \in \mathcal{S}_f$ has an identity and a position in $\mathbb{R} \times \mathbb{R}$ for each of its anchors. We write $s.\jmath$ to denote the occurring symbol. Further, we consider the set $\mathcal{A}_f$ of occurrences of predicate arrows (cf. item 4) that connect a symbol occurrence $s \in \mathcal{S}_f$ to a symbol occurrence s' at a frame (transitively) containing f. Also, $a \in \mathcal{A}_f$ has an identity and we denote its source symbol occurrence as $a.s$ and its target symbol occurrence as $a.s'$.

To translate a snapshot (cf. Algorithm 1) we recursively translate the snapshot frame. To translate a frame f we (i) derive constraints that capture the meaning of the (object) symbols $\jmath$ with occurrence s at f, $s \in \mathcal{S}_f$. If $s.\jmath$ is a box, we use as constraint the formula of the content of s here; (ii) We reflect the relative placement of symbols of f; (iii) encode that the symbols of f are within f; and (iv) reflect predicate arrows $a \in \mathcal{A}_f$ between (a) symbols of f and (b) symbols at f or at frames containing f.

For an example, let us consider the first snapshot at Fig. 12. We highlight the currently translated elements by a white background and grey out its surroundings.

(1) of Fig. 12 shows the initial snapshot. (2) The top-level frame gets translated to *"There are three lanes next to each other. In the top lane is a s-box swb and within it, φ_{swb} holds. In the middle lane is a car. In the bottom lane is a n-box nwb and within it $\neg\varphi_{nwb}$ holds. On the x-axis, first comes the n-box's rear, then the s-box's rear, then the car's rear, then the car's front, then the s-box's*

Fig. 12. Steps of snapshot translation

front, then the n-box's front." (3) The s-box *swb* is translated to $\varphi_{swb} =$ *"There is a bike and directly in front of it is a n-box within which* $\neg\varphi'_{nwb}$ *holds."* (4) The n-box at the top lane is translated to $\varphi'_{nwb} =$ *"There is a car faster than the car at the middle lane.".* (5) The content of the bottom n-box gets $\varphi_{nwb} :=$ *"There is a bike, and in front of it a car.".* Put together: *There are three lanes next to each other. In the top lane, somewhere within area A1, is a bike and directly in front of it is no car faster than the car in the middle lane. In the middle lane is a car. In the bottom lane nowhere is first a bike and then a car. We also derive the following order of anchors on the x-axis: Area A1 is included by the x-positions of area A3, the bottom n-box. The x-position of the car is included in the x-positions of A1.*

To track an object along a snapshot sequence, we introduce in the next section the bulletin board, which is a visual means to assign to all occurrences of a symbol the same identity across all snapshots of an SC. Symbols with identities have a global scope. Hence the translation procedure of Algorithm 1 takes a set $\mathcal{S}_B$ containing symbols with a unique identifier as its input. We use $\mathcal{S}_f$, $\mathcal{A}_f$ as before. Additionally, we denote by $\mathcal{S}_f^{\text{NB}}$ the set of n-box occurrences at frame f, $\mathcal{S}_f^{\text{SB}}$ denotes the set of s-box occurrences at f, and $\mathcal{S}_f^0$ is the set $\mathcal{S}_f \setminus (\mathcal{S}_f^{\text{NB}} \cup \mathcal{S}_f^{\text{SB}})$. At line 3 a quantifier opens a local scope for each symbol occurrence $s \in \mathcal{S}_f \setminus \mathcal{S}_B$[5] and binds an object variable $o_{s.id}$. Predicates on these object variables are added at lines 4 to 9 where the local scope ends. We do not quantify an object variable $o_{s.id}$ if $s \in \mathcal{S}_B$ as these variables will be globally quantified (cf. Sect. 4.7). At line 4, we require an object $o_{s.id}$ is alive (cf. Sect. 3), when s is placed at a frame. The predicate $\mathsf{O}_{s.s}(o_{s.id})$ at line 5 encodes constraints encoding the features visualized by $s.s$ (cf. item 2). These constraints are defined in the s-dictionary. At line 6, we capture the placement of symbol occurrences s of frame f, $\mathcal{S}_f$, relative to (i) symbol occurrences in the same frame $s' \in \mathcal{S}_f$; and (ii) the symbol occurrence that spans the frame, $\mathcal{S}_{spans(f)}$. $\mathcal{S}_{spans(f)}$ contains either the box symbol that spans f or is empty if f is the top most frame. $\mathsf{T}_{s,s'}(o_{s.id}, o_{s'.id})$ translates the relative placement of symbols to constraints on the placement of objects. That is, if $s.pos \bowtie s'.pos$, then basically $\mathsf{T}_{s,s'}(o_{s.id}, o_{s'.id}) = o_{s.id}.pos \bowtie o_{s'.id}.pos$ with $\bowtie \in \{<, \leq, =, \geq, >\}$. For the sake of brevity, we refrain from giving a detailed definition of $\mathsf{T}_{s,s'}$, which takes the sets of anchors into account that are defined for $s.s$ and $s'.s$. At line 7 the predicates at arrows between two symbols s and s' get translated to predicates on $o_{s.id}$ and $o_{s'.id}$. Lines 8 and 9 fill in the content of box symbols, where an n-box's content formula gets negated. We slightly simplified the algorithm by treating boxes simply as objects, which we interpret to trivially

---

[5] In abuse of notation $\mathcal{S}_f \setminus \mathcal{S}_B$ denotes $\{s \in \mathcal{S}_f \mid \forall s \in \mathcal{S}_B : s \neq s.s\}$.

be alive and have y, $\bar{y}$, $\underline{x}$, and $\bar{x}$. To summarize, Algorithm 1 translates a given snapshot sn, considered as the outer most frame, and a set of symbols $\mathcal{S}_B$, into a multi-sorted first-order formula φ_{sn} with free variables $o_{s.id}$ for each $s \in \mathcal{S}_B$.

Algorithm 1. Translation of a Frame of the Spatial View

---

1 **Function** translateFrame

2 **input :** frame f, set of of bound symbols $\mathcal{S}_B$ **output:** first-order formula φ_f

3 $\varphi_f \leftarrow \bigwedge_{s \in \mathcal{S}_f \setminus \mathcal{S}_B} \exists o_{s.id} \in \mathsf{type}_{sdict}(s.s):$ //object variable o_s for symbol occurrence s

4      $\bigwedge_{s \in \mathcal{S}_f} \mathtt{alive}(o_{s.id})$ //o_s is required to be alive

5    $\wedge \bigwedge_{s \in \mathcal{S}_f^o} \mathsf{O}_{s.s}(o_{s.id})$ //features of $s.s$

6    $\wedge \bigwedge_{s,s' \in \mathcal{S}_f \times (\mathcal{S}_f \cup \mathcal{S}_{spans(f)})} \mathsf{T}_{s,s'}(o_{s.id}, o_{s'.id})$ //relative placement

7    $\wedge \bigwedge_{l \in \mathcal{A}_f} \mathsf{P}(o_{(l.s).id}, o_{(l.s').id})$ //arrow predicates

8    $\wedge \bigwedge_{s \in \mathcal{S}_f^{SB}} \mathtt{translateFrame}(s)$ //nested somewhere-box constraints

9    $\wedge \bigwedge_{s \in \mathcal{S}_f^{NB}} \neg\mathtt{translateFrame}(s)$ //nested nowhere-box constraints

10 **if** f is negated **then return** $\neg\varphi_f$; **else return** φ_f;

4.4 Snapshot Charts and Their Visualization

Now we show how snapshots are used within *snapshot charts* (*SC*s) to describe an evolution over time. SCs are annotated snapshot graphs, that are directed graphs with snapshots as nodes. Within an SC, a snapshot describes (invariant) properties that hold for a while, i.e., a time span greater zero. Like the pages of a flip book, a sequence of snapshots then describes a story that evolves over time. Contiguously one snapshot holds until the next. At SCs we have a new dimension that was missing at snapshots, namely time. Hence, an SC translates to a temporal logic formula. Next, we give an overview of the visual syntax elements of SCs.

4.5 Overview on Syntactical Elements in SCs

1. SCs provide visualizations for snapshot graphs. The simplest snapshot graph is a snapshot node, i.e., a node that represents a single snapshot. Snapshot graphs can be composed via sequential or parallel composition, choice, and negation. Figure 13 illustrates for two snapshots how the resulting snapshot graphs are visualized. Snapshots are connected via arrows to avoid ambiguities. But we may omit the arrows, if this is unambiguous.
2. An SC can specify an implication. Therefore, we provide a dedicated visualization called the *premise-consequence chart*. Their most general form provides the pattern *"the past and the future imply a future consequence"*. This pattern basically allows to express that the future is implied by what happened before, and also by what *will* happen. So, roughly, "If I *have* felt sick and still

feel sick, and if I *will* sneeze, then I *will* get a tissue." matches this pattern. The visualization of this pattern is illustrated in Fig. 14. Roughly, the SC expresses "*If* first (A and next B) happened and now B holds, and if next (C and next D) will happen, *then* (E and next F) will happen".

3. Snapshot graphs can be annotated with timing constraints. The *hour glass* allows to denote durations for snapshot (sub)sequences and *time pins* provide a means to synchronize concurrent developments. Figure 15 shows an example SC with an hour glass that takes the time of the second snapshot. So we can express that the car indicates for less then 2 s, and then drives across the lane separator. Figure 16 shows an example SC where a time pin is used to denote that the two concurrent developments (one at the top, one at the bottom) synchronize. The time pin declares the switching time between $sn_{1.1}$ and $sn_{1.2}$ at the top as $sync_1$ (snapshots at the top are $sn_{1.1}$ and $sn_{1.2}$, at the bottom are $sn_{2.1}$ to $sn_{2.3}$). The dotted line with label $sync_1$ at the bottom snapshot sequence on top of $sn_{2.3}$ denotes that $sn_{2.3}$ happens during a time interval that includes $sync_1$.

4. In order to track an object along a snapshot sequence, object symbols can be fixed to represent the same object identity along an evolution. To this end, we provide two syntactical means. We allow labeling objects with identifiers as, e.g., in Fig. 17. We also use a *bulletin board* (b-board) to declare that a symbol represents the same object along the subsequent path of an SC (cf. Fig. 18).

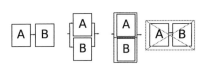

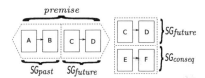

Fig. 13. Sequence, choice, parallel composition, and negation of two snapshots.

Fig. 14. An SC specifying a *"past and future imply future consequence"* pattern.

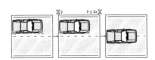

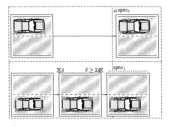

Fig. 15. The hour glass specifies a dwell time.

Fig. 16. Two concurrent snapshot sequences with time pin and hour glass.

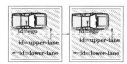 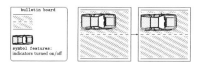

Fig. 17. An SC with identifiers.   **Fig. 18.** An SC and its bulletin board

4.6 Snapshot Charts Semantics

Via Algorithm 2 we define how SCs can be translated to a multi-sorted first-order real-time formula. The algorithm distinguishes the following elements.

Snapshot Graphs. Algorithm 2 inductively translates an annotated snapshot graph SG_{id} into a formula φ_{id} by composing node formulas following the graph's structure. A snapshot graph of just one node, SG_o, gets translated to a *node formula* of the form $\varphi_o = \Box_{[b_o,e_o)}\varphi_{sn_o} \wedge b_o < e_o \wedge \psi$, where φ_o is generated by Algorithm 1 for sn_o, and ψ encodes the annotated timing constraints as explained in the following. φ_o expresses that the constrains encoded by sn_o invariantly hold from time b_o up to e_o. The node formulas are composed so that they contiguously hold along a graph's path. This is realized by substituting the end time variable e_1 and the start time variable b_2 of concatenated subgraphs $SG_1; SG_2$ to the same time variable. Therefore, we assume that each (sub)graph has a unique id. Algorithm 2 constructs a formula $\varphi_{id} = \texttt{translateSG}(SG_{id})$ where the start and end time variables are uniquely referable as b_{id} and e_{id}. More precisely, Algorithm 2 builds a list of variable substitutions ξ_{id} along with the formula φ_{id}, that rename the start and end time variables appropriately. For a formula φ, a substitution list $\xi_1^\frown\xi_2$ means that first ξ_1 is applied and on its result ξ_2.

Figure 19 illustrates the translation process on an exemplary snapshot graph, which is shown in Fig. 19(a). We assume that snapshots sn_i have already been translated to formulas φ_i by Algorithm 1. As a short hand, we write in the following $\Box_{[b<e)}\varphi$ for $\Box_{[b,e)}\varphi \wedge b < e$. *Figure 19(b):* The graph is considered as sequence of subgraphs A, B, which are translated to φ_A, φ_B. φ_{SG} gets $\exists t_{SG} \in Time : \varphi_A \wedge \varphi_B$ with $\xi_{SG} = [e_A \backslash t_{SG}, b_B \backslash t_{SG}]$. *Figure 19(c):* A is the choice of snapshots sn_1 and sn_2, hence $\varphi_A = \Box_{[b_1<e_1)}\varphi_1 \vee \Box_{[b_2<e_2)}\varphi_2$ with $\xi_A = [b_1\backslash b_A, e_1\backslash e_A, b_2\backslash b_A, e_2\backslash e_A]^\frown\xi_{SG}$. B is the concurrency of sn_5 with subgraph C. So Algorithm 2 sets $\varphi_B = \Box_{[b_5<e_5)}\varphi_5 \wedge \varphi_C$ with $\xi_B = [b_5\backslash b_B, e_5\backslash e_B, b_C\backslash b_B, e_C\backslash e_B]^\frown\xi_{SG}$. *Figure 19(d):* Since C is the sequence of sn_3 and sn_4, φ_C gets $\exists t_C \in Time : \Box_{[b_3<e_3)}\varphi_3 \wedge \Box_{[b_4<e_4)}\varphi_4$ with $\xi_C = [b_3\backslash b_C, e_3\backslash t_C, b_4\backslash t_C, e_4\backslash e_C]^\frown\xi_B$. To sum up, according to Algorithm 2 φ_{SG} translates to $\exists t_{SG} : (\Box_{[b_{SG}<t_{SG})}\varphi_1 \vee \Box_{[b_{SG}<t_{SG})}\varphi_2) \wedge (\Box_{[t_{SG}<e_{SG})}\varphi_5 \wedge (\exists t_C : (\Box_{[t_{SG}<t_C)}\varphi_3 \wedge \Box_{[t_C<e_{SG})}\varphi_4))$.

Timing Constraints. A timer can be started when a snapshot is entered, and stopped at the end of a snapshot—these need not necessarily be the same snapshot. The start and stop of a timer is denoted via ⊠ and ⊠. At the start hour glass a name for the timer is specified, say δ, and at the end hour glass a constraint on δ is specified, say ψ. Let the timer be started at snapshot sn_m and

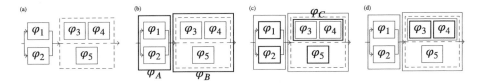

Fig. 19. Steps of snapshot graph translation

stopped at a snapshot sn_n. To translate the timer constraint into the formula φ_{SG}, we insert the constraint on the respective time variables at an appropriate position within φ_{SG}. Algorithm 2 introduces variables for the start and end time of δ (which is also the start of sn_m and the end of sn_n), say b_m and e_n. We replace δ in ψ by $e_n - b_m$, $\psi' := \psi[\delta \backslash e_n - b_m]$, and ψ' gets a conjunct of the node formula of sn_n, $\square_{[b_n, e_n)} \varphi_n \wedge \psi'$.

A time pin φ can be placed at the start of a snapshot node sn_m and be labeled with an identifier, say π. At a concurrent snapshot (sub)graph we can synchronize (1) the switching time of a snapshot sn_n with π. This is annotated by placing a dotted vertical line labeled with π at sn_n's start. We can also synchronize (2) sn_n to be active at least at time π. This is annotated by placing the synchronization bar (dotted horizontal bar) labeled π above sn_n. (1) means that the start time of sn_m, b_m equals the start time of sn_n, b_n, so $\psi := (b_n = b_m)$ gets a conjunct of the node formula of sn_n. (2) means that the time π is somewhere between the start time of sn_n, b_n, and end time of sn_n, e_n. So, $\psi := (b_n < b_m < e_n))$ gets a conjunct of the node formula of sn_n, $\square_{[b_n, e_n)} \varphi_{sn_n} \wedge \psi$.

Object Identities. Identities introduced via b-board or id-labels are translated along the same lines. Hence, we only discuss the b-board here. Let $\mathcal{S}_B$ be the set of symbols at the b-board, each having a unique identifier $\jmath.id$. A symbol $\jmath \in \mathcal{S}_B$ is required to be visually unique, also under all modifications according to Item 2 in Sect. 4.2. Occurrences of a particular symbol $\jmath$ (e.g., a car symbol) refer to a particular object across different snapshots in which $\jmath$ occurs.

Upon the translation into a formula, we globally bind an object variable via quantification for each symbol $\jmath$ of the b-board. Therefore, if $\jmath$ (modified or non-modified) occurs in a snapshot sn at a frame f, then each symbol occurrence $s \in \mathcal{S}_f$ with $s.\jmath = \jmath$ gets the same id as $\jmath \in \mathcal{S}_B$, $s.id = \jmath.id$. That way, Algorithm 1 generates snapshot formulas that all refer to the same object variable, $o_{\jmath.id}$, for a symbol occurrence s with $s.\jmath = \jmath$. Further, the translation of snapshots via Algorithm 1 gets as input $\mathcal{S}_B$, so that object variables $o_{\jmath.id}$ do not get quantified locally within a snapshot formula. These free variables are globally bound by existential/universal quantifiers according to the header information (cf. Sect. 4.7).

Translation Scheme. To keep it short, we consider any SC in the sequel as a special case of a premise-consequence chart. The translation first determines the constituent annotated snapshot graphs and, if the SC is not a full *"past and future imply a future consequence"* pattern, sets omitted parts to be True. Next, these snapshot graphs are translated according to Algorithm 2. Time annotations and identities are considered when translating a snapshot node. The method translateAnnotatedSN$(sn, \cdot)$ returns basically $\varphi_{id} := \Box_{[b_{id}, e_{id}]}$translateFrame$(sn, \mathcal{S}_B) \wedge b_{id} < e_{id}$ but, additionally, annotations are encoded according to the paragraphs on timing constraints and object identities.

Given that we have already translated $\bullet$ SG$_{past}$ to φ_{past} and $\bullet$ SG$_{fut.}$ to $\varphi_{fut.}$ and $\bullet$ SG$_{cons.}$ to $\varphi_{cons.}$. We compose these sub-formulas into the formula φ_{SC} with free variables b_{SC}, t_{SC}, e_{SC}, which, respectively, represent the start time, switching time between past and future/consequence, and the end time.

$$\varphi_{SC} = \varphi_{past} \wedge \varphi_{fut.} \Rightarrow \varphi_{fut.} \wedge \varphi_{cons.} \text{ with}$$
$$\xi = [b_{past} \backslash b_{SC}, e_{past} \backslash t_{SC}, b_{fut.} \backslash t_{SC}, e_{fut.} \backslash e_{SC}, b_{cons.} \backslash t_{SC}, e_{cons.} \backslash e_{SC}].$$

So φ_{SC} means that, for a switching time t_{SC}, if first φ_{past} holds up to t_{SC} and from t_{SC} $\varphi_{fut.}$ holds, then also $\varphi_{cons.}$ holds from t_{SC}. Since in snapshot graphs with synchronization between future and consequence, the SG$_{fut.}$ is repeated as being concurrent to SG$_{cons.}$ (cf. Fig. 13), $\varphi_{fut.}$ has also two occurrences of $\varphi_{cons.}$ (in order to closely resemble the graph).

Algorithm 2. Translation of an Annotated Snapshot Graph

---

1 **Function** translateSG
   input : Annotated snapshotgraph SG$_{id_0}$ with id id_0, Substitution ξ
   output: temporal first-order formula

2 **if** $SG_{id_0} = SG_{id_1}; \ldots; SG_{id_n} \wedge n > 1$ **then** //SG$_{id_0}$ describes sequence
3   Let t_{id_0} be an unused time variable name.
4   Let ξ' be $[e_{id_1} \backslash t_{id_0}, b_{id_2} \backslash t_{id_0}]^\frown \xi$.
5   **return** $\exists t_{id_0}:$ translateSG$(SG_{id_1}, \xi') \wedge$ translateSG$(SG_{id_2}; \ldots; SG_{id_n}, \xi')$;

6 **if** $SG_{id_0} = SG_{id_1} \| SG_{id_2}$ **then** //SG$_{id_0}$ describes choice
7   Let ξ' be $[b_{id_1} \backslash b_{id_0}, b_{id_2} \backslash b_{id_0}, e_{id_1} \backslash e_{id_0}, e_{id_2} \backslash b_{id_0}]^\frown \xi$.
8   **return** (translateSG$(SG_{id_1}, \xi') \vee$ translateSG(SG_{id_2}, ξ'));

9 **if** $SG_{id_0} = SG_{id_1} \& SG_{id_2}$ **then** //SG$_{id_0}$ describes concurrency
10   Let ξ' be $[b_{id_1} \backslash b_{id_0}, b_{id_2} \backslash b_{id_0}, e_{id_1} \backslash e_{id_0}, e_{id_2} \backslash b_{id_0}]^\frown \xi$.
11   **return** (translateSG$(SG_{id_1}, \xi') \wedge$ translateSG(SG_{id_2}, ξ'));

12 **if** $SG_{id_0} = \neg SG_{id_1}$ **then** //SG$_{id_0}$ describes negation
13   Let ξ' be $[b_{id_1} \backslash b_{id_0}, e_{id_1} \backslash e_{id_0}]^\frown \xi$.
14   **return** $\neg$translateSG(SG_{id_1}, ξ');

15 **return** translateAnnotatedSN(SG_{id_0}, ξ); //SG$_{id_0}$ is a (time annotated) snapshot node

---

4.7   TSCs, Satisfaction

As we consider—in this paper—TSCs without an LSC part, an SC together with a header constitutes a complete TSC. Also, we discuss here only the two headers used in the example that are of type (A) act.m = always and qnt.m = all and (B) act.m = initial and qnt.m = exists. The translation of other headers can be found in [4].

A TSC of type (A) means that always the SC has to hold (activation mode always) and all trajectories and objects have to satisfy the SC (quantification mode all). A TSC of type (A) is hence translated to $\varphi_{TSC} = \mathbf{A}\forall o_{id_1} \in T_1 \ldots \forall o_{id_n} \in T_n : \Box \forall e_{TSC}, t_{SC} \in Time : \varphi_{SC}[b_{SC}\backslash 0, e_{SC}\backslash e_{TSC}]$, where $\mathcal{S}_B = \{s_1, \ldots, s_n\}$ is the set of symbols of the TSC's bulletin board, $T_i = \text{type}_{sdict}(s_i)$ and $id_i = s_i.id$.

So, all trajectories and all objects that could match the referred object(symbol)s with identities have to satisfy the SC at all times. As φ_{SC} has the form $\varphi_{past} \wedge \varphi_{fut.} \Rightarrow \varphi_{fut.} \wedge \varphi_{cons.}$, the universal quantification of (i) e_{TSC}, the end time, and (ii) t_{SC}, the switching time between past and future, means that whenever the premise of $\varphi_{past} \wedge \varphi_{fut.}$ is satisfied for a pair of t_{SC}, e_{TSC}, then also the consequence has to hold between t_{SC} and e_{TSC}. We used a universal TSC in Sect. 2, page 5, to describe a lane change rule.

A TSC of type (B) means that the SC has to bear right from the start (activation mode initial) and there is at least one trajectory with objects that satisfy the SC (quantification mode exists). A TSC of type (B) is hence translated to $\varphi_{TSC} = \mathbf{E}\exists o_{id_1} : T_1 \ldots \exists o_{id_n} \in T_n : \exists e_{TSC}, t_{SC} \in Time : \varphi_{SC}[b_{SC}\backslash 0, e_{SC}\backslash e_{TSC}]$. At Sect. 2 we used existential TSCs of the form $\varphi_{SC} = \varphi_{cons.}$ to describe scenarios—there φ_{past} and $\varphi_{fut.}$ were both omitted (True).

Let a specification Spec be given in form of a set of TSCs, $\mathbb{TSC}_S$, together with a world model WM. For this paper, we consider specifications where the behavior of an autonomous car, called ego, is specified. The world WM, given as the parallel composition of hybrid automaton instances H_i, has a distinct H_j that represents ego. In the specification H_{ego}, reflects the physical laws of a mechanical car but leaves the controller open. So H_{ego} neither controls safety distances nor obeys traffic rules. An implementing system I specifies a controller for ego. So I equals WM except for H_{ego}, which is replaced by an automaton H^I_{ego} whose controller is implemented. The controller has the task to ensure that ego obeys the TSC specification. We say I *implements a TSC specification* Spec, iff $I \models \bigwedge_{TSC \in \mathbb{TSC}_S} \varphi_{TSC}$.

5   Related Work

Live Sequence Charts (LSCs) are a visual specification language for the description of system traces and communication [2]. The key elements are instances and messages sent between them. Indeed, TSCs have been developed with LSCs in mind. We plan to integrate LSCs into TSCs in order to specify communications, such that TSCs extend the LSC formalism by providing a visualisation of the continuous evolution via sequences of snapshot invariants.

Multi-Lane Spatial Logic is a spatial interval logic based on the view of each car. It was introduced in [13] to simplify reasoning about safety of road traffic by abstracting from the car dynamics. MLSL has been shown to be undecidable in various relaxations and restrictions. Nevertheless, sound proof systems for reasoning about safety of traffic situations have been presented [14,17,19]. In [9] it has been shown that it is decidable whether truth of an arbitrary MLSL formula can be safely determined for a given sample size under a reasonable model of technical observation of the traffic situation. In contrast to MLSL, TSCs do not determine the level of abstraction, but leave open the specification of the world model. The efficient analysis of TSC specifications is future work though. In particular, it seems promising to develop approaches that exploit the results of MLSL for TSCs.

OpenSCENARIO [22] together with OpenDRIVE [20] and OpenCRG [21] forms a set of exchange formats tailored for describing traffic scenarios. These formats aim at becoming a standard and serve as a means to imperatively describe the behavior of the environment and, optionally, of the ego vehicle. The static road networks are basically described as graphs of lanes labeled with geometric shapes. Dynamic content is described as a storyboard with trigger-action pairs. OpenSCENARIO corresponds to existential TSCs (quantification mode = exists) and, hence, are not suitable for the specification phase. Even the specification of existential scenarios is limited in comparison to TSCs. In the current state— to the best of the authors' knowledge—OpenSCENARIO lacks elements to (1) distinguish between possible (existential) and expected (universal) behavior; (2) distinguish between past and future behavior, and consequences; (3) express "don't cares," "somewhere," or "nowhere"; and (4) explicitly express alternative and concurrent behavior.

Realizability of cooperative driving tasks has been addressed in [6]. In particular, a formal approach has been developed for the verification of time probabilistic requirements (such as collision freedom) of given maneuvering and communication capabilities of the car based on a formal specification. Future work will investigate algorithms for deciding consistency and realizability of TSC specifications under robustness assumptions. While we do not believe that formally synthesized controllers for the ego vehicle will be used for implementation purposes, they can be used in the concept analysis phase of autonomous vehicles expected to master additional traffic scenarios.

(Probabilistic) Timed Property Sequence Charts (PTPSCs) extend Property Sequence Charts. Both are a scenario-based notation to represent temporal properties of concurrent systems that aims to balance expressive power and simplicity of use [23]. PTPSCs provide pre-charts, borrowed from LSCs, *clock resets* and *clock constraints*. Additionally, (sets of) messages can be assigned probabilities which impact the reception of the messages. TPSCs can be automatically translated into timed-Büchi automata and, hence, are suitable for runtime verification. Hypothesis testing can be used to also check the probabilistic part [24] by inspecting several sample runs. However, PTPSCs provide no means to graphically describe spatial constraints, branching, or concurrency, so that the planned addition of probabilities to TSCs is a worthwhile contribution.

Visual Logic (VL) was developed by Kemper and Etzien to specify sequences of traffic situations on the highway, aiming to bridge the gap between engineers, psychologists, and scientists [16]. Like TSCs, VL aims to provide an intuitive visual formalism with a formal semantics. VL combines LSCs and a visual formalism via which spatial relations of traffic scenarios are captured. Kemper and Etzien define the semantics of VL via a translation into *timed automata*. Conceptually, TSCs can be considered a extension of VL: TSCs share the motivation and borrow from the visual formalism of VL, and we plan to integrate LSCs as well. While VL allows sequences of snapshots only, TSCs allow SCs with a complex graph structure. Our visual formalism generalizes distance arrows of VL to predicate arrows. The concept of nowhere- and somewhere-boxes is new, as well as the possibility to define anchors. Further, TSCs allow time annotations and identity labels. The "past and presence implies a future consequence" pattern is new.

6   Conclusion and Future Work

This paper is a first stepping stone in a concerted effort of providing a design flow for highly autonomous vehicles supporting concept development, specification, and verification and validation. The way towards achieving this goal involves both foundational challenges and industrial acceptance.

On the foundation side, we have to extend TSCs to deal with cooperation and imperfect perception; the problem of partial information requires one to differentiate between the ego car's beliefs about its environment, including the intentions of other traffic participants, and ground truth. Conceptually, TSCs allow rich specifications at the level of SCs and the world model (and hence are generally undecidable [12]). When used as specification formalism throughout the design process, appropriate restrictions can be imposed when necessary. In the future we will also look into efficient methods for generating simulation runs to cover TSCs, as well as automatic methods for checking consistency and completeness relative to a given world model, building in particular on the results of [8,10] on decidability for robust satisfaction. On the industrial side, we will work with traffic psychologists to revisit the language design, while we continue to test the approach on non-trivial sample use cases, and participate actively in the ongoing standardization activities for OpenSCENARIO.

We hope that this line of research will ultimately contribute to making highly autonomous driving safe and enjoyable.

References

1. Damm, W., Finkbeiner, B.: Does it pay to extend the perimeter of a world model? In: Butler, M., Schulte, W. (eds.) FM 2011. LNCS, vol. 6664, pp. 12–26. Springer, Heidelberg (2011). https://doi.org/10.1007/978-3-642-21437-0_4
2. Damm, W., Harel, D.: LSCs: breathing life into message sequence charts. Formal Methods Syst. Des. **19**(1), 45–80 (2001). https://doi.org/10.1023/A:1011227529550

3. Damm, W., Horbach, M., Sofronie-Stokkermans, V.: Decidability of verification of safety properties of spatial families of linear hybrid automata. In: Lutz, C., Ranise, S. (eds.) FroCoS 2015. LNCS (LNAI), vol. 9322, pp. 186–202. Springer, Cham (2015). https://doi.org/10.1007/978-3-319-24246-0_12

4. Damm, W., Kemper, S., Möhlmann, E., Peikenkamp, T., Rakow, A.: Traffic sequence charts - from visualization to semantics. Reports of SFB/TR 14 AVACS 117, SFB/TR 14 AVACS, October 2017

5. Damm, W., Kemper, S., Möhlmann, E., Peikenkamp, T., Rakow, A.: Traffic sequence charts - a visual language for capturing traffic scenarios. In: Embedded Real Time Software and Systems - ERTS2018, February 2018

6. Damm, W., Peter, H., Rakow, J., Westphal, B.: Can we build it: formal synthesis of control strategies for cooperative driver assistance systems. Math. Struct. Comput. Sci. **23**(4), 676–725 (2013). https://doi.org/10.1017/S0960129512000230

7. Damm, W., Westphal, B.: Live and let die: LSC based verification of UML models. Sci. Comput. Program. **55**(1–3), 117–159 (2005). https://doi.org/10.1016/j.scico.2004.05.013

8. Fränzle, M.: What will be eventually true of polynomial hybrid automata? In: Kobayashi, N., Pierce, B.C. (eds.) TACS 2001. LNCS, vol. 2215, pp. 340–359. Springer, Heidelberg (2001). https://doi.org/10.1007/3-540-45500-0_17

9. Fränzle, M., Hansen, M.R., Ody, H.: No need knowing numerous neighbours. In: Meyer, R., Platzer, A., Wehrheim, H. (eds.) Correct System Design. LNCS, vol. 9360, pp. 152–171. Springer, Cham (2015). https://doi.org/10.1007/978-3-319-23506-6_11

10. Fränzle, M.: Analysis of hybrid systems: an ounce of realism can save an infinity of states. In: Flum, J., Rodriguez-Artalejo, M. (eds.) CSL 1999. LNCS, vol. 1683, pp. 126–139. Springer, Heidelberg (1999). https://doi.org/10.1007/3-540-48168-0_10

11. Harel, D., Marelly, R.: Come, Let's Play: Scenario-Based Programming Using LSC's and the Play-Engine. Springer, New York (2003). https://doi.org/10.1007/978-3-642-19029-2

12. Henzinger, T.A., Kopke, P.W., Puri, A., Varaiya, P.: What's decidable about hybrid automata? J. Comput. Syst. Sci. **57**(1), 94–124 (1998)

13. Hilscher, M., Linker, S., Olderog, E.-R., Ravn, A.P.: An abstract model for proving safety of multi-lane traffic manoeuvres. In: Qin, S., Qiu, Z. (eds.) ICFEM 2011. LNCS, vol. 6991, pp. 404–419. Springer, Heidelberg (2011). https://doi.org/10.1007/978-3-642-24559-6_28

14. Hilscher, M., Schwammberger, M.: An abstract model for proving safety of autonomous urban traffic. In: Sampaio, A., Wang, F. (eds.) ICTAC 2016. LNCS, vol. 9965, pp. 274–292. Springer, Cham (2016). https://doi.org/10.1007/978-3-319-46750-4_16

15. ITU-T: ITU-T recommendation Z.120: Message Sequence Chart (MSC) (2011). https://www.itu.int/rec/T-REC-Z.120-201102-I

16. Kemper, S., Etzien, C.: A visual logic for the description of highway traffic scenarios. In: Aiguier, M., Boulanger, F., Krob, D., Marchal, C. (eds.) Complex Systems Design and Management, pp. 233–245. Springer, Cham (2014). https://doi.org/10.1007/978-3-319-02812-5_17

17. Linker, S., Hilscher, M.: Proof theory of a multi-lane spatial logic. Log. Methods Comput. Sci. **11**(3) (2015). http://lmcs.episciences.org/1580

18. Lynch, N., Segala, R., Vaandrager, F.: Hybrid I/O automata. Inf. Comput. **185**(1), 105–157 (2003). http://www.sciencedirect.com/science/article/pii/S0890540103000671

19. Ody, H.: Undecidability results for multi-lane spatial logic. In: Leucker, M., Rueda, C., Valencia, F.D. (eds.) ICTAC 2015. LNCS, vol. 9399, pp. 404–421. Springer, Cham (2015). https://doi.org/10.1007/978-3-319-25150-9_24

20. VIRES Simulationstechnologie GmbH: OpenDRIVE (2015). http://www.opendrive.org. Accessed 07 Sept 2017

21. VIRES Simulationstechnologie GmbH: OpenCRG (2016). http://www.opencrg.org. Accessed 07 Sept 2017

22. VIRES Simulationstechnologie GmbH: OpenSCENARIO (2017). http://www.openscenario.org. Accessed 07 Sept 2017

23. Zhang, P., Grunske, L., Tang, A., Li, B.: A formal syntax for probabilistic timed property sequence charts. In: 2009 IEEE/ACM International Conference on Automated Software Engineering, pp. 500–504, November 2009

24. Zhang, P., Li, W., Wan, D., Grunske, L.: Monitoring of probabilistic timed property sequence charts. Softw.: Pract. Exp. **41**(7), 841–866 (2011). https://doi.org/10.1002/spe.1038

Enabling Flow Preservation and Portability in Multicore Implementations of Simulink Models

Caroline Brandberg and Marco Di Natale[✉]

Scuola Superiore Sant'Anna, Pisa, Italy
caroline.brandberg@santannapisa.it, marco.dinatale@sssup.it

Abstract. Model-Based Design plays an important role in the development of embedded software. Automatic code generation from models is needed to minimize the possibility of introducing errors by manual coding, thereby preserving the validation and verification done on the model. Automatic code generation also eases traceability back to the model as required in most certification processes. The generated code must preserve the model semantics (or at least its properties of interest) and use the platform resources in the most efficient (or cost-effective) way. Achieving correctness and efficiency becomes harder in new multicore platforms. Commercially available multitask code generators from Simulink introduce variations to the model semantics that are dependent on the deployment option and the generated code is specific to a given platform configuration (hardware and OS), which makes reuse and portability more difficult. In this paper, we report on the early stages of a project that will improve on the portability of currently available code generation options from Simulink.

1 Introduction

Model-Based Design (MBD) is today widely used in the embedded systems industry throughout the development cycle; from design, to analysis, to implementation. Among the tools supporting MBD, Simulink by the MathWorks (in its corrent 2017a version) allows the definition of models using a graphical editor, their analysis by simulation or model-checking, and the automatic generation of a code implementation on selected platform options, including programmable HW and multicores.

Automatic code generation is a key requirement for any formal MBD process. There are many benefits from code generation, but first and foremost, it enables consistency and traceability between the model and the executable code. Consistency in the sense that it preserves the semantics of the model reducing the risk of introducing unwanted errors, otherwise any verification and validation done on the model would be lost. Automatically generated code is today very efficient in terms of speed and size. Analysis by Thales and Visteon show how the generated code can be both faster [20] and smaller in size [13] than hand-written code.

© Springer International Publishing AG, part of Springer Nature 2018
M. Lohstroh et al. (Eds.): Lee Festschrift, LNCS 10760, pp. 206–222, 2018.
https://doi.org/10.1007/978-3-319-95246-8_12

The necessary move from single-core to multicore platforms brings new challenges to the task of providing semantics-preserving and efficient code implementations of Simulink models. With respect to semantics preservation, the objective is to preserve the block rate activation specifications, the partial order of execution of blocks (which implies flow preservation) and to guarantee the code execution within the deadlines imposed by the preservation of the synchronous assumption or the flow of communication data. Commercial Simulink generators for multicore platforms do not account for the enforcement of the order of execution constraints. When a Simulink model is defined as mapped for execution on a multicore platform, the model semantics (at simulation time) changes in an attempt at matching the semantics of the generated code, which consists of a set periodic and asynchronous task executions on the cores. The tasks are executing the subsystems in the model according to the mapping directives provided by the user. Furthermore, the Rate Transition communication mechanism that is used in single core platforms to guarantee preservation of data flows (at least in selected conditions [31]) does not provide the same guarantees when code is executed in multicores and therefore needs to be extended [31].

With respect to efficiency, in a multicore implementation the generated code should allow for a bounded worst case execution time and effective memory placement; and use at best the system resources and the API provided by the platform (OS and drivers). With respect to this last objective, another limitation of current commercial code generators is that the available code generation options target individual platform configurations (HW/OS) making portability and extensibility challenging, especially for new platforms and/or unsupported operating systems. Currently, multicore generation from Simulink is at its early developments and only the Windows API is fully supported (Linux and VXWorks are not officially supported but custom code generators are available from third party open projects).

Finally, commercial OS mostly support a *partitioned* scheduling model (as opposed to *global* scheduling). While this seems a sensible choice as supported by recent comparisons between the two scheduling models [6], it also places high relevance into the design stage in which the partitioning of functions into cores and the design of tasks are defined.

In this work, we describe the development of a new multicore code generation facility for Simulink that is meant to preserve the order of execution of blocks and data flows as defined for a "purely functional" (that is, without any platform mapping) model, and is more easily retargetable to a wide selection of platform configurations. The latter objective is obtained by providing an abstract OS-level API that is tailored for the synchronous-reactive model of execution of Simulink. The abstract API consists of a limited subset of functions, rich enough to fulfill its purpose and yet simple enough to be easily remapped to a set of OS of practical use. With our API, the code generation process will produce code that is independent of the operating system and can later re-target any preferred choice. We provided examples of retargeting for Windows, Linux and PikeOS [26] and are in the process of extending our examples to other standards such as AUTOSAR (formerly OSEK). While clearly not fully comprehensive, this list provides sufficient coverage of today's available commercial options and confidence that the approach can be further extended to other platforms.

2   Related Work

In the early 90s, the first synchronous languages, Esterel [5], Lustre [14] and Signal [17] were developed. These languages are based on a formal semantics and introduced into software development a programming paradigm based on a timely ordered execution of event-driven (possibly periodic) processing steps. The synchronous languages find today a commercial implementation in the SCADE (Safety Critical Application Development Environment) tool (now at Suite 6 [4]), which provides certified code generation; a simulator; and verification through plug-ins.

In parallel, the development of controls has been strongly influenced by the Simulink/Stateflow [27] tool, widely used for the modeling and simulation of control systems. Even though the SCADE semantics is formally documented whereas Simulink only provides a set of execution rules through its user manual, it is possible to define a suitable restriction of Simulink that can adhere to a synchronous formal semantics and be even formally translated into SCADE/Lustre was created [7,24,28].

Code generation from synchronous languages has been extensively studied for the case of a single cyclic executable implementing the model [15]. The issue of preserving the semantics when implementing synchronous programs on single-core platforms is further discussed in [8], where they present a semantic-preserving inter-task communication protocol. Further optimization of flow preservation techniques is discussed in [10,29,30]. The complexity of flow-preservation increases when moving from single- to multi-core platforms, as discussed in [31]. The general issue of the composition of possibly heterogeneous models with the need to preserve determinism in the execution on actual platforms is discussed at lenght in [11] and solutions for the case of discrete event systems are proposed in the PTIDES project [33].

In the context of concurrent implementation of models, prior research has been dedicated to find an optimal assignment of model blocks to threads, and later threads to cores. The mapping of functional blocks into threads is discussed in [10] where an MILP optimization framework is used. Further, [3,32] discusses approaches to find the best possible mapping of threads to cores. Also, the optimal placement of memory in multi-core platforms has been discussed in [23,25].

The generation of code from models for multicore platforms is the subject of the case study on the Rosace architecture [22]. However, in this case the Simulink model is translated manually in a Prelude program, which is finally executed onto a Tilera multicore (a system based on a NoC). The paper presents a very interesting case study but does not provide details into the problem of preserving the original Simulink semantics.

In general Simulink could benefit from a more formal treatment of several semantics issues (including those related to platform mapping), that have been carefully examined and discussed in the context of the Ptolemy [11] and Metropolis [12] projects. Since the user base of Simulink is extremely large and includes control designers and developers in several industries, we believe a discussion on the issue of portability and semantics preservation for multicore implementation is potentially very fruitful.

Our work also builds on the very general concept of abstraction layers and abstract operating systems. There has been a very large amount of work done to make applications portable across operating systems. Among the most popular efforts is the POSIX standard [2] which provides portability between Unix bases systems. Posix compliance is often achieved by OS vendors by simply implementing the Posix API by an abstraction layer. OSEK [21] and later AUTOSAR [1] are other standards, which provides an OS abstraction for the automotive industry. However, to the best of our knowledge, there has been no API explicitly designed for the needs of a synchronous reactive model implementation.

3   System Model

In this work, we discuss a framework for the generation of portable code for multicore platforms from Simulink models. Currently, the semantics of a Simulink model depends on the implementation assumptions (as explained later) and the generated code makes use of OS-specific primitives. In our work, we propose an implementation that abstracts from both dependencies. In the next section we discuss the execution semantics of a Simulink model that is amenable for code generation when no platform mapping is defined (the model is simulated as a purely functional model). Following, we discuss the semantics changes that apply when a multicore mapping is defined and our proposal for an implementation generation that restores the execution semantics of the purely functional model (independent from the selected platform and the implementation choices, such as the task model and the task allocation on the cores).

3.1   Simulink Model and Platform-Independent Execution Semantics

A Simulink system consists of a network of blocks. A block b_j can be abstracted as a function operating on a set of (continuous time) input signals and producing a set of output signals. We denote inputs of block b_j by $i_{j,p}$ ($\overline{i_j}$ as vector) and outputs by $o_{j,q}$ ($\overline{o_j}$). Each blocks may also have a state S_j. Simulink provides three types of blocks: continuous, discrete and triggered. Discrete blocks are activated periodically with a period T_i. Continuous blocks process signals in continuous time, but for control systems that require code generation, they actually evaluated at the system base rate T_B, which is an integer divisor of any system period. Triggered blocks are activated by a function or signal transition. Each time a block is activated, a new set for its output signal values and a new state are computed, based on the input values and the block state.

$$(\overline{o_j}, S_j^{\text{New}}) = f_s(\overline{i_j}, S_j). \tag{1}$$

A block for which the output values are directly dependent on the input is called direct feedthrough. These blocks may not execute before their input is available. This implies a constraint on the order of execution of blocks. The set of topological dependencies implied by the direct feedthrough defines a partial order of execution among blocks. The partial order must be accounted for in the simulation and in the run-time execution of the model. If two blocks b_i and b_j are in an input-output feedthrough relationship (the output of b_j depends on its input coming from one of the outputs of b_i, and b_j is of type feedthrough), we denote $b_i \rightarrow b_j$. Let $b_i(k)$ represent the k-th occurrence of block b_i, and a sequence of activation times $a_i(k)$ is associated to b_i. Given $t \geq 0$, we define $n_i(t)$ to be the number of times that b_i has been activated before or at t.

In case $b_i \rightarrow b_j$, if $i_j(k)$ denotes the input of the k-th occurrence of b_j, then the SR semantics specify that this input is equal to the output of the last occurrence of b_i that is no later than the k-th occurrence of b_j, that is,

$$i_j(k) = o_i(m), \text{ where } m = n_i(a_j(k)). \tag{2}$$

This constraint is called *flow preservation*. Any code implementation that is flow preserving ensures that the produced values are the same as they appear at simulation time (even if the time at which they are produced in the actual code implementation may be different).

The Simulink code generation can target single- or multi-task. When targeting multi-task, each rate within the model will be mapped into tasks, which will be executed by a real-time operating system under fixed-priority scheduling.

Semantics Preservation Constraints. The model of execution of Simulink dictates the constraints on the code generation for a given platform (in our case of interest for a multicore platform). Code generating targeting multi-task needs to consider properties such as preemption and scheduling. In our work we only target periodic Simulink systems (an extension to triggered subsystems is possible, but not discussed here).

- **Task model.** Periodic subsystems must be executed by tasks so that their activation rate is preserved.
- **Order of execution.** The order of execution of subsystems must be preserved, according to the partial order dictated by the feedthrough semantics.
- **Communication and flow preservation.** The correspondence of values defined in Eq. (2) must be preserved.

When a model has loops, code generation is possible on condition that each loop includes at least one block for which the output values do not depend on the inputs (a Moore type machine). In this case, this block is executed first, and then the other blocks in the loop are executed in order following the feedthrough dependencies.

For example, in the sample system of Fig. 1 with two subsystems S_1 and S_2, the order of execution of the blocks would be b_2 first (a delay block, non-feedthrough), then b_3, then all the blocks in the subsystem S_1, then b_1, in order.

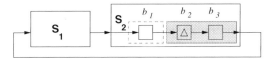

Fig. 1. Execution order in case of loops with non-feedthrough blocks (b_2, b_3, S_1, b_1).

Please note that this prevents a "modular" code generation in which the subsystems are the atomic units for generation and a single function is associated to each of them. Clearly, the correct order of execution cannot be enforced if all the blocks in S_1 are implemented as a single code function, and all the blocks in S_2 as another function (the situation is not too different from the problem highlighted in [18]).

3.2 Code Generation Facility in Simulink

The code generation process from Simulink models is summarized in Fig. 2. The model is first compiled. As a result of this process, all blocks are assigned a periodic execution rate, and an order of execution is defined using the set of partial orders from the feedthrough dependencies. The results are saved in a file with extesion .rtw that defines the serialization of the compiled model as a set of nested text records.

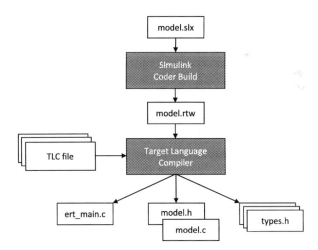

Fig. 2. AOS mapping

The information in the .rtw file is then processed by the Target Language Compiler (TLC): a template based model-to-text transformation tool that produces the executable code based on a set of templates in the TLC template language.

Code can be generated at the system level or for each subsystem individually. In case of a system-level generation, the code can include a main program and the multithreaded implementation of the model. In this case (of interest for us), the fundamental structure of the generated code is the following. One file is generated as the main file, containing the thread structure and all the scheduling-related code. In addition, there will be one file containing all the application code. In this file, each subsystem can be implemented as inlined code or as a separate function. In the end, all the computations being performed at the same rate on one of the cores (and invoked as the body of one of the threads) are available as a single Step function.

3.3   Simulation of Multicore Models

Since its version 2014b, Simulink allows the definition of the mapping of subsystems in a model to the cores of a multicore execution platform. Each subsystem is executed as one or more (periodic) tasks (a single task if the subsystem is single rate, each task for each subsystem rate if it is multirate). Figure 3 shows a sample model (from The Mathworks Simulink set of Examples) with three subsystems implemented as four tasks on two cores.

If a multicore mapping is implemented, the simulation tries to keep into account the task model and the simulation results are different from those obtained simulating the model without mapping information. This is potentially a problem, because it makes the simulation semantics dependent on the task and platform implementation. On the other hand, a simulation that considers the implementation details could help move the system analysis closer to the actual execution code behavior.

4   Current Multicore Code Generation and Simulation Semantics

Currently, the code generator produces a multithreaded/multitask implementation in which each task is activated by a core-level dispatcher. Each core dispatcher is periodically triggered by a timer event at the greatest common divisor of the task periods under its control. According to a simple period multiplication, the core dispatcher activates its core tasks using synchronization events (Fig. 4).

If a model is mapped for implementation on a multicore as a set of periodic tasks (as in Fig. 3), the model execution semantics is changed in an attempt to match the deployment information, the parallel execution on the cores and the asynchronous execution of the periodic functions implementing the subsystems. The order of execution among blocks defined by the feedthrough dependencies for the functional model is changed. This is necessary also because of the modular code generation. Consider the example model of Fig. 3. The model has a loop that includes a delay block, as shown in Fig. 5. The delay block should be executed before the subsystem labeled as Fcn3, and, in turn, this subsystem should be

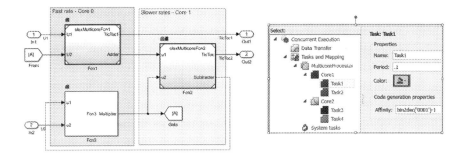

Fig. 3. Model with subsystems mapped as tasks executing on the cores

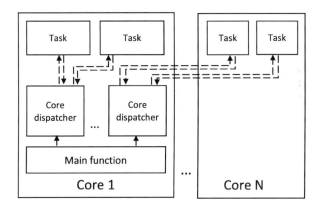

Fig. 4. Runtime activation of threads as generated by Simulink for multicore platforms

executed before the Subtract block inside Fcn2. However, since in the generated multicore code each subsystem is implemented by a single function and task, it is clearly impossible to enforce such order of execution.

The situation is made even worse because the simulated execution cannot predict the actual code execution times and the scheduling delays, and, as a result, it cannot predict the order of execution of the (now) periodic asynchronous tasks on different cores. Hence, the values obtained at simulation time do not match the corresponding values produced by the generated code when executed on the host. Furthermore, multiple runs of the same code may easily produce different results. This is acknowledged as part of the code generation options for multicore models (time determinism and therefore flow preservation cannot be guaranteed).

Figure 6 shows how the set of values that are obtained from the same functional model for two outputs (the output of the adder port of the subsystem Fcn1 on the top left of the Figure, and the output of the subsystem Fcn3 that is fed back into the input port U2 of Fcn1) are different when the model is first simulated as a purely functional model (on the left) and when the model is simulated after the subsystems are mapped onto tasks and the tasks on the two cores (on the right).

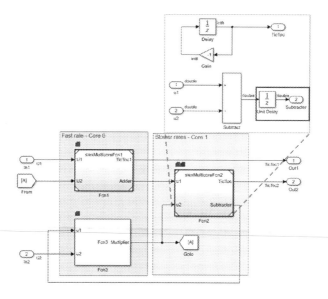

Fig. 5. The details of the example multicore model with the delay block in the cycle

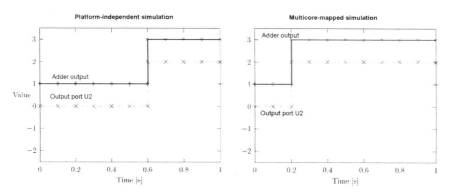

Fig. 6. Simulation results with and without multicore mapping

Unfortunately, two runs of the code implementation of the model can also result in different sets of values, as shown by the graphs of Fig. 7.

There are several reasons for this. The first is dropping the order of execution constraints of the blocks inside the subsystems in favor of a concurrent asynchronous execution model. The second reason (directly connected with the first) is the modular code generation that requires that one function and one task is generated for each mapped subsystem.

In Sect. 6, we show how these restrictions are the consequence of a choice made by the developers of the current code generators, and can be removed. We show how it is possible to modify the code generation options and to enforce an order of execution among tasks in such a way that the generated code behaves

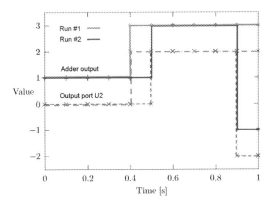

Fig. 7. The execution of the generated code is not deterministic and does not match the simulation values

in the value domain as the functional model (without any platform mapping) restoring time determinism and flow preservation. In addition, our customized code generation makes use of a generic API that enables retargetability to a number of possible operating system, easing portability. The produced code contains function calls for task creation, priority setting, timer and dispatcher events plus a set of additional service operations.

5 Abstract Operating System

Our objective is to improve the code generation for multicore platforms by making the generated code independent from the platform specifics (OS and HW architecture), and correct with respect to the semantics preservation requirements presented in the previous section. This requires two main intermediate results:

- Design an abstract OS API that provides the main concepts for concurrency, communication and synchronization that are needed for the semantics-preserving implementation of Simulink models on multicores.
- Define a code generation pattern that is semantics preserving and write a set of Target Language Compiler (TLC) files for it.

The advantages of our proposed approach are the following. Every time a new platform is introduced, meaning a new hardware configuration, or a new operating system, or even a new subsystem to task mapping definition, the user can trust that the model execution behavior will be unchanged. In addition, if a new operating system is introduced, the user does not have to wait for a new code generator to be available, nor it has to write its own generation templates using the (not widely known) TLC language. To port the generated code to a new OS, the designer only needs to port the functions of the abstract API to the selected OS. This porting is usually very simple and consists of writing a few lines of code (or even a macro translation) for each function. We show data about the complexity of the porting of the abstract API to Windows and Linux at the end of this section.

5.1   OS Abstraction

The three main concepts needed for the abstract OS API are the following:

– Support for thread creation and management
– Support for synchronization based on events. Two types of events are required
  • Timer Events: for periodic activations
  • Condition Event: for the enforcement of the order of execution (activation) of the tasks by the dispatcher
– Communication mechanisms that can enforce data consistency and flow preservation (see [31]).

File Structure. The extensions provided are summarized in Fig. 8, where the (darker and lighter) gray boxes illustrate our contribution. The abstract OS API is defined in a generic header file AOS.h. Another header file AOS_cfg.h provides the other declarations and macros that are needed for mapping the abstract API onto the target OS functions. The actual definition of the abstract OS functions in terms of the concrete OS functions (besides the macros), is implemented in the file AOS_cfg.c. The additional implementation is a custom TLC file that produces the code implementation of the system using the AOS functions. In the following, we outline the abstract API.

Thread Management. A thread is defined by a set of attributes stored in a thread description structure (of type AOSThreadInfoType). Among them are: the thread priority, affinity, and the thread handle (or entry point). Some of these attributes are OS-dependent and will be themselves represented by an abstract type (to be redefined in the OS-specific files).

The main functions for thread management are summarized in the following list. All the API functions start with AOS which is an abbreviation of Abstract Operating System.

Thread functions

```
AOSStatusType AOSCreateThread(AOSThreadInfoType *threadInfo);
AOSThreadType AOSGetCurrentThread();
AOSThreadMaskType AOSGetCoreAffinityMask(int *coreAffinity,
        int thread_index,
        int nbrOfCoresPerThread);
AOSStatusType AOSSetThreadPriority(AOSThreadType thread,
      AOSThreadPriorityType prio);
void AOSThreadTerminate();
AOSStatusType AOSDeleteThread(AOSThreadInfoType *thread);
AOSStatusType AOSWaitForThreadToTerminate(AOSThreadInfoType
    *threadInfo);
```

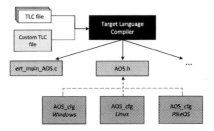

Fig. 8. AOS mapping

The meaning of the functions can be easily derived from the signature. They are used for thread creation, setting the priority and the affinity of the thread, to signal the thread termination or to delete it and, finally, for waiting for a thread to terminate.

Each thread, is scheduled by the core dispatchers. To enable event signaling from the system to its subsystem, two conditional events are associated to each thread. The first event is used to send a start event from the dispatcher to the thread. The second event is used to signal the thread termination from the thread to the dispatcher to check for time overruns.

Events. As for the task management, the meaning of most functions is intuitive and can easily be derived from the signature. Events can be timer or condition events. An abstract type AOSEventType is defined for them. A timer event is used to trigger the periodic execution of the core dispatchers. Condition events are used for starting threads and signaling their completion and to enforce an order of execution among threads. The events management API is summarized in the following.

Event functions

```
AOSStatusType AOSWaitEvent(AOSEventType *event);
AOSStatusType AOSPeekEvent(AOSEventType *event);
AOSStatusType AOSDeleteEvent(AOSEventType *event);
```

Generic event functions are used to wait for a (timer or condition) event, to check for its being set and to delete an event object.

Timer functions

```
AOSStatusType AOSCreateTimer(AOSEventType *event);
AOSStatusType AOSSetTimer(AOSEventType *event,
                          int sec,
                          int nsec,
                          boolean_T periodic);
AOSStatusType AOSSendSignalTimer(AOSEventType *event);
```

Timer functions allow to create a timer object, set to expire (as one shot or periodic) at future times and also to explicitly send a timer event signal.

Condition functions

```
AOSStatusType AOSCreateCondition(AOSEventType *event,
                       boolean_T initialState);
AOSStatusType AOSSetCondition(AOSEventType *event);
```

Similarly, two functions can be used to create a condition object and to set its corresponding condition event. Finally, an additional set of API functions is available for monitoring, error management and system termination cleanup.

We wrote a TLC program (TLC code is used to customize code generation in Simulink) to generate code from a Simulink model that makes use of our abstract API. The TLC code was developed using as a template similar template files that are used to generate code for Linux, Windows and VxWorks.

In addition, we implemented the mapping between the abstract operating system API and three operating systems: PikeOS [26], Linux and Windows.

As outlined in Fig. 8, the mapping consist of a header and a source file. For these three OS mappings, the header file required between 100 and 150 lines and the source file between 120 and 350 lines, including comments and empty lines. The longest mapping function is the function for creating a thread, which is 57 lines long in the case of a PikeOS mapping. Even in this case, creating a thread and providing the correct attributes does not require special skills and can be easily performed. Other functions require just a single line (or macro), as for the mapping of the function *AOSGetCurrentThread*.

```
/* Mapping to Windows */
#define AOSGetCurrentThread()    GetCurrentThread()

/* Mapping to PikeOS */
#define AOSGetCurrentThread()    p4_my_thread()

/* Mapping to Linux */
#define AOSGetCurrentThread()    pthread_self()
```

The extension was compared to the standard code generation for the Windows OS. The speed overhead was measured using the Measure-Command, where the results showed that the implementation using the AOS API had no significant overhead. The overhead in terms of size is shown in Table 1.

Table 1. Section sizes of object files

	Default	AOS API
.text	74699	76155
.rdata	28888	29010
.data	4096	4096

Our abstract OS generation process and the remapping code have been tried on one of the example models provided by The MathWorks in the Simulink release for the assignment of task to cores for multi-core programming [16].

We generated code for Linux and Windows. The result of the execution of the generated code was always the same as the execution of the code generated for the model without any platform mapping. In addition, we compared the execution time of the Windows version with and without out abstract API and remapping layer. The overhead of the mapping layer seems to be negligible for the example model we tried. The largest time difference in our runs was in the order of less than $2 * 10^{-5}$ as a fraction of the total model execution time. Considering that the model performs an extremely limited set of computations (and therefore the impact of the OS calls is significant), and that is several runs our AOS implementation actually performed better than the native Windows API code, we may conclude that the approach is at the very least feasible.

The entire implementation is now available as open source on the Matlab Central repository [1].

6   Flow Preserving Implementation

Finally, we outline the actions that are required to generate code that preserves the causality order of blocks and the execution semantics of a purely functional (that is, without platform mapping) model. The approach is applicable to any mapping of subsystems into tasks and then cores.

The first step consists in analyzing the model to find loops among subsystems that go across the core boundary.

For each such loop, the subsystems in it are examined to find at least one subsystem that has a non-feedthrough dependency between the input and output ports that are part of the loop. Such subsystem must always exist because the model is guaranteed to have no algebraic loops (code generation is otherwise not allowed). For this subsystem, all the internal (to the subsystem) paths between the input and output port contain at least one block of type non-feedthrough, that is, that there exists a cut, consisting only of non-feedthrough blocks in the signal graph between the input and output port.

Assume the subsystem is denoted as S_i (as shown in the figure), and let the input and output ports that are part of the loop be labeled as i_i and o_i.

Assume all the blocks that are in the loop from o_i back to i_i belonging to outer subsystems are ordered for execution (according to the partial order defined by their feedthrough dependencies) as in $b_p, \ldots, b_q$. Consider the graph of all the data dependencies that go from the input port to the output port. This graph must have at least one cut consisting of non-feedthrough blocks (such as $b_{i,j}, b_{i,k}$ and $b_{i,z}$ in the figure). Let $b_{i,n}$ be the writer block for the output port in the loop.

Denote as $\mathcal{B}_a$ an execution order for all the blocks in the dependency graph between $b_{i,1}$ and the blocks in the cut (excluded) that is consistent with their partial execution order. Also, denote as $\mathcal{B}_b$ an execution order for all the blocks in the cut and the following blocks in the graph until $b_{i,n}$, that is consistent with their partial execution order.

---

[1] https://it.mathworks.com/matlabcentral/fileexchange/65247-aos-api.

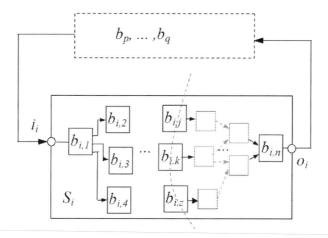

Fig. 9. Splitting subsystems in tasks

An execution order for the block output update functions that is consistent with the set of all the partial orders on the blocks executions is

$$[\mathcal{B}_b \to b_{i,n}] \to [b_p \to \ldots \to b_q] \to [b_{i,1} \to \mathcal{B}_a]$$

Hence, a possible task model for the implementation of this system consists of splitting the blocks of S_i in two tasks, one $\tau_{i,1}$ implementing the blocks in $[\mathcal{B}_b \to b_{i,n}]$, the other $\tau_{i,2}$ implementing the blocks in $[b_{i,1} \to \mathcal{B}_b]$.

Splitting the subsystem requires navigating the graph of signals from the output port to the first set of non-feedthrough blocks realizing a cut in the graph of the paths to the input port in the loop. For details on how to possibly partition subsystems, please refer to [9,19] discussing similar problems in the context of modular code generation. In the simple system of Fig. 9, the loop in the bottom part of the figure can be broken by partitioning the subsystem Sub2 in such a way that all the delay block on the bottom right is split and associated to a separate subsystem.

After the subsystems are partitioned, the new set of subsystems is now free from cyclic dependencies. A new set of tasks can be generated from them and allocated to cores. In the new set, the feedthrough dependencies among subsystems are a directed graph and they can be preserved in the generated code by using the event signaling mechanism of our abstract API to enforce the correct task execution order (as also recommended in [31]).

7   Conclusion and Future Work

In this paper, we presented an implementation for generating code from Simulink to an abstract operating system. The generated code can be remapped to the preferred operating system by simply rewriting a thin layer of code for API translation. We also extended the API with mechanisms to guarantee data consistency and flow preservation when executing on multi-core platforms as well as support for inter-core communication. Enforcing the order of execution that guarantees causality in multicores requires changing the code generation paradigm and changing the model to split subsystems breaking the feedthrough dependencies.

Acknowledgments. This work has been sponsored by The MathWorks.

References

1. AUTOSAR. http://www.autosar.org. Accessed 23 Mar 2017
2. POSIX - Austin Joint Working Group. http://standards.ieee.org/develop/wg/POSIX.html. Accessed 31 Mar 2017
3. Al-bayati, Z., Sun, Y., Zeng, H., Di Natale, M., Zhu, Q., Meyer, B.: Task placement and selection of data consistency mechanisms for real-time multicore applications. In: 2015 IEEE Real-Time and Embedded Technology and Applications Symposium (RTAS), pp. 172–181. IEEE (2015)
4. Ansys: SCADE suite product web page. http://www.esterel-technologies.com/products/scade-suite/. Accessed 23 Mar 2017
5. Boussinot, F., De Simone, R.: The Esterel language. Proc. IEEE **79**(9), 1293–1304 (1991)
6. Brandenburg, B., Gul, M.: Global scheduling not required: simple, near-optimal multiprocessor real-time scheduling with semi-partitioned reservations. In: Proceedings of the 37th IEEE Real-Time Systems Symposium (RTSS 2016), pp. 99–110, December 2016
7. Caspi, P., Curic, A., Maignan, A., Sofronis, C., Tripakis, S., Niebert, P.: From simulink to SCADE/Lustre to TTA: a layered approach for distributed embedded applications. In: ACM Sigplan Notices, vol. 38, pp. 153–162. ACM (2003)
8. Caspi, P., Scaife, N., Sofronis, C., Tripakis, S.: Semantics-preserving multitask implementation of synchronous programs. ACM Trans. Embed. Comput. Syst. (TECS) **7**(2), 15 (2008)
9. Deng, P., Cremona, F., Zhu, Q., Di Natale, M., Zeng, H.: A model-based synthesis flow for automotive CPS. In: Proceedings of the ACM/IEEE Sixth International Conference on Cyber-Physical System, Seattle, pp. 198–207, April 2015
10. Di Natale, M., Guo, L., Zeng, H., Sangiovanni-Vincentelli, A.: Synthesis of multitask implementations of simulink models with minimum delays. IEEE Trans. Industr. Inf. **6**(4), 637–651 (2010)
11. Eker, J., Janneck, J., Lee, E.A., Liu, J., Liu, X., Ludvig, J., Sachs, S., Xiong, Y.: Taming heterogeneity - the Ptolemy approach **91**(1), 127–144 (2003)
12. Balarin, F., Watanabe, Y., Hsieh, H., Lavagno, L., Passerone, C., Sangiovanni-Vincentelli, A.L.: Metropolis: an integrated electronic system design environment. Computer **36**(4), 45–52 (2003)
13. Grantley, H.J., Ye, W.: Stuart: multi-target modelling for embedded software development for automotive applications. https://es.mathworks.com/tagteam/20307_91197v00_Multi-Target_Modeling_2004-01-0269.pdf. Accessed 23 Mar 2017
14. Halbwachs, N., Caspi, P., Raymond, P., Pilaud, D.: The synchronous data flow programming language LUSTRE. Proc. IEEE **79**(9), 1305–1320 (1991)
15. Halbwachs, N.: Synchronous programming of reactive systems. In: Hu, A.J., Vardi, M.Y. (eds.) CAV 1998. LNCS, vol. 1427, pp. 1–16. Springer, Heidelberg (1998). https://doi.org/10.1007/BFb0028726
16. TMW Inc.: Assigning tasks to cores for multicore programming. http://www.mathworks.com. Accessed 23 Mar 2017

17. LeGuernic, P., Gautier, T., Le Borgne, M., Le Maire, C.: Programming real-time applications with SIGNAL. Proc. IEEE **79**(9), 1321–1336 (1991)
18. Lublinerman, R., Tripakis, S.: Modularity vs. reusability: code generation from synchronous block diagrams. In: Proceedings of the Design, Automation and Test in Europe Conference (DATE 2008). ACM (2008)
19. Lublinerman, R., Tripakis, S.: Modular code generation from triggered and timed block diagrams. In: Real-Time and Embedded Technology and Applications Symposium (RTAS 2008), June 2008
20. Nigel Holliday, T.M.E.: Software development with real-time workshop embedded coder. https://it.mathworks.com/solutions/aerospace-defense/presentations.html. Accessed 23 Mar 2017
21. OSEK OS: VDX operating system specification 2.2.1. OSEK Group (2003)
22. Pagetti, C., Saussie, D., Gratia, R., Noulard, E., Siron, P.: The ROSACE case study: from simulink specification to multi/many-core execution. In: Proceedings of the Real-Time and Embedded Technology and Applications Symposium (RTAS 2014) (2014)
23. Rixner, S., Dally, W.J., Kapasi, U.J., Mattson, P., Owens, J.D.: Memory access scheduling. In: ACM SIGARCH Computer Architecture News, vol. 28, pp. 128–138. ACM (2000)
24. Scaife, N., Sofronis, C., Caspi, P., Tripakis, S., Maraninchi, F.: Defining and translating a safe subset of simulink/stateflow into lustre. In: Proceedings of the 4th ACM International Conference on Embedded Software, pp. 259–268. ACM (2004)
25. Sharifi, A., Kultursay, E., Kandemir, M., Das, C.R.: Addressing end-to-end memory access latency in noc-based multicores. In: 2012 45th Annual IEEE/ACM International Symposium on Microarchitecture (MICRO), pp. 294–304. IEEE (2012)
26. SysGO AG: Pike OS web page. https://www.sysgo.com/products/pikeos-hypervisor/. Accessed 23 Mar 2017
27. The MathWorks: Simulink and StateFlow user manuals. http://www.mathworks.com. Accessed 23 Mar 2017
28. Tripakis, S., Sofronis, C., Caspi, P., Curic, A.: Translating discrete-time simulink to lustre. ACM Trans. Embed. Comput. Syst. (TECS) **4**(4), 779–818 (2005)
29. Tripakis, S., Sofronis, C., Scaife, N., Caspi, P.: Semantics-preserving and memory-efficient implementation of inter-task communication on static-priority or EDF schedulers. In: Proceedings of the 5th ACM International Conference on Embedded Software, pp. 353–360. ACM (2005)
30. Wang, G., Di Natale, M., Mosterman, P.J., Sangiovanni-Vincentelli, A.: Automatic code generation for synchronous reactive communication. In: 2009 International Conference on Embedded Software and Systems, ICESS 2009, pp. 40–47. IEEE (2009)
31. Zeng, H., Di Natale, M.: Mechanisms for guaranteeing data consistency and flow preservation in AUTOSAR software on multi-core platforms. In: 2011 6th IEEE International Symposium on Industrial Embedded Systems (SIES), pp. 140–149. IEEE (2011)
32. Zhu, Q., Zeng, H., Zheng, W., Natale, M.D., Sangiovanni-Vincentelli, A.: Optimization of task allocation and priority assignment in hard real-time distributed systems. ACM Trans. Embed. Comput. Syst. (TECS) **11**(4), 85 (2012)
33. Zou, J., Matic, S., Lee, E.A., Feng, T.H., Derler, P.: Execution strategies for PTIDES, a programming model for distributed embedded systems. In: Proceedings of the IEEE Real-Time and Embedded Technology and Applications Symposium (RTAS), April 2009

A Semantic Account of Rigorous Simulation

Adam Duracz[1], Eugenio Moggi[2], Walid Taha[3(✉)], and Zhenchao Lin[4]

[1] Rice University, Houston, TX, USA
adam.duracz@rice.edu
[2] DIBRIS, Genova University, Genova, Italy
moggi@unige.it
[3] Halmstad University, Halmstad, Sweden
walid.taha@hh.se
[4] Zhejiang University, Hangzhou, China
cszclin@gmail.com

Abstract. Hybrid systems are a powerful formalism for modeling cyber-physical systems. Reachability analysis is a general method for checking safety properties, especially in the presence of uncertainty and non-determinism. Rigorous simulation is a convenient tool for reachability analysis of hybrid systems. However, to serve as proof tool, a rigorous simulator must be correct w.r.t. a clearly defined notion of reachability, which captures what is *intuitively* reachable in finite time.

As a step towards addressing this challenge, this paper presents a rigorous simulator in the form of an operational semantics and a specification in the form of a denotational semantics. We show that, under certain conditions about the representation of enclosures, the rigorous simulator is correct. We also show that finding a representation satisfying these assumptions is non-trivial.

Keywords: Reachability analysis · Correctness
Programming languages

1 Introduction

The crux of the intellectual problem with Cyber-Physical Systems (CPS) is that, for the models that we use for the physical world, such as ODEs or DAEs, there is a huge body of knowledge that has built up since the 19th century on how to model physical systems using these abstractions. In the computing world, we also developed a lot of abstractions over a much shorter history, from the 1930s or so, to talk about computing. And those two classes of abstractions don't play together. Generally, one has a notion of time, the other doesn't. How do you make these systems play

Funded by USA National Science Foundation and Swedish Knowledge Foundation. Most of the work on this paper was done when the authors were at Halmstad Univ.

together? This is a big intellectual challenge. We are basically trying to take two fabulously developed sets of theories that have diverged, and bring them back together.—Edward A. Lee, 2012.[1]

No sooner had the term CPS been coined by Helen Gill in 2006 [17] that Lee began, with such characteristic eloquence, to tirelessly inspire multitudes of researchers, including the authors, to address the challenges of modeling Cyber-Physical Systems. For us, the following issues are of particular interest:

1. A mathematics that can cope with both continuous and discrete changes.
2. The possibility of extending to an heterogeneous setting modeling methods and practices developed only for the continuous or the discrete setting.
3. Software tools that can support modeling in an heterogeneous setting.

Hybrid automata [4,12] and the more general hybrid systems [11] appear to address the first issue. Reachability analysis is an important tool to address safety in both the continuous and discrete setting, and its extension to a broader setting is highly desirable. Other features make reachability analysis attractive. First, it can incorporate both symbolic and numerical methods for solving continuous dynamics, allowing a trade-off between speed and generality. Second, given the broad applicability of the notions of "safe sets" and "bad sets", reachability can be used to analyze the designs of a wide range of cyber-physical systems. Third, because of its similarity to numerical simulation, it has an intuitive appeal for a broad audience and a more gradual learning curve than other formal methods.

Motivated by these observations, the Acumen modeling language [1,10,22,24,25,28] allows users to describe hybrid systems that can then be simulated either "traditionally" or "rigorously".

Rigorous simulation [8] uses a time-bounded reachability algorithm that proceeds in fixed size time steps, scanning the time domain from zero to a user-specified end time, and at each step computes an *over-approximation* of the states reachable in that time interval. In [10] rigorous simulation has been used to analyze early-stage designs of Advanced Driver Assistance Systems (ADAS).

1.1   Problem

Validated numerics, including directed rounding and other rigorous methods for programming with floating point numbers, address the question of correctness of numerical methods, and show how interval methods can be used to overcome this problem [21,23]. However, two other steps are needed to establish correctness of a rigorous simulator (or some other tool for reachability analysis).

– to give a mathematical definition of the set of reachable states, and
– to prove that the tool computes an over-approximation of this set.

---

[1] Edward A. Lee, First Halmstad Colloquium, Halmstad Univ., February 10th, 2012. Minutes 1:17-1:20 in video http://bit.ly/HC-EAL, paraphrased slightly for clarity.

For a discrete system reachability is given by the reflexive and transitive closure $\rightarrow^*$ of the transition relation $\rightarrow$ describing how the state of the system changes at each tick of the clock. What is needed is a generalization, that copes with real time and continuous state spaces.

The category **Top** of topological spaces and continuous maps is an obvious choice, in fact: a set amounts to a discrete space, an Euclidean space (more generally a metric space) comes with the topology generated by its *open balls*, a complete lattice can be equipped with Alexandrov topology or Scott topology.

1.2   Contributions and Organization of This Paper

The main contributions of this paper are the denotational semantics used as a reference to define correctness criteria, the definition of a rigorous simulator in the form of an operational semantics *parameterized* wrt an abstract data-type of timed enclosures, a modular strategy for proving the correctness of an operational semantics with respect to the denotational semantics. The strategy captures our intuitive understanding of how implementation and specification should relate. At the same time, this approach places demands on the abstract data-type of timed enclosures. The rest of the paper is organized as follows:

– Section 2 gives an overview, driven by examples, of rigorous simulation.
– Section 3 gives the denotational semantics of a minimal modeling language, where a *model* is interpreted by a hybrid system [11]. We endorse hybrid systems for their simplicity and generality, in particular they fully support non-determinism, which is essential to model *known unknowns* and *don't care*. Then, we define (time-bounded) reachability in the form of a monotonic map induced by a (timed) transition relation.
– Section 4 describes a rigorous simulator as a small-step operational semantics manipulating *timed enclosure*. We make few connections with Sect. 3, in order to exemplify a possible interpretation of *timed enclosure*.
– Section 5 gives an interpretation for all entities used by the operational semantics and proves correctness in the form of an *assume-guarantee* result.

2   Hybrid Systems and Rigorous Simulation

In a modeling language hybrid systems can be described as collections of guarded jumps and guarded flows. To use a programming language metaphor, they are if-statements saying when the system should change discretely or continuously. Without going into syntactic details, we can illustrate some key concepts of rigorous simulation with two examples:

1. Saw Tooth: This is a system that climbs continuously at speed a per second until it reaches the height of b, at which point it resets to zero, from where it can resume its continuous climbing behavior. As defaults we will take parameters $a = 1$ and $b = 1$; and as initial value for height $x_0(0) = 0$.

2. Bouncing Ball: This is a system that starts at a certain height and a certain speed and it is subject to a downwards acceleration g until it hits the ground at height zero, at which point it loses energy and bounces with a speed equal to a fraction c of its speed. As defaults we will take parameters $g = 1$ and $c = 0.5$; and as initial values for height $x_0(0) = 1$ and for speed $x_1(0) = 0$.

2.1 Basic Concepts

Rigorous simulation proceeds through time by discrete steps. An key concept in rigorous simulation (or reachability analysis) is that of an *enclosure*, i.e., a machine-representable entity that over-approximates the set of states reached within a time interval $[0, h]$ by the system being simulated (or analyzed). Whereas traditional simulation (assumes that the system is deterministic and) produces a *point approximation* for the state reached at the end of a time step, Acumen's rigorous simulation produces a set of *triples*.

The **first plot in** Fig. 1 illustrates the results for the first two time steps in a simulation of the saw tooth example. To make the visual representation easy to read, we start the system with an initial value that is not a point but a set of possible values, namely, the interval $[0, 0.1]$. Each triple consists of three intervals: the first (black box) over-approximates the set of values at the start, the second (pink box) over-approximates the set of values taken by x_0 during the entire time step, and the third (black box) over-approximates the set of values at the end, or equivalently at the start of the next time step. This plot displays two triples that over-approximate the *trajectory* $x_0(t) = t$ with $t < b$. The second interval in a triple always contains the other two, which give more precise bounds for the start and the end, and help main precision across steps.

A powerful feature of rigorous simulation is the ability to start, work, and compute with sets values. We started with a set of initial values because it is easier to see on the visualization. One can also start with a single initial value, but this exact value can be harder to see. The **second plot in** Fig. 1 is produced when we start with the value zero. Visualizing triples in this manner allows us to distinguish between uncertainty due to the size of the time step and uncertainty in the set of values being passed from one step to the next. Visualizing triples enables the user to pinpoint the sources of uncertainty in results, be it uncertainty about inputs, due to underlying numerics, or due to the fact that an algorithm is stepping discretely through time. For example, if we allow the Saw Tooth system start from a single initial value and run longer, we can observe some important artifacts of how rigorous simulation deals with discrete events.

In general, the exact time when an event occurs in a continuous system may not be representable nor computable. This means that a rigorous simulation algorithm must reason about what happens when an event occurs at some unknown time within the time step. The **third plot in** Fig. 1 runs the simulation longer and shows the results after the first jump in the saw tooth system. The results give a hint of how events are handled. In essence, we consider all values taken by $x_0(t)$ from the start to the end of the time step. Then, we compute the result of

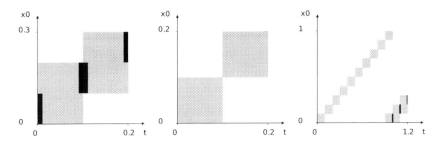

Fig. 1. Simulation steps, triples, flows, and jumps (Color figure online)

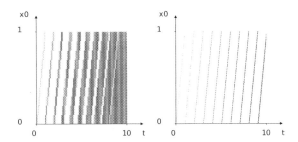

Fig. 2. Jumps, uncertainty, and simulation step size

the jump from that set. The only question that remains is how long the system can evolve after that point and until the end of the time step. We must work with the worst case, i.e., it can evolve for anywhere between zero and the length of the time step. The result is that the final value at the end of the time step is often "blurred" with uncertainty.

The reader may be alarmed that this means that uncertainty can quickly accumulate due to simulation. This is only half true. Errors can also decrease during a simulation. The **two plots in** Fig. 2 give the simulation of the saw tooth system for ten seconds, one with step size 0.1, the other with step size 0.01. The plots show that a smaller step size can slow the rate at which error is added, but it is unlikely to stop it. There are two features of rigorous simulation that can stop and even reduce error. The first is explicit constraints. For example, in the saw tooth example, even though the each event adds uncertainty, the value of x_0 remains bounded between 0 and 1. This is due to exploiting the information present in the guards to the events using, for examples, the contractor techniques advocated by Jaulin [6,13]. The second is that when the system being studied has stable dynamics, this dynamics can be used to absorb the uncertainties due to simulation, and the error can eventually become smaller. This means that, as long we are designing stable systems, accurate rigorous simulation should be possible for good designs [9].

2.2 Zeno Behavior

More challenging problems for rigorous simulation arise from the interaction between continuous and discrete dynamics, including Zeno [14,15,26,27] and

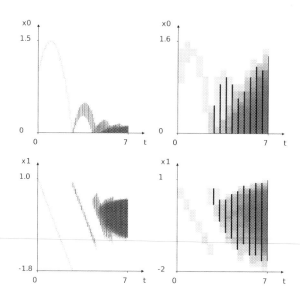

Fig. 3. Rigorous simulation past Zeno point. Two valid but divergent simulations. (Color figure online)

chattering behavior [2,3,18,19]. In these behaviors there is an infinite number of discrete events (jumps) in a finite amount of time, thus the simulator has to handle an unknown number of jumps within a single time step. Previous work involving some of the authors [15,16] showed how such systems can nevertheless be rigorously simulated using enclosures, i.e., by demonstrating that "no transition can take the system outside a given enclosure". The bouncing ball is a classic example of a system that can exhibit Zeno behavior.

The **plots on the left** of Fig. 3 display the height x_0 and the speed x_1 of the ball for the first simulation. Triples generated during a simulation step can overlap, which leads to a red (darker pink) color. In general, a simulation step can generate many triples, due to a wide range of uncertainties, including whether or not a guard is true. For example, the third "falling band" for speed starts before the end of the second falling band. This is because in some of the possible trajectories the ball has already bounced twice, while in some others not. Such uncertainty is natural in the presence of discrete events, and increases close to Zeno points. This increase is captured by the increased intensity of the red color. In this example, the maximum height that the ball reaches after each bounce forms a geometric series. The Zeno point for this example is reached before $t = 7$. Thus, this simulation successfully goes beyond the Zeno point. What is not achieved, however, is to stop the increase of uncertainty. Increasing uncertainty is confirmed by the (slowly) increasing size of the enclosure for both variables as we get closer to $t = 7$. The **plots on the right** of Fig. 3 confirm this divergence. They show the simulation results for the same system with the same initial conditions but with a bigger time step. Because this system is self-similar as we approach the Zeno point, using a proportionally larger time step is

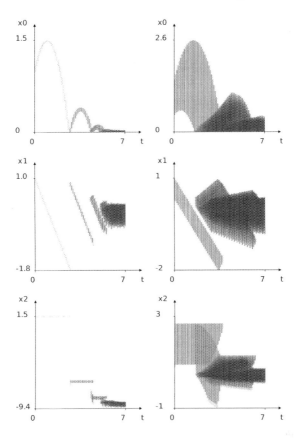

Fig. 4. Rigorous simulation past Zeno point - valid and convergent enclosures

equivalent to zooming in around the Zeno point. The second diagram confirms that the overall size of the enclosures is increasing.

The **plots in** Fig. 4 show how adding an extra variable x_2 for the (kinetic plus potential) energy of the system (which changes at bounces and stays constant otherwise) allows to achieve contracting enclosures for the system. To illustrate the robustness of this phenomena, the plots on the right show a simulation for the system but with larger time steps *and* much larger uncertainty about the initial value of the height and speed at the start of simulation. As the graph shows, the enclosures still converge. This is confirmed by the falling energy levels, which strongly limit the set of possible values for height and speed.

3   Denotational Semantics

We define the criteria that a simulator for hybrid systems on an Euclidean space $\mathbb{S} \triangleq \mathbb{R}^n$ must satisfy to be considered *rigorous*, namely it must *over-approximate* the *safe evolution map* E_h (see Definition 3) of the system over an initial segment $[0, h]$ of the continuous time-line $\mathbb{T} \triangleq \{d : \mathbb{R} | d \geq 0\}$.

In this section we use the cartesian closed category **Po** of complete lattices and monotonic maps, in particular E_h is such a map. **Po** is also the natural setting for defining and comparing *abstract interpretations* [7]. We assume familiarity with the category **Top** of topological spaces and continuous maps, some topological notions (such as open, close and compact subset) and the definition of derivative (in the context of Euclidean spaces).

In the rest of the paper, we write $x : X$ for membership $x \in X$, $\mathsf{P}(X)$ for the set of subsets of X, $\mathsf{P}_f(X)$ for the set of finite subsets of X, and make limited use of the category $\mathbf{Set}_p$ of sets and partial maps.

Definition 1 (HS [11]). *A **Hybrid System** (HS for short) is a pair (F, G) of binary relations on $\mathbb{S}$, respectively called **flow** and **jump** relation, its **support** is given by $\mathsf{S}(F, G) \triangleq \{s | \exists s'.s\, F\, s' \vee s\, G\, s' \vee s'\, G\, s\}$. Finally, $\mathbb{H}(\mathbb{S}) \triangleq \mathsf{P}(\mathbb{S}^2)^2$ denotes the complete lattice of HS on $\mathbb{S}$ ordered by component-wise inclusion.*

As customary in mathematical logic, we must interpret syntactic entities by mathematical entities. This *semantic* link is essential to relate the transformations implemented by a computer program (like a simulator) to some mathematical function.

For our purposes it is useful to split the syntax in two layers:

- The upper layer considers modes q as primitive entities, and it suffices to define our denotational and operational semantics and to prove correctness
- The lower layer gives the concrete syntax for modes, which usually depends on the expressions handled by the libraries used, while the cardinality of X determines the Euclidean space $\mathbb{R}^n$ used by the denotational semantics.

mode	$q \in Q ::= \ldots$
model	$m \in M ::= q \mid m_1, m_2$

variable	$x \in X$ finite set
real exp	$e ::= x \mid f(e_i | i : \#f)$
bool exp	$b ::= p(e_i | i : \#p) \mid b_1 \wedge b_2 \mid b_1 \vee b_2$
mode	$q \in Q ::= \text{if } b \text{ flow } (x' = e_x | x : X) \mid \text{if } b \text{ jump } (x^+ = e_x | x : X)$

More generally, flows and jumps could be boolean expressions (with variables $X, \dot{X}$ and X, X^+ respectively) denoting binary relations on $\mathbb{R}^n$.

We interpret a mode $q : Q$ by a HS $[\![q]\!] : \mathbb{H}(\mathbb{S})$, and extend the interpretation to models m and sets Q of modes by taking component-wise union, e.g.

$$[\![m_1, m_2]\!] \triangleq [\![m_1]\!] \cup [\![m_2]\!] = (F_1 \cup F_2, G_1 \cup G_2) \text{ when } [\![m_i]\!] = (F_i, G_i) : \mathbb{H}(\mathbb{S})$$

Example 1. We describe a simple system with a parameter $b : [0, 1]$, namely a timer v with a timeout u, that exhibits a Zeno behaviour when $b : (0, 1)$. Its description as a model m_T is q_0, q_1, q_2, where

$q_0 = \text{if } 0 < v < u \text{ flow } v' = 1, u' = 0$	timer increases as time flows
$q_1 = \text{if } 0 < v = u \text{ jump } v^+ = 0, u^+ = bu$	timer reset to 0 and timeout updated
$q_2 = \text{if } v = u = 0 \text{ jump } v^+ = 0, u^+ = 1$	timeout reset to 1

Its description as a HS $\mathcal{H}_T = (F, G) = [\![m_T]\!]$ on $\mathbb{R}^2$ is

$$F = \{((v, u), (1, 0))|0 < v < u\} \quad G = \{((u, u)(0, bu))|0 < u\} \uplus \{((0, 0), (0, 1))\}$$

For cardinality reasons it is impossible to have finitary representations for all elements of an Euclidean space $\mathbb{S}$. In a complete lattice, like $\mathsf{P}(\mathbb{S})$, the order allows us to tell when (the interpretation of) a representation approximates an element. Similar considerations motivate the use of interval arithmetic.

Definition 2 (TR). *The **transition relation** $\xrightarrow[(F,G)]{}$: $\mathsf{P}(\mathbb{S} \times \mathbb{T} \times \mathbb{S})$ of a HS is $s \xrightarrow[(F,G)]{d} s' \overset{\Delta}{\Longleftrightarrow} d = 0 \wedge s\,G\,s'$ or $d > 0 \wedge \exists f : \mathbf{Top}([0, d], \mathbb{S})$ such that*

- *the derivative $\dot{f}$ of f is defined and continuous in $(0, d)$*
- *$s = f(0)$, $s' = f(d)$ and $\forall t : (0, d).f(t)\,F\,\dot{f}(t)$.*

In the later case we say that f realizes the transition.

The transition relation allows to define the *safe evolution map,* which computes an over-approximation of the states reachable at a given time by a HS, even when the HS has Zeno behaviors.

Definition 3 (Safe evolution). *Let $\mathsf{C}(\mathbb{S})$ be the complete lattice of **closed subsets** of a topological space $\mathbb{S}$ (ordered by inclusion). The time-bounded **transition** map $\mathsf{T}_h : \mathbf{Po}(\mathbb{H}(\mathbb{S}) \times \mathsf{P}([0], h] \times \mathbb{S}), \mathsf{P}([0, h] \times \mathbb{S}))$ and **safe evolution** map $\mathsf{E}_h : \mathbf{Po}(\mathbb{H}(\mathbb{S}) \times \mathsf{P}([0, h] \times \mathbb{S}), \mathsf{C}([0, h] \times \mathbb{S}))$ are given by*

- $\mathsf{T}_h(H, I) \overset{\Delta}{=} \{(t + d, s')|\exists s : \mathbb{S}.(t, s) : I \wedge s \xrightarrow[H]{d} s' \wedge t + d \leq h\}$
- $\mathsf{E}_h(H, I) \overset{\Delta}{=}$ *the smallest* $E : \mathsf{C}([0, h] \times \mathbb{S})$ *such that* $I \cup \mathsf{T}_h(H, E) \subseteq E$.

Remark 1. The map $\mathsf{T}_h(\mathcal{H}, -)$ corresponds to the binary relation $R_{\mathcal{H}}$ on $[0, h] \times \mathbb{S}$ st $(t, s)R_{\mathcal{H}}(t', s') \overset{\Delta}{\Longleftrightarrow} (0 \leq t \leq t' \leq h) \wedge s \xrightarrow[\mathcal{H}]{t'-t} s'$. In fact $\mathsf{T}_h(\mathcal{H}, I) = R_{\mathcal{H}}(I)$. $R_{\mathcal{H}}^*(I)$, where $R_{\mathcal{H}}^*$ is the reflexive and transitive closure of $R_{\mathcal{H}}$, captures only what is reachable from I in finitely many transitions, but may fail to capture what is reachable in finite time. The safe evolution map $\mathsf{E}_h(\mathcal{H}, I)$ avoids this pitfall by requiring E to be a closed subset (see [20]). An equivalent definition of $\mathsf{E}_h(\mathcal{H}, I)$ in terms of $R_{\mathcal{H}}$ is the smallest $E : \mathsf{P}([0, h] \times \mathbb{S})$ such that $I \cup R_{\mathcal{H}}(E) \cup \overline{E} \subseteq E$, and E is closed because $E \subseteq \overline{E}$ is always true.

  In a metric space there is another reason to use $\mathsf{C}(\mathbb{S})$ instead of $\mathsf{P}(\mathbb{S})$. If the accuracy to *discriminate* among points in $\mathbb{S}$ is δ, then a subset $S : \mathsf{P}(\mathbb{S})$ cannot be distinguished from the open subset $B(S, \delta) \overset{\Delta}{=} \{s'|\exists s : S.d_{\mathbb{S}}(s, s') < \delta\}$. But $S \subseteq \overline{S} \subseteq B(S, \delta)$, where $\overline{S}$ is the *closure* of S, i.e., the smallest $S' : \mathsf{C}(\mathbb{S})$ containing S. Therefore, one cannot distinguish two subsets of $\mathbb{S}$ with the same closure, no matter how small δ is.

Example 2. Let $\mathcal{H}$ be $\mathcal{H}_T$ in Example 1, then

- The transition relation $\xrightarrow{\quad}_{\mathcal{H}}$ is $(v, u) \xrightarrow{\ d\ } (v+d, u)$ when $0 \le v < v+d \le u$, $(u, u) \xrightarrow{\ 0\ } (0, bu)$ when $0 < u$, and $(0, 0) \xrightarrow{\ 0\ } (0, 1)$; in particular, one has $(0, u) \xrightarrow{\ u\ } (u, u) \xrightarrow{\ 0\ } (0, bu)$ when $0 < u$.
- The relation $R_{\mathcal{H}}$, which determines the map $\mathsf{T}_h(\mathcal{H}, -)$, is

$$\{((t, v, u), (t+d, v+d, u)) | 0 \le t < t+d \le h \wedge 0 \le v < v+d \le u\} \uplus$$
$$\{((t, u, u), (t, 0, bu)) | 0 \le t \le h \wedge 0 < u\} \uplus \{((t, 0, 0), (t, 0, 1)) | 0 \le t \le h\}$$

thus $s_0 R_{\mathcal{H}}^* s_n \overset{\triangle}{=} (t_n, 0, b^n u)$ when $0 < b, u$ and $t_n = \sum_{i:n} b^i u \le h$, but the Zeno point $s_\omega = (t_\omega, 0, 0)$ is not reachable, even when $t_\omega = \sum_{i:\omega} b^i u \le h$.
- The set $E = \mathsf{E}_h(\mathcal{H}, I)$ includes $R_{\mathcal{H}}^*(I)$, $s_\omega : E$ when $\forall n : \omega.s_n : E$, because s_ω is the limit of a sequence $(s_n | n : \omega)$ in E, and $R_{\mathcal{H}}^*(s_\omega) \subseteq E$ when $s_\omega : E$.

However, if $\mathcal{H}$ is modified so that the $(0, 0) \xrightarrow{\ 0\ } (0, 1)$ is removed or replaced by $(0, 0) \xrightarrow{\ 0\ } (0, 0)$, then the system cannot progress, i.e., $R_{\mathcal{H}}^*(s_\omega) = \{s_\omega\}$.

A minimal requirement for a simulator used for *safety analysis* should be *partial correctness* wrt E_h. Namely, given a symbolic description m of a HS and a representation *over-approximating* a set $I : \mathsf{P}(\mathbb{S})$ of initial states the simulator should either fail or compute an *over-approximation* of $\mathsf{E}_h([\![m]\!], [0] \times I)$, or of the bigger set $\mathsf{E}_h([\![m]\!], [0] \times \overline{I})$ (see the above considerations on indistinguishability).

The following result is relevant to prove correctness in Sect. 5.

Lemma 1. *Let F_i and G_j denote the HS $(F_i, \varnothing)$ and $(\varnothing, G_j)$ on $\mathbb{S}$, then*

1. $\xrightarrow{\quad}_{F_i \cup G_j} = \xrightarrow{\quad}_{F_i} \cup \xrightarrow{\quad}_{G_j}$
2. $\xrightarrow{\quad}_{G_0 \cup G_1} = \xrightarrow{\quad}_{G_0} \cup \xrightarrow{\quad}_{G_1}$
3. $\xrightarrow{\quad}_{F_0 \cup F_1} = \xrightarrow{\quad}_{F_0} \cup \xrightarrow{\quad}_{F_1}$, *if* $\overline{\mathsf{S}(F_0)}$ *and* $\overline{\mathsf{S}(F_1)}$ *are disjoint subsets of* $\mathbb{S}$

where $\overline{S}$ *is the **closure** of* $S : \mathsf{P}(\mathbb{S})$, *i.e., the smallest* $S' : \mathsf{C}(\mathbb{S})$ *such that* $S \subseteq S'$.

Proof. We prove only the last claim. If $f : \mathbf{Top}([0, d], \mathbb{S})$ realizes $s \xrightarrow[F_0 \cup F_1]{\ d\ } s'$, then the image of f is a subset of $\overline{\mathsf{S}(F_0 \cup F_1)} = \overline{\mathsf{S}(F_0)} \uplus \overline{\mathsf{S}(F_1)}$. By taking the inverse image of the two disjoint closed subsets we get a partitioning of $[0, d]$ in two disjoint closed subsets, but $[0, d]$ is connected, so one of them is empty. $\square$

Remark 2. The lemma says that the transition relation of the union of two HS $\mathcal{H}_0$ and $\mathcal{H}_1$ (on the same state space) is the union of their transition relations only if the flow relations of the two HS are *apart*, i.e., $\overline{\mathsf{S}(F_0)}$ and $\overline{\mathsf{S}(F_1)}$ are disjoint.

If $s \xrightarrow[F]{\ d\ } s'$, then s and s' belong to the same connected component of $\overline{\mathsf{S}(F)}$.

Given a flow relation F and a connected component C of $\overline{\mathsf{S}(F)}$, let F_C be the restriction of F to C. By definition the flow relations F_C are pairwise apart and $F = \bigcup_C F_C$, thus $\xrightarrow{\quad}_{F} = \bigcup_C \xrightarrow{\quad}_{F_C}$. Therefore, the connected components of $\overline{\mathsf{S}(F)}$ could be viewed as the *control modes* of a hybrid automaton [5].

4   Operational Semantics

The operational semantics uses some auxiliary domains and maps, which form an abstract data-type (ADT). To establish correctness of the operational semantics this ADT must satisfy certain properties. Here we give properties of the ADT that do not refer directly to the denotational semantics, in Sect. 5 we give more properties that make direct reference to the denotational semantics.

Enclosures. D is a countable set of **enclosures** d interpreted as closed subsets $[\![d]\!] : \mathsf{C}(\mathbb{S})$. We assume that D is closed wrt binary intersection $d_1 \cap d_2$, contains the empty enclosure $\varnothing$, and the **cover relation** $d \leq_{\mathsf{D}} [d_i | i : n] \stackrel{\triangle}{\Longleftrightarrow} [\![d]\!] \subseteq \bigcup_{i:n} [\![d_i]\!]$ is decidable (we drop the subscript when it is clear from the context). The inclusion relation on D is definable as $d' \subseteq d \stackrel{\triangle}{\Longleftrightarrow} d' \leq [d]$ and $\leq$ extends to a pre-order on D^*, namely $D' \leq D \stackrel{\triangle}{\Longleftrightarrow} \forall d' : D'.d' \leq D$.

A possible choice for D is the set of *P-boxes* in $\mathbb{R}^n$, i.e., cartesian products of n closed intervals $[x, y]$, whose endpoints are in a countable subset P of $\mathbb{R}$, eg the subset of rational numbers or the finite subset of floating point numbers.

Timed Enclosures. The operational semantics uses only an ADT Z of **timed enclosures**, representing over-approximations for closed subsets of $\mathbb{T} \times \mathbb{S}$. An *Acumen-like* implementation is $\mathsf{Z} \subset \mathsf{D} \times \mathsf{D} \times \mathsf{D}$ containing *initial* $e(z) = b(z) = \varnothing$ and *proper* $i(z), e(z) \subseteq b(z)$ triples, where $i(z)$, $b(z)$ and $e(z)$ denotes the three components of a $z : \mathsf{Z}$. The interpretation $[\![z]\!]_h : \mathsf{P}(\mathsf{C}([0, h] \times \mathbb{S}))$ is given by

$$C : [\![z]\!]_h \stackrel{\triangle}{\Longleftrightarrow} C(0) \subseteq [\![i(z)]\!] \wedge (\forall t : (0, h).C(t) \subseteq [\![b(z)]\!]) \wedge C(h) \subseteq [\![e(z)]\!]$$

where $C(t) \stackrel{\triangle}{=} \{s | (t, s) : C\}$ when $C : \mathsf{C}([0, h] \times \mathbb{S})$.

Z inherits from D intersection, defined component-wise, and the **cover relation** $z \leq_{\mathsf{Z}} [z_i | i : n] \stackrel{\triangle}{\Longleftrightarrow} \forall C : [\![z]\!]_h.\exists C' : \prod_{i:n} [\![z_i]\!]_h.C = \bigcup_{i:n} C'_i$ (the derived notions of inclusion and the pre-order $\leq$ on Z^* are defined as in the case of D).

Theorem 1. *The following decision procedure $\leq'$ is sound for the cover relation on Z, i.e., $z \leq' Z \implies z \leq_{\mathsf{Z}} Z$, and the converse holds when $\forall d : \mathsf{D}.[d]$ is convex*

$$z \leq' Z \stackrel{\triangle}{\Longleftrightarrow} \text{if } b(z) = \varnothing \text{ (i.e., } z \text{ is initial) then } i(z) \leq_{\mathsf{D}} [i(z') | z' : Z]$$
$$\text{else } b(z) \leq_{\mathsf{D}} [b(z') | z' : Z \wedge b(z') \cap i(z) \subseteq i(z')] \text{ and}$$
$$b(z) \leq_{\mathsf{D}} [b(z') | z' : Z \wedge b(z') \cap e(z) \subseteq e(z')]$$

Proof. Soundness means $C : [\![z]\!]_h \wedge z \leq' [z_i | i : n] \implies \exists C' : \prod_{i:n} [\![z_i]\!]_h.C = \bigcup_{i:n} C'_i$. The case "$z$ initial" is trivial, otherwise fix $0 < 0' < h' < h$ and let $C'_i \stackrel{\triangle}{=} C \cap \bigcup(\{[0, h'] \times b(z_i) | b(z_i) \cap i(z) \leq i(z_i)\} \cup \{[0', h] \times b(z_i) | b(z_i) \cap e(z) \subseteq e(z_i)\})$. $\square$

Remark 3. In general $[\![z]\!]_h$ is downward closed and closed wrt finite unions, but may not have a biggest element, except when z is $(d, \varnothing, \varnothing)$ or (d, d, d).

Jumping. Jump: $\mathbf{Set}_p(Q \times D, D)$ interprets jumps. $\mathsf{Jump}(q, d) \uparrow$ when it cannot compute an enclosure of the states reachable by jumping with q from d. We assume the following properties.

O.J Jump is *strict*, i.e., $\mathsf{Jump}(q, \varnothing) = \varnothing$, and
   monotonic in d, i.e., $d' \subseteq d \wedge \mathsf{Jump}(q, d) \downarrow \implies \mathsf{Jump}(q, d') \subseteq \mathsf{Jump}(q, d)$.

Flowing. $\mathsf{Flow}_h: \mathbf{Set}_p(Q \times D, Z)$ interprets flows for time step h. $\mathsf{Flow}_h(q, d) \uparrow$ when it cannot compute a timed enclosure of the states reachable by flowing with q from d. We assume the following properties.

O.F Flow_h is *strict, monotonic* in d, and
   the flow starts from d, i.e., $z = \mathsf{Flow}_h(q, d) \implies z = \mathsf{Flow}_h(q, d \cap i(z))$.

Jump and Flow_h are extended from D to Z as follows (and the extensions inherit the properties assumed for the original maps, like strictness and monotonicity).

 − $\mathsf{Jump}(q, z) = z' \xLeftrightarrow{\Delta} z' = (\mathsf{Jump}(q, i(z)), \mathsf{Jump}(q, b(z)), \mathsf{Jump}(q, e(z)))$
 − $\mathsf{Flow}_h(q, z) = z' \xLeftrightarrow{\Delta}$ if $b(z) = \varnothing$ then $z' = z'_i$ else $z' = (i(z'_i), d'_b, d'_b)$ where
   $z'_i \stackrel{\Delta}{=} \mathsf{Flow}_h(q, i(z))$ and $d'_b \stackrel{\Delta}{=} b(\mathsf{Flow}_h(q, b(z)))$.

Operational Rules. Fix a finite set $Q : \mathsf{P}_f(Q)$ of modes.
   A Q-**set** is a sequence $W : (Z \times \mathsf{P}_f(Q) \times \mathsf{P}_f(Q) \times \mathsf{P}_f(Q))^*$ such that

$$\forall (z, Q_a, Q_d, Q_c) : W.\varnothing \subset z \wedge Q_a \uplus Q_d \uplus Q_c \subseteq Q$$

 − W is **initial** $\xLeftrightarrow{\Delta} \forall (z, Q_a, Q_d, Q_c) : W.Q_a = Q$.
 − W is **terminal** $\xLeftrightarrow{\Delta} \forall (z, Q_a, Q_d, Q_c) : W.Q_a = \varnothing$.

For defining the operational semantics we make the following assumptions

O.# $\forall q : Q.(\forall z : Z.\mathsf{Jump}(q, z) = \varnothing) \vee (\forall z : Z.\mathsf{Flow}_h(q, z) = \varnothing)$, thus Q is partitioned in flows Q_F (i.e., modes that cannot jump) and the rest Q_J (that cannot flow)
O.Q $\forall q, q' : Q.\forall z, z' : Z.z' = \mathsf{Flow}_h(q, z) \wedge q \neq q' \implies \mathsf{Flow}_h(q', z') = \varnothing$, this says at the level of timed enclosures that flows in Q are *apart* (see Remark 2).

The binary relation $\xrightarrow{Q}$ on Q-sets is defined by the following rules

jump $W, (z, Q_a \uplus q, Q_d, Q_c), W' \xrightarrow{Q} W, (z, Q_a, q \uplus Q_d, Q_c), W', (z', Q - q, \varnothing, \varnothing)$
   if $\varnothing \subset \mathsf{Jump}(q, z) = z'$
flow $W, (z, Q_a \uplus q, Q_d, Q_c), W' \xrightarrow{Q} W, (z, Q_a, q \uplus Q_d, Q_c), W', (z', Q - q, \varnothing, \varnothing)$
   if $\varnothing \subset \mathsf{Flow}_h(q, z) = z'$
done $W, (z, Q_a \uplus q, Q_d, Q_c), W' \xrightarrow{Q} W, (z, Q_a, q \uplus Q_d, Q_c), W'$
   if $\mathsf{Flow}_h(q, z) = \mathsf{Jump}(q, z) = \varnothing$

cover $W, (z, Q_a \uplus q, Q_d, Q_c), W' \xrightarrow[Q]{} W, (z, Q_a, Q_d, q \uplus Q_c), W'$
$\quad$ if $z \leq [z' | (z', Q'_a, Q'_d, Q'_c) : W, W' \wedge q \in Q'_d]$.

Remark 4. The side conditions of (jump), (flow) and (done) are mutually exclusive by (O.#). The following rule is derivable by exploiting (O.#) and (O.Q)

flow* $W, (z, Q_a \uplus q, Q_d, Q_c), W' \xrightarrow[Q]{} W, (z, Q_a, q \uplus Q_d, Q_c), W', (z', Q_J, Q_F - q, \varnothing)$
$\quad$ if $\varnothing \subset \mathsf{Flow}_h(q, z) = z'$, where Q_J and Q_F are defined in assumption (O.#).

The assumptions (O.#) and (O.Q) can be recast in terms of D

O.#* $\forall q : Q.(\forall d : \mathsf{D}.\mathsf{Jump}(q, d) = \varnothing) \vee (\forall d : \mathsf{D}.\mathsf{Flow}_h(q, d) = \varnothing)$
O.Q* $\forall q, q' : Q.\forall d : \mathsf{D}.\forall z' : \mathsf{Z}.z' = \mathsf{Flow}_h(q, d) \wedge q \neq q' \implies \mathsf{Flow}_h(q', b(z')) = \varnothing$

but the operational rules (and the proof of correctness) treat Z as an ADT, thus one can adopt a different implementation of Z without invalidating correctness, provided all assumptions are cast in terms of Z.

5 Correctness

The operational semantics is defined on top of the ADT Z for timed enclosures, thus its correctness is an assume-guarantee result of the form "if the ADT Z satisfies certain properties, then the operational semantics is correct".

Assumptions. We fix $Q : \mathsf{P_f}(Q)$, define $(F_q, G_q) = [\![q]\!] : \mathbb{H}(\mathbb{S})$ (see Sect. 3), and make the following assumptions, in addition to (O,#) and (O.Q) of Sect. 4.

A.Z $\forall z : \mathsf{Z}.[\![z]\!]_h \subseteq \mathsf{C}([0, h] \times \mathbb{S})$ is downward closed and has a top element $C(z)$
A.# $\forall q : Q.F_q = \varnothing \vee G_q = \varnothing$, i.e., $[\![q]\!]$ is either a jump or a flow
A.Q $\forall q, q' : Q.q \neq q' \implies \overline{S(F_q)} \cap \overline{S(F_{q'})} = \varnothing$, i.e., $\overline{[\![Q]\!]}$ is a hybrid automaton
$\quad$ (see Remark 2), since $\overline{S(\overline{F})} = \overline{S(F)}$
A.J $\forall q : Q.\forall z, z' : \mathsf{Z}.\mathsf{Jump}(q, z) = z' \wedge C : [\![z]\!]_h \implies \mathsf{E}_h(\overline{G_q}, \mathsf{T}_h(\overline{G_q}, C)) : [\![z']\!]_h$
A.F $\forall q : Q.\forall z, z' : \mathsf{Z}.\mathsf{Flow}_h(q, z) = z' \wedge C : [\![z]\!]_h \implies \mathsf{E}_h(\overline{F_q}, \mathsf{T}_h(\overline{F_q}, C)) : [\![z']\!]_h$.

In the sequel we write $q(C)$ for $\mathsf{T}_h([\![q]\!], C)$ and $q^+(C)$ for $\mathsf{E}_h([\![q]\!], q(C))$, where $q : Q$ and $C : \mathsf{C}([0, h] \times \mathbb{S})$. By Lemma 1 the assumptions (A.#) and (A.Q) imply $\overrightarrow{[\![Q']\!]} = \bigcup_{q:Q'} \overrightarrow{[\![q]\!]}$, or equivalently $\mathsf{T}_h([\![Q']\!], C) = \bigcup_{q:Q'} q(C)$, when $Q' \subseteq Q$.

Remark 5. The assumptions (A.J) and (A.F) refer to the extensions of Jump and Flow_h to Z. Section 4 implements Z using a simpler ADT D, but the operational rules refer only to Z, thus correctness holds, as far as the assumptions on Z hold. **Warning:** the simple implementation of Z in terms of D defined in Sect. 4 satisfies a weaker property than (A.Z), see Remark 3, thus we cannot claim correctness for an operational semantics using that implementation.

To state correctness we have to define the semantics of Q-sets W, this is done coherently with the semantics of timed enclosures $z : \mathsf{Z}$.

Definition 4. *The semantics* $[\![W]\!]_h : \mathsf{P}(\mathsf{C}([0, h] \times \mathbb{S}))$ *for a Q-set W is*

- $[\![(z, Q_a, Q_d, Q_c)]\!]_h \triangleq [\![z]\!]_h : \mathsf{P}(\mathsf{C}([0,h] \times \mathbb{S}))$
- $[\![W]\!]_h \triangleq \{\bigcup_{i:n} C_i | C : \prod_{i:n} [\![W(i)]\!]_h\}$, with $n = |W|$ and $W(i)$ i-th item in W.

Correctness says that the operational semantics computes over-approximations of the safe evolution map. However, the computation may fail to terminate, there is no bound on the accuracy of the over-approximations, termination and accuracy may depend on the order in which the operational rules are applied.

Theorem 2 (Correctness). If $W \xrightarrow{*}_{Q} W'$ with W initial and W' terminal, then $\forall C : [\![W]\!]_h . \mathsf{E}_h(\overline{[\![Q]\!]}, C) : [\![W']\!]_h$.

Correctness relies on a lemma saying that $\xrightarrow{}_{Q}$ preserves *well-formed Q-sets*.

Definition 5. For $i : n = |W|$ let $(z(i), Q_a(i), Q_d(i), Q_c(i)) = W(i)$ and $Q(i) = Q_a(i) \uplus Q_d(i) \uplus Q_c(i)$, then W is a **well-formed Q-set** $\iff \exists p : n \rightharpoonup n \times Q$ such that

1. $p(i) = (j, q) \implies j < i$, i.e., n forms a forest with arcs $j \xrightarrow{q} i$
2. $p(i) = p(j) \implies i = j$
3. $i : n \wedge p(i) \uparrow \implies Q(i) = Q$
4. $p(i) = (j, q) \wedge q : Q_J \implies q : Q_d(j) \wedge \mathsf{Jump}(q, z(j)) = z(i) \wedge Q(i) = Q - q$
5. $p(i) = (j, q) \wedge q : Q_F \implies q : Q_d(j) \wedge \mathsf{Flow}_h(q, z(j)) = z(i) \wedge Q(i) = Q - q$
6. $q : Q_d(j) \implies \mathsf{Jump}(q, z(j)) = \mathsf{Flow}_h(q, z(j)) = \varnothing \vee \exists i : n.p(i) = (j, q)$
7. $q : Q_c(j) \implies z(j) \leq [z(i)|i : n \wedge q : Q_d(i)]$.

In particular, an initial W is well-formed by taking p such that $\forall i : n.p(i) \uparrow$.

The partial map $p : n \rightharpoonup n \times Q$ records how items were added to W, i.e., $p(i) = (j, q)$ means that $W(i)$ was added by applying (flow) or (jump) to remove q from $Q_a(j)$.

Lemma 2. If W is well-formed and $W \xrightarrow{}_{Q} W'$, then W' is well-formed.

Proof. By case analysis on the operational rule used to derive $W \xrightarrow{}_{Q} W'$. The proof relies on the assumption (O.#) and the side-conditions of the operational rules. In particular, the witness p' that W' is well-formed is given by the witness p for W in the cases (done) and (cover), while it is an extension of p in the cases (jump) and (flow). □

Lemma 3. If W is well-formed and terminal, then $\mathsf{E}_h(\overline{[\![Q]\!]}, D) : [\![W]\!]_h$, where $D = \bigcup\{C(z(i))|i : n \wedge p(i) \uparrow\}$ with $n = |W|$ and p witness that W is well-formed.

Proof. Define $C' : [\![W]\!]_h$ such that $D \subseteq C'$ and $\mathsf{T}_h(\overline{[\![Q]\!]}, C') = \bigcup_{q:Q} q(C') \subseteq C'$, therefore $\mathsf{E}_h(\overline{[\![Q]\!]}, D) \subseteq C'$ belongs to $[\![W]\!]_h$, because $[\![W]\!]_h$ is downward closed.

For $i : n$ let $\varnothing \subset C_i \triangleq C(z(i))$ the top element in $[\![W(i)]\!]_h$ by (A.Z), $C \triangleq \bigcup_{i:n} C_i$ the top element in $[\![W]\!]_h$, $C'_i \triangleq C_i$ when $p(i) \uparrow$, $C'_i \triangleq q^+(C_j)$ when $p(i) = (j, q)$, and $C' \triangleq \bigcup_{i:n} C'_i$, then the following properties hold

1. $D \subseteq C'$, by definition of D and C'
2. $C' \subseteq C$, because W is well-formed and $C'_i = q^+(C_j) \subseteq C_i$ when $p(i) = (j, q)$, by (A.#), (A.J), (A.F) and definition of C_i
3. $\forall j : n. \forall q : Q_d(j).q^+(C_j) \subseteq C'$, because W is well-formed and $q^+(C_j) = \varnothing$ or $\exists i : n.p(i) = (j, q) \wedge q^+(C_j) = C'_i$
4. $\forall i : n. \forall q : Q_c(i).q^+(C_i) \subseteq C'$, because $C_i \subseteq \bigcup \{C_j | j : n \wedge q : Q_d(j)\}$ by W well-formed, and $q^+(C_i) = \bigcup \{q^+(C_j) | j : n \wedge q : Q_d(j)\} \subseteq C'$ by point 3
5. $\forall i : n. \forall q : Q(i).q(C_i) \subseteq C'$, by the points 3 and 4, because $q(C_i) \subseteq q^+(C_i)$ and $Q(i) = Q_d(i) \uplus Q_c(i)$ by W terminal
6. $\forall q : Q.q(C') \subseteq C'$. We prove $\forall i : n. \forall q : Q.q(C'_i) \subseteq C'$ by case analysis on $i : n$:
   - if $p(i) \uparrow$, then $Q(i) = Q$ and $C'_i = C_i$, thus $\forall q : Q.q(C'_i) \subseteq C'$ by point 5
   - $p(i) = (j, q)$, then $Q(i) = Q - q$ and $C'_i = q^+(C_j)$, thus $q(C'_i) \subseteq C'_i \subseteq C'$ by definition of C'_i, and $\forall q' : Q - q.q'(C'_i) \subseteq C'$ by point 5. □

6 Conclusions and Future Work

The main contribution of the paper is an assume-guarantee proof of correctness (see Sect. 5) for the rigorous simulator defined in Sect. 4, where the assumptions concern an ADT Z of timed enclosures. The proof may serve as a blueprint for similar results. For instance, one could replace safe evolution with a variant which is *robust* wrt arbitrary small over-approximations of the hybrid system and the set of initial states (see [20]), or strengthen the correctness guarantees by specifying the accuracy of the over-approximation computed by the rigorous simulator (this means that accuracy becomes a parameter for the simulator, the auxiliary maps Jump and Flow$_h$, and the statement of correctness).

We showed that a simple implementation of Z, defined in terms of an ADT D (see Sect. 4), does not satisfy the assumption that the interpretation $[\![z]\!]_h$ has a top element, or more precisely that $[\![z]\!]_h$ is a principal ideal in $\mathsf{C}([0, h] \times \mathbb{S})$ ordered by inclusion. Thus, an important next step will be to determine whether there can be an implementation of Z satisfying all assumptions. It will also be interesting to see if there is an alternative proof of correctness that rely on the weaker assumption that $[\![z]\!]_h$ is only an ideal.

We sketch an implementation of Z satisfying all assumptions required by the proof of correctness, in particular for each $z : \mathsf{Z}$ the ideal $[\![z]\!]_h$ has a top element $E(z)$ and $[\![z]\!]_h = \{C : \mathsf{C}([0, h] \times \mathbb{S}) | C \subseteq E(z)\}$. The basic idea is that $E(z)$ is a convex bounded polytope P in $\mathbb{T} \times \mathbb{R}^n$ such that $P(t)$ is a box in $\mathbb{R}^n$ for each $t : \mathbb{T}$. More formally, we take as $z : \mathsf{Z}$ sequences of inequalities of the form $a \le t \le b$ (where $0 \le a, b \le h$) or $a + a't \le x_i \le b + b't$ with rational coefficients and involving $n+1$ variables, namely t for time and x_i for the i-th state variable.

A sequence z of inequalities defines a closed convex subset $E(z)$ of $\mathsf{C}([0, h] \times \mathbb{S})$ consisting of the points satisfying all inequalities (thus $E(z)$ is a polytope), and it is bounded when z includes an inequality $a \le t \le b$ and at least one inequality for each x_i. Finally, the inclusion and cover relation for convex polytopes described by conjunctions of linear inequalities with rational coefficients are decidable, because they are Turing-reducible to linear programming.

References

1. Acumen (2016). http://acumen-language.org
2. Aljarbouh, A., Caillaud, B.: On the regularization of chattering executions in real time simulation of hybrid systems. In: Baltic Young Scientists Conference, p. 49 (2015)
3. Aljarbouh, A., Zeng, Y., Duracz, A., Caillaud, B., Taha, W.: Chattering-free simulation for hybrid dynamical systems. In: 2016 IEEE International Conference on Computational Science and Engineering, IEEE International Conference on Embedded and Ubiquitous Computing, and International Symposium on Distributed Computing and Applications to Business, Engineering and Science. IEEE Computer Society (2016)
4. Alur, R., Courcoubetis, C., Halbwachs, N., Henzinger, T.A., Ho, P.H., Nicollin, X., Olivero, A., Sifakis, J., Yovine, S.: The algorithmic analysis of hybrid systems. Theoret. Comput. Sci. **138**, 3–34 (1995)
5. Alur, R., Courcoubetis, C., Henzinger, T.A., Ho, P.-H.: Hybrid automata: an algorithmic approach to the specification and verification of hybrid systems. In: Grossman, R.L., Nerode, A., Ravn, A.P., Rischel, H. (eds.) HS 1991-1992. LNCS, vol. 736, pp. 209–229. Springer, Heidelberg (1993). https://doi.org/10.1007/3-540-57318-6_30
6. Chabert, G., Jaulin, L.: Contractor programming. Artif. Intell. **173**(11), 1079–1100 (2009)
7. Cousot, P., Cousot, R.: Abstract interpretation frameworks. J. Log. Comput. **2**(4), 511–547 (1992)
8. Duracz, A.: Rigorous simulation: its theory and applications. Ph.D. thesis. Halmstad University Press (2016)
9. Duracz, A., Bartha, F.A., Taha, W.: Accurate rigorous simulation should be possible for good designs. In: 2016 International Workshop on Symbolic and Numerical Methods for Reachability Analysis, SNR, pp. 1–10. IEEE (2016)
10. Duracz, A., Eriksson, H., Bartha, F.A., Zeng, Y., Xu, F., Taha, W.: Using rigorous simulation to support ISO 26262 hazard analysis and risk assessment. In: 12th International Conference on Embedded Software and Systems, ICESS, pp. 1093–1096. IEEE (2015)
11. Goebel, R., Sanfelice, R.G., Teel, A.: Hybrid dynamical systems. IEEE Control Syst. **29**(2), 28–93 (2009)
12. Henzinger, T.A.: The theory of hybrid automata. In: Logic in Computer Science, pp. 278–292. IEEE Computer Society, New Brunswick (1996)
13. Jaulin, L., Kieffer, M., Didrit, O., Walter, E.: Applied Interval Analysis: With Examples in Parameter and State Estimation, Robust Control and Robotics. Springer, London (2001). https://doi.org/10.1007/978-1-4471-0249-6
14. Johansson, K.H., Egerstedt, M., Lygeros, J., Sastry, S.: On the regularization of Zeno hybrid automata. Syst. Control Lett. **38**(3), 141–150 (1999)
15. Konečný, M., Taha, W., Bartha, F.A., Duracz, J., Duracz, A., Ames, A.D.: Enclosing the behavior of a hybrid automaton up to and beyond a Zeno point. Nonlinear Anal.: Hybrid Syst. **20**, 1–20 (2016)
16. Konečný, M., Taha, W., Duracz, J., Duracz, A., Ames, A.: Enclosing the behavior of a hybrid system up to and beyond a Zeno point. In: 1st IEEE International Conference on Cyber-Physical Systems, Networks, and Applications, CPSNA, pp. 120–125 (2013)

17. Lee, E.A., Seshia, S.A.: Introduction to Embedded Systems: A Cyber-Physical Systems Approach. MIT Press, Cambridge (2016)
18. Lee, E.A., Zheng, H.: Operational semantics of hybrid systems. In: Morari, M., Thiele, L. (eds.) HSCC 2005. LNCS, vol. 3414, pp. 25–53. Springer, Heidelberg (2005). https://doi.org/10.1007/978-3-540-31954-2_2
19. Lygeros, J.: Lecture notes on hybrid systems. In: Notes for an ENSIETA Workshop (2004). Sect. 4.2
20. Moggi, E., Farjudian, A., Duracz, A., Taha, W.: Safe & robust reachability analysis of hybrid systems. Theor. Comput. Sci. (2018). https://doi.org/10.1016/j.tcs.2018.06.020
21. Moore, R.E.: Interval Analysis, vol. 4. Prentice-Hall, Upper Saddle River (1966)
22. Taha, W., Brauner, P., Zeng, Y., Cartwright, R., Gaspes, V., Ames, A., Chapoutot, A.: A core language for executable models of cyber-physical systems (preliminary report). In: 32nd International Conference on Distributed Computing Systems, pp. 303–308. IEEE (2012)
23. Tucker, W.: Validated Numerics: A Short Introduction to Rigorous Computations. Princeton University Press, Princeton (2011)
24. Zeng, Y., Bartha, F., Taha, W.: Compile-time extensions to hybrid ODEs. In: Ábrahám, E., Bogomolov, S. (eds.) Proceedings of 3rd International Workshop on Symbolic and Numerical Methods for Reachability Analysis, Uppsala, Sweden. Electronic Proceedings in Theoretical Computer Science, vol. 247, pp. 52–70. Open Publishing Association (2017)
25. Zeng, Y., Chad, R., Taha, W., Duracz, A., Atkinson, K., Philippsen, R., Cartwright, R., O'Malley, M.: Modeling electromechanical aspects of cyber-physical systems. J. Softw. Eng. Robot. **7**(1), 100–119 (2016)
26. Zhang, J., Johansson, K.H., Lygeros, J., Sastry, S.: Zeno hybrid systems. Int. J. Robust Nonlinear Control **11**(5), 435–451 (2001)
27. Zheng, H., Lee, E.A., Ames, A.D.: Beyond Zeno: get on with It!. In: Hespanha, J.P., Tiwari, A. (eds.) HSCC 2006. LNCS, vol. 3927, pp. 568–582. Springer, Heidelberg (2006). https://doi.org/10.1007/11730637_42
28. Zhu, Y., Westbrook, E., Inoue, J., Chapoutot, A., Salama, C., Peralta, M., Martin, T., Taha, W., O'Malley, M., Cartwright, R., et al.: Mathematical equations as executable models of mechanical systems. In: Proceedings of the 1st ACM/IEEE International Conference on Cyber-Physical Systems, pp. 1–11. ACM (2010)

On Determinism

Stephen A. Edwards$^{(\boxtimes)}$

Columbia University, New York, USA
sedwards@cs.columbia.edu

Abstract. The notion of deterministic execution of concurrent systems
has appeared in many guises throughout Edward A. Lee's œuvre, but
few really grasp how powerful, important, subtle, and flexible the concept
really is. Determinism can be thought of as an abstraction boundary that
delineates where control is passed from a system designer to the implementation. This paper surveys some of the many forms of determinism
available in the models of computation Lee and others have proposed.

1 Introduction

Edward Lee and I have been chasing determinism for much of our careers, but
the term means different things to different people. The dictionary definition
of "determinism" is roughly the doctrine that nobody has free will, but our
definition is more subtle. First, we concern ourselves with engineered systems
instead of human beings[1]. Second, and more importantly, our notion of determinism actually permits a limited amount of free will—a system may make choices
(both when it is implemented or when it is running) provided those choices do
not affect the system's observed outputs. For example, we consider a combinational digital logic circuit to be deterministic even though the delays of its gates,
and hence its detailed temporal behavior, may vary. The system specification
only constrains the Boolean input/output relationship of the network; the physical behavior of an implementation of the network may vary provided the I/O
relationship is respected.

  In an attempt to more precisely characterize the notion of determinism, consider a quasi-formalism:[2] let $M = (S, I, O, C, E, B, p)$ be a *model of computation*
(MoC) where S is the set of all legal system specifications (i.e., supplied by a
designer), C be the set of all legal choices that can be made in implementing any
system, I and O be the sets of inputs and outputs accounted for by the model
of computation, E and B be the sets of environmental inputs and behaviors not
accounted for by the model of computation, and $p : S \times C \to (I \times E \to O \times B)$ be

---

[1] At least I do; ignoring people is more-or-less why I entered engineering. That hasn't
  worked out too well.

[2] A quasi-formalism because the notions of these sets are far too abstract to be a
  proper formalism. In particular, the sets E and B are difficult to define because they
  are meant to represent "everything else," but this requires a careful definition of the
  universal set, which is not obvious.

© Springer International Publishing AG, part of Springer Nature 2018
M. Lohstroh et al. (Eds.): Lee Festschrift, LNCS 10760, pp. 240–253, 2018.
https://doi.org/10.1007/978-3-319-95246-8_14

the system implementation function for the model of computation, which takes a system specification and implementation choices and returns a system that transforms known and unaccounted-for inputs into known and unaccounted-for outputs. A model of computation M is *deterministic* if for all $s \in S$, $c \in C$, $i \in I$, and $e \in E$, there is some function $d : S \times I \to O$ such that

$$p(s, c)(i, e) = \big(d(s, i), b\big). \tag{1}$$

In other words, the outputs that the model of computation accounts for *only* depend on the system specification and the inputs accounted for by the model of computation. Implementation choices and the environment may only affect the behavior of the system outside of these outputs.

By design, the above takes a very abstract view of what inputs and outputs, environmental or otherwise, may be. For example, inputs and outputs may be vectors of Boolean values, sequences of Boolean vectors over time, events tagged with timestamps [37], continuous-valued signals [38], and many more. In fact, a crucial choice in the design of a model of computation is whether such physical properties such as time, space, and voltage are considered part of a system's inputs and outputs versus being relegated to the environment. For example, in most classical models of computation in computer science (e.g., Turing machines), physical time is ignored; termination or the lack thereof was the only real concern. While such a view brings many theoretical benefits, it hinders the control of physical systems, which invariably depend strongly on time.

Example 1. Consider the model of computation embodied in an AND/INVERTER graph (AIG), a streamlined, abstract model of combinational Boolean logic networks proposed by Kuehlmann et al. [31] and used, for example, in Brayton and Mishchenko's ABC tool [10] to verify and synthesize digital logic circuits.

An AIG is a directed acyclic graph with three types of vertices: a vertex with two incoming arcs represents a logical AND gate; a primary input (i.e., from the environment) is modeled as a vertex with zero incoming arcs; and one particular vertex with no incoming arcs represents the constant "0." Vertices with a single or more than 2 incoming arcs are not allowed, but there is no constraint on the number of outgoing arcs from a vertex. Certain vertices are also considered outputs. Each arc has a Boolean inversion attribute that indicates whether the value flowing through it is to be complemented. For a particular assignment of input values to input vertices, the output from the network is an assignment of Boolean values to the output vertices that comes from an assignment of Boolean values to every AND vertex that satisfies all of them, i.e., each vertex takes on the logical AND of the values of the vertices along its incoming arcs, inverted according to the attribute on each arc.

It is easy to see such the output of such a network is deterministic. Since the graph is directed and acyclic, its vertices can be topologically ordered starting from the primary inputs, and the value of each vertex can be established in that order. The invariant is that a vertex's value is evaluated after its two fan-in vertices have been evaluated.

In this MoC, S is the set of all AIGs; I is an assignment of a Boolean value to each primary input vertex, and O is the assignment of Boolean values to each output vertex that is consistent with the inputs and the network. Choices C that can be made during the implementation of the system include which logic gates to use, their speed, and how they are connected. Any circuit that ultimately gives the same input-output relationship is considered correct; its structure in not limited by the structure of the AIG. Environmental inputs might include fluctuations in supply voltage that could affect the delays of certain gates and noise coupled into the circuit from outside. The behavior B may describe the voltages on each of the wires in the circuit as a function of time, or approximations to this, such as times at which the signals change.

The AIG MoC is deterministic in the sense of (1). An underlying assumption is that the choices C are correct (i.e., produce a working circuit) and that the environmental inputs E ultimately do not affect the output O.

Example 2. Consider the model of computation represented by the C programming language. In this MoC, S is the set of all legal C programs; C is the set of all choices a compiler may make during the compilation process, e.g., which instructions to choose, which registers to use, etc.

Defining I and O, the inputs specified by the model of computation, is a little subtle. I includes command-line arguments, environment variables, the standard input stream, files in the filesystem, etc. O includes the return value, the standard output stream, files the program writes to the filesystem, etc.

Defining E and B are more subtle still. E can include things such as the type and speed of the processor in which the C program is being run, the time of day at which the program is run, and load and scheduling policy of the operating system under which it is run. B includes things such as the time it takes to execute the program, the amount of power consumed by the computer while the program is running, and many others.

While programmers traditionally think of C as being deterministic, and most C programs behave deterministically once compiled, certain C constructs have unspecified behavior, meaning the C standard defines multiple possible behaviors but does not specify which must be chosen. Constructs may also have undefined behavior, meaning the standard imposes no requirements whatsoever, and implementation-defined behavior.

For example, C's argument evaluation order is unspecified. This readily leads to nondeterministic behavior when argument evaluation has interacting side-effects, such as in the (nonsensical) function call `foo(a=1, a=2)`. When the function `foo()` executes, the variable `a` will be either 1 or 2, but the C standard does not prescribe which (i.e., it is an implementation choice).

The C standard (e.g., ISO/IEC 9899:2011) attempts to legislate away the problems of nondeterminism by restricting the set of legal C programs S to those that are *strictly conforming*: i.e., programs that do not produce output that depends on unspecified, undefined, or implementation-defined behavior.

Understandably, C programmers are taught to eschew unspecified, undefined, and implementation-defined behavior, but this approach is only partially effective. Although good C programmers are aware of and avoid such issues, in reality programmers rely on the C compiler at their disposal to test the legality of a program and under this definition, the legality of a C program is technically undecidable. For example, while I was pleased to discover the version of GCC on my desktop machine (5.4) will produce a warning for the `foo(a=1, a=2)` example given the `-Wsequence-point` option, GCC failed to warn when the effects were moved to functions, i.e., `foo(one(), two())`.

Time is another thorny issue. The C standard provides the standard library function `time()` that returns the current calendar time. If programs that can call `time()` are part of S, the C MoC is deterministic only if I includes the current time and fine details about the execution rate of the program.

A central tenet of determinism is that there are choices (c) to be made in the implementation of a system (s) that may affect its behavior (b), but they do not affect the output characterized by the model of computation.

I know of only a few mathematical approaches to determinism. Although there may be others, the deterministic MoCs I know of all use these. Below, I discuss these approaches and the models that use them.

2   The Banach Fixed-Point Theorem

Of the various fixed-point theorems at the root of deterministic MoCs, the Banach Fixed-Point Theorem is the easiest to state and understand. We start with a set (space) X for which there is a *metric* $d : X \times X \to \mathbb{R}$ that represents a distance between two points $x, y \in X$, i.e., $d(x,x) = 0$, $d(x,y) > 0$ if $x \neq y$, $d(x,y) = d(y,x)$, and $d(x,y) \leq d(x,z) + d(z,y)$ (the triangle inequality).

Theorem 1 *(Banach [1]). If X is a space with metric d and $f : X \to X$ is a contraction mapping on X, i.e., there exists a Lipschitz constant $K < 1$ such that $d\big(f(x), f(y)\big) \leq Kd(x,y)$, then there is a unique fixed-point x^*, i.e., $f(x^*) = x^*$, where $x^* = \lim_{n \to \infty} f^n(x)$ for any $x \in X$.*

Two amazing things are happening here: that two points, after being mapped, come closer together is enough to ensure a unique fixed point, and that this fixed point can be found by starting anywhere and simply iterating. Intuitively, the Lipschitz constant K provides a bound on how iterations of f must behave, in particular telling us that they must grow closer.

In the MoC setting, the space X is typically the output from the system, the mapping f corresponds to taking some small step in running the system (e.g., evaluating a single logic gate), and the fixed point x^* corresponds to a "stable" state of the system in which nothing more can or will be done to evaluate it. Determinism corresponds exactly to the fixed point being unique.

Lee et al. use Theorem 1 to show how discrete-event simulation models could be made deterministic. In such a model, a signal (i.e., communication history between processes) is modeled as a set of events—value-time pairs. The central challenge is choosing a suitable metric for what is otherwise a rather unwieldy space of possible behaviors X. Lee's earlier work [33] uses the Cantor metric $d(x, y) = 1/2^t$, where the time of each event is represented by a real number and t is the earliest time at which events in the two signals x and y differ. Later, Lee et al. [15,16] adopt superdense time, in which each event is tagged by a real number-natural number pair to more delicately model simultaneous events. This complicates the metric, but Lee et al. show Theorem 1 can still be applied to establish determinism.

3   The Kleene/Knaster-Tarski Fixed-Point Theorem

The Banach Fixed-Point theorem relies on a metric that assigns real numbers to every pair of points in a space, which may be awkward in certain settings. Fortunately, another fixed-point theorem demands far less structure, making it easier to apply to MoCs. I state the theorem first then explain its details and implications.

Theorem 2 *(Kleene/Knaster-Tarski). Let $(X, \sqsubseteq)$ be a complete partial order with minimum element $\bot \in X$ and $f : X \to X$ a continuous function. f has a unique least fixed point $\bigsqcup \{ f^n(\bot) \mid n \in \{1, 2, \ldots\} \}$.*

Theorem 2, apparently a "folk theorem" variously attributed to Kleene and Knaster-Tarski [32,53], instead of a metric, relies on a partial order relation, written $\sqsubseteq$ and sometimes pronounced "approximates," that is reflexive ($x \sqsubseteq x$), antisymmetric (if $x \sqsubseteq y$ and $y \sqsubseteq x$, then $x = y$), and transitive (if $x \sqsubseteq y$ and $y \sqsubseteq z$, $x \sqsubseteq z$). The relation is partial because it may be the case that neither $x \sqsubseteq y$ nor $y \sqsubseteq x$, i.e., x and y may be incomparable. The usual subset relation $\subseteq$ is one such partial order. This mathematical machinery has been published in many places; Winskel [56] is my favorite; see also Scott [47] and Davey and Priestley [21].

Theorem 2 further requires the partial order to be *complete*: any (increasing) chain $C = \{c_1, c_2, \ldots\}$ (where $c_1 \sqsubseteq c_2 \sqsubseteq \cdots$) must have a least upper bound $\bigsqcup C \in D$ satisfying $c_k \sqsubseteq \bigsqcup C$ (i.e., $\bigsqcup C$ is an upper bound) and $\bigsqcup C \sqsubseteq b$ for any b such that $c_k \sqsubseteq b$ (i.e., $\bigsqcup C$ is the least such bound). Intuitively, increasing sequences in the space can not increase forever.

Finally, Theorem 2 requires a *continuous* function (sometimes termed "Scott continuous" after Dana Scott [46], who pioneered their use for modeling recursion in denotational semantics). Continuity is analogous to the usual definition for real-valued functions: the limit of the function is the function at the limit, i.e., for all chains C, $\bigsqcup \{ f(c) \mid c \in C \} = f(\bigsqcup C)$. Informally, nothing strange happens when you actually reach a limit. Moreover, continuity implies monotonicity, i.e., $x \sqsubseteq y$ implies $f(x) \sqsubseteq f(y)$.

The sketch of the proof of Theorem 2 is quick and illuminating. Montonicity implies $\bot \sqsubseteq f(\bot) \sqsubseteq f^2(\bot) \sqsubseteq \cdots$ is a chain. Because $\sqsubseteq$ is complete, this chain C has a unique least upper bound $\bigsqcup C$. Finally, because f is continuous, $\bigsqcup C$ is a fixed point because $f(\bigsqcup C) = \bigsqcup \{ f(c) \mid c \in C \} = \bigsqcup C$.

Put another way, iterating f produces a nondecreasing sequence that approaches a unique least upper bound, which happens to be the least fixed point. Theorem 2 only guarantees a unique least fixed point; f may have other, greater fixed points.

Perhaps most famously, Kahn [30] uses Theorem 2 to show his process networks are deterministic. Kahn networks consist of sequential processes that communicate through unbounded FIFO channels. Each process may compute, emit a token to an output channel, or wait for the next token on an input channel. Kahn models the contents of each channel as D^{ω}: the set of finite and infinite sequences over the set of tokens D, and the domain X is a vector of channels. Kahn shows that each process behaves as a continuous function under his restrictions, e.g., monotonicity follows from blocking reads: additional input tokens can never make a process "unemit" tokens or "change its mind" about a token emitted earlier; continuity follows because a process can't "wait forever" before generating an output. Kahn defines the behavior of his networks as the least fixed point of the function composed from the functions of all the processes, which is therefore unique. Furthermore, the proof of Theorem 2 tells us that this fixed-point may be reached (or at least approximated) by simply running the processes.

In the vocabulary of (1), Kahn networks have S as the Kahn network, I and O are the sequences of tokens on the channels, C and E include implementation choices, e.g., with respect to scheduling the execution of the processes, and B includes the timing of the tokens on the channels.

Kahn's networks and its underlying mathematics have spawned a host of variants. Lee's Synchronous Dataflow (SDF) [35] is a restriction of Kahn networks to regular, statically known communication patterns, thus piggybacks on Kahn's result to guarantee determinism. Many slight variants have been proposed, including cyclo-static dataflow [8] and Boolean dataflow [14]. Lee and Parks [36] discuss many of these models. Lee and Matsikoudis [34] show how dataflow actors with firing rules behave like Kahn processes (i.e., continuous functions over streams). My own SHIM formalism [22,24] falls somewhere between the rigid, predictable communication patterns of Lee's SDF and Kahn's Turing-complete process networks by restricting processes communicate via rendezvous to bound buffer sizes. Lately, I have devised yet another deterministic dataflow formalism derived from Kahn, this time synthesizing deterministic hardware from bounded-buffer dataflow networks [25].

Kahn relies on the ability of Theorem 2 to cope with infinite domains, but finite domains often suffice.

For example, Theorem 2 also provides determinism to cyclic combinational logic circuits and related block diagram languages. In classical three-valued circuit simulation, the domain X is a finite vector of finite elements: three-valued wire values where the unknown value (usually written "X" in the engineering literature) is the least element $\perp$ and $\perp \sqsubseteq 0$ and $\perp \sqsubseteq 1$ where 0 and 1 are incomparable.

Three-valued digital logic simulation has been around since at least the 1950 s. Muller [43] was one of the earliest to consider it in light of the works of Kleene and others. Eichelberger [26] showed how to use it to detect switching hazards in circuits. Bryant [11] used this logic to simulate switching networks built from MOS transistors that could include such oddities as pass gates and dynamic logic families. Later, researchers including Brzozowski and Seger [12,13], Malik [40] and Shiple and Berry [48] connected three-valued simulation to the analysis of logic circuits with loops and time models, ultimately showing it is a precise abstraction of logic gate networks with unknown timing [42].

Berry [5] adopted what is essentially three-valued logic simulation semantics for later versions of his Esterel language [6] to resolve some longstanding questions about which programs were self-contradictory. He also noted the connection between three-valued simulation, Theorem 2, and constructive logic, dubbing this treatment the constructive semantics of Esterel [4].

My own thesis work, which Lee oversaw, produced a block-diagram language [23] whose deterministic semantics amounted to three-valued simulation abstracted further to allow general monotonic functions to operate on arbitrary data, not just Boolean. August and his group at Princeton used this approach in their Liberty processor simulation environment [44]. More recently, Lee and Zheng [39] sewed this model together with discrete-event simulation.

Theorem 2 is often applied in a setting where the behavior and/or implementation of a system may be one of a family of functions f that arise from evaluating parts of a system at different rates. For example, implementing an SDF graph usually involves scheduling the rates and execution order of the processes, which generally affects the function f [7]. Fortunately, it turns out that such restructuring does not affect the fixed point. Bekić [3] shows, for example, that a system may be split apart and the parts run asynchronously but their results ultimately merged without affecting the fixed point. See also Winskel [56, Chap. 10].

Such an asynchronous approach to computing a function is usually termed "chaotic iteration," and is a common way to compute large functions on parallel hardware. Cousot and Cousot [20] and Wei [55] observe the connection between this approach and Theorem 2. Bourdoncle [9] shows how wisely partitioning the graph of a system can reduce the amount of effort involved in evaluating it without affecting the result.

4   Church-Rosser, Confluence, and the Lambda Calculus

Church's lambda calculus [2,17,18] is a remarkable piece of mathematics in that it is deceptively simple yet somehow all-encompassing. The basis of functional programming including McCarthy's LISP [41], Sussman and Steele's Scheme [50], Milner's ML [27], and Haskell [28], it reduces computation to little more than substituting arguments for variables in functions, which, amazingly, is enough to make it as powerful as Turing machines [54]. Expositions of the lambda calculus abound. Berendregt [2] is the all-inclusive reference, but I much prefer Peyton Jones [29, Chap. 2] as a place to start. Stoy [49] also provides a readable treatment.

Unlike Theorems 1 and 2, the lambda calculus only guarantees that a fixed point is unique *if it exists*. This is a side-effect of the "batch mode" bias in the lambda calculus: it was intended to model computation that produces a result only when it terminates.

Another big difference of the lambda calculus compared to Theorems 1 and 2 is its explicit use of choice in the evaluation "function." The lambda calculus proceeds not by applying a particular function f, but by applying a rewriting procedure that may make choices that produce different (intermediate) results.

A *lambda expression* is either x (a variable), $(\lambda x.M)$ (a lambda abstraction—a model of a function), or $(M\ N)$ (application of the expression M to argument N), where M, N, ... are lambda expression and x, y, ... are variables.

For example, $(\lambda x.x)$ represents the identity function; $(\lambda x.(\lambda y.x))$ is a function that takes an argument x and returns a function that takes an argument y, ignores it, and returns x, which can be used to represent the Boolean "true." To improve the readability of lambda expressions, parentheses are dropped where ambiguity can be resolved by taking the body of a lambda abstraction to extend as far to the right as possible and taking juxtaposition as associating left-to-right, e.g., $(\lambda x.x\ y\ z)\ w$ means $((\lambda x.((x\ y)\ z)))\ w)$.

A *reducible expression* or *redex* is a lambda expression of the form $((\lambda x.M)\ N)$, i.e., where a lambda abstraction is being applied and thus computation is to be performed. For example, $(\lambda z.z)\ y$ is a redex in which the identity function is being applied to y, but $(\lambda x.x)$, $x\ y$, and $x\ (\lambda x.x)$ are not redexes.

The one interesting computational step in the lambda calculus is β-reduction, in which a redex is replaced with a version of the body of the lambda abstraction in which every instance of the variable is replaced with the argument:

$$((\lambda x.M)\ N) \to_\beta M[x := N] \quad (\beta)$$

where $M[x := N]$ means a copy of M in which all free[3] instances of x have been replaced with the argument N. So for example, $(\lambda x.\lambda y.x)\ (\lambda z.z) \to_\beta \lambda y.\lambda z.z$.

In general, β-reduction can be applied anywhere in a lambda expression, not just at the top level as prescribed by the (β) rule. To do this, the $\to_\beta$ rule is extended with three others that allow β-reduction to be performed inside the body of a lambda abstraction, or on either the left or right side of an application:

$$\frac{M \to_\beta M'}{(\lambda x.M) \to_\beta (\lambda x.M')}\ (\text{body})$$

$$\frac{M \to_\beta M'}{(M\ N) \to_\beta (M'\ N)}\ (\text{left}) \qquad \frac{N \to_\beta N'}{(M\ N) \to_\beta (M\ N')}\ (\text{right})$$

In general, the (β), (left), and (right) rules may each apply to a lambda expression, which introduces choice. For example, applying (β) to $(\lambda x.\lambda y.y)\ ((\lambda w.w\ w)\ (\lambda z.z\ z))$ produces $\lambda y.y$ since x does not appear in the body of the λx expression. However, the (right) rule also applies to this expression,

---

[3] I am sidestepping all the fussy bookkeeping necessary to deal with reused variable names because it is ultimately bland, mathematically speaking. See, e.g., Peyton Jones [29, Chap. 2].

which allows the argument to the λx expression to be reduced before it is substituted, giving

$$\frac{(\lambda w.w\, w)\, (\lambda z.z\, z) \to_\beta (\lambda z.z\, z)\, (\lambda z.z\, z)}{(\lambda x.\lambda y.y)\, ((\lambda w.w\, w)\, (\lambda z.z\, z)) \to_\beta (\lambda x.\lambda y.y)\, ((\lambda z.z\, z)\, (\lambda z.z\, z))}\,.$$

A model of computation in which a choice may be taken is at the heart of nondeterminism. Superficially, it would seem that allowing a model to take different steps that produces different results (as the above example illustrated) would produce a nondeterministic model, but this turns out not to be the case for the lambda calculus, as Church and Rosser originally showed.

As defined above, determinism constrains the relationship between the inputs and outputs of a model of computation, but not choices and behavior of how the system implements the I/O relationship. In the lambda calculus, a redex represents work yet to be done, i.e., a function that can still be evaluated; any expression that contains a redex is not (yet) at the point where it will generate an output.

A lambda expression is in *normal form* if it contains no redex, i.e., if β-reduction cannot be applied. "Execution" of a lambda expression amounts to applying β-reduction (i.e., $\to_\beta$) until the expression reaches normal form, which is considered the "output" of a lambda expression.

It turns out the lambda calculus is deterministic due to a remarkable result by Church-Rosser: if a lambda expression can be β-reduced into normal form, there is only one such normal form. In other words, making choices about which redex to reduce cannot affect the ultimate result. There are lambda expressions that do not have a normal form, perhaps the simplest of which is $(\lambda x.x\, x)\, (\lambda y.y\, y)$ (β-reduction can be applied indefinitely yet the expression does not effectively change). These are analogous to non-terminating programs on, say, Turing machines.

The proof of determinism works in two steps. First, β-reduction is *confluent*:

Theorem 3 *(Church-Rosser [19]). Let $\to_{\beta*}$ represent one or more applications of the $\to_\beta$ relation. If $M \to_{\beta*} N_1$ and $M \to_{\beta*} N_2$, then there exists an M' such that $N_1 \to_{\beta*} M'$ and $N_2 \to_{\beta*} M'$.*

The second, easier step observes confluence implies an expression's normal form, if any, is unique:

Corollary 1. *No lambda expression can be β-reduced to two different normal forms.*

Proof. Suppose $M \to_{\beta*} N_1$, $M \to_{\beta*} N_2$, and both N_1 and N_2 are in normal form. By Theorem 3, this means there exists M' such that $N_1 \to_{\beta*} M'$ and $N_2 \to_{\beta*} M'$. However, since both N_1 and N_2 are in normal form, they contain no redexes, so it must be that $N_1 = N_2$.

The proof of Theorem 3 is not obvious because β-reduction can substantially restructure an expression. Reducing a redex may make others disappear, e.g., since $(\lambda x.y)\ M \to_\beta y$, any redex in M goes away. Reducing a redex may also make copies of a redex, e.g., since $(\lambda x.x\ x\ x)\ M \to_\beta M\ M\ M$, any redex in M is copied three times. "Reducing" the lambda expression $(\lambda x.x\ x\ x)\ (\lambda y.y\ y\ y)$ actually makes it increase without bound. In general, this makes β-reduction non-monotonic, precluding a proof like that for Theorem 2.

The usual proof of Theorem 3 demonstrates confluence by showing it is possible, after any single β-reduction of a redex, to reach the configuration obtained by reducing *all* redexes "in parallel." Induction on this step completes the proof, which Tait and Martin-Löf developed in the early 1970 s but did not publish. Barendregt [2] recites this proof and others, but I prefer Pollack's [45] treatment of Takahashi's presentation [51, 52].

The rules for maximal parallel β-reduction are deterministic:

$$x \Rightarrow x \quad \text{(p-var)} \qquad \frac{M \Rightarrow M' \quad N \Rightarrow N'}{(\lambda x.M)\ N \Rightarrow M'[x := N']}\ \text{(p-}\beta\text{)}$$

$$\frac{M \Rightarrow M'}{\lambda x.M \Rightarrow \lambda x.M'}\ \text{(p-}\lambda\text{)} \qquad \frac{M \Rightarrow M' \quad N \Rightarrow N' \quad M \text{ is not a lambda}}{M\ N \Rightarrow M'\ N'}\ \text{(p-app)}$$

The (p-var) rule is the base case, which leaves unbound variables unchanged. The (p-λ) rule handles a lambda term by rewriting its body. Finally, (p-β) and (p-app) handle applications. The (p-β) rule performs the usual β-reduction on redexes, but only *after* reducing all redexes in the body M and the argument N. The (p-app) rule applies to every other application term (e.g., when M is an application or a variable) and reduces all redexes in both of its sub-expressions.

However, reducing all redexes according to these deterministic, maximally parallel rules does not necessarily produce a normal form; reductions may expose new ones that were not initially "visible" to the parallel β-reduction rules. For example, reducing $((\lambda w.\lambda x.w)\ y)\ z$ to normal form takes two steps. The first:

$$\frac{\dfrac{\dfrac{w \Rightarrow w}{\lambda x.w \Rightarrow \lambda x.w}\ \text{(p-}\lambda\text{)} \quad y \Rightarrow y}{(\lambda w.(\lambda x.w))\ y \Rightarrow \lambda x.y}\ \text{(p-}\beta\text{)} \quad z \Rightarrow z}{((\lambda w.(\lambda x.w))\ y)\ z \Rightarrow (\lambda x.y)\ z}\ \text{(p-app)}$$

Determinism in the lambda calculus, therefore, has parallels with acyclic digital electronic logic circuits: the implementation may choose to do more work than necessary, but the outcome of needless work does not affect the ultimate result. In a lambda expression, "more work" would be performing β-reductions on terms that are eventually ignored. Similarly, a circuit may "glitch" and transition more than necessary because of multiple paths with different delays to a particular logic gate. However, because an acyclic circuit is finite and contains finitely many paths, glitching always converges, whereas it impossible in general to guarantee β-reduction will converge because the model is Turing-complete.

For practical reasons, most functional languages (e.g., LISP, Scheme, and ML) have adopted the applicative execution policy familiar to most programmers, i.e., function arguments are evaluated before the function is invoked. In the lambda calculus, this corresponds to reducing the argument to a lambda term to normal form before performing β-reduction. However, other languages, notably Haskell, adopts a more lazy strategy in which evaluation is deferred. The result is that certain programs coded in Haskell (e.g., those that manipulate infinite lists) will terminate while the same programs in other functional languages do not. However, if a Haskell program is coded in an applicative function language and still terminates, Church-Rosser ensures the result is the same.

5   Conclusion

I presented a very abstract model of models of computation that gives us a starting point for speaking about the determinism of MoCs, provided some examples and their relationship to the model, and discussed three well-known theorems that provide determinism to many models of computation.

The goal of determinism is to provide implementation flexibility (e.g., to optimize metrics such as speed or cost) without these choices affecting how a designer understands the behavior of the system. Technically speaking, I define a deterministic model of computation as one in which the relationship between the defined inputs and outputs of the system is a function that is unaffected by choices made during its implementation or operation.

The Banach Fixed-point Theorem (Theorem 1) shows a contracting function in a metric space converges to a fixed point. Lee et al. used this for arguing the determinism of certain discrete-event models.

The Kleene-Knaster-Tarski Theorem (Theorem 2) relies on a partial order with well-defined limits and a continuous function, which also happens to be monotonic. In this setting, iterations starting from the least defined element $\perp$ in the space converge to a unique least fixed point. Kahn [30] used this to show his process networks were deterministic and many variants since then, including Lee's SDF [35], have also relied on this result to ensure a parallel, asynchronous implementation of a system remains deterministic.

The lambda calculus has the Church-Rosser Theorem (Theorem 3), which states the ultimate result of computation (the normal form of a lambda expression) is unique if it exists. Reducing an expression to normal form involves making choices (either statically, as part of the implementation choices, or dynamically), but Church-Rosser says these choices only affect performance, not the ultimate result. This theorem provides determinism guarantees to many functional languages and can also be used in a parallel setting.

It is my hope that this survey has clarified your understanding of the meaning and utility of determinism in MoCs, perhaps providing inspiration of how to ensure determinism in the next MoC you devise.

Acknowledgements. The National Science Foundation funded this work (CCF-1162124); the suggestions of two anonymous reviewers definitely improved this paper.

References

1. Banach, S.: Sur les opérations dans les ensembles abstraits et leur application aux équations intégrales. Fundamenta Mathematicae **3**(1), 133–181 (1922)
2. Barendregt, H.P.: The Lambda Calculus: Its Syntax and Semantics. Studies in Logic and the Foundations of Mathematics, vol. 103, Revised ed, North-Holland (1984)
3. Bekić, H.: Definable operations in general algebras, and the theory of automata and flowcharts. In: Jones, C.B. (ed.) Programming Languages and Their Definition. LNCS, vol. 177, pp. 30–55. Springer, Heidelberg (1984). https://doi.org/10.1007/BFb0048939
4. Berry, G.: The constructive semantics of pure Esterel. Draft book (1999)
5. Berry, G.: The foundations of Esterel. In: Proof, Language and Interaction: Essays in Honour of Robin Milner. MIT Press (2000)
6. Berry, G., Gonthier, G.: The esterel synchronous programming language: design, semantics, implementation. Sci. Comput. Program. **19**(2), 87–152 (1992)
7. Bhattacharyya, S.S., Murthy, P.K., Lee, E.A.: Synthesis of embedded software from synchronous dataflow specifications. J. VLSI Sig. Process. Syst. **21**(2), 151–166 (1999)
8. Bilsen, G., Engels, M., Lauwereins, R., Peperstraete, J.A.: Cycle-static dataflow. IEEE Trans. Signal Process. **44**(2), 397–408 (1996)
9. Bourdoncle, F.: Efficient chaotic iteration strategies with widenings. In: Bjørner, D., Broy, M., Pottosin, I.V. (eds.) Formal Methods in Programming and Their Applications: International Conference Proceedings. LNCS, vol. 735. Springer, Heidelberg (1993). https://doi.org/10.1007/BFb0039704
10. Brayton, R.K., Mishchenko, A.: ABC: an academic industrial-strength verification tool. In: Touili, T., Cook, B., Jackson, P. (eds.) CAV 2010. LNCS, vol. 6174, pp. 24–40. Springer, Heidelberg (2010). https://doi.org/10.1007/978-3-642-14295-6_5
11. Bryant, R.E.: Boolean analysis of MOS circuits. IEEE Trans. Comput.- Aided Des. Integr. Circ. Syst. CAD **6**(4), 634–649 (1987)
12. Brzozowski, J.A., Seger, C.-J.H.: Asynchronous Circuits. Springer, New York (1995). https://doi.org/10.1007/978-1-4612-4210-9
13. Brzozowski, J.A., Yoeli, M.: On a ternary model of gate networks. IEEE Trans. Comput. **C–28**(3), 178–184 (1979)
14. Buck, J.T.: Static scheduling and code generation from dynamic dataflow graphs with integer-valued control streams. In: Proceedings of the Asilomar Conference on Signals, Systems and Computers, Pacific Grove, California, pp. 508–513, October 1994
15. Cataldo, A., Lee, E., Liu, X., Matsikoudis, E., Zheng, H.: Discrete-event systems: generalizing metric spaces and fixed point semantics. Technical report UCB/ERL M05/12, University of California, Berkeley, April 2005
16. Cataldo, A., Lee, E., Liu, X., Matsikoudis, E., Zheng, H.: A constructive fixed-point theorem and the feedback semantics of timed systems. In: Workshop on Discrete Event Systems, 10–12 July 2006
17. Church, A.: A set of postulates for the foundation of logic. Ann. Math. **33**(2), 346–366 (1932)
18. Church, A.: The Calculi of Lambda-Conversion. Princeton University Press, Princeton (1941)
19. Church, A., Rosser, J.B.: Some properties of conversion. Trans. Am. Math. Soc. **39**(3), 472–482 (1936)

20. Cousot, P.: Asynchronous iterative methods for solving a fixed point system of monotone equations in a complete lattice. Rapport de Recherche IMAG-RR-88, Laboratoire d'Informatique, Université Scientifique et Médicale de Grenoble, Grenoble, France, September 1977

21. Davey, B.A., Priestley, H.A.: Introduction to Lattices and Order. Cambridge University Press, Cambridge (1990)

22. Edwards, S.A.: Concurrency and communication: lessons from the SHIM project. In: Lee, S., Narasimhan, P. (eds.) SEUS. LNCS, vol. 5860, pp. 276–287. Springer, Heidelberg (2009). https://doi.org/10.1007/978-3-642-10265-3_25

23. Edwards, S.A., Lee, E.A.: The semantics and execution of a synchronous block-diagram language. Sci. Comput. Program. **48**(1), 21–42 (2003)

24. Edwards, S.A., Tardieu, O.: SHIM: A deterministic model for heterogeneous embedded systems. IEEE Trans. Very Large Scale Integr. (VLSI) Syst. **14**(8), 854–867 (2006)

25. Edwards, S.A., Townsend, R., Kim, M.A.: Compositional dataflow circuits. In: Proceedings of the International Conference on Formal Methods and Models for Codesign (MEMOCODE), Vienna, Austria, September 2017

26. Eichelberger, E.B.: Hazard detection in combinational and sequential switching circuits. IBM J. Res. Dev. **9**(2), 90–99 (1965)

27. Gordon, M.J., Milner, A.J., Wadsworth, C.P.: Edinburgh LCF. LNCS, vol. 78. Springer, Heidelberg (1979). https://doi.org/10.1007/3-540-09724-4

28. Hudak, P., Jones, S.P., Wadler, P.: Report on the programming language Haskell: a non-strict purely functional language (version 1.2). ACM SIGPLAN Not. **27**(5), 1–164 (1992)

29. Jones, S.P.: The Implementation of Functional Programming Languages. Prentice Hall, New Jersey (1987)

30. Gilles, K.: The semantics of a simple language for parallel programming. In: Information Processing 74: Proceedings of IFIP Congress 74, Stockholm, Sweden, pp. 471–475, August 1974

31. Kuehlmann, A., Paruthi, V., Krohm, F., Ganai, M.K.: Robust Boolean reasoning for equivalence checking and functional property verification. IEEE Trans. Comput.-Aided Des. Integr. Circuits Syst. **21**(12), 1377–1394 (2002)

32. Jean-Louis, J.-L., Nguyen, V.L., Sonnenberg, E.A.: Fixed point theorems and semantics: a folk tale. Inf. Process. Lett. **14**(3), 112–116 (1982)

33. Lee, E.A.: Modeling concurrent real-time processes using discrete events. Ann. Softw. Eng. **7**, 25–45 (1999)

34. Lee, E.A., Matsikoudis, E.: The semantics of dataflow with firing. In: From Semantics to Computer Science: Essays in Memory of Gilles Kahn, Chap. 4, pp. 71–94. Cambridge University Press, Cambridge (2008)

35. Lee, E.A., Messerschmitt, D.G.: Synchronous data flow. Proc. IEEE **75**(9), 1235–1245 (1987)

36. Lee, E.A., Parks, T.M.: Dataflow process networks. Proc. IEEE **83**(5), 773–801 (1995)

37. Lee, E.A., Sangiovanni-Vincentelli, A.: A framework for comparing models of computation. IEEE Trans. Comput.-Aided Des. Integr. Circuits Syst. **17**(12), 1217–1229 (1998)

38. Lee, E., Varaiya, P.: Structure and Interpretation of Signals and Systems. Addison-Wesley, Reading (2003)

39. Lee, E.A., Zheng, H.: Leveraging synchronous language principles for heterogeneous modeling and design of embedded systems. In: Proceedings of the International Conference on Embedded Software (EMSOFT), Austria, pp. 114–123, September 2007

40. Malik, S.: Analysis of cyclic combinational circuits. In: Proceedings of the International Conference on Computer Aided Design (ICCAD), Santa Clara, California, pp. 618–625, November 1993

41. McCarthy, J.: Recursive functions of symbolic expressions and their computation by machine, part I. Commun. ACM **3**(4), 184–195 (1960)

42. Mendler, M., Shiple, T.R., Berry, G.: Constructive Boolean circuits and the exactness of timed ternary simulation. J. Formal Methods Syst. Des. **40**(3), 283–329 (2012)

43. Muller, D.E.: Treatment of transition signals in electronic switching circuits by algebraic methods. IRE Trans. Electron. Comput. **EC–8**(3), 401 (1959)

44. Penry, D.A., August, D.I.: Optimizations for a simulator construction system supporting reusable components. In: Proceedings of the 40th Design Automation Conference, Anaheim, California, pp. 926–931, June 2003

45. Pollack, R.: Polishing up the Tait-Martin-Löf proof of the Church-Rosser theorem. In: Proceedings De Wintermöte, Göteborg, Sweden. Department of Computing Science, Chalmers University, January 1995

46. Scott, D.: Continuous lattices. In: Lawvere, F.W. (ed.) Toposes, Algebraic Geometry and Logic. LNM, vol. 274, pp. 97–136. Springer, Heidelberg (1972). https://doi.org/10.1007/BFb0073967

47. Scott, D.: Data types as lattices. SIAM J. Comput. **5**(3), 522–587 (1976)

48. Shiple, T.R., Berry, G., Touati, H.: Constructive analysis of cyclic circuits. In: Proceedings of the European Design and Test Conference, Paris, France, pp. 328–333, March 1996

49. Stoy, J.: Denotational Semantics: The Scott-Strachey Approach to Programming Language Theory. MIT Press, Cambridge (1977)

50. Sussman, G.J., Steele Jr., G.L.: Scheme: an interpreter for extended lambda calculus. Technical report AIM-349, MIT AI Lab, Cambridge, Massachusetts (1975)

51. Takahashi, M.: Parallel reductions in λ-calculus. J. Symb. Comput. **7**(2), 113–123 (1989)

52. Takahashi, M.: Parallel reductions in λ-calculus. Inf. Comput. **118**(1), 120–127 (1995)

53. Tarski, A.: A lattice-theoretical fixpoint theorem and its applications. Pac. J. Math. **5**(2), 285–309 (1955)

54. Turing, A.M.: Computability and λ-definability. J. Symb. Logic **2**(4), 153–163 (1937)

55. Wei, J.: Parallel asynchronous iterations of least fixed points. Parallel Comput. **19**(8), 886–895 (1993)

56. Winskel, G.: The Formal Semantics of Programming Languages: An Introduction Foundations of Computing. MIT Press, Cambridge (1993)

Lossy Channels in a Dataflow Model of Computation

Pascal Fradet, Alain Girault[(✉)], Leila Jamshidian, Xavier Nicollin, and Arash Shafiei

Univ. Grenoble Alpes, Inria, CNRS, Grenoble INP, LIG,
38000 Grenoble, France
alain.girault@inria.fr

Abstract. In this paper, we take into account lossy channels and retransmission protocols in dataflow models of computation (MoCs). Traditional dataflow MoCs cannot easily cope with lossy channels, due to the strict notion of iteration that does not allow the re-emission of lost or damaged tokens. A general dataflow graph with several lossy channels will indeed require several phases, each of them corresponding to a portion of the initial graph's schedule. Correctly identifying and sequencing these phases is a challenge. We present a translation of a dataflow graph, written in the well-known Synchronous DataFlow (SDF) MoC of Lee and Messerschmitt, but where some channels may be lossy, into the Boolean Parametric DataFlow (BPDF) MoC.

1 Introduction

The Internet of Things (IoT) has led to the deployment of billions of small devices that are interconnected mainly by wireless communication protocols. A lot of IoT applications use a form of dataflow communication between the nodes, so it seems a good idea to use a dataflow Model of Computation (MoC) to program such applications. One great advantage is the possibility to perform formal reasoning at compile time, ensuring bounded memory, absence of deadlock, schedulability, and performance properties. The problem is that IoT applications are subject to communication losses, which can arise for various reasons: e.g., electromagnetic interferences, low bandwidth, power shortage (frequent in tiny devices which are typical of the IoT). There are many communication protocols, such as Automatic Repeat Request (ARQ) protocols, to deal with lossy channels and to achieve reliable transmission. These techniques are all based on *retransmissions*.

Traditional dataflow MoCs cannot easily cope with lossy channels, due to the strict notion of iteration that does not allow the retransmission of lost or damaged tokens. Consider a simple dataflow graph of the form

$$X \to Y \rightsquigarrow Z \to T$$

Grenoble INP—Institute of Engineering Univ. Grenoble Alpes

© Springer International Publishing AG, part of Springer Nature 2018
M. Lohstroh et al. (Eds.): Lee Festschrift, LNCS 10760, pp. 254–266, 2018.
https://doi.org/10.1007/978-3-319-95246-8_15

where $\rightsquigarrow$ denotes a lossy channel. Executing such a graph consists in executing X, Y, Z, and T consecutively. But if Z reads corrupted data it has to produce immediately data which most probably depends on its input. Furthermore, if Z then asks for a retransmission, then executing Y again would entail reading new data from X. The partial re-executions asked by ARQ protocols do not fit within the standard dataflow model.

In this paper, we propose to use the Boolean Parametric DataFlow (BPDF) MoC [2] to deal with lossy channels and the necessary retransmissions when tokens are damaged or lost. BPDF extends the classical Synchronous DataFlow (SDF) MoC of Lee and Messerschmitt [6] with *Boolean parameters* on the dataflow edges, which permits to *disable* and *enable* edges. By carefully controlling the Boolean conditions, we can model the execution phases of dataflow graphs with lossy channels.

Section 2 presents the necessary background, namely the SDF and BPDF MoCs. SDF with lossy channels and its translation into BPDF are described in Sect. 3. Section 4 suggests several future work directions. Finally, Sect. 5 summarizes our contributions and concludes.

2 Background

Since our goal is to extend SDF with a notion of lossy channel and to show how to translate this model into BPDF, we present these two MoCs in turn.

2.1 Synchronous DataFlow (SDF)

Formally, an SDF graph $G = \langle \mathcal{V}, \mathcal{E}, \iota, \rho \rangle$ consists of:

- a finite set of actors (computation nodes) $\mathcal{V}$;
- a finite set of edges $\mathcal{E} \subseteq \mathcal{V} \times \mathcal{V}$; edges can be seen as unbounded FIFO channels; if $e = (X, Y)$, also written XY, is an edge, then e is an *outgoing edge* of X, and an *incoming edge* of Y.
- a function $\iota : \mathcal{E} \to \mathbb{N}$ that returns, for each edge, its number of initial tokens (possibly zero);
- a function $\rho : \mathcal{E} \to \mathbb{N}_{>0} \times \mathbb{N}_{>0}$ that returns, for each edge a tuple containing the *production rate* of its source actor and the *consumption rate* of its sink actor.

The execution of an actor (called *firing*) first consumes data tokens from all its incoming edges (its inputs), then computes, and finishes by producing data tokens to all its outgoing edges (its outputs). The number of tokens consumed (resp. produced) at a given incoming (resp. outgoing) edge at each firing is called its consumption (resp. production) rate and is specified by function ρ. An actor can fire only when all its incoming edges have enough tokens, *i.e.*, at least the number specified by the corresponding rate (edges may have a non-null number of initial tokens, defined by function ι). For instance, Fig. 1 shows a simple SDF graph G with three actors A, B, C.

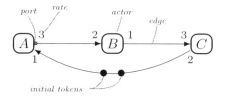

Fig. 1. A simple SDF graph with 3 actors and 3 edges.

Each edge carries zero or more tokens at any moment. The state of a dataflow graph is the vector of the number of tokens present at each edge. The initial state of a graph is defined as the vector of the number of initial tokens on its edges. For instance, the initial state of the graph of Fig. 1 is the vector $[0; 0; 2]$.

Because all rates in SDF are fixed values, a static schedule can be produced and a number of analyses can be performed at compile time (*e.g.*, boundedness, liveness, throughput, latency, ...).

An *iteration* of an SDF graph is a non empty sequence of firings that returns the graph to its initial state[1]. For the SDF graph in Fig. 1, firing actor A twice (consuming 2 tokens and producing 6 tokens), actor B thrice (consuming 6 tokens and producing 3 tokens), and finally actor C once (consuming 3 tokens and producing 2 tokens) forms an iteration. We write $\#X$ the number of firings of actor X in the iteration.

The *basic repetition vector* $\mathbf{Z} = [\#A = 2, \#B = 3, \#C = 1]$ indicates the number of firings of actors per (minimal) iteration, and the iteration is noted (A^2, B^3, C). The repetition vector is obtained by solving the system of *balance equations*: each edge $X \xrightarrow{p \ q} Y$ is associated with the balance equation $\#X.p = \#Y.q$, which states that all produced tokens during an iteration must be consumed within the same iteration. If non-null solutions exist, the graph is said to be consistent [6], and the smallest solution defines the basic repetition vector. Consistency ensures that the graph can be executed infinitely in bounded memory.

Deadlock analysis must check that the graph G admits a schedule that is always live, called an *admissible schedule*. A simple algorithm to find such a schedule performs a symbolic execution of the SDF graph [6]. Among the admissible schedules, we distinguish *flat single appearance schedules* [4] (FSAS) where, once factorized (*i.e.*, any sequence $A; \ldots; A$ of n firings of A is replaced by A^n), each actor appears exactly once. The SDF graph G of Fig. 1 admits only one FSAS: $\{A^2; B^3; C\}$. An acyclic SDF graph always admits a FSAS, while a cyclic SDF graph admits a FSAS if and only if each cycle includes at least one *saturated* edge, that is, an edge XY that contains enough initial tokens to fire Y at least $\#Y$ times.

---

[1] We only consider here the *minimal* iteration. Any multiple of the minimal iteration is also a valid iteration.

2.2 Boolean Parametric DataFlow (BPDF)

The Boolean Parametric DataFlow (BPDF) MoC [2,5] extends SDF with two features: *integer parameters* for rates, similar to [3], and *Boolean parameters* annotating edges. Only the second feature is of interest for the present paper, so we focus on it.

The general idea is that any edge of a BPDF graph can be labeled with a Boolean expression built from the following grammar:

$$\mathcal{B} ::= tt \mid ff \mid b \mid \neg \mathcal{B} \mid \mathcal{B}_1 \wedge \mathcal{B}_2 \mid \mathcal{B}_1 \vee \mathcal{B}_2 \tag{1}$$

where tt is true, ff is false and b denotes *Boolean parameters*. Each Boolean parameter b is modified by a single actor called its *modifier*. Each modifier has annotations of the form "$b@\pi_w$" where b is the Boolean parameter to be set and π_w is the *period* of the Boolean parameter, that is, the exact number of firings of its modifier between two successive assignments[2].

Formally, a BPDF graph is a tuple $G = \langle \mathcal{V}, \mathcal{E}, \iota, \rho, P_b, \beta, M, \pi_w \rangle$ (for the sake of simplicity, integer parameters are omitted here) where:

- $\mathcal{V}$ (actors), $\mathcal{E}$ (edges), ι (initial tokens), and ρ (rates) are defined as in SDF graphs (see Sect. 2.1);
- P_b is the set of Boolean parameters;
- $\beta : \mathcal{E} \rightarrow \mathcal{B}$ returns, for each edge, its Boolean expression;
- $M : P_b \rightarrow \mathcal{V}$ returns, for each Boolean parameter, its modifier;
- $\pi_w : P_b \rightarrow \mathbb{N}_{>0}$ returns, for each Boolean parameter, its writing period.

In general, a Boolean parameter can take several values during an iteration of a BPDF graph. However, in the context of this paper, Boolean parameters take only one value per iteration. In other words, $\forall b \in P_b, \pi_w(b) = \#M(b)$. Figure 2 shows a BPDF graph with three actors and two Boolean parameters.

An edge labeled by a Boolean expression is *disabled* whenever its expression evaluates to false and *enabled* otherwise. An edge not labeled by a Boolean expression is seen as labeled by tt and thus behaves exactly as in SDF. When an edge XY is disabled, X fires but does not emit any token to Y (but emits tokens on its enabled outgoing edges) and Y fires but does not read any token from X (but reads tokens from all its enabled incoming edges). When an actor X is such that all its edges are disabled, it still fires; such firings are referred as *dummy*. However, a modifier of one or more Boolean parameters may still update their value during a dummy firing.

A *user* of a Boolean parameter b is an actor with one of its edge labeled by a Boolean expression that depends on b. Formally, the set of users of b is defined as:

$$Users(b) = \{X \in \mathcal{V} \mid \exists Y \in \mathcal{V} : b \in \beta(XY) \vee b \in \beta(YX)\}$$

Once a new value for b is produced, it is propagated to all users of b.

---

[2] Obviously, an assignment does not necessarily change the value.

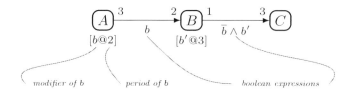

Fig. 2. A simple BPDF graph.

Whenever it fires, a BPDF actor X performs the following steps:

1. Read the value of each Boolean parameter b for which $X \in Users(b)$ (only at its first firing in the iteration);
2. Consume tokens on the enabled incoming edges, which must have enough tokens (otherwise the actor is blocked);
3. Compute its new internal state and outputs;
4. Produce tokens on the enabled outgoing edges;
5. If X is the modifier of a Boolean parameter b and the current firing corresponds to its period ($\pi_w(b)$), then the value of b is propagated to all its users (*Users(b)*). In this paper, $\pi_w(b)$ is restricted to be equal to $\#M(b)$ so such propagations take place only during the last firing of each modifier in the iteration.

In constrast, an SDF actor only performs steps 2, 3, and 4, and of course all its edges are always enabled.

Consistency analysis in BPDF requires to check, as in SDF, rate consistency. We ignore the Boolean expressions and solve the system of balance equations to check that there exists a non-null solution. In general, a second condition called period safety, should be checked (see [2]). However, in this paper, since Booleans parameters are changed at most once by iteration the second condition is trivially true. Liveness has also to be checked using a refinement of the algorithm used in SDF (see [2]). It is easy to check that the BPDF graph of Fig. 2 is consistent, live, and that its iteration is (A^2, B^3, C).

In general, integer parameters prevent the generation of static schedules for BPDF graphs [1]. In the context of this paper, we do not consider integer parameters and we are able to generate static schedules. For instance, the only FSAS of the BPDF graph of Fig. 2 is $\{A^2; B^3; C\}$. Note that A and B are the modifiers of b and b' respectively, whereas A is a user of b, and B and C are users of b and b'. Therefore, the first firing of A reads the value of b produced in the *previous* iteration, whereas the second (and last) firing produces the value of b that will be used in the *next* iteration. Similarly, the first firing of B reads the values of b and b' produced in the *previous* iteration, while the third (and last) firing of B produces the value of b' that will be read in the *next* iteration. Finally, the first (and only) firing of C reads the values of b and b' produced in the *previous* iteration.

3   From Lossy SDF to BPDF

We call *lossy SDF* the SDF model enriched with the information on whether edges are lossy or not. Informally a lossy SDF graph should behave exactly as if all its channels were non lossy. Its high-level semantics is therefore given by the SDF semantics. One assumption needs to be formulated though: on each lossy channel, tokens are eventually transmitted correctly. If this cannot be guaranteed, a maximum number of retransmissions can be specified for each lossy channel, with a default token value (and, in that case, the semantics departs from SDF's).

We show in this section how a lossy SDF graph can be translated automatically into a BPDF graph with an equivalent semantics.

The intuitive semantics of lossy SDF can be implemented based on selective retransmissions. Consider the same simple dataflow graph as in the introduction

$$X \rightarrow Y \rightsquigarrow Z \rightarrow T$$

where $\rightsquigarrow$ denotes a lossy channel. We saw that the standard dataflow execution does not suit potential re-executions. Our solution is to divide the execution of this graph in three phases: first the X-Y part where X fires and Y only reads (called the *upstream* phase), then the Y-Z part where Y only writes and Z only reads (called the *lossy* phase), and finally the Z-T part where Z only writes and T fires (called the *downstream* phase). This division allows re-executions of Y-Z until the token sent by Y is correctly received by Z. Of course when there are multiple lossy channels or cycles in the graph, many phases should be considered and combined. We present how to implement such phases in BPDF using Boolean conditions to enable/disable individual edges.

3.1   Translation of a Simple SDF Graph with One Lossy Channel

Consider the SDF graph of Fig. 3, where the edge BC is lossy, indicated by a curly arrow. Its iteration is (A^2, B^3, C^3, D^3) and its only FSAS is $\{A^2; B^3; C^3; D^3\}$.

Fig. 3. A simple SDF graph with one lossy channel BC.

To account for the lossy channel BC, this graph is executed into three consecutive phases:

1. **Upstream phase:** First $\{A^2; B^3\}$ where B reads the tokens produced by A but does not send any token to C;
2. **Lossy phase:** Then $\{B^3; C^3\}$ which may be repeated until all tokens sent by B are correctly received by C; in this phase, B does not read any token on channel AB;
3. **Downstream phase:** Finally $\{C^3; D^3\}$ where C does not read tokens from the edge BC and sends the tokens to D.

The BPDF graph implementing these three phases is shown in Fig. 4. Its FSAS is $\{A^2; B^3; C^3; D^3\}$. The first phase is when $b = tt \wedge b' = tt$. The Boolean expressions of both edges BC and CD evaluate to ff. The actor B fires three times and reads its incoming tokens from A but does not send any. Since both C and D are disconnected their three firings are dummy. The second phase corresponds to $b = \mathit{ff} \wedge b' = tt$. Now the firings of A and D are dummy, B does not read any tokens from A, and C does not write any token to D. The only exchange of tokens takes place between B and C. This phase can be repeated as long as $b = \mathit{ff} \wedge b' = tt$. The third phase is when $b = \mathit{ff} \wedge b' = \mathit{ff}$, yielding the iteration $\{A^2; B^3; C^3; D^3\}$ where the firings of A and B are dummy firings, and the only exchange of tokens takes place between C and D. This three phase cycle can now be repeated by returning to $b = tt \wedge b' = tt$.

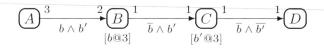

Fig. 4. The translation into BPDF of the graph of Fig. 3.

The Boolean parameter b could be set by any actor in the graph. Here we have chosen B to set b, thereby controlling the end of the first phase which always occurs after one iteration. In contrast, the Boolean parameter b' must mandatorily be set by actor C, because C is the only actor capable of asserting when the tokens produced by B have been received correctly. We assume that the communication system layer provides information about token corruption and/or loss. This can be performed by using error-detecting codes and/or time out mechanisms. For instance, one of the Automatic Repeat-Request (ARQ) protocols, *e.g.*, Stop-and-Wait ARQ, Go-Back-N ARQ, or Selective Repeat ARQ, can be used [10]. In general, the SDF graph will include several lossy channels, yielding more than three phases and requiring more Boolean parameters, as we see in the next section.

3.2   General Translation Algorithm

In this section, we propose a general translation from a lossy SDF graph into an equivalent BPDF graph. By "equivalent", we mean that the semantics of the resulting BPDF graph must coincide with the semantics of the original lossy SDF graph.

Let $G = \langle \mathcal{V}, \mathcal{E}, \iota, \rho \rangle$ be the initial SDF graph and let $\mathcal{L} \subseteq \mathcal{E}$ be the subset of lossy channels. We assume that G admits a sequential FSAS denoted by S_G. The translation from G into a semantically equivalent BPDF graph proceeds as follows:

1. We number the actors from 1 to n ($n = |\mathcal{V}|$) according to their order of appearance in S_G. They are now uniquely identified as $V_1, V_2, \ldots V_n$.

2. S_G also induces a total order on the edges of $\mathcal{E}$. An edge AB occurs before another XY, if A occurs before X in the FSAS S_G and AB occurs before AC if B occurs before C in S_G. Formally,

$$\forall (V_i V_j), (V_k V_\ell) \in \mathcal{E}, (V_i V_j) < (V_k V_\ell) \Leftrightarrow (i < k) \vee (i = k \wedge j < \ell)$$

We number all edges from 1 to p ($p = |\mathcal{E}|$) which are now uniquely identified as $E_1, E_2, \ldots, E_p$.

3. The total order on $\mathcal{V}$ can be projected onto $\mathcal{L}$, yielding a total order on $\mathcal{L}$, so we can number lossy channels from 1 to $|\mathcal{L}| = q$. All lossy channels in $\mathcal{L}$ are now uniquely identified as $L_1, L_2, \ldots L_q$. Moreover, for each $j \in [1, q]$, there exists a unique $i \in [1, p]$ such that $L_j = E_i$. We denote this index $i = \varphi(j)$.

4. Then, G is translated into the BPDF graph $G' = \langle \mathcal{V}, \mathcal{E}, \iota, \rho, P_b, \beta, M, \pi_w \rangle$ such that:
   - Actors $\mathcal{V}$, edges $\mathcal{E}$, production/consumption rates ρ, and number of initial tokens ι remain the same as in G.
   - For each lossy channel L_i, we introduce two Boolean parameters b_i and b_i'. The resulting set of Boolean parameters is defined as: $P_b = \{b_i, b_i' | 1 \leq i \leq q\}$.
   - For all $1 \leq i \leq p$, we set $\beta(E_i) = bc_1 \wedge bc_2 \wedge bc_3$ with:
     - bc_1 accounts for all lossy channels that are *after* E_i in S_G: $bc_1 = \bigwedge_{j=u}^{q} (b_j \wedge b_j')$ with $u = \min\{j \in [1, q] \mid \varphi(j) > i\}$.
     - bc_2 accounts for the fact that E_i may be itself a lossy channel: if $\exists j \in [1, q]$ such that $E_i = L_j$, then $bc_2 = \overline{b_j} \wedge b_j'$ else $bc_2 = tt$.
     - bc_3 accounts for all lossy channels that are *before* E_i in S_G: $bc_3 = \bigwedge_{j=1}^{\ell} (\overline{b_j} \wedge \overline{b_j'})$ with $\ell = \max\{j \in [1, q] \mid \varphi(j) < i\}$.
   - For all $1 \leq i \leq q$ and $L_i = S_i R_i$, we set $M(b_i) = S_i$ and $M(b_i') = R_i$ with $\pi_w(b_i) = \#M(b_i)$ and $\pi_w(b_i') = \#M(b_i')$.

The BPDF actors connected by a lossy channel $S \rightsquigarrow R$ must also be instrumented. The receiver R needs to detect when the received tokens are correct so that it can change the phase by propagating a new Boolean value. As already mentioned, we assume that the communication system marks tokens as correct or incorrect. The sender S needs to keep a copy of its transferred tokens in order to resend them when necessary. It knows not to resend tokens when the phase changes.

3.3   Sequencing the Phases

The BPDF graph of Fig. 4 runs according to three phases. These three phases are summarized in the following table on the left (dummy firings are omitted):

Phase	Partial schedule	b_1	b_1'
1 (upstream)	$\{A^2; B^3\}$	tt	tt
2 (lossy)	$\{B^3; C^3\}^*$	ff	tt
3 (downstream)	$\{C^3; D^3\}$	ff	ff

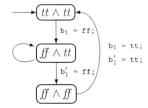

On the right we have shown the labeled transition system (LTS) of the three phases. We adopt the convention that all the Boolean parameters are initially equal to tt, so its initial state is phase 1, corresponding to $tt \wedge tt$. To implement these three phases, the modifiers of the two Boolean parameters must implement the following pseudo-code:

Actor B	Actor C
`if (phase==1) then b₁=ff;`	`if (phase==2) then b'₁=ff;`
`if (phase==3) then b₁=tt;`	`if (phase==3) then b'₁=tt;`

Note that an actor can easily determine the current phase by looking at the current values of the Boolean parameters.

We now address the general case. A BPDF graph with q lossy channels has at most $2q+1$ phases, because we totally order the edges according to its FSAS. We have chosen to implement these $2q + 1$ phases with $2q$ Boolean parameters (the b_is and b'_is), although one may think that $\lceil log_2(2q+1) \rceil$ Booleans would be enough. Yet, there is a restriction that, for each lossy channel $L_i = S_i R_i$, only R_i can control the end of the lossy phase of L_i, because only R_i can tell whether or not the tokens sent by S_i have been received correctly. It follows that at least q Boolean parameters are required for this, one for each lossy channel (the b'_is). Yet, the remaining q Booleans could be optimized (the b_is). This could be the topic of future work.

The sequencing of the phases for a general graph can be represented by a similar LTS as the one shown above for the graph of Fig. 4. To implement such an LTS, we must provide the pseudo-code for each actor that modifies one (or more) Boolean parameter(s). For each lossy channel $L_i = S_i R_i$, recall that we have two Boolean parameters, b_i and b'_i, respectively modified by S_i and R_i, such that S_i controls the switching from phase $2i - 1$ to $2i$ while R_i controls the switching from phase $2i$ to $2i + 1$. After the last phase, each modifier must also reset its Boolean parameters to tt to return to the initial phase. As a consequence, S_i and R_i must implement the following pseudo-code:

S_i	R_i
`if (phase==2*i-1) then bᵢ=ff;`	`if (phase==2*i)   then b'ᵢ=ff;`
`if (phase==last)   then bᵢ=tt;`	`if (phase==last) then b'ᵢ=tt;`

As we have said, the maximum number of phases with q lossy channels is $2q+1$. Yet, there are several cases when this number can be reduced. For instance when there are two lossy channels in sequence, say XY and YZ, then Y will update both the Boolean b'_i corresponding to XY and the Boolean b_{i+1} corresponding to YZ. As a consequence, there is one phase less because two Booleans are set to *ff* at the same firing of Y. Another typical case is when there is a fork of two lossy channels, say XY and XZ. As in the previous case, X sets two Booleans to *ff* during its firing, so there is one less phase. It follows that the precise number of phases must be computed prior to obtain the value of `last` used in the above table.

Finally, a particular case occurs when the first lossy channel L_1 is also the first edge E_1. In this case, there is no real first phase, because when all the Boolean parameters are equal to *tt* and all the edges of the BPDF graph are disabled, so each actor performs a dummy firing. A similar case occurs when the last lossy channel L_q is also the last edge E_p. In this case there is no real last phase since all the actors perform only a dummy firing. Of course, these special situations could be optimized out.

3.4   Cyclic Graphs

Cyclic lossy SDF graphs pose a problem because the backward edges appear both in the upstream phases so that the destination actor can consume the initial tokens, *and* in the downstream phase so that the source actors can produce the initial tokens for the next iteration of the graph.

Recall that we have assumed that each cycle contains at least one saturated edge (see Sect. 2.1).

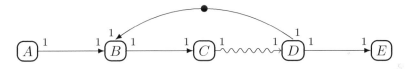

Fig. 5. An SDF graph with a cycle and a lossy channel.

Consider the example of Fig. 5. For the sake of simplicity, all the production and consumption rates are equal to 1. Assuming the FSAS $\{A; B; C; D; E\}$, its translation into BPDF is shown in Fig. 6.

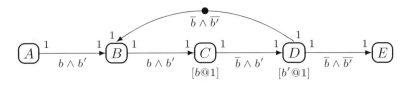

Fig. 6. The BPDF graph obtained by translating the SDF graph of Fig. 5.

As we can see, the backward edge DB (which is saturated thanks to the initial token) belongs only to the *downstream* phase, hence it is not executed during the upstream phase. It follows that, when B fires during the upstream phase, it cannot read any initial token from the backward edge DB because this edge is disabled. To solve this issue, we consider that all initial tokens are in fact stored directly in the *internal memory* of the destination actor of the edge to which they belong. In the case of Fig. 6, this means that the initial token of the backward edge DB is stored in the internal memory of actor B. As a consequence, during the upstream phase, B reads the token sent by A and the initial token stored in its internal memory, and sends a token to C. During the lossy phase D reads the token sent by C until this token is correctly received. Finally, during the downstream phase D sends a token to E and a token to B on the backward edge, this last token being in fact directly written in the internal memory of B.

4   Future Work

This work is still in progress and we present in this section a number of issues that remain open.

Influence of the Chosen FSAS. The translation algorithm is based on an arbitrary FSAS of the considered graph G. An interesting question is what is the influence of this choice whenever G admits several FSASs.

Let us first remark that the choice of the FSAS can change the number of phases. Consider for instance the SDF graph G of Fig. 7(a) with one lossy channel, with its translation into BPDF G' shown in Fig. 7(b).

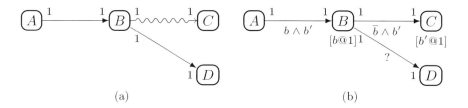

(a)   (b)

Fig. 7. (a) A graph G that admits two FSASs. (b) Its translation G'.

The Boolean expression attached to BD is marked with a '?' because it depends on the FSAS of G. Indeed, G admits two FSASs: $\{A; B; C; D\}$ and $\{A; B; D; C\}$. With the first FSAS, BD belongs to the downstream phase, thereby getting the Boolean expression $\bar{b} \wedge \bar{b'}$. With the second FSAS, BD belongs to the upstream phase, thereby getting $b \wedge b'$. The second FSAS results in two phases against three phases for the first FSAS. A follow up question is the impact of the reduction of the number of phases. More generally, we should strive to choose a FSAS that optimizes performance criteria.

Parallel Schedules. Another topic of future work is how to consider *parallel schedules*. So far, we start from a sequential FSAS to sequence the phases. This is adequate when the SDF graph is sequential, but not when it is parallel. An idea to preserve the parallelism in phases would be to identify, for each lossy channel L_j, its *upstream cone* $UC(L_j)$ and its *downstream cone* $DC(L_j)$. Intuitively, the upstream cone of XY is the set of all predecessor edges of X. This is a classical graph traversal problem. Each edge E_i in the resulting BPDF graph will therefore get the Boolean expression $\beta(E_i) = bc_1 \wedge bc_2 \wedge bc_3$ where:

- bc_1 accounts for all the lossy channels L_j such that E_i belongs to $UC(L_j)$;
- bc_2 accounts for the fact that E_i may be itself a lossy channel;
- bc_3 accounts for all the lossy channels L_j such that E_i belongs to $DC(L_j)$.

This would result in a BPDF graph with more parallelism than with the algorithm proposed in Sect. 3.2, because the phases would not be totally ordered as in Sect. 3.3. This would allow the generation of parallel code (for which there is a huge literature, *e.g.*, [7] to cite just one).

A related topic is to handle joins of lossy channels in parallel instead of sequentially. Consider, for instance, a set of lossy channels $\{X_1Y, \ldots X_nY\}$. The phases of the lossy channels X_iY can actually be run in parallel: Y would handle all the Boolean parameters b_i', setting them from tt to ff as soon as the tokens from the corresponding actors X_i are received correctly, and moving to the next phase only when the predicate $\bigwedge_{i=i}^{n} \overline{b_i'}$ becomes tt.

Optimization and Performance Evaluation. When the initial graph contains q lossy channels, we use $2 * q$ Boolean parameters to make up the phases in the BPDF graph. As explained in Sect. 3.3, this could be optimized.

The general topic of the performance evaluation of the BPDF graphs raises many issues because the number of token retransmissions necessary for each lossy channel cannot be known in advance. Therefore, the *exact* worst case response time cannot be computed. Instead, we may compute the *expected* worst case response time, based on the probability distribution of the damaged/lost tokens on each lossy channel.

5   Conclusion

Modeling lossy channels in a dataflow MoC is relevant for the future IoT applications where mobile devices communicate through wireless channels that are subject to packet loss or damage. In order to model dataflow applications with unreliable communications, we have presented a translation from an SDF graph with lossy channels into the Boolean Parametric DataFlow (BPDF) MoC. This translation isolates the necessary phases of execution of the graph to cope with the retransmissions caused by lost or damaged tokens transmitted over the lossy communication links, and to sequence correctly those phases.

There are a few dataflow MoCs that could express such phases. For instance, we could adopt the Scenario Aware DataFlow MoC (SADF) [9] or its FSM extension [8]. However, this has the inconvenient that all phases must be made explicit, resulting in a potential state space explosion if many lossy channels must be modeled. For this reason, we have chosen BPDF [2,5], which uses Boolean parameters to encode the phases and to keep them implicit.

A final issue is the interaction between actors and the system in charge of detecting the lost and/or damaged tokens sent over the lossy channels. We have assumed a communication system layer that implements the error-detecting code (in charge of detecting damaged tokens), a timeout mechanism (in charge of detecting lost tokens) and some ARQ protocol in charge of propagating the Boolean parameters from their modifier to all their users. These hypotheses should be validated by an actual implementation.

Acknowledgments. The authors are grateful for the numerous discussions with Prof. Edward Lee, the invitations to visit Berkeley, and all the good moments spent at various conferences around the world. In more than one way, the work presented in this paper originated in those discussions.

References

1. Bebelis, V., Fradet, P., Girault, A.: A framework to schedule parametric dataflow applications on many-core platforms. In: International Conference on Languages, Compilers and Tools for Embedded Systems, LCTES 2014, Edinburgh, UK. ACM, June 2014
2. Bebelis, V., Fradet, P., Girault, A., Lavigueur, B.: BPDF: a statically analyzable dataflow model with integer and boolean parameters. In: International Conference on Embedded Software EMSOFT 2013. ACM, September 2013
3. Bhattacharya, B., Bhattacharyya, S.: Parameterized dataflow modeling for DSP systems. IEEE Trans. Sig. Process. **49**(10), 2408–2421 (2001)
4. Bhattacharyya, S., Murthy, P., Lee, E.: Software Synthesis from Dataflow Graphs. Kluwer Academic Pub, Hingham (1996)
5. Bouakaz, A., Fradet, P., Girault, A.: A survey of parametric dataflow models of computation. ACM Trans. Des. Autom. Electron. Syst. **22**(2), 38 (2017)
6. Lee, E., Messerschmitt, D.: Synchronous data-flow. Proc. IEEE **75**, 1235–1245 (1987)
7. Sih, G., Lee, E.: A compile-time scheduling heuristic for interconnection constraint heterogeneous processor architectures. IEEE Trans. Parallel Distrib. Syst. **4**(2), 175–187 (1993)
8. Skelin, M., Geilen, M., Catthoor, F., Hendseth, S.: Parametrized dataflow scenarios. In: International Conference on Embedded Software EMSOFT 2015, Amsterdam, Netherlands, pp. 95–104. IEEE, October 2015
9. Stuijk, S., Geilen, M., Theelen, B., Basten, T.: Scenario-aware dataflow: modeling, analysis and implementation of dynamic applications. In: IC-SAMOS 2011, pp. 404–411. IEEE (2011)
10. Tanenbaum, A., Wetherall, D.: Computer Networks, 5th edn. Pearson, New York City (2011). http://www.worldcat.org/oclc/698581231

If We Could Go Back in Time...
On the Use of 'Unnatural' Time
and Ordering in Dataflow Models

Marc Geilen[(✉)]

Eindhoven University of Technology, Eindhoven, The Netherlands
m.c.w.geilen@tue.nl

Abstract. Model-based design methods have become common practice
for the design, analysis, and synthesis of embedded and cyber-physical
systems. Different models of computation are used (for example state-
based models, dataflow models, differential equations, hybrid-models).
In real-time and cyber-physical systems it is common to incorporate in
such models some representation of time, physical, logical or otherwise.
We are used to time progressing in forward direction. This assumption
is built into the very definition of many of our favorite models of computation. Execution times or delays are usually non-negative. Time stamps
usually increase monotonically. Tasks can depend on past activations of
other tasks, but not on future activations. Tasks are temporally causal.
In this paper we explore the possibilities and the potential benefits of
liberating our models from these assumptions, allowing time go backward in our models. We will use the dataflow model of computation for
our exploration and show that there are potential benefits to negative
execution times, negative delays on channels, and non-monotone events
in event traces.

1 Introduction

This Festschrift marks an excellent opportunity to reflect on the passing of wall-
clock time and on the events that have happened, what happened before, what
came after and what are the causal and temporal relationships between those
events. We make model abstractions with which we describe, analyze, and simulate real-life systems or according to which we synthesize physical system realizations. The models serve as mathematical abstractions of real-world artifacts.
When we define such models we are inclined to incorporate properties that we
believe to be true in the physical world and to forbid behaviors that seem unnatural. We argue in this paper that such behaviors can sometimes be very convenient
assets in a model and may lead to cleaner and simpler models for relevant real-
world systems. We will discuss such models and their semantics and analysis in
the context of the timed data flow framework, the synchronous data flow (SDF)
model of [1], extended with time [2] and several forms of dynamic behavior [3–5].
For brevity, we refer to timed synchronous data flow as SDF in the remainder

© Springer International Publishing AG, part of Springer Nature 2018
M. Lohstroh et al. (Eds.): Lee Festschrift, LNCS 10760, pp. 267–286, 2018.
https://doi.org/10.1007/978-3-319-95246-8_16

of the paper. SDF has an intuitive graphical representation and is expressive enough for the use case in this paper. We do not argue that the model is better than other models. The concepts we discuss may also apply to other models of computation.

Many different timed models of computation, such as timed SDF, time Petri nets [6], and timed automata [7], describe activities with quantified durations. Such durations are sometimes allowed to be zero, but not negative. Physical activities are *causal*, effects cannot occur earlier than their causes. In Sect. 3 we show that actors in SDF need not always represent physical activities and negative durations, and non-causal actors can be very convenient modeling assets.

Besides temporal dependencies, many models also capture ordering relations between events. In SDF, executions of an actor have a logical order, and, similarly, the data items communicated on channels have a fixed logical order; for instance, for samples of a signal, the order in which they were sampled. Causality is often also assumed on the logical order of events. Events can depend on logically earlier events, but not on future events. A bare channel in SDF denotes a dependency on the same logical data item, while the addition of *initial tokens* (also called *delays*) on the edges modifies the dependency to logically earlier data items. There is no possibility in SDF to represent dependencies on logically *future* data items. In pipelined systems, for instance, logically future events may be processed temporally simultaneously, or even earlier, when they occur in earlier pipeline stages. In Sect. 4 we show that it may be useful to have the possibility in SDF to represent dependencies on logically future data items by means of anti-tokens.

Many models that have both logical ordering and temporal ordering among events do not allow for both orderings to be inconsistent. The operational semantics of SDF [8] does not allow the temporal ordering of actor firings to deviate from their logical order. This would not be compatible, for instance, with the FIFO semantics usually given to the channels. In that case logically later tokens will 'overtake' earlier tokens and the functionality of the application will be broken. This struggle is observed in some of the more dynamic dataflow models, such as CSDF [9], where actor execution times vary. We see such restrictions also in other models [6,10], especially when they aim to address also the synthesis of implementations, for instance Ptides [11]. In Sect. 5 we explore the possibilities to allow non-monotone event orderings. We see that for timed dataflow models this allows us to strengthen their natural relation to classical linear systems analysis techniques.

Models that violate such rudimentary causality assumptions seem unnatural at first, to the extent that we feel the need to a priori exclude them, forbid the user to even express them. We explore what happens if we resist those urges, and find that it may turn out to be useful and beneficial, because they lead to models that make accurate predictions about real-life systems.

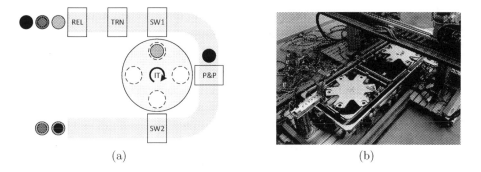

Fig. 1. A simple cyber-physical system (Color figure online)

2 Preliminaries

This section introduces preliminaries needed for the paper, in particular on the use case, on the timed data flow model and its semantics, and on max-plus linear systems.

2.1 A Cyber-Physical Use Case

As a use case we study the simple cyber-physical system shown in Fig. 1(a); a small product assembly line inspired by the experimental setup in our lab [12], shown in Fig. 1(b). From the top-left side in the diagram, different pieces enter the system. We consider three different types of pieces: bottom pieces (shown in gray), red top pieces (red) and black top pieces (black). Bottom pieces need to be combined with a top piece in the assembly line. Bottom pieces will be released (REL) into the machine and advance on a conveyor belt, passing the turner (TRN) unchanged and move on to the switch (SW1) that pushes them onto the *indexing table* (IT). On the indexing table, a bottom piece rotates once clock-wise to the second position where the pick and place unit (P&P) assembles it with a top part. Then the indexing table rotates again and a switch (SW2) pushes the bottom piece onto the conveyor belt and the assembled product is unloaded at the bottom left of the machine. Top pieces are released from the same place (REL), but pass the switch SW1 to advance to the pick and place unit that will assemble them with a bottom piece. Finally, we assume that black tops will pass the turner untouched, but red tops need to be turned around by the turner, which takes some additional amount of time.

Using the system, the following constraints need to be respected. The peripherals (REL, TRN, SW1, P&P, SW2) can only handle one piece at a time. (The conveyor belt can transport multiple pieces simultaneously.) Moreover, we assume that the indexing table shall always fill all index slots with bottom pieces and does not leave index positions open.

2.2   Synchronous Data Flow

We use timed synchronous data flow (SDF) [1,2] as the model of computation for this paper. Figure 2 shows an example of an SDF model. The details of the particular model are discussed in the next section. The circles are *actors*. The directed edges between actors are *channels*. From an operational point of view, channels carry *tokens* from one actor to another in the direction of the edge and the tokens represent the actor's enabling conditions. Actors *fire* or execute only when their firing conditions are met, i.e., when there is a token on each of its input edges, for instance, each of the white actors in Fig. 2 are enabled. An actor firing takes a fixed amount of time, after which it produces new tokens on its outgoing edges, thus enabling new actors to fire. In this paper we consider SDF models with open input and output edges, for instance, the red actor labeled Rel and the blue actor labelled Load. Tokens on these edges are provided, respectively, by or to the environment.

The SDF model has several very attractive properties. SDF models are deterministic; their behavior is easy to analyze compared to non-deterministic models. Their behavior repeats in periodic patterns. They are also monotone. This excludes timing anomalies and allows performance analysis based on worst-case identification and SDF models with constant (hence deterministic) execution times can serve as proven conservative abstractions of dataflow behavior with non-deterministically varying execution times [10]. Stronger than being monotonic, they are, in fact, *linear* systems, so they enjoy the nice properties of linear systems, such as *homogeneity* and the *superposition* principle (discussed in the next section).

We often think of actors from an operational point of view as producers and consumers of tokens. We can similarly describe the dependency as an equation. Let $Rel[k]$ denote the start time of the k'th firing of actor REL and similarly $Belt1[k]$ for actor Belt1, then the edge from actor REL to Belt1 represents the following constraint.

$$Belt1[k] \geq Rel[k] + e(Rel) \text{ for all } k \in \mathbb{N}$$

where $e(Rel)$ is the execution time of actor REL. In general we write $e(A)$ to denote the execution time of an actor A. Initial tokens on edges can be used to create dependencies on *earlier* firings of some actor. For instance, an edge from some actor A to an actor B with m initial tokens expresses the following constraint.

$$B[k] \geq A[k - m] + e(A) \text{ for all } k \in \mathbb{N}$$

with the convention that $A[k - m] = 0$ if $k - m < 0$. (Or similarly, sometimes, as we will see, $A[k - m] = -\infty$ if $k - m < 0$).

In general there can be many solutions to these equations that are all valid executions. There is however a unique 'fastest' execution in which all actors fire as soon as they are enabled. This execution is usually called a *self-timed* execution.

2.3 Max-Plus Linear Systems

An important property of timed data flow models is that they are *linear* systems, although not in the classical linear algebra, but in a linear algebra that is called *max-plus algebra* [13]. It uses the set $\mathbb{R}$ of real numbers, extended with the value $-\infty$. It uses two operators $\oplus$ and $\otimes$ that take the roles of addition and multiplication in traditional linear algebra, respectively, with the following definitions.

$$x \oplus y = \max(x, y)$$
$$x \otimes y = x + y$$

for the additional element $-\infty$ the operators are, naturally, defined as follows.

$$-\infty \oplus x = x \oplus -\infty = x$$
$$-\infty \otimes x = x \otimes -\infty = -\infty$$

Self-timed firing times of dataflow actors can be described in max-plus-linear equations. The firing time is determined by the maximum (max-plus sum $\oplus$) of all its dependencies and its completion time is computed from its firing time by max-plus multiplication, $\otimes$ (addition) of its execution time. As such, timed data flow models are max-plus-linear systems and enjoy many of the special properties of regular linear systems, such as the aforementioned homogeneity and superposition. Homogeneity means that if some input signal x leads to an output signal y, then the same input multiplied by a scalar constant c, $c \otimes x$ leads to an output that is also scaled with the same constant: $c \otimes y$. Since the $\otimes$ operator is addition this means that if the input signal is delayed in time then the output is delayed by the same amount of time. The second property is superposition, which states that if input x_1 gives output y_1 and input x_2 gives output y_2, then input $x_1 \oplus x_2$ gives output $y_1 \oplus y_2$. Recall that the operator $\oplus$ amounts to taking the maximal of the two signals. Note that superposition can also be exploited to determine the response to multiple external input signals individually. We will see in Sect. 5 how we can also use the classical concept of *impulse response* for time-invariant systems.

3 Negative Execution Times

Actors in dataflow models traditionally, and generally often, represent operations or computations, and the execution times of the actors typically represent the time that these operations take, or upper bounds thereof. Hence, they are usually assumed to be positive numbers. The same can be observed in other timed models such as timed automata [7] or Time Petri Nets [6]. In more abstract models actors can be used to represent different kinds of constraints on the occurrence of events, for instance, a reconfiguration time or set up time. Those constraints are still often positive. It may, however, be beneficial to not a priori, in the *definition* of the model of computation, exclude the possibility of negative time

272   M. Geilen

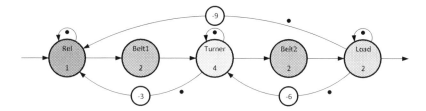

Fig. 2. Dataflow model of a conveyor belt (Color figure online)

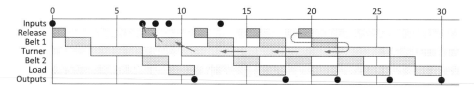

Fig. 3. Gantt chart of the conveyor belt model and a critical path (Color figure online)

constraints or actor firings with negative delays. We argue that these degrees of
freedom are very useful, and in fact even necessary, to make a faithful model of
the assembly line use case.

We first concentrate on modeling the initial part of the assembly line (Fig. 1),
up to switch SW1. We extend the scope of the model later. The SDF model of this
part is shown in Fig. 2. Most of the model is rather straightforward. We assume
that pieces arrive from the environment through the open input dependency to
the actor Rel, that models the release component. The release takes one time
unit, represented by the firing duration of the actor (we write the firing duration
inside the actor in the figures). After the release, the piece is transported by
the conveyor belt for two time units. This is represented by the yellow actor
Belt1. There is a dependency from Rel to Belt1 to model the transfer. Similarly,
it continues with the Turner, Belt2, and Load actors representing all the stages
that the piece passes. An interesting and challenging dependency that needs to
be modeled is the constraint to not release a new piece too soon so as to not
interfere with the operation of turner TRN on the previous piece. We can model
this, as usual, with a dependency from the turner operation represented by actor
Turner, to the release operation, actor Rel with a single initial token to indicate
that the dependency is to the *previous* piece. This would enforce the following
constraint.

$$Rel[k] \geq Turner[k-1] + e(Turner) \text{ for all } k \in \mathbb{N}$$

This is safe. The next piece is released only after the turner is done with the
previous piece. However, it is too pessimistic to release the new piece only when
the turner is ready (i.e., when the Turner actor produces a token) since the piece
will spend some time on the conveyor belt before it actually reaches the turner.
Once a piece is released onto the conveyor belt, it moves for two time units until

reaching the turning actuator. The constraint on the starting of the release that accurately captures the requirement is the following.

$$Rel[k] \geq Turner[k-1] + e(Turner) - e(Rel) - e(Belt1) \text{ for all } k \in \mathbb{N}$$

This equation can be realized by adding an extra actor with an execution time totaling $-e(Rel) - e(Belt1)$, which is -3, in between the actors. This is the inserted white actor in Fig. 2. The two equations for the two edges we now have are (with $D[k]$ the firing times of the negative delay actor):

$$Rel[k] \geq D[k] - 3$$
$$D[k] \geq Turner[k-1] + e(Turner)$$

Together they establish the required equation:

$$Rel[k] \geq Turner[k-1] + e(Turner) - 3$$

In exactly the same way, constraints are added to ensure that the turner does not turn too early for the Load actor with a delay of -6 and that the Rel actor is not too early for Load with a delay of -9. Leading to two additional feedback paths. For usability it could be interesting to add syntax to directly express the constraint between actors, eliminating an additional consistency check. However, the solution with negative execution times requires fewer modification of the model of computation.

The operational semantics of such an actor with a negative delay is non-causal: it produces its output before consuming the input token that causes that output. Luckily, we do not need to implement this actor. We observe only that it accurately represents the desired constraint, and that, as we will see, (most of) the existing analysis techniques still work and deliver results that are meaningful for the physical system. The schedule we obtain is valid and optimal.

Figure 3 shows a Gantt chart of the execution of the model. The arrivals of pieces as inputs to the model are shown by black dots in the first row. Products 3–5 arrive too quickly to be immediately released onto the conveyor belt as they would collide in the turner. Including an actor with a delay of -3 between the turner and the release holds off the release just enough for the piece to arrive just in time at the turner. The red arrows show the critical path that determines the start time of the release of the last product. It fires at time 19 although the product was available from time 13. The critical dependency is on the firing of Turner for the previous product, which completed at time 22. Then it follows the dependencies from the self-loop of the Turner, and finally, the Belt1, Rel, and the arrival of the second product.

The maximal throughput that the model can sustain is determined by its critical cycle. One of the critical cycles in the model is the cycle through Release, Belt1, Turner, and the -3-delay. This cycle has a cycle ratio (total execution time by number of tokens) of 4, which is the maximum cycle ratio in the graph. It limits the throughput to $\frac{1}{4}$, when the turner is continuously busy.

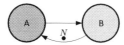

Fig. 4. A typical dataflow model of a bounded FIFO buffer

The classical performance analysis methods based on cycle-mean or cycle-ratio analysis [2], or on max-plus spectral analysis [14] need no modifications to incorporate negative execution times. Operational semantics based analysis [8] would require some modifications, since a normal discrete-event simulation does not handle non-causal behavior. Note that dependency related properties, such as deadlock freedom or consistency are independent of actor execution times and hence are not affected.

4   Anti-tokens

4.1   Motivation

Initial tokens in dataflow models can be used to shift dependencies between actor firings. In particular, this is needed to model cyclic dependencies between actors without creating deadlocks, for example, when a computation depends on internal state left by the previous computation, or when computations on previous data items need to complete to free up buffer space to write to. Figure 4, for instance, shows a typical way to model a FIFO communication buffer of size N. The two edges capture the two relevant constraints. The first, from A to B, due to data dependence:

$$B[k] \geq A[k] + e(A)$$

and the second, due to the buffer capacity constraint (to not overrun the buffer).

$$A[k] \geq B[k - N] + e(B)$$

Firings of actor A become dependent on firings of B on *previous* data items.

Sometimes systems exhibit constraints in which task executions for a given data item k depend on the availability of *future* data items. An example is a data-driven, asynchronous, pipelined data path in an FPGA accelerator as shown in Fig. 5(a). In order for a data item k to progress through the data path, future data items need to be ready to occupy the earlier pipeline stages. For actor D these dependencies have the following form.

$$D[k] \geq A[k + 1] + e(A) \qquad\qquad D[k] \geq x[k + 2]$$
$$D[k] \geq B[k + 1] + e(B) \qquad\qquad D[k] \geq y[k + 2]$$

If having N initial tokens leads to a dependency of item k on item $k - N$, then perhaps this can be modeled by -1 or -2 initial tokens on such channels?

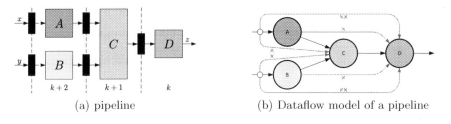

(a) pipeline   (b) Dataflow model of a pipeline

Fig. 5. A pipeline structure and its dataflow model

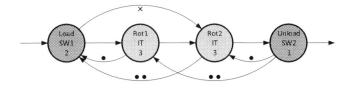

Fig. 6. Dataflow model of an indexing table

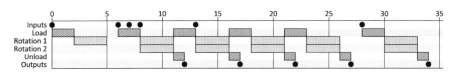

Fig. 7. Gantt chart of the indexing table model

Indeed, it can. We say that there are, respectively, one and two *anti-tokens* on the channel. Converting the equations into a dataflow graph, we arrive at the graph shown in Fig. 5(b). The anti-tokens in the model are depicted by the '×' symbol. The small white actors have an execution time of 0, and are merely used to copy the input tokens onto multiple edges, because edges can only connect two actors in SDF. Negative token counts in dataflow graphs have been used before, for instance, in [15,16] to create conservative abstractions of multi-rate behavior or of out-of-order computation of data items, where the negative token counts are arrived at from conservative equations. In work on retiming, negative token counts also appear at intermediate stages as invalid retimings [17,18].

4.2 Modelling the Indexing Table

A situation similar to the pipeline occurs in the indexing table of the assembly line of Fig. 1. We assume that all positions on the indexing table need to be filled with bottom pieces. We make a simple model of a bottom piece passing switch SW1, then passing two rotation operations (skipping the assembly at the pick-and-place unit for the moment) and being unloaded from the indexing table by switch SW2. The model is shown in Fig. 6. As we can see from the model, there are a number of additional dependencies that need to be modeled. (Note that some redundant dependencies have been removed from the model for clarity, such as self-edges on all the actors.) SW1 can only activate when there is an input piece and the rotations of previous pieces have finished: the first-stage rotation of the previous piece and the second stage rotation of the piece before that one. The first-stage rotation requires the switch to be done with loading the piece, but also needs the unloading of the before-previous piece to be completed. (Note that it also needs the first-stage rotation of the previous piece to be complete, but that dependency is redundant because the loading of the pieces already depended on it.) The second stage rotation of the piece depends on the completion of the unload of the previous piece. It additionally depends on the loading of the *next* piece. The last one is a dependency we cannot naturally model with a dataflow graph until we allow the use of anti-tokens. Note how the model uses an anti-token on the edge from the loading to the second rotation to express this dependency.

Figure 7 shows an example Gantt chart for the model in which we observe a manifestation of this dependency. The fifth piece arrived at time 13, was loaded at time 21, and started its first rotation on the table at time 23. After that rotation (26), however, it had to wait in the indexing table, because the next piece had not yet arrived. The next piece arrives only at time 28, after which it is loaded, and only then the second rotation of piece five starts.

Such a forward dependency cannot be directly expressed without the use of anti-tokens. By absence of anti-tokens, this problem is often circumvented by modeling the system in an ongoing pipelined execution, i.e. starting with some initial piece inside the indexing table, or with data in the pipeline for the pipeline model. This is undesirable, however, since the first output no longer corresponds to the first input of the system, but to some 'dummy' data that needs to be disregarded. We can indeed get rid of the anti-token in the model by firing actor Load, or both Load and Rot1. This is usually called *retiming* of the model [17,18]. However, then there is a piece in the model initially, and the first piece to leave the table is not the first piece that enters the model.

The operational semantics of a dataflow model with anti-tokens is similar to the original operational semantics. Actors fire when the firing condition is met (with regular tokens). Tokens and anti-tokens annihilate each other when they meet, i.e., when an actor produces tokens onto a channel that contains anti-tokens. One may assume that anti-tokens do not move and channels cannot contain both tokens and anti-tokens.

Analysis of data flow graphs with anti-tokens is not substantially different from the analysis of traditional graphs. Deadlock or liveness [19,20] analysis on single-rate graphs, for instance, is done by checking for cycles in the graph without tokens. Now we need to check that the net number of tokens minus the number of anti-tokens is positive[1].

---

[1] Interestingly, if there are only cycles with negative token counts the equations also permit a solution in which all actors fire in reverse logical order, but the operational semantics does not allow such behavior to get started.

Proposition 1. *A single rate dataflow graph with anti-tokens is live if and only if on every cycle the total number of tokens minus the total number of anti-tokens is positive.*

Proof. The proof is similar to the classical case [19,21]. We first observe that the token count of all cycles remain invariant when actors fire. If there is a cycle with a non-positive net token count, then the graph is not live, because in an infinite execution in which all actors on the cycle fire infinitely often the tokens meet the anti-tokens, and since there are at least as many anti-tokens as tokens, all tokens will disappear from the cycle and the actors on the cycle can no longer fire. Conversely, if the graph is not live, then a state can be reached in which a set of actors are in a cyclic dependency, i.e., none of the edges on the cycle have any tokens. Hence, the cycle token count cannot be positive to start with.

For multi-rate dataflow graphs the PASS analysis of [2,21] can be used to establish deadlock freedom or liveness. Consistency analysis does not consider any initial tokens, and, consequently, it does not change for graphs with anti-tokens. Another common analysis is throughput analysis. We have argued in Sect. 3 that negative execution times do not pose a particular problem for the cycle ratio approach to throughput analysis. Also, anti-tokens do not pose any problem.

Proposition 2. *Any live SDF graph with anti-tokens can be converted to a graph without anti-tokens, with the same throughput through retiming.*

Proof. Since the graph is live, we can fire any actor an arbitrary number of times. For every edge with n anti-tokens, after firing the actor that produces onto that edge at lease n times, all anti-tokens have disappeared. If this is done for all edges with anti-tokens, the resulting graph is a graph free of anti-tokens, obtained from the original graph through retiming.

Proposition 3. *Maximal throughput for single rate SDF graphs with negative execution times and anti-tokens, is the reciprocal of the Maximum Cycle Ratio of the graph considering the ratio of execution time over number of tokens.*

Proof. Since cycle ratios are invariant under retiming, we can use retiming to obtain a graph without anti-tokens and identical cycle ratios to the original graph. The throughput computation can be reduced to cycle time computation of a max-plus matrix [13,14]. The cycle time computation applies equally to matrices with negative elements.

We have shown that the existing analysis algorithms for single rate dataflow graphs are straightforwardly adapted for negative execution times and anti-tokens. Analysis algorithms for multi-rate graphs are mostly (either implicitly or explicitly) based on a transformation into an equivalent single-rate graph. Because of this also multi-rate graph with negative execution times and anti-tokens can mostly be analyzed with the traditional methods.

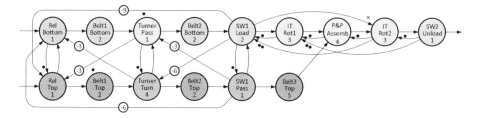

Fig. 8. Dataflow model of a static assembly line (Color figure online)

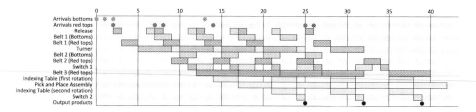

Fig. 9. Gantt chart of the assembly line model (Color figure online)

4.3   A Complete Model: Static Assembly Line

We can integrate the partial models discussed before into a complete model of the assembly line, shown in Fig. 8. It alternatingly handles red top pieces and bottom pieces to assemble them. It is straightforwardly constructed from the conceptual solutions discussed separately before. Note that it includes both anti-tokens and actors with negative execution times. The Gantt chart of its operation is shown in Fig. 9. The darker shaded bars of the same color represent operations on the red top pieces. The lighter shaded ones on the bottom pieces. The operation starts upon the arrival of the first top piece at time 2. Initially the turner is fully loaded, but eventually the critical cycle of the alternation of pick and place assembly and rotation of the indexing table slows the process done. We can see that the releases of the parts are adjusted accordingly: not immediately when the piece arrives, but as early as possible not causing any conflicts.

4.4   A Dynamic Assembly Line

In this section we complete our model of the assembly line as a dynamic dataflow model. We relax the static order of top and bottom pieces. We could further imagine that besides the red top pieces also black top pieces may arrive that do not need to be turned around. Such a non-deterministic sequence of operations can be modeled with a dynamic timed dataflow model such as the scenario-aware dataflow (SADF) model of computation [5,22] or mode-controlled dataflow [23].

SADF models pieces of dataflow behavior that can occur in non-deterministic orders by separate dataflow graphs. These pieces of dataflow behavior are called *scenarios*. The internal behavior of scenarios is still entirely deterministic and follows familiar dataflow semantics. Dependencies between subsequent scenarios are expressed through dataflow tokens that are produced in one scenario and consumed in another scenario. The possible orders in which scenarios can occur are separately specified with a finite state machine. The separation in non-deterministic sequences of deterministic scenarios makes that the model can be analyzed efficiently compared to entirely non-deterministic models such as timed automata that will suffer more from the state-space explosion effect. The pieces of dataflow behavior of subsequent scenarios can be active concurrently, typically in a pipelined way. With the generalization to anti-tokens in this paper, dependencies can be specified even from future scenarios to past scenarios. Where traditional dataflow models are linear systems in max-plus algebra, SADF graphs are comparable to *switched linear systems* in traditional system theory.

The SADF model of the dynamic assembly line is shown in Fig. 10. It has three different scenarios, the *bottom* scenario (Bot, Fig. 10(a)), which represents the bottom part being assembled into a complete product; the *red top* scenario (Red, Fig. 10(b)), describing the red top part progressing up to the assembly, and the *black top* scenario (Blck, Fig. 10(c)), which is the same as the *red top* scenario except it describes the trajectory of black pieces.

In each scenario dataflow graph, the horizontal pipelines follow the main flow of the product. The vertical edges represent the various dependencies that govern the execution of the scenario. The dependencies relate the execution of the

Table 1. Scenario dependencies

Input dependencies					
Nr.	From	To	Dist.	Prod. scen	Cons. scen
i	TRN	REL	1	{Bot, Red, Blck}	{Bot, Red, Blck}
ii	SW1	REL	1	{Bot, Red, Blck}	{Bot, Red, Blck}
	SW1	TRN	1	{Bot, Red, Blck}	{Bot, Red, Blck}
iii	SW1	IT	−1	{Bot}	{Bot}
iv	IT	SW1	1	{Bot}	{Bot}
v	P&P	IT	1	{Bot}	{Bot}
vi	IT	P&P	1	{Bot}	{Bot}
	IT	SW1	2	{Bot}	{Bot}
vii	SW2	IT	1	{Bot}	{Bot}
	SW2	IT	2	{Bot}	{Bot}
viii	Belt3	P&P	0	{Red, Blck}	{Bot}
ix	REL	REL	1	{Bot, Red, Blck}	{Bot, Red, Blck}
x	TRN	TRN	1	{Bot, Red, Blck}	{Bot, Red, Blck}
xi	SW1	SW1	1	{Bot, Red, Blck}	{Bot, Red, Blck}
xii	SW2	SW2	1	{Bot, Red, Blck}	{Bot, Red, Blck}

scenario to previous or future scenarios. The dependencies have been labelled i–viii. Dependency i, for instance, represents the dependency from the turner to the release, as discussed in Sect. 3. Table 1 summarizes all dependencies, the scenarios that produce the tokens, the scenarios that consume the tokens, and the dependency distance (the number of initial tokens). There are four dependencies (ix–xii) that are not visualized in Fig. 10 for clarity. They are dependencies on single actors (REL, TRN, SW1 and SW2) to prevent them from firing multiple times simultaneously (autoconcurrency). The possible scenario sequences are specified by the automaton in Fig. 10(d). It defines a non-deterministic alternation between bottom pieces and arbitrary top pieces. The model works for arbitrary sequences, although some (for instance three bottom pieces in a row) will deadlock.

Note the anti-token on the dependency iii from SW1 to IT among Bot scenarios. SW1 consumes the token that is produced in the Bot scenario that *follows* it. As in the static model, this dependency on future scenarios does not lead to a deadlock. We have seen earlier that we can get rid of anti-tokens by retiming. A similar approach can be applied here to arrive at a model in which dependencies only exist from past to future scenarios. To achieve this we need to

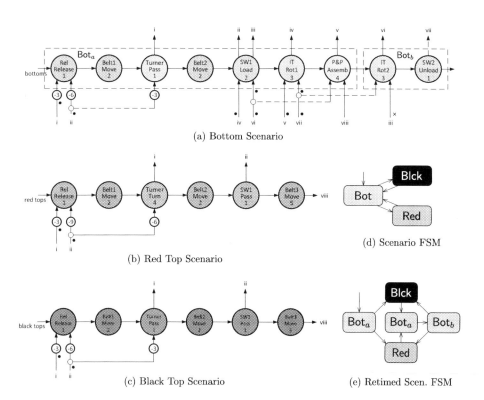

(a) Bottom Scenario

(b) Red Top Scenario

(d) Scenario FSM

(c) Black Top Scenario

(e) Retimed Scen. FSM

Fig. 10. Scenario-aware data flow model of a dynamic assembly line (Color figure online)

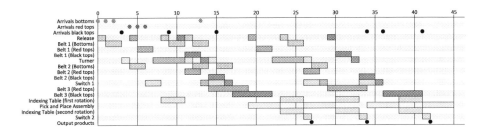

Fig. 11. Gantt chart of the SADF model of the dynamic assembly line (Color figure online)

split the scenario Bot into the two parts enclosed by dashed boxes in Fig. 10(a), Bot_a and Bot_b. Then a retiming of the model is possible, leading to the scenario FSM shown in Fig. 10(e). The second execution of the Bot_a scenario is now executed before the first execution of the Bot_b scenario and therefore the producing scenario comes before the consuming scenario, and the model does not need anti-tokens.

Figure 11 shows a Gantt chart of one particular scenario sequence of the model (Bot, Red, Bot, Blck, Bot, Red, Bot, Blck). Different shades are used to distinguish firings of the same actor in different scenarios. Darker shades are again the top pieces and the darkest shade represents the black top pieces.

Similar to the static dataflow case, the classical throughput analysis technique [14] handles negative execution times without modification. With such a model we can, for instance, find the most productive sequence of operations that produces equal amounts of red and black products [24] via a combination of model-checking and performance analysis that avoids the state-space explosion one would suffer with, for instance, analyses based on timed automata.

5 Non-monotone Event Sequences

The input pieces to the assembly model arrive at certain moments in time. The actors in the model fire at specific points in time that satisfy all the timing constraints, and the tokens exchanged between actors are produced and consumed at certain points in time. In dataflow, and in many other models, such sequences of events are modeled as a sequence of *timestamps* or *dater functions* [10,11,25]. Many of these models implicitly or explicitly adopt the requirement that the ordering of events is identical to, or for partial orders, consistent with, the ordering of the timestamps. Sometimes, 'exotic' time domains, such as *super-dense time* are used [26,27] for this purpose. We usually do this because it seems natural, but we will discuss the possible benefits of resisting this constraint and we will see that there are important advantages to this.

One of the most widely used models for sequences of events is the tagged signal model [25]. It represents signals as a mapping from some time or other (possibly partially) ordered domain of choice to the co-domain of signal values.

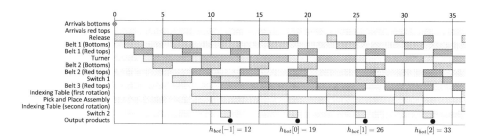

Fig. 12. Impulse response of the static assembly line model

In that model, events have no other ordering than inherited from the tags. We can think of our event sequences as having a logical ordering that is separate from the ordering derived from the timestamps. [15] introduces a model where events are explicitly labeled with both a logically and a temporally ordered tag in order to apply the abstraction-refinement theory of [10] to realizations that compute tokens out of logical order. The logical order could also have been obtained from the ordering of events in the event sequence without an additional tag.

Ptides [11] considers synthesis of systems from timed models in which events are also labelled with time stamps. Temporal causality information is exploited for distributed execution without synchronization through empty messages. The execution strategy allows independent events to be processed out of timestamp order, although actors must process their own event in timestamp order.

5.1   Impulse Response Analysis

Linear time-invariant (LTI) systems are fully characterized by their impulse responses. This principle also applies to dataflow models. For max-plus linear systems, the *impulse* function δ takes the value $-\infty$ for all k, except $\delta[0] = 0$ ($-\infty$ and 0 being, respectively, the zero and unit element of the algebra). The response of the system to an impulse input signal exposes all dependencies on that particular, single, input token $\delta[0]$, since all other tokens (before, but also *after*) are available since time $-\infty$. Figure 12 shows the impulse response h_{bot} of the static assembly line of Fig. 8 to a bottom input. Only one input is visible. All other inputs occur at time $-\infty$. Looking at the output event sequence, we have the sequence $h_{bot} = [\ldots, -\infty, 12, 19, 26, 33, \ldots]$. Note that the impulse response is not logically causal, $h_{bot}[-1] = 12$ already depends on input 0 (but it is temporally causal; an input at time 0 leads to an output 12 time units later).

As in traditional LTI systems, any input event sequence can be described as a linear combination of scaled and shifted impulse functions. We then know that the output of the system is the same linear combination of shifted impulse response functions and can be computed from a convolution of the input event sequence and the system's impulse response. Moreover, when there are two inputs, we know from the superposition principle that the response is the (max-plus) sum of the responses to the separate input sequences. Without further analysis or simulation, we directly conclude that if the impulse responses for tops and bottoms are $h_{top}[k]$ and $h_{bot}[k]$, respectively, (they can be determined independently from the input sequence and independently from each other), and $t[k]$ and $b[k]$ are the arrival sequences of the tops and bottoms, then the outputs will be produced at the times given by the function

$$o = (t \otimes h_{top}) \oplus (b \otimes h_{bot})$$

Note that single-rate dataflow systems (like the example in this paper) are time-invariant systems. Multi-rate dataflow models may not be time-invariant, but their responses are periodic with an iteration of the graph and similar techniques can be applied.

The impulse response analysis focuses on the *arrival times* of tokens and assumes infinite sequences of tokens, both into the future and into the past. If we consider finite sequences, we additionally need to consider how many output tokens can be produced from the provided inputs. We have already seen that output tokens depend on the current and all previous bottom inputs, but also on one future bottom input. Therefore, when m bottom pieces are offered at the input, at most $m - 1$ outputs can be produced. This can be observed from the dataflow graph in Fig. 8 by a path from the bottoms input to the output with a single anti-token on it. The same holds for the tops input.

5.2 Generalizing Dataflow Semantics

A second reason to embrace the non-monotonic event sequences is that it can solve or circumvent some of the recurring difficulties in the semantics of dataflow models with autoconcurrency (the ability of actors to fire multiple times concurrently), especially in combination with varying execution times, such as in CSDF, or in an interpretation of timed SDF with non-deterministic execution times. In essence the problem is the following. It is possible for two concurrent firings of the same actor that the firing that started last will complete first. Communication between actors is traditionally modeled as a FIFO channel. If this situation happens, then one data item has 'overtaken' another data item, the logical ordering has changed, and the functional correctness of the application may be compromised.

Various measures are taken in different dataflow models to escape from this problem. CSDF, for instance, forbids autoconcurrency of its actors altogether [9]. Other models restrict the possible behaviors to those in which no overtaking occurs [28], assume that execution times are constant, as most works do, or add indices to firings [15]. All such problems disappear from the semantics when we decouple the logical ordering of tokens (the order in which they appear in the event sequence) from the ordering in time in which they are produced or consumed. Functional correctness is guaranteed as long as the logical ordering is preserved by the semantics. Also the implementation then needs to support out-of-order production and consumption. A very common implementation of FIFO communication through a cyclic buffer is compatible with this generalization if it allows random access to the reading and writing intervals [29]. If adaptation is not possible or too expensive, additional constraints can be introduced that guarantee in-order production and consumption, although this may come at a cost of performance.

6 Conclusion

We have seen that it may be worthwhile to extend the dataflow model of computation and its semantic framework with some constructs that initially seem unnatural and therefore useless and undesirable, but that upon closer inspection can be very useful, enable more elegant models and allow the application of linear system theory. Moreover, the additions do not significantly complicate the prevalent semantics and analysis techniques. There may be some implementation challenges however, in particular, to maintain a correct logical ordering of data when executions are out of order, for instance, in the realization of data dependencies between actors. The use of anti-tokens may require additional administration of validity of data.

References

1. Lee, E., Messerschmitt, D.: Synchronous data flow. IEEE Proc. **75**, 1235–1245 (1987)
2. Sriram, S., Bhattacharyya, S.S.: Embedded Multiprocessors: Scheduling and Synchronization. Marcel Dekker Inc., New York (2009)
3. Buck, J.: Scheduling dynamic dataflow graphs with bounded memory using the token flow model. Ph.D. thesis. EECS Department, University of California, Berkeley (1993)
4. Girault, A., Lee, B., Lee, E.: Hierarchical finite state machines with multiple concurrency models. IEEE Trans. Comput. Aided Des. Integr. Circ. Syst. **18**, 742–760 (1999)
5. Theelen, B.D., Geilen, M., Basten, T., Voeten, J., Gheorghita, S.V., Stuijk, S.: A scenario-aware data flow model for combined long-run average and worst-case performance analysis. In: Proceedings of the Fourth ACM and IEEE International Conference on Formal Methods and Models for Co-Design 2006, MEMOCODE 2006, pp. 185–194 (2006)
6. Berthomieu, B., Diaz, M.: Modeling and verification of time dependent systems using time Petri nets. IEEE Trans. Softw. Eng. **17**, 259–273 (1991)
7. Alur, R., Dill, D.L.: A theory of timed automata. Theoret. Comput. Sci. **126**, 183–235 (1994)
8. Ghamarian, A., Geilen, M., Stuijk, S., Basten, T., Moonen, A., Bekooij, M., Theelen, B., Mousavi, M.: Throughput analysis of synchronous data flow graphs. In: Proceedings of the 6th International Conference on Application of Concurrency to System Design, ACSD 2006, pp. 27–30. IEEE Computer Society Press, Los Alamitos (2006)
9. Bilsen, G., Engels, M., Lauwereins, R., Peperstraete, J.: Cyclo-static dataflow. IEEE Trans. Signal Process. **44**, 397–408 (1996)

10. Geilen, M., Tripakis, S., Wiggers, M.: The earlier the better: a theory of timed actor interfaces. In: Proceedings of the 14th International Conference on Hybrid Systems: Computation and Control, HSCC 2011, pp. 23–32. ACM, New York (2011)
11. Derler, P., Feng, T.H., Lee, E.A., Matic, S., Patel, H.D., Zhao, Y., Zou, J.: PTIDES: a programming model for distributed real-time embedded systems. Technical report UCB/EECS-2008-72. EECS Department, University of California, Berkeley (2008)
12. Adyanthaya, S., Ara, H.A., Bastos, J., Behrouzian, A.R.B., Sánchez, R.M., van Pinxten, J., van der Sanden, B., Waqas, U., Basten, T., Corporaal, H., Frijns, R., Geilen, M., Goswami, D., Hendriks, M., Stuijk, S., Reniers, M.A., Voeten, J.: xCPS: a tool to explore cyber physical systems. SIGBED Rev. **14**, 81–95 (2016)
13. Heidergott, B., Olsder, G.J., van der Woude, J.: Max Plus at Work. Princeton University Press, Princeton (2006)
14. Geilen, M., Stuijk, S.: Worst-case performance analysis of synchronous dataflow scenarios. In: Proceedings of the International Conference on Hardware-Software Codesign and System Synthesis, CODES + ISSS 2010, Scottsdale, Az, USA, 24–29 October 2010, pp. 125–134 (2010)
15. Hausmans, J.P.H.M., Bekooij, M.J.G.: A refinement theory for timed-dataflow analysis with support for reordering. In: Proceedings of the 13th International Conference on Embedded Software, EMSOFT 2016, pp. 20:1–20:10. ACM, New York (2016)
16. de Groote, R., Hölzenspies, P.K.F., Kuper, J., Broersma, H.: Back to basics: homogeneous representations of multi-rate synchronous dataflow graphs. In: 2013 Eleventh ACM/IEEE International Conference on Formal Methods and Models for Codesign, MEMOCODE 2013, pp. 35–46 (2013)
17. O'Neil, T.W., Sha, E.H.M.: Retiming synchronous data-flow graphs to reduce execution time. IEEE Trans. Signal Process. **49**, 2397–2407 (2001)
18. Zhu, X.Y., Basten, T., Geilen, M., Stuijk, S.: Efficient retiming of multirate DSP algorithms. IEEE Trans. Comput. Aided Des. Integr. Circ. Syst. **31**, 831–844 (2012)
19. Commoner, F., Holt, A.W., Even, S., Pnueli, A.: Marked directed graphs. J. Comput. Syst. Sci. **5**, 511–523 (1971)
20. Ghamarian, A.H., Geilen, M.C.W., Basten, T., Theelen, B.D., Mousavi, M.R., Stuijk, S.: Liveness and boundedness of synchronous data flow graphs. In: Proceedings of the Formal Methods in Computer Aided Design, FMCAD 2006, pp. 68–75. IEEE Computer Society, Washington, DC (2006)
21. Lee, E.A., Messerschmitt, D.G.: Static scheduling of synchronous data flow programs for digital signal processing. IEEE Trans. Comput. **C−36**, 24–35 (1987)
22. Stuijk, S., Geilen, M., Theelen, B., Basten, T.: Scenario-aware dataflow: modeling, analysis and implementation of dynamic applications. In: Proceedings of International Conference on Embedded Computer Systems, SAMOS 2011, pp. 404–411 (2011)
23. Moreira, O.: Temporal analysis and scheduling of hard real-time radios running on a multi-processor. Ph.D. thesis. Eindhoven University of Technology (2012)
24. van der Sanden, B., Bastos, J., Voeten, J., Geilen, M., Reniers, M., Basten, T., Jacobs, J., Schiffelers, R.: Compositional specification of functionality and timing of manufacturing systems. In: 2016 Forum on Specification and Design Languages, FDL, pp. 1–8 (2016)
25. Lee, E., Sangiovanni-Vincentelli, A.: A framework for comparing models of computation. IEEE Trans. Comput.-Aided Des. Integr. Circ. Syst. **17**, 1217–1229 (1998)
26. Cataldo, A., Lee, E., Liu, X., Matsikoudis, E., Zheng, H.: A constructive fixed-point theorem and the feedback semantics of timed systems. In: 2006 8th International Workshop on Discrete Event Systems, pp. 27–32 (2006)

27. Maler, O., Manna, Z., Pnueli, A.: Prom timed to hybrid systems. In: de Bakker, J.W., Huizing, C., de Roever, W.P., Rozenberg, G. (eds.) REX 1991. LNCS, vol. 600, pp. 447–484. Springer, Heidelberg (1992). https://doi.org/10.1007/BFb0032003

28. Poplavko, P., Basten, T., Bekooij, M., Meerbergen, J.v., Mesman, B.: Task-level timing models for guaranteed performance in multiprocessor networks-on-chip. In: Proceedings of the International Conference on Compilers, Architecture and Synthesis for Embedded Systems, CASES 2003, San Jose, USA, 30 October–1 November 2003, pp. 63–72. IEEE Computer Society Press, Los Alamitos (2003)

29. Bijlsma, T.: Automatic parallelization of nested loop programs - for non-manifest real-time stream processing applications. Ph.D. thesis, University of Twente (2011)

Compressed Sensing
in Cyber Physical Social Systems

Radu Grosu[1(✉)], Elahe Ghalebi K.[1], Ali Movaghar[2], and Hamidreza Mahyar[1]

[1] Fakultät für Informatik, Technische Universität Wien, Vienna, Austria
{radu.grosu,elahe.ghalebi,hamidreza.mahyar}@tuwien.ac.at
[2] Department of Computer Engineering, Sharif University of Technology,
Tehran, Iran
movaghar@sharif.edu

Abstract. We overview the main results in Compressed Sensing and Social Networks, and discuss the impact they have on Cyber Physical Social Systems (CPSS), which are currently emerging on top of the Internet of Things. Moreover, inspired by randomized Gossip Protocols, we introduce TopGossip, a new compressed-sensing algorithm for the prediction of the top-k most influential nodes in a social network. TopGossip is able to make this prediction by sampling only a relatively small portion of the social network, and without having any prior knowledge of the network structure itself, except for its set of nodes. Our experimental results on three well-known benchmarks, Facebook, Twitter, and Barabási, demonstrate both the efficiency and the accuracy of the Top-Gossip algorithm.

1 Introduction

Looking back at the time Bill Gates was one of his brilliant students, Christos Papadimitriou concluded that one of the greatest challenges of the academic community is to recognizing when an IT revolution is on its way. He did not see the PC revolution coming, but his student did. Since then several other revolutions happened, such as the Internet and the Mobiles revolutions. Another imminent revolution is now in the making: The CPSS/IoT revolution.

The worldwide academic institutions have a responsibility to ask the following important questions: Are we prepared for the CPSS/IoT revolution? Do we have the proper modeling, analysis, and control techniques? Do we have adequate infrastructure, software tools, and courses? The answer is unfortunately "No, and we have to act now." Two of the initiatives in this direction are the Terra Swarm Research Center at UC Berkeley, and the CPSS/IoT Ecosystem Project at TU Wien.

Cyber Physical Social Systems (CPSS) are spatially-distributed, time-sensitive multi-scale, networked embedded systems, connecting the physical world to the cyber and social worlds through sensors and actuators. The Internet of Things (IoT) is the backbone of CPSS. It connects the (terra) swarm of

© Springer International Publishing AG, part of Springer Nature 2018
M. Lohstroh et al. (Eds.): Lee Festschrift, LNCS 10760, pp. 287–305, 2018.
https://doi.org/10.1007/978-3-319-95246-8_17

Sensors and Actuators to the nearby Gateways through various protocols, and the Gateways to the Fog and the Cloud. The Swarm resembles the billions of human skin and muscle cells, providing real-time information about the physical environment and acting upon it. The Fog resembles the human spine, providing fast and adequate response to imminent situations. The Cloud resembles the human brain, providing large storage and analytic/decision capabilities.

CPS research is strongly anchored within the academia. There are many important CPS conferences around the world, with CPS Week as their flagship. Social networks (SN) are a relatively new field, and CPSS is currently emerging. IoT however, went pretty much under the radar of academia. This was not the case in industry. With a $15 trillion business forecast for the next 20 years, 50 billion devices connected by 2020, and 50 terabytes of data per day from the avionics industry alone, all big IT and industrial players are dedicating immense resources to IoT. It is more than telling that the IoT World Congress in 2016, had talks by CEOs, but almost no talk of any academic researcher. This is now changing. For example, CPS Week 2017 included an IoT conference, too.

What drives this excitement and sense of urgency within the industry? Four pillars: connectivity, monitoring, prediction, and optimization. Connectivity has already been enabled by the technological developments over the past years. The next step, which is expected to radically change every aspect of our society, is monitoring, prediction, and optimization. The huge number of sensors to be deployed in areas such as manufacturing, transportation, energy and utilities, buildings and urban planning, health care, environment, or jointly in smart cities, will allow the collection of terabytes of information (Big-Data), which can be processed for predictive purposes. Moreover, the huge number of actuators will enable the optimal control of these areas and drive market advantages.

For example, the predictive maintenance of assets is expected to save up to 12% in scheduled repairs, reducing maintenance costs up to 30%, and eliminating breakdowns up to 70%, according to a GE survey [1]. According to the same survey, 73% of companies are already investing more than 20% of their overall technology budget in big-data analytics, and more than two in 10 are investing more than 30%. Moreover, three-fourths of executives expect that spending level to increase just in the next year. Across the industries surveyed, 80% to 90% of companies indicated that big-data analytics is either the top priority for the company or in the top three. A staggering 89% say that companies not adopting big-data analytics in the next year risk losing market share and momentum.

While the industrial excitement is a very important technological driver for the development of CPSS/IoT, it is important to mention that monitoring, prediction, and optimization in CPSS/IoT, are all Grand Challenges of the twenty first century. Research and breakthroughs in all these areas are necessary, in order to make the expectations a reality. One such breakthroughs is compressed sensing (CS) [9,14], which allows monitoring at sub-Shannon/Nyquist rates. This has the potential to make the state-estimation aspect in CPSS/IoT tractable.

Compressed sensing was originally introduced in signal processing. It was long observed that signals used in everyday applications are sparse in some basis. For example, photographs or radiology images are sparse in the Fourier or the wavelet domain. As a consequence, one can compress a signal at the source of a transmission, and decompress it at the destination. Compressed sensing simplifies this process, by directly taking compressed photographs or radiology images, and recovering them at the destination with optimization techniques that take advantage of the signal's sparsity. If a signal was sampled before at the Shannon/Nyquist rate, in compressed sensing such a signal can be undersampled (in a random fashion though), orders of magnitudes below this rate.

From a CPS perspective one can therefore undersample signals transmitted by temperature, CO_2, etc., sensors, in time, and of video-camera sensors, both in time and space. This dramatically increases monitoring performance for a single sensor. But what about the Terra-swarm of sensors? Can we apply the same techniques? Unfortunately, many sensor networks are not deployed on a regular grid, but rather on an arbitrary graph. As a consequence, compressed sensing had to be extended to this more general setting. This uses combinatorial (graph-based), instead of geometric (lattice-based) techniques [19,36,42].

Interestingly enough, the combinatorial approach found its application in SN, too [27,41]. In this context, a main challenge is to determine the top-k most influential nodes in an SN. For quantifying influence various centrality metrics have been proposed. Among them the most popular is arguably the betweenness centrality C_B [11,40]. Given an arbitrary node u and two nodes v, w, distinct from each other and from u, the betweenness centrality of u with respect to v and w, $C_{B,v,w}(u)$, is the number of geodesics (shortest paths) between v and w that pass through u, divided by the total number of geodesics between v and w. Now $C_B(u)$ is the sum of all $C_{B,v,w}(u)$, for all pairs of nodes v and w in the SN.

Computing the k maximal-C_B nodes under the full knowledge of the vertices V and edges E of an unweighted SN, was shown to have $O(|V||E|)$ time complexity in [8]. For the huge SNs that occur in practice, this is intractable. Moreover, for privacy reasons, it is not realistic to assume that, say an advertising company (AC), has the full knowledge of an SN. As a consequence, one would like to employ techniques that both scale up and maintain privacy.

In order to address these two important problems, we propose in this paper a new technique for computing the k nodes with largest C_B. We call it TopGossip, because it was inspired by the randomized gossip protocols. TopGossip addresses scalability issues by employing a local betweenness-centrality measure, called ego betweenness centrality eC_B. This applies $C_{B,v,w}(u)$ only for nodes v, w that are immediate neighbors of u. It has been shown in [15], that ego-betweenness eC_B is in practice very strongly correlated with betweenness centrality C_B.

TopGossip addresses privacy concerns, by requiring that each node u, woken up by the AC, computes is own eC_B, adds it to a token it got from one of its neighbors, and passes it either to another neighbor, chosen in a random fashion, or to the AC. The AC then sums up the tokens it got, and creates this way a compressed-sensing measurement. By employing thereafter sparse optimization techniques, the AC is able to recover the top-k most influential nodes.

In summary, the AC only needs to know the set of nodes V of the SN, and the nodes have to know their neighbors and the AC. Like in randomized gossip protocols, the nodes can work in a distributed fashion. The computation time of TopGossip is $O(m |V|)$, where m is proportional to k.

Our experimental results on three well-known SN benchmarks, Facebook, Twitter, and a synthetic Barabási-Albert network, demonstrate that TopGossip is more accurate than the best previous work we are aware of.

The rest of the paper is organized as follows. In Sect. 2 we overview CS, given its importance in CPSS/IoT, and its use in TopGossip. In Sect. 3 we then discuss SN and our main problem, computing the top-k most influential nodes in an SN. In Sect. 4 we introduce TopGossip, our novel CS algorithm for solving this problem. This uses a small number of measurements, and operates with local knowledge of the SN structure, only. In Sect. 5 we evaluate the performance of our algorithm, and in Sect. 6 we present our conclusions.

2   Compressed Sensing

The swarm of a CPSS/IoT, such as in smart farming or smart city, will generate/consume terabytes of information. This information will have to be sensed/actuated in real time, in order to control the CPSS, by estimating its state, and issuing (optimal) control actions. But how will this be possible?

The answer lies in a dramatic sub-Shannon/Nyquist sensing and actuation rate of the swarm signals, in both time and space. This is always sound, provided the signals are sparse in some basis. Now, if only a few signals were sparse, this would not be such great news. However, the opposite is true. Most natural signals are indeed sparse, as their structure lets one predict their values from only a few samples. The least sparse signals are, quite counter-intuitively, the random signals, because it is very hard to predict their values.

A hint that such an approach was possible came early on from various areas, such as geophysics, signal processing, and group testing [13]. For example, in their hunt for oil reserves, seismologists were able to acquire much better images of the underground layers, than the Shannon/Nyquist sampling theorem would have predicted. Moreover, they developed a very successful greedy algorithm, called Orthogonal Matching Pursuit (OMP) with time-frequency dictionaries for this purpose [31]. Variants of this algorithm are still in use nowadays.

Very intuitive depictions of the sparse-recovery phenomenon were presented in [20,25]. We reproduce in Fig. 1, one from [25]. Let x denote the discrete frequency-domain signal shown in Fig. 1(a). Assume x is properly sampled (according to Shannon/Nyquist), with say n frequencies, i.e., x is a vector of dimension n. Signal x is 3-sparse, with $3 \ll n$, as it only contains three frequencies, with amplitude different from zero. By applying the *inverse Fourier transform* to x we obtain the discrete time-domain signal y shown in Fig. 1(b):

$$y(t) = \mathcal{F}^{-1}(x)(t) = \frac{1}{n} \sum_{\nu=1}^{n} e^{i2\pi\nu t/n} x(\nu) \qquad (1)$$

where the dimension of y is chosen to be the same as the one of x. The inverse Fourier transform can be represented as a square matrix F, with

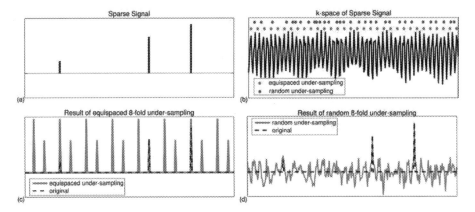

Fig. 1. (a) A sparse signal in the frequency domain. (b) Under-sampling its time domain representation, with a rate that is eight times lower than the Shannon/Nyquist rate, either equally spaced (red), or random (blue). (c) If the sample is equally spaced, then the Fourier transform introduces aliases, which are indistinguishable from the real frequencies. (d) If the sample is random, then the main frequencies can be recovered. Note that the recovery of the least-amplitude frequency, requires noise removal first [25] (Color figure online)

$F_{t,\nu} = e^{i2\pi\nu t/n}/n$. One can then write that $y = Fx$. Let T be one of the *time under-samplings* in Fig. 1(b), with $|T| = m \ll n$, and let $\mathcal{A} = F_T$ and $\hat{y} = y_T$ be the restrictions of F and y to T, respectively. Then one can write that $\hat{y} = \mathcal{A}x$, where $\mathcal{A}$ is called the *measurements matrix*, and $(\hat{y}_i, \mathcal{A}_i)$ a *linear measurement*.

Recovering x from $\hat{y} = \mathcal{A}x$ is hopeless, as there are fewer constraints than indeterminates. As a consequence, the system has infinitely many solutions. However, if one looks for the sparsest solution, that is, for the one that has the least number of nonzero elements, then this equation has a unique solution. This is true also for the more realistic case, where the signal x or the measurements $\hat{y}$ are noisy, with noise of magnitude no larger than say ϵ.

Definition 1 (Sparse approximation problem [14]). *Let ℓ_0 be the pseudo-norm counting the number of nonzero elements, and ℓ_2 be the Euclidean norm. Then the sparse approximation problem can be formulated as follows:*

$$\operatorname*{argmin}_{x} \| x \|_0 \quad \text{subject to} \quad \| \hat{y} - \mathcal{A}x \|_2 \ \leq \ \epsilon \tag{2}$$

Unfortunately, solving (2) is NP hard, as there is no known efficient way of traversing the space of sparse vectors. Fortunately however, there are two approaches which make the search tractable: a *geometric* approach and a *combinatorial* approach. We discuss them both below.

Geometric Approach. In the geometric approach, the underlying Shannon/Nyquist structure of a signal is assumed to be a *regular grid*. For example, in Fig. 1(a) and (b), the underlying signals x and y are defined on equally spaced frequency and time values, respectively. In image processing, one also considers 2D or 3D images, defined over equally spaced spatial grids.

Moreover, in the geometric context, one assumes that the measurement matrix $\mathcal{A}$ is essentially not increasing the ℓ_2 norm of the vector x, that is, $\mathcal{A}$ is in some sense an *isometric* transformation. More formally:

Definition 2 (Restricted Isometry Property (RIP) [9]). *An $m \times n$ measurement matrix $\mathcal{A}$ with unit norm, i.e., $\sum_{j=1}^{n} \mathcal{A}_{i,j} = 1$ for $i = 1, \ldots, m$, is said to satisfy the restricted isometry property $(RIP_{k,\delta})$ of order k, whenever:*

$$(1 - \delta)\frac{m}{n}\| x \|_2^2 \le \| \mathcal{A}x \|_2^2 \le (1 + \delta)\frac{m}{n}\| x \|_2^2 \qquad (3)$$

holds simultaneously for all k-sparse vectors $x \in \mathbb{R}^n$, for a sufficiently small δ.

The $RIP_{k,\delta}$ property is sometimes also called the *uniform uncertainty principle*. Measurement matrices $\mathcal{A}$ satisfying $RIP_{k,\delta}$ are injective, that is, they do not map distinct k-sparse signals x and x' to the same measurement $\hat{y}$. The unit norm restriction is motivated by physical characteristics of real sensing systems, which limit the amount of energy allocated to each linear measurement.

Under the $RIP_{k,\delta}$ assumption, the ℓ_0 norm in the sparse approximation problem, can be safely replaced with the ℓ_1 norm. This reduces the NP-Hardness of the reconstruction problem to a tractable, linear programming problem, with $O(n^3)$ complexity. One talks in this case about *compressed sensing* [9,14].

Definition 3 (Compressed sensing problem [9]). *Let ℓ_1 be the absolute value norm, i.e., $\| x \|_1 = \sum_{i=1}^{n} |x_i|$, ℓ_2 be the Euclidean norm, and $\mathcal{A}$ be as in Definition 3. Then the compressed sensing problem can be formulated as follows:*

$$\underset{x}{\operatorname{argmin}} \| x \|_1 \quad \text{subject to} \quad \| \hat{y} - \mathcal{A}x \|_2 \le \epsilon \qquad (4)$$

The explicit construction of the measurement matrix requires that $\mathcal{A}$ is *dense* and *stochastic*. In general, the entries of $\mathcal{A}$ are assumed to be identically distributed realizations of certain zero-mean random variables (e.g., uniform, normal) with variance $1/n$, and where $(m \ge ck \log n)$ for some constant c. In Fig. 1(d), $\mathcal{A}$ is a stochastic Fourier matrix, whose rows T were uniformly sampled.

Since $O(n^3)$ might be intractable for very large signals, various greedy algorithms were developed, to efficiently solve the linear-program problem. One algorithm was already mentioned, the orthogonal matching pursuit, but many other variations have been developed in the meantime [13].

Combinatorial Approach. In the combinatorial approach, the underlying Shannon/Nyquist structure of a signal is assumed to be a *graph*. This extension is motivated in the *IoT setting* by the modern sensors/actuators networks being deployed, for example, in traffic-management or in environmental applications.

A graph-based underlying structure was also traditionally assumed in the more theoretical work on *group testing*. In contrast to the IoT setting, where the signals of interest have a very rich co-domain, such as speed, temperature, or pressure, in group testing the signals are Boolean, and represent the adjacency matrix, or some other property, of the graph. The same is true in SN, where one is interested in finding out the top-k *influencers* of the SN. As a consequence, different methods were developed in each case, which we discuss below.

Graph-Based Transforms. Discrete signal processing on graphs, in particular the graph-Fourier and graph-Wavelet transforms, are mainly addressed within what is called *algebraic signal processing* [34]. We shortly discuss them below.

Consider a signal $x : V \rightarrow \mathbb{R}$ defined on a graph $G = (V, E)$, with V being the set of vertices, and E the set of edges. Graph G may be either directed or undirected. In latter case, the adjacency matrix Adj corresponding to E is symmetric.

The *graph-Fourier basis* of x on G, is defined in [36] as $F = U^{-1}$, where U is the generalized-eigenvectors basis of Adj, under the Jordan decomposition $Adj = U\,J\,U^{-1}$. The block-diagonal matrix J, is the *Jordan normal form* of Adj. In case Adj is symmetric, J is diagonal, as all eigenvalues of Adj are distinct and real. The *graph-Fourier transform* of x is then $y = F\,x$.

Earlier definitions of the graph-Fourier transform, consider U as the eigenvectors basis of the *Laplacian matrix* $L = D - Adj$, where D is the *degree* diagonal matrix, with $D_{i,i}$, representing the degree of vertex i in Adj [42].

It is worth noting that the graph Laplacian is a second-order operator for signals on graphs, quantifying correlations, whereas the Adjacency matrix transform represents power spectral densities. Moreover, the Laplacian-based definition is not applicable to directed graphs or graphs with negative weights.

Both graph-Fourier transforms are useful for signals $x : V \rightarrow \mathbb{R}$, where x has interesting $\mathbb{R}$ structure, and $y = Fx$ is sparse. However, the eigenvalues J, and the eigenvectors U themselves, are not related to the particular vertices in the graph anymore, but rather quantify the cycles properties of Adj. A transform that is defined with respect to the ring-like neighborhood of the vertices $i \in V$ (all vertices between k-hops and l-hops away from vertex i), is the *graph-Wavelet transform*. For space reasons, we refer the interested reader to [12, 19].

Once the transform matrix F is defined, one can construct stochastic measurement matrices, by uniformly choosing a graph under-sampling T and restricting F and y to T, as discussed at the beginning of this section.

Expander-Graphs Transforms. Work on expander-graph transforms was originally developed within *group-testing* [10] and *coding theory* [38]. Group-testing however, was mainly restricted to the Boolean domain, and to Boolean operations. This work was extended in [41] to CS over graphs [27, 28], where the signal values of x were allowed to range over $\mathbb{R}$. The same is true for the proposed approach in the next section for identifying top-k influencers in an SN.

The three main ideas in the expander-graph (EG) approach are as follows. First, the measurement matrix $\mathcal{A}$ is considered to be Boolean. Second, $\mathcal{A}$ has to

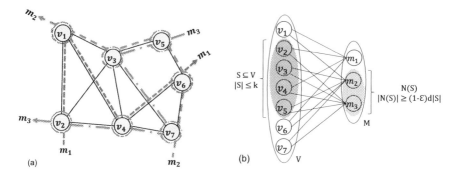

Fig. 2. (a) Measurements m_1, m_2, and m_3, as random walks in graph G. (b) The measurements represented as a bipartite graph $B = (V, M, E)$, with V the vertices in G, M the random walks in G, and $E_{m,v}$ the membership of vertex v to the walk m.

be consistent with the underlying graph structure G of the signal x. Third, the signal x quantifies in most cases some global property of interest of G.

The EG approach in [41] to creating a measurement matrix $\mathcal{A}$ for a graph G, that is consistent with G, is shown in Fig. 2. The main idea is to define a linear measurement m_i, as a random walk through G. In Fig. 2(a) we show three such walks, and in Fig. 2(b) the same information as a bipartite graph, where edges represent the membership of vertices to walks.

Definition 4 (Bipartite graph). *A bipartite graph $B = (V, M, E)$ is a graph whose vertices are partitioned into V and M, and whose edges E only connect V to M. This graph is called* left-regular of degree d, *if each vertex in V has degree d. One writes for such graphs $B = (V, M, E, d)$.*

The 3×7 bi-adjacency matrix of the bipartite graph in Fig. 2(b) is shown below. It represents a consistent measurement matrix $\mathcal{A}$.

$$\mathcal{A} = \begin{array}{c} \\ m_1 \\ m_2 \\ m_3 \end{array} \begin{array}{c} \begin{array}{ccccccc} v_1 & v_2 & v_3 & v_4 & v_5 & v_6 & v_7 \end{array} \\ \left(\begin{array}{ccccccc} 1 & 1 & 0 & 1 & 0 & 1 & 0 \\ 1 & 0 & 1 & 0 & 1 & 1 & 1 \\ 0 & 1 & 1 & 1 & 1 & 0 & 1 \end{array} \right) \end{array} \tag{5}$$

In order for $\mathcal{A}$ to be useful in compressed sensing, one needs to impose additional constraints on $\mathcal{A}$ that are in some sense similar to the $\text{RIP}_{k,\delta}$ used in the geometric approach. Such properties are called $\text{RIP}_{p,k,\delta}$ properties.

Definition 5 (p-Restricted Isometry Property [4]). *An $m \times n$ matrix $\mathcal{A}$ satisfies the p-restricted isometry property of order k ($RIP_{p,k,\delta}$), whenever:*

$$(1 - \delta)\|x\|_p \leq \|\mathcal{A}x\|_p \leq (1 + \delta)\|x\|_p \tag{6}$$

holds simultaneously for all k-sparse vectors $x \in \mathbb{R}^n$, in an ℓ_p norm with p satisfying $p \in [1, 1 + O(1)/\log n]$, for a sufficiently small δ.

This property holds for particular kinds of left-regular bipartite graphs of degree d, called bipartite expander graphs. Their definition is given below. The main intuition of why such graphs would satisfy the $\text{RIP}_{p,k,\delta}$ property, is that any vertex subset $S \subseteq V$ of such graphs participates in sufficient measurements.

Definition 6 (Unbalanced Expander Graph). *Let $B = (V, M, E, d)$ be a left-regular bipartite graph of degree d. If for some small ε and any $S \subseteq V$ of size $|S| \leq k$, the neighborhood $N(S)$ of S satisfies $|N(S)| \geq (1 - \varepsilon)\, d\, |S|$, then B is called a (k, d, ϵ)-unbalanced bipartite expander graph of degree d.*

In constructing an unbalanced bipartite expander graph, the goal is to make $|M|$, d and ϵ as small as possible, while making k as close to $|M|$ as possible.

Theorem 1 ($\text{RIP}_{p,k,\delta}$ and (k, d, ϵ)-expanders [4]). *Consider an $m \times n$ matrix $\mathcal{A}$ that is the bi-adjacency matrix of a (k, d, ϵ)-unbalanced bipartite expander graph $B = (V, M, E, d)$, with $|V| = n$, $|M| = m$, left degree d, such that $1/\epsilon$ and and d are smaller than n. Then the scaled matrix $A/d^{1/p}$ satisfies the $\text{RIP}_{p,k,\delta}$, for $p \in [1, 1+1/\log n]$ and $\delta = C\,\epsilon$, for some constant $C > 1$.*

3   Social Networks

In cyber-physical systems, the cyber part is often partitioned between regular components (the computers) and super components (the humans). For example, in smart mobility, the physical components are the cars, the regular cyber components are the traffic controllers, and the super components are the drivers, with their own GPS preferences. The drivers themselves form a social network which has a considerable impact on the smart-mobility system. To account for the role of humans, one speaks about cyber-physical-social systems.

Online social networks have hundreds of millions of users nowadays. For example, Facebook alone has more than 1.59 billion active users per month [16]. As a consequence, Facebook users have a tremendous power to influence the opinions of other users, with respect to what they read, watch, or buy, or even for whom they vote. But do all users have the same power? The answer is no. There is usually a very small set of most influential users, and these are typically targeted by advertising agencies. But how can they find out who are these users; by searching the huge underlying network graph?

Social network (SN) analysis addresses exactly this problem [11,29,30,40]. In order to quantify the notion of influence (or centrality), researchers have proposed various measures, reflecting different points of view [2,5,6,11,17,21, 24,32,35]. Some of them, such as degree centrality (C_D), where $C_D(u)$ is simply the degree of node u, focus on the local properties of an SN, while others, such as betweenness centrality (C_B), consider the global properties of an SN.

Betweenness centrality is arguably the most popular, and will be the focus of this paper, too. For every SN node u, and nodes v, w, distinct from each other

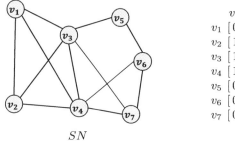

$$
\begin{array}{c}
\begin{array}{ccccccc}
v_1 & v_2 & v_3 & v_4 & v_5 & v_6 & v_7
\end{array} \\
\begin{array}{c}
v_1 \\ v_2 \\ v_3 \\ v_4 \\ v_5 \\ v_6 \\ v_7
\end{array}
\begin{bmatrix}
0 & 1 & 1 & 1 & 0 & 0 & 0 \\
1 & 0 & 1 & 1 & 0 & 0 & 0 \\
1 & 1 & 0 & 1 & 1 & 0 & 1 \\
1 & 1 & 1 & 0 & 0 & 1 & 1 \\
0 & 0 & 1 & 0 & 0 & 1 & 0 \\
0 & 0 & 0 & 1 & 1 & 0 & 1 \\
0 & 0 & 1 & 1 & 0 & 1 & 0
\end{bmatrix}
\end{array}
$$

SN $Adj(SN)$

Fig. 3. An SN with 7 nodes and 12 links, and its adjacency matrix. Adj may be viewed as a two dimensional Boolean signal, e.g., an image with only black and white pixels

and from u, the betweenness centrality of u with respect to v and w, $C_{B,v,w}(u)$, is the number geodesics (shortest paths) between v and w that pass through u, divided by the total number of geodesics between v and w. Now $C_B(u)$ is the sum of all $C_{B,v,w}(u)$, for all pairs of nodes v and w in the SN.

Definition 7 (Betweenness centrality [11]). *Let $G = (V, E)$ be the underlying graph of an SN, with V its set of nodes, and E its set of (undirected) edges. Then the betweenness centrality $C_B(u)$ of a node $u \in V$ is defined as follows:*

$$
C_B(u) = \sum_{v,w \in V, v \neq w} \frac{\sigma_{vw}(u)}{\sigma_{vw}} \tag{7}
$$

where σ_{vw} is the total number of geodesics (shortest paths) between nodes $v, w \in V$, $u \neq v \neq w$, and $\sigma_{vw}(u)$ is the number of such geodesics that pass through node u.

The fastest known exact algorithm for computing C_B for all nodes in an unweighted and undirected SN, under the full knowledge of its vertices V and edges E, requires $O(|V| + |E|)$ space, and an asymptotic run time of $O(|V||E|)$ [8]. For the huge SNs that occur in practice, this is intractable. Moreover, for privacy reasons, it is not realistic to assume that, say an advertising company (AC), has the full knowledge of an SN. As a consequence, one would like to employ techniques that both scale up and maintain privacy.

In order to address these two important problems, we propose in this paper a new technique for computing the k nodes with largest C_B. We call it TopGossip, because it was inspired by the randomized gossip protocols.

TopGossip addresses scalability issues by employing a local centrality measure, called an ego betweenness centrality measure eC_B. This centrality measure applies $C_{B,v,w}(u)$ only for the nodes v, w that are immediate neighbors of u. It has been shown in [15], that the ego-betweenness centrality measure eC_B is in practice very strongly correlated with the betweenness centrality C_B.

Definition 8 (Ego betweenness centrality [15]**).** *Let* $G = (V, E)$ *be the underlying graph of an undirected SN, with vertices* V *and edges* E. *Then the ego betweenness centrality* $eC_B(u)$ *of a node* $u \in V$ *is defined as follows:*

$$eC_B(u) = \sum_{v,w \in E(u), v \neq w} \frac{\sigma_{vw}(u)}{\sigma_{vw}} \tag{8}$$

where σ_{vw} *is the total number of geodesics (shortest paths) between* $v, w \in V$, $u \neq v \neq w$, *and* $\sigma_{vw}(u)$ *is the number of such geodesics that pass through node* u.

For example, consider the SN and its adjacency matrix in Fig. 3. The C_D, eC_B and C_B for all nodes are given in Table 1. The table shows that nodes v_3 and v_4 have the largest centrality. Hence, one may safely conclude that these nodes are the most important in the SN. Note also that eC_B/C_B are better measures than C_D, as $C_D(v_1) = C_D(v_2) = 3$, but their eC_B/C_B value is 0.

Table 1. Centrality measures for the sample network in Fig. 3

Centrality	v_1	v_2	v_3	v_4	v_5	v_6	v_7
Degree C_D	3	3	5	5	2	3	3
eBetweenness eC_B	0	0	5	3.5	1.0	2.0	0.5
Betweenness C_B	0	0	4	3.3	0.3	1	0.3

Let us now discuss how to efficiently compute eC_B. We use node v_4 in Fig. 3 as a running example. The adjacency matrix Adj_{v_4} of v_4 (also called its ego) is shown in Fig. 4. It contains all the nodes of Adj except for node v_5 which is not a neighbor of v_4. The neighbors of v_4 which are directly connected to each other have a geodesic (shortest path) of length 1. As a consequence, there is no geodesic between them that also passes through v_4, as this would have length 2. The other pairs are not directly connected, so they are candidates for $eC_B(v_4)$. We obtain these candidates in matrix $(1 - Adj_{v_4})$, above its main diagonal (since the matrix is symmetric, we disregard entries below the diagonal).

Matrix $(1 - Adj_{v_4})$ serves as a mask, used to get rid of the uninteresting entries in matrix $Adj_{v_4}^2$. Note that an entry $(Adj_{v_4}^2)_{ij}$ contains the number of paths of length two between nodes v_i and v_j. The masking operation is achieved through the Hadamard (point wise) product $Adj_{v_4}^2 \circ (1 - Adj_{v_4})$. Since there is only one path through v_4 for each pair of distinct neighbors, one has now to add the inverses of the non-zero entries above the diagonal in the product matrix, to get $eC_B(v_4) = 1 + 1 + 1/2 + 1/2 + 1/2 = 3.5$. The complexity of this operation for node v_4 is $O(m^3)$ where $m = C_D(v_4) + 1$. For all nodes in V the complexity is going to be dominated by the nodes with largest degree C_D.

Most companies are interested in the k nodes with largest C_B, for small k, only. This is reasonable, since a node with large C_B is more influential than one with low C_B. For example, Samsung was willing to give free Galaxy mobiles to a few influencers, dissatisfied with their iPhones. Similarly, travel agencies

$$
\begin{array}{ccccc}
& \begin{smallmatrix} v_1\ v_2\ v_3\ v_4\ v_6\ v_7 \end{smallmatrix} & \begin{smallmatrix} v_1\ v_2\ v_3\ v_4\ v_6\ v_7 \end{smallmatrix} & \begin{smallmatrix} v_1\ v_2\ v_3\ v_4\ v_6\ v_7 \end{smallmatrix} & \begin{smallmatrix} v_1\ v_2\ v_3\ v_4\ v_6\ v_7 \end{smallmatrix} \\
\begin{smallmatrix} v_1 \\ v_2 \\ v_3 \\ v_4 \\ v_6 \\ v_7 \end{smallmatrix}
& \begin{bmatrix} 0&1&1&1&0&0 \\ 1&0&1&1&0&0 \\ 1&1&0&1&0&1 \\ 1&1&1&0&1&1 \\ 0&0&0&1&0&1 \\ 0&0&1&1&1&0 \end{bmatrix}
& \begin{bmatrix} 1&0&0&0&1&1 \\ 0&1&0&0&1&1 \\ 0&0&1&0&1&0 \\ 0&0&0&1&0&0 \\ 1&1&1&0&1&0 \\ 1&1&0&0&0&1 \end{bmatrix}
& \begin{bmatrix} 3&2&2&2&1&2 \\ 2&3&2&2&1&2 \\ 2&2&4&3&2&1 \\ 2&2&3&5&1&2 \\ 1&1&2&1&2&1 \\ 2&2&1&2&1&3 \end{bmatrix}
& \begin{bmatrix} 3&0&0&0&1&2 \\ 0&3&0&0&1&2 \\ 0&0&4&0&2&0 \\ 0&0&0&5&0&0 \\ 1&1&2&0&2&0 \\ 2&2&0&0&0&3 \end{bmatrix} \\
& Adj_{v_4} & 1 - Adj_{v_4} & Adj^2_{v_4} & Adj^2_{v_4} \circ (1 - Adj_{v_4})
\end{array}
$$

Fig. 4. Given the SN in Fig. 3, the matrix Adj_{v_4} is the projection of the SN to the immediate neighborhood of v_4. The matrix $1 - Adj_{v_4}$ sets to 0 all the direct connections between nodes (with geodesic 1), and sets to 1 the others (with geodesic 2). The matrix $Adj^2_{v_4}$ contains for every entry, the number of paths of length 2 (geodesics) between every pair of nodes. The Hadamard (pointwise) product $Adj^2_{v_4} \circ (1 - Adj_{v_4})$, zeroes out all the noninteresting entries above and below the diagonal of $Adj^2_{v_4}$. Since the matrix is symmetric, one only has to consider the entries above the diagonal. Moreover, since there is at most one geodesic of length 2 passing through v_4 for each pair of nodes, one has to add the inverses of the entries. Hence $eC_B(v_4) = 1 + 1 + 1/2 + 1/2 + 1/2 = 3.5$.

and hotels give free vacations to the topmost influencers, to boost their ratings, and so do fashion companies with their products. Transportation/IT companies are interested in locating the most important bottle-necked junctions/routers in their transportation/data networks. Finally, community-detection applications use the nodes with highest C_B in order to detect communities [22,23,37].

Since C_B and eC_B are strongly correlated in practical applications, one may approximately determine the k users with largest C_B, by determining the k users with largest eC_B. If every user u would send its $eC_B(u)$ to the AC, this could efficiently sort the eC_Bs in time $O(|V| \log |V|)$, and take the top-k users. This approach scales up, but it may jam the AC when all V users simultaneously send their eC_B to the AC. The approach also addresses part of the privacy concerns in an SN, as the AC only gets $eC_B(u)$, and not the actual friends of user u.

TopGossip addresses the potential jamming of the AC, and introduces additional privacy-preserving measures, by using compressed sensing. This works intuitively as follows. Each user u is woken up by the AC, computes its own $eC_B(u)$, adds it to a token it got from one of its neighbors v, and passes it either to another neighbor w, chosen in a random fashion, or to the AC. The AC then sums up the tokens it got, and creates this way a compressed-sensing measurement. Note that a user u does not directly reveal its $eC_B(u)$ to the AC or its neighbor w, and these are not supposed to know it either. However, by employing sparse optimization techniques, the AC is still able to recover the top-k most influential users. More details are discussed in the next section.

4   Gossip-Inspired Compressed Sensing

We now discuss TopGossip, our new approach for determining the top-k influencers within a social network (SN), in detail. TopGossip uses the expander-graph transform approach to compressed sensing, as in Sect. 2. Top-Gossip is also inspired by the randomized gossip protocols analyzed in [7].

Intuitively, TopGossip helps the AC to construct a (k, d, ϵ)-expander matrix $\mathcal{A}$ of size $m \times n$ and a measurement vector y of size n, where $d < m$, $m \propto k \log |V|$, and $n = |V|$, in a distributed fashion. For this purpose, each user u maintains a sparse copy $\hat{\mathcal{A}}^u$ and $\hat{y}^u$. Its goal is to set precisely $d = |I|$ entries $\hat{\mathcal{A}}^u_{i,u}$ to one, and to sum up its $eC_B(u)$ to the corresponding entries in $\hat{y}^u_i$, for all $i \in I$.

A user u is woken up either by one of its neighbors v in a measurement i, or by the AC. If u is woken up by v, it first checks if $\hat{\mathcal{A}}^u_{*,u}$ already has d ones, or if $\hat{\mathcal{A}}^u_{i,u} = 1$. If this is the case, it ignores v. Otherwise, u receives from v a row $\hat{\mathcal{A}}^v_{i,*}$ and $\hat{y}^v_i$. It then adds $\hat{\mathcal{A}}^u_{i,*}$ to $\hat{\mathcal{A}}^v_{i,*}$, sets $\hat{\mathcal{A}}^u_{i,u}$ to 1, and adds $\hat{y}^u_i$ to $\hat{y}^v_i + eC_B(u)$.

The AC wakes up the users uniformly at random, and without replacement, every time a clock with a Poisson distribution ticks. When u is woken up by the AC, it may have already participated in $I = \{i \,|\, \hat{\mathcal{A}}^u_{i,u} = 1\}$ measurements. To reduce the communication overhead with the AC, it aims to prolong these measurements. For each $i \in I$, it first computes the set $R = N - U$ where N is the set of its neighbors, and U is the set of users that already participated in measurement i. Then it repeatedly samples uniformly at random one neighbor w from R and attempts to communicates with it. If R is empty or it had no success communicating with a neighbor, it adds i to the set O.

Once it has finished with I, it samples uniformly at random and without replacement $d - |I|$ measurements from the set $\bar{I} = \{i \,|\, \hat{\mathcal{A}}^u_{i,u} = 0\}$. For each measurement i it first sets $\hat{\mathcal{A}}^u_{i,u}$ to 1, and $\hat{y}^u_i$ to $eC_B(u)$. It then repeatedly tries to communicate with one of its neighbors, uniformly at random. If it does not succeed, it adds i to the set O. After it has finished the two iteration loops, it sends to the AC the rows $\hat{\mathcal{A}}^u_{i,*}$ and measurements $\hat{y}^u_i$, for all $i \in O$.

The longer the measurements in $\hat{\mathcal{A}}^u_{i,*}$, are, the less are the users communicating with the AC, and the more are they communicating with each other. However, the precise communication pattern depends on the structure of the SN.

After the AC has awoken all users in V, it may safely conclude that it has now received sufficient information to construct $\mathcal{A}$ and y. Note that in practice, each user and the AC may have its own clock with a Poisson distribution, so that the AC will not necessarily have to awake each user. The AC only needs to robustly determine when all users have taken their own round. At this point, the AC adds all rows $\hat{\mathcal{A}}^u_{i,*}$ and all measurements $\hat{y}^u_i$ together, and assembles them into the matrix $\mathcal{A}$ and the vector y. It then uses sparse optimization to approximately recover the sparse vector x from the linear measurement $y = \mathcal{A} x$.

The corresponding pseudo-code is shown in Algorithm 1. For readability, we use a global array of measurement matrices $\hat{\mathcal{A}}$ and a global array of measurement vectors $\hat{y}$, where each element of the arrays represent a private copy of a user. We also replace the communication actions with updates in these arrays. One can easily infer how this code can be changed to include communications. We also provide the edges E in addition to V as an input, but E is used only locally by each user, who is supposed anyway to know his contacts.

Algorithm 1. TopGossip Algorithm for Compressed Sensing in SN

Input: V, E, k, m, d, ϵ **Output:** x

1: $\hat{\mathcal{A}}_{n \times m \times n} = 0_{n \times m \times n}$;   Measurement matrices, one for each user
2: $\hat{y}_{n \times m} = 0_{n \times m}$;   Measurement vectors, one for each user
3: $O_{m \times n} = 0_{m \times n}$;   Output matrix, one column for each user

4: **function** free(w,m) $\{$**return** $(\hat{\mathcal{A}}^w_{m,w} = 0) \ \wedge \ |\{i \,|\, \hat{\mathcal{A}}^w_{i,w} = 1\}| < d\}$;

5: **forall** $(u \in 1 : n : \text{unifAtRandom})$ $\{$ Awake each user u

6:    $I = \{i \,|\, \hat{\mathcal{A}}^u_{i,u} = 1\}$; $\overline{I} = \{i \,|\, \hat{\mathcal{A}}^u_{i,u} = 0\}$;

7:    **forall** $(m \in I : \text{unifAtRandom})$ $\{$ Old communications
8:      $\text{neigh} = E(u) - \{v \,|\, \hat{\mathcal{A}}^u_{m,v} = 1\}$; $w = 0$;
9:      **forall** $(x \in \text{neigh} : \text{unifAtRandom})$ **if** $(\text{free}(x,m))$ $\{w = x; \text{ break}\}$;   Try
10:     **if** $(\text{neigh} = \emptyset \ \vee \ w = 0)$ $O_{m,u} = 1$;   Failure
11:     **else** $\{$ $\hat{\mathcal{A}}^w_{m,*} \mathrel{+}= \hat{\mathcal{A}}^u_{m,*}$; $\hat{\mathcal{A}}^w_{m,w} = 1$; $\hat{y}^w_m \mathrel{+}= \hat{y}^u_m + eC_B(w)\}\}$;   Success

12:    **forall** $(m \in \overline{I} : \text{unifAtRandom} : d - |I| \text{ times})$ $\{$ New communications
13:      $\text{neigh} = E(u)$; $w = 0$; $\hat{\mathcal{A}}^u_{m,u} = 1$; $\hat{y}^u_m = eC_B(u)$;
14:      **forall** $(x \in \text{neigh} : \text{unifAtRandom})$ **if** $(\text{free}(x,m))$ $\{w = x; \text{ break}\}$;   Try
15:      **if** $(\text{neigh} = \emptyset \ \vee \ w = 0)$ $O_{m,u} = 1$;   Failure
16:      **else** $\{$ $\hat{\mathcal{A}}^w_{m,*} \mathrel{+}= \hat{\mathcal{A}}^u_{m,*}$; $\hat{\mathcal{A}}^w_{m,w} = 1$; $\hat{y}^w_m \mathrel{+}= \hat{y}^u_m + eC_B(w)\}\}\}$;   Success

17: $\mathcal{A}_{m \times n} = 0_{m \times n}$;   Measurement matrix of the AC
18: $y_{m \times 1} = 0_{m \times 1}$;   Measurement vector of the AC

19: **forall** $(m \in 1 : m)$ $\{$ $\text{out} = \{i \,|\, O_{m,i} = 1\}$;
20:    **forall** $(u \in \text{out})$ $\{$ $\mathcal{A}_{m,*} \mathrel{+}= \hat{\mathcal{A}}^u_{m,*}$; $y_m \mathrel{+}= \hat{y}^u_m$ $\}\}$ Update $\mathcal{A}$ and y
21: $\underset{x}{\text{argmin}} \ \|x\|_1$ subject to $\|y - \mathcal{A}x\|^2_2 \leq \epsilon$ Top-k eC_B recovered in x

---

The matrix O remembers the "communications" with the AC, and it is used to construct the measurement matrix $\mathcal{A}$ and the measurement vector y. The AC uses sparse optimization at the end to approximately recover x, with the LASSO objective function $\|\mathcal{A}x - y\|^2_2 \leq \epsilon$ [39]. LASSO is very popular because it works even in the presence of noise or truncated values in $\mathcal{A}$ and y.

Algorithm 1 has the following important properties. First, it results in the bi-adjacency matrix $\mathcal{A}$ of a left-regular bipartite graph $B = (V, M, E, d)$ of degree d. This cannot be guaranteed in [41], for example, as a vertex v might not be visited by any of the m random walks, and this would violate d regularity.

Theorem 2 (Regular bipartite graph). *Matrix $\mathcal{A}$, constructed by Algorithm 1, is the bi-adjacency matrix of a left-regular bipartite graph $B = (V, M, E, d)$ of degree d, with V as the vertices in G, and M as the set of measurements.*

Proof. By construction, each vertex $v \in V$ is selected in exactly d measurements.

Second, our measurement matrix $\mathcal{A}$ is consistent with the SN graph structure, because for each user, we select only its neighbors.

Theorem 3 (Consistency of the graph). *Matrix A, constructed by Algorithm 1, is consistent with the structure of the underlying graph G of the SN.*

Proof. A vertex changes the entries of neighboring vertices, only. Hence, a row of $\mathcal{A}$ may contain several disconnected random walks. This could be problematic in a directed graph. However, it is not in an undirected connected graph, because the ends of the disconnected walks are, in fact, connected in the graph. It is just that a particular measurement misses the connecting pieces (paths).

Third, matrix $\mathcal{A}$ is not only a d-regular bipartite graph, but it is, in fact, an expander graph for appropriately chosen k and ϵ.

Theorem 4 (Expander property). *Matrix $\mathcal{A}$, constructed by Algorithm 1, is the bi-adjacency matrix of a (k, d, ϵ)-unbalanced bipartite expander graph.*

Proof. Given the sparsity factor k of the vector x to be approximated, we can choose m proportional to $k \log n$, and ϵ as discussed in Sect. 2.

Fourth, from the expansion property of $\mathcal{A}$ we can immediately prove that $\mathcal{A}$ satisfies the p-restricted isometry property.

Theorem 5 (RIP property). *The measurement matrix $\mathcal{A}$, constructed by Algorithm 1, satisfies the p-restricted isometry property $RIP_{p,k,\delta}$.*

Proof. $\mathcal{A}$ corresponds to a (k, d, ϵ)-unbalanced bipartite expander graph. Hence Theorem 1 holds, and therefore $\mathcal{A}$ satisfies the $RIP_{p,k,\delta}$, for a small δ.

Fifth, since $RIP_{p,k,\delta}$ holds, sparse approximation can be reduced to compressed sensing, which can be solved by linear programming, or by any associated greedy algorithm, such as the LASSO algorithm [39] we are using.

Theorem 6 (Compressed sensing). *The measurement matrix $\mathcal{A}$, constructed by Algorithm 1, reduces sparse approximation to compressed sensing.*

Proof. Since the measurement matrix $\mathcal{A}$ satisfies $RIP_{p,k,\delta}$, the sparse approximation problem 1 can be solved by compressed sensing as in (4).

Sixth, the time complexity of constructing $\mathcal{A}$ by Algorithm 1 is $O(d^2 |V|)$. As a consequence, we are able to compute the top-k C_B-influencers in a much shorter time than $O(|E| |V|)$, which is required by the exact algorithm of Brandes.

Theorem 7 (Approximate betweenness). *The complexity of TopGossip, our gossip-inspired compressed-sensing algorithm for identifying the top-k influencers in a social network with n users is $O(d^2 n)$ time, where $d \ll n$.*

Proof. The most time consuming part of TopGossip is in constructing $\mathcal{A}$. As one can see in Algorithm 1, the outer `while` loop repeats at most n times, and the inner `while` loop repeats at most d times. There is also a `for` loop over the selected neighbors, which has at most d members. Overall, the time complexity of constructing the measurement matrix $\mathcal{A}$ is $O(d^2 n)$, where $d \ll n$.

5   Experimental Results

We evaluate the performance of TopGossip in determining the top-k influencers experimentally, on one synthetic and two real-world networks, respectively. Although we use the local ego-betweenness centrality eC_B, our results are compared to the global betweenness centrality C_B. As we will see, we obtain very good results, which confirms on our examples the correlation between eC_B and C_B.

Synthetic Network. The synthetic network we use is: *(1) A scale-free network* (power-law graph) based on the model in [3], with 500 nodes, 2979 links, average degree of 11.916, and modularity of 0.243, where each node created six links.

Real-World Networks. The real-world networks we use are: *(2) A Facebook-like social network* [33] from an online community for students at the UC Irvine. This network contains 1899 users that sent and received at least one message, and the total number of 59835 messages passed over 20296 links among the users. *(3) A part of the twitter network* [18], with 3656 nodes and 188712 links.

$$Precision = TruePositives/(TruePositives + FalsePositives)$$
$$Recall = TruePositives/(TruePositives + FalseNegatives)$$
$$F\text{-}measure = 2 \times (Precision \times Recall)/(Precision + Recall)$$

Evaluation Method. We use precision and recall to evaluate the accuracy of TopGossip. Intuitively, *precision* is the number of correctly identified influencers divided by the number of identified influencers either correctly or incorrectly. Similarly, *recall* the number of correctly identified influencers divided by the number of true influencers either identified or overlooked. We incorporate both metrics by using the *F-measure*. Formally, these are defined as follows:

Compared Methods. We compare TopGossip with two methods: *(1) RW*, a combinatorial, graph-based approach for compressed sensing, recovering k-sparse graph signals, where each measurement is a random walk in a given graph [41]. *(2) CS-TopCent*, a combinatorial, graph-based, compressed-sampling approach for SN, detecting the top-k influencers without prior knowledge of the SN's topological structure, and by using indirect measurements, only [26].

Results. Figure 5 depicts the accuracy (in terms of the F-measure) of TopGossip, RW, and CS-TopCent, in identifying the top-k influencers in an SN. The horizontal axis shows the sparsity level k, and the vertical axis shows the F-measure of each method for a certain sparsity. As one can see from Fig. 5, TopGossip performs better than RW and TopCent, by having higher F-measure in all tests. We can also observe that TopGossip works well even on very low sparsity levels. The results demonstrate the close correlation between the top-k influencers lists identified by TopGossip and the global betweenness centrality.

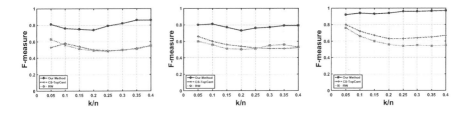

Fig. 5. Accuracy of TopGossip (in blue), RW (in green), and CS-TopCent (in red), in terms of their F-measure, for varying percentage of sparsity, in three different networks: (left) Facebook, (middle) Twitter, and (right) Barabási-Albert synthetic, scale-free (Color figure online)

6 Conclusions and Outlook

In this paper we have reviewed the recent developments in compressed sensing and in social networks, and discussed their impact on the cyber physical social systems, which currently emerge on top of the Internet of things.

We have also introduced TopGossip, a new, on-the-fly, compressed sensing algorithm, that extracts the top-k influencers in an SN. TopGossip only uses local information and only has complexity $O(d^2n)$, where n is the number of nodes in the SN, $d < m$ corresponds to the sparsity k, and $m \ll n$ is the number measurements. We demonstrated the accuracy of TopGossip on three classic examples from the SN community: Facebook, Twitter, and Barabási-Albert.

In future work we would like the apply the compressed sensing approach to both the social and cyber-physical parts of a cyber physical social system and exploit the synergies between the two. A cyber-physical-social-systems application that looks very promising in this respect is smart mobility.

Acknowledgments. This work was partially supported by the following awards: AT-HRSM CPSS/IoT Ecosystem, NSF-Frontiers Cyber-Cardia, US-AFOSR Arrive, EU-Artemis EMC2, EU-Ecsel Semi40, EU-Ecsel Productive 4.0, AT-FWF-NFN RiSE, AT-FWF-LogicCS-DC, AT-FFG Harmonia, AT-FFG Em2Apps, and TUW-CPPS-DK.

References

1. GE Industrial Internet insights report. Technical report (2015). www.ge.com/digital/sites/default/files/industrial-internet-insights-report.pdf
2. Bae, J., Kim, S.: Identifying and ranking influential spreaders in complex networks by neighborhood coreness. Phys. A **395**, 549–559 (2014)
3. Barabasi, A.L., Albert, R.: Emergence of scaling in random networks. Science **286**(5439), 509–512 (1999)
4. Berinde, R., Gilbert, A., Indyk, P., Karloff, H., Strauss, M.: Combining geometry and combinatorics: a unified approach to sparse signal recovery. In: Allerton Conference on Communication, Control, and Computing (2008)
5. Bonacich, P.: Power and centrality: a family of measures. Am. J. Sociol. **92**, 1170–1182 (1987)

6. Borgatti, S.P.: Identifying sets of key players in a social network. Comput. Math. Organ. Theory **12**, 21–34 (2006)
7. Boyd, S., Ghosh, A., Prabhakar, B., Shah, D.: Randomized gossip algorithms. IEEE Trans. Inf. Theory **45**(6), 2508–2530 (2006)
8. Brandes, U.: A faster algorithm for betweenness centrality. J. Math. Sociol. **25**, 163–177 (2001)
9. Candes, E.J., Tao, T.: Decoding by linear programming. IEEE Trans. Inf. Theory **51**(12), 4203–4215 (2005)
10. Cheraghchi, M., Karbasi, A., Mohajer, S., Saligrama, V.: Graph constrained group testing. IEEE Trans. Inf. Theory **58**(1), 248–262 (2012)
11. Costa, L., Rodrigues, F., Travieso, G., Villas-Boas, P.: Characterization of complex networks: a survey. Adv. Phys. **56**, 167–242 (2007)
12. Crovella, M., Kolaczyk, E.: Graph wavelets for spatial traffic analysis. In: Twenty-Second Annual Joint Conference of the IEEE Computer and Communications Societies, vol. 3, pp. 1848–1857. IEEE (2003)
13. Davenport, M., Duarte, M., Eldar, Y., Kutyniok, G.: Introduction to compressed sensing. In: Compressed Sensing: Theory and Applications. Cambridge UP (2012)
14. Donoho, D.: Compressed sensing. IEEE Trans. Inf. Theory **52**(4), 1289–1306 (2006)
15. Everett, M., Borgatti, S.P.: Ego network betweenness. Soc. Netw. **27**, 31–38 (2005)
16. Facebook Climbs To 1.59 Billion Users And Crushes Q4 Estimates With 5.8B Revenue (2016). http://techcrunch.com/2016/01/27/facebook-earnings-q4-2015
17. Freeman, L.: A set of measures of centrality based on betweenness. Sociometry **40**, 35–41 (1977)
18. Gephi platform for interactive visualization and exploration of graphs (2017). http://rankinfo.pkqs.net/twittercrawl.dot.gz
19. Hammond, D., Vandergheynst, P., Gribonval, R.: Wavelets on graphs via spectral graph theory. Appl. Comput. Harmon. Anal. **30**, 129–150 (2011)
20. Haupt, J., Bajwa, W., Rabbat, M., Nowak, R.: Compressed sensing for networked data: a different approach to decentralized compression. IEEE Sig. Process. Mag. **25**(2), 92–101 (2008)
21. Huang, X., Vodenska, I., Wang, F., Havlin, S., Stanley, H.E.: Identifying influential directors in the United States corporate governance network. Phys. Rev. E **84** (2011)
22. Lee, M., Choi, S., Chung, C.: Efficient algorithms for updating betweenness centrality in fully dynamic graphs. Inf. Sci. **326**, 278–296 (2016)
23. Liu, J.G., Ren, Z.M., Guo, Q.: Ranking the spreading influence in complex networks. Phys. A **392**, 4154–4159 (2013)
24. Lu, L., Zhou, T., Zhang, Q.M., Stanley, H.: The h-index of a network node and its relation to degree and coreness. Nat. Commun. **7**, 10168 (2016)
25. Mackenzie, D.: Compressed sensing makes every pixel count. What's Happening Math. Sci. **7**, 114–127 (2009)
26. Mahyar, H.: Detection of top-k central nodes in social networks: a compressive sensing approach. In: IEEE/ACM International Conference on Advances in Social Networks Analysis and Mining, ASONAM, pp. 902–909, August 2015
27. Mahyar, H., Rabiee, H.R., Hashemifar, Z.S.: UCS-NT: an unbiased compressive sensing framework for network tomography. In: IEEE International Conference on Acoustics, Speech, and Signal Processing, pp. 4534–4538 (2013)
28. Mahyar, H., Rabiee, H.R., Hashemifar, Z.S., Siyari, P.: UCS-WN: an unbiased compressive sensing framework for weighted networks. In: Conference on Information Sciences and Systems, CISS. pp. 1–6, March 2013

29. Mahyar, H., Rabiee, H.R., Movaghar, A., Ghalebi, E., Nazemian, A.: CS-ComDet: a compressive sensing approach for inter-community detection in social networks. In: IEEE/ACM ASONAM, pp. 89–96, August 2015

30. Mahyar, H., Rabiee, H.R., Movaghar, A., Hasheminezhad, R., Ghalebi, E., Nazemian, A.: A low-cost sparse recovery framework for weighted networks under compressive sensing. In: IEEE International Conference on Social Computing and Networking, SocialCom, pp. 183–190, December 2015

31. Mallat, S., Zhang, Z.: Matching pursuits with time-frequency dictionaries. IEEE Trans. Sig. Process. **41**(12), 3397–3415 (1993)

32. Newman, S.: Networks: An introduction, 1st edn. Oxford University Press, Oxford (2010)

33. Opsahl, T., Panzarasa, P.: Clustering in weighted networks. Soc. Netw. **31**(2), 155–163 (2009)

34. Püschel, M., Moura, J.: Algebraic signal processing theory. arXiv/0612077v1, pp. 1–67 (2006)

35. Sabidussi, G.: The centrality index of a graph. Psychometrika **31**, 581–603 (1966)

36. Sandryhaila, A., Moura, J.: Discrete signal processing on graphs: frequency analysis. IEEE Trans. Sig. Process. **62**(12), 3042–3054 (2014)

37. Singh, B., Gupte, N.: Congestion and decongestion in a communication network. Phys. Rev. E **71**(5), 055103 (2005)

38. Sipser, M., Spielman, D.: Expander codes. IEEE Trans. Inf. Theory **42**(6), 1710–1722 (1996)

39. Tibshirani, R.: Regression shrinkage and selection via the LASSO. J. R. Stat. Soc. B **58**, 267–288 (1994)

40. Xu, S., Wang, P.: Identifying important nodes by adaptive leaderrank. Phys. A **469**, 654–664 (2017)

41. Xu, W., Mallada, E., Tang, A.: Compressive sensing over graphs. In: IEEE INFOCOM, pp. 2087–2095, April 2011

42. Zhu, X., Rabbat, M.: Approximating signals supported on graphs. In: IEEE International Conference on Acoustics, Speech and Signal Processing, pp. 3921–3924 (2012)

Embedded Software Design Methodology Based on Formal Models of Computation

Soonhoi Ha$^{(\boxtimes)}$ and EunJin Jeong

Seoul National University, Seoul, Korea
{sha,chjej202}@snu.ac.kr
http://peace.snu.ac.kr

Abstract. The current practice of embedded software design resorts to
test or simulation to verify the correctness of the design, which is very
time-consuming and incapable of covering all cases. Existent software
engineering techniques are not concerned about real-time performance
and resource requirements that embedded systems should satisfy for correct operation. In this work, we propose a new methodology to design
dependable software for embedded systems. The key idea of the proposed methodology is to define a universal execution model (UEM) of
heterogeneous multiprocessor embedded systems and to design the software based on the UEM that hides the underlying system architecture
from the programmer. UEM puts restrictions on how to communicate
and synchronize tasks that conventional operating systems deal with.
We define the UEM by extending well-known formal models such as
Synchronous Dataflow (SDF) and finite state machine (FSM). There are
several benefits to use formal models for software design. First, we can
detect critical design errors such as deadlock and buffer overflow by static
analysis of formal models. Second, we can estimate the resource requirement and real-time performance at compile time. Last, not the least, we
can synthesize the target code from the UEM automatically minimizing
the manual coding efforts. By preserving the semantics of the UEM, the
synthesized code will be correct by construction. The key challenge lies in
the expression capability of the proposed UEM. Preliminary experiments
with several non-trivial applications prove the viability of the proposed
methodology.

Keywords: SW design methodology · Universal execution model
SDF

1 Introduction

The application domain of embedded computers as special purpose computers
is steadily increasing as virtually all things are becoming smart or intelligent.
The complexity of embedded computers is also incessantly increasing as can be
observed in automotive electronic systems, intelligent robots, medical devices, as
well as mobile devices. Since everyday life will depend on embedded computers

© Springer International Publishing AG, part of Springer Nature 2018
M. Lohstroh et al. (Eds.): Lee Festschrift, LNCS 10760, pp. 306–325, 2018.
https://doi.org/10.1007/978-3-319-95246-8_18

extensively in the future, it is crucial to make them dependable to avoid serious damages caused by an error or failure of the. For instance, in 2013, the US Department of Justice issued a ruling that imposed a fine of 12 billion dollars to a car manufacturer for sudden acceleration incident that was caused by a software defect in the electronic control unit. Thus it is needless to say how significant is to increase the dependability of embedded computer systems, particularly dependability of the software.

The user of an embedded computer system anticipates that the system works correctly any time, even with the non-zero possibility of hardware component failure. Above all, the correctness of the software should be ensured under the normal operating condition. Unfortunately, it is a well-known fact that it is not possible to detect all errors of a sequential program even though extensive research efforts have been made to develop static analysis techniques to solve this problem. Ensuring functional correctness of parallel programs is much more difficult since the program may have non-deterministic behavior at run-time due to unpredictable access order to shared resources. To make matters worse, embedded systems impose extra constraints on memory space, energy budget, real-time performance, and so on. For real-time applications, we need to guarantee that the real-time constraints are satisfied under the worst-case scenario of the system behavior.

The current practice of software design resorts to test or simulation to verify the functional correctness. To improve the functional safety of automotive electronics systems, for instance, the ISO26262 standard defines how to perform unit test and integration test. However, verification by test or simulation is very time consuming and incapable of covering all possible behaviors. Thus there is non-zero possibility to face an unexpected software behavior at run-time that has not been visited in the test or simulation phase.

There have been various methodologies proposed in software engineering to increase the design productivity and maintainability of software, including structural programming, object-oriented programming, model-driven development, component-based development, and so on. Each methodology has its advantages and disadvantages depending on the application area and the hardware platform. Most of those approaches use a test-based or a simulation-based method to verify the correctness. Nay more, they do not consider the memory space constraints, energy budget, and real-time performance requirements that should be satisfied in the embedded system. It is the designer's responsibility to meet those constraints. A common way to satisfy the real-time performance is to over-design the system with a significant safety margin (at least 50% for instance) over the worst-case values measured in the test phase.

In short, how to verify the correctness of embedded software is still an open problem, a stronghold that could not be conquered by existent methodologies. In this work, we propose a new methodology to make an embedded software correct by construction by designing embedded applications with formal models of computation at the OS level. It is motivated by the observation that a parallel application consists of a set of tasks, or threads, at the operating system (OS) level regardless of the initial specification. A task, or thread, is a unit of mapping

and scheduling and there are various ways of communication and synchronization between tasks. In the proposed methodology, we define a set of rules on
task synchronization and communication that tasks are enforced to follow. To
be concrete, we make computation tasks follow a dataflow model where tasks
communicate with each other through channels, disallowing implicit communication through shared variables. By using a restricted form of dataflow model
such as Synchronous Data Flow (SDF) [1] for application specification, we can
perform static analysis to check the possibility of deadlock or channel buffer
overflow. Moreover, we can estimate the worst-case performance and resource
requirement at compile-time.

The proposed methodology separates design and implementation of embedded software. The designed software based on formal models of computation
is mostly independent of the hardware platform, except for a minimal set of
platform-dependent tasks Parallelizing an application is easily performed by
mapping tasks onto processors, and inter-processor interface code is automatically synthesized in the proposed methodology. By keeping the semantics of
formal models, the implemented software is free from a class of errors that can
be detected by static analysis performed at compile time. It is distinguished from
the current practice of embedded software development that is tightly coupled
with a given hardware platform. Parallelizing an application is performed manually considering the features of the given hardware platform. Since an embedded
application is tailored to a specific platform, it is not easy to port an application
to a different hardware platform.

The proposed methodology concerns about the execution of tasks at the OS
level and above, assuming that each task is already verified and its execution
profile is given a priori. It is complementary to the existing methodologies in
that test-based verification or formal verification should be used to verify each
task. Defining a set of rules on task synchronization and communication can be
understood as defining a universal execution model[1] (UEM) for multi-processor
embedded systems. Even though we aim to make the proposed execution model
be *universal*, because the baseline model is a data flow model, it fits better for
computation-oriented applications than database-oriented applications.

Figure 1 shows the vertical software structure based on the UEM. The UEM
is positioned on top of the OS layer, hiding the low-level details of the architecture from the application programmers. The UEM layer consists of three layers
internally. The UEM execution engine serves the role of middleware that executes the UEM tasks on the target architecture, which is platform-dependent.
To the application programmer, the UEM layer provides a set of APIs (application programming interface) for communication and synchronization between
tasks. Thus, the application programmer can design an embedded software on
top of the UEM without knowing the actual hardware platform on which the program runs. In the middle, a set of UEM tasks is generated from the application

---

[1] The term *universal* is not based on any formal proof but on our goal to make the
model independent of underlying hardware platforms.

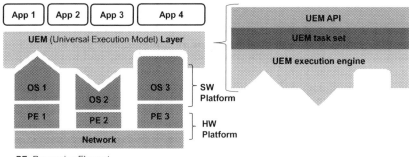

Fig. 1. Vertical software structure based on the UEM (universal execution model)

program. The UEM execution engine customized to a specific architecture aims to emulate the UEM efficiently.

The key challenge of the proposed methodology lies in the expression capability of the proposed UEM. Since the existent formal models of computation exhibit limitation on expression capabilities, several extensions have been made to the existent models in UEM. Preliminary experiments with several non-trivial applications prove the viability of the proposed methodology.

2 Dataflow Specification of an Application

In the proposed UEM, an application is specified by an extended synchronous dataflow (SDF) model. We first review the baseline SDF model and explain how the SDF model is extended.

2.1 Synchronous Data Flow

In the SDF model [1], an application is specified with a dataflow graph, $G(V, E)$, where V is a set of nodes and E is a set of arcs. A node $v \in V$ represents a function module, or a task, and an arc $e \in E$ is a FIFO channel between two tasks. Communication between two tasks is performed by explicit message passing via a FIFO channel. Figure 2(a) shows an example SDF graph where the number annotated on the arc indicates the number of data samples, called a sample rate, to produce or consume per task execution. If unspecified, the sample rate is 1 by default. The input sample rate and the output sample rate on an arc are represented as $cons(e)$ and $prod(e)$, respectively. In the SDF model, a task becomes executable only when all input arcs have no fewer samples than the specified sample rate in the associated arcs.

By comparing the input and the output sample rates on each arc, e, we can determine the relative execution rates between the source task, denoted by $src(e)$, and the destination task, denoted by $dest(e)$. For instance, the execution rate of task C should be twice higher than that of task A in Fig. 2(a), in order

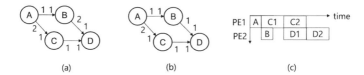

Fig. 2. (a) An example SDF graph with annotated sample rates on the arcs, (b) an inconsistent SDF graph that has a buffer overflow error, and (c) a mapping and scheduling result of the SDF graph onto two processing elements

to make the number of samples produced from the source task the same as the number of samples consumed by the destination task. This constraint can be formulated as the following equation, called balance equation: $prod(e) \times R(src(e)) = cons(e) \times R(dest(e))$ where $R(v)$ indicates the repetition counts of task v. An SDF graph is said to be consistent if we can find the repetition counts of all tasks to satisfy the balance equations of all arcs. Otherwise, the graph is called sample rate inconsistent, shortly inconsistent. The SDF graph shown in Fig. 2(b) is inconsistent, which may incur a buffer overflow error on arc AC. An iteration of an SDF graph is defined by the set of task executions with minimum repetition counts. The minimum repetition counts of tasks in the SDF graph of Fig. 2(a) are $R(A) = R(B) = 1$ and $R(C) = R(D) = 2$.

Since we can compute the minimum repetition counts of all tasks and the graph shows the dependency relationship between tasks, we can perform task scheduling at compile time, which is to determine where and in what order tasks will be executed on a given hardware platform. By constructing a static schedule of tasks at compile time, we can detect the critical software faults such as buffer overflow and deadlock. Figure 2(c) illustrates a parallel scheduling result by mapping tasks onto two processing elements. From the parallel scheduling result, we can estimate the buffer size and the real-time performance of the graph if the execution time of each task is bounded. Note that even though there may exist numerous schedules for a given application, determinism of the execution behavior is guaranteed, meaning that the execution result is independent of the schedule.

In summary, by using the SDF model, we can verify the satisfaction of real-time requirement and resource constraints with static scheduling. Moreover, we can detect buffer overflow and deadlock errors at compile time. While the SDF model has the aforementioned benefits from its static analyzability, it has a severe limitation to be used as a general model for behavior specification. It is not possible to specify the dynamic behavior of an application since the sample rate may not change dynamically. To overcome this limitation while preserving the static analyzability of the SDF model, several extensions have been proposed, including CSDF (cyclo-static dataflow) [2], SADF (scenario-aware dataflow) [3], and PSDF (parameterized SDF) [4]. In the proposed methodology, we use the FSM model in combination with the SDF model to express the dynamic behavior of an application at the task level.

2.2   Dynamic Behavior Specification

In case an application has a finite number of different behaviors, called modes of operation, the behavior of each mode is expressed by an SDF graph, and mode transitions are specified by a tabular specification of an FSM, called Mode Transition Machine (MTM) [5]. It is similar to FSM-SADF [3]. An MTM describes the mode transition rules for the SDF graph, defined as a tuple {*Modes, Variables, Transitions*} where *Modes* and *Variables* represent a set of modes and a set of mode variables respectively, and *Transitions* is a set of transitions that consists of the current mode, a Boolean function of conditions, and the next mode. A Boolean function of the transition condition is defined by a simple comparison operation between a mode variable and a value.

An example of MTM-SDF specification is shown in Fig. 3 in which an application has two modes of operation, S1 and S2. The input and output sample rates of a task may vary, depending on the mode. In this example, the MTM is quite simple since it needs to distinguish two modes of operation by a single mode variable. Since the granularity of a task is large and the dynamic behavior inside a task is not visible in the UEM, an MTM is not complex in general. At compile time, the SDF graph is scheduled separately for each mode of operation. We assume that all modes share the same initial buffer states. Then, mode change can be made at the iteration boundary safely without any inconsistency of buffer states between modes.

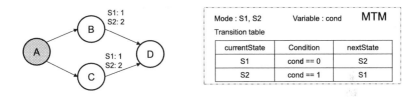

Fig. 3. Extended SDF graph with an MTM with 2 modes

Mode transition is enabled by setting the mode variable. There are two ways of setting the mode variable. It can be set by a hidden supervisor, which will be explained in the next section. Alternatively, it can be set by a designated task. A stream-based application usually starts with parsing a header information that determines the mode of operation, followed by processing a stream of data. In this case, the SDF task that parses the header information is designated as a special task that may change the mode variable. In the example of Fig. 3, task A can be designated as the special task that determines the mode of operation.

When mode transition occurs, the SDF schedule is changed accordingly. If the mode change is enabled by the hidden supervisor, it is activated at the iteration boundary of the SDF graph. If it is enabled by a designated task, mode change occurs right after the task finishes its execution. For consistency of operation, in this case, the schedules of all modes should have the same task schedule before the designated task. In case the designated task is the first task in the SDF schedule, this restriction is satisfied easily.

2.3   Library Task

In the dataflow specification, use of shared variables among tasks is not allowed since the access order to a shared variable may vary depending on the execution order of tasks and the application behavior will be non-deterministic. In many embedded applications, however, it is popular to use a global data structure that is shared among tasks. In the UEM, another extension is made to the SDF graph by introducing a special type of task, called library task, to allow the use of shared resources in the SDF model [6].

A library task is a mappable object that defines a set of service functions to a shared resource among tasks. Figure 4 shows an SDF graph that consists of three normal SDF tasks ($T1$ - $T3$) and two library tasks ($L1$ - $L2$). For connection with a library task, we introduce new types of ports, library master port and library slave port that are represented by a red circle and a blue square, respectively in the figure. An arc between a library master port and a library slave port is not a data channel, but represents a client-server relation. A library task plays the role of a server with a single slave port that can be connected to multiple masters that request the predefined services of the library task. Unlike a normal SDF task, a library task is not invoked by input data but by a function call inside an SDF task; it is a passive object.

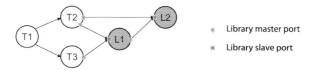

Fig. 4. Extended SDF graph with library tasks (Color figure online)

There are several use cases of library task depending on the kind of a shared resource. A library task can be used as a monitor that handles the access conflict to the shared variables at a high level. If a shared resource is a hardware device, the library task is a thread-safe device driver that provides a set of Application Programming Interfaces (APIs) to access the device. In a server-client application, the server task can be specified by a library task that may be shared by multiple clients. Another use case of a library task is to make a vertically layered software structure by providing a set of APIs of the software layer below the application layer. Figure 4 depicts three layers of software structure.

In case multiple masters access a shared variable that a library task manages, it is unavoidable that the return value of a library function depends on the execution order of the master tasks, which is anathema to any deterministic model. By the use of a library task, however, we explicitly specify the possibility of such non-determinism. In case the library task has no state or returns the same value to the master tasks regardless of the calling order, the library task is classified as deterministic. Otherwise, the developer should be aware that the library task does not guarantee deterministic behavior in the sense that the return value to a master task depends on the scheduling order of master tasks. Nonetheless, the same behavior can be repeated if the same scheduling order is followed since the SDF model allows us to construct a static schedule of tasks. Then the application behavior becomes deterministic if the static schedule of tasks is followed at run-time.

2.4 Loop Structure (SDF/L)

A compute-intensive application usually spends most of its execution time in loop structures and how to parallelize them is the main challenge for accelerating the application. Even though dataflow models, including the SDF model, are good at exploiting the task-level parallelism of an application, it is difficult to exploit the parallelism of loop structures since they are not explicitly specified in existent dataflow models. In SDF, a loop structure is implicitly expressed by sample rate changes as illustrated in Fig. 2(a). Among many possible schedules, a looped schedule $AB2(CD)$ can be constructed. In case 2 executions of (CD) can be parallelized with 2 output samples from A and B, a user may want to construct a parallel schedule as illustrated in Fig. 5(b). However, identifying such a loop structure and parallelizing it is not easy because existent parallel scheduling techniques usually aim to exploit task-level parallelism only.

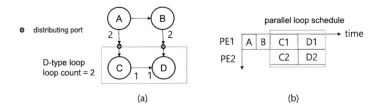

(a)   (b)

Fig. 5. SDF graph with a loop structure

Recently, we proposed a novel extension to specify a loop structure as a super node to make the SDF graph hierarchical [7]. The extended SDF graph with loop structures is called an SDF/L graph. Figure 5(a) is the SDF/L graph representation of the application of Fig. 2(a).

In the SDF/L model, two types of loop structures are distinguished, data loop (D-type) and convergent loop (C-type), and two types of input ports, distributing port and broadcasting port. In a D-type loop (data loop), each iteration of the loop consumes new input data from each distributing input port. The number of iterations is determined by the sample rate change of the associated input channel. The loop structure of Fig. 5(a) is a D-type loop.

On the other hand, Fig. 6 shows an SDF graph that has a C-type loop. For a C-type loop. The C-type loop has two attributes, loop_count and exit_flag. The former is the maximum iteration count and the second is set by a designated

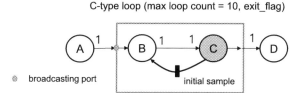

Fig. 6. SDF graph with a C-type loop structure

task, task C in this figure. The number of iteration is dynamically decided by the result of computation that will set the exit-flag. All input ports of a C-type loop should be broadcasting ports from which input samples are reused in all iterations of the loop; the sample rate of the output connection is equal to the sample rate of the input connection.

In summary, in UEM the SDF model is extended to express dynamic behavior with an MTM, to allow the use of shared resources with a library task, and to explicitly specify the loop structures hierarchically. Refer to the corresponding references for more detailed explanation of each extension. Note that these extensions preserve the static analyzability of the SDF model. We perform static scheduling for each mode of operation. In the SDF/L model, static scheduling can be performed hierarchically from the bottom layer. A loop structure is encapsulated as a regular SDF task at the upper layer.

3   Universal Execution Model (UEM)

Figure 7 shows the overall software architecture of the UEM that is layered hierarchically. Each application that is specified by an aforementioned extended SDF model is encapsulated as a dataflow process at the upper layer. We can group a set of dataflow processes in case whose execution states are inter-related. For each application group, a control process is defined in the dynamic behavior of an application group is specified formally by an FSM (finite state machine).

Figure 8(a) represents a multi-mode multimedia terminal (MMMT) application group that contains 8 dataflow processes and 1 control process. Among 8 dataflow processes, 4 processes with pink color have internal dataflow graphs while the other 4 processes with yellow color are single sequential tasks. This application group has the following 4 different modes of operation: Menu, Video player, MP3 player, and Video phone. The *UserInput* task receives a user input to select a mode of operation and sends it to the control process. Based on the selected model, the control process enables a set of applications that run concurrently to serve the mode of operation.

Figure 8(b) shows the FSM specified inside the control process The FSM consists of 4 states that correspond to the modes of operation. In the Video play mode, it enables 2 dataflow processes, H264 decoder and MP3 player. During execution, the mode transition may occur from the Video play mode to Video phone mode if a call is received from the Interrupt task. Then, the control process

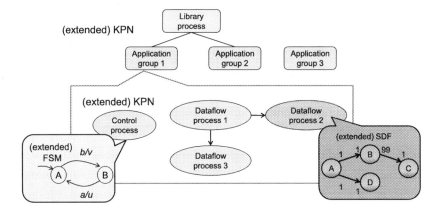

Fig. 7. Software architecture of the UEM

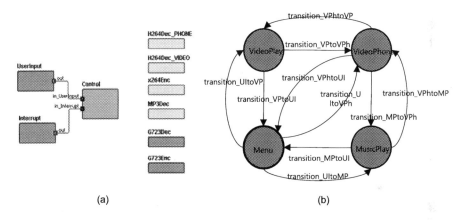

Fig. 8. A multi-mode multimedia terminal application group (a) specification, and (b) the control task specification (Color figure online)

suspends the dataflow tasks of the Video play mode and enables 4 dataflow processes, H264 decoder, x264 encoder, G723 Decoder, and G723 Encoder. After the call is completed, it resumes the suspended dataflow processes of the Video play mode. We can perform model checking to verify the behavior of the control task satisfies the specification at compile time.

In case there are multiple application groups, we can add another layer as shown in Fig. 7. At the top level, each application group is represented by an extended KPN. A process in the KPN (Kahn process network) [8] model allows only blocking read, which makes the KPN determinate, meaning that the execution result is independent of the execution order of processes. To allow shared resources among KPN processes, we extend the KPN with library processes, similarly to the extended SDF model with library tasks.

3.1 Dataflow Task Code Template

In the proposed methodology, a programmer is supposed to specify the system behavior following the software architecture of Fig. 7, starting from dataflow specification of tasks at the bottom layer. As a unit of mapping and scheduling, a dataflow task is a sequential program that should be written with the UEM APIs, based on the coding guidelines defined in the UEM. Figure 9 shows the task code template that consists of three sections, TASK_INIT, TASK_GO, and TASK_WRAPUP. In the current implementation, it is assumed that the task is written in C programming language that is most popular for embedded SW design.

```
TASK_INIT {/* task initialization code */
          port_in = PORT_INITIALIZE(TASK_ID, "in");
          port_out = PORT_INITIALIZE(TASK_ID, "out");}
TASK_GO {
          MQ_RECEIVE(port_in, ...)
          /* main body of the task */
          MQ_SEND(port_out, ...) }
TASK_WRAPUP { /* task wrapup code */ }
```

Fig. 9. A code template of a dataflow task that uses generic APIs for communication

The TASK_INIT section contains the code that will be executed in the initialization stage of the task such as initialization of internal variables and data structures associated with ports. The TASK_GO section is the main body of the task that will be executed repeatedly when it is scheduled by the operating system. The TASK_WRAPUP section is executed just before the task is terminated.

In the TASK_GO section, the task reads the input data from its input ports, perform computation, and sends the output data to the output ports. To make it independent of the hardware architecture and FIFO channel implementation, generic APIs are defined for communication via ports and port initialization as shown in Table 1.

The UEM assumes that there is a hidden supervisor that manages the tasks. We define a set of services that a task can request to the supervisor using a special API, SYS_REQ. The first argument of this API is the service name. Remind that a task may vary its internal behavior depending on the mode of operation in the extended SDF model as explained in the previous section. To change its internal definition, a task can ask the supervisor of what is the current mode; Mode = SYS_REQ(GET_CURRENT_MODE_NAME). A designated task can set the mode by using the following API; SYS_REQ(SET_MTM_PARAM, task_name, var_name, value).

Table 1. UEM application programming interfaces

Task type	API	Description
Common	PORT_INITIALIZE(task_id, port_name)	Initialize a port
	MQ_RECEIVE(channel_id, buffer, buffer_length)	Read data from the FIFO-type channel
	MQ_SEND(channel_id, buffer, data_length)	Write data to the FIFO-type channel
	MQ_AVAILABLE(channel_id)	Check if there is data in the input FIFO
	BUF_RECEIVE(channel_id, buffer, buffer_length)	Read data from the buffer-type channel
	BUF_SEND(channel_id, buffer, data_length)	Write data to the buffer-type channel
	SYS_REQ(service_name, arguments)	Request a service to the hidden supervisor. The first argument of the API designates the service name
Dataflow	LIBCALL(master_port, function_name, function_arguments)	Call a library function from the library task connected through the library master port
Library	LIBFUNC(return_type, function_name, function_arguments)	Define a library function

3.2 Control Task Code Template

A control task is supposed to specify its internal behavior with an FSM. The FSM code template is defined as shown in Fig. 10, which can be automatically generated from the graphic FSM editor in our design environment. In each state, the programmer may use SYS_REQ API to define the control action, which is similar to action scripts of the statechart in STATEMATE [9].

The control services that a control task can request to the supervisor are listed in Fig. 11. The first category is to control the execution status of an application

```
while(1){
    MQ_AVAILABLE(all_ports);                              // 1-1. Check the existence of a new event
    SYS_REQ(CHECK_TASK_STATE, "task_name", ...); // 1-2. Check the termination of a task
    if(available) MQ_RECEIVE(selected port);              // 2. read the new event
    if(some event or task state is triggered)   break;   // 3. Break a loop to make transition
}
switch( current_state ) {
    case ID_STATE_S1:
        if(selected port==1 && input data==2) {          // 4. check the transition condition
            current_state = ID_STATE_S2;
            SYS_REQ(SET_PARAM_INT, "task_name", "param_name", data, 0, 0);
        }                                // 5. send the control message through the system port
        break;
    case ID_STATE_S2: { }
    case ID_STATE_S3: { }
    ....
}
```

Fig. 10. An example code template of a control task in UEM

and the second category is to change or monitor a specific parameter of an application. The third category is defined to specify the timing requirements of the system explicitly.

Category	APIs	Description
Execution Status Control	SYS_REQ(RUN_TASK, task_name);	Run the task
	SYS_REQ(STOP_TASK, task_name);	Terminate the task
	SYS_REQ(SUSPEND_TASK, task_name);	Suspend the task
	SYS_REQ(RESUME_TASK, task_name);	Resume the task
	status=SYS_REQ(CHECK_TASK_STATE, task_name);	Get the current state of the task
Parameter Control	p_value = SYS_REQ(GET_PARAM_INT/FLOAT, task_name, param_name);	Get the value of a task parameter
	SYS_REQ(SET_PARAM_INT/FLOAT, task_name, param_name);	Change a value of a task parameter
Timing Control	SYS_REQ(SET_THROUGHPUT, task_name, thr_val);	Set throughput requirement
	SYS_REQ(SET_DEADLINE, src_task, dst_task, lat_val);	Set deadline requirement to the task chain (src_task to dst_task)

Fig. 11. Control actions that a control task can request to the supervisor

3.3   Library Task Code Template

Figure 12 illustrates code templates associated with a library task. A library task has two separate files associated: a library header file and a library code file. The library header file declares the library functions, while the library code file defines the function bodies. The prototype of a library function is defined by a directive, LIBFUNC(), that will be translated into a regular function definition automatically by the CIC translator.

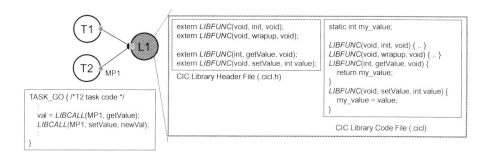

Fig. 12. Code templates associated with a library task

A library task defines init and wrapup functions like a normal SDF task for initialization and finalization of the library task. A caller task uses LIBCALL directive to call a library function as shown in Fig. 12. The first parameter of LIBCALL() is the name of the library master port, the second is the function name, and the others are the arguments. If the function has a return value, it can be taken from the LIBCALL invocation. Note that pointers may not be used for arguments and return values to make the SDF graph portable to a variety of target architectures. For shared address space architectures, however, the developer may use pointers for efficient implementation, giving up portability. A library task may have a persistent internal state, simply called a state. Then the access to the state should be protected by synchronization primitives, Lock() and Unlock() to avoid data race problems.

4   Automatic Code Generation

Based on the mapping and the scheduling result, we can generate the target code automatically from the UEM assuming that the task code inside each node of a SDF graph and the control task is given and correct. It remains as a future work to check the correctness of each task.

We can synthesize the communication and interface code between tasks as well as the scheduling code automatically. Since the HW/SW interface code and the task synchronization code are particularly error-prone, automatic synthesis of those codes will alleviate the burden of the programmer significantly. Moreover, by keeping the SDF semantics, the synthesized code is guaranteed to be free of buffer overflow and deadlock error. Then, functional verification of embedded software can be performed by verifying the functional correctness of each task only. Since each task is a sequential code, we can use the state-of-the-art verification techniques of a sequential code, which is complementary to the proposed methodology.

Another benefit of automatic code generation from the UEM is that we can add extra software modules to enhance the reliability or the safety of the software. Even though the software is designed based on the UEM without consideration of any possibility of hardware failure, we apply fault-tolerant techniques to insert extra codes to the generated target code, while satisfying the real-time requirements and the resource constraints.

If the efficiency of the automatically generated code is much worse than the manually optimized code, people may prefer manual coding even with the higher risk of error to automatic code synthesis because embedded systems are usually cost-sensitive. Since the internal code of each task is assumed to be optimized, the overhead will be associated with inter-task communication if exists. For efficient code generation, we may use several techniques that have been developed to minimize the buffer size when constructing a static schedule of an SDF graph [10,11].

Note that code generation is specific to the system architecture that runs the application. Then a key challenge in the proposed methodology is how difficult is to make the UEM compiler to synthesize the software automatically for a given architecture. If the difficulty of making the UEM compiler is higher than that of developing the software manually for a given architecture, the proposed technique will be of no use. For UEM compilation, following the well-established procedure of traditional compilation, we separate the platform-independent part and the platform-dependent part of UEM compilation. By pre-defining the HW-specific interface as software component libraries, we simplify the platform-dependent part maximally. From our experience, we expect that it will take less than a month to make a UEM compiler for a new hardware platform.

5   Preliminary Experiments

The proposed methodology has been applied to the development of a parallel embedded software design framework, called HOPES [12]. Specification and parallel scheduling of the MMMT application group in Fig. 8(a) can be found in [12]. The reference also presents the scheduling and mapping result of a lane detection algorithm for a CPU-GPU heterogeneous system. In this section, we present two more examples that use library tasks.

5.1   A Cryptographic System

Figure 13 shows the captured screen of HOPES that specifies a cryptographic system following the UEM software architecture. The pink task represents two dataflow processes that have an extended SDF graph inside as displayed in the figure. Two tasks, *Encryption* and *Decryption*, call library functions inside to request the service of a library task, *CrytographyLibrary* that provides a set of service functions for cryptography. The *Control* task activates the *Sender* task if it receives a user input and the *Sender* task packs the input data, encrypts the packed message, and transfers the encrypted message. If the control task is triggered by an incoming message, it decrypts, unpacks and displays it.

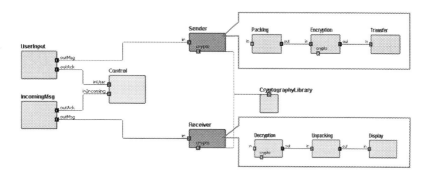

Fig. 13. A cryptographic system example (Color figure online)

5.2   Cooperating Robots

Figure 14 specifies a multi-robot system where multiple robots accomplish a mission, sharing the information. The mission in this experiment is to find all color papers scattered on the floor whose boundary is marked by black tapes. While each robot searches color papers in the region independently, the found papers are reported to the library task to avoid the redundant labor of robots. When all papers are found, the robots go back to the initial position. Each robot performs a group of applications that are depicted in the figure. An application group consists of 8 tasks: 3 sensor tasks, 4 actuator tasks, and 1 control task.

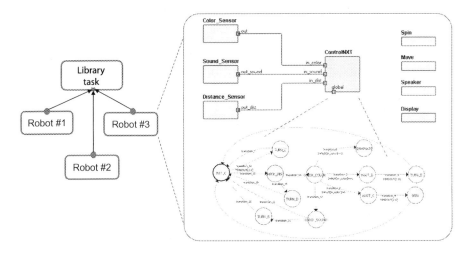

Fig. 14. A cooperative robots example (Color figure online)

In this experiment, three different types of robots used: *TI Evalbot, NXT LEGO*, and *iRobot Create*. The robots have different hardware platforms and operating systems as shown in Fig. 15. The library task is mapped to *iRobot Create* that is most powerful. The figure also shows the distribution of code size. In addition to the task code given by the user, the scheduler code, data structure, and communication codes are automatically generated. In this example, the task code takes about 21.9% of the total code size on average. Since the coding error probability is known to be dependent on the code size in general, it can be said that automatic code synthesis increases the design productivity of this control oriented application.

	TI Evalbot	NXT LEGO	iRobot Create
OS	uC-OS III	NXT-OSEK	Linux (Ubuntu)
Proc.	LM3S9B92 (80MHz)	Atmel® 32-bit ARM (48MHz)	Intel i3-4000M (2.4GHz)
Mem.	96KB	64KB	4GB
Total code size	2721	3301	2996
Given task code	580	604	787
Scheduler code	1171	928	931
Other code	970	1,769	1,278

Fig. 15. Robot hardware specs and synthesized code size

6   Related Work

Defining a universal execution model is not a unique idea of the proposed methodology. Several executions models have been proposed in various application domains, to make the software independent of the hardware platform and so portable to different types of architecture easily. A good example is the AUTOSAR (AUTomotive Open Software Architecture) methodology that defines the open and standardized software architecture for automotive electronic control units [13]. AUTOSAR defines a set of APIs assuming that the software components communicate with each other through virtual sockets. Thus, software developer can design software using the APIs, without knowledge of the underlying hardware platform, which is the same as the proposed technique that provides the UEM APIs to the programmer. After mapping of software components onto the ECUs is determined, the runtime environment supervises the execution of software components and communication between them. Since the AUTOSAR is not based on formal models of computation, however, this methodology resorts to test-based methods for software verification.

The proposed methodology has been evolved from a hardware/software codesign methodology where the behavior specification of a system is made separately from architecture specification. In this codesign methodology, formal models of computations are widely for behavior specification since they make it easy to explore the wide design space of architecture configuration and mapping of the application to the processing elements. In case the hardware platform is given, the design space is reduced to find an optimal mapping of the application and the software code for each processing element is automatically generated based on the mapping and scheduling decision. In other words, the HW/SW codesign methodology becomes an embedded SW design methodology if the hardware platform is fixed.

Nonetheless, the proposed methodology differs from conventional model-based codesign environments such as Daedalus [14] and DAL [15]. While they use the KPN model for behavior specification, the UEM model is defined as the execution model at the operating system level, combining three different models of computation. Its model composition rule is different from that of Ptolemy [16] which allows hierarchical composition of models without limitation on the depth of hierarchy and the kinds of models. Last, not the least, a major difference between the codesign methodology and the software design methodology is the granularity of the atomic actor. The atomic actor is as large as a function module that can be implemented as a hardware component in the codesign methodology, while it is larger in the software design methodology as a sequential task that is a unit of mapping and scheduling at the operating system level.

7   Conclusion

For the design of embedded software, we have to ensure not only the functional correctness but also satisfaction of several constraints on real time performance and resource limitation. In this work, a novel methodology to make an embedded software correct by construction is proposed by designing embedded applications with formal models of computation. Unlike the conventional model-based design, formal models of computation are applied to the software architecture of tasks that are mapped and scheduled by the operating systems. Thus, the proposed software architecture can be understood as a universal execution model (UEM) of underlying hardware platforms. We define the UEM by *extending* well-known formal models, Synchronous Dataflow (SDF) for the computation parts of the system and finite state machine (FSM) for the control structure of the system. At the top level, an extended KPN (Kahn process network) is used to define the interaction between applications. To be concrete, the SDF model is extended to specify dynamic behavior by combining a FSM model, called MTM (mode transition machine), to allow the use of shared resources by defining a new type of task, called library tasks, and to express loop structures explicitly by defining a loop super node to make the SDF model hierarchical.

There are several benefits to use formal models for software design. First, we can detect critical design errors such as deadlock and buffer overflow by static analysis of formal models. Second, we can estimate the resource requirement and real-time performance at compile time. Last, not the least, we can synthesize the target code from the UEM automatically minimizing the manual coding efforts. By preserving the semantics of the UEM, the synthesized code will be correct by construction. The key challenge lies in the expression capability of the proposed UEM. Preliminary experiments with several non-trivial applications prove the viability of the proposed methodology.

8   Epilogue

I am very grateful that I was involved in the development of Ptolemy [16] from its birth during my doctoral study. Under the supervision of Prof. E.A. Lee, I developed and implemented several models of computations and their hierarchical structure. Naturally, I became an advocate of formal models of computation and their mixture for system specification and simulation. After joining the faculty of SNU (Seoul National University, Korea), I switched my gear to the HW/SW codesign of embedded systems and had developed a HW/SW codesign environment, called PeaCE (Ptolemy extension as a Codesign Environment) [17] for the first 12 years. As the name implies, the baseline of the environment is Ptolemy classic. Since our aim was to synthesize the system automatically from the behavior specification, we had to restrict the use of formal models and their composition. Our choice was to use SDF and FSM models since they offer good static analyzability and the refinement path from specification to implementation is well established. To overcome the limitation of expression capability, we have proposed several extensions to those models. The viability of the proposed approach was proven with a design of a simple smartphone application.

As the number of processors integrated into a chip increases and platform based design becomes popular, parallelizing software becomes more challenging than partitioning an application into hardware and software. Since the PeaCE environment was not well engineered from the start, graduate students had difficulty of maintaining the environment. So we decided to develop a new design environment, HOPES [18], from scratch, focusing on the development of parallel embedded software based on the formal models of computation, keeping the spirit of Ptolemy and PeaCE. Since a hardware component can be regarded as a special processing element that can perform a designated task only, the HOPES environment can be used as a HW/SW codesign environment. By increasing the granularity of a task, it is easier to use formal models for behavior specification. Another 12 years have passed. We are now renovating the HOPES environment. Our goal is to make the HOPES environment as a software engineering tool that can be adopted in the industries.

Acknowledgments. This research was supported by the National Research Foundation of Korea (NRF) grant funded by the Korea government (MSIP) (No. NRF-2016R1A2B3012662). The ICT at Seoul National University provided research facilities for this study.

References

1. Lee, E.A., Messerschmitt, D.G.: Synchronous data flow. Proc. IEEE **75**, 1235–1245 (1987)
2. Bilsen, G., Engels, N., Lauwereins, R., Peperstraete, J.: Cyclo-static dataflow. IEEE Trans. Signal Process. **44**, 397–408 (1996)
3. Stuijk, S., Geilen, M., Theelen, B.D., Basten, T.: Scenario-aware dataflow: modeling, analysis and implementation of dynamic applications. In: Proceedings of International Conference on Embedded Computer Systems: Architecture, Modeling, and Simulation, vol. 72, pp. 404–411 (2011)
4. Bhattacharya, B., Bhattacharyya, S.: Parameterized dataflow modeling for DSP systems. IEEE Trans. Signal Process. **49**, 2408–2421 (2001)
5. Jung, H., Lee, C., Kang, S., Kim, S., Oh, H., Ha, S.: Dynamic behavior specification and dynamic mapping for real-time embedded systems: HOPES approach. ACM Trans. Embed. Comput. Syst. **13**, 135:1–135:26 (2014)
6. Park, H., Jung, H., Oh, H., Ha, S.: Library support in an actor-based parallel programming platform. IEEE Trans. Ind. Inform. **7**, 340–353 (2011)
7. Hong, H., Oh, H., Ha, S.: Hierarchical dataflow modeling of iterative applications. In: Proceedings of Design Automation Conference, vol. 39 (2017)
8. Kahn, G.: The semantics of a simple language for parallel processing. In: Proceedings of the IFIP Congress (1974)
9. Harel, D., Naamad, A.: The STATEMATE semantics of statecharts. ACM Trans. Softw. Eng. Methodol. **5**, 293–333 (1996)
10. Shin, T., Oh, H., Ha, S.: Minimizing buffer requirements for throughput constrained parallel execution of synchronous dataflow graph. In: Proceedings of Asia and South Pacific Design Automation Conference (2012)
11. Oh, H., Ha, S.: Memory-optimized software synthesis from dataflow program graphs with large size data samples. EURASIP J. Appl. Signal Process. **2003**, 514–529 (2003)

12. Ha, S., Jung, H.: HOPES: programming platform approach for embedded systems design. In: Ha, S., Teich, J., et al. (eds.) Handbook of Hardware/Software Codesign, pp. 951–981. Springer, Dordrecht (2017). https://doi.org/10.1007/978-94-017-7267-9_1

13. Pelz, G., Oehler, P., Fourgeau, E., Grimm, C.: Automotive system design and AUTOSAR. In: Boulet, P. (ed.) Advances in Design and Specification Languages for SoCs, pp. 293–305. Springer, Boston (2005). https://doi.org/10.1007/0-387-26151-6_21

14. Nikolov, H., et al.: Daedalus: toward composable multimedia MP-SoC design. In: Proceedings of Design Automation Conference, pp. 574–579 (2008)

15. Schor, L., Bacivarov, I., Rai, D., Yang, H., Kang, S.-H., Thiele, L.: Scenario-based design flow for mapping streaming applications onto on-chip many-core systems. In: Proceedings of CASES, pp. 71–80 (2012)

16. Buck, J.T., Ha, S., Lee, E.A., Messerschmitt, D.G.: Ptolemy: a framework for simulating and prototyping heterogenous systems. Int. J. Comput. Simul. **4**, 155–182 (1994)

17. Ha, S., Kim, S., Lee, C., Yi, Y., Kwon, S., Joo, Y.: PeaCE: a hardware-software codesign environment for multimedia embedded systems. ACM Trans. Des. Autom. Electron. Syst. **12**, 24:1–24:25 (2007)

18. Kwon, S., Kim, Y., Jeun, W., Ha, S., Paek, Y.: A retargetable parallel programming framework for MPSoC. ACM Trans. Des. Autom. Electron. Syst. **13**, 39:1–39:18 (2008)

Anytime Algorithms in Time-Triggered Control Systems

Hermann Kopetz[(✉)]

Vienna University of Technology, Vienna, Austria
h.kopetz@gmail.com

Abstract. The deterministic temporal behavior of a time-triggered computer platform provides an ideal base for the implementation of a real-time control system. The temporal predictability requires that the durations of the time-slots for the execution of the control algorithms can be specified *a priori* at design time. Since the indeterminism of state of the art hardware makes it difficult to arrive at a tight worst-case-execution-time (WCET) bound for the execution of a conventional control algorithm we propose to use anytime algorithms in a time-triggered control systems. An anytime algorithm trades precision for execution time. In a real-time control system we would like to have both, *good algorithmic precision* and a *low response time*—but these are conflicting goals. In this paper we propose a novel method for the design of the slot length for the execution of an anytime algorithm in a time-triggered control that on the one side is sufficient to achieve the required precision and on the other side will not introduce an extensive latency that has a detrimental effect on the quality and stability of a closed-loop control system.

Keywords: Control systems · Time-triggered systems · Anytime algorithms

1 Introduction

In a cyber-physical control system, a cyber-system interacts periodically with a controlled object in the physical world in order to realize the desired behavior of the controlled object. These periodic interactions occur at two different periodic instants: (i) the point of observation (or *sampling point*) where the cyber system observes the state of the controlled object, and (ii) the point of actuation, where the cyber-system sets the state of controlled variables in actuators that act in the physical world in order to influence the future physical behavior of the controlled object.

In most cases, the cyber-physical control system is realized by a distributed computer system consisting of node-computers with sensors, node-computers that execute control algorithms, and node-computers with actuators. The node-computers exchange messages using a real-time communication system. In a time-triggered (TT) control system, where a global notion of time is available at all node-computers, it is assumed that the periodic sampling instants, the periodic actuation instants and the periodic instants when messages are sent and received by the TT communication system are specified *a priori* on the global time-line. In most cases, the temporal distance, i.e., the

© Springer International Publishing AG, part of Springer Nature 2018
M. Lohstroh et al. (Eds.): Lee Festschrift, LNCS 10760, pp. 326–335, 2018.
https://doi.org/10.1007/978-3-319-95246-8_19

duration, between two successive sampling and two successive actuation points (also called the sampling time) is assumed to be constant in a given mode of operation.

We call the sequence of all computational and communication actions between a sampling point and the corresponding actuation point a *frame*. In a frame, RT (real-time)-transactions [1, p. 24] have to be executed. The constant duration between the end points of a RT transaction (i.e. the sampling instant and the actuation instant) is called the *response time* of a RT-transaction.

In a distributed real-time system, a RT-transaction consists of a sequence of computational actions and communication actions. The *a priori* specification of the behavior of the time-triggered communication system provides the start instant and the termination instant for every communication action. It follows that a computational action within a node computer must deliver a result within an *a priori* specified global time interval, the *time-slot* for a TT computation action. It is a challenge in the design of a hard real-time system to develop algorithms that meet this temporal requirement. These algorithms must compute the best answers they can provide in the restricted time that is available.

There are two possible approaches to tackle this challenge: the use of *WCET (worst-case-execution-time) algorithms* or the use of *any-time algorithms*.

Many algorithms are required to run to completion before they deliver a useful result. We call these algorithms *WCET* (worst case execution time) *algorithms*. In the WCET approach algorithms are developed where the worst-case execution time (WCET) bound for the algorithm execution on the given hardware base can be established *a priori* (at design time) for all data points of the input domain. This produces a conservative design, because the WCET approach has to fight two enemies, an enemy from below and an enemy from above. The enemy from below refers to temporal indeterminism that is inherent in modern hardware architectures [2]. The enemy from above refers to algorithmic issues, e.g., the complexity of a computationally expensive algorithm that makes it hard or even impossible to establish a WCET bound for all data points of the given input domain.

In the anytime approach [3], the algorithm must guarantee to provide a *satisficing result* before the deadline and will continually improve this result until the deadline is reached. A result is a *satisficing result* [4] if it is *adequate* (but not necessarily optimal) in the particular situation and meets all safety assertions. An anytime algorithm consists of a *core segment* followed by an *enhancing segment*. The execution of the core segment is guaranteed to provide a first *satisficing* result quickly. Continuous improvements of the satisficing result are provided by the repeated execution of the enhancing segment until the deadline is reached.

In the anytime approach, a WCET bound for the core segment must be established. As a consequence, the core segment must deploy algorithms that are amenable to WCET analysis [5]. The size of the time-interval between the average execution time of the core segment and the WCET of the core segment is used to improve the quality of the result. The WCET bound for the core segment can be derived either from an analytical analysis of the core-segment code [2] of the algorithm or from experimental observations of the execution times of the algorithm in the given application context (or from both). In a safety critical system a violation of this WCET bound is tantamount to a serious failure that must be masked by a redundant mechanism.

In real-time control systems, there is a tradeoff between the *precision of an algorithm* and the *response time (latency) of the control system*. It is the purpose of this paper to present a method for the design of the durations of the time-slots for any-time algorithms in distributed time-triggered real-time control systems that optimizes this tradeoff. The paper starts with a short introduction of time-triggered control systems and model-based control in Sects. 2 and 3. In Sect. 4, we discuss anytime algorithms and introduce the concept of the *precision profile* of an anytime algorithm. Section 5 presents a method for finding the optimal duration of the time-slots in a time-triggered control system. The paper closes with a conclusion in Sect. 6.

2 Time-Triggered Systems

2.1 Basic Concepts

A computer system is *time-triggered (TT)* if the periodic signals for starting a computational action or a communication action are derived from the progression of the global physical time. TT systems require the availability of a—preferably fault-tolerant—global time base of specified precision. In a frame-based sampled system, the duration of the RT transactions corresponds to the duration of a frame. An *a priori* supplied *time schedule* that is contained in the TT operating system of every node specifies at which periodically recurring instants within a frame the trigger signals for the start of communication and computational actions within a RT transaction have to be generated by the operating system of the node.

In a TT communication system, data is exchanged according to *state semantics* (i.e., similar to the semantics of a variable in a programming language). In *state semantics* outgoing data is not consumed on reading and a new version of incoming data overwrites the old version. Since there is no message queue if the communication is based on *state semantics*, the duration of a TT communication action is constant and known *a priori*. Examples for TT communication protocols are the time-triggered protocol (TTP) or TTEthernet [1, p. 183].

The advantages of TT real-time systems are the guaranteed response time of all real-time transactions and the *support of composition* in multi-criticality systems. In a TT system, any indirect temporal interference of functionally independent RT tasks of a multi-criticality system is *avoided by design*. The indirect temporal interference between RT tasks in a *priority driven event triggered system* has a significant impact on the performance of all but the highest priority task and thus prevents the smooth temporal composition of the tasks.

The *time-schedule* of a TT system must specify the durations of the time-slots for the communication and computational actions. If the size of the messages and the bandwidth of the communication system are known, it is straightforward to calculate the length of the time slot for a communication action. The determination of the length of the time slot for the computational actions is more involved and is discussed in this paper.

2.2   An Example

Consider the example of a driver assistance system depicted in Fig. 1. At a periodic instant derived from the progression of the global time (the start of a new frame), the *laser node*, the *camera node* and the *radar node* observe the environment simultaneously. After preprocessing of the acquired raw data in the sensor nodes, the preprocessed data is sent to a *sensor fusion and trajectory-planning* node to calculate setpoints for the *engine controller*, the *steering controller* and the *brake controller* in order that the planned trajectory is carried out in the near future. A monitor node accepts the acquired data and the proposed trajectory to check whether all safety assertions are satisfied. The time-triggered temporal control structure of this data flow graph is developed at design time and is encoded in the time-schedule that is stored in the operating system of every node of this TT distributed system.

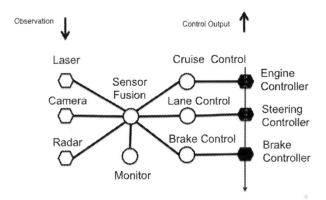

Fig. 1. Example of a driver assistance system

The *accuracy* of the scene analysis of a vision system depends on the available time budget for processing the raw data [6]. The longer the time-slots allocated to the computational actions in the three sensor nodes, the better the *analysis accuracy*. However, in a highly dynamic environment, such as in this example of a driver assistance system, a long duration of the time-slots reduces the accuracy of the model predictions, since the world may have changed since the last sampling point. These conflicting requirements on the length of the time slot are investigated in the following section.

3   Model-Based Control

3.1   Basic Concepts

A *control system* consists of a *controlled object* (often called the *plant*) and a *controller* that observes the controlled object at the beginning of every periodic frame and outputs *controller outputs* (e.g., the set points for the actuators) to the controlled objects at the end of a frame. In a *model-based control system* (MBC), the controller contains an approximate model of the behavior of the controlled object in its open environment. This model is used for calculating the *controller outputs* during each frame.

The state-space of the model in the controller encompasses four types of variables

- *Independent variables of the control system that are set by the operator.* The values of these variables specify the objectives and constraints of the control system and are thus determined by an authority outside the control system.
- *Independent variables of the controlled object that are set by the controller* (i.e. the *controller outputs* or setpoints for the actuators). The model in the controller calculates new values of these variables during each frame.
- *Observable state variables*—observable variables denoting the state of the controlled object and the state of the environment at the instant of observation. i.e. the start of a frame.
- *Hidden state variables* that are part of the model in the controller. The hidden state variables are of eminent importance, since they carry the knowledge acquired in one frame to the following frame.

At the instant *beginning of a frame*, let us say *frame$_k$*, of a periodic frame-based control system, the *observable state variables* are observed by the controller. During a frame, new values for the *independent variables of the controlled object* (the *setpoints*) and *predicted (anticipated) values* of the observable and the hidden state variables are calculated by the model in the controller for the instant *end of frame$_k$* (that is also the *beginning of frame$_{k+1}$*). The difference between the *predicted value* of an *observable state variable* at the *end of frame$_k$* and the *observed value* of this *variable* at the *end of frame$_k$*, the *model error*, is an important input to the model for the calculations of the controller outputs in the following frame. After every frame, the prediction horizon is shifted one frame further into the future. For this reason model-based control is sometimes called *receding horizon control*.

3.2   An Example

The following simple example of an *open system*, the *temperature control* of the liquid in a reservoir for water purification, is introduced in order to clarify the preceding concepts. The temperature of the liquid in the reservoir can be raised by setting the actuator valve that controls the flow of hot water through a pipe system that is contained in the reservoir. *Environmental dynamics*, e.g., *wind* or *rain*, lower the temperature of the liquid. It is the objective of the control system to keep the *variable temperature* of the liquid in the reservoir at a preset value.

In the model of this control system, the single *physical quantity temperature of the liquid* is thus represented by three different variables:

ts_k: the desired (but in some operational situations not achievable) value of the *independent variable temperature* submitted by the operator for the instant *beginning of frame k*.

to_k: the value of the variable temperature observed at the instant *beginning of frame k*.

tp_k: the anticipated value of the controlled variable temperature predicted by the model for the instant *beginning of frame k* (which is also the *end of frame k−1*).

We call the difference

$$me_k = /tp_k - to_k/$$

the *model error me_k* at the instant *beginning of frame k*.

3.3   Model Error

The *model error* is caused by two different phenomena:

(i)   Reality has *changed* since the last instant of observation. The impact of unidentified or unanticipated processes in the environment (*environmental dynamics*) of an open system increases with the length of a frame (and the timeslots allocated to a computational action).

(ii) Imperfections of the model: The model is not a *true* image for the behavior of reality. For example, nonlinearities that exist in reality have not been properly modeled.

The predictive power of the model can be improved if sensors for the observation of additional state variables in the environment are installed. If, in the above example, a temperature sensor for the outside air and a rain-sensor are provided, some effects of the *environmental dynamics* can be considered in the model. If the model were *perfect* in anticipating the future behavior of the controlled object—i.e. a true image of the behavior of the controlled object in the given open environment—then the *model error* would disappear. However, a perfect model of an open system is unattainable [7, 8].

The model error will increase if we move further away from the instant where the *observable state variables* of the system have been observed. Figure 2 depicts a qualitative *model error profile*, i.e. the dependence of the standard deviation of the model error as a function of the duration of a frame.

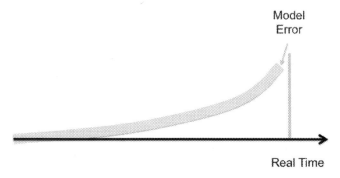

Fig. 2. *Model error profile* as a function of frame duration.

4   Anytime Algorithms

4.1   Basic Concepts

The execution time slot given to a WCET algorithm must be large enough to allow the algorithm to run to completion for all data points of its input domain on the available hardware base, otherwise a *timing error* may occur occasionally. Since, in most cases, the (data dependent) difference between the WCET and the average execution time is considerable [2], the WCET approach results in a conservative design with long frame durations. During the long frame duration, the size of the *model error* can become significant.

In 1991 Liu et al. [9] introduced the concept of *imprecise computations* in real-time systems in order to avoid the excessive frame durations required until a precise (final) result of a WCET algorithm is available. In some real-time scenarios it is preferable to provide algorithms that generate an *imprecise result* that is available at an earlier instant.

An *anytime algorithm* is an algorithm that returns an imprecise, but still useful result whenever it is interrupted after a mandatory minimal duration. The precision of the result depends on the amount of computation the algorithm is able to perform in the available time-slot until interruption. Dean and Boddy [10] introduced the term *anytime algorithm* in 1988 in the context of their work on time-dependent planning in the area of Artificial Intelligence.

A good example for an anytime algorithm is Newton's method for finding successively better approximations for the roots of an equation. Anytime algorithms are widely used in search problems or scene analysis problems where the determination of a WCET is infeasible.

There have been a number of proposals [11–14] to deploy anytime algorithms instead of WCET algorithms in the domain of real-time control. Proposals for the design of anytime algorithms in control systems can be found in this literature.

4.2   Precision Profile

Characteristic for an anytime algorithm is the *precision error* of the result at the instant of interruption. In a simple system the *precise result* is the single numerical value that is provided if the algorithm runs to completion. The *precision error* (PE) is then the difference between the result provided at the instant of interruption and the precise result. The *precision profile* of an anytime algorithm depicts the dependence of the precision error on the provided computational resources. In most cases, the precision error is significantly reduced in the first few iterations of an anytime algorithm.

In a complex system, where the result is a data structure comprising many variables, the concept of *precision error* is more involved. It requires a careful analysis of the utility of the result in the context of the given application to arrive at a reasonable definition of the *precision error*.

The performance of the available computer hardware determines the mapping of the computational resources to the domain of real-time. If the performance of the hardware platform for the execution of the anytime algorithms is known, then the precision profile can be presented as a function of real-time, as shown in Fig. 3.

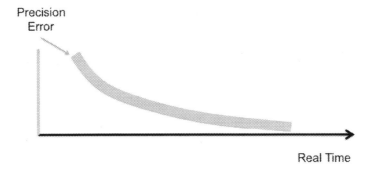

Fig. 3. *Precision profile* of an anytime algorithm as a function of slot duration for a computational action.

5 Design Method

In this final Section we propose a method for the determination of the duration of the time slot for a computational action in a time-triggered control system.

5.1 Precision Profile and Model Error Profile

After an anytime algorithm for a control system has been developed, the first step is concerned with the determination of the *precision profile* of the anytime algorithm on the provided execution platform and the *error profile* of the model in the given application context. These profiles must be established experimentally by executing the algorithm repeatedly with different input data for different slot durations.

At the beginning of each slot, the values of all input-data elements of the model must be collected and stored by the monitor system of Fig. 1 for later *off-line* analysis. Furthermore, the monitor system collects the predicted and the observed values of the model variables at the end of each slot.

The collected data is then analyzed *off-line* as follows: The collected input data set of the model at the beginning of a slot is used to calculate *off-line* (without real-time constraints) the *precise result* of the anytime algorithm for the prediction of the values of the model variables. The *precise result* is a result where the anytime algorithm has run to completion or an *a priori* specified small precision bound of the result has been verified.

The difference between this *precise result* of the anytime algorithm and the result delivered by the anytime algorithm at the point of interruption (at the end of the given slot) yields to the *precision error* of the anytime algorithm for this input data set.

The difference between this *precise result* for the predicted value of a variable at the end of a slot and the *observed value* of this variable at the end of a slot yields the *model error*. By probing a large number of points of the input domain of the algorithm in the given application a *slot error set* of the *precision error* and *model error* can be experimentally established for the given slot duration.

334   H. Kopetz

This procedure is repeated for different slot durations in order to determine the *slot error sets* for a plurality of slot durations. We call the totality of all slot error sets *the precision error set* of the anytime algorithm in the given application context.

5.2   Optimal Slot Duration

If we extend the slot duration, on the one side, the precision error is expected to be reduced, but, on the other side, the model error is expected to be increased. There must be an optimal slot duration that minimizes the *total error*, i.e. the sum of the *precision error* of the anytime algorithm and the *model error* in the given application context. To find the *optimal slot duration* where the total error is minimized we analyze the *precision error set* by statistical techniques.

In a simple control system, such as the example of the water purification system of Sect. 3.2, the application of standard statistical techniques may suffice for the analysis of the experimentally collected *precision error set*. If the *standard deviation* σ of the *precision error* of an anytime algorithm follows the form

$$\sigma(t) = A \exp(-Bt)$$

where t represents the slot duration of the enhancing segment of the anytime algorithm, then the parameters A and B can be chosen to find the best fit to the experimental data.

In a complex control system, such as the driver assistance system of Fig. 1, at first an application specific measure for the control quality of a trajectory has to be established. This measure will be a function of a number of application specific parameters, such as safe distance from obstacles, speed of traversal, etc., that characterize the optimal trajectory. The analysis of the *precision error set* will require advanced statistical data analysis techniques that take account of all these parameters in order to find the optimal slot duration (Fig. 4).

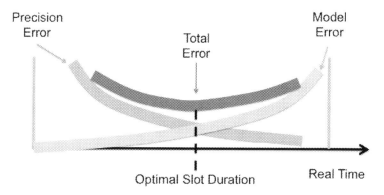

Fig. 4. Optimal slot duration

6   Conclusion

In a time-triggered control system the durations of the time-slots for the computational actions must be specified *a priori*. There are two contradicting requirements that must be considered when devising these durations: on the one side, the durations should be small in order to minimize the *model error*, on the other side, the duration should be large enough in order that a *satisficing result* can be provided for all data points of the input domain. The concept of an anytime algorithm, that is guaranteed to provide a first satisficing result for all data points of the input domain and improves this result iteratively until the deadline arrives is ideally suited for the application in time-triggered control systems. This paper presented a method for the selection of the slot durations in time-triggered control systems.

References

1. Kopetz, H.: Real-Time Systems—Design Principles for Distributed Embedded Applications. Springer, Heidelberg (2011). https://doi.org/10.1007/978-1-4419-8237-7
2. Wilhelm, R., et al.: The worst-case execution time problem—on overview of methods and a survey of tools. ACM Trans. Embed. Comput. Syst. (TECS) **7**(3), 36 (2008)
3. Zilberstein, S.: Using anytime algorithms in intelligent systems. AI Mag. **7**(3), 73–83 (1996)
4. Simon, H.A.: The architecture of complexity. Proc. Am. Philos. Soc. **106**(6), 467–482 (1962)
5. Puschner, P., Burns, A.: Writing temporally predictable code. In: Proceedings of the Workshop on Object Oriented Dependable Real-Time Systems (WORDS 2002), pp. 85–91. IEEE Press (2002)
6. Liu, B., He, X.: Learning dynamic hierarchical models for anytime scene labeling. In: Leibe, B., Matas, J., Sebe, N., Welling, M. (eds.) ECCV 2016. LNCS, vol. 9910, pp. 650–666. Springer, Cham (2016). https://doi.org/10.1007/978-3-319-46466-4_39
7. Rosen, R.: Anticipatory Systems, pp. 313–370. Springer, Heidelberg (2012). https://doi.org/10.1007/978-1-4614-1269-4
8. Lee, E.: Fundamental limits of cyber-physical systems modeling. ACM Trans. Cyber-Phys. Syst. **1**(1), 3 (2016)
9. Liu, J., et al.: Algorithms for scheduling imprecise computations. In: van Tilborg, A.M., Koob, G.M. (eds.) Foundations of Real-Time Computing. Scheduling and Resource Managemen, pp. 203–249. Springer, Heidelberg (1991). https://doi.org/10.1007/978-1-4615-3956-8_8
10. Dean, T., Boddy, M.: An analysis of time-dependent planning. Proc. AAAI **88**, 49–54 (1988)
11. Bhattacharaya, R., et al.: Anytime control algorithm: model reduction approach. J. Guidance Control Dyn. **27**(5), 767–776 (2005)
12. Mangraham, R., et al.: Anytime algorithms for GPU architectures. In: Proceedings of RTSS 2011, pp. 47–56. IEEE Press (2011)
13. Pant, Y.V., et al.: Co-design of anytime computation and robust control. In: Proceedings of RTSS 2015, pp. 43–52. IEEE Press (2015)
14. Jha, D.K., et al.: Data-driven anytime algorithms for motion planning with safety guarantees. In: Proceedings of the 2016 American Control Conference (ACC), pp. 5716–5721. IEEE Press (2016)

Autonomous Retailing: A Frontier for Cyber-Physical-Human Systems

Jie Liu[✉]

Microsoft AI and Research, One Microsoft Way, Redmond, WA 98052, USA
jie.liu@microsoft.com

Abstract. Retail is one of the largest economic sectors, accounting for almost \$5 trillion in sales in the US alone. With the proliferation of e-commerce, mobile devices, and digitally engaging shopping journeys, retail is going through profound transformations that will change everyone's life. The future of retail will inevitably integrate online and in-store shopping, and promises to enhance customers' shopping experience. Physical stores, which still account for 85% of retail sales, and 95% of grocery sales, must be repositioned to coexist with online and mobile shopping channels.

Autonomous retailing is a retail process where a physical store is aware of all elements involved—products, people, and activities—without explicit help from human workers. Autonomous stores allow shoppers to pick up products and walk out of the store, without going through a checkout lane. Although the concept is more than a decade old, Amazon Go, a recent effort to realize frictionless checkout, brings it a huge step closer to reality. Autonomous stores are an example of cyber-physical-human systems that incorporate advanced artificial intelligence (AI) through abound embedded sensors and computation. Natural human activities bring significant challenges to system provisioning, sensing, and inference, but also provide input for the system to learn from and adapt to. In this article, we discuss the design space and technical challenges of autonomous retailing and motive it as a frontier of cyber-physical-human system research.

1 Introduction

In 1916, Piggly Wiggly opened the first self-serving supermarket in Memphis, TN. Shoppers no longer needed to ask store workers behind the counters to retrieve every product for purchasing. Friction in the shopping process, caused by factors such as delays and psychological barriers due to the inability to examine and compare products, were greatly reduced. Merchants could offer greater product selection and manage larger store footprints with less workers. In the next 100 years, various technologies, such as shopping carts, Universal Product Code (UPC) bar codes, credit cards, self-checkout counters, and mobile payment, were invented and adopted to further reduce shopping friction and store efficiency. But, the final bottleneck of checking out at the end of shopping trips remained.

© Springer International Publishing AG, part of Springer Nature 2018
M. Lohstroh et al. (Eds.): Lee Festschrift, LNCS 10760, pp. 336–350, 2018.
https://doi.org/10.1007/978-3-319-95246-8_20

In 2018, Amazon opened its Amazon Go store in Seattle WA. In Amazon Go, all activities of shoppers are monitored by the store. Whenever a product is picked up from the shelf, the store knows what exactly it is and who picks it, a change of ownership is logged right away. At the end of the trip, no store worker tallies the amount or checks the basket. Shoppers simply walk out of the store with a mobile payment confirmation on the phone. "No lines, no checkout..."

We call this shopping experience where sales no longer require the involvement of sales staff *Autonomous Retailing*. Autonomous retailing is not a new concept. For example, Metro AG tested a RFID-enabled autonomous checkout store in 2003 [16]. IBM illustrated a similar experience in a RFID commercial in 2006. However, Amazon Go is the first known attempt to bring the concept to reality at scale. Since then, several retailers and technology providers, such as BingoBox,[1] Alibaba Tao Cafe,[2] and Standard Cognition,[3] have demonstrated similar proofs of concept. As e-commerce continues to disrupt brick-and-mortar stores with convenience, choice, and savings, the latter must reinvent themselves through digital transformations. In other words, a brick-and-mortar store must focus on reducing friction and offer a superb experience to its shoppers, through sensing, intelligence, and actuation. Future stores will become cyber-physical environments for human users.

Due to physical constraints and human behavior dynamics, autonomous stores must employ a large number of sensing and processing units. It faces all challenges that are intrinsic to TerraSwarm-like systems [2]. Furthermore, the level of correctness required by retail transactions, together with the possibilities of human exploitation of potential vulnerabilities, make them a pinnacle of Cyber-Physical-Human system ambitions, as much as autonomous vehicles.

In this article, we discuss autonomous retailing from shopper and technology perspectives, such as different levels of autonomy, core design space, and critical technology enablers. Although full autonomy is still hard to achieve at scale with its current cost structure, we believe subsets of those technologies can already help brick-and-mortar retailers reduce operation cost and improve shopper experiences.

2   Levels of Autonomy

Retailing is about a single relationship change, which we call *Transfer Of Ownership* (TrOO) – the ownership of a product changing from the store to a shopper and, occasionally, in the reverse order, if the shopper changes her mind. Currently, TrOO only happens at the checkout counter, assisted by store workers. This creates the main bottleneck in physical shopping, and is the top complaint in shopping experience surveys.

---

[1] "In China, Amazon's 'store of the future' is already open," (https://www.techinasia.com/china-version-amazon-go-bingobox-funding).

[2] "Alibaba's self-service Tao Cafe takes e-shopping offline," (http://news.xinhuanet.com/english/2017-07/11/c_136434967.htm).

[3] https://www.standardcognition.com/.

There are many ways to mitigate and ultimately remove this bottleneck, and give shoppers increasing freedom in the stores. Just like self-driving cars, autonomous retailing is not an "all-or-nothing" concept. Depending on how much cognitive load, deliberate shopper involvements and shopper-staff interaction take place, there is a spectrum of experiences and solutions. We classify them into six *Levels of Autonomy*, as shown in Table 1.

L0 [Monitored Autonomy]: Self-checkout stations are common in stores today. They facilitate the same scan and pay process, conducted by store workers in the past, but now by shoppers themselves. Typically, there is still a store worker that oversees 4 to 6 self-checkout stations to make sure all items are scanned, to check for age-limited items, and to provide any necessary help. During busy times, shoppers still need to wait in lines for an available station, especially since shoppers are much less efficient at using these stations than store workers using regular checkout machines are.

L1 [Deliberate Autonomy]: Instead of lining up at a checkout station at the end of a trip, shoppers scan products in aisles while purchase decisions are made. This is sometimes called *scan and go*. In typical cases, the scanner can be a dedicated store device or consumers' own mobile phones. Whether a shopper indeed scanned every purchased product is *not* known automatically. At the end of the trip, store workers will by default check baskets before shoppers leave the store to ensure correctness. This checking can be a full audit or on a random subset of the products. The store environment by itself, cannot differentiate who scanned every product and who, intentionally or unintentionally, forgot some.

Although bar code scanning is the predominate form in scan-and-go implementation today, the notion of scanning can be generalized to include any deliberate showing of a product to a device. Products can be identified, through optical tags, such as bar code, QR code, or invisible watermarks (DW Code) [8], through RF tags such as RFID or NFC, or directly through the shape and look of the packaging by computer vision.

L2 [Assisted Autonomy]: At this level, the store can recognize certain human activities automatically. Although shoppers still need to scan every product they wish to purchase, the store can detect unscanned items in shopping baskets and remind shoppers accordingly. At the end of a trip, if the store believes that all products have been scanned properly, the shopper can walk out without being checked. Otherwise, the shopper will be routed to a store worker. With the reminders assisted by the stores, the cognitive load of remembering to scan every product is reduced.

L3 [Partial Autonomy]: When the store gets smarter, it can recognize and track certain products and their belongings throughout the store. Shoppers' deliberation of showing products to devices is reduced. As long as a shopper only visits certain part of the store, or uses certain shopping devices (like smart shopping carts), no worker auditing is necessary at the exit.

L4 [Conditional Autonomy]: At this level, the shopping and checkout processes are fully automated, as long as shoppers do not intentionally cheat the

Table 1. Levels of autonomous retailing

Level	Description	TrOO	Characteristics
L0	Monitored Autonomy	Scanning under worker monitoring	Current self-checkout requires shoppers to go to the checkout counters and scan each product under the monitoring of store workers
L1	Deliberate Autonomy	Unmonitored, deliberate scanning	Shoppers are equipped with scanning devices, such as hand-held bar code scanners or consumer phones, and are expected to deliberately scan each product before putting them into baskets. Their baskets are checked before leaving the store for confirmation
L2	Assisted Autonomy	Getting reminded if not scanned	While scanning every product is still required for correct checkout, the store system assists the shoppers by reminding them if any product is not scanned
L3	Partial Autonomy	Certain TrOO automated	The store is partially equipped with technology capable of recognizing products automatically without shoppers having to manually scan them. As long as shoppers only pick up items from a particular subset of products and/or from particular areas within the store, the checkout is automatic without auditing
L4	Conditional Autonomy	All TrOO automated under conditions	Shoppers enjoy autonomous checkout in ordinary situations where shoppers do not intentionally trick or cheat the system. Examples of conditions: limitations on the number of concurrent shoppers, on product selections or packaging, etcetera
L5	Full Autonomy	All TrOO automated always	The store charges shoppers correctly under all conditions, even when shoppers conduct malicious exploitations

system. The correctness of checkout may still depend on whether or not shoppers are honest, and the automated checkout process may impose limitations on the range of available products. No stop-and-check at the exit by store workers is necessary in most cases. Shopping will feel like picking up items from one's own pantry room.

L5 [Full Autonomy]: This is the ultimate autonomous retail capability where shop lifting is virtually impossible. All ownership changes are understood and reflected in the transactions.

Remarks:

- This classification is abstract by design, irrespective of implementation details. For example, difficulties vary greatly depending on whether products are tagged with unique identifiers or whether users are assisted with additional devices.
- Although it may be easiest to think in terms of a grocery store example with shelved products, shopping carts, and baskets, the same key elements are present in most types of open retail spaces.
- Levels of autonomy tie closely to the type of products that the store sells. For example, computer vision is not good at differentiating different instances of clothes with high accuracy yet. Achieving L3 and above at apparel stores can be very different from how this may be achieved at convenience stores.
- There are two major quantum leaps in this classification. One is to reduce and remove product scanning, between L2 and L3; and the other is to increase the tolerance of malicious behavior, between L4 and L5. Amazon Go appears to be at L4 and is approaching L5, considering its limited store size and product selection.
- Scanning serves two purposes: one is to identify the product, and the other is to associate a product instance with the customer who intends to buy it. By eliminating the scanning step, the store must identify and track shoppers during their entire visit, and any shopping activity that is related to the handling of products must be understood.

3   Cyber-Physical Intelligence

Autonomous retailing at L2 and beyond are clearly cyber-physical environments that need sophisticated sensing and processing capabilities to function correctly. In this section, we discuss the key tasks that must be performed by autonomous stores, and the technologies that enable them. We use grocery shopping as an example scenario throughout, but the tasks and technologies apply to other types of retailing as well.

Retailing is concerned with three key pieces of information, as shown in Fig. 1: the identity of a shopper (and ultimately her payment account), the type or model of a product (thus its price), and the possession/ownership relationship between customer and product. Where and how these three pieces of information are established, and how accurate they are, reflect the intelligence level of the store and shoppers' experience in it.

Recent advances in autonomous retailing are, to a great extent, empowered by advances in deep learning [5] and computer vision. It is possible for deep neural-networks (DNN) to classify and recognize faces, objects, and human activities at high accuracy and speed [3,10]. However, computer vision has its limitations in the real world, due to occlusion, variability in lighting conditions, sizes and

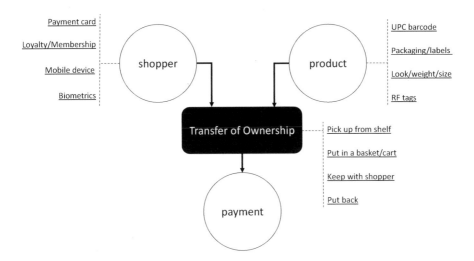

Fig. 1. Key entities and relationship in the retail process.

forms of objects, and the complexity of sensing and processing. These challenges put high demands on deployment density, computing power, and network performance, and leave many corner cases unsolved.

3.1   Core Sensing and Inference Requirements

Shopper Identification. A shopper's identity is typically established through linkage with an identifier in the digital domain, such as a credit card number, a loyalty ID, or a GUID in a mobile phone app. Thus identifying shoppers may require them to present, and sometimes to prove the legitimacy of, their digital representation.

Biometric identification methods, such as face, iris, and fingerprint recognition, are becoming mature technologies thanks to advances in deep learning. There are two ways of using biometric identification in autonomous retailing:

- Verification. The verification problem [4] is to test if a biometric measurement is indeed from a given customer. The algorithm only gives yes-no answers with an associated confidence level. Biometric verification is a mature technology. It is widely used in device authentication such as Touch ID on iOS devices and Windows Hello on PCs.
- Recognition. The recognition problem is to identify a person within a potential set of candidates, or return "unrecognized" if the person is not in the set. With a dataset smaller than a few thousand, the recognition correctness, measured by the true identity being within a top 5 returned results, is beyond 99%. The recognition problem is considerably harder and time consuming than the verification problem, especially with large datasets.

Collecting and managing biometrics at the scale of potential customers creates a legal and operational burden for retailers. One simplification is to only identify in-store shoppers by assigning them unique but anonymous IDs when they enter the store, and only keep the ID persistent through the trip. This requires the recognition system to quickly enroll new faces and retrain the recognizer in real time.

Product Recognition. At L3+, an intelligent store must recognize some to all products in it to facilitate transactions. Although UPC bar codes uniquely represent a product, they cannot be reliably read without deliberate scanning.

Recently, computer vision technologies made huge advances in image recognition [7,9]. However, to obtain transaction-level accuracy on the handling of arbitrary products poses many challenges, such as (1) near-identical packaging with only textual differences; (2) very small objects that can easily be occluded by hands or other objects; (3) very large objects that can only be partially captured by a camera; (4) unpackaged goods such as product, fruits, and meat where certain types are almost identical by look, and (5) bulk items.

In addition, as stores introduce new or seasonal products, product recognition models must be updated, and sometimes completely re-trained.

Like people recognition, identifying products from a large set of candidates is less accurate and slower than from a small set of candidates. Product layout, shopper location, and even past purchases can be used to reduce the search space and improve accuracy.

Tagging is a way to compensate the inaccuracy of product recognition from computer vision alone. Retail industry has explored various tagging technologies from RF to invisible patterns:

- **UHF RFID.** Ultra High Frequency RFID (UHF RFID) operates in the 860 MHz to 960 MHz band. UHF RFID uses RF waves to communicate between the RFID reader and tags. They have been used extensively in retail environments and warehouses. While the RF waves have a relatively large range (several meters), the UHF RFID systems have fundamental weaknesses in product tracking. First, RF signal propagation is heavily affected by environmental factors such as the presence of human bodies, water, and metal. Secondly, it is hard to confine RF signals to a well-defined space. The most successful use case of RFID is in apparel retail stores and pallet-level inventory control. These products have RF-friendly-built materials that are ill-suited for other recognition methods.
- **HF RFID (NFC).** High Frequency RF ID (HF RFID) operates at 13.56 MHz and uses inductive coupling (magnetic field) to communicate between readers and tags. Inductive-coupling-based communication has several important features when used for product tracking. The HF RFID detection range is relatively short (a few inches) and is well defined. This short range enables accurate tracking of the product locations. In addition, magnetic fields can easily penetrate different materials such as the human body,

liquid, and even some types of metal. This makes product tracking immune against environmental changes, packaging, and the product itself.
- **DW Codes.** Digital Watermark (DW) Codes [8] are image-based encodings that are invisible to the human eye, yet can be detected and interpreted by post processing of images captured with a camera. They are commercialized by Digimarc Inc., and has recently become a GS1 standard[4] for product identification, just like UPC bar codes. Under good lighting conditions and with sufficient image resolution, they can be decoded like bar codes. Since they are invisible to the human eye, they can be replicated throughout product packaging for easy identification. The standardization of DW Codes happened only recently, and their adoption by the product manufacturers has been relatively slow. Once they are proven to substantially reduce the cost of autonomous retailing, retailers may have more incentive to adopt them.

It is worth pointing out that recognizing products, tagged or not, is much easier when the products are displayed on shelves or racks, rather than being handled by a person. The human body—hands in particular—are likely to obstruct light and RF propagation.

Product Ownership. Beyond identifying shoppers and products, the store must also establish relationships between them. Due to the elimination of the checkout process at the end of a shopping trip, the semantics of TrOO may be different in an autonomous store than in a regular store. In most stores today, a shopper does not *own* a product, until she checks out at the exit, since there is simply no visibility into how the product is handled before the shopper checks out.

In L3+ autonomous retailing, when product scanning is removed from shopping process, the TrOO can not be viewed as an atomic action any more. It is better understood as an transaction process. When the product is picked up from the shelf by a shopper, a transaction concerning that particular product is initiated. It may take multiple cameras and sensors (spread across multiple locations) a period of time to confirm which product it is. In that process, if the shopper changes her mind and puts the product back, then the associated transaction is canceled. When, at the end of the trip, the shopper decides to pay for all products, all transactions in the trip are committed.

With the transactional model in mind, key activities to be sensed and inferred in the store are product pickups and returns. One possible way is to track shoppers' hands and their movements. Alternatively, if we can continuously track the accurate location of each person and each product, and infer that certain products consistently move with a certain person until she exits, we can infer that the products are bought by that person.

Neither precise hand motion tracking and accurate location tracking is easy in real retail environment without very dense sensor instrumentation. TrOO represents the hardest technical problem in this cyber-physical environment.

---

[4] GS1 is the standard body for managing retail bar codes. https://www.gs1.org/.

3.2   Critical Spots and Moments

There are a few particular locations in the store where, and moments in the shopping process during which, the state of transactions can change. The instrumentation in these spots and the timing of information extraction and processing is worth careful examination. These design choices also induce the following possible subsystems in autonomous stores.

– Store entrance. This is the spot to best identify shoppers and assign them an ID as they walk into the store. Shoppers may also be most open to engagement if there is any need for setting up, for example, by launching a store app, confirming loyalty/club membership, or possibly choosing a preferred payment method for this shopping session. One can employ biometric sensing or deliberate shopper log in (e.g., using a mobile app) at the entrance to establish the identity of the shopper.
– Shelf edge. Most transaction states change at the shelf edge when shoppers pick up products, or put products back on the shelves. Crowed shelf edges are challenging to the task of assigning ownership; a customer may reach in front of another to pick up a product. Similarly, counting exactly how many products are picked up at one time is difficult to achieve using computer vision alone. One way to complement cameras and computer vision at shelf edges is to incorporate weight sensors, which can tell if, and how many, items are removed from or added to the shelf.
– Shopping carts. For stores that provide them, shopping carts are natural association points between shoppers and their potential purchases. Socially, it is widely accepted that products in a shopping cart belong to the shopper who uses it. If a shopping cart can register every product that is put in or removed from it, it is an ideal place for L3+ autonomy.
– Store exit. This is the spot that all transactions are closed and payments are processed. When the system has any unresolved uncertainty, it is also the last chance for a store worker to help or to intervene.

4   Human Factors

An autonomous store is not just a physical environment in isolation. Both store workers and shoppers add significant complexity and are a source of dynamism. Human activities are the most complex to recognize, even in this constrained context. But both shopper activities and worker assistance also let the store system to continuously learn and improve its intelligence levels.

4.1   Human Challenges

The thesis of autonomous retailing is to minimize shopping friction. However, human shoppers themselves can be a source of friction when no single, automated process can cover all corner cases.

Signal Obstruction. Human bodies are terrible media for most sensing signals, such as RF, sound, and light. They can wear, carry, or hold additional objects, and form groups to block signals from arbitrary angles. As they move around in the space, it is hard to provision a sensing system that can handle all possible corner cases. The system must be able to tolerate and track uncertainty over space and time and resolve them opportunistically or intentionally later.

Groups and Accounts. In most retail environments, it is fairly common for a family to shop together. Members of a group may part ways within the store and reconvene later, carrying different items. In this scenario, not all persons, especially kids, are expected or able to pay. So the group may use a single payment account. However, checking whether everyone entering the store has payment authority, or people who entered separately belong to the same group, brings friction to the shopping experience. Handling group shoppers correctly may require defining an alternative shopper experience, and educating shoppers.

Vulnerability Exploitation. Another unique complexity in retail stores is the potential dishonesty of shoppers. The average shrinkage in the retail industry is about 1.45% [1]. That means 1.45% of transaction amounts are not paid for. However, this statistic is based on stores with human attendance and regular checkout counters. For autonomous stores, if a vulnerability is discovered, for example, certain human gestures are not recognized correctly, then malicious shoppers can actively exploit it for personal gains. For this reason, the barrier from L4 to L5 is very high. There must be a safety net that bounds the store's losses under all corner cases, even unforeseen attacks.

4.2   Human Assistance

While humans bring challenges to autonomous retailing, they also provide hope for progressive store intelligence. Human intelligence compliments store intelligence in several ways. Store workers can catch potential errors the automated system makes, and correct them before a customer checks out. For example, the levels of autonomy directly map to the degree of effort from store workers is necessary to assure checkout correctness, ranging from full auditing (in theory) in L0 to L2, partial auditing in L3 and L4, and, finally, completely human free in L5.

In addition to assistance at the end of a trip, humans can also help complex sensing and inference tasks in the inference loop. For example, in the shelf-edge disambiguation case illustrated in Fig. 2, by looking from the top, it is hard to correctly infer which customer picked up what product from computer vision alone. To involve human assistance, the store system can stream the video to back-end human monitors who can point out which case it is. Machine intelligence can then integrate human input into further inference.

A key requirement for an autonomous store is to understand its own intelligence boundaries. That is, how confident it is about inference results, what it needs to do in order to reduce uncertainty, and what raw data or evidence is relevant to present to human assistants [15].

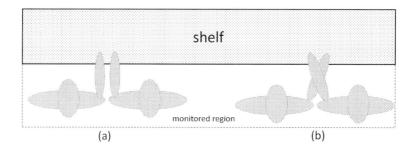

Fig. 2. Ambiguity illustrated by two shoppers at the shelf edge. Without fine grained joint skeletal tracking, it is difficult to tell who picked up what product.

Human labels, through verified checkout, barcode scanning, or behind-the-scene disambiguation, offer ground truths for autonomous stores to learn and improve their intelligence. Modern AI are primarily data driven. Increasing levels of autonomy guide a progressive process of gradually improving a system's capacity to handle complex corner cases.

5   TerraSwarm Thinking

A mass-market retail store can have tens of thousands of types of products, hundreds of thousands of individual items, and hundreds of shoppers at peak time. Shoppers, products, and store layout change over time. Even putting the capital cost consideration aside, such a system must coordinate a large number of distributed sensors with different modalities, orchestrate local and central decisions, and react at different time scales. To some extent, these challenges present themselves in any TerraSwarm-style systems (consider smart grids, smart cities, and health care applications), but the transaction-level correctness required for retailing, the large scale of deployment, and trickiness of tracking the physical maneuvers of humans, make this problem unique.

Let us take the shelf-edge inference pipeline (Fig. 3) as an example. In order to correctly recognize the product, the count, and the picking up/placing back action, one may turn the shelf into a smart shelf with pressure sensors on each layer and with cameras pointing to the shelves to identify and count products. If the products are small and hard to be recognized by computer vision alone, one may add an NFC reader on the shelves and label the bottom of each product with NFC tags. In order to infer product ownership changes (like disambiguating between the two situations illustrated in Fig. 2), one may use depth sensors (like Kinect) to track the arm movements for people within certain range of the shelf. Whenever a product leaves the shelf, the sensor identifies the hand and traces along the arm to the human body. The smart shelf system needs to further interact with a shopper identification system that may use face detection and recognition [10]. Now imagine scaling this design up to over 1000 shelves in a typical grocery store.

From system design point of view, autonomous retailing also offer many research challenges.

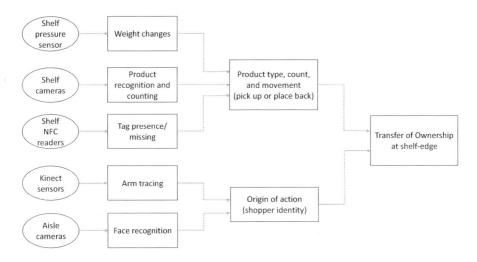

Fig. 3. Example of sensors and fusion at shelf edges for TrOO inference.

5.1   Uncertainty as a First Class Citizen

As discussed in previous sections, natural conditions (e.g. lighting and RF background noise) and human activities make sensor data noisy and unreliable. Machine learning based inference results themselves have to be probability distributions. For example, face recognition algorithms are typically evaluated in terms of the correctness of the top-5 outputs. These uncertainties need to be carried over space and time. Opportunistically or intentionally, additional sensor observations may be used to help resolve uncertainty. The decisions at the end of each shopping trip, which determine the amounts charged to customers, have to be deterministic.

Introducing uncertainty as a first-class citizen requires probabilistic models of computation. For example, a particle filter provides a way to represent and process non-parametric, uncertain information with deterministic calculations. Each data object in the system is represented by a set of particles distributed over possible values. These particles can go through different processing paths based on their values. In any probabilistic model, prior knowledge is key to set up an initial probability distribution. Fortunately, human activity and shopping behaviors are habitual. A person may be left-handed or right-handed, which is a useful prior for tracking product picking. A person may have developed strong preferences for particular categories of groceries [17], which can serve as a useful prior for predicting their shopping paths and product selection.

5.2   Belief Fusion

Several inference tasks in autonomous stores involve large amount of data (like streaming video feeds), large models (like deep neural-nets), and heavy computation. While distilling high-level information from raw sensor data, the system architecture, i.e., where and when inference is done requires careful thinking.

There is a spectrum of architecture designs. At one end of the spectrum, all data are streamed to the cloud for processing. The benefit is that the cloud is not resource constrained, and it now has a global view of measurements. Model and algorithm updates are also easy since nothing needs to be pushed back to the nodes. Indeed, for many low data rate Internet of Things solutions, this is the default cloud + IoT architecture [11,12]. We call this approach *(global) sensor fusion*.

On the other end of the spectrum, each node or subsystem makes a *decision*, which is a deterministic event assertion, locally. For example, a camera will assert the identity of a person in its field of view from face or gait recognition. Upper level aggregation and inference assumes that the assertions are right. We call this approach *Decision Fusion*. The benefit of decision fusion is that the raw data are distilled into high level information as soon as possible, so the data that needs to be communicated among different tiers of the system is minimal. However, by doing so, important hypothesis and probabilities may be discarded too early and cause irreversible wrong decisions.

A trade-off in between is *belief fusion* or belief propagation [14], where uncertainty is carried with data until a decision has to be made. Sensors and intermediate inference may deliver incomplete or inconsistent partial results. Hypotheses are validated over space, time, and sensing modality to refine and revise beliefs. Updates are then diffused to correct other derived hypotheses. This approach is more resource efficient than sensor fusion, and more flexible and reliable than decision fusion. The challenge is to potentially maintain a large set of hypothesis and inference and to expand and trim them as new evidence come in.

Embedded ML. Clearly, the more we can push inference towards the source of the information, the more likely we can create strong beliefs of reality and maintain fewer hypotheses. Modern inference is primarily data driven and uses big models. For example, a generic object recognition network like a 50-layer ResNet [7] has 25.5M wights and 3.9G multipliers and accumulators. Their resource requirements are beyond most embedded systems.

Embedded machine learning is to trade off accuracy with resource requirements. For example, by using fixed-point multipliers and adders, and trimming down the connections between layers of neural-networks, one can compress full blown DNN by up to 50X without loss of accuracy [6]. These are promising techniques on bringing intelligence into the real world through embedded platforms.

Security and Data Integrity. An autonomous store has a large attack surface, from both the digital side and the physical side. It is also a public space. Breaching such system give attackers physical material gains. Among possible attacks, data integrity attacks, which try to fool the sensors so that the system will make seemingly correct but wrong decisions, is uniquely damaging and hard to discover. Researchers have shown that simple eye wear can mislead facial recognition software [13], while hijacking and replaying camera feeds can cover up traces of human activity. These challenges call for new security and data integrity research to be done for cyber-physical-human systems.

6 Conclusions

Over the past 50 years, embedded computing systems have moved from a marginal research topic to an interdisciplinary research area that impacts almost every aspects of human life. First, with sensors and actuators, embedded systems motivated real-time computing for mission-critical tasks. Next, connectivity and networking give embedded systems the scale of Internet of Things and cyber-physical systems, and thus give rise to TerraSwarm-type challenges. In this third wave of AI and data, we believe intelligent embedded systems will make our physical environment smarter. Autonomous retailing is an iconic challenging scenario for the next wave of cyber-physical-human systems. While there are several attempts to showcase proofs of concept, we believe that, to achieve fully autonomous environments at acceptable cost, years of fundamental and applied research are required still.

References

1. Bamfield, J.: Changing retail, changing loss prevention (2013). https://sm. asisonline.org/ASIS%20SM%20Documents/GRTB_Changing_Retail_Changing_ Loss_Prevention_2013.pdf
2. Blaauw, D., Dutta, P., Fu, K., Guestrin, C., Jafari, R., Jones, D., Kubiatowicz, J., Kumar, V., Lee, E.A., Murray, R., Pappas, G., Rabaey, J., Rowe, A., Sangiovanni-Vincentelli, A., Sechen, C.M., Seshia, S.A., Tajana Simunic Rosing, B.T., Wawrzynek, J., Wessel, D.: The terraswarm research center (2012). http:// www.terraswarm.org/docs/TerraSwarm_Whitepaper_103112.pdf
3. Cao, Z., Simon, T., Wei, S., Sheikh, Y.: Realtime multi-person 2D pose estimation using part affinity fields. CoRR abs/1611.08050 (2016). http://arxiv.org/abs/1611. 08050
4. Chen, D., Cao, X., Wen, F., Sun, J.: Blessing of dimensionality: high-dimensional feature and its efficient compression for face verification. In: Proceedings of the IEEE Conference on Computer Vision and Pattern Recognition, pp. 3025–3032 (2013)
5. Goodfellow, I., Bengio, Y., Courville, A.: Deep Learning. The MIT Press, Cambridge (2016)
6. Han, S., Mao, H., Dally, W.J.: Deep compression: compressing deep neural network with pruning, trained quantization and Huffman coding. In: 4th International Conference on Learning Representations, ICLR 2016 (2016)
7. He, K., Zhang, X., Ren, S., Sun, J.: Deep residual learning for image recognition. In: The IEEE Conference on Computer Vision and Pattern Recognition (CVPR), June 2016
8. Holub, V., Filler, T.: Feature-based watermark localization in digital capture systems. In: Proceedings of SPIE, Electronic Imaging, Media Watermarking, Security, and Forensics, San Francisco, CA, February 2014

9. Krizhevsky, A., Sutskever, I., Hinton, G.E.: Imagenet classification with deep convolutional neural networks. In: Pereira, F., Burges, C.J.C., Bottou, L., Weinberger, K.Q. (eds.) Advances in Neural Information Processing Systems 25, pp. 1097–1105. Curran Associates, Inc. (2012). http://papers.nips.cc/paper/4824-imagenet-classification-with-deep-convolutional-neural-networks.pdf

10. Li, H., Lin, Z., Shen, X., Brandt, J., Hua, G.: A convolutional neural network cascade for face detection. In: Proceedings of the IEEE Conference on Computer Vision and Pattern Recognition, pp. 5325–5334 (2015)

11. Microsoft: Microsoft azure IoT services reference architecture (2016). https://azure.microsoft.com/en-us/updates/microsoft-azure-iot-reference-architecture-available/

12. Services, A.W.: AWS IoT developer guide (2017). http://docs.aws.amazon.com/iot/latest/developerguide/iot-dg.pdf

13. Sharif, M., Bhagavatula, S., Bauer, L., Reiter, M.K.: Accessorize to a crime: real and stealthy attacks on state-of-the-art face recognition. In: Proceedings of the 2016 ACM SIGSAC Conference on Computer and Communications Security, CCS 2016, pp. 1528–1540. ACM, New York (2016). https://doi.org/10.1145/2976749.2978392

14. Sudderth, E.B., Ihler, A.T., Isard, M., Freeman, W.T., Willsky, A.S.: Nonparametric belief propagation. Commun. ACM **53**(10), 95–103 (2010). https://doi.org/10.1145/1831407.1831431

15. Veloso, M., Biswas, J., Coltin, B., Rosenthal, S.: CoBots: robust symbiotic autonomous mobile service robots. In: Proceedings of the 24th International Conference on Artificial Intelligence, IJCAI 2015, pp. 4423–4429. AAAI Press (2015). http://dl.acm.org/citation.cfm?id=2832747.2832901

16. Violino, B.: Metro opens store of the future (2003). http://www.rfidjournal.com/articles/view?399

17. Wan, M., Wang, D., Goldman, M., Taddy, M., Rao, J., Liu, J., Lymberopoulos, D., McAuley, J.: Modeling consumer preferences and price sensitivities from large-scale grocery shopping transaction logs. In: Proceedings of the 26th International Conference on World Wide Web, WWW 2017, pp. 1103–1112. International World Wide Web Conferences Steering Committee, Republic and Canton of Geneva, Switzerland (2017). https://doi.org/10.1145/3038912.3052568

The Relativity Example: Is Terminological Innovation a Good Idea?

David G. Messerschmitt[(✉)][(iD)]

Department of Electrical Engineering and Computer Sciences,
University of California, Berkeley, Berkeley, USA
`messer@eecs.berkeley.edu`

Abstract. Relativistic kinematics and its impact on timekeeping in distributed systems design and operation is emerging as a sub-discipline as bandwidths and clock rates increase and timing accuracy requirements grow more stringent. In a recent tutorial paper [3] we have proposed a new terminology for some of the concepts of relativistic kinematics, along with some new formulations of the theory that better fit the distributed systems application. We describe our motivations, justifications, and philosophy in defining a terminology that is self-consistent and meaningful in this new system context, even as it breaks with a century of scientific literature. We argue that this unusual attempt at terminological innovation is practical in the case of a design paradigm that is only emerging, and justified by the contextual needs and pedagogical opportunities. Only time will tell whether this new terminology becomes established and entrenched.

1 Introduction

Human knowledge expands exponentially, and one pragmatic response is to find simpler and more effective ways of explaining existing concepts to each new cohort of students and practitioners. Another response is increasing specialization, so that for example design disciplines often apply domain-specific abstractions and simplifications rather than rely literally on related and foundational disciplines.

We encountered this opportunity in our recent research into relativistic modeling in the design of distributed systems [3]. Engineering design of distributed systems overwhelmingly neglects relativistic effects. Even though such effects are omnipresent, they are often sufficiently small to be safely neglected. However, as bandwidths and clock rates inevitably increase, and as system requirements on timing precision inevitably become more stringent, it eventually becomes necessary to take into account relativistic effects. Beginning notably with the Global Positioning System (GPS), within a growing number of system applications the relativistic influences of gravity and motion on timekeeping increasingly can no longer be neglected.

M. Lohstroh et al. (Eds.): Lee Festschrift, LNCS 10760, pp. 351–359, 2018.
https://doi.org/10.1007/978-3-319-95246-8_21

1.1   Terminology of Relativity

We therefore undertook the challenge of developing a foundation for the emerging discipline of relativistic timekeeping in a distributed system context. One aspect of this is the terminology used to describe the modeling variables of interest. As defined by Wikipedia:

> *Terminology* is the study of terms and their use. *Terms* are words and compound words or multi-word expressions that in specific contexts are given specific meanings – these may deviate from the meanings the same words have in other contexts and in everyday language.

Since relativistic effects are just emerging in the practice and literature of a distributed system context, there would be an opportunity to remake the terminology of relativity for this context. Unfortunately this means a break with some century-old terminology in the scientific literature, which we will call the *legacy* terminology. Arguably this break is both justifiable and not too disruptive for a new and emerging sub-discipline. We decided to undertake this. Here we outline the rationale for this rather unusual step, and also consider some obvious disadvantages.

2   What Makes a Good Terminology

The following are some of the considerations we addressed in developing a terminology.

Alignment with the Literature. The default is clearly to make use of terminology already appearing in the literature, making it straightforward to explore more deeply. For this reason the use of terminology inconsistent with the literature should clearly be avoided unless there is compelling justification.

Meaningful in Context. As relativistic modeling becomes more the norm in system design, it is appropriate to consider a terminology that aligns with the special considerations of that application domain. As there is relatively little design-based literature to establish a tradition, there is an opportunity to define a new domain-specific terminology.

The physics domain in which the legacy terminology arose is experimental and observational science, where the observer is typically considered (or approximated) to be inertial (not accelerated), and the phenomenon being observed (like particles in a collider or astronomical bodies) do not possess the ability to observe time or position (although some of their physical interactions are governed by an externally observable time or position). A system design context differs markedly in that typically there are no inertial observers, but rather the system nodes are manufactured (as opposed to natural) and specifically endowed with observational capability (such as time and position) and the ability to share those observations with other nodes through an endowed communications capability.

Internal Consistency. The legacy terminology that has arisen since Einstein's original paper in 1905 has been incrementally appended by a number of authors. As a result we claim that the legacy terminology of relativity is not globally thought out, particularly with respect to internal consistency of the terminological conventions that have evolved.

Metaphorical. An approach that has proven valuable for ease and depth of understanding is to relate domain-specific concepts back to some situation that is familiar in everyday circumstances. This is the *metaphor* as a design description, a familiar example of which is the "desktop" metaphor that inspired the windowed computer user interface [2]. Research in linguistics and psychology suggest that the metaphor can be a significant aid to easy and in-depth understanding of a new concept:

> ... conceptual metaphor theories suggest that cognition is dominated by metaphor-based thinking, whereby the structure and logical protocols of one or more domains, combined in various ways, guide or structure thinking in another. ... The theory has been widely discussed and tested, and enjoys a raft of supporting evidence in linguistics and cognitive psychology [1].

Cognitive science has a related model of brain structure called neural reuse:

> An emerging class of theories concerning the functional structure of the brain takes the reuse of neural circuitry for various cognitive purposes to be a central organizational principle. According to these theories, it is quite common for neural circuits established for one purpose to be exapted (exploited, recycled, redeployed) during evolution or normal development, and be put to different uses, often without losing their original functions [1].

These theories suggest an opportunity to make use of concepts ingrained in everyday experience to more readily absorb a new set of concepts (like relativity) that are outside of everyday experience, even to the extent of possibly repurposing some neural circuitry.

The legacy terminology has avoided any opportunity to be metaphorical. Rather, it evolved during the early theoretical development of the field where applications (and even experimentation or observation) were not yet prominent. The mathematical constructs employed were the primary inspiration for a terminology which has survived to this day.

3   Relativistic Kinematics

As an illustration we now summarize the new terminology of relativity [3]. The scope is specifically kinematics, which is the study of motion and the relevant variables of motion. The context is the design of distributed systems where nodes experience relative motion, and observations of time and position are affected by that motion. The models of interest in this circumstance come from relativistic kinematics. Gravity is not subsumed by kinematics, but we have simplified the effect of gravity on clocks by modeling gravity in the absence of motion. This avoids the greater sophistication (and mathematical baggage) of the general theory of relativity, but also neglects any interaction between motion and gravity.

We now briefly describe some of the new terminology we have designed according to the principles of Sect. 2. Then we relate that terminology to overlapping terminology widely employed in the scientific literature, and in the process make the case for why the unusual step of defining a new terminology was justified.

3.1   A Traveler-Map-Denizen Metaphor

We have chosen to relate the terminology of relativistic kinematics to the everyday experience of navigating (following or determining position vs time) using a map and available instrumentation, such as a clock and an accelerometer (which relies on that clock).

A *map* is a 3-D coordinate system that allows a node to position itself, either passively ("what is my current position?") or actively ("at what position do I want to arrive, and how do I get there?"). Technically a map is an inertial frame, implying that any observer at a fixed position on the map (said to be *at rest*) does not experience acceleration.[1]

A *clock* is a technological construct that measures time (typically based on a harmonic oscillator). There are two distinct types of observers, who are assumed to carry two distinct types of clocks. A *denizen*, who carries along a *denizen's clock*, is at rest at some position on the map. All denizens' clocks (which measure time t) run at the same clock-rate, although there is an issue of consistent initialization, which is the issue of *clock synchronization*. Denizens' clocks are said to be synchronized when they can cooperatively and correctly measure the speed of light by observing and comparing the times of photon emission and detection based on the knowledge of the distance that photon had to travel.

A *traveler* and a *traveler's clock* are allowed to change position on the map with time. This may mean that a traveler is experiencing acceleration, or it may mean that the traveler is moving with a fixed velocity. A clock carried by the traveler measures time τ, which is called the *traveler's time*. Two traveler's clocks will experience different clock rates (except when the two travelers have no relative velocity) and a traveler's clock will experience a different clock rate from the denizens clocks (except when the traveler is temporarily at rest relative to the map).

---

[1] The development of special relativity in introductory texts focuses on the transformation between two inertial frames in relative motion. Generally this is not of concern or interest in a distributed system, so we limit attention to a single (but arbitrary) inertial frame.

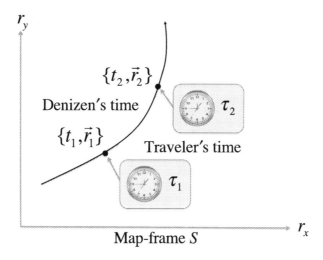

Fig. 1. An illustration of the trajectory of a traveler (adopted from [3]), which is a curve in the spatial coordinate system parameterized by time. Each map-position r along the trajectory is associated with two times τ and t.

3.2   The Trajectory

Typically a quantification of the changing position of a traveler is of interest, both for purposes of navigation and for purposes of characterizing the effect of that changing position on the clock-rate of the traveler's clock. The changing position is embodied in a *traveler's trajectory*, which is illustrated by plotting it on a map (as illustrated in Fig. 1). The trajectory is a continuous curve that captures all the map-positions that the traveler visits.

For purposes of capturing motion variables such as velocity and acceleration, it is convenient to parameterize the map-position by the time at which the traveler visits that position. However, there are two candidates for that time. The traveler's time τ at a map-position r on the trajectory is that time measured by a traveler's clock as the traveler passes that position. The denizen's time t at a map-position r is the time measured by a denizen's clock presumed to be at rest at that position at the instant the traveler passes by. Such a denizen's clock is notional, meaning that it is unlikely to exist as a physical entity but nevertheless we can predict theoretically what time it would measure if it were to exist. To get a consistent picture of the trajectory from the denizens' perspective, all such notional denizens' clocks along the trajectory are presumed to be synchronized.

Both time parameterizations of the trajectory are useful for distributed-system design. The traveler's time τ is that measured by clocks that are typically carried by system nodes. The denizens' time t is not normally measured during a system operation, but it is essential for characterizing the times of emission and detection of photons that pass between system nodes in the course of navigation and communication. This is because we rely on a postulate of special relativity that the speed of light (as measured by synchronized denizens' clocks) is a fixed value c irrespective of the choice of a map-frame.

Having a trajectory parameterized by two clocks is awkward, so we choose the traveler's clock as the single time parameterization. This choice makes sense since a clock carried by the traveler is oblivious to what map we have chosen, and is thus independent of that choice (such is not the case of the denizens' clocks). In this view, both the map-position r and the denizens' time t at which the traveler passes that position are parameterized by the traveler's time τ. Mathematically the trajectory consists of the 4-D description $\{t(\tau), r(\tau)\}$, where both time and position are parameterized by traveler's time τ. This description of the trajectory is called a *worldline*.

3.3 Motion Variables

There is a basic ambiguity in the measurement and instrumentation of motion variables like velocity and acceleration, because there are two different time bases by which we could measure those motion variables. Two different sets of motion variables are listed in Table 1, one based on the traveler's clock and the other on the totality of denizens' clocks.[2]

Table 1. Motion vectors and their magnitudes [3]

Motion variable	Traveler's	Denizens'
Time	τ	t
Time-speed	$\gamma = \mathrm{d}t/\mathrm{d}\tau$	$\gamma = \mathrm{d}t/\mathrm{d}\tau$
Map-position	r	r
Map-velocity	$w = \dfrac{\mathrm{d}r}{\mathrm{d}\tau}$	$u = \dfrac{\mathrm{d}r}{\mathrm{d}t}$
Map-speed	$w = \|w\|$	$u = \|u\|$
Map-acceleration	$b = \dfrac{\mathrm{d}w}{\mathrm{d}\tau}$	$a = \dfrac{\mathrm{d}u}{\mathrm{d}t}$
Map-acceleration magnitude	$b = \|b\|$	$a = \|a\|$
Self-acceleration	α	
Self-acceleration magnitude	α	

Denizens' Perspective. The scientific literature consistently and almost universally adopts the denizens' perspective on motion, measuring velocity and acceleration using the notional denizens' clocks as the time base for measuring these quantities. This choice has its origins in the mathematical development in the field, and follows a tradition established by Einstein from the beginning. It is also a sensible choice for laboratory and observational science, where physically

---

[2] In this table and throughout [3] we follow the common convention that motion variables like t and r are implicitly parameterized by τ.

realized clocks are typically inertial and the objects of study (natural entities like particles and astronomical bodies) are associated with notional (but not physical) clocks.

Traveler's Perspective. However, for distributed system design, where the nodes are manufactured entities, the situation reverses. The physically realized clocks are carried by travelers, and denizens' clocks are often notional constructs required for the limited purpose of predicting photon trajectory timing. For this reason in [3] we developed an alternative treatment of relativistic kinematics based on the *traveler's perspective*, always retaining the tools for an optional conversion to the denizens' perspective where needed.

The traveler's perspective also has the significant advantage that it is much simpler, easier to understand, and more intuitive. In particular, in the denizens' perspective *relativistic effects* (deviations from classical mechanics) are ubiquitous, and are often somewhat confounding and difficult to justify and explain. This is because motion variables are based on a frame-dependent measure of time, the denizen's time t. A notable example of such a relativistic effect is the well-known "light-speed limit", in which denizen's map-speed (magnitude of velocity) must be strictly less than the speed of light.

From the traveler's perspective (where traveler's time is used as the basis of measurements) relativistic effects are largely absent (except in the obvious case where a conversion to the denizens' perspective is undertaken). For example, the traveler's map-speed (magnitude of map-velocity) has no upper limit (although it has to be finite). This alignment with classical kinematics is good justification, in our opinion, to adopt the traveler's perspective in all introductory treatments of special relativity, including in the sciences as well as engineering.

There is one (and only one) instance of relativistic effects entering the traveler's perspective. In Table 1 we have listed a self-acceleration vector α, which is the acceleration measured by the traveler using an instrument (an accelerometer) carried by the traveler. Such an instrument can be based, for example, on releasing a small weight and observing whether it remains stationary relative to the traveler (zero acceleration), falls behind the traveler (positive traveler's self-acceleration), or moves out ahead of the traveler (negative traveler's self-acceleration).

In the traveler's perspective, the traveler's map-acceleration magnitude b (which is the acceleration observed when the traveler follows map-position and uses its own traveler's clock as a reference) is always greater than the traveler's self-acceleration magnitude a (which is measured by an accelerometer carried along with the traveler). This *acceleration boost* is one of nature's gifts to a relativistic traveler, because it indicates that progress toward a destination map-position is much more rapid (when measured by the traveler's clock) than would be expected classically.[3]

---

[3] Due to the light-speed limit, from the denizens' perspective progress toward the destination is slower than the classical prediction. The difference in perspective is attributable to using different clocks.

3.4   Justification for a New Terminology

In introducing the new traveler's perspective, while not entirely abandoning the denizens' perspective, we faced the challenge of naming the added motion variables, and distinguishing those names from the legacy denizens' motion variables. Thus it was inevitable that we needed to introduce some new terms. Was this best accomplished with some "extension" to the legacy terminology, or a new terminology based on the map-traveler-denizen metaphor?

The terminology we adopted is listed in Table 2. This terminology clearly differentiates between motion variables instrumented using the traveler's clock (traveler's velocity and acceleration) and the denizens' clocks (denizens' velocity and acceleration). It also differentiates between accelerations measured relative to map-coordinates (map-acceleration) and that measured by an accelerometer without reference to a map (self-acceleration). The terminology is admittedly somewhat cumbersome, involving three-word phrases, but that is arguably inevitable with so many distinct (and meaningful) motion variables in this more complete relativistic model.

Table 2. Terminology comparison [3]

Traveler-map-denizen	Conventional
τ = Traveler's time	Proper time
t = Denizens' time	Coordinate time
γ = Time-speed	Lorentz factor
w = Traveler's map-velocity	Proper velocity
α = Traveler's self-acceleration	Proper acceleration
b = Traveler's map-acceleration	Not considered
u = Denizens' map-velocity	Coordinate velocity
a = Denizens' map-acceleration	Coordinate acceleration

We also adopted a consistent usage of the term *speed*, which we apply to the derivative of any scalar variable (or vector magnitude) with respect to traveler's time τ. Instances of this in Tables 1 and 2 are time-speed and map-speed. Other instances of speeds occur in [3], such as image-speed and gravity-speed.

Disadvantages of the Legacy Terminology. We have outlined two justifications for our terminological innovation: The challenges associated with integrating a novel traveler's perspective, and the cognitive benefits of a metaphorical approach.

There are some additional disadvantages we can ascribe to the legacy terminology, which is listed in the second column of Table 2 for comparison.[4] One is the disconnect between the terms (like "proper" and "coordinate" and "Lorentz") and any physical or logical or familiar construct in the context of the design of distributed systems. Another is the inconsistencies that arise in a terminology arising over a number of decades with contributions from a number of authors. This is most evident in the usage of the term "proper":

- Generally this is taken to mean a "measurement made by an instrument carried along with the observer", which is the case with "proper time" and "proper acceleration". In the case of "proper velocity" such a measurement requires the observation of map-position, which requires more instrumentation and infrastructure than can be carried with the observer alone.
- The "proper acceleration" is not directly related to the derivative of the "proper velocity" as one would expect.

4 Conclusion

Are the advantages of a remaking of terminology for an emerging design discipline sufficiently compelling to overcome the disconnect from the legacy terminology? Clearly this could only be considered in the context of a body of knowledge that is early undergoing a transition from scientific endeavor to design practice. It is left to the reader to decide if this was a step forward or a step backward. The true test, however, will be whether this (or similarly unconventional) terminology becomes established in design practice, or alternatively the weight of scientific precedence is too difficult to overcome.

References

1. Anderson, M.L.: Neural reuse: a fundamental organizational principle of the brain. Behav. Brain Sci. **33**(4), 245–266 (2010)
2. Kaptelinin, V., Czerwinski, M.: Beyond the Desktop Metaphor: Designing Integrated Digital Work Environments. The MIT Press, Cambridge (2007)
3. Messerschmitt, D.G.: Relativisitc timekeeping, motion, and gravity in distributed systems. Proc. IEEE **105**(8), 1511 (2017). http://ieeexplore.ieee.org/document/7982857/

---

[4] The term "proper velocity" is not in common usage, but has been introduced in a couple of recent papers. This is an instance where this author is not entirely alone in recognizing the utility of a traveler's perspective.

Hierarchical System Design with Vertical Contracts

Pierluigi Nuzzo[1]([✉]) and Alberto L. Sangiovanni-Vincentelli[2]

[1] Department of Electrical Engineering, University of Southern California,
Los Angeles, CA 90089, USA
`nuzzo@usc.edu`
[2] Department of Electrical Engineering and Computer Sciences,
University of California at Berkeley, Berkeley, CA 94720, USA
`alberto@eecs.berkeley.edu`

Abstract. We propose the notions of *heterogeneous refinement* and *vertical contracts* as additions for any contract framework to provide full methodological support for multi-view and multi-layer system design with heterogeneous models. We rethink the relation of contract refinement in the context of layered design and discuss how it can be extended, via heterogeneous refinement and vertical contracts, to deal with hierarchies of models that present heterogeneous architectures as well as behaviors expressed by heterogeneous formalisms. We then show via design examples that such an extension can, indeed, encompass a richer set of design refinement relations, including support for synthesis methods and optimized mappings of specifications into implementations.

Keywords: System design · Embedded systems
Cyber-physical systems · Design automation · Platform-Based Design
Contract-based design · Assume-guarantee contracts
Vertical contracts

1 Preamble

It is both a pleasure and an honor to dedicate this paper to Edward A. Lee, a friend and colleague over many years. During his entire academic career, Edward has been a staunch evangelist for system level design based on rigorous methodologies and for tools that could be proven correct. His work on models of computation and on Ptolemy is an epitome of this approach. Our work on contracts was inspired by his views. We are very pleased that he picked this notion to carry it to new heights with his elegant application of vertical contracts to component-based software design for the Internet of Things [27]. For this reason, we chose vertical contracts as the focus of this work. We count on working with Edward for many, many years to come and discover new research directions together.

© Springer International Publishing AG, part of Springer Nature 2018
M. Lohstroh et al. (Eds.): Lee Festschrift, LNCS 10760, pp. 360–382, 2018.
https://doi.org/10.1007/978-3-319-95246-8_22

2   Introduction

Methodologies such as component-based design [2] and contract-based design [48] have emerged as unifying formal compositional paradigms for the design of complex systems. Contracts are mathematical objects that model the interface between components and levels of abstraction in a design, and establish the foundations for assume-guarantee reasoning about composability and abstraction/refinement relationships between subsystems. Contracts enable modular and hierarchical verification of global properties of a system, whose satisfaction can be proven based on the satisfaction of local properties of the components. Contracts support stepwise refinement, where hierarchical specifications can be used to reason about component decompositions, even if the component implementations are not yet available. Contracts facilitate component reuse, as any components satisfying a contract directly inherit its guarantees.

Overall, contracts have shown to be effective for specifying and reasoning about components and their aggregations, especially when component models belong to the same level of abstraction (e.g., algorithm, software, architecture) or adopt the same formalism. However, there is no universal modeling formalism that can capture every aspect of complex, heterogeneous systems, such as cyber-physical systems (CPSs), and guarantee, at the same time, tractable analysis. Designers usually "decompose" a system into different semantic domains, by adopting the most convenient formalisms to represent different portions of the design or different *viewpoints* [8, 46] (e.g., system function, safety, timing, energy) at different abstraction levels. They then leverage the most suitable tools to analyze and synthesize these models separately. A set of challenges remain for contract-based design when system models are to be formulated and manipulated along the design flow and across different abstraction levels. For example, in control applications, control laws are typically derived and initially evaluated using control-oriented models, in which details of the implementation and the physical dynamics are simplified or neglected. These details are usually modeled and evaluated using other formalisms and tools. Each model represents some aspect of system design and occludes others, by making simplifying assumptions that are often undocumented or informally captured at best. The heterogeneity of these models poses challenges when assessing the performance and correctness of the entire system.

While contract theories promise to encompass any kind of formalism and decomposition, it is not always clear how they can effectively support the correct transition between heterogeneous abstraction levels. In fact, the notions of contract abstraction and refinement are traditionally defined in the context of a single formalism, e.g., using language inclusion or simulation relations. In system design, abstractions should, instead, be able to bridge heterogeneous formalisms (i.e., *semantically heterogeneous* models), and heterogeneous decomposition architectures (i.e., *structurally heterogeneous* models), to make system analysis and synthesis tractable, by consistently combining different verification and synthesis results. These difficulties are exacerbated by the fact that different formal theories of components and contracts have been proposed in the literature, for example, *interface theories* [1,2,49] and *assume-guarantee (A/G) contracts* [7], and research efforts toward understanding the relationships between them have only started to appear [8,32].

This paper investigates a path toward a comprehensive contract framework for multi-view, multi-layer design. We propose the notions of *heterogeneous refinement* and *vertical contracts* as additions for any contract framework to provide full methodological support for hierarchies of models exposing both structural and semantic heterogeneity. Heterogeneous refinement extends the classical relation of contract refinement to contracts expressed using different formalisms. However, being exclusively based on behavior mappings, heterogeneous refinement does not subsume any notion of architectural decomposition, and cannot express *per se* refinements between specifications and implementations of systems presenting heterogeneous modeling architectures and structures. This motivates the introduction of vertical contracts, which can relate a contract and its vertical heterogeneous refinement, including different viewpoints, independently of their structures. Vertical contracts subsume heterogeneous refinements and help formalize a richer set of design refinement relations, including support for synthesis methods and optimized mappings of specifications into implementations.

Some of the results of this paper appeared in previous publications in the context of CPSs [8,36,41,48] as well as analog and mixed-signal systems [33,39]. In this paper, we expand on our previous formulations and show via examples how the proposed extensions can be used to represent any logical decomposition of complex system verification and synthesis problems into arbitrary conjunctive and disjunctive combinations of smaller sub-problems. While our results apply to any design methodology and contract theory, for simplicity, we choose two exemplar multi-layer design and contract frameworks, namely, Platform-Based Design (PBD) [47] and A/G contracts, respectively, to illustrate them. We then start by providing an overview of these frameworks below.

3   Preliminaries

3.1   Platform-Based Design

Platform-Based Design (PBD) was introduced in the late 1980s as a rigorous framework to reason about system design that could be shared across industrial domain boundaries [47] and support multi-layer optimization and multiple viewpoints. PBD concepts have been, indeed, applied to a variety of very different domains, from automotive to System-on-Chip, from building automation to synthetic biology.

In PBD, the design process is articulated as a sequence of steps. At each step, *top-down refinements* of high-level specifications are mapped into *bottom-up abstractions* and characterizations of potential implementations. Each abstraction layer is defined by a design *platform*, which is the set of all architectures that can be built out of a *library* (collection) of *components* according to *composition rules*. The bottom-up phase of the design flow consists in building the component library. In the top-down phase, high-level requirements are formalized and a *design refinement* step called *mapping* is performed, where the requirements are mapped to the implementation library components. Mapping is the mechanism that allows moving from a level of abstraction to a lower one using the available components within the library. For example, mapping may be cast as an optimization problem where a set of performance metrics and quality factors are optimized over a space constrained by both system requirements and component feasibility constraints. The different viewpoints of the system and of the components, such as the functional viewpoint as well as the extra-functional viewpoints (e.g., safety, timing, energy) can all be considered in the mapping phase. When some constraint cannot be satisfied using the available library components or the mapping result is not satisfactory for the designer, additional elements can be designed and inserted into the library. After each mapping step, the current representation of the design platform serves as a specification for the next mapping step, until the final implementation is reached.

In such a layered design methodology, providing formal guarantees about the correctness of each design refinement step is crucial to improve on both design quality and productivity, by decreasing the overall verification and testing effort and the number of design iterations. In this respect, contract frameworks can play a key role [41].

3.2 Assume-Guarantee Contracts

The notion of contracts originates in the context of compositional *assume-guarantee reasoning* [12]. In a contract framework, design and verification complexity is reduced by decomposing system-level tasks into more manageable sub-problems at the component level, under a set of assumptions. Contract frameworks were widely developed in the context of software engineering and object oriented programming [30]. More recently, they have been extended to *reactive systems*, i.e., systems that maintain an ongoing interaction with their environment, and *cyber-physical systems (CPSs)* [8,26,35,37,41,48], i.e., systems in which computation, communication, and control are tightly connected in feedback loops with physical processes. We use the design of reactive and cyber-physical systems as the motivation for the examples in this paper, since it typically requires a richer set of modeling formalisms and architectures [38,40]. We further choose the A/G contract framework [7,8] to illustrate our approach, since it is centered around a generic notion of *behaviors* which can encompass all kinds of models encountered in CPS design, from hardware and software models to representations of physical phenomena. We start our overview of A/G contracts with a simple, generic representation of a component and we associate to it a set of properties that the component satisfies expressed with contracts. The contracts will be used to verify the correctness of the compositions and of the refinements.

We call a *component* an element of a design, characterized by a set of *variables* and a set of *behaviors* over its variables.[1] Components can be connected together under constraints on the values of certain variables. We use $[\![M]\!]$ to denote the set of behaviors of component M. A system can then be assembled by *composition* and interconnection of components, where the behaviors of the composition is described as the *intersection* of the behaviors of its components, i.e., $[\![M_1 \times M_2]\!] = [\![M_1]\!] \cap [\![M_2]\!]$. A *contract* $\mathcal{C}$ for a component M is a triple (V, A, G), where V is the set of component variables, and A and G are sets of behaviors over V. A represents the *assumptions* that M makes on its environment, and G represents the *guarantees* provided by M under the environment assumptions. A component M satisfies a contract $\mathcal{C}$ whenever M and $\mathcal{C}$ are defined over the same set of variables, and all the behaviors of M are *contained* in the guarantees of $\mathcal{C}$ once they are composed (i.e., intersected) with the assumptions, i.e., when $[\![M]\!] \cap A \subseteq G$ or, equivalently, when $[\![M]\!] \subseteq G \cup \overline{A}$, $\overline{A}$ being the complement of A. We denote this *satisfaction* relation by writing $M \models \mathcal{C}$, and we say that M is a (legal) *implementation* of $\mathcal{C}$. However, a component E can also be associated with a contract $\mathcal{C}$ as an *environment*. We say that E is a (legal) environment of $\mathcal{C}$, and write $E \models_E \mathcal{C}$, whenever E and $\mathcal{C}$ have the same variables and $[\![E]\!] \subseteq A$. Further, we say that a contract is *consistent* when it is feasible to develop implementations for it, i.e., when $G \cup \overline{A} \neq \emptyset$, where $\emptyset$ is the empty set. A contract is *compatible* if there exists a legal environment E for its implementations, i.e., if and only if $A \neq \emptyset$.

Contract *saturation* is used to compute operations and relations between contracts. A contract $\mathcal{C} = (V, A, G)$ is *saturated* if the *union* of its guarantees G and the complement of its assumptions A is coincident with G, i.e., $G = G \cup \overline{A}$. Any contract $\mathcal{C}$ can be turned into a saturated form $\mathcal{C}'$ by taking $A' = A$ and $G' = G \cup \overline{A}$. $\mathcal{C}$ and $\mathcal{C}'$ have identical variables, identical assumptions, and possess identical sets of environments and implementations. Such two contracts $\mathcal{C}$ and $\mathcal{C}'$ are then *equivalent*. To capture a notion of replaceability, contracts can be ordered by establishing a *refinement* relation. Given two saturated contracts $\mathcal{C}$ and $\mathcal{C}'$, we say that $\mathcal{C}$ refines $\mathcal{C}'$, written $\mathcal{C} \preceq \mathcal{C}'$, if and only if $A \supseteq A'$ and $G \subseteq G'$. Refinement amounts to relaxing assumptions and reinforcing guarantees, therefore "strengthening" the contract. Since $\mathcal{C}$ admits fewer implementations than $\mathcal{C}'$ but more environments than $\mathcal{C}'$, we can replace $\mathcal{C}'$ with $\mathcal{C}$. Moreover, we can compute the *conjunction* of $\mathcal{C}_1$ and $\mathcal{C}_2$, written $\mathcal{C}_1 \wedge \mathcal{C}_2$, by taking their greatest lower bound (GLB) with respect to the refinement relation; that is, $\mathcal{C}_1 \wedge \mathcal{C}_2$ is the "weakest" contract that refines both $\mathcal{C}_1$ and $\mathcal{C}_2$. For saturated contracts on the same variable set V, we have $\mathcal{C}_1 \wedge \mathcal{C}_2 = (V, A_1 \cup A_2, G_1 \cap G_2)$. The conjunction of contracts can be defined to compose multiple viewpoint specifications for the same component that need to be satisfied simultaneously.

Finally, similar to composition of components, *composition* of contracts can be used to construct composite contracts out of simpler ones. Then, the contract

---

[1] A more general definition of component distinguishes between *variables* and *ports* [36]. For simplicity, in this paper, we use the same term variables to denote both component variables and ports.

composition $C_1 \otimes C_2$ is defined as the minimum of the set of all contracts C such that, if $M_1 \models C_1$, $M_2 \models C_2$, and $E \models_E C$, then $M_1 \times M_2 \models C$ and $E \times M_{1(2)} \models_E C_{2(1)}$, i.e., any legal environment E for C provides a legal environment for both C_2, when composed with M_1, and C_1, when composed with M_2. For $C_1 = (V, A_1, G_1)$ and $C_2 = (V, A_2, G_2)$ saturated contracts over the same set of variables, $C_1 \otimes C_2$ can be computed as (V, A, G) where $A = (A_1 \cap A_2) \cup \overline{(G_1 \cap G_2)}$ and $G = G_1 \cap G_2$. Importantly, contract refinement is preserved by composition, which is a desirable property to insure that subsystems can be independently implemented (refined), while guaranteeing that they are compatible for subsequent integration and satisfy the requirements.

3.3 Proposed Approach and Related Work

We would like to use contracts to formalize and reason about refinement relations between designs at different abstraction levels in a layered process, as in PBD, to fully support multi-level and multi-view design in a compositional way. To do so, we first observe that the definitions summarized above can be effectively used to compute operations and relations between contracts if all the assumptions and the guarantees are expressed using the same formalism. Since this is not always the case in layered design, we extend the contract framework with relations and operations that support abstraction and refinement between pairs of heterogeneous formalisms or modeling architectures. In model-based verification, heterogeneous abstractions have been used in the past for specific pairs of formalisms, such as hybrid abstractions of nonlinear systems [14,20], linear hybrid automata abstractions of linear hybrid systems [17], discrete abstractions of hybrid systems [3,4,11]. By embedding heterogeneous refinement within a generic A/G contract framework, our work aims to provide a compositional formulation that virtually applies to any pair of formalisms.

Heterogeneous reactive systems can be compared and composed using the tagged-signal semantics [24]. This approach uses system traces or behaviors as a mathematical framework for creating relations between the semantics of different modeling formalisms. A formal framework that addresses the semantic heterogeneity of CPS by relating the semantics of different models using behaviors and their mappings has also been developed recently by Rajhans et al. [45]. In a similar spirit, we use mathematical functions between behavior domains as the semantic mappings between heterogeneous behaviors and contracts. However, in addition to supporting system analysis, our intent is to also support different forms of design refinement, such as refinement by synthesis and optimized mapping. Further, we aim to provide a formulation that can incorporate the concept of *orthogonalization of concerns*, such as the separation of communication vs. computation, function vs. architecture, and behavior vs. performance [22].

At some point in the design flow, specifications must be realized by using resources, including, e.g., computing units or communication media (networks, buses, and protocols). When deploying an application over a computing platform, in addition to the functional viewpoint, non-functional viewpoints (e.g., safety, timing, energy) are of importance as well. While it is still convenient to keep the separation between the specification layer used for initial prototyping and the supporting execution layer for deployment, the actual satisfaction of design requirements will heavily depend on the execution platform. It is often the case that the two layers have distinct structural decompositions. Moreover, combining different viewpoints of the lower-level platform (e.g., timing and functional) may be necessary to effectively prove the correctness of the refinement of a single viewpoint (e.g., functional) of the higher-level platform. We introduce vertical contracts to capture notions of design refinement that depend on the *mapping of the application into the execution platform*. We refer to this type of contracts, bridging distinct abstraction levels, as vertical contracts, and distinguish them from *horizontal contracts*, traditionally employed to specify and reason about design elements at the same abstraction level.

Finally, ontologies have been used in the past as a knowledge-management approach to combine verification or analysis results across heterogeneous models in a consistent way. For instance, lattice-based ontologies can be used to infer semantic relationships between elements of heterogeneous models [25]. Rather than treating verification activities as knowledge to be combined, our work aims to use logical combinations of verification and synthesis tasks, mediated by contracts, to develop complex hierarchies. In a similar spirit, the temporal logic of actions proof system deploys a proof manager that breaks down a complex verification task logically into proof obligations that are proved using theorem provers and satisfiability modulo theory solvers [10]. However, this framework is primarily aimed towards software systems, whereas our objective is to rather develop a "design manager," supporting more general (e.g., continuous, hybrid) dynamics and non-deductive analysis techniques as well as synthesis and optimization methods.

4 Heterogeneous Refinement

We rely on the fact that A/G contracts are defined out of sets of behaviors to develop a formal framework that can work with every formalism, while being at the same time independent of the specifics of any of them. Therefore, as a first step, we use *behavior mappings* to introduce a new relation, *heterogeneous refinement*, which extends the classical relation of contract refinement to contracts expressed using different formalisms.

The notion of contract refinement introduced in Sect. 3 can be generalized to the case of two contracts, C_1 and C_2, expressed by different formalisms. In this case, before a refinement relation can be defined, we need to map the behaviors expressed by one of the contracts to the domain of the other contract via a transformation $\mathcal{M}$. Let B_1 and B_2 be two sets of behaviors, possibly defined in the different formalisms $\mathcal{B}_1$ and $\mathcal{B}_2$, respectively. Behavior formalisms may include, for instance, event traces, continuous signals, or hybrid trajectories. We define mappings between different behavior domains in terms of *abstraction functions* as follows.

Definition 1 (Behavior Abstraction Function). *Given two behavior domains B_1 and B_2 in possibly different behavior formalisms $\mathcal{B}_1$ and $\mathcal{B}_2$, a behavior abstraction function is a function $\mathcal{M} : B_1 \rightarrow B_2$ that associates each behavior $\beta_1 \in B_1$ with one and only one behavior $\beta_2 = \mathcal{M}(\beta_1) \in B_2$.*

Because multiple behaviors in B_1 can be associated with the same behavior in B_2, an abstraction function is not an isomorphism, in general; in fact, it results in loss of information when mapping sets of behaviors from the concrete domain B_1 to the abstract domain B_2. Abstraction functions are often problem-specific and they are usually assumed informally any time two different models M_1 and M_2 of the same system are created using different formalisms; we aim to facilitate the explicit and rigorous definition of these abstraction functions.

Let us assume that behaviors in B_1 and B_2 are defined, respectively, over the sets of variables V_1 and V_2. Then, while mapping behaviors in B_1 to behaviors in B_2, $\mathcal{M}$ will also establish a mapping between the variable sets V_1 and V_2; this mapping will be, in general, a relation $R_\mathcal{M} \subseteq V_1 \times V_2$. In the following, we use the notation $\mathcal{M}(B_1')$ to denote the image of a behavior set $B_1' \subseteq B_1$ via the mapping $\mathcal{M}$, i.e., $\mathcal{M}(B_1') = \{b_2 | b_2 = \mathcal{M}(b_1), \forall b_1 \in B_1'\}$. Furthermore, for a subset of variables $V_1' \subseteq V_1$, we use the notation $R_\mathcal{M}(V_1')$ to denote the subset of variables in V_2 associated with the variables in V_1', i.e., $R_\mathcal{M}(V_1') = \{v_2 \in V_2 | \exists v_1 \in V_1' : (v_1, v_2) \in R_\mathcal{M}\}$. Similarly, we denote the inverse image of a behavior set $B_2' \subseteq B_2$ via the mapping $\mathcal{M}$ as $\mathcal{M}^{-1}(B_2')$, i.e., $\mathcal{M}^{-1}(B_2') = \{b_1 | \mathcal{M}(b_1) \in B_2'\}$, and the subset of variables in V_1 associated with the set of variables $V_2' \subseteq V_2$ as $R_\mathcal{M}^{-1}(V_2')$, i.e., $R_\mathcal{M}^{-1}(V_2') = \{v_1 \in V_1 | \exists v_2 \in V_2' : (v_1, v_2) \in R_\mathcal{M}\}$. Based on these definitions, we introduce the notion of heterogeneous refinement as follows.

Definition 2 (Heterogeneous Refinement). *Let B_1 and B_2 be two behavior domains, including, respectively, behaviors over the variable sets V_1 and V_2, and possibly expressed using different formalisms $\mathcal{B}_1$ and $\mathcal{B}_2$; let $\mathcal{M}$ be a behavior abstraction function from B_1 to B_2. Given contracts $\mathcal{C}_1 = (V_1, A_1, G_1)$ and $\mathcal{C}_2 = (V_2, A_2, G_2)$, both in saturated form, and such that $A_1, G_1 \subseteq B_1$, $A_2, G_2 \subseteq B_2$, and $V_1 = R_\mathcal{M}^{-1}(V_2)$, we say that $\mathcal{C}_1$ refines $\mathcal{C}_2$ via $\mathcal{M}$, written $\mathcal{C}_1 \preceq_\mathcal{M} \mathcal{C}_2$, if and only if $A_1 \supseteq \mathcal{M}^{-1}(A_2)$ and $G_1 \subseteq \mathcal{M}^{-1}(G_2)$.*

Example 1. Let $\mathcal{C}_{dis} = (\{powered\}, \mathrm{T}, \Diamond_{[0,3)}powered)$ be the contract specifying the dynamics of a load in an electrical system, which is powered at startup. $\mathcal{C}_{dis}$ offers a discrete-time discrete-state abstraction of the dynamics, prescribing that, in all contexts, the Boolean variable *powered* must be asserted, i.e., evaluates to true, within three time units. Assumptions and guarantees are captured by formulas in Metric Temporal Logic (MTL) [23], where T stands for the Boolean value *true*, and $\Diamond$ for the temporal operator *eventually*. On the other hand, let $\mathcal{C}_{con}(\tau, v_f) = (\{v\}, \mathbb{R}, v(t) = v_f(1 - e^{-\frac{t}{\tau}}), t \in \mathbb{R}, t \geq 0)$ be the contract describing the voltage level of the electrical load as a continuous function of time t, parameterized by the time constant $\tau \in \mathbb{R}^+$ and steady-state voltage $v_f \in \mathbb{R}^+$. The load responds as a first-order dynamical system with time constant τ and

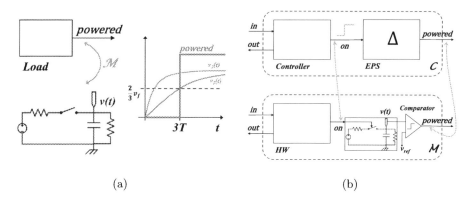

Fig. 1. Specification and implementation platform examples used to illustrate heterogeneous refinement (a) and vertical contracts (b).

steady-state voltage v_f. Then, given a time step T, we can reason about refinement between $\mathcal{C}_{con}$ and $\mathcal{C}_{dis}$ using the transformation $\mathcal{M}$, mapping continuous time and voltage levels into discrete ones:

$$\mathcal{M} : \begin{cases} powered := \left(v \geq \frac{2}{3}v_f\right) \\ \qquad k := \left\lfloor \frac{t}{T} \right\rfloor \end{cases} . \tag{1}$$

The variable *powered* is asserted if and only if the voltage is greater than or equal to two thirds of the steady-state value, while the discrete time index k is obtained by discretizing t according to the quantization step T. Resting on this mapping, we can then conclude that $\mathcal{C}_{con} \preceq_{\mathcal{M}} \mathcal{C}_{dis}$ if and only if $v(3T) > \frac{2}{3}v_f$, i.e., if and only if the system time constant satisfies $\tau < \frac{3T}{\ln 3}$. This condition is illustrated in Fig. 1a, where $v_2(t)$ (in green) satisfies the constraint on τ and refines the guarantees of $\mathcal{C}_{dis}$, whereas $v_1(t)$ (in blue) does not, since it reaches the desired value $\frac{2}{3}v_f$ exactly at time $t = 3T$ ($k = 3$), while the interval in the guarantees of $\mathcal{C}_{dis}$ is right-open.

As shown in Example 1, heterogeneous refinement allows reasoning about replaceability between contracts in different formalisms. Moreover, similarly to homogeneous refinement, it is also preserved by composition, as stated by the following proposition.

Proposition 1 (Compositional Heterogeneous Refinement). *Let B and B' be behavior domains over the variable sets V and V', expressed in formalisms $\mathcal{B}$ and $\mathcal{B}'$, respectively; let $\mathcal{M} : B \to B'$ be a behavior abstraction function, with $B' = \mathcal{M}(B)$ and $V = R_\mathcal{M}^{-1}(V')$. Let $\mathcal{C}_1, \mathcal{C}_2$ be A/G contracts defined in the behavior domain B, and $\mathcal{C}_1', \mathcal{C}_2'$ be A/G contracts defined in the domain B', all in saturated form. If $\mathcal{C}_1 \preceq_\mathcal{M} \mathcal{C}_1'$, $\mathcal{C}_2 \preceq_\mathcal{M} \mathcal{C}_2'$, and $\mathcal{C}_1'$ is compatible with $\mathcal{C}_2'$, then $\mathcal{C}_1$ is also compatible with $\mathcal{C}_2$ and $\mathcal{C}_1 \otimes \mathcal{C}_2 \preceq_\mathcal{M} \mathcal{C}_1' \otimes \mathcal{C}_2'$.*

Proof. Let $\mathcal{C}'_1 = (V', A'_1, G'_1)$ and $\mathcal{C}'_2 = (V', A'_2, G'_2)$, with $A'_1, G'_1, A'_2, G'_2 \subseteq B'$, and $\mathcal{C}_1 = (V, A_1, G_1)$ and $\mathcal{C}_2 = (V, A_2, G_2)$, with $A_1, G_1, A_2, G_2 \subseteq B$. By hypothesis, we have $G_1 \subseteq \mathcal{M}^{-1}(G'_1), G_2 \subseteq \mathcal{M}^{-1}(G'_2), A_1 \supseteq \mathcal{M}^{-1}(A'_1), A_2 \supseteq \mathcal{M}^{-1}(A'_2)$. Therefore, for the guarantees of $\mathcal{C}_1 \otimes \mathcal{C}_2$ we obtain

$$G_{12} = G_1 \cap G_2 \subseteq \mathcal{M}^{-1}(G'_1) \cap \mathcal{M}^{-1}(G'_2) = \mathcal{M}^{-1}(G'_1 \cap G'_2) = \mathcal{M}^{-1}(G'_{12}). \quad (2)$$

On the other hand, for the assumptions of $\mathcal{C}'_1 \otimes \mathcal{C}'_2$ we obtain

$$
\begin{aligned}
\mathcal{M}^{-1}(A'_{12}) &= \mathcal{M}^{-1}\left((A'_1 \cap A'_2) \cup \overline{G'_1 \cap G'_2} \right) \\
&= \left(\mathcal{M}^{-1}(A'_1) \cap \mathcal{M}^{-1}(A'_2) \right) \cup \mathcal{M}^{-1}(\overline{G'_1 \cap G'_2}) \\
&= \left(\mathcal{M}^{-1}(A'_1) \cap \mathcal{M}^{-1}(A'_2) \right) \cup \overline{\mathcal{M}^{-1}(G'_1 \cap G'_2)} \\
&\subseteq (A_1 \cap A_2) \cup \overline{G_1 \cap G_2} = A_{12}, \quad (3)
\end{aligned}
$$

where we use (2) in the last step of (3).[2] By definition of heterogeneous refinement, (2) and (3) allow us to conclude $\mathcal{C}_1 \otimes \mathcal{C}_2 \preceq_{\mathcal{M}} \mathcal{C}'_1 \otimes \mathcal{C}'_2$. Moreover, by compatibility of $\mathcal{C}'_1$ and $\mathcal{C}'_2$, and by B' being the image of B under $\mathcal{M}$, we have that $\mathcal{M}^{-1}(A'_{12})$ is not empty, hence A_{12} is not empty, which means that $\mathcal{C}_1$ is also compatible with $\mathcal{C}_2$.   □

By the proposition above, compatible contracts can be independently refined, which is key to enable top-down incremental design with heterogeneous formalisms, by iteratively decomposing a system-level contract $\mathcal{C}$ in formalism $\mathcal{B}'$ into sub-system contracts $\mathcal{C}_i$ in formalisms $\mathcal{B}$ for further development and subsequent integration.

Heterogeneous Refinement and Galois Connections. An alternative formalization of heterogeneous refinement can also consider abstractions whose structure is more complex than that of the functions in Definition 1, such as abstractions based on *Galois connections* or *conservative approximations* [42]. A Galois connection (α, γ) can relate concrete and abstract representations of a system via an abstraction function α and a concretization function γ, such that γ is the closest possible approximation of an inverse for α. Galois connections are central to the theory of abstract interpretation proposed by Cousot and Cousot [13]. Moreover, they can be seen as related, but complementary, to conservative approximations [42]. We plan to further investigate effective embeddings of these kinds of abstractions into our framework.

In this respect, Benveniste et al. [9] show that an abstraction $\bar{\alpha}$ on contracts can be systematically derived from a Galois connection (α, γ) on components. There are, however, obstructions in building a corresponding concretization map to directly lift Galois connections on components to Galois connections on contracts [9]. Nonetheless, the proposed abstraction $\bar{\alpha}$ has already many desirable

---

[2] We also use the fact that $\mathcal{M}^{-1}(\overline{A'}) = \overline{\mathcal{M}^{-1}(A')}$ for any subset A' of the universal set B'. In fact, we have $B = \mathcal{M}^{-1}(B') = \mathcal{M}^{-1}(A' \cup \overline{A'}) = \mathcal{M}^{-1}(A') \cup \mathcal{M}^{-1}(\overline{A'}), \emptyset = \mathcal{M}^{-1}(A' \cap \overline{A'}) = \mathcal{M}^{-1}(A') \cap \mathcal{M}^{-1}(\overline{A'})$, which jointly lead to $\mathcal{M}^{-1}(\overline{A'}) = \overline{\mathcal{M}^{-1}(A')}$.

properties. It is monotonic with respect to the refinement orders and allows proving contract consistency and compatibility entirely in the abstract, usually simpler, domain. $\overline{\alpha}$ is also compositional with respect to contract conjunction, i.e., $\overline{\alpha}(\mathcal{C}_1 \wedge \mathcal{C}_2) = \overline{\alpha}(\mathcal{C}_1) \wedge \overline{\alpha}(\mathcal{C}_2)$. Under appropriate conditions, $\overline{\alpha}$ is also compositional with respect to contract composition, i.e., $\overline{\alpha}(\mathcal{C}_1 \otimes \mathcal{C}_2) \succeq \overline{\alpha}(\mathcal{C}_1) \otimes \overline{\alpha}(\mathcal{C}_2)$. Consistency checking on abstracted contracts can then be performed in a modular way with respect to both conjunction and composition. On the other hand, compatibility checking is only proven to be modular with respect to conjunction.

The approach in this paper is different from the above effort. The above work targets compositional verification of contract compatibility and consistency entirely based on abstractions. We aim, instead, to extend contract refinement to allow preserving key properties of interest when passing from an abstract domain to a concrete domain. Our contract refinements are compositional, in that composition is monotonic with respect to the refinements (see, e.g., Proposition 1). When applied to A/G contracts, the abstraction $\overline{\alpha}$ [9] abstracts both assumptions and guarantees via the map α, i.e., $\overline{\alpha}(A, G) = (\alpha(A), \alpha(G \cup \overline{A}))$. Conversely, heterogeneous refinement operates on assumptions and guarantees in a covariant-contravariant fashion, by widening the assumptions and tightening the guarantees as we transition from the abstract to the concrete domain (see, e.g., Definition 2). In our framework, complex verification and synthesis tasks need not be performed, compositionally, entirely in the abstract domain; heterogeneous refinements would rather bridge and combine, in a consistent way, proofs and proof techniques that are effective in different domains.

5   Vertical Contracts

Since it is based on behavior mappings, heterogeneous refinement does not subsume any notion of architectural decomposition; therefore, it is not enough to express refinement between the specification contracts and the implementation contracts of systems when they relate to heterogeneous modeling architectures and present heterogeneous structures. As a second step, we then equip our framework with a new notion of contract composition that can relate a contract and its vertical heterogeneous refinement, including different viewpoints, independently of their modeling structures. Compatibility and consistency of the resulting *vertical contract* will then be checked to assess design correctness.

Consider the problem of mapping a specification platform of a system at level $l+1$ into an implementation platform at level l in PBD. In general, the specification platform architecture (i.e., interconnection of components) may be defined in an independent way, and may not directly match the implementation platform architecture. Such a *heterogeneous architectural decomposition* will also reflect on the contracts associated with the components and their aggregations. For instance, the contract describing the specification platform $\mathcal{C}$ may be defined as the conjunction of K different viewpoints, each characterized by its own architectural decomposition into I_k contracts, i.e., $\mathcal{C} = \bigwedge_{k \in K} \left(\bigotimes_{i \in I_k} \mathcal{C}_{ik} \right)$. On the other hand, the contract describing the implementation platform $\mathcal{M}$ may be better represented as a composition of J contracts, each defined out of a conjunction of its different viewpoints, i.e., $\mathcal{M} = \bigotimes_{j \in J} \left(\bigwedge_{n \in N_j} \mathcal{M}_{jn} \right)$. We denote by $\mathbb{C} = \{ \mathcal{C}_{ik} | k \in K, i \in I_k \}$ and $\mathbb{M} = \{ \mathcal{M}_{jn} | j \in J, n \in N_j \}$, respectively, the architectural decompositions of $\mathcal{C}$ and $\mathcal{M}$, i.e., the set of all the contracts and viewpoints that are used to describe them.

Because there may not be, in general, a direct matching between contracts and viewpoints of $\mathcal{M}$ and $\mathcal{C}$, checking that $\mathcal{M} \preceq \mathcal{C}$ in a compositional way, by reasoning on the elements of $\mathcal{M}$ and $\mathcal{C}$ independently, as discussed in Sect. 3 (for classical refinement) and Sect. 4 (for heterogeneous refinement), may not be effective or even possible. However, we would still like to capture the fact that the actual satisfaction of all the design requirements and viewpoints by a deployment depends on the supporting execution platform, the underlying physical system, and on the way in which system functionalities are mapped into them. To formalize this mapping of system functionalities into architecture primitives, we first introduce the compact notation $\mathrm{Ag}(\mathbb{C})$ or, equivalently, $\mathrm{Ag}(\mathcal{C}_1, \ldots, \mathcal{C}_n)$ to represent a generic aggregation of contracts and viewpoints $\mathcal{C}_1, \ldots, \mathcal{C}_n$ from a set $\mathbb{C} = \{ \mathcal{C}_1, \ldots, \mathcal{C}_n \}$ via composition or conjunction operations. For example, $\mathrm{Ag}_1(\mathcal{C}_1, \ldots, \mathcal{C}_4) := (\mathcal{C}_1 \otimes \mathcal{C}_2) \wedge (\mathcal{C}_3 \otimes \mathcal{C}_4)$ and $\mathrm{Ag}_2(\mathcal{C}_1, \ldots, \mathcal{C}_4) := \mathcal{C}_1 \wedge ((\mathcal{C}_2 \wedge \mathcal{C}_3) \otimes \mathcal{C}_4)$ define two different aggregation operators on $\mathcal{C}_1, \ldots, \mathcal{C}_4$. We then introduce the notion of *architecture mapping* as follows.

Definition 3 (Architecture Mapping). *Let $\mathcal{C}_1$ and $\mathcal{C}_2$ be two contracts with architectural decompositions $\mathbb{C}_1$ and $\mathbb{C}_2$, respectively. An* architecture mapping *between $\mathcal{C}_1$ and $\mathcal{C}_2$ is a relation $\mathcal{V} \subseteq 2^{\mathbb{C}_1} \times 2^{\mathbb{C}_2}$ such that $(\mathbb{V}_1, \mathbb{V}_2) \in \mathcal{V}$ if and only if there exist aggregation operators Ag_1 and Ag_2 and a behavior abstraction function $\mathcal{A}$ such that $\mathrm{Ag}_1(\mathbb{V}_1) \preceq_{\mathcal{A}} \mathrm{Ag}_2(\mathbb{V}_2)$.*

The intent of architecture mapping is to associate heterogeneous aggregations of contracts and viewpoints in an implementation contract $\mathcal{C}_1$ with their specification counterparts $\mathcal{C}_2$ and *vice versa*, where $\mathcal{C}_1$ and $\mathcal{C}_2$ may be expressed in different formalisms. We can then reason about refinement between an implementation contract $\mathcal{M}$ and a specification contract $\mathcal{C}$ by resorting to a contract which specifies the composition of a model and its vertical refinement, even though they are not directly connected, by connecting them indirectly through an architecture mapping $\mathcal{V}$. For example, $\mathcal{V}$ can be implemented by synchronizing pairs of events, as if co-simulating a model and its refinement, or by a set of constraints over the variables of $\mathcal{M}$ and $\mathcal{C}$. We can then model the interaction between the specification and the implementation platforms using a conjunction operation, as defined below.

Definition 4 (Vertical Contract). *Let $\mathcal{C}$ and $\mathcal{M}$ be two contracts, possibly describing the specification and implementation platforms of a system, and let $\mathcal{V}$ be an architecture mapping between $\mathcal{M}$ and $\mathcal{C}$. We call* vertical contract under $\mathcal{V}$ *the composite contract $\mathcal{C} \wedge_{\mathcal{V}} \mathcal{M}$, i.e., the conjunction of $\mathcal{C}$ and $\mathcal{M}$ subject to the mapping constraints established by $\mathcal{V}$.*

Assumptions and guarantees in $\mathcal{C} \wedge_{\mathcal{V}} \mathcal{M}$ combine as defined in Sect. 3, and $\mathcal{C} \wedge_{\mathcal{V}} \mathcal{M}$ is assured to refine $\mathcal{C}$ by construction. We can then replace $\mathcal{C}$ with $\mathcal{C} \wedge_{\mathcal{V}} \mathcal{M}$. However, being a conjunction, it can still be a source of inconsistencies. Therefore, to guarantee that the design can be implemented, the consistency of $\mathcal{C} \wedge_{\mathcal{V}} \mathcal{M}$ must be checked or enforced by the designer. Checking consistency on the composite contract can be, however, easier than checking $\mathcal{M} \preceq \mathcal{C}$, since some of the assumptions made by the specification platform on the implementation platform can be discharged by the guarantees of the implementation platform, and *vice versa*, when computing $\mathcal{C} \wedge_{\mathcal{V}} \mathcal{M}$ subject to the mapping constraints defined by $\mathcal{V}$. We exemplify the use of vertical contracts by referring to the model of a simple system in Fig. 1b.

Example 2. The specification platform architecture at the top of Fig. 1b consists of two interconnected components. At startup, the *Controller* interacts with an external subsystem through its *in* and *out* ports to perform some high-priority task. Then, it switches on a safety-critical electric power system *EPS*, by asserting its output *on*, and makes sure that the system is actually powered, i.e., the signal *powered* is asserted, by the deadline t_d.

At the application level, to conveniently explore different control strategies, the designer abstracts the physical system *EPS* using a simple delay block, which propagates the value of its input *on* to its output *powered* with a delay Δ. We therefore obtain $t_{pow} - t_{on} = \Delta$, where t_{pow} and t_{on} are, respectively, the times at which *powered* and *on* are asserted, and Δ is selected to accommodate the delay of the physical platform. Then, the designer implements the required functionality by allocating the *Controller* to its higher priority task, while guaranteeing a worst case switch-on time $t_{on}^{max} = t_d - \Delta$ to meet the deadline on the *powered* signal.

While the functional platform described above is very convenient to explore different control strategies, it is not sufficient to determine the correctness of the final design. In fact, the satisfaction of the timing viewpoints heavily relies on the assumptions on the delay of the physical system, which can only be discharged by the implementation platform. The architecture of the implementation platform is shown at the bottom of Fig. 1b. The functionality of the *Controller* is mapped to a hardware execution platform *HW*, while the *EPS* is modeled by a cascade of a first-order filter with time constant τ, represented in the figure as an electrical network, and an ideal *Comparator* block, with reference voltage v_{ref}. In this case, the filter and *Comparator* blocks (and their contracts) are associated with the *EPS* block (and its contract) via an architecture mapping $\mathcal{V}$. If the filter output voltage v is larger than v_{ref}, the *Comparator* asserts its output *powered*. The reference v_{ref} corresponds to 90% of the final value v_f reached by v at steady state.

To show that the implementation platform refines the specification platform, hence satisfies the system requirements, we formalize the interaction between the two levels in terms of the vertical contract $\tilde{\mathcal{C}}^t \wedge_{\mathcal{V}} \tilde{\mathcal{M}}^t$ between the following timing contracts under the constraints established by $\mathcal{V}$:

– $\tilde{\mathcal{C}}^t = (\{t_{on}, t_{pow}\}, t_{on} \leq (t_d - \Delta), t_{pow} \leq t_d)$, the specification contract, states that the requirement on t_{pow} is satisfied if on is asserted by at least an interval Δ before the deadline t_d.

– $\tilde{\mathcal{M}}^t = (\{t_{on}, t_{pow}\}, \mathrm{T}, t_{pow} = t_{on} + \tau \ln 10)$, the implementation contract, exposes the timing behavior of the *powered* signal. $\tilde{\mathcal{M}}^t$ states that, whenever on is asserted, *powered* will be asserted with a delay $\tau \ln 10$, due to the physical system (a first-order filter).

Assumptions and guarantees are expressed using predicates on real variables. Then, to check the correctness of the refinement, a binding mechanism between the two contracts, each linked to its own platform, can now be provided by the conjunction of $\tilde{\mathcal{M}}^t$ and $\tilde{\mathcal{C}}^t$ and the architecture mapping between them. Proving the consistency of this conjunction is instrumental to prove the correctness of the overall system. $\tilde{\mathcal{C}}^t \wedge_{\mathcal{V}} \tilde{\mathcal{M}}^t$ ensures that both contracts are jointly satisfied, and refines $\tilde{\mathcal{C}}^t$ by construction. Therefore, all we need to check is that $\tilde{\mathcal{M}}^t$ does not create inconsistencies in $\tilde{\mathcal{C}}^t \wedge_{\mathcal{V}} \tilde{\mathcal{M}}^t$, in the sense that $(\forall t_{on} : \exists t_{pow} : G_{\tilde{\mathcal{M}}^t} \cap G_{\tilde{\mathcal{C}}^t})$ is true,[3] where $G_{\tilde{\mathcal{M}}^t}$ and $G_{\tilde{\mathcal{C}}^t}$ are the guarantees of the two contracts in saturated form. In our case,

$$\forall t_{on} : \exists t_{pow} : (t_{pow} = t_{on} + \tau \ln 10) \wedge ((t_{on} > t_d - \Delta) \vee (t_{pow} \leq t_d))$$
$$= \forall t_{on} : (\exists t_{pow} : t_{pow} = t_{on} + \tau \ln 10) \wedge (t_{on} > t_d - \Delta) \vee (t_{on} \leq t_d - \tau \ln 10)$$
$$= \forall t_{on} : (t_{on} > t_d - \Delta) \vee (t_{on} \leq t_d - \tau \ln 10)$$

leads to the condition $\tau \ln 10 \leq \Delta$. Intuitively, this amounts to requiring that, if t_{on} and t_{pow} have to synchronize so that $\tilde{\mathcal{M}}^t$ refines $\tilde{\mathcal{C}}^t$ and the overall system satisfies the timing requirement on t_{pow}, then the delay implemented by the physical system in $\tilde{\mathcal{M}}^t$ must be smaller than or equal to the one defined by the application platform in $\tilde{\mathcal{C}}^t$. This inequality can be used at design time, as a practical guideline to dimension either the specification platform, by increasing its margin Δ, or the implementation platform, by decreasing its time constant τ, to deploy a correct design.

The approach illustrated above was previously used to formalize mechanisms for mapping a specification over an execution platform in the design of analog and mixed-signal integrated circuits [33,39] and in the METROPOLIS [5] framework and its successors [6,19]. In the context of analog and mixed-signal integrated circuits, we leveraged effective approximations of implementation constraints to formulate vertical contracts representing different viewpoints (e.g., timing, energy, noise), and then checking their compatibility or consistency during design space exploration. More recently, a similar approach has also been advocated in the context of AUTOSAR [8].

---

[3] We are actually interested in checking consistency $\forall t_{on} : t_{on} \leq (t_d - \Delta)$, which is the set of legal environments for $\tilde{\mathcal{C}}^t$. In fact, we want to show that, for each t_{on} satisfying the assumptions of the specification contract $\tilde{\mathcal{C}}^t$, there exists an implementable t_{pow}, according to the implementation contract $\tilde{\mathcal{M}}^t$, which also satisfies the deadline t_d, as required by $\tilde{\mathcal{C}}^t$. When $t_{on} > (t_d - \Delta)$, $\tilde{\mathcal{C}}^t \wedge \tilde{\mathcal{M}}^t$ is trivially consistent, since the guarantees of $\tilde{\mathcal{C}}^t$ are vacuously true.

Alternatively, when vertical contract assumptions and guarantees cannot be effectively expressed by compact models, compatibility and consistency of vertical contracts can be checked by co-simulation of the application and implementation platforms under a mapping mechanisms, such as the one in the METRONOMY framework [19], in which tuples of signals in the two platforms are synchronized. In the context of Example 2, this technique can be applied by unifying both occurrences and values of the *on* and *powered* signals, as shown in red in Fig. 1b, and then checking that the synchronized models satisfy the requirements. In the following, we further illustrate the usage of vertical contracts in combination with heterogeneous refinement in PBD. More application examples will be discussed in Sect. 7.

6   Vertical Contracts in Platform-Based Design

In PBD, horizontal contracts are used to formalize the conditions for correctness of element integration at the same level of abstraction, while vertical contracts formalize the conditions for lower levels of abstraction to be consistent with the higher ones, and for abstractions of available components to be faithful representations of the actual parts. If vertical contracts are satisfied, the mapping mechanism of PBD can be used to produce design refinements that are correct by construction. Informally, vertical contracts are often decomposed into bottom-up and top-down contracts [33,48]. For instance, when analyzing the behavior of complex CPSs, simplified macro-models are typically used to capture the relevant behaviors of the components at higher levels of abstraction. Therefore, guarantees should be provided on the accuracy of the macro-models with respect to models at lower levels of abstraction. These guarantees can be captured via *bottom-up vertical contracts*. On the other hand, in a top-down design approach, *top-down vertical contracts* can be used to encode top-level requirements that system architects introduce to craft the behavior of a chosen architecture according to the desired functionality. In the following, we show how these concepts can be formalized using the notions of heterogeneous refinement and vertical contracts introduced in Sects. 4 and 5.

For reasoning about a system M at level $l + 1$, let $\mathcal{C}_B^{l+1}$ be a bottom-up vertical contract used to capture what is expected to be offered by possible implementations of M at level l, so as to be able for M to perform its intended function at level $l + 1$, as expressed by a top-down vertical contract $\mathcal{C}_T^{l+1}$. The correctness of the design using M at level $l+1$ will then depend on the existence of an implementation of M meeting this bottom-up vertical contract. Moreover, $\mathcal{C}_B^{l+1}$ adds to the horizontal contract $\mathcal{C}_H^{l+1}$, which is also attached to M, to capture the conditions imposed on its context at level $l+1$ for its correct integration. Such a breakdown into $\mathcal{C}_H^{l+1}$, $\mathcal{C}_B^{l+1}$, and $\mathcal{C}_T^{l+1}$ can be used to enforce orthogonalization of concerns, by separating function ($\mathcal{C}_T^{l+1}$) from communication ($\mathcal{C}_H^{l+1}$) and from implementation ($\mathcal{C}_B^{l+1}$). In this setup, $\mathcal{C}_T^{l+1}$ captures the top-level requirements on M, while $\mathcal{C}_H^{l+1}$ and $\mathcal{C}_B^{l+1}$ can be regarded as two different viewpoints, used to specify the conditions imposed, respectively, on the integration environment at level $l + 1$ and the implementation platform at level l.

We now assume that the system M at level $l + 1$ is to be implemented by an aggregation of subsystems $M_1, \ldots, M_n$ at level l, and show how the afore-mentioned structural decomposition can be leveraged to generate a hierarchy of verification (or synthesis) tasks during the design flow.

Top-Down Design Step. When using budgeting in a *top-down approach*, the designer assigns responsibilities to the subsystems implementing M, by deriving top-down contracts $\mathcal{C}_{T1}^l, \ldots, \mathcal{C}_{Tn}^l$, al level l, for each of them. These contracts must jointly establish M's bottom-up vertical contract $\mathcal{C}_B^{l+1}$ by construction, and can be derived, for instance, by using synthesis methods. In this example, we assume that levels l and $l+1$ may use, in general, different behavior formalisms, which are related by a mapping $\mathcal{M}$. We can then formalize the condition stated above as follows:

$$\bigotimes_{i=1}^{n} \mathcal{C}_{Hi}^l \bigwedge \bigotimes_{i=1}^{n} \mathcal{C}_{Ti}^l \preceq_{\mathcal{M}} \mathcal{C}_B^{l+1}, \tag{4}$$

where we highlight the fact that the execution of this cross-layer design step must assume that the integration of the different subsystems is successful, as prescribed by the horizontal contracts.[4]

Bottom-Up Design Step. Alternatively, when using a *bottom-up approach*, the top-down vertical contracts of $M_1, \ldots, M_n$ at level l are given, and we need to establish that the bottom-up contract of M at level $l + 1$ is satisfied by check-ing (4). Horizontal contracts can also be used this time as additional premise in the verification of refinement. The verification step in (4) can be performed in different ways. In particular, a convenient way could be to resort to a vertical contract, in the sense of Sect. 5, and prove that it is consistent. Given $\mathcal{C}_B^{l+1} = (V_B^{l+1}, A_B^{l+1}, G_B^{l+1})$, and $\mathcal{M}^{-1}(\mathcal{C}_B^{l+1}) := (R_{\mathcal{M}}^{-1}(V_B^{l+1}), \mathcal{M}^{-1}(A_B^{l+1}), \mathcal{M}^{-1}(G_B^{l+1}))$, such a vertical contract can be defined as follows:

$$\mathcal{M}^{-1}(\mathcal{C}_B^{l+1}) \wedge \bigotimes_{i=1}^{n} \mathcal{C}_{Hi}^l \bigwedge \bigotimes_{i=1}^{n} \mathcal{C}_{Ti}^l,$$

which refines $\mathcal{C}_B^{l+1}$ by construction.

In both the top-down and bottom-up approaches, the design finally proceeds with the additional verification steps required for each component M_i to demon-strate that, based on the expected capabilities of its realization, as expressed by its bottom-up vertical contract, the functionality of the component as expressed by its top-down vertical contract can be achieved, i.e.,

$$\forall i \in \{1, \ldots, n\} : \mathcal{C}_{Bi}^{l+1} \wedge \mathcal{C}_{Hi}^{l+1} \preceq \mathcal{C}_{Ti}^{l+1}. \tag{5}$$

---

[4] We observe that the structural decomposition adopted in (4) is just an example. Another alternative could be to represent the left-hand side contract as $\bigotimes_{i=1}^{n}(\mathcal{C}_{Hi}^l \wedge \mathcal{C}_{Ti}^l)$.

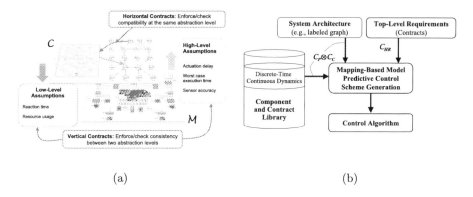

Fig. 2. Role of horizontal and vertical contracts in system design (a) and mapping flow for automatic generation of model predictive control schemes (b).

Again, as shown in (5), these proofs can take the horizontal contracts of the components as additional supportive argument. Moreover, they can be performed by leveraging the vertical contracts $\mathcal{C}_{Ti}^{l+1} \wedge \mathcal{C}_{Bi}^{l+1} \wedge \mathcal{C}_{Hi}^{l+1}$, for each component M_i, and proving their consistency.

7 Application Examples

Vertical contracts can be applied to reason about hierarchical design of embedded controllers, in that they can formalize the agreement between control, software, and hardware engineers when specifying both system functionality and timing requirements [15,41,48]. In PBD, such an agreement is encoded in terms of top-down and bottom-up vertical assumptions and guarantees. In a typical scenario, as represented in Fig. 2a, a controller takes as assumptions several aspects that include the timing behavior of the control tasks and of the communication between tasks, e.g., delay, jitter, as well as the accuracy and resolution of the computation (vertical assumptions in $\mathcal{C}$). On the other hand, the controller provides guarantees in terms of the amount of requested computation, activation times, and data dependencies (vertical assumptions in $\mathcal{M}$). Several controller design guidelines previously proposed in the literature can then be derived by formulating and requiring consistency of vertical contracts across the hardware, software, and control layers, as done in Example 2. In the following, we discuss how vertical contracts can be used to formalize the hierarchical design of embedded controllers combining synthesis and optimization methods.

7.1 Contract-Based Design of Hierarchical Controllers

Embedded controllers in complex, safety-critical CPSs, such as large power distribution networks or robotic systems, often rely on hierarchical architectures. The high-level controller, e.g., a task planner or supervisory controller, is in charge of high-level decisions and can benefit from discrete abstractions and synthesis techniques, such as reactive synthesis from linear temporal logic [43,44] (LTL) specifications, to provide a high degree of assurance on the system functionality [34,35]. However, several real-time performance requirements (e.g., timing constraints), mostly related to the dynamics of the physical plant and the hardware implementation of the controller, cannot be effectively captured by discrete models. A low-level controller, e.g., a trajectory planner, is usually in charge of satisfying these requirements, and leverages virtual prototyping techniques based on the analysis of simulation traces in the absence of tractable algorithmic synthesis methods. In this scenario, vertical contracts can be used to formalize and orchestrate the hierarchical design process.

As an example, let contract C_C express the controller requirements, where the assumptions A_C encode the allowable behaviors of the environment (including aspects of the physical plant) and the guarantees G_C encode the desired behaviors of the controller in closed-loop with its plant. We assume that C_C can be expressed as the conjunction between a contract C_{syn}, for which a synthesis method can be effectively applied to generate high-level controller implementations, and a contract C_{ver}, which can only be checked by a verification or simulation routine, which we call an *oracle*. We refer the reader to our previous work [31,35] for an instance of this design problem, where C_{syn} is expressed using LTL, C_{ver} is expressed using signal temporal logic (STL) [29], and the oracle is a contract monitoring routine operating on simulation traces. $C_{syn} \wedge C_{ver}$ is then a *vertical contract* for the controller, where C_{syn} and C_{ver} refer to different controller representations, possibly involving different viewpoints (e.g., functional and timing).[5] To guarantee the consistency of $C_{syn} \wedge C_{ver}$ and refine it towards an implementation, the design process can be decomposed in the following steps.

As a first step, C_{syn} can be used together with discrete models of the plant and the environment (which can also be captured, for instance, by LTL formulas) to synthesize a reactive control strategy in the form of one (or more) state machines using algorithmic synthesis techniques. The resulting high-level controller will satisfy C_{syn} by construction. As a second step, the synthesized state machine is embedded into a high-fidelity hybrid model of the system. The entire system is simulated and the satisfaction of C_{ver} is assessed by monitoring simulation traces, while possibly optimizing a set of system parameters and costs. In this step, a mapping methodology can be used to perform joint design exploration of the high-level and low-level controllers together with the execution platform, while guaranteeing that their specifications, captured by the vertical contract, are consistent and the architecture mapping constraints are satisfied. The low-level controller is then refined in this step and the resulting optimal hierarchical architecture is returned as the final design.

For instance, let $C_{ver} = (S, \phi_e, \phi_e \rightarrow \phi_s)$ be a vertical contract that must be checked by simulation, where ϕ_e and ϕ_s are temporal logic formulas. Then, given an array of costs C, the mapping problem can be cast as a *multi-objective*

---

[5] For simplicity, we drop the symbol of the architecture mapping V from the expressions of the vertical contracts in this section and in the following ones.

robust optimization problem, to find a set of configuration parameter vectors κ^* that are Pareto optimal with respect to the objectives in C, while guaranteeing that the system satisfies ϕ_s for all possible traces s satisfying the environment assumptions ϕ_e. More formally,

$$\min_{\kappa \in \mathcal{K}, \pi \in \Pi} \quad C(\kappa, \pi)$$

$$\text{s.t.} \begin{cases} \mathcal{F}(s, \kappa) = 0 \\ s \models \phi_s(\pi) \qquad \forall \; s \text{ s.t. } s \models \phi_e(\pi) \end{cases} \tag{6}$$

where π is a set of parameters that can be used to capture degrees of freedom that are available in the system specifications, and whose final value can also be determined as a result of the optimization process. For a given parameter value κ', s' is the set of system traces that are obtained by simulating the hybrid dynamical model $\mathcal{F}(.)$ of the system. A multi-objective optimization algorithm with simulation in the loop can then be implemented to find the Pareto optimal solutions κ^*. While this may be expensive in general, it becomes the only affordable approach in many practical cases. Finn et al. [16] propose a mixed discrete-continuous optimization scheme to solve an instance of problem (6), and apply it to the design space exploration of an aircraft environmental control system.

In this hierarchical control design methodology, guaranteeing that several functional, safety, and reliability requirements are already satisfied by construction after the synthesis step helps decrease the execution time. Finally, the joint execution of the controller with the plant in the mapping step effectively implements the synchronization mechanism introduced in Sect. 5, which is instrumental in: (i) checking the consistency of the vertical contract, (ii) discharging the timing discretization assumptions made during the synthesis steps, and (iii) ultimately verifying the satisfaction of both the functional and timing viewpoints.

7.2   Generation of Model Predictive Control Schemes

By using a formalization of the design requirements and the plant dynamics in terms of constraints over real numbers, it is possible to formulate the control problem as an optimization problem that is solved using a receding horizon approach to determine a correct control strategy that can also optimize some performance metrics. In this scenario, vertical contracts can support the automatic generation of model predictive control schemes [18].

A representation of the design flow following a PBD approach is shown in Fig. 2b. Both the plant P and the controller C can be specified by an aggregation of contracts from a library $\mathcal{L}$. We denote the composition of the plant and controller contracts under feedback interconnection as $\mathcal{C}_P \otimes \mathcal{C}_C$. The top-level requirements are instead specified by a system-level application contract $\mathcal{C}_{RH}$. The refinement (mapping) between $\mathcal{C}_{RH}$ and $\mathcal{C}_P \otimes \mathcal{C}_C$ is then modeled as the vertical contract $\mathcal{C}_{RH} \wedge (\mathcal{C}_P \otimes \mathcal{C}_C)$ given by the conjunction of the architecture and application contracts under the architecture mapping constraints. We are interested in an optimal control law subject to the constraint that $\mathcal{C}_{RH} \wedge (\mathcal{C}_P \otimes \mathcal{C}_C)$ is consistent, i.e., there exists an implementation satisfying both the guarantees of $\mathcal{C}_{RH}$ and $\mathcal{C}_P \otimes \mathcal{C}_C$ in the context of their assumptions. To this aim, an optimal control problem can be formulated as an optimized mapping problem, an instance of (6), over a time horizon H.

If a discrete-time abstraction of the hybrid system dynamics is available, e.g., relying on linear difference equations over the components' variables and parameters (e.g., for time-varying properties), or linear constraints on real variables that must hold at each time step or at steady state (e.g., for time-invariant properties), then it is possible to express behaviors, assumptions, and guarantees, and implement the algebra of contracts using conjunctive or disjunctive combinations of linear constraints over the reals. The control law will be a discrete-time continuous-valued trace and the formulation in (6), which is returned as the final design, translates into a mixed integer linear (or quadratic) program that can be effectively solved by state-of-the-art optimization algorithms. This approach has been effective for generating model predictive control schemes for integrated energy management in smart grids [21,28] as well as aircraft power distribution networks [26].

8   Conclusions

The design of complex engineering systems requires reasoning about hierarchies of models characterized by both semantic and structural heterogeneity. Heterogeneous refinement and vertical contracts provide a viable foundation to effectively reason about the relationships between these models for multi-view and multi-layer design. They have been demonstrated on examples form hierarchical controller design and the generation of model predictive control schemes. Both the formalization and concretization of these concepts are, however, in their infancy. Future work includes, for example, the investigation of links between vertical contracts and alternative notions of abstraction based on approximations or the theory of abstract interpretation. We believe that novel and effective formalization efforts and applications will emerge as we strive to embed more and more cognitive capabilities in our design tools.

References

1. de Alfaro, L., Henzinger, T.A.: Interface automata. In: Proceedings of the Symposium Foundations of Software Engineering, pp. 109–120. ACM Press (2001)
2. de Alfaro, L., Henzinger, T.A.: Interface theories for component-based design. In: Henzinger, T.A., Kirsch, C.M. (eds.) EMSOFT 2001. LNCS, vol. 2211, pp. 148–165. Springer, Heidelberg (2001). https://doi.org/10.1007/3-540-45449-7_11
3. Alur, R., Henzinger, T., Lafferriere, G., Pappas, G.: Discrete abstractions of hybrid systems. Proc. IEEE **88**(7), 971–984 (2000)
4. Alur, R., Dang, T., Ivančić, F.: Counterexample-guided predicate abstraction of hybrid systems. Theor. Comput. Sci. **354**(2), 250–271 (2006)

5. Balarin, F., Hsieh, H., Lavagno, L., Passerone, C., Sangiovanni-Vincentelli, A.L., Watanabe, Y.: Metropolis: an integrated electronic system design environment. Computer **36**(4), 45–52 (2003)
6. Balarin, F., Davare, A., D'Angelo, M., Densmore, D., Meyerowitz, T., Passerone, R., Pinto, A., Sangiovanni-Vincentelli, A., Simalatsar, A., Watanabe, Y., Yang, G., Zhu, Q.: Platform-based design and frameworks: metropolis and metro II. In: Nicolescu, G., Mosterman, P.J. (eds.) Model-Based Design for Embedded Systems, Chap. 10, p. 259. CRC Press, Taylor and Francis Group, Boca Raton, London, New York, November 2009
7. Benveniste, A., et al.: Multiple viewpoint contract-based specification and design. In: de Boer, F.S., Bonsangue, M.M., Graf, S., de Roever, W.-P. (eds.) FMCO 2007. LNCS, vol. 5382, pp. 200–225. Springer, Heidelberg (2008). https://doi.org/10.1007/978-3-540-92188-2_9
8. Benveniste, A., Caillaud, B., Nickovic, D., Passerone, R., Raclet, J.B., Reinkemeier, P., Sangiovanni-Vincentelli, A., Damm, W., Henzinger, T., Larsen, K.G.: Contracts for System Design. Rapport de recherche RR-8147, INRIA, November 2012
9. Benveniste, A., Nickovic, D., Henzinger, T.: Compositional contract abstraction for system design. Research Report RR-8460, INRIA, January 2014
10. Chaudhuri, K., Doligez, D., Lamport, L., Merz, S.: The TLA$^+$ proof system: building a heterogeneous verification platform. In: Cavalcanti, A., Deharbe, D., Gaudel, M.-C., Woodcock, J. (eds.) ICTAC 2010. LNCS, vol. 6255, p. 44. Springer, Heidelberg (2010). https://doi.org/10.1007/978-3-642-14808-8_3. http://dl.acm.org/citation.cfm?id=1881833.1881837
11. Chutinan, A., Krogh, B.: Verification of infinite-state dynamic systems using approximate quotient transition systems. IEEE Trans. Autom. Control **46**(9), 1401–1410 (2001)
12. Clarke, E.M., Grumberg, O., Peled, D.A.: Model Checking. The MIT Press, Cambridge (2008)
13. Cousot, P., Cousot, R.: Abstract interpretation: a unified lattice model for static analysis of programs by construction or approximation of fixpoints. In: Symposium on Principles of Programming Languages (POPL), pp. 238–252. ACM Press (1977)
14. Dang, T., Maler, O., Testylier, R.: Accurate hybridization of nonlinear systems. In: Proceedings of the Hybrid Systems: Computation and Controlm, HSCC 2010, pp. 11–20. ACM, New York (2010). https://doi.org/10.1145/1755952.1755956
15. Derler, P., Lee, E.A., Tripakis, S., Törngren, M.: Cyber-physical system design contracts. In: Proceedings of the International Conference Cyber-Physical Systems, pp. 109–118 (2013). https://doi.org/10.1145/2502524.2502540
16. Finn, J., Nuzzo, P., Sangiovanni-Vincentelli, A.: A mixed discrete-continuous optimization scheme for cyber-physical system architecture exploration. In: Proceedings of the IEEE/ACM International Conference on Computer-Aided Design, pp. 216–223, November 2015
17. Frehse, G.: PHAVer: algorithmic verification of hybrid systems past HyTech. Int. J. Softw. Tools Technol. Transfer **10**, 263–279 (2008)
18. Garcia, C.E., Prett, D.M., Morari, M.: Model predictive control: theory and practice – a survey. Automatica **25**(3), 335–348 (1989). http://www.sciencedirect.com/science/article/pii/0005109889900022
19. Guo, L., Zhu, Q., Nuzzo, P., Passerone, R., Sangiovanni-Vincentelli, A., Lee, E.A.: Metronomy: a function-architecture co-simulation framework for timing verification of cyber-physical systems. In: Proceedings of the International Conference Hardware-Software Codesign and System Synthesis, pp. 24:1–24:10, October 2014

20. Henzinger, T., Ho, P.H., Wong-Toi, H.: Algorithmic analysis of nonlinear hybrid systems. IEEE Trans. Autom. Control **43**(4), 540–554 (1998)
21. Jin, B., Nuzzo, P., Maasoumy, M., Zhou, Y., Sangiovanni-Vincentelli, A.: A contract-based framework for integrated demand response management in smart grids. In: Proceedings of the International Conference Embedded Systems for Energy-Efficient Built Environments, pp. 167–176. ACM (2015)
22. Keutzer, K., Malik, S., Newton, R., Rabaey, J., Sangiovanni Vincentelli, A.: System level design: orthogonalization of concerns and platform-based design. IEEE Trans. Comput.-Aided Des. Integr. Circ. Syst. **19**(12), 1523–1543 (2000)
23. Koymans, R.: Specifying real-time properties with metric temporal logic. Real-Time Syst. **2**(4), 255–299 (1990)
24. Lee, E.A., Sangiovanni-Vincentelli, A.: A framework for comparing models of computation. IEEE Trans. Comput.-Aided Des. Integr. Circ. Syst. **17**(12), 1217–1229 (1998)
25. Leung, M.-K., et al.: Scalable semantic annotation using lattice-based ontologies. In: Schürr, A., Selic, B. (eds.) MODELS 2009. LNCS, vol. 5795, pp. 393–407. Springer, Heidelberg (2009). https://doi.org/10.1007/978-3-642-04425-0_31
26. Li, J., Nuzzo, P., Sangiovanni-Vincentelli, A., Xi, Y., Li, D.: Stochastic contracts for cyber-physical system design under probabilistic requirements. In: Proceedings of the International Conference Formal Methods and Models for Co-design, September 2017
27. Lohstroh, M., Lee, E.A.: An interface theory for the internet of things. In: Calinescu, R., Rumpe, B. (eds.) SEFM 2015. LNCS, vol. 9276, pp. 20–34. Springer, Cham (2015). https://doi.org/10.1007/978-3-319-22969-0_2
28. Maasoumy, M., Nuzzo, P., Sangiovanni-Vincentelli, A.: Smart buildings in the smart grid: contract-based design of an integrated energy management system. In: Khaitan, S.K., McCalley, J.D., Liu, C.C. (eds.) Cyber Physical Systems Approach to Smart Electric Power Grid. PS, pp. 103–132. Springer, Heidelberg (2015). https://doi.org/10.1007/978-3-662-45928-7_5
29. Maler, O., Nickovic, D.: Monitoring temporal properties of continuous signals. In: Lakhnech, Y., Yovine, S. (eds.) FORMATS/FTRTFT 2004. LNCS, vol. 3253, pp. 152–166. Springer, Heidelberg (2004). https://doi.org/10.1007/978-3-540-30206-3_12
30. Meyer, B.: Applying "design by contract". Computer **25**(10), 40–51 (1992)
31. Nuzzo, P., Finn, J.B., Iannopollo, A., Sangiovanni-Vincentelli, A.L.: Contract-based design of control protocols for safety-critical cyber-physical systems. In: Proceedings of the Design, Automation and Test in Europe Conference, pp. 1–4, March 2014
32. Nuzzo, P., Iannopollo, A., Tripakis, S., Sangiovanni-Vincentelli, A.L.: Are interface theories equivalent to contract theories? In: International Conference on Formal Methods and Models for Co-design, pp. 104–113, October 2014
33. Nuzzo, P., Sangiovanni-Vincentelli, A., Sun, X., Puggelli, A.: Methodology for the design of analog integrated interfaces using contracts. IEEE Sens. J. **12**(12), 3329–3345 (2012)
34. Nuzzo, P., Sangiovanni-Vincentelli, A.L., Murray, R.M.: Methodology and tools for next generation cyber-physical systems: the iCyPhy approach. In: Proceedings of the INCOSE International Symposium, vol. 25, pp. 235–249. Wiley Online Library, July 2015
35. Nuzzo, P., Xu, H., Ozay, N., Finn, J., Sangiovanni-Vincentelli, A., Murray, R., Donzé, A., Seshia, S.: A contract-based methodology for aircraft electric power system design. IEEE Access **2**, 1–25 (2014)

36. Nuzzo, P.: Compositional design of cyber-physical systems using contracts. Ph.D. thesis, EECS Department, University of California, Berkeley, August 2015. http://www.eecs.berkeley.edu/Pubs/TechRpts/2015/EECS-2015-189.html

37. Nuzzo, P., Lora, M., Feldman, Y., Sangiovanni-Vincentelli, A.: CHASE: contract-based requirement engineering for cyber-physical system design. In: Proceedings of the Design, Automation and Test in Europe Conference Dresden, Germany (2018, to appear)

38. Nuzzo, P., Sangiovanni-Vincentelli, A.: System design in the cyber-physical era. In: Nanoelectronics: Materials, Devices, Applications, pp. 363–396 (2017). https://doi.org/10.1002/9783527800728.ch15

39. Nuzzo, P., Sangiovanni-Vincentelli, A.: Robustness in analog systems: design techniques, methodologies and tools. In: Proceedings of the IEEE Symposium Industrial Embedded Systems, pp. 194–203, June 2011

40. Nuzzo, P., Sangiovanni-Vincentelli, A.: Let's get physical: computer science meets systems. In: Bensalem, S., Lakhneck, Y., Legay, A. (eds.) ETAPS 2014. LNCS, vol. 8415, pp. 193–208. Springer, Heidelberg (2014). https://doi.org/10.1007/978-3-642-54848-2_13

41. Nuzzo, P., Sangiovanni-Vincentelli, A., Bresolin, D., Geretti, L., Villa, T.: A platform-based design methodology with contracts and related tools for the design of cyber-physical systems. Proc. IEEE **103**(11), 2104–2132 (2015)

42. Passerone, R., Burch, J.R., Sangiovanni-Vincentelli, A.L.: Refinement preserving approximations for the design and verification of heterogeneous systems. Formal Methods Syst. Des. **31**(1), 1–33 (2007). https://doi.org/10.1007/s10703-006-0024-z

43. Piterman, N., Pnueli, A., Sa'ar, Y.: Synthesis of reactive(1) designs. In: Emerson, E.A., Namjoshi, K.S. (eds.) VMCAI 2006. LNCS, vol. 3855, pp. 364–380. Springer, Heidelberg (2005). https://doi.org/10.1007/11609773_24

44. Pnueli, A.: The temporal logic of programs. In: Symposium Foundations of Computer Science, vol. 31, pp. 46–57, November 1977

45. Rajhans, A., Bhave, A., Ruchkin, I., Krogh, B.H., Garlan, D., Platzer, A., Schmerl, B.: Supporting heterogeneity in cyber-physical systems architectures. IEEE Trans. Autom. Control **59**(12), 3178–3193 (2014)

46. Reineke, J., Tripakis, S.: Basic problems in multi-view modeling. In: Ábrahám, E., Havelund, K. (eds.) TACAS 2014. LNCS, vol. 8413, pp. 217–232. Springer, Heidelberg (2014). https://doi.org/10.1007/978-3-642-54862-8_15

47. Sangiovanni-Vincentelli, A.: Quo vadis, SLD? Reasoning about the trends and challenges of system level design. Proc. IEEE **95**(3), 467–506 (2007)

48. Sangiovanni-Vincentelli, A., Damm, W., Passerone, R.: Taming Dr. Frankenstein: contract-based design for cyber-physical systems. Eur. J. Control **18-3**(3), 217–238 (2012)

49. Tripakis, S., Lickly, B., Henzinger, T.A., Lee, E.A.: A theory of synchronous relational interfaces. Trans. Program. Lang. Syst. **33**(4), 14 (2011)

Abstraction and Refinement in Hierarchically Decomposable and Underspecified CPS-Architectures

Bernhard Rumpe and Andreas Wortmann[✉]

Software Engineering, RWTH Aachen University, Aachen, Germany
{rumpe,wortmann}@se-rwth.de

Abstract. Model-driven development of cyber-physical systems (CPS) requires modeling techniques based on a well-founded theory that supports addressing development techniques, such as decomposition, refinement and the different notions of time required by its components. Based on an elaborated theory for the modeling of underspecification with respect to nondeterminism, hierarchical composition, refinement that is compatible with composition, and finally proven correct evolution patterns, we discuss how such a theory can be practically applied for the development of CPS. Through an orchestrated efficient simulation, we can identify potential bottlenecks, function failures, hardware risks, *etc.* early. All models as well as the simulation take advantage of the compositionality and the timing refinement properties of the theory. In summary, we discuss how the elaborated theory shapes the simulation and the results.

1 Motivation

Rigorous model-driven development requires a well-defined set of integrated modeling notations that allows to define a set of possible implementations as well as a well-founded theory that is able to capture important aspects of the system while at the same time. It should (a) be as *abstract* as possible, (b) allow to specify known properties and to leave unknown properties unspecified, and (c) assist the core techniques in a development process.

A typical development process today has to provide various forms of *underspecification* to allow describing known properties and open issues, to support *refinement* along the development process from abstract requirements to very fine-grained technical specifications, and to *compose* specifications. It is not the composition itself, that is of prime importance, but the ability to *decompose* the problem, solve the smaller problems independently through a chain of refinements, and ultimately compose the solutions. This in particular implies that decomposition and refinement must be compatible. This full compatibility of the composition and refinement is important, because only then a decomposition of the problem leads to component specifications that can be independently

© Springer International Publishing AG, part of Springer Nature 2018
M. Lohstroh et al. (Eds.): Lee Festschrift, LNCS 10760, pp. 383–406, 2018.
https://doi.org/10.1007/978-3-319-95246-8_23

developed and refined. Ultimately, their implementations can be composed being sure that the properties specified originally still hold.

There are not many theories that can serve as the foundation for the development of systems, which potentially consist of a physical and a software part, are inherently distributed, and need to cope with a dynamically changing context, while having to fulfill tasks under given time constraints. Much has been said and written about cyber-physical systems (CPS) [33,34] and how those systems can be described and developed [13,16,30]. Only few theories, such as FOCUS [8] and consideration of superdense time [36,39], can actually serve the challenges discussed above. The more development techniques a theory assists, the more complex it necessarily has to be. Many earlier theories, such as CSP [25], CCS [43], Petri Nets [50], or the π-calculus [44] yield specific advantages, but unfortunately yield shortcomings in other techniques. Especially the existence of techniques for decomposition and refinement as well as their compatibility are crucial.

In this article, we summarize stream based theory, that emerges from FOCUS [5,8,31,53] and has been elaborated by Manfred Broy and his group over several decades in a larger set of publications. Model-driven development [15,65] can facilitate engineering of CPS [29], but requires implementing the underlying theory properly. Consequently, we also present how the theory is implemented in a tool suite called *MontiArc* [9,18,20], that allows to model various aspects of CPS and to simulate CPS with a focus on the interactions within and to the systems context. We briefly discuss, how this theory and its techniques for time and time refinement are realized and we sketch, how MontiArc models are used for example in robotic applications [24,52]. The key idea of the orchestrated efficient simulation that MontiArc provides, is to early identify potential bottlenecks, function failures, hardware risks, *etc.* All models as well as the simulation take advantage of the compositionality and the timing refinement properties of the theory.

In the following, Sect. 2 summarizes parts of the FOCUS theory, before Sect. 3 presents the MontiArc tool suite with its architecture description language and simulation framework. Afterwards, Sect. 4 discuss the benefits of this approach and Sect. 5 highlights related work. Section 6 concludes.

2   Theory of Streams

This section contains a condensed form of stream theory. Literature, such as [7,8,53] gives more detailed motivation and discussion of the properties. Ultimately, employing stream theory as the foundation for model-driven development enables modeling architectures for software-intensive CPS as depicted in Fig. 1 under consideration of time as required by its different components.

2.1   Streams and Stream Processing Functions

We consider *components* that only interact through explicit, directed, and typed *communication ports*. Such a component can be atomic or decomposed into *sub-components.* When composing components, ports are connected through directed *channels.*

A *channel observation* is modeled as *stream* M^ω of finite or infinitely messages over a message alphabet M. Progress of time is modeled by an explicit $\checkmark$ (called *"tick"*) message assuming that each occurrence of the message denotes the start of the next time slice. Thus $M^\omega_{\checkmark}$ describes a timed observation of a certain time interval (count the ticks!). A complete observation therefore has to contain infinitely many ticks. Within a time slice any finite sequence of messages including the empty sequence may occur. This models the order of messages, but abstracts away from the concrete time. Time synchronous systems are modeled as $\mathbb{N} \to M$, which is the core embedding in the AutoFocus tool suite [2,3,6,26–28]. If messages are optional, $\mathbb{N} \to M \cup \{\bot\}$ is used and $\bot$ is a pseudo message describing the absence of a real message.

There are various forms of mappings of one timing domain into the other as well as many operations on streams [53]. It is possible to choose the form of streams that fit the modeling interests best, but we mostly use M^ω in the following. In [53], we also embed dense time [39] and Edward Lee's superdense streams [35,36] into the framework.

Ticks partition time into slices, each with a finite sequence of events. The semantics of integrated behavior thus follows the concept of superdense time [35, 39], which, distinguishes between a discrete "time continuum" (the global FOCUS time) and "untimed causally-related actions" (a behavior model's actions within the time slice of a component).

One stream describes one behavior observation. A specification of allowed behaviors is therefore described by a *set of streams* in $\wp(M^\omega)$. It is a general

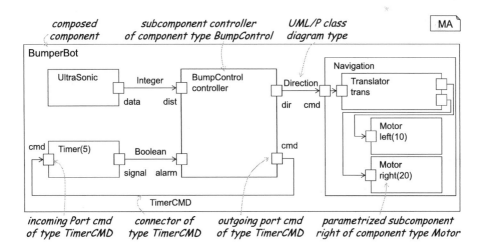

Fig. 1. A MontiArc software architecture of a mobile robot. The composed component `BumperBot` contains four sub-components of different types to read sensor data, interpret it, and actuate two motors. The robot explores uncharted territory and avoids obstacles in the process.

principle to use sets as a mechanism for specification and especially *underspec-ification*, because using a set we can precisely define the allowed properties. Furthermore, *consistency* of a specification corresponds to non-emptiness of a set and *refinement* of a specification corresponds to set inclusion. A set A refines another set B exactly, if $A \subseteq B$. Refinement thus is transitive and reflects that the more information we have the less (mis-)behaviors are possible.

It is not the channel that is of primary interest, but the component and its behavior. The signature of a component is a pair (I, O) of port names from P describing the input and the output. Each port $p \in P$ is typed by the set of messages M_p. An observation set of channels $I \subset P$ then is described by a type-preserving mapping of each $i \in I$ to M_i^ω. In short, this mapping is called $\overrightarrow{I}$.

The behavior of a component can then be modeled as a mathematical object of sort $\overrightarrow{I} \to \overrightarrow{O}$ that maps input behaviors to output behaviors. Please note, that this function completely embeds temporal behavior, because the mapping does not map a single message but has the full observation on its inputs available to determine the full observation on the outputs. However, to be implementable a component may not predict the future, *i.e.*, the output in one time slice may not depend on the input of a later time slice. In the untimed case, *monotonicity* and *continuity*, and in the timed case, *weak* and *strong causality*, are mathematically precise constraints that describe if a function is *realizable*. Fortunately, the forms of streams defined above each form a well-founded CPO (complete partial order) based on prefix ordering that allows defining these constraints.

A realizable function of sort $\overrightarrow{I} \to \overrightarrow{O}$ describes exactly one possible implementation of the component. We call those *stream processing functions*. Again, we generalize to specifications by using the power set construction, regarding each *component specification* as element of $\wp(\overrightarrow{I} \to \overrightarrow{O})$. Refinement again is defined as subset.

2.2   Composition

Several techniques for modification for components exist, such as *renaming* ports or *hiding* output ports, but of particular interest is *composing* two component specifications, denoted with $\otimes$. Specification composition is defined by point-wise specification of functions and two functions f, g are connected through the channels with same names (and inverted directions). $f \otimes g$ basically is function composition and thus very well understood. Its new output signature is $O = O_f \cup O_g$ and input $I = (I_f \cup I_g) \setminus O$ and thus does not hide connected channels.

Other forms of composition include explicitly named pairs of channels that shall be connected, automatic hiding of connected channels, as well as specialized variants, such as parallel and sequential composition or feedback. All are grounded on the same composition principle. As composition is associative and commutative, it can be generalized to composing any forms of architectures.

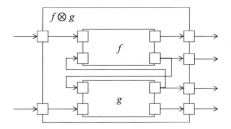

Fig. 2. General form of composition.

Composition is well defined in each of the individual streams' domains. And because it is defined pointwise for specifications, properties of the resulting composed specification can be inferred from properties of the individual specifications. For example, the composition is a consistent specification exactly when both components have a consistent specification (Fig. 2).

But most importantly, composition and refinement are compatible, *i.e.*, given three specifications S, S', T, where S' is a refinement of S, then

$$S' \subseteq S \quad \longrightarrow \quad S' \otimes T \subseteq S \otimes T.$$

Therefore, refinement of any decomposed component leads to a refinement of the overall composition. Refinement means that details on the implementation are decided and more information added and thus less behavior possible. The compatibility of refinement with composition means that once the system is decomposed, each component can be developed and refined independently.

Because decomposition can be applied hierarchically, a complex CPS can be decomposed into individual, atomic, and manageable components.

2.3   Description Styles for Components

A mathematical theory such as streams for describing CPS needs to be backed up by more pragmatic styles of denoting specifications. The stream theory does not directly qualify as a specification technique, but serves as a semantic domain [23] for an appropriate set of concrete modeling notations.

Neither infinite streams, nor stream processing functions, nor sets over both should directly be used in mathematical definitions. Instead a structural modeling technique should be available to define the internal decomposition of components. A hierarchy of such structural decompositions finally leads to an *architecture* comprising ports, channels, components and their composition. MontiArc's main modeling sublanguage allows to describe system architectures based on streams. Message types and potentially other, internally used, forms of types must be defined using an appropriate data structure language, *e.g.*, UML class diagrams [17,60]. Behavior of components can be defined in a relational form, using for example the assumption/guarantee style composed of two logic specifications [8], where the assumption restricts the allowed input and the guarantee relates input to output.

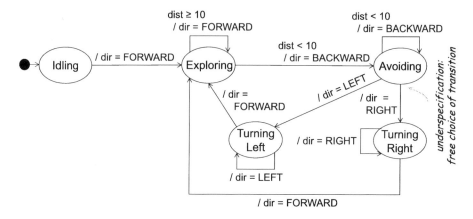

Fig. 3. State machine describing the behavior of the `BumpControl` component of the `BumperBot` software architecture (*cf.* Fig. 1).

State Machines. Today, state machines are used in various forms, which include Statecharts [21,22], finite or infinite automata, Büchi automata [64], I/O-automata [1,37], or I/O$^\omega$-automata [53,58,59] allow to describe behavior in a stepwise manner, based on an internal state. Dependent on the form of the state machine, different specific properties, such as liveness or completeness, can potentially be described. The important concept of underspecification, which we above realize through power sets, can partially be used within the automaton language directly, using alternate transitions. Indeed is nondeterminism in the state machine specification technique perfectly corresponding to underspecification in the development process and if the developer does not decide, which of the alternatives to be taken, actually the implementation may choose nondeterministically.

Figure 3 depicts a state machine leveraging nondeterminism to specify the behavior of the component `BumpControl` of the `BumperBot` software architecture illustrated in Fig. 1: based on stimuli received through input `dist`, it describes how the systems explores an area until finding an obstacle (states `Exploring` and `Avoiding`). Afterwards it can drive backward, turn left, or turn right (states `Avoiding`, `Turning Left`, and `Turning Right`) until it selects to continue exploring. All decisions following entering state `Avoiding` are based on nondeterministic choice, which is suitable to underspecify CPS properties in different design stages.

I/O$^\omega$ automata are still not a concrete modeling language, but are conceptually rather close. Such an automaton is a tuple $(S, M_{in}, M_{out}, \delta, I)$ with a potentially infinite set of states S, input and output alphabet M_{in} and M_{out}, a state transition function $\delta \subseteq S \times M_{in} \times S \times M_{out}^\omega$ and initial state and output pairs $I \subseteq S \times M_{out}^\omega$. An I/O$^\omega$ automaton can easily be mapped to a set of stream processing functions [58].

If the automaton is total, then the component specification is consistent (*i.e.*, a nonempty set of functions). If the automaton is deterministic, then exactly one function is in the semantics. If the automaton is not total, then several choices, such as error completion, full underspecification or ignoring input messages that cannot be handled are available. This all holds for the untimed and timed cases.

Furthermore, there are a larger set of modifications on automata available, such as removing one of several alternate transitions or splitting states, that by application are correct refinements [53,59]. These modifications allow an evolutionary development of atomic component specifications. One of the advantages of state machines is that they can always be directly interpreted as implementation (with more or less choices) and thus used in simulations.

Architectures. The composition operation $\otimes$ allows to build hierarchically composed systems. To explicitly understand the architecture, it can be modeled explicitly. A static architecture is minimally modeled by (A, sub, σ, β), where A denotes the set of components (respectively component identifiers), $sub : A \rightarrow \wp(A)$ the hierarchy of compositions, for $a \in A$, $\sigma(a) = (I_a, O_a)$ is the signature of the component and $\beta(a)$ denotes a behavioral specification of the component in form of a set of stream processing functions $\wp(\overrightarrow{I_a} \rightarrow \overrightarrow{O_a})$. Signatures as well as behavior can now be derived bottom-up through the composition operator as well as specified top-down using for example functional or state based specifications.

It is possible, to use several specification techniques describing different aspects of the same component. Dependent on the form of development process, it may make sense to start with an incomplete assumption/guarantee specification, complete it into a state machine and then hierarchically refine the structure and decompose the overall behavior into a number of interacting components. Semantically, we always know, whether the development steps have been correct, because either they are refinements or we can compare the semantics of a composed architecture and the semantics of a state machine on the basis of the sets of stream processing functions that they define.

2.4 Refinement

It is worth to have a deeper look at refinement. *Refinement* is defined as relation between mathematical models that exhibits useful properties. Model B generally is a refinement of A, when implementations allowed by B are all correct implementations of A. In its simplest form, A and B are sets of implementations themselves and refinement is realized by the subset equation. This holds for stream specifications as well as for specification of components, which are sets of stream processing functions.

The notion of refinement can be extended in two ways: (1) instead of using a pure semantic relation, constructive transformation techniques are defined, and (2) if the signature of the components changes then signature mappings for abstraction and refinement need to be added.

Constructive transformations T can be used instead of using a pure semantic relation $R(.,.)$. They by definition lead to the appropriate refinement. That means for all models A we have $R(A, T(A))$. A sequence of transformations always leads to a refinement of the system. As a consequence, refinement needs to be transitive. The refinement techniques need to be chosen and defined according to the methodical steps that the developer needs. While the refinement relation is defined in a general form concrete transformation steps should be handy, simple and understandable and thus many kinds of small transformation steps are useful.

Refinement of State Machines Through Transformation. We demonstrate the general principle of constructive transformations for refinement on the already mentioned refinement concept for state machines as defined in [59]. We repeat the list of concrete refinement steps from [53] in Table 1.

Table 1. Refinement transformations preserving or refining semantics of automata models $A = (S, M_{in}, M_{out}, \delta, Init)$ to $T(A) = (S', M'_{in}, M'_{out}, \delta', Init')$

Transformation	Condition and Description
$Init' \subseteq Init$	Removing initial non-determinism
$\delta' \subseteq \delta$	Removing non-deterministic transitions (with same input in same state); constraint: only for reduction of nondeterminism
$\delta' \supseteq \delta$	Add transitions: removing partiality of accepted input; constraint: not allowed to introduce alternatives to existing transitions
$S' \subseteq S, \delta' \subseteq \delta$	Removing states not reachable with any finite or infinite transition sequence
$S' \supseteq S$	Adding states
$S \rightsquigarrow S'$	S replaced by S' with a total, surjective relation that respects δ' from S to S' (adapting δ' and $Init'$)
$Init \rightsquigarrow Init'$	Changing initial state where initial output is infinite
$\delta \rightsquigarrow \delta'$	Changing destination state where output is infinite
$M_{in} \subseteq M'_{in}$	Extending input alphabet: semantics preserved for inputs of M_{in}^{ω} that do not contain any of the new messages
$S' = S_{\perp}, \delta \subseteq \delta'$	Chaos complete: adding error state $\perp$, making transition relation total using target state $\perp$, and allowing any output
$\delta \supseteq \delta'$	Compactify: transforming transitions with infinite output to self-loops

In each case $T(A)$ is a refinement of the original state machine A, if we ensure that the context conditions (*i.e.*, well-formedness rules and the application rules for the transformation) are met. Refinement here means, that the semantics

$[\![A]\!]$ and $[\![T(A)]\!]$, which of both sets of stream processing functions, are in the appropriate relation: $[\![A]\!] \supseteq [\![T(A)]\!]$.

As discussed, $(S, M_{in}, M_{out}, \delta, Init)$ is still not a concrete modeling syntax, but it exhibits many more concepts of a concrete modeling language. It will therefore be easier to map a concrete state machine modeling language to these concepts and then understand, what the appropriate evolution steps on state machines are to ensure refinement.

Refinement of Architectures. There also is an evolutionary calculus available that allows to modify the given structure of a decomposed component in a controlled way, such that the overall behavior defined by the outside specification is not altered or only refined, when modifying the component internally [48,49]. We call this *glass-box refinement*. This contrasts both, the black-box refinement, where only specifications are considered, as well as the decomposition refinement, where a black-box is decomposed into an architecture of communicating components using a composition operator.

A *decomposition refinement* actually is a modification of the architecture (A, sub, σ, β) in such a way that a so far atomic component $a \in A$ becomes decomposed by a set of new components. Glass-box refinement allows to modify components and their interconnections and thus leads to calculus like the one presented in Table 2, taken from [48,49], where also the context conditions are precisely defined.

In addition, the papers [40,41,51,56] also have explored to use architecture definitions as incomplete views. That means while syntactically equivalent to an architectural definition, the view only depicts certain components, omits uninteresting channels and also boundaries, how these components are embedded into an architecture. A view based specification therefore corresponds well to the independent modeling of a feature in a high-level form independent of any technical architecture. And those features can in the development process be merged into a complete architecture allowing, *e.g.*, an efficient form of variant management. Again a variety of refinement techniques are possible on views.

Refinement of Component Signatures Using Mappings. If the signature of the discussed components change or the set of messages in a set of streams changes, then the specifications are not directly comparable. This happens at many architectural modifications, *e.g.*, if new inputs or outputs are added or a port is renamed. In this case an *abstraction mapping* and a *representation mapping*—we call them α and ρ—are necessary to relate the two specifications respectively their semantics. Details of these mappings differ depending on the form of refinement. Again it is mandatory that signature refinements are transitive, which is achieved through function composition on chains of refinement and abstraction mappings.

As simple refinement for two sets of messages M, N is defined using an injective $\rho : M \to N$ and $\alpha(\rho(m)) = m$ for $m \in M$. Then ρ is an encoding of the old messages into a potentially more technical representation and α is

Table 2. Refinement transformations preserving or refining semantics of architecture models $S = (A, sub, \sigma, \beta)$ to $T(S) = (A', sub', \sigma', \beta')$

Transformation	Condition and Description
$\beta'(a) \subseteq \beta(a)$	*Behavioral refinement* of the specification for component $a \in A$, usually under an invariant Φ that is valid on any system execution that has this architecture
$A' = A \cup N$	*Architectural decomposition* of an atomic component $a \in A$, *i.e.*, $sub(a) = \emptyset$, by a set of new components $N \not\subseteq A$, where $sub'(a) = N$, $sub'(N) = \emptyset$ and $sub' = sub$ otherwise
$\sigma'_o(a) = \sigma_o(a) \cup \{c\}$	Adding output channel to a component that has previously been hidden internally *i.e.*, $c \in \sigma_o(sub(a))$
$\sigma'_o(a) = \sigma_o(a) \setminus \{c\}$	Removing an output channel that is not used by sibling components, nor further exported, *i.e.*, for parent p with $a \in sub(p)$: $c \notin \sigma_i(sub(p))$ and $c \notin \sigma_o(p)$
$\sigma'_i(a) = \sigma_i(a) \cup \{c\}$	Adding input channel that is now available, but unused
$\sigma'_i(a) = \sigma_i(a) \setminus \{c\}$	Removing an input channel of a component. This is only allowed, when the component does not rely on the input channel under an invariant Φ. This can either be checked syntactically (absence of use of c) or needs a proof
$A' = A \cup \{a\}$	Adding a component a is always uncritical. The component may be added at any level of the hierarchy and read all available channels. It's output isn't used (yet) and thus the modification is uncritical. (sub' includes a, β' extended on a as well)
$A' = A \setminus \{a\}$	Removal of a component a is allowed, when the component has no impact, *i.e.*, doesn't emit any channel – $\sigma_o(a) = \emptyset$ – or it's channels are not used anymore (see removing output channels)
$A' = A \setminus \{a\}$	*Expanding component structure* of $a \in A$, where $sub'(p) = sub(p) \setminus \{a\} \cup sub(a)$, leading to an expansion of the internal structure of a into it's father component p
$A' = A \cup \{a\}$	*Folding a sub-component structure* by introducing new component $a \in A$ and embedding a subset $C \subseteq sub(p)$ in component a, for instance, $sub'(p) = sub(p) \cup \{a\} \setminus C$ and $sub(a) = C$

the corresponding abstraction. All messages in $N \setminus \rho(M)$ are not needed and should therefore not occur in system executions. However, components may react robustly on those messages, for example by ignoring them.

Components a using M as input on a port p may be refined accordingly. With $\rho^c(a)$ and $\alpha^c(a)$, we denote the specifications resulting from the signature change of component a induced by ρ and α. Because specifications are sets of stream processing functions, ρ^c and α^c are mappings between sets, resulting in $\alpha^c(\rho^c(a)) = a$. The latter equality ensures the faithfulness of the encoding representation.

There are many possible forms to extend encodings. We, for example, can use a surjective, but not necessarily injective abstraction α, allowing that many messages in N represent the same abstract message in M. Then ρ is a relation, but still $(\alpha \otimes \rho)(m)$.

We could represent an abstract message in M by a sequence of messages in N. This can be described by $\rho : M^\omega \to N^\omega$ and again $\alpha(\rho(s)) = s$ for $s \in M^\omega$. Again, the encoding does not discuss, what happens with illegitimate sequences of messages, *i.e.*, $s \notin \rho(M^\omega)$, which gives additional freedom when further refining the resulting specification. However, illegitimate sequences of messages should not even occur in a system execution, because through proper refinement of an architecture, the emitting component obeys the same encodings as the receiving component.

If the encoding covers even several channels, *e.g.*, when mapping an 32-bit integer into 32 separate binary channels, then ρ and α will be applied on sets of channels.

Through these various generalizations and the possibility to build chains of encodings $\rho_1(\rho_2(...))$, we finally are able to map abstractly defined components to concrete components and relate their specifications in form of an *U-simulation* (see [4]). U-simulation uses the idea that the input is mapped down via ρ to a concrete representation and the output is mapped back via α: The refinement of component a is therefore $\rho^c(a) = \alpha \circ a \circ \rho$. This technique is useful, when a single component is to be refined and shall be used in the original, unchanged context.

If a complete architecture is to be refined, then it is sufficient to define representation mappings for all channels using ρ and apply the representation mapping to all components in an architecture. However, ρ also needs to have an inverse relation with certain properties, to ensure that an encoding is complete and faithful. [4] calls this *refinement under the representation specification ρ* or *downward simulation*. In that article, upward simulation and U^{-1}-simulation are defined also.

Relatively simple forms of refinement, namely the renaming of a channel or the replacement of a set of messages by an equivalent one are easily subsumed under these forms of interaction refinement. Several of the above discussed glass-box modifications for a given architecture can also be derived by applying abstraction and representation mappings on the architectures.

Refinement of Time. Time is a very special concept. It is worth to take a deeper look at the possibilities of modifying specifications, that incorporate time. Above we introduced the tick ✓ to model the progress of time. Precisely, in a stream two consecutive ticks represent the beginning and end of a time slice. All time slices in a stream are of equal length, although we do not necessarily need to know the length explicitly. Furthermore, in all streams on all channels ticks model the same progress of time.

Initially, the tick was introduced mainly to model delay. With the tick it became possible to describe, for example, the *merge* function inductively, which previously was not possible. When real-time functions became more important *e.g.*, in the domain of CPS, the tick was also used to represent equidistant progress of time. Formally, the tick is handled like any other message in a stream, which means that stream processing functions may react on progress of time. In particular, we may model timeouts by counting the ticks, which implements clocks.

Timed streams, therefore, have a very similar power of description compared to the concept of superdense event structures [35, 36]. All messages within a time slice are known to consecutively follow each other, but nothing is said about the actual progress of time between them. While in the superdense event structure [36], each event has a precise time stamp, in streams only the time slice (and the relative order of events) are known. If real-time comes into play, but the exact timing is not necessary, it should be possible to define time slices small enough to accommodate timed behavior specifications. This abstraction might be useful in specifications especially for underspecification.

Assuming, that a given specification uses a time slice of size t. When refining the specification to be able to more precisely describe expected behavior, we might be interested in *refining time* as well, splitting each time slot into n sub-slots. Formally, such a refinement is defined by an abstraction mapping $\alpha : M_{\checkmark}^{\omega} \to M_{\checkmark}^{\omega}$ that filters each consecutive $n-1$ ticks, while emitting each n-th tick. The representation ρ is therefore a relation allowing many different forms of splits for the time slice, *i.e.,* injecting ticks at different places in a stream. Time refinement can also be chained, allowing a hierarchy of time slices.

For simulation purposes, it is interesting to relax the constraint that all ticks model the same time slices. First, we may use channels, where the observed behavior differs from channel to channel. We may even allow timed and untimed channels within the same architecture, which allows us to model system structures and component behaviors as abstract as desired. Formally, we assume a minimal and potentially very small time slice t that is available in the whole system. Each channel is then accompanied with a natural number n (or ∞) describing the size of its time slice as multiple $n * t$. For a simple mathematical description, we may use $\checkmark_n$ to denote ticks on a channel with multiplicity n.

A component can then accept a variety of timed channels, allowing to be internally decomposed into sub-components of different (synchronous) clocks as well as introducing specification components the main purpose of describing how timing behavior is handled.

There is a lot more theory available, *e.g.,* there are interesting techniques to refine time in a state based specification, where each transition describes an event (including timing events) or describes a time slice [4, 58].

Equipped with the above summarized theory, we are in the following looking at the simulation environment provided by MontiArc and how several of the above described techniques are practically realized.

3   Architecture Models in MontiArc

MontiArc [9,18,20] is an extensible component & connector ADL [42] allowing to describe the architecture of hierarchically composed components. MontiArc, furthermore, comprises languages for definition of data types and the behavior or of components. MontiArc's components realize stream processing functions that can implement the above discussed timing paradigms. All MontiArc languages are realized as textual modeling languages with the MontiCore [32] language workbench, which supports MontiArc's language extension mechanisms [9]. MontiArc and its variants have been applied to the software engineering of automotive software [19], cloud systems [45], and robotics applications [52] in industrial [24] and academic contexts [54,55].

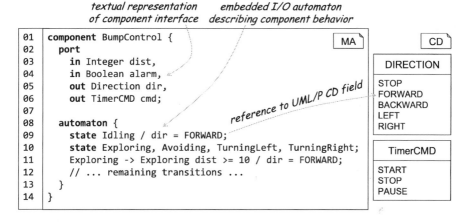

Fig. 4. Textual representation of the component BumpControl controlling the behavior of the BumperBot architecture using an embedded I/O$^\omega$ automaton emulating the behavior depicted in Fig. 3.

Components, such as BumperBot of Fig. 4 directly correspond to sets of stream processing functions. MontiArc architectures support refinement and composition. The outermost component BumperBot defines the system boundary and through instantiation relations and establishment of connectors between its subcomponents defines a software architecture in the sense of (A, sub, σ, β) (cf. Sect. 2.3). With MontiArc, A is the set of components transitively used by the outermost component, sub is characterized by the instantiation relation of the contained components, σ is defined by their incoming and outgoing ports, and β is defined by the behavior models employed by the instantiated components. To this end, MontiArc components yield interfaces of typed, directed input and output ports through which they receive and emit streams of messages to from and to the environment (ll. 2–6). Components also are either composed or atomic: composed components comprise connectors that realize aforementioned communication channels (cf. Sect. 2.1) and through which they define

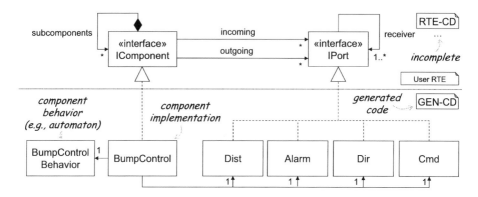

Fig. 5. Quintessential interfaces of MontiArc's run-time environment and how they are related to the generated implementation of component `BumpControl` of Fig. 1.

their sub-components' composition (*cf.* Sect. 2.2). Atomic components feature local variables and an I/O^ω automaton describing component behavior (ll. 8–13). An I/O^ω automaton comprises a finite set of states (ll. 9–10), initial variable values, a set of initial states with optional outputs (l. 9), and a set of transitions (ll. 11 ff). Every transition has a source state, a pattern of values read on input ports (inputs) and local variables, a target state, values written to output ports (outputs), and values assigned to local variables (assignments). Inputs, outputs, and assignments may refer to values read from input ports and to values of variables. Embedding other behavior modeling languages is possible [52]. For detailed definitions and well-formedness rules see [20,57].

3.1   Transforming MontiArc Models to Executable Java

MontiArc leverages MontiCore's template-based code generation framework [61] to translate component models into executable Java artifacts. To this end, MontiArc parses textual models into abstract syntax trees (ASTs), checks their well-formedness, and applies FreeMarker [63] templates to transform ASTs into Java classes that are compatible to a run-time environment featuring component simulation. This section illustrates this transformation and the next section presents how the Java classes are employed for simulation.

The code generator of MontiArc aims to minimize memory footprint of architectures and operates in the context of a run-time environment (RTE) that provides functionality required by every generated architecture. To this end, it provides various interfaces that generated component code as well as parts of the RTE rely upon. Its quintessential interfaces for describing component structure are `IComponent` and `IPort`, which are implemented by generated component implementations and their ports as depicted in Fig. 5.

Components interact with their environment through sets of incoming and outgoing ports only and can comprise sub-components (composed components only) or behavior implementations (atomic components only) that realize, for instance, the embedded automata. Each emitting port is connected to a set of receiving ports. This conforms to the FOCUS property that a sender can transmit data to multiple receivers. As sending ports are directly connected to receiving ports, MontiArc does not require to reify connectors (channels) as Java classes. This reduces the number of required objects at runtime and increases scheduling flexibility. Component implementations take care of creating and initializing their sub-components hierarchically according to the corresponding architecture model.

At the core of MontiArc's simulation capabilities is its scheduling infrastructure, which enables simulation of hierarchical architectures of components following different timing paradigms. Each component may carry its own scheduler. Default schedulers are provided, which interact in such a way, that time progress is ensured and all messages are scheduled in their time slot.

Figure 6 depicts its infrastructure but omits the associations already depicted in Fig. 5. Aside from `IComponent` and `IPort`, the schedulers use the following classes and interfaces:

- Interfaces `IOutPort` and `IInPort`: Both interfaces implement `IPort` and enable component developers to send and receive messages respectively.
- Interface `ISimComponent` provides two methods to the scheduler to activate components. Via method `handleMessage(port, message)`, the scheduler invokes processing the passed data `message` on port `port`. The method `handleTick()` to make a component increase its internal clock and emit $\sqrt{}$ messages on each outgoing port.
- Abstract class `AComponent` serves a common superclass for generated component classes (such as `BumpControl`) and comprises the component name as well as an error handler.
- Interface `IOutSimPort` provides methods to register receivers (*i.e.*, establish connectors).
- Interface `IInSimPort` enables to setup the containing component and related scheduler to outgoing port instances.
- Additional scheduling-related methods to manipulate the state of ports are provided but omitted in the Figure (*e.g.*, put to sleep, wake up, *etc.*).
- Interface `IScheduler` features the `setupPort(inPort)` method to set up a concrete scheduler and the `registerPort(inPort, msg)` method to trigger scheduling of a certain port and message.
- Interface `IPort` unifies the use of incoming and outgoing ports throughout the generated architecture.
- Interface `IForwardPort` defines incoming ports for decomposed components and forwards messages to the connected incoming ports of the corresponding sub-components.
- Class `Port` is the default port implementation for simulation. To conserve memory, `Port` instances are created for incoming ports of atomic components only. Through `IPort`, instances of the connected incoming ports can be used as outgoing ports and dedicated objects for outgoing port are unnecessary.

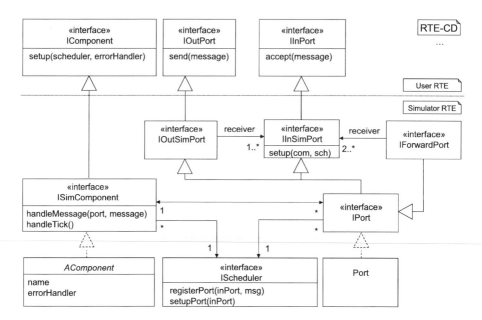

Fig. 6. Quintessential classes and interfaces of MontiArc's simulation run-time environment as presented in [18].

Leveraging interfaces to describe MontiArc's scheduling facilitates extending its simulator for different scheduling purposes and timing paradigms. The next section describes how this infrastructure is employed to realize various timing paradigms with MontiArc.

The default scheduling can be individually replaced by specific schedulers, that either know more about the implementation and the order of how messages are processed, or can for example in the simulation be used to experiment with different possible orders to understand how parallel processing respectively interleaving affects the overall outcome. Default scheduling is underspecified in the order of executing the messages (within a given time frame).

The default scheduling is also able to manage cycles of communicating components. Such a cycle needs to be broken up in order to allow progress. In accordance to the theory of Sect. 2, we break each cycle at components that are strongly causal. Strong causality means that the output of a time slice is determined by the inputs of the previous time slice, which means that the component introduces delay, and the calculation of the following components can start already based on the predetermined result of the strongly causal component. If there is a cycle where no component is a strongly causal, the feedback composition will not be well-defined and the simulation would correspondingly get stuck (respectively issues a halting error).

The scheduling order of messages introduces certain form of nondeterminism that may for example occur, if several messages in different channels arrive in the same time slot and are individually processed based on a potentially changed internal state. Introducing our own schedulers allows to control this form of nondeterminism. Furthermore, for an intensive set of tests of the component interaction, different schedules should be experimented with.

The very same challenge occurs, if the component itself is underspecified, allowing different potential implementations. This is for example the case for nondeterministic state machines, where alternative transitions can be taken with different reactions and different target states. For an extensive simulation, this form of nondeterminism is also to be controlled and scheduled using different alternatives. A typically possible way to control these forms of nondeterminism is to externalize the choice. I.e. instead of nondeterminism, the choice can be controlled by an additional external *oracle*, which may for example be a stream of binary suggestions. I.e. mathematically, we replace and set of stream processing functions $\wp(\overrightarrow{I} \rightarrow \overrightarrow{O})$ by a single deterministic function with an additional input channel $\overrightarrow{\mathbb{B}} \times \overrightarrow{I} \rightarrow \overrightarrow{O}$). The binary decisions $\mathbb{B}$ can be extended to finite or even unbounded choice if necessary. A given architecture can be adapted accordingly, such that each underspecified component and each scheduler receive appropriate oracles. The adapted architecture can be well used for extensive tests in simulations.

3.2   Simulating Time in MontiArc Architectures

Simulating time of logically distributed and concurrent components in a single thread requires explicit scheduling, where the schedulers are responsible for message processing and the simulation of time. As discussed above, each component can yield an individual scheduler and a larger variety of scheduling schemes is possible. Each scheduler decides which sub-component executes next and the schedulers synchronize incoming data and ticks received on the incoming ports of components. One strategy is to merge incoming events to a *simulated timed input trace*. This trace is then propagated to scheduled components, which internally process each event and also process timing progress through √-events.

As different applications favor different communication timing strategies – embedded applications might favor global clocks whereas cloud systems might benefit from event-driven communication – MontiArc supports all paradigms of time described in Sect. 2. As complex architectures can be composed from components realizing different time paradigms, MontiArc supports registering different schedulers for each composed component. It also provides a default scheduler supporting all three timing paradigms through temporal unification. This is presented in the following.

The foundation of MontiArc simulations are the timed streams discussed in Sect. 2. The timing paradigm of a component determines how the tick messages and data messages of those streams are translated to events, which are propagated to the component implementation. For composed components comprising sub-components of different timing paradigms, the distinct timing behavior is unified to the underlying timed stream paradigm automatically. This entails not forwarding time events to untimed components and forwarding only a single message per time interval to time-synchronous components. Where special translations between different timing paradigms of sub-components are required, the models have to be adapted to enable proper interaction. This can be achieved by introducing upscaling and downscaling sub-components [8] that translate between different timings in terms of a behavior refinement and serve as adapters between sub-components with different time paradigms.

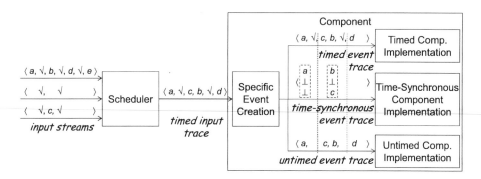

Fig. 7. Unification of time-synchronous streams, timed streams, and untimed streams into timed input traces.

MontiArc's default scheduler unifies time in composed components as depicted in Fig. 7: upon receiving a bundle of streams of the component to be scheduled, the scheduler synchronizes these streams into a timed input trace. For each completed time interval in all received input streams, a time event ($\sqrt{}$) is present in the produced input trace produced by the scheduler. All data events are propagated to the components input trace in order of their occurrence also. The scheduler then uses the timed input trace to trigger the scheduled component. Time events are raised at the component using its `handleTick()` method, data events are raised using its `handleMessage()` method. The `Specific Event Creation` part of a component then creates timing paradigm specific events that are passed to the concrete implementation of a component.

Unless modeled differently, MontiArc components communicate in a timed fashion. Timed components react to the progress of time as well as data messages on each incoming port. Hence, timed components can produce arbitrary many output messages in a single time slice. Their output is produced in the same time interval in which the triggering input occurred. The `Specific Event Creation` of timed components forwards the received timed input trace from the scheduler to the component implementation. Hence, the timing domain specific event trace directly corresponds to the timed input trace.

Time-synchronous components process up to one input event per time slice and also send up to one message per outgoing port as a reaction to the received input event. Input events of time-synchronous components are tuples holding exactly one message (which may be the empty message $\bot$) per input channel.

The propagation of messages from timed input streams to time-synchronous event traces defines the semantics of time-synchronous components operating over timed streams. The `Specific Event Creation` takes care of creating corresponding tuples to liberate component developers from addressing synchronization.

Untimed components are unaware of timing events, but react to data events only. To this end, the `Specific Event Creation` filters the tick ($\sqrt{}$) messages produced by the scheduler as part of the timed input event trace and forwards the result to untimed components accordingly.

Components receiving streams of any timing paradigm can refine the time indicated by these streams as required through decomposing time slices into smaller slices processed by their subcomponents as presented in Sect. 2.4. This corresponds to subcomponents operating in a superdense time where the time continuum can be decomposed until (through architecture decomposition) atomic component perform multiple untimed causally-related actions in a single time slice. Details on realizing the different timing paradigms in MontiArc [18, 20] as well as its implementation and tutorials[1] are available.

One of the big advantages of $\sqrt{}$s in the simulation are that the modeled time in the simulation becomes explicit and thus is decoupled from the time necessary to execute the simulation. The simulation can therefore run much larger time frames than it needs to execute the simulation, e.g. necessary for climatic simulations, or vice versa can simulate very tiny timeslots, such as typical for physical atomic processes. Furthermore, when distributing the simulation to many computational cores, then individual cores can run different time frames and can even partially look far into the future, as long as they don't rely on other older parts of the simulation from other cores.

With code generation, hierarchical component instantiation, and extensible scheduling for different timing paradigms in place, MontiArc is suitable to address many challenges arising from engineering software-intensive CPS.

4   Discussion

MontiArc supports simulating logically distributed systems of stream processing functions according to different timing paradigms. This enables exploring and validating MontiArc architecture in an agile way. Together with its extensible ADL MontiArc is suitable for rapidly prototyping system models.

The MontiArc simulation realizes the FOCUS architecture and communication model. Outgoing ports directly transmit messages to connected incoming ports and records of these transmissions correspond to FOCUS streams that describe the timed communication between sender and receiver. As the MontiArc simulation aims to minimize the memory footprint of architectures at runtime and streams are rarely needed during the execution of a simulation, streams are, by default, not recorded to reduce the amount of allocated memory. However,

---

[1] See http://www.monticore.de/languages/montiarc/.

for analysis and testing, the relevant ports can be flexibly replaced with test ports that explicitly record transmitted messages in a stream data structure for analysis during or after the simulation execution.

Despite the simulation being executed in a single thread with synchronous blocking method calls, atomic components can be implemented in an event-based fashion. To this end, the MontiArc runtime system prescribes interacting interfaces for components and ports that enable its schedulers to stimulate components with incoming events. Although the message transmission and event propagation by the scheduler require some real time, no simulation time has passed when the control flow returns to a component. Consequently, MontiArc's simulation is logically asynchronous and event-based, which is suitable to a wide range of software-intensive CPS.

5   Related Work

A study on architecture description languages discovered over 120 different languages for different kinds of systems operating in different domains [38]. Of these, various languages serve modeling the structure and behavior of software-intensive CPS, including automotive systems [12], avionics [14], consumer electronics [46], and robotics [62]. The languages focus on different aspects and challenges of architecture engineering from academic and industrial perspectives. Overall, architecture description languages rarely are grounded in a well-defined theory. Many prominent ADLs rely on theories realized implicitly through their tooling.

In contrast, AutoFOCUS 3 [26] is a tool suite for developing reactive embedded systems that also bases its semantics on FOCUS [8]. In contrast to MontiArc, AutoFOCUS 3 cannot leverage the language composition of an underlying language workbench and, hence, does not feature MontiArc's powerful language embedding mechanisms [9]. Further prominent examples of ADLs with well-founded semantics are the π-ADL [47], LEDA [10], and PiLar [11], all of which rest on the π-calculus [44], which lacks the powerful properties of FOCUS regarding composition of refined components.

6   Conclusion

We have presented how the FOCUS theory of stream processing functions can be leveraged to facilitate the model-driven development of cyber-physical systems through early simulation under consideration of different timing paradigms. To this end, we summarized refinement and composition in FOCUS and showed how automata can employ underspecification to support model-driven specification in early design stages. Based on this theory, we presented the MontiArc architecture modeling tool suite and explained how its code generation and simulation capabilities support engineering software-intensive cyber-physical systems with underspecification and different timing requirements through simulation. We believe that this combination of well-founded theory and practical modeling technique facilitates software engineering of cyber-physical systems.

References

1. de Alfaro, L., Henzinger, T.A.: Interface automata. SIGSOFT Softw. Eng. Notes **26**(5), 109–120 (2001)
2. Aravantinos, V., Voss, S., Teufl, S., Hölzl, F., Schtäz, B.: Autofocus 3: tooling concepts for seamless, model-based development of embedded systems. In: 8th International Workshop on Model-based Architecting of Cyber-physical and Embedded Systems, pp. 19–26 (2015)
3. Bauer, A., Romberg, J., Schätz, B.: Integrierte entwicklung von automotive-software mit autofocus. Informatik - Forschung und Entwicklung **19**, 194–205 (2005)
4. Broy, M.: (Inter-)action refinement: the easy way. In: Broy, M. (ed.) Program Design Calculi. NATO ASI F, vol. 118, pp. 121–158. Springer, Heidelberg (1993). https://doi.org/10.1007/978-3-662-02880-3_5
5. Broy, M., Dederich, F., Dendorfer, C., Fuchs, M., Gritzner, T., Weber, R.: The design of distributed systems - an introduction to FOCUS. Technical report, TUM-I9202, SFB-Bericht Nr. 342/2-2/92 A (1993)
6. Broy, M., Huber, F., Schätz, B.: Autofocus - ein werkzeugprototyp zur entwicklung eingebetteter systeme. Informatik-Forschung und Entwicklung **14**(3), 121–134 (1999)
7. Broy, M., Rumpe, B.: Modulare hierarchische modellierung als grundlage der software- und systementwicklung. Informatik-Spektrum **30**(1), 3–18 (2007)
8. Broy, M., Stølen, K.: Specification and Development of Interactive Systems. Focus on Streams, Interfaces, and Refinement. Springer, Heidelberg (2001). https://doi.org/10.1007/978-1-4613-0091-5
9. Butting, A., et al.: Systematic language extension mechanisms for the montiarc architecture description language. In: Anjorin, A., Espinoza, H. (eds.) ECMFA 2017. LNCS, vol. 10376, pp. 53–70. Springer, Cham (2017). https://doi.org/10.1007/978-3-319-61482-3_4
10. Canal, C., Pimentel, E., Troya, J.M.: Specification and refinement of dynamic software architectures. In: Donohoe, P. (ed.) Software Architecture. ITIFIP, vol. 12, pp. 107–125. Springer, Boston, MA (1999). https://doi.org/10.1007/978-0-387-35563-4_7
11. Cuesta, C.E., de la Fuente, P., Barrio-Solírzano, M., Beato, M.E.G.: An "abstract process" approach to algebraic dynamic architecture description. J. Log. Algebraic Program. **63**, 177–214 (2005)
12. Debruyne, V., Simonot-Lion, F., Trinquet, Y.: EAST-ADL—an architecture description language. In: Dissaux, P., Filali-Amine, M., Michel, P., Vernadat, F. (eds.) Architecture Description Languages. ITIFIP, vol. 176, pp. 181–195. Springer, Boston, MA (2005). https://doi.org/10.1007/0-387-24590-1_12
13. Derler, P., Lee, E.A., Vincentelli, A.S.: Modeling cyber-physical systems. Proc. IEEE **100**(1), 13–28 (2012)
14. Feiler, P.H., Gluch, D.P.: Model-Based Engineering with AADL: An Introduction to the SAE Architecture Analysis & Design Language. Addison-Wesley, Boston (2012)
15. France, R., Rumpe, B.: Model-driven development of complex software: a research roadmap. In: Future of Software Engineering (FOSE 2007), pp. 37–54, May 2007
16. Giese, H., Rumpe, B., Schätz, B., Sztipanovits, J.: Science and engineering of cyber-physical systems (Dagstuhl seminar 11441). Dagstuhl Rep. **1**(11), 1–22 (2012)

17. OM Group: OMG Unified Modeling Language (OMG UML), Infrastructure version 2.3 (10-05-03) (2010)
18. Haber, A.: MontiArc - Architectural Modeling and Simulation of Interactive Distributed Systems. Aachener Informatik-Berichte, Software Engineering, Band, vol. 24. Shaker Verlag, September 2016
19. Haber, A., Rendel, H., Rumpe, B., Schaefer, I.: Evolving delta-oriented software product line architectures. In: Calinescu, R., Garlan, D. (eds.) Monterey Workshop 2012. LNCS, vol. 7539, pp. 183–208. Springer, Heidelberg (2012). https://doi.org/10.1007/978-3-642-34059-8_10
20. Haber, A., Ringert, J.O., Rumpe, B.: Montiarc - architectural modeling of interactive distributed and cyber-physical systems. Technical report AIB-2012-03, RWTH Aachen University, February 2012
21. Harel, D.: Statecharts: a visual formalism for complex systems. Sci. Comput. Program. **8**, 231–274 (1987)
22. Harel, D., Pnueli, A.: On the development of reactive systems. In: Apt, K.R. (ed.) Logics and Models of Concurrent Systems. NATO ASI F, vol. 13, pp. 477–498. Springer, Heidelberg (1985). https://doi.org/10.1007/978-3-642-82453-1_17
23. Harel, D., Rumpe, B.: Meaningful modeling: what's the semantics of "semantics"? IEEE Comput. **37**(10), 64–72 (2004)
24. Heim, R., Mir Seyed Nazari, P., Ringert, J.O., Rumpe, B., Wortmann, A.: Modeling robot and world interfaces for reusable tasks. In: Intelligent Robots and Systems Conference (IROS 2015), pp. 1793–1798. IEEE (2015)
25. Hoare, C.A.R.: Communicating sequential processes. In: Hansen, P.B. (ed.) The Origin of Concurrent Programming, pp. 413–443. Springer, New York (1978). https://doi.org/10.1007/978-1-4757-3472-0_16
26. Hölzl, F., Feilkas, M.: 13 AUTOFOCUS 3 - a scientific tool prototype for model-based development of component-based, reactive, distributed systems. In: Giese, H., Karsai, G., Lee, E., Rumpe, B., Schätz, B. (eds.) MBEERTS 2007. LNCS, vol. 6100, pp. 317–322. Springer, Heidelberg (2010). https://doi.org/10.1007/978-3-642-16277-0_13
27. Huber, F., Schätz, B.: Rapid prototyping with AutoFocus. In: Wolisz, A., Schieferdecker, I., Rennoch, A. (eds.) Formale Beschreibungstechniken für verteilte Systeme, GI/ITG Fachgespräch, pp. 343–352. GMD Verlag, St. Augustin (1997)
28. Huber, F., Schätz, B., Schmidt, A., Spies, K.: AutoFocus—a tool for distributed systems specification. In: Jonsson, B., Parrow, J. (eds.) FTRTFT 1996. LNCS, vol. 1135, pp. 467–470. Springer, Heidelberg (1996). https://doi.org/10.1007/3-540-61648-9_58
29. Jensen, J.C., Chang, D.H., Lee, E.A.: A model-based design methodology for cyber-physical systems. In: 2011 7th International on Wireless Communications and Mobile Computing Conference (IWCMC), pp. 1666–1671. IEEE (2011)
30. Karsai, G., Sztipanovits, J.: Model-integrated development of cyber-physical systems. Softw. Technol. Embed. Ubiquit. Syst. **5287**, 46–54 (2008)
31. Klein, C., Rumpe, B., Broy, M.: A stream-based mathematical model for distributed information processing systems - SysLab system model. In: Workshop on Formal Methods for Open Object-based Distributed Systems. IFIP Advances in Information and Communication Technology, pp. 323–338. Chapmann & Hall (1996)
32. Krahn, H., Rumpe, B., Völkel, S.: MontiCore: a framework for compositional development of domain specific languages. Int. J. Softw. Tools Technol. Transf. (STTT) **12**(5), 353–372 (2010)

33. Lee, E.A.: Cyber-physical systems-are computing foundations adequate. In: Position Paper for NSF Workshop On Cyber-Physical Systems: Research Motivation, Techniques and Roadmap, vol. 2 (2006)
34. Lee, E.A.: Cyber physical systems: design challenges. In: 2008 11th IEEE International Symposium on Object Oriented Real-Time Distributed Computing (ISORC), pp. 363–369. IEEE (2008)
35. Lee, E.A.: CPS foundations. In: 2010 47th ACM/IEEE Design Automation Conference (DAC), pp. 737–742. IEEE (2010)
36. Lee, E.A.: Constructive models of discrete and continuous physical phenomena. IEEE Access **2**, 1–25 (2014)
37. Lynch, N.A., Tuttle, M.R.: An introduction to input/output automata. CWI Q. **2**, 219–246 (1989)
38. Malavolta, I., Lago, P., Muccini, H., Pelliccione, P., Tang, A.: What industry needs from architectural languages: a survey. IEEE Trans. Softw. Eng. **39**(6), 869–891 (2013)
39. Manna, Z., Pnueli, A.: Verifying hybrid systems. In: Grossman, R.L., Nerode, A., Ravn, A.P., Rischel, H. (eds.) HS 1991-1992. LNCS, vol. 736, pp. 4–35. Springer, Heidelberg (1993). https://doi.org/10.1007/3-540-57318-6_22
40. Maoz, S., Ringert, J.O., Rumpe, B.: Synthesis of component and connector models from crosscutting structural views. In: Meyer, B., Baresi, L., Mezini, M. (eds.) Joint Meeting of the European Software Engineering Conference and the ACM SIGSOFT Symposium on the Foundations of Software Engineering (ESEC/FSE 2013), pp. 444–454. ACM, New York (2013)
41. Maoz, S., Ringert, J.O., Rumpe, B.: Verifying component and connector models against crosscutting structural views. In: Software Engineering Conference (ICSE 2014), pp. 95–105. ACM (2014)
42. Medvidovic, N., Taylor, R.N.: A classification and comparison framework for software architecture description languages. IEEE Trans. Softw. Eng. **26**, 70–93 (2000)
43. Milner, R.: Communication and Concurrency, vol. 84. Prentice Hall, Upper Saddle River (1989)
44. Milner, R.: Communicating and Mobile Systems: the π Calculus. Cambridge University Press, Cambridge (1999)
45. Navarro Pérez, A., Rumpe, B.: Modeling cloud architectures as interactive systems. In: Model-Driven Engineering for High Performance and Cloud Computing Workshop. CEUR Workshop Proceedings, vol. 1118, pp. 15–24 (2013)
46. van Ommering, R., van der Linden, F., Kramer, J., Magee, J.: The Koala component model for consumer electronics software. Computer **33**(3), 78–85 (2000)
47. Oquendo, F.: π-ADL: an architecture description language based on the higher-order typed π-calculus for specifying dynamic and mobile software architectures. ACM SIGSOFT Softw. Eng. Notes **29**, 1–14 (2004)
48. Paech, B., Rumpe, B.: State based service description. In: Proceeding of the IFIP TC6 WG6.1 International Workshop on Formal Methods for Open Object-Based Distributed Systems, FMOODS 1997, pp. 293–302. Chapman & Hall Ltd., London (1997)
49. Philipps, J., Rumpe, B.: Refinement of pipe-and-filter architectures. In: Wing, J.M., Woodcock, J., Davies, J. (eds.) FM 1999. LNCS, vol. 1708, pp. 96–115. Springer, Heidelberg (1999). https://doi.org/10.1007/3-540-48119-2_8
50. Reisig, W.: Petri Nets: An Introduction, vol. 4. Springer, Heidelberg (2012). https://doi.org/10.1007/978-3-642-69968-9

51. Ringert, J.O.: Analysis and Synthesis of Interactive Component and Connector Systems. Aachener Informatik-Berichte, Software Engineering, Band, vol. 19. Shaker Verlag (2014)

52. Ringert, J.O., Roth, A., Rumpe, B., Wortmann, A.: Language and code generator composition for model-driven engineering of robotics component & connector systems. J. Softw. Eng. Rob. (JOSER) **6**(1), 33–57 (2015)

53. Ringert, J.O., Rumpe, B.: A little synopsis on streams, stream processing functions, and state-based stream processing. Int. J. Softw. Inform. **5**(1–2), 29–53 (2011)

54. Ringert, J.O., Rumpe, B., Schulze, C., Wortmann, A.: Teaching agile model-driven engineering for cyber-physical systems. In: International Conference on Software Engineering: Software Engineering and Education Track (ICSE 2017), pp. 127–136. IEEE (2017)

55. Ringert, J.O., Rumpe, B., Wortmann, A.: A case study on model-based development of robotic systems using montiarc with embedded automata. In: Giese, H., Huhn, M., Philipps, J., Schätz, B. (eds.) Dagstuhl-Workshop MBEES: Modellbasierte Entwicklung eingebetteter Systeme, pp. 30–43 (2013)

56. Ringert, J.O., Rumpe, B., Wortmann, A.: From software architecture structure and behavior modeling to implementations of cyber-physical systems. In: Software Engineering Workshopband (SE 2013). LNI, vol. 215, pp. 155–170 (2013)

57. Ringert, J.O., Rumpe, B., Wortmann, A.: Architecture and behavior modeling of cyber-physical systems with MontiArcAutomaton. No. 20 in Aachener Informatik-Berichte, Software Engineering. Shaker Verlag (2014)

58. Rumpe, B.: Formale Methodik des Entwurfs verteilter objektorientierter Systeme. Herbert Utz Verlag Wissenschaft, München, Deutschland (1996)

59. Rumpe, B.: Modellierung mit UML. Springer, Heidelberg (2004). https://doi.org/10.1007/978-3-642-22413-3

60. Rumpe, B.: Modeling with UML: Language, Concepts, Methods. Springer, Heidelberg (2016). https://doi.org/10.1007/978-3-319-33933-7

61. Schindler, M.: Eine Werkzeuginfrastruktur zur agilen Entwicklung mit der UML/P. Aachener Informatik-Berichte, Software Engineering, Band, vol. 11. Shaker Verlag (2012)

62. Schlegel, C., Steck, A., Lotz, A.: Model-driven software development in robotics: communication patterns as key for a robotics component model. In: Chugo, D., Yokota, S. (eds.) Introduction to Modern Robotics. iConcept Press (2011)

63. Tedd, L.A., Radjenovic, J., Milosavljevic, B., Surla, D.: Modelling and implementation of catalogue cards using freemarker. Program **43**(1), 62–76 (2009)

64. Thomas, W.: Automata on infinite objects. In: Handbook of Theoretical Computer Science, vol. B, pp. 133–191. Elsevier (1990)

65. Völter, M., Stahl, T., Bettin, J., Haase, A., Helsen, S., Czarnecki, K., von Stockfleth, B.: Model-Driven Software Development: Technology, Engineering, Management. Wiley Software Patterns Series. Wiley, Hoboken (2013)

Cyber-Physical Systems Education: Explorations and Dreams

Sanjit A. Seshia$^{(\boxtimes)}$

Department of Electrical Engineering and Computer Sciences,
University of California, Berkeley, Berkeley, USA
`sseshia@eecs.berkeley.edu`

Abstract. The field of cyber-physical systems (CPS), as a well-defined intellectual discipline, is entering its second decade. The past decade has seen several explorations in CPS education, accompanied by related research projects and technologies. This article reviews some of these explorations that the author has been involved with, and tries to extrapolate these to "dreams" for what the future may bring.

1 Prologue

In 2006, the term "cyber-physical systems" was coined by Helen Gill at the U.S. National Science Foundation to capture an emerging discipline concerned with the integrations of computation with physical processes. A nascent research community started to emerge, building on the momentum cutting across fields such as embedded systems, real-time systems, hybrid systems, control theory, sensor networks, and formal methods. Discussions began about developing curricula for training students interested in working in the broad area of cyber-physical systems.

During the 2006–2007 academic year, a small group of UC Berkeley faculty in the Electrical Engineering and Computer Sciences (EECS) Department, including Edward Lee, Claire Tomlin, and myself, met to discuss the creation of an undergraduate curriculum in CPS. Berkeley had already been a pioneer in research and graduate education in CPS for several years, but there were still no undergraduate courses focusing on CPS. A major challenge was the breadth of topics needed to cover the area. A further challenge was to achieve a balance between theoretical content and practical, lab-based coursework. From the discussion, the basic contours of an undergraduate course emerged, and over the next decade it developed into a broader "expedition" in CPS education.

A major expedition to explore the unknown is best undertaken by a team. This has been true of some of the major expeditions in history, such as the Lewis and Clark expedition, and it is true of expeditions in research and teaching. In my case, I have been fortunate to undertake this expedition in CPS education with Edward Lee and several others. It has comprised several smaller explorations along "trails" in CPS education. This article is my attempt to report on these explorations, the results they obtained, and what we learned from them, and to extrapolate them to "dreams" for the future of CPS education.

© Springer International Publishing AG, part of Springer Nature 2018
M. Lohstroh et al. (Eds.): Lee Festschrift, LNCS 10760, pp. 407–422, 2018.
https://doi.org/10.1007/978-3-319-95246-8_24

2   Trail I: EECS 149

During the Spring 2008 semester, Edward Lee and I co-taught the first offering of *Introduction to Embedded Systems*, the undergraduate course in CPS we created at Berkeley [14].[1] I will refer to this course by its number in the Berkeley course catalog, EECS 149. We limited enrollment and advertised the class as being for "advanced and adventurous" undergraduates. A small class of about 20 students showed up. Over the course of the next 13 weeks, we explored a selection of topics in CPS together, blending theoretical topics with experimental work. It was a rewarding experience in many ways—perhaps most satisfyingly, two of the students in that class, Jeff Jensen and Trung Tran, went on to work closely with us on further developing the laboratory and online content for the course.

There were a few key decisions we faced in designing a new undergraduate course in CPS. At the time, we ended up making choices that just seemed natural to us. Ten years on, I believe these choices have proved crucial in developing a durable and unique CPS curriculum at Berkeley, one which is also starting to have a promising impact at institutions around the world.

Diversity of Topics and Backgrounds: The field of CPS draws from several areas in computer science, electrical engineering, and other engineering disciplines, including computer architecture, embedded systems programming languages, software engineering, real-time systems, operating systems and networking, formal methods, algorithms, theory of computation, control theory, signal processing, robotics, sensors and actuators, and computer security. How do we integrate this bewildering diversity of areas into a coherent whole?

One approach would be not to attempt such an integration. Instead, one could have a collection of courses that together cover all the key areas in CPS. However, we felt that this approach would have two major shortcomings. First, the reader can observe that the collection of areas could essentially end up covering a whole undergraduate program in electrical engineering and computer science! Second, in CPS there is a pressing need for people who understand the *intersection* between the various areas. We believed that the treatment of the subject of CPS would be best achieved by carefully selecting a collection of topics from the various areas and then presenting a unified treatment that emphasizes how they interact in the modeling, design, and analysis of CPS.

A related challenge was to deal with the diversity of backgrounds students bring to a course in CPS. Over the years, we have had students from computer science, electrical and computer engineering, mechanical engineering, civil engineering, and even bioengineering. Presenting a unified treatment of the various topics in CPS helps mitigate this challenge somewhat, by reducing the dependence on any specific collection of topics one might encounter in a specific engineering program.

---

[1] At the time, the term "cyber-physical systems" was still in its infancy, so we decided to use "embedded systems" instead since, at least at Berkeley, we believed that they were essentially equivalent—two names for the same class of systems.

Balancing Theory and Practice: Many courses on embedded systems focus on the collection of technologies needed to get computers to interact properly with the physical world, including sensor calibration, interfacing with sensors and other input/output devices, programming in assembly or low-level languages, etc. Others focus more on applications, such as building a robotic system such as an autonomous vehicle or an Internet-of-Things (IoT) application. Still others focus entirely on theoretical topics, such as models of computation for CPS, or formal modeling and verification. With EECS 149, we decided very early on to blend theoretical topics with practical, lab-based work. Further we decided to build some flexibility into the lab work, splitting it into a 6-week structured lab sequence followed by a capstone design project whose topic students could choose for themselves. In particular, from the very beginning, a programmable, somewhat-customizable mobile robotic platform called the Cal Climber (see Fig. 1)[2] was chosen for the structured lab sequence, with the following assignment:

> *Design a controller to drive the Cal Climber. On level ground, your robot should drive straight. When an obstacle is encountered, such as a cliff or an object, your robot should navigate around the object and continue in its original orientation. On an incline, your robot should navigate uphill, while still avoiding obstacles. Use the accelerometer to detect an incline and as input to a control algorithm that maintains uphill orientation.*

Fig. 1. Cal Climber laboratory platform (early prototype)

This simple assignment allowed us to interleave basic conceptual and theoretical topics with the lab sequence: for example, students learned about modeling and interfacing with sensors and actuators in class as they interfaced to an accelerometer in the lab; they learned about programming with interrupts in class as they worked with an interrupt-driven controller in the lab, and they learned about modeling with state machines, composition, and hierarchy in class as they programmed their controller with StateCharts in the lab. We have found this interleaved presentation to help students gain an appreciation for theory

---

[2] In the initial years, this platform was the iRobot Create, the programmable version of the Roomba vacuum cleaner. Later, we moved to the very similar Kobuki platform.

in lab work and for motivating theoretical topics in class. We have seen students continue making these connections in their capstone projects, with very satisfactory learning outcomes.

A further aspect of balancing theory with practice is the emphasis in the course on formal methods and model-based design. *Formal methods* is a field of computer science and engineering concerned with the rigorous mathematical specification, design, and verification of computational systems [1,33]. We decided early on to make formal methods and model-based design a key component of the course. In part, this is due to our research backgrounds involving extensive work on these topics. However, we took this step with some trepidation—after all, it is known from earlier experiments in undergraduate education that an emphasis on formal modeling and proof can be a bit "dry" and difficult for students. However, our overall experience has been very promising. Students realized the value of formal modeling, e.g., in reducing the number of design iterations needed to succeed in their capstone projects. This positive experience has extended beyond the community of Berkeley students to include students in the online course we offered a few years ago (see Sect. 4). Similarly, the integration of formal methods with practical lab work forced us to prune down the subject to a core set of formal methods topics that we found to be most relevant to an introductory course in CPS.

A more detailed discussion of the philosophy underlying the course, especially on the lab component and its integration with theoretical content, appears in [4,19].

3   Trail II: The Lee and Seshia Textbook

By the fall of 2009, we had offered EECS 149 twice already. The course, as noted earlier, was unique in its coverage of a broad set of topics and its integration of theory and practical content. Edward Lee and I could not find a single book that could cover all the content we wanted to teach. Therefore, we started to develop our own course notes. Gradually the notes grew into something more coherent, and we decided to put them together as a textbook. In 2010–2011, this effort culminated in the publication of the first edition of *Introduction to Embedded Systems: A Cyber-Physical Systems Approach* [16].

In earlier articles and the book's preface [15–17,19], we have discussed at length the various design decisions made in writing the textbook, and how this book differs from other CPS textbooks. Therefore, we discuss here aspects that have not been covered in depth elsewhere.

Definition of CPS: A textbook on cyber-physical systems must define what that class of systems is. CPS have been informally described as integrations of computation with physical processes. Some definitions emphasize the networked aspect of these systems. Still others make distinctions between CPS and other terms such as the Internet of Things (IoT), embedded systems, the Industrial Internet, Industry 4.0, etc.

We chose an inclusive approach, formulating the following definition:

A *cyber-physical system* (CPS) is an integration of computation with physical processes whose behavior is defined by *both* cyber and physical parts of the system.

This definition defines CPS as being about the *intersection*, not the union, of the physical and the cyber. It is not sufficient to separately understand the physical components and the computational components; we must instead understand their interaction. Note that we do not define the CPS as being networked or having other specific characteristics. We believe that the terms CPS, embedded systems, IoT, Industry 4.0, etc. are essentially equivalent, describing the same class of systems while emphasizing different characteristics of those systems.

Emphasis on Models and Software: Mirroring the EECS 149 course, we decided to focus the book on the interplay of software and hardware with the physical processes with which they interact. Most specifically, we chose not to focus on the design of hardware components of CPS. These aspects are clearly important in any actual CPS design. However, with increasing commoditization of hardware, including processors, sensors, and actuators, we believe that the major intellectual challenge in CPS lies in how we can most effectively design algorithms, models and software to harness a combination of hardware, sensors, actuators, and networking components to achieve a design objective. Moreover, industry trends (e.g., in automotive systems) clearly indicate an explosive growth in the software in CPS – both in terms of opportunities and complexity. For these reasons, our textbook places an emphasis on rigorous mathematical models coupled with software design and implementation for the design of CPS. Such modeling and programming must be informed by hardware, no doubt. To that end, we present ways to effectively model relevant properties of hardware components so as to use those properties in making higher-level design choices.

Organization: We made two key decisions in the organization of course content in the textbook. First, we decided to split the book into three parts, focusing respectively on *Modeling*, *Design*, and *Analysis*. Figure 2 gives the organization of the current edition with the dependencies between chapters. The three parts are relatively independent of each other and are meant to be read concurrently. For example, in EECS 149, we interleave a discussion of programming with interrupts and threads (Part II on Design) with one on modeling with interacting state machines (Part I on Modeling). This enables students to see the connections between the more theoretical content on modeling with the more applied content on design and implementation. Moreover, it has enabled others to use the textbook for their own customized purposes—we are aware of more applied classes focusing mainly on Part II, whereas more theoretical classes on formal methods use portions of Parts I and III. Finally, we decided not to include details of laboratory exercises in this textbook. A separate lab book, co-authored with Jensen and in collaboration with National Instruments, was published online [5]. One reason for this separation is the difficulty in replicating a lab setup across

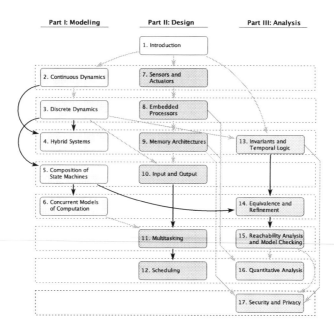

Fig. 2. Organization of the Lee and Seshia textbook (2nd edition)

institutions. We have found a far greater number of institutions using our textbook as compared to the lab book, and this is in part due to the various hardware and space dependencies, as well as support systems required to successfully replicate the lab content.

Publishing: We decided to try a publishing experiment with the first edition of this book. Rather than going with a traditional, established publisher, we decided to use a "print-on-demand" online publisher. This allowed us, amongst other things, to keep a free PDF version online while also providing readers with the option of purchasing a paper copy. Moreover, the paper copy was able to be sold at a much lower price that we believed would be the case with traditional publishers. Six years on, we believe this experiment made the right choices. As of this writing, our textbook has been adopted at around 300 institutions in over 50 countries—some of these, we are fairly sure, would not have been possible without the free PDF version being available online. Additionally, we found that many readers do purchase a paper copy even though a free PDF is available. Our most recent (second) edition is now published by MIT Press at what appears to be an affordable price and with a PDF available online for free. Having the PDF available online also made it easier for us to use the book in the online version of EECS 149 on edX, since enrollees around the world could consult the version they could most easily get their hands on.

4 Trail III: MOOCs and Exercise Generation

The advent of massive open online courses (MOOCs) [23] has promised to bring world-class education to anyone with Internet access. Additionally, it has placed a renewed focus on the development and use of computational aids for teaching and learning. MOOCs present a range of problems to which the field of formal methods has much to contribute. These include *automatic grading*, *automated exercise generation*, and *virtual laboratory environments*. In automatic grading, a computer program verifies that a candidate solution provided by a student is "correct", i.e., that it meets certain instructor-specified criteria (the specification). In addition, and particularly when the solution is incorrect, the automatic grader (henceforth, *auto-grader*) should provide feedback to the student as to where he/she went wrong. Automatic exercise generation is the process of synthesizing problems (with associated solutions) that test students' understanding of course material, often starting from instructor-provided sample problems. Finally, for courses involving laboratory assignments, a virtual laboratory (henceforth, lab) seeks to provide the remote student with an experience similar to that provided in a real, on-campus lab.

In 2011–2012, we started to brainstorm about an online version of EECS 149, and what technologies we could develop to aid in creating such an online course. We first looked at the task of automatic exercise generation. The term "automatic" may seem to indicate a goal of completely automating the process of creating problems and solutions. However, we felt that it would be unrealistic and also somewhat undesirable to completely remove the instructor from the problem generation process, since this is a creative process that requires the instructor's input to emphasize the right concepts. Automation is best employed in those aspects of problem generation that are tedious for an instructor. Additionally, in the MOOC setting, generating customized problems for students is impossible without some degree of automation. Finally, creating many different versions of a problem can help to reduce cheating by blind copying of solutions.

Examining problems from all three parts of the Lee and Seshia textbook [16], Sadigh et al. [26] take a *template-based approach* to automatic problem generation. Specifically, several existing exercises in the book are shown to conform to a template. The template identifies common elements of these problems while representing the differentiating elements as parameters or "holes". In order to create a new problem, the template essentially must be instantiated with new parameter values. However, it is often useful to create new problems that are "similar" in difficulty to existing hand-crafted problems. To facilitate this, new problems are generated using a bounded number of *mutations* to an existing problem, under suitable constraints and pruning to ensure well-defined results. An instructor can then select results that look reasonable to him or her.

For brevity, we outline some of the main insights reported in [26] as they relate to the application of formal methods. The first insight relates to the structure of exercises After investigating the exercises from certain relevant chapters (Chaps. 3, 4, 9, 12, 13) of Lee and Seshia [16], we found that more than 60% of problems fit into the model-based category, where the problem tests concepts involving relationships between models, properties and traces. Figure 3 is an illustration of the three entities, and their characteristics. At any point, given one or two of these entities, we can ask about instances of the unknown entity. Table 1 groups exercises into different classes based on what is given and what is to be found. Each group represents an interaction between models, properties and traces. The first column shows the given entity, and the second column is the unknown entity. The third column shows some of the variations of the same class of problem.

Table 2 states a solution technique for each problem category listed in Table 1. Note that major topics investigated in formal methods such as model checking, specification mining, and synthesis can be applied to various tasks in exercise generation. Moreover, since textbook problems are typically smaller than those arising in industrial use, their size is within the capacity of existing tools for synthesis and verification.

5   Trail IV: EECS 149.1x and CPSGrader

During 2012–2013, we began a concerted effort to develop a MOOC version of EECS 149. Berkeley had joined edX as a university partner, and a large campus effort was underway to engage with the emerging landscape on large-scale online education. However, taking EECS 149 online was not going to be easy.

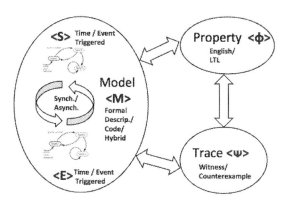

Fig. 3. Models, properties and traces: entities in exercises in Lee and Seshia textbook [16] (reproduced from [26])

One the one hand, with the growing interest in CPS from academia and industry, there was a clear demand for making educational resources in CPS more widely accessible. Having materials from EECS 149 and the Lee-Seshia textbook available freely online made it easier to offer a free MOOC to the broader community. On the other hand, a major challenge was posed by the lab component of the course. Lab-based courses that are not software-only, such as EECS 149, pose a particular technical challenge for MOOCs. A key component of learning in lab-based courses is working with hardware, getting "one's

Table 1. Classification of model-based problems in Lee and Seshia [16], first edition, version 1.06 (reproduced from [26])

Given	Find	Variations	Exercise #
$\langle \phi \rangle$	$\langle M \rangle$	(i) $\phi \in$ English or LTL (ii) Use hybrid systems for M (iii) Modify pre-existing M	3.1, 3.2, 3.3, 4.1, 4.2, 4.3, 4.4, 4.5, 4.6, 4.8, 9.4, 9.6, 13.2, 13.3
$\langle M \rangle$	$\langle \psi \rangle$	(i) Reachable trace (ii) Describe output	3.3, 3.5, 4.2
$\langle M \rangle$	$\langle \phi \rangle$	Models can be given in code or formal description	3.2, 12.3
$\langle M \rangle$ & $\langle \psi \rangle$	$\langle \psi \rangle$	Given input trace $\rightarrow$ find output trace	9.5
$\langle M \rangle$ & $\langle \phi \rangle$	$\langle \psi \rangle$	Find counterexample or witness trace	3.4, 4.3, 12.1

Table 2. Techniques to find solutions for model-based problems (reproduced from [26])

Given	Find	Solution technique
$\langle \phi \rangle$	$\langle M \rangle$	Constrained synthesis or repair
$\langle M \rangle$	$\langle \psi \rangle$	Simulation of model
$\langle M \rangle$	$\langle \phi \rangle$	Specification mining
$\langle M \rangle$ & $\langle \psi \rangle$	$\langle \psi \rangle$	Simulation with guidance
$\langle M \rangle$ & $\langle \phi \rangle$	$\langle \psi \rangle$	Model checking

hands dirty". It appears extremely difficult, if not impossible, to provide that experience online. And yet, it is undeniably useful to provide a learning experience that approximates the real lab as well as possible. Indeed, in industrial design one often prototypes a design in a simulated environment before building the real artifact. Thus, we decided to build a virtual laboratory environment for EECS 149, and blend that with suitable theoretical content to create the MOOC version.

Working with Lee and Jensen, and a team at National Instruments, my research group and I developed courseware and technologies for an online course in CPS. In Spring 2013, we presented a paper sketching out our main ideas for a virtual lab in CPS [6]. In 2013–2014, we began an effort that culminated in two key contributions: EECS 149.1x [18], the online version of EECS 149 offered on edX in 2014, and CPSGrader, an automatic grading and feedback system for virtual laboratory environments [9]. We describe both these efforts in more detail below.

5.1 CPSGrader

In an ideal world, we would provide an infrastructure where students can log in remotely to a computer which has been preconfigured with all development tools and laboratory exercises and gives the students a view into how their solution is executing in the real lab setting; in fact, pilot projects exploring this approach have already been undertaken (e.g., see [22]). However, in the MOOC setting, the large numbers of students makes such a remotely-accessible physical lab expensive and impractical. A virtual lab environment, driven by simulation of real-world environments, appears to be the only solution at present.

To this end, we developed CPSGrader, which combines virtual lab software with automatic grading and feedback for courses in the areas of cyber-physical systems and robotics [8–10]. CPSGrader has been successfully used in both the on-campus *Introduction to Embedded Systems* at UC Berkeley [14] and its online counterpart on edX [18]. Recall that in the lab component of this course, students program the Cal Climber [5] robot (see Fig. 1) to perform certain navigation tasks like obstacle avoidance and hill climbing. Students can prototype their controller to work within a simulated environment based on the LabVIEW Robotics Environment Simulator by National Instruments (see Figs. 4 and 5).

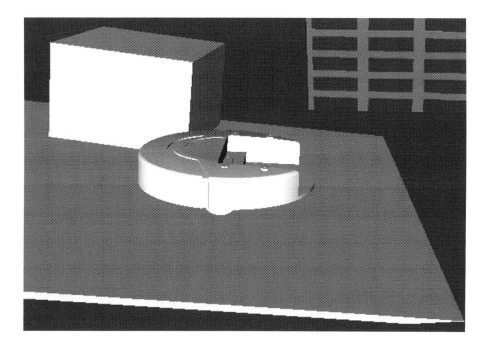

Fig. 4. Cal Climber in the LabVIEW robotics environment simulator

The virtual lab dynamical model is a complex, physics-based one, which, due to its complexity and dependence on third party components, we decided to treat as a black box. CPSGrader employs simulation-based verification, arguably the main scalable formal approach in this setting. Correctness and the presence of certain classes of mistakes are both checked using *test benches* formalized in *Signal Temporal Logic* (STL) [21]. However, coming up with these STL properties can be tedious and error-prone, even for instructors well-versed in formal methods. Therefore, in Juniwal et al. [10], we showed how these temporal logic testers can be synthesized from examples. Our approach can be viewed as an instance of machine learning from student solutions that have the fault (positive examples) and those that do not (negative examples). An active learning framework has also been developed to ease the burden of labeling solutions as positive or negative [8]. In machine learning terminology, this can be thought of as the *training* phase. The resulting test bench then becomes the *classifier* that determines whether a student solution is correct, and, if not, which fault is present. CPSGrader was used successfully in the edX course EECS149.1x offered in May–June 2014 [18], an experiment we describe in more detail in Sect. 5.2.

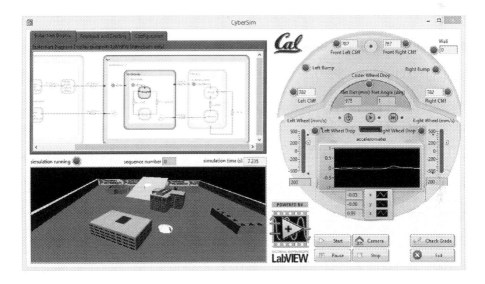

Fig. 5. Simulator with auto-grading functionality used in EECS 149.1x

There are several interesting directions for future work, including developing quantitative methods for assigning partial credit, mining temporal logic testers to capture new classes of student mistakes, and online monitoring of these testers to improve responsiveness.

5.2   EECS 149.1x

Over a 7-week period in May-June 2014, we offered *EECS 149.1x: Cyber-Physical Systems* free to the public on the edX platform. To our knowledge, this was the first MOOC covering a breadth of topics in CPS offered on any of the major platforms. We simplified some of the course content from the material in EECS 149, since we could not rely on students in the MOOC having the same pre-requisite background that UC Berkeley students possess. The course included 49 lectures comprising nearly 11 h of video content. It also included 6 weekly lab assignments that somewhat mirrored the 6-week structured lab sequence in EECS 149. The Cal Climber lab was turned into an entirely online lab to be performed using the virtual lab software we created—CyberSim and CPSGrader—described in the preceding section. In addition, we had an optional "hardware track" for those students who were open to purchasing and assembling the hardware components themselves. The theoretical course topics covered in the lectures included inline quizzes but no separate homework assignments—the lab sequence was integrated with the theoretical course content. We organized the lectures into the following ten modules: Introduction to CPS; Memory Architectures; Interrupts; Modeling Continuous Dynamics; Sensors and Actuators; Modeling Discrete Dynamics; Extended and Hybrid Automata; Composition of State Machines; Hierarchical State Machines, and Specification & Temporal Logic.

The impact in MOOCs can be difficult to quantify, but here are some numbers from EECS149.1x. The course attracted a peak enrollment of 8767, of which 2213 ended up submitting at least one lab assignment. Of these, the number who passed the course was 342 (4% of peak enrollment). Around the 6th week of the course, we conducted an anonymized survey of the students still engaged in the MOOC. This produced some very interesting and encouraging data, which I summarize here:

- We seemed to attract a population of students who had already taken other MOOCs – 54% of those who stayed until the 6th week had taken 3 or more MOOCs.
- Of those who had taken at least one other MOOC, over 80% of the students rated our course as good or better than the one(s) they had previously taken.
- A majority of the students were new to model-based design with a language like LabVIEW, but even so, 73% found it to be a useful experience to do the lab assignment in two different languages, C and LabVIEW.
- 86% of the students rated CPSGrader as being useful in their lab assignments – an encouraging sign for the use of such tools for personalized education.
- A small fraction of students did the optional hardware track. Of these, over 90% found that if their solution passed CPSGrader in the virtual lab, it worked on the real hardware! This statistic was a really encouraging piece of data for the CPSGrader project. We had been using CyberSim in the on-campus lab for a couple of years, but saw no such correlation. However, using CPSGrader seems to have pushed students to debug the corner cases that also improved the reliability of their solution on the real hardware.
- We polled the students on the lecture modules they liked most, both from the viewpoint of relevance to lab assignments and from a theoretical standpoint. This poll was motivated in part for us to learn whether a general, non-Berkeley student population, including several students working in industry, would be

receptive to the large formal methods content in the MOOC. To our pleasant surprise, we found that the modules on Hierarchical State Machines and Composition of State Machines were in the top three topics found relevant to the lab, while the module on Formal Specification and Temporal Logic ranked in the top three theoretical topics. This provides some real-world validation that relevance of and receptiveness to formal methods in a general student population.

In summary, creating the online version of EECS 149 was a lot of fun, and a tremendously rewarding experience. It is a first step towards creating a strong learning experience for "lab-based MOOCs" in science and engineering. The CPSGrader software is available open source and is architected to work with any simulator. Moreover, its success points the way to a broader application of formal methods for enhancing science and engineering education.

6   Dreams for the Future

As I think about the future of CPS education, and of engineering education in general, two sets of articles come to mind. The first is a pair of thought-provoking articles written by Lee and Messerschmitt as the twentieth century drew to a close. One article discussed the future of engineering education, focusing, in particular, on electrical and computer engineering [12]. The other article presented an innovative viewpoint on what higher education might look like in the year 2049 [13]. The other set of articles has to do with the recent studies and opinions about the impact of automation and information technology (IT) on jobs (e.g., [2, 31, 32]).

A few threads emerge. First, with rapid technological change, and increasing automation, the need for lifelong learning becomes ever more important. Second, humans will increasingly need to collaborate with intelligent machines in their jobs. How should we design engineering and CPS education for such a future?

I will approach this question from the viewpoint of leveraging the work described in the preceding four sections.

The landscape for CPS education in the near future looks very exciting, with opportunities for further innovation. For inspiration, we can look to the emerging areas for research and industrial practice in CPS. There are at least three such areas that are not adequately covered by EECS 149 and the textbook: (i) networking and distributed CPS; (ii) human-CPS (CPS that work in concert with humans), and (iii) CPS that make extensive use of machine learning. All three are active areas of research by the CPS community, and are finding broad applications in the real world. For example, the TerraSwarm research center has developed a number of innovations in the area of networked, distributed CPS (see, e.g., [3, 11, 28]), and some of these ideas have had a direct impact on the material in EECS 149. Similarly, the CPS community is starting to bring the strong formal approach to modeling, design and analysis that underlies EECS 149 to the design of human-CPS, including modeling human cognition, perception, situational awareness, and action (see, e.g., [20, 24, 25, 28, 29]). Additionally, even as machine learning becomes more pervasive in CPS, recent advances in formal design and analysis of learning-based CPS (e.g., [7, 27, 30]) point the way to teaching a principled approach to designing such systems to students and practitioners. Currently, in EECS 149, we cover these topics mainly through the capstone design projects. Over the next decade, we see them making their way into the core curriculum, although much research remains to be done.

Some institutions around the world are seeing rapid growth in the number of students who want to take classes and major in computer science and related areas. CPS/IoT is already starting to be one of these areas. These institutions are seeing pressure on campus teaching resources due to burgeoning enrollments. Technologies for personalized education can play a role in reducing this pressure while ensuring that instructor attention is used more effectively. They can also play a role in broadening access to CPS education.

It is much harder to predict what role CPS education can play to mitigate the impact of automation and IT on jobs. It is clear that technology is only part of the solution (e.g., see [2, 32]). Even so, technologies for personalized education, such as CPSGrader, can help by providing students with personalized feedback on their work, even in online courses. Virtual lab technologies can enable students to build up expertise in a vocational topic which can then make them more attractive to prospective employers. However, the experience with several MOOCs so far has shown that the students who benefit the most are the ones who were most motivated and best prepared in the first place. How can one ensure that students who need more help can benefit as well? For this, we need more work to develop structures such as the virtual "village" discussed by Lee and Messerschmitt [13], where technologies like CPSGrader are integrated with a community of mentors and peers forming a support system for the students.

Acknowledgments. I thank the anonymous reviewers for their feedback. The work described in this article was supported in part by the National Science Foundation, by a gift from National Instruments, and by TerraSwarm, one of six centers of STARnet, a Semiconductor Research Corporation program sponsored by MARCO and DARPA.

References

1. Clarke, E.M., Wing, J.M.: Formal methods: state of the art and future directions. ACM Comput. Surv. (CSUR) **28**(4), 626–643 (1996)
2. Committee on Information Technology, Automation, and the U.S. Workforce: Information technology and the U.S. workforce: Where are we and where do we go from here? http://www.nap.edu/24649
3. Lee, E.A., et al.: The swarm at the edge of the cloud. IEEE Des. Test **31**(3), 8–20 (2014)
4. Jensen, J.C., Lee, E.A., Seshia, S.A.: An introductory capstone design course on embedded systems. In: Proceedings of International Symposium on Circuits and Systems (ISCAS), pp. 1199–1202, May 2011
5. Jensen, J.C., Lee, E.A., Seshia, S.A.: An Introductory Lab in Embedded and Cyber-Physical Systems. LeeSeshia.org, Berkeley (2012)

6. Jensen, J.C., Lee, E.A., Seshia, S.A.: Virtualizing cyber-physical systems: bringing CPS to online education. In: Proceedings First Workshop on CPS Education (CPS-Ed), April 2013

7. Jha, S., Seshia, S.A.: A theory of formal synthesis via inductive learning. Acta Inform. **54**(7), 693–726 (2017)

8. Juniwal, G.: CPSGrader: auto-grading and feedback generation for cyber-physical systems education. Master's thesis, EECS Department, University of California, Berkeley, December 2014. http://www.eecs.berkeley.edu/Pubs/TechRpts/2014/EECS-2014-237.html

9. Juniwal, G., Donzé, A., Jensen, J.C., Seshia, S.A.: CPSGrader website. http://www.cpsgrader.org

10. Juniwal, G., Donzé, A., Jensen, J.C., Seshia, S.A.: CPSGrader: synthesizing temporal logic testers for auto-grading an embedded systems laboratory. In: Proceedings of the 14th International Conference on Embedded Software (EMSOFT), October 2014

11. Latronico, E., Lee, E.A., Lohstroh, M., Shaver, C., Wasicek, A., Weber, M.: A vision of swarmlets. IEEE Internet Comput. **19**(2), 20–28 (2015)

12. Lee, E.A., Messerschmitt, D.G.: Engineering and education for the future. IEEE Comput. **31**, 77–85 (1998)

13. Lee, E.A., Messerschmitt, D.G.: A highest education in the year 2049. Proc. IEEE **87**(9), 1685–1691 (1999)

14. Lee, E.A., Seshia, S.A.: EECS 149 course website. http://chess.eecs.berkeley.edu/eecs149

15. Lee, E.A., Seshia, S.A.: An introductory textbook on cyber-physical systems. In: Proceedings of Workshop on Embedded Systems Education (WESE), October 2010

16. Lee, E.A., Seshia, S.A.: Introduction to Embedded Systems - A Cyber-Physical Systems Approach, 1st edn. LeeSeshia.org, Berkeley (2011)

17. Lee, E.A., Seshia, S.A.: Introduction to Embedded Systems - A Cyber-Physical Systems Approach, 2nd edn. MIT Press, Cambridge (2016)

18. Lee, E.A., Seshia, S.A., Jensen, J.C.: EECS149.1x Course Website on edX. https://www.edx.org/course/uc-berkeleyx/uc-berkeleyx-eecs149-1x-cyber-physical-1629

19. Lee, E.A., Seshia, S.A., Jensen, J.C.: Teaching embedded systems the Berkeley way. In: Proceedings of the Workshop on Embedded and Cyber-Physical Systems Education, WESE 2012, Tampere, Finland, p. 1, 12 October 2012

20. Li, W., Sadigh, D., Sastry, S.S., Seshia, S.A.: Synthesis for human-in-the-loop control systems. In: Ábrahám, E., Havelund, K. (eds.) TACAS 2014. LNCS, vol. 8413, pp. 470–484. Springer, Heidelberg (2014). https://doi.org/10.1007/978-3-642-54862-8_40

21. Maler, O., Nickovic, D.: Monitoring temporal properties of continuous signals. In: Lakhnech, Y., Yovine, S. (eds.) FORMATS/FTRTFT -2004. LNCS, vol. 3253, pp. 152–166. Springer, Heidelberg (2004). https://doi.org/10.1007/978-3-540-30206-3_12

22. Massachusetts Institute of Technology (MIT): The iLab Project. https://wikis.mit.edu/confluence/display/ILAB2/Home. Accessed Feb 2014

23. Pappano, L.: The Year of the MOOC, November 2012. http://www.nytimes.com/2012/11/04/education/edlife/massive-open-online-courses-are-multiplying-at-a-rapid-pace.html

24. Sadigh, D.: Safe and interactive autonomy: control, learning, and verification. Ph.D. thesis, EECS Department, University of California, Berkeley, August 2017. http://www2.eecs.berkeley.edu/Pubs/TechRpts/2017/EECS-2017-143.html

25. Sadigh, D., Sastry, S., Seshia, S.A., Dragan, A.D.: Information gathering actions over human internal state. In: Proceedings of the IEEE/RSJ International Conference on Intelligent Robots and Systems (IROS), pp. 66–73, October 2016

26. Sadigh, D., Seshia, S.A., Gupta, M.: Automating exercise generation: a step towards meeting the MOOC challenge for embedded systems. In: Proceedings of Workshop on Embedded Systems Education (WESE), October 2012

27. Seshia, S.A.: Combining induction, deduction, and structure for verification and synthesis. Proc. IEEE **103**(11), 2036–2051 (2015)

28. Seshia, S.A., Hu, S., Li, W., Zhu, Q.: Design automation of cyber-physical systems: challenges, advances, and opportunities. IEEE Trans. CAD Integr. Circ. Syst. **36**(9), 1421–1434 (2017)

29. Seshia, S.A., Sadigh, D., Sastry, S.S.: Formal methods for semi-autonomous driving. In: Proceedings of the Design Automation Conference (DAC), pp. 148:1–148:5, June 2015

30. Seshia, S.A., Sadigh, D., Sastry, S.S.: Towards Verified Artificial Intelligence. ArXiv e-prints, July 2016

31. Vardi, M.Y.: Humans, machines, and the future of work. In: Ada Lovelace Symposium 2015 - Celebrating 200 Years of a Computer Visionary, Ada Lovelace Symposium 2015, Oxford, UK, p. 2, 10 December 2015

32. Vardi, M.Y.: The moral imperative of artificial intelligence. Commun. ACM **59**(5), 5 (2016)

33. Wing, J.M.: A specifier's introduction to formal methods. IEEE Comput. **23**(9), 8–24 (1990)

Power is Overrated, Go for Friendliness! Expressiveness, Faithfulness, and Usability in Modeling: The Actor Experience

Marjan Sirjani[1,2](✉)

[1] School of Innovation, Design and Engineering, Mälardalen University,
Västerås, Sweden
[2] School of Computer Science, Reykjavik University, Reykjavík, Iceland
marjan.sirjani@mdh.se

Abstract. Expressive power of a language is generally defined as the breadth of ideas that can be represented and communicated in a language. For formal languages, the expressive power has been evaluated by checking its Turing completeness. In a modeling process, apart from the modeling language, we have two other counterparts: the system being modeled and the modeler. I argue that faithfulness to the system being modeled and usability for the modeler are at least as important as the expressive power of the modeling language, specially because most of the modeling languages used today are highly expressive. I call faithfulness and usability together "friendliness". I show how we used the actor-based language Rebeca in modeling different applications, where it is friendly, and where it is not. I discuss how the friendliness of Rebeca may help in the analysis of models and allows for system synthesis on the basis of models.

Foreword

People have different ways of thinking. What seems simple, clear, and understandable to me may seem highly complicated and convoluted to others. When we tell a story in our words we make a different model of the same concept, and this new model may give a better insight to certain audiences. That is why people talk about the same concept again and again in different ways. I see three counterparts involved when you tell a story: the audience, the way you tell the story, and the story itself. I got to learn that all three can be equally important. Edward has a wealth of knowledge and a wide range of expertise. One of his several qualities is the way he tells stories; he says what I want to say in a much better way! This gives me more courage to write, even if others have already told my story. After all, I may say it in a better way, at least for a certain audience.

© Springer International Publishing AG, part of Springer Nature 2018
M. Lohstroh et al. (Eds.): Lee Festschrift, LNCS 10760, pp. 423–448, 2018.
https://doi.org/10.1007/978-3-319-95246-8_25

1   Introduction

Why yet another modeling language? I've seen this question on so many occasions, especially asked by people in the formal methods community. The main reason that this question is asked is because the tradition in theoretical computer science is to compare two languages based on their expressive power. Expressive power is generally defined as the breadth of ideas that can be represented and communicated in a language. One way that has been used for evaluating the expressive power of a language is checking for Turing completeness. Turing completeness was not enough and the community moved towards other ways of comparing expressiveness, mostly based on mutually encoding the formalisms into each other. But most of the modeling languages we work with are highly expressive, and may have equivalent expressive powers. So, why yet another modeling language?

Turing completeness and most of the other ways of comparing languages check computability, and nowadays, interaction; the focus here is on the machine world. I can see two other major counterparts in modeling, the system that is modeled and the modeler. A modeling language has to be evaluated by its faithfulness to the system it is modeling, and usability for the modeler. I call usability and faithfulness together friendliness, friendliness to the system and friendliness to the modeler. What theoretical computer scientists are missing is the friendliness of the languages.

Since the main complexity of the modeling job is the computation part, it is natural to focus on that part. Moreover, people tend to focus on parts that they understand better and are more familiar with. When we are working with more and more complicated applications with heterogeneous components and different technologies, then I believe friendliness of our modeling languages will become at least as important as their expressive power.

We also have to remember that the goal of building a model is usually analysis and/or building or synthesizing the system based on the model. Therefore, analyzability is crucial. Expressive power and friendliness both affect analyzability and synthesizability. Sometimes faithfulness criteria may guide us to a less expressive language, and that may help in improving the analyzability (similar to domain-specific languages). Moreover, friendliness can give us a good traceability, from the model to the system. If we find a problem in the model, then we can trace it back into the system more easily. Thus, apart from expressiveness, friendliness can be a criterion for choosing the modeling language we want to use.

I have to add that there are different communities that consider modeling in all its aspects. For example, modeling is an important part in software engineering. The object-oriented paradigm came with the winning slogan of *decreasing the semantic gap* between the real world and the program, i.e., increasing faithfulness. If we focus on expressive power we would be still programming in assembly languages.

Faithfulness and Usability. Faithfulness is about the similarity of the model and the system. In most places it is defined as the degree of detail incorporated in the model [21]. What I mean in this paper by faithfulness of a modeling language is whether and how the structures and features that are supported by the modeling language match the needs of the domain of the system being modeled, and how much this helps in having a more natural mapping between the model and the system. More precisely, we can define faithfulness based on the definition of model of computation. A collection of rules that govern the execution of the (concurrent) components and the communication between components is called a model of computation (MoC) [23]. We say a modeling language is faithful to a system if the model of computation supported by the language matches the model of computation of (the features of interest of) the system. Faithfulness can be seen as the key motivation behind domain-specific languages.

Sometimes I use the term *"model"* when you expect to see *"modeling language"*. This is where I mean the model of computation. The structures, features, and flow of control provided and imposed by your modeling language can shape your model. As they say, language can shape your thoughts.

In synthesis, we make a model, prior to building the system itself, to help us build the system. In the model we incorporate all the properties of interest. Faithfulness then is defined as how faithful the system is to the model. This is what is common in engineering domains. In analysis, if the system already exists, we make an (abstract) model of the system to help us perform different kinds of analysis. This is the type of modeling that scientists are more familiar with. We can look at faithfulness in both directions: faithfulness of the system towards the model, and the model towards the system.

In ISO 9241 [16], usability is defined as the extent to which a product can be used by specified users to achieve specified goals with effectiveness, efficiency and satisfaction, in a specified context of use. Effectiveness is accuracy and completeness with which users achieve specified goals. Efficiency is resources expended in relation to the accuracy and completeness with which users achieve goals. Satisfaction is freedom from discomfort and positive attitudes towards the use of the product. In this paper, I do not discuss usability in an extensive manner. I can only explain my experience through the years, as we have not yet run any scientific experiment that evaluates the usability of different modeling languages.

Edward and Modeling. The first time that I have seen a truly convincing answer to the question "why yet another modeling language?", was a text by Edward in the Ptolemy book [23] "An important part of a science, quite complementary to the scientific method, is the construction of models. Models are abstractions of the physical reality, and the ability of a model to lend insight and predict behavior may form the centerpiece of a hypothesis that is to be validated (or invalidated) by experiment. The construction of models is itself more an engineering discipline than a science. It is not, fundamentally, the study of a system that preexists in nature; it is instead the human-driven construction of an artifact that did not previously exist. A model itself must be engineered.

Good models can even reduce the need for measurement, and therefore reduce the dependence on the scientific method." The keywords for me were "engineering" and "human-driven construction," which bring in the modeler and show its importance, and "the ability of a model to lend insight" which, I think, can depend on the faithfulness as much as the expressiveness of the modeling language.

Actors and Friendliness. In this paper, I will explain how the actor-based [2] language Rebeca [30–33] is used for modeling and analysis of different domains of applications, and where and how it has been more faithful and usable, and where it has multiple shortcomings. I will not cover a comparison between modeling each of the applications using Rebeca versus modeling the same application using other modeling languages. The interested reader can find the comparisons in corresponding papers published on each application. For each application domain I will explain the mapping between the entities and concepts in the real world, and the ones in the Rebeca model. The interesting and important properties that have to be verified or analyzed in each domain is not always trivial. For each application, I will explain the property that is checked and the analysis that is done.

In the next section there is a short description of Rebeca and Timed Rebeca. In Sect. 3, I will explain how we used Timed Rebeca in modeling sensor networks and check the schedulability [18,19]. In Sect. 4, I will describe how extensions of Rebeca are used for analyzing different network protocols [36,37]. In Sect. 5, I view Network on Chip (NoC) as an example of track-based traffic systems and show how we used Timed Rebeca in evaluating different routing algorithms [26–28]. In Sect. 6, I will give a short overview of friendliness, analyzability and other features of Rebeca.

The goal of this paper is not to present a novel technique or a new model, it is to tell an already-told story in a different way. The message is where and how friendliness of a language can help in modeling and analysis, and the target audience are mainly those who are looking for a modeling language for analyzing their application.

Disclaimer: Most of the technical material in this paper is taken from published or draft papers. In some places the sentences are copied without using quotation marks.

2   The Actor-Based Language, Rebeca

Rebeca (Reactive Object Language) [30,32] is an actor-based language based on Hewitt and Agha's actors [2,13]. Actors are units of concurrency, with no shared variables, communicating via asynchronous messages. There is no explicit receive statement, and send statements are non-blocking. Rebeca is an imperative language, with Java-like syntax. In each actor there is only a single thread of execution and one message queue. The actor takes a message from the top of its message queue, and executes the corresponding method (called *message server*) non-preemptively. If you see messages as events, then a Rebeca model can be seen as an event-driven model. The execution of message servers is also similar to *atomic asynchronous call-backs* in the context of JavaScript.

In Timed Rebeca (the real-time extension of Rebeca) [1,25,33], we have a message bag instead of a message queue, where messages are tagged with their time-stamps (sometimes I use message buffer as a more general term instead of message queue or bag). We consider synchronized local clocks throughout the model for all the actors (you can read it as a global time). The sender tags a message with its own local time, at the time of sending. This can be seen as *model time* in Ptolemy.

A Rebeca model consists of a number of *reactive classes*, each describing the type of a certain number of *actors* (called *rebecs*, we use both terms, rebec and actor, interchangeably in the Rebeca context). Each reactive class declares the size of its message buffer, a set of *state variables*, and the messages to which it can respond. The local state of each actor is defined by the values of its state variables and the contents of its message buffer. Each actor has a set of *known rebecs* to which it can send messages. Reactive classes have constructors, with the same name as their reactive class. They are responsible for initializing the actor's state variables and putting initially-needed messages in the message buffer of that actor. See Fig. 1 for an abstract syntax of Timed Rebeca.

$$Model ::= Class^* \; Main$$
$$Main ::= \textbf{main} \; \{ \; InstanceDcl^* \; \}$$
$$InstanceDcl ::= className \; rebecName(\langle rebecName \rangle^*) : (\langle literal \rangle^*);$$
$$Class ::= \textbf{reactiveclass} \; className \; \{ \; KnownRebecs \; Vars \; MsgSrv^* \; \}$$
$$KnownRebecs ::= \textbf{knownrebecs} \; \{ \; VarDcl^* \; \}$$
$$Vars ::= \textbf{statevars} \; \{ \; VarDcl^* \; \}$$
$$VarDcl ::= type \; \langle v \rangle^+;$$
$$MsgSrv ::= \textbf{msgsrv} \; methodName(\langle type \; v \rangle^*) \; \{ \; Stmt^* \; \}$$
$$Stmt ::= v = e; \; |v =?(e, \langle e \rangle^+); \; |Call; \; |\textbf{delay}(t); \; |if(e)\{Stmt^*\}[else\{Stmt^*\}]$$
$$Call ::= rebecName.methodName(\langle e \rangle^*) \; [\textbf{after}(t)] \; [\textbf{deadline}(t)]$$

Fig. 1. Abstract syntax of Timed Rebeca (from [20]). Angled brackets ⟨...⟩ are used as meta parenthesis, superscript + for repetition at least once, superscript * for repetition zero or more times, whereas using ⟨...⟩ with repetition denotes a comma separated list. Brackets [...] indicates that the text within the brackets is optional. Identifiers *className*, *rebecName*, *methodName*, *v*, *literal*, and *type* denote class name, rebec name, method name, variable, literal, and type, respectively; and *e* denotes an (arithmetic, boolean or nondeterministic choice) expression.

The way an actor responds to a message is specified in a *message server*. The state of an actor can change during the executing of its message servers through assignment statements. An actor makes decisions through conditional statements, communicates with other actors by sending messages, and performs periodic behavior by sending messages to itself. Since communication is asynchronous, each actor has a *message buffer* from which it takes the next incoming message. An actor takes the first message from its message buffer, executes its corresponding message server in an isolated environment, takes the next message (or waits for the next message to arrive), and so on. A message server may have a *nondeterministic assignment* statement which is used to model the nondeterminism in the behavior of a message server. Finally, the `main` block is used to instantiate the actors of the model. Note that Rebeca does not support dynamic actor creation, and all the actors of a model must be defined in the main block.

Timed Rebeca adds three primitives to Rebeca to address timing issues: *delay*, *deadline* and *after*. A *delay* statement models the passage of time for an actor during execution of a message server. Note that all other statements of Timed Rebeca are assumed to execute instantaneously. The keywords *after* and *deadline* are used in conjunction with a method call. The term `after(n)` indicates that it takes n units of time for a message to be delivered to its receiver. The term `deadline(n)` expresses that if the message is not taken in n units of time, it will be purged from the receiver's message bag automatically.

Actors in Ptolemy and Rebeca. Actors in Ptolemy are more like components in software engineering terminology. In Ptolemy, actors have ports, they read and write to and from their ports, while in Rebeca actors send messages to each other knowing each others names (like objects in object-oriented languages). Ptolemy actors may have more than one port, while in Rebeca there is only one message buffer.

Note that in Ptolemy you have *directors* that coordinate the behavior of actors. Through that coordination you are able to impose an order on the execution of actors and make the model deterministic. You can also make different models of computation. Rebeca and Timed Rebeca can be seen as specific models of computation in Ptolemy.

Rebeca is initially designed for analysis, and hence supports features for making a model of an existing system. The language allows non-deterministic assignments, and the model checking tools consider non-deterministic order of execution (or an interleaved model of concurrency). Ptolemy is initially designed for synthesis, and hence there are powerful techniques to avoid non-determinism. When synthesizing, you desire, and you do your best to make your model function deterministically, no matter how the environment (and the underlying technology on which your system will be built) is non-deterministic.

Both languages can be used in different ways, you are able to make a deterministic model in Rebeca, and a non-deterministic one in Ptolemy. Rebeca models can be used for synthesizing (after analyzing your abstract designs), and Ptolemy models are analyzed (before synthesizing your system).

3   Wireless Sensor Network Applications and Schedulability

Wireless sensor and actuator networks (WSANs) are built from a collection of nodes that gather data from their surroundings to achieve specific application objectives. A WSAN application is a distributed system where multiple nodes are used to monitor properties like temperature, humidity, pressure, or position, and perform various tasks like anomaly detection and target tracking. WSANs can provide low-cost continuous monitoring. However, building WSAN-applications is particularly challenging because of the complexity of concurrent and distributed programming, networking, real-time requirements, and power constraints. It can be hard to find a configuration that satisfies these constraints while optimizing resource use [18]. WSAN applications are sensitive to timing, with soft deadlines at each step of the process that are required to ensure correct and efficient operation.

Several software platforms have been developed specifically for WSANs [3]. Among these, the most accepted platform is the TinyOS [34], which is an open-source operating system designed for wireless embedded sensor networks. TinyOs is based on an event-driven execution model that enables fine-grained power management strategies.

A sensor node is a node in a wireless sensor network that is capable of performing some processing, gathering sensory information and communicating with other connected nodes in the network. Each sensor node consists of independent concurrent entities, including CPU, sensor, and radio systems. These sensor nodes are connected via a wireless communication device which uses a transmission control protocol. Interactions between entities, both within a node and across nodes, are concurrent and asynchronous.

Modeling Sensor Nodes and Communication Medium in Rebeca.[1] We consider sensor nodes in WSAN applications, and we also model the network between these nodes. A sensor node is responsible for monitoring; it collects data, performs necessary processing, and then sends the data to another node via the network. A sender node has concurrent components performing the *sensing, data processing*, and *data transmission*. In addition to processing the data provided by the sensor component, there are also *miscellaneous* tasks that the processing unit in a node has to handle. So, we have four actors (concurrent and asynchronously executing objects) which all are located in a sensor node (see Fig. 2 for a visual mapping of real-world entities to actors in the Rebeca model, and see Fig. 3 for the Rebeca code):

- Sensor actor for sensing,
- CPU actor for processing,
- Communication Device actor for transmission (CD), and
- Misc actor for performing miscellaneous tasks.

---

[1] In some places I say Rebeca when I mean Timed Rebeca.

In some applications a sensor node works as a router and passes the data that it has received, this is done by the Communication Device.

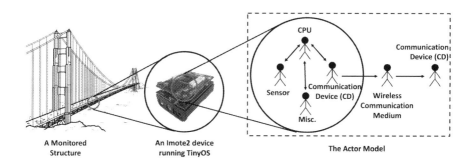

Fig. 2. Modeling the behavior of a WSAN application in its real-world installation in the actor model (from [18])

We have a fifth actor named Wireless Medium that models the communication medium. Wireless Medium informs the Communication Device of the status of the network and performs broadcasting of the data. Each of these two tasks are modeled as a message server (i.e. event handler) in Rebeca. The details of the communication protocol, like the implementation of the Media Access Control (MAC) level, is modeled in the Communication Device actor. Different protocols that are modeled in the Communication Device actor trigger two events in the Wireless Medium: one requesting the status of the network, and another requesting the data be broadcast. As a result, different implementations of communication protocols can be replaced without significantly impacting the remainder of the model. During the application design phase, different components, services, and protocols may be considered. For example, TDMA [10] as a MAC-level communication protocol may be replaced by B-MAC [22] with minimal changes.

Timed Rebeca Code. Figure 3 shows an abstract version of the Timed Rebeca code of the WSAN application. The main activity of this model is started by executing `sensorLoop` (line 16) of the `Sensor` actor (line 10). In this loop, based on the specified sampling rate, data is acquired by `Sensor` and it is sent to `CPU` (line 18). There is the same behavior in `Misc` (line 21). These two actors send messages to `CPU` (line 22). The actor `CPU` handles the messages received from `Sensor` and `Misc` by the `sensorEvent` and `miscEvent` message servers respectively (lines 28 and 40). The message server `sensorEvent` starts the processing of the acquired data by sending a `sensorTask` message (line 29). In `sensorTask` (line 31), the schedulability of processing of acquired data is checked, it is packed into one packet, and the packed data is sent by the communication device of this node if it reaches the limit which is specified by `bufferSize` (lines 36–37).

```
 1 env int samplingRate = 25;
 2 env int numberOfNodes = 6;
 3 env int bufferSize = 2;
 4 env int sensorTaskDelay = 2;
 5 env int OnePacketTransmissionTime = 7;
 6 env int miscTaskDelay = 10;
 7 env int tmdaSlotSize = 10;
 8 env int miscPeriod = 120;
 9 env int packetMaximumSize = 112;
10 reactiveclass Sensor(10) {
11     knownrebecs { CPU cpu; }
12     Sensor() { self.sensorFirst(); }
13     msgsrv sensorFirst() {
14         self.sensorLoop() after(?(10,
                   20, 30));
15     }
16     msgsrv sensorLoop() {
17         int period = 1000 /
                   samplingRate;
18         cpu.sensorEvent(period);
19         self.sensorLoop()
                   after(period);
20 }  }
21 reactiveclass Misc(10) { ... }
22 reactiveclass CPU(10) {
23     knownrebecs {
24         CommunicationDevice senderDev,
                   receiverDev;
25         Sensor sensor;}
26     statevars { int
                   collectedSamplesCounter; }
27     CPU() { collectedSamplesCounter =
                   0; }
28     msgsrv sensorEvent(int period) {
29         self.sensorTask(period,
                   currentMessageWaitingTime);
30     }
31     msgsrv sensorTask(int period, int
                   lag) {
32         int tmp = period - lag -
                   currentMessageWaitingTime;
33         assertion(tmp >= 0);
34         delay(sensorTaskDelay);
35         collectedSamplesCounter += 1;
36         if (collectedSamplesCounter ==
                   bufferSize){
37             senderDev.send(receiverDev,
                   0, 1);
38             collectedSamplesCounter =
                   0;
39 }  }
40     msgsrv miscEvent() {
             delay(miscTaskDelay); }
41 reactiveclass CommunicationDevice
         (10) {
42     knownrebecs { WirelessMedium
             medium; }
43     statevars {
44         byte id;
45         int sendingData;
46         int sendingPacketsNumber;
47         CommunicationDevice
                   receiverDev;}
48     CommunicationDevice(byte myId) {
49         id = myId;
50         sendingData = 0;
51         sendingPacketsNumber = 0;
52         receiverDev = null;}
53     msgsrv send(CommunicationDevice
             receiver, int data, int
             packetsNumber) {
54         assertion(receiverDev == null);
55         sendingPacketsNumber =
                   packetsNumber;
56         receiverDev = receiver;
57         sendingData = data;
58         medium.getStatus();}
59     msgsrv receiveStatus(boolean
             result) { ... }
60     msgsrv receiveResult(boolean
             result) { ... }
61     msgsrv
             receiveData(CommunicationDevice
             receiver, int data, int
             receivingPacketsNumber) { ...
             }
62 reactiveclass WirelessMedium(5) {
63     statevars {
64         CommunicationDevice senderDev;
65         CommunicationDevice
                   receiverDev;
66         int maxTraffic;}
67     WirelessMedium() {
68         senderDev = null;
69         receiverDev = null;
70         maxTraffic = (125 * 1024) / 8;
71     }
72     msgsrv getStatus() { ... }
73     msgsrv
             broadcast(CommunicationDevice
             receiver, int data, int
             packetsNumber){ ... }
74     msgsrv broadcastingIsCompleted() {
75         senderDev = null;
76         receiverDev = null;
77 }  }
78 main {
79   WirelessMedium medium():();
80   CPU cpu (sensorNodeSenderDevice,
             receiver, sensor):();
81   Sensor sensor(cpu):();
82   Misc misc(cpu):();
83   CommunicationDevice
             sensorNodeSenderDevice(medium):
             ((byte)1);
84   CommunicationDevice
             receiver(medium):((byte)0);}
```

Fig. 3. The Rebeca model of a WSAN application (based on the code in [17])

The communication protocol between nodes is implemented in the actor `CommunicationDevice` (line 41). The Rebeca model for TDMA and B-MAC communication protocols can be found in [18]. In the current implementation shown in Fig. 3, before sending data, the availability of the communication device is checked, then the needed messages are scheduled for sending data.

The effect of the wireless communication and transmission conflict is modeled by the actor `WirelessMedium` (line 62). Communication devices send `broadcast` messages (line 73) to the wireless medium to send data to other communication devices, and the receivers of broadcast data send `broadcastingIsCompleted` (line 74) to signal successful reception of the data.

Faithfulness. In the WSAN example, all the counterparts that are running concurrently in the system are modeled as actors: sensor, CPU, communication device, Misc, and wireless medium. The focus is on the schedulability of tasks. Each actor asks the CPU for execution of some tasks and the question is whether or not the CPU can handle all the tasks without missing any deadlines. So, what has been modeled accurately are different services that are requested to run on the CPU, and their timing. We also had to model the communication medium as an actor because the status of the network affects the overall behavior. TinyOS and Rebeca match perfectly in their MoC. There are no "wait" or "receive" statements, event-handlers are executed non-preemptively, and there are no priority queues.

Usability. As for usability of Rebeca in modeling WSAN applications, we can claim effectiveness, efficiency, and satisfaction. Users can achieve their goal of schedulability analysis in a complete and accurate way (effectiveness). The model can capture all the necessary details, and the model checking tool provides necessary information more accurately than alternative techniques of simulation or mathematical analysis. Efficiency relates to the time that the modeler needs to achieve her goals. For a software engineer or a computer scientist, writing Java or C-like code is simpler and takes less time compared to writing mathematical formulas. Also, comparing to simulation tools, by using Rebeca we build more abstract models, and hence we spend less time. Based on our experience, the majority of software engineers and computer scientists prefer program-like syntax, and hence Rebeca stimulates a positive attitude and satisfaction. Moreover, Faithfulness fosters usability. A natural, and in most cases one-to-one mapping of the constructs in WSAN applications into the Rebeca model makes the process effective, efficient, and with minimal hassle.

Reusability, and Modeling Different Protocols. For modeling different protocols, we only need to change the code of the `Communication Device` actor. By using Rebeca, we preserve the modular design of the protocol, so, we improve reusability. When we use other paradigms for modeling network protocols, like process algebra or automata, we usually need to spread out the functionality of one module of the system throughout different modules of the model. This will jeopardize reusability.

The TDMA protocol defines a cycle, over which each node in the network has one or more chances to transmit a packet or a series of packets. If a node has data available to transmit during its allotted time slot, it may be sent immediately. Otherwise, packet sending is delayed until its next transmission slot.

The periodic behavior of a TDMA slot is handled by a message server which sets and unsets a flag to show whether the node is in its allotted time slot or not. Upon entering into its slot, a device checks for pending data to send and schedules a message to be sent at the end of the time slot. On the other hand, when CPU sends a packet (message) to a Communication Device, the message is added to the other pending packets which are waiting for the next allotted time slot.

In contrast to TDMA, in B-MAC, RCD tries to detect free channel status and send data upon receiving a request from CPU. In the case of detecting a free channel, the data is sent immediately. This way, collisions may occur; Communication Device has to wait for some amount of time and resend data. B-MAC protocol does not need complicated and expensive synchronization methods. It also avoids data fragmentation. It would be more complicated to coordinate long messages and B-MAC expects short messages, which is common for information of WSAN nodes.

Schedulability Analysis. In the application we require that all the periodic tasks (sample acquisition, data processing, and radio packet transmission) are completed before the next iteration starts. This defines the deadline for each task. The goal is to have a higher sampling rate or a larger number of nodes without violating schedulability constraints.

The configuration of this model is specified by the values of the environment variables (lines 1 to 7 in Fig. 3). Based on these values, there are six nodes in the environment (line 2) and the sampling rate of the nodes is 25 samples per 1000 units of time (line 1). Each node packs two acquired data elements in one packet (line 3). The time spent for the internal activities of a node is specified in lines 4 to 6.

The Afra model checking tool verifies whether the schedulability properties hold in all reachable states of the system. If there are any deadline violations, a counterexample will be produced. A counterexample shows the sequence of states from an initial configuration that results in the violation. This information can be used to change the system parameters in order to avoid such situations, for example, by increasing the TDMA time slot length or reducing the sampling rate.

TCTL model checking can be used to check the utilization of resources. For example, we can check the utilization of the communication medium.

Scalability Challenges. One way of modeling WSAN using actor model is to instantiate actors for each node in the network. That may cause state explosion when doing the model checking. A main challenge is to find an effective and correct abstraction technique. In TDMA, the packet transmission of one sensor node does not interfere with the other sensor nodes. Having more sensor nodes only results in having shorter time slots, so the presence of sensor nodes can be abstracted and modeled by making time slots shorter. Using this abstraction, we only have to model one node which is in communication with the central node. Verification of WSAN applications against schedulability and deadlock-freedom properties then become feasible for networks in any size [19].

In B-MAC, the presence of sensor nodes can be abstracted and modeled as the possible number of collisions before a data communication is performed successfully [19]. Using this abstraction, only one sensor node which is in communication with the central node has to be considered for networks in any size. Any data transmission of this sensor node may encounter a collision. The maximum number of the collisions is the number of sensor nodes in the model. In the Rebeca code for Communication Device, for each data transmission we have a non-deterministic choice between a successful transmission or a collision. During model checking, in the case of collision, data transmission with zero, one, ..., up to n collisions are considered where n is the number of sensor nodes.

4   Mobile Ad-Hoc Network Protocols and Finding Possible Faults

A Mobile Ad-hoc Network (MANET) is a wireless network consisting of mobile routers (and associated hosts) connected by wireless links, the union of which forms an arbitrary topology. The routers are free to move randomly and organize themselves arbitrarily, so, the network's wireless topology may change rapidly and unpredictably.

MANETs have different applications from military to managing disastrous situations where there is no network infrastructure and nodes can freely change their locations. Mobility is the main feature of MANETs which makes them powerful and at the same time error-prone in practice. The process of protocol design is not straightforward. Since there is no base station or fixed network infrastructure, every node acts as a router and keeps the track of the previously seen packets to efficiently forward the received messages to desired destinations. In essence, MANETs need routing protocols in order to provide a way of communication between two indirectly-connected nodes. In the protocol, there has to be an algorithm for each node to continuously maintain the information required to properly route traffic.

MANETs are wireless sensor networks; but the differences between WSANs, discussed in Sect. 3, and MANETs are that in WSANs there is usually one sink (or base station) which collects the data, and there are fixed routes in the network (except when we have failures of nodes). In MANETs, nodes are continuously moving in any direction, and there is no fixed route between two nodes.

Routing protocols for MANETs are devised in a completely distributed manner and adaptive to topology changes, so, building reliable and efficient routing protocols is complicated and also crucial. The Ad-hoc On Demand Distance Vector (AODV) protocol is one of the most prominent routing protocol in MANETs. The AODV protocol has evolved as new failure scenarios were experienced or errors were found in the protocol design.

Modeling MANETs in Rebeca. One of the challenges in modeling MANETs is representing the connectivity of pairs of nodes in the network. Two nodes are connected if they are within the wireless communication range. As the nodes are moving the network topology is changing all the time. Rebeca is extended in [37] to wRebeca, to address local broadcast and dynamically changing topology. In order to abstract the data link layer services, the wireless communications in the framework, namely local broadcast, multicast, and unicast, are considered to be reliable. Therefore, a node can broadcast/multicast/unicast a message successfully to the nodes within its communication range, and the message delivery is guaranteed for the connected nodes to the sender. In the case of unicast, if the sender is located in the receiver communication range, it will be notified, otherwise it assumes that the transmission was unsuccessful so it can react appropriately.

Each node in the network is modeled as an actor, and the routing protocol is represented through the message servers of the actor. The network topology and its mobility are captured while analyzing the model, and are not explicitly modeled in the Rebeca code.

Rebeca Code. The wRebeca model of an abstract version of AODV is given in Fig. 4. There is one reactive class, *Node*, representing the nodes in the network. In this protocol, routes are built upon route discovery requests and maintained in nodes routing tables for further use. In message server *rec-newpkt* (line 14), whenever a node intends to send a data packet, it looks in its routing table to see if it has a valid route to the intended destination. In case it finds a route, it sends the data packet through the next-hop specified in that route (line 16–17). Otherwise, it starts a route discovery by broadcasting a route request, *rec-rreq*, after increasing its sequence number (line 18–21).

In message server *rec-rreq* (line 23), whenever a node receives a new routing packet, it updates its routing table with new information. The forward messages contain the route back to the *source*, while the backward messages carry the route information towards a *destination*. While the forward packet proceeds towards the destination, a *backward path*, a path to *source* from *destination*, is constructed. In message server *rec-rreq*, every node, upon receiving a packet, looks up the destination in its routing table, and if it has a route available, replies by sending a *rec-rrep* message (line 31). Otherwise, it continues route discovery by re-sending the *rec-rreq* message, after increasing the hop-count. There is an upper limit for the hop-count, after which the algorithm gives up on that route. The *unicast* message (line 31) will be delivered successfully (*succ* in line 32) if the receiver node is in the access range, or the delivery can fail (*unsucc* in line 36) if the receiver node is not in the access range.

```
1  reactiveclass Node()                    42        }
2  {                                        43      } else {
3    statevars                              44        hops_ = hops_ + 1;
4    {                                      45        if(hops_<maxHop) {
5      int sn, ip;                          46          rec-rreq(hops_, dip_, dsn_,
6      int[] dip, dsn, route_state,                        oip_, osn_, self,
          hops, nhops,                                      maxHop);
7    }                                      47  } } }}
8    Node(int i, boolean starter)           48  msgsrv rec-rrep(int hops_ ,int dip_
9    {                                      49          ,int dsn_ ,int oip_ ,int sip_)
10     /* initializing the route table      49  {
          variables*/                       50    boolean gen_msg = false;
11     if(starter==true) {                  51    /* evaluate and update the routing
12       unicast(self,rec-newpkt(7,2));              table, decide whether a new
13     } }                                            rreq should be generated */
14   msgsrv rec-newpkt(int data ,int        52    if(gen_msg == true)
          dip_)                             53    { if(ip == oip_ )
15   {                                      54      { /* this node is the originator
16     if(route_state[dip_]==1) {                      of the corresponding RREQ,
17       /* valid route to dip forward                 a data packet may now be
          packet */                                     sent */ }
18     } else {                             55      else {
19       /* no valid route to dip send a    56        hops_= hops_+1;
          new rout discovery request        57        unicast(nhop[oip_],
          */                                             rec-rrep(hops_, dip_,
20       sn++;                                             dsn_, oip_, self))
21       rec-rreq(0, dip_, dsn[dip_],        58        succ:
          self, sn, self, 5);               59        {
22     } }                                   60          route_state[oip_]=1;
23   msgsrv rec-rreq (int hops_, int         61          break;
          dip_ , int dsn_ , int oip_ ,       62        }
          int osn_ , int sip_, int           63        unsucc:
          maxHop)                            64        {
24   {                                       65          if(route_state[oip_] == 1) {
25     boolean gen_msg = false;              66            /* error recovery procedure
26     /* evaluate and update the routing                    */
          table, decide whether a new        67          }
          rreq should be generated */        68          route_state[oip_] = 2;
27     if (gen_msg == true) {                69  } } } }
28       if (ip == dip_) {                   70  msgsrv rec-rerr(int source_ ,int
29         sn = sn+1;                                sip_, int[] rip_rsn)
30         /* unicast the RREP towards       71  {
          oip of the RREQ */                 72    /* regenerate rrer for invalidated
31         unicast(nhop[oip_],rec-rrep(0            routes */
          , dip_ , sn , oip_ ,               73  } }
          self))                             74  main
32       succ:                               75  {
33       {                                   76    Node node0(node1,node3):(0,true);
34         route_state[oip_] = 1; break;     77    Node node1(node0,node3):(1,false);
35       }                                   78    Node node2(node3):(2,false);
36       unsucc:                             79    Node node3(node2,node0,node1):
37       {                                             (3,false);
38         if(route_state[oip_] == 1) {      80    constraints
39           /* error recovery procedure     81    { and(con(node0,node1),
          */                                               con(node2,node3)) }
40         }                                 82  }
41         route_state[oip_] = 2;
```

Fig. 4. The AODV specification given in wRebeca (based on the code in [35])

In message server *rec-rrep* (line 48), whenever a node receives a message it updates its routing table accordingly to construct the *backward path*. When it reaches the source, a bidirectional route has been formed and the data packet can be sent towards the destination through the next-hops in the routing tables. In addition to the above message servers, there is message server *rec-rerr* (line 70) that is called whenever a node fails to send a packet through a *valid* route, in order to inform other interested nodes in the broken route about the failure. Due to the mobility of the nodes this may happen often.

Faithfulness. For MANETs, we modeled the network nodes as actors. Nodes send asynchronous messages to each other, and the protocol is modeled by message servers. The MoCs match perfectly, except that Rebeca in its core form does not support broadcast or multicast. But broadcast and multicast are both asynchronous and non-blocking from the sender side, and we do not need any explicit receive statement in the receiver side. The crucial rules of the MoC stay unchanged, i.e., the main transition rule, which takes a message and triggers the message server, is not changed. Moreover, mobility of the nodes is captured at the level of the state transition system at the time of analysis. This keeps the model simple. Different properties of the protocols can be checked using the model checking tool.

Usability. Usability of Rebeca in modeling network protocols depends on the goal. The modeling process can be performed efficiently and with satisfaction. Each node is running concurrently and, generally, there is asynchronous communication. Each node can be mapped to an actor. Communication protocols are usually written as algorithms or pseudo-code in an imperative form and can be naturally mapped to message servers in Rebeca. The effectiveness of the modeling depends on the goal: what kind of analysis has to be done and what properties must be checked. Based on the properties we need to check, we have to model different features of the system. We need reduction techniques to tackle state space explosion in the analysis phase. Compared to alternative modeling paradigms, faithfulness of the model brings in usability.

Reusability and Modeling Different Network Protocols. Different versions of the AODV are modeled in wRebeca. For each version, the parts of the message servers related to updating the routing table are revised. The local data in the routing table must be adjusted based on the information that should be maintained for each version. Most of the code can remain unchanged.

Analyzing Wireless Ad-Hoc Networks Protocols. The goal in [37] is to find the conceptual mistakes in the protocol design rather than problems caused by an unreliable communication. A customized model checking tool is developed [11] and the loop-freedom property is checked while generating the state space. The reason for violating the property was to maintain multiple uncon-firmed next hops for a route without checking them to be loop-free. Furthermore, the monotonic increase of sequence numbers and packet delivery properties are checked via model checking. The wRebeca team found a loop creation scenario in AODVv2 protocol (version 11) in 2016, and reported it to the AODV group. The AODV group confirmed the possibility of loop creation and released a new revised version of the protocol and the authors are acknowledged[2]. Henceforth, new versions of the protocol are verified using wRebeca.

Scalability Challenges. While building the state space for analyzing a MANET protocol a few abstraction techniques are used. The first technique considers the network with a fixed topology, ignoring the mobility of nodes. Then the actors that have the same neighbors and local states are considered identical. This way many states can be merged as the actors are no longer dis-tinguished by their identifiers. It is shown in [37] that the reduced transition system is strongly bisimilar to the original one, and the state space reduction is considerable. This technique is beneficial for finding an error during the design of a new version of a protocol. If we know that a certain topology leads to mal-functioning of a previous version of the protocol, we can check the new version of the protocol using that certain topology.

The above technique ignores the mobility of nodes and will not work if we have a dynamic topology. As an example of an effective design decision, in [37], changes in the topology are not captured at the level of the wRebeca model. Instead, for analyzing the protocols, arbitrary changes in the underlying topology are considered while generating the state space. These random changes make the state space grow exponentially. To tackle the state space explosion, the states which are only different in their topologies are combined, and the topology-sensitive behaviors are captured by adding appropriate labels on the transitions. It is proved in [37] that the reduced transition system is branching bisimilar to the original one, and consequently a set of properties such as ACTL-X is preserved. Another way used to restrict the random changes in the topology, is to allow the modeler to specify constraints over the topology in the model.

5   Network on Chips and Routing

System-on-chip (SoC) designs provide integrated solutions to challenging design problems in the telecommunications, multimedia, and home electronics domains [5]. An SoC can be viewed as a micronetwork of components. The network is the abstraction of the communication among components and must satisfy quality-of-service requirements - such as reliability, performance, and energy bounds. Network on Chip (NoC) (an SoC paradigm) is a network of computational, storage and I/O resources, interconnected by a network of switches. Computing resources communicate with each other using addressed data packets routed to

---

[2] The acknowledgment is at https://tools.ietf.org/html/draft-ietf-manet-aodvv2-16.

their destination [12]. In NoC designs, functional verification and performance evaluation in the early stages of the design process are suggested as ways to reduce the fabrication cost.

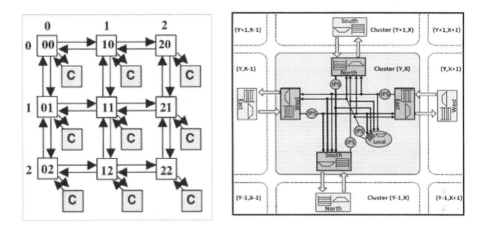

Fig. 5. A 2D mesh NoC (on the left), and a router in ASPIN [29] (on the right)

Modeling NoC in Rebeca. As an example of a NoC, we modeled and analyzed ASPIN (Asynchronous Scalable Packet switching Integrated Network), which is a fully asynchronous two-dimensional NoC design [29]. In an ASPIN design, each core is placed in a two-dimensional mesh and has (at most) four adjacent cores and four internal buffers for storing the incoming packets (one for each direction). Figure 5 shows the 2D mesh consisting of nine clusters (on the left), and a zoom-in picture of each cluster (on the right). The four (pairs of input and output) internal buffers are shown in the figure.

Different routing algorithms have been proposed for the two-dimensional NoC design. Here, we consider the XY-routing algorithm. Using the XY-routing algorithm, packets are moving along the X direction first, and then along the Y direction to reach their destination cores. In ASPIN, packets are transferred through channels, using a four-phase handshake communication protocol. The protocol uses two signals, namely *Req* and *Ack*, to implement this four-phase handshaking protocol. This way, to transfer a packet, first the sender sends a request by raising the *Req* signal along with the data and waits for an acknowledgment, which is the raising of the *Ack* signal by the receiver. In the third phase, when the sender gets the *Ack* from the receiver it will lower the *Req* signal. Finally, in the fourth phase. when the receiver notices that the *Req* signal is lowered it will lower the *Ack* signal. After successful communication all of the signals return to zero.

```
1    env byte inBufSize = 2;
2    env byte writeT = 2;
3    env byte readT = 6;
4    env byte flitNum = 2;
5    ...
6    reactiveclass Manager(60){
7      knownrebecs{
8        Router r00, r10, r01, r11;
9      }
10     statevars{}
11     Manager(){testScenario(); }
12     void testScenario(){
13       r00.inReq(4,1,1,1) after (184);
14       r00.inReq(4,1,1,1) after (274);
15       r01.inReq(4,1,1,2) after (18);
16       r01.inReq(4,1,1,2) after (110);
17     }
18   }
19   reactiveclass Router(60) {
20     knownrebecs {
21       Router N, E, S, W;
22     }
23     statevars {
24       byte Xid, Yid, received;
25         boolean[5] inBufFull,
                 outBufFull;
26       }
27   //---Comunication---
28     msgsrv inReq (byte inPort, byte
           Xtarget, byte Ytarget, byte
           id){
29       if (inBufFull[inPort] == false ){
30         sendInAck((byte)(inPort + 2)%4,
             inAD);
31         self.process(inPort, Xtarget,
             Ytarget,id, false,
             false)after((writeD *
             inBufSizeTest)+ readD);
32         ...
33       } else { ... }
34     }
35     msgsrv process(byte inPort, byte
           Xtarget, byte Ytarget,byte id,
           boolean isPushed, boolean
           justPush) { ...}
36         ...
37   //---Routing Algorithm---
38     byte XYrouting(byte Xtarget, byte
           Ytarget){
39       if (Xtarget > Xid) //East
40       else if (Xtarget < Xid) //west
41       else if (Ytarget > Yid) //South
42       else if (Ytarget < Yid) //North
43       else outPort = 4; //the local
             buffer, arrived at destination
44       return outPort;
45     }
46   //---Scheduling Algorithm---
47     byte RRSched(byte outPort){
48       byte[5] priorities = {4, 3, 1, 0,
           2};
49       //turn = Number of the last input
           port which was its turn
50       //passedFlit = Number of passed
           flits which was sent from
           "turn" to outPort
51       if(BufFull[outPort]) return;
52       if (passedFlit == 0){  // this
           flit is the header
53       for(byte i=0 ; i<5 ; i++){
54         //turn= according to priorities,
             choose next input port
             which is waiting for outPort
55         outReqEnable[turn] = false;
56         //Save turn for outPort
57         passedFlit ++;
58         if(passedFlit == flitNum){
59           passedFlit = 0;
60         }
61         //save passedFlit for outPort
62       }
63       }else{// body of the packet
64         outReqEnable[turn] = false;
65         passedFlit ++;
66         if(passedFlit == flitNum){
67           passedFlit = 0;
68         }
69         //save passedFlit for outPort
70       }
71     }
72   -----------------------------------
73     //Other auxiliary Functions &
           Message Servers
74   }
75   main {
76     Manager m(r00,r01,r10,r11):();
77     Router
           r00(m,r01,r10,r01,r10):(0,0);
78     Router
           r10(m,r11,r00,r11,r00):(1,0);
79     Router
           r01(m,r00,r11,r00,r11):(0,1);
80     Router
           r11(m,r10,r01,r10,r01):(1,1);
81   }
```

Fig. 6. The Rebeca model of an ASPIN NoC (based on the code in [27])

Timed Rebeca Code. The simplified version of the Timed Rebeca model of ASPIN is shown in Fig. 6, which contains two different reactive classes: `Manager` and `Router`. The `Manager` (line 11) does not exist in real NoC systems, it is used here to model different scenarios of packet generation. In Fig. 6, in function *testScenario*, two packets are generated, each contains two flits (lines 13–14 and 15–16). One packet is sent from the r00 router to r11 at the time 184 (the first flit), and 274 (the second flit), and the other packet is sent from r01 router to r11 at the time 18 (the first flit), and 110 (the second flit).

Each `Router` has four known rebecs which are its four neighbors (line 21). Its state variables include a composite id which is its X-Y position, buffer variables which show that the buffers are enabled or full, and a counter for the number of received packets (lines 24–25). Packets move through channels according to the four-phase handshake communication protocol. The delivery of a packet is attempted by sending an `inReq` message to a router. The receiver router accepts the packet if its input buffer is free. Upon accepting a packet, an acknowledgment is sent to its sender and an internal message is scheduled to process this packet. The time needed to do some of the processing or routing is modeled using *delay* or *after* constructs in the code. The processing of a packet takes place in message server `process` (line 35). If there is a packet ready for processing, based on the routing algorithm, one of the *outPorts* is selected to send the packet to the appropriate neighbor. Routing is based on the XY-algorithm, and the output port for routing a packet is computed by the function `XYrouting` (line 38). The scheduling algorithm is implemented in the function `RRSched` (line 47). The 2D-mesh of this model is formed in the `main` block of the model by setting known rebecs based on the locations of the routers (lines 77–80).

Faithfulness. ASPIN is a GALS NoC design, with synchronous behavior within each node and asynchronous message passing between nodes. So, we model each node (router and the core) as an actor, and the MoCs of ASPIN and Rebeca match, and a faithful model of NoC can be built. One can observe that within a router different ports can be running concurrently, but we did not model each port as an actor to avoid state space explosion. Reading from each input port and putting the packet into the correct output port is done using a round-robin scheduling policy which is modeled in the code. We do not lose any interesting property with this abstraction.

Usability. In a high level of abstraction NoC can be mapped to Rebeca efficiently. We showed that despite the high level of abstraction the results are consistent with hardware simulation results in the literature, so, the approach is effective. In the NoC project, extended versions of the model including the communication protocol and more detailed versions of the scheduling algorithm are developed in later phases. Adding more details (like buffer length, packet length and flit number, packet generation delay, more precise communication protocol) results in more precise measurements, showing effectiveness. Naturally, debugging the Rebeca code becomes more difficult when the code becomes more detailed. On the positive side, more details can be added to the model in an iterative and incremental way which is not a capability supported by all available hardware simulation tools. Our analysis technique is based on model-checking, it captures the simultaneity of the events (which is modeled using interleaving), while hardware simulation tools are not capable of that. As for satisfaction, a hardware designer may not be comfortable with programming in a C- or Java-like language.

Reusability and Modeling Different Routing Algorithms. Modeling different routing algorithms in Rebeca can be done efficiently; we have to change the routing function in the code. The rest of the code can be reused. Routing algorithms can be classified into deterministic and adaptive routings. In a deterministic routing there can only be one path between a source and a destination, whereas in an adaptive routing more than one possible path may exist and the algorithm considers the conditions of the dynamic network to decide in which direction a packet should be transferred. The XY algorithm is a deterministic algorithm, Odd-Even routing is an adaptive one, and DyAD routing chooses dynamically between a deterministic or an adaptive algorithm, based on the different network congestion conditions.

Odd-Even routing algorithm is based on Odd-Even turn model [9]. According to Odd-Even turn model north-to-west and south-to-west turns are prohibited in routers located in an odd column and east-to-south and east-to-north turns are prohibited in routers located in an even column. The restrictions are enforced to ensure deadlock freedom. For routing a packet, each router decides between two legitimate downstream neighbors based on the number of the empty slots in their input buffer. The neighbor with more empty slots will be selected. In this algorithm, each router keeps track of the number of packets in input buffer of each of its neighbors. In the Rebeca model [28], whenever the size of an input buffer of a router changes, it informs its corresponding upstream neighbor by sending a message.

In DyAD routing, each router monitors the occupation ratio of its input buffers (except for the local buffer). Whenever one of the buffers reaches a pre-defined congestion threshold a mode flag is set to inform the corresponding neighboring about the congestion. On the other hand, each router periodically checks mode flag of its neighbors to decide whether to work with deterministic or adaptive routing. According to [15], if at least one of the neighboring routers were congested the router would decide to work with adaptive routing; otherwise it would work with deterministic routing. To model a DyAD router in Rebeca we add a mode flag to our model [28]. The mode flag becomes true if the size of the corresponding input buffer reaches the congestion threshold.

Analyzing NoC Design, and Evaluating Different Routing Algorithms.
Timing analysis of NoCs is required to discover possible deadline misses for packets traveling through the network. Based on the results of such analysis, suitable design decisions can be made. In asynchronous systems, lack of a reference clock

leads to an interleaved execution of processes. Therefore, in GALS NoCs, a sent packet might be delayed by different numbers of disrupting packets and may have various end-to-end latencies. For analysis of such systems, it is essential to consider all possible behaviors of the system rather than specific traces.

The timed version of ASPIN is modeled and analyzed in [26] using simulation and model checking. Afra toolset was used for checking deadlock freedom, and message arrival, and for estimating the maximum end-to-end packet latency in the model. In the Rebeca model, we considered hardware features like switching strategy, communication protocols, and buffer and link delays. Packet latencies are computed with different design parameters, specially buffer sizes. Different routing algorithms are analyzed and compared.

The model is validated through comparing the extracted results to that of HSPICE [14], under both manual and real traffic [26]. Note that in HSPICE simulator, the lowest level of simulation in hardware domain is performed, and all the details of transistors and wires are considered.

Scalability Challenges. Clearly we cannot generate all the possible scenarios of packet injection in the network. We use PARSEC benchmarks [6] for choosing our scenarios. PARSEC is a well-known set of scenarios for packet generation in network on chip. For performance estimation, the Black-Scholes scenario from this benchmark has been selected.

For estimating maximum end-to-end packet latency, in order to analyze large NoCs, a scalable approach is proposed based on compositional verification [26]. The compositional approach is specific for the XY-routing algorithm. The method computes the maximum end-to-end latency in GALS NoCs with XY-routing algorithm in two steps. It breaks the path of a packet to its destination into horizontal and vertical sub-paths and then performs latency estimation in each sub-path separately. At the end, the results for each sub-path are combined to get latency estimation of the whole path. To do so, possible paths for each packet should be investigated precisely to find out which packets may make disruption for the transferring packet. To check the correctness of the method, these disruptions are considered in the scenarios and then the results are compared to that of HSPICE.

6   Discussion

Here we discuss the points raised in the introduction section, mainly faithfulness, usability, and analyzability.

Faithfulness. When we make a Rebeca model of a given system (or based on a given specification), first we want to know the set of actors that build the model. We start by finding the modules that are running concurrently in the system and communicate asynchronously via message passing. Each of these modules will be represented by an actor in the model. Each actor may represent a module that may contain different sub-modules that are not executed concurrently, or are communicating synchronously (like in Globally Asynchronous, Locally Synchronous systems). Networks of nodes which communicate through asynchronous messages build systems with a model of computation perfectly matching Rebeca. This is the case for all the three examples provided in Sects. 3 to 5.

The level of abstraction in modeling depends on the properties of the model we are interested in. For different aspects to be checked we have to model different features of the system.

Usability. As for usability, we focused on effectiveness, efficiency, and satisfaction. Rebeca is usable for software engineers and programmers. They are familiar with the Java-like syntax of Rebeca and with the object-oriented style of programming. For concurrent programming, programmers are mostly using thread-based programming, and the event-based model of computation may not be as widely used by all the programmers. Usually it would be enough to tell them that each actor is one thread of execution and message servers run atomically with no preemption. To be completely fair, it is worth mentioning that designing the code with an event-driven style may not be straightforward for all the programmers, but it is learned fairly quickly. Hardware and electrical engineers are more familiar with event-driven computation. But based on our observation, electrical engineers prefer a component-based system, like what they get with Simulink.

Reusability and Design Patterns. In Sects. 3, 4, and 5 we have subsections on how the Rebeca code can be reused or extended for similar applications in the same domain. Based on our experience on the NoC design, we proposed a generic pattern for track-based traffic control systems and used it for building a coordinated actor model for adaptive air traffic control systems [4]. We used Timed Rebeca in modeling mobile agents, using this pattern, but different in the analysis part. We came up with a light-weight approach in planning using this model [8].

Analyzability and Synthesis. Based on the asynchrony and isolation of actors, we designed specialized reduction techniques in model checking Rebeca and Timed Rebeca. In some cases, like for analyzing SystemC codes, we needed to extend Rebeca to have wait statements and global variables [24]. In these cases the MoC is no longer the same and most of our reduction techniques will no longer work.

So far, synthesis has not been the focus of our research. But in the cases that Rebeca models represent the network protocol, then the implementation of the protocol can be just a refinement of the Rebeca code.

Traceability and Compositionality. Isolated units of concurrency make the model modular. Also, effective compositional verification techniques are introduced. But there are no compositional semantics for Rebeca, mainly because of the message buffers. Traceability is high between the model and the system. But at the level of semantics and transition systems, we are dealing with similar problems like for other modeling languages.

Expressiveness and Rebeca Extensions. The discussion in this paper is based on the assumption that we have a language that is expressive enough for the domain of our interest. We had to extend Rebeca to increase its expressiveness where necessary. Timed and probabilistic extensions of Rebeca were introduced because the expressive power of Rebeca was not enough to capture the notions of time and probability. An ongoing project is extending Rebeca to model cyber-physical systems by supporting actors with continuous behavior, and for that we need the capability of defining linear differential equations. Different extensions of Rebeca build an actor family of languages [7].

Future Trends. Modeling cyber-physical systems using an extension of Rebeca and building analysis techniques for this domain is a current ongoing project. Rebeca supports dynamic creation and topology in theory, but in none of the techniques have we carefully considered this dynamicity. Recently, the possibility of passing rebec names and hence having dynamic topology is added to the Rebeca tools. This is mostly necessary for modeling and analyzing autonomous and self-adaptive systems which are another domain of interest. For the techniques, in the future, we plan to focus more on synthesis, and also testing.

Acknowledgements. My work is supported in part by DPAC Project (Dependable Platforms for Autonomous Systems and Control) at Mälardalen University, Sweden, and by the project Self-Adaptive Actors: SEADA? (nr 163205-051) of the Icelandic Research Fund.

I would like to thank the Rebeca team, everyone who worked in the team since 2001, and helped us to gain the insight and the experience, and be where we are now. Special thanks go to Ehsan Khamespanah for refactoring the model checking tool of Rebeca and extending and maintaining it for years. For writing this paper I had to bug the leaders of the three projects explained in the three Sects. 3, 4, and 5; many thanks to Ehsan Khamespanah, Fatemeh Ghassemi, and Zeinab Sharifi. I would also like to thank Reinhard Wilhelm for challenging me on the explanation of the main concepts discussed in this paper. The discussion significantly improved the paper. Thanks to Hossein Hojjat for his careful comments throughout the paper, thanks to Paolo Masci for reading the paper and giving me the right pointers for the standard definitions of usability, thanks to Mohammad Reza Mousavi who kept me on my toes when talking about expressiveness, thanks to Tom Henzinger for his reassuring words, thanks to Alessandro Papadopoulos whose comments made me add some final notes to the paper, and thanks to Hans Hansson, Jan Friso Groot, Mohsen Vakilian and Amin Shali for finding the paper thought provoking and enjoyable. Last but not least thanks to Edward for inspiring me and being the drive and support to finally write this paper.

References

1. Aceto, L., Cimini, M., Ingólfsdóttir, A., Reynisson, A.H., Sigurdarson, S.H., Sirjani, M.: Modelling and simulation of asynchronous real-time systems using Timed Rebeca. In: FOCLASA, pp. 1–19 (2011)
2. Agha, G.: Actors: A Model of Concurrent Computation in Distributed Systems. MIT Press, Cambridge (1990)
3. Akyildiz, I., Vuran, M.C.: Wireless Sensor Networks. Wiley, New York (2010)
4. Bagheri, M., Akkaya, I., Khamespanah, E., Khakpour, N., Sirjani, M., Movaghar, A., Lee, E.A.: Coordinated actors for reliable self-adaptive systems. In: 13th International Conference on Formal Aspects of Component Software, FACS 2016 (2016)
5. Benini, L., Micheli, G.D.: Networks on chips: a new SoC paradigm. IEEE Comput. **35**(1), 70–78 (2002). https://doi.org/10.1109/2.976921
6. Bienia, C., Kumar, S., Singh, J.P., Li, K.: The PARSEC benchmark suite: characterization and architectural implications. In: Proceedings of the 17th International Conference on Parallel Architectures and Compilation Techniques, PACT 2008, pp. 72–81. ACM (2008). https://doi.org/10.1145/1454115.1454128
7. de Boer, F.S., et al.: A survey of active object languages. ACM Comput. Surv. **50**(5), 76:1–76:39 (2017). https://doi.org/10.1145/3122848
8. Castagnari, C., de Berardinis, J., Forcina, G., Jafari, A., Sirjani, M.: Lightweight preprocessing for agent-based simulation of smart mobility initiatives. In: Cerone, A., Roveri, M. (eds.) SEFM 2017. LNCS, vol. 10729, pp. 541–557. Springer, Cham (2018). https://doi.org/10.1007/978-3-319-74781-1_36
9. Chiu, G.M.: The odd-even turn model for adaptive routing. IEEE Trans. Parallel Distrib. Syst. **11**(7), 729–738 (2000). https://doi.org/10.1109/71.877831
10. El-Hoiydi, A.: Spatial TDMA and CSMA with preamble sampling for low power ad hoc wireless sensor networks. In: Proceedings of the Seventh IEEE Symposium on Computers and Communications (ISCC 2002), pp. 685–692 (2002). https://doi.org/10.1109/ISCC.2002.1021748
11. Ghassemi, F., Fokkink, W.: Model checking mobile ad-hoc networks. Formal Methods Syst. Des. **49**(3), 159–189 (2016). https://doi.org/10.1007/s10703-016-0254-7
12. Guerrier, P., Greiner, A.: A generic architecture for on-chip packet-switched interconnections. In: 2000 Design, Automation and Test in Europe (DATE 2000), pp. 250–256 (2000). https://doi.org/10.1109/DATE.2000.840047
13. Hewitt, C.: Description and theoretical analysis (using schemata) of PLANNER: a language for proving theorems and manipulating models in a robot. Technical report, MIT Artificial Intelligence Technical Report (1972)
14. HSPICE: HSPICE homepage: https://www.synopsys.com/verification/ams-verification/circuit-simulation/hspice.html
15. Hu, J., Marculescu, R.: DyAD: smart routing for networks-on-chip. In: Proceedings of the 41st Annual Design Automation Conference, DAC 2004, pp. 260–263. ACM (2004). https://doi.org/10.1145/996566.996638
16. ISO: Ergonomics of human-system interaction part 210: Human-centred design for interactive systems. Technical report, ISO 9241-210:2010, International Organization for Standardization (2010). https://www.iso.org/obp/ui/#iso:std:iso:9241:-210:ed-1:v1:en
17. Khamespanah, E., Khosravi, R., Sirjani, M.: An efficient TCTL model checking algorithm and a reduction technique for verification of timed actor models. In: Science of Computer Programming (2017). http://www.rebeca-lang.org/wiki/pmwiki.php/Rebeca/Publications

18. Khamespanah, E., Mechitov, K., Sirjani, M., Agha, G.: Schedulability analysis of distributed real-time sensor network applications using actor-based model checking. In: Bošnački, D., Wijs, A. (eds.) SPIN 2016. LNCS, vol. 9641, pp. 165–181. Springer, Cham (2016). https://doi.org/10.1007/978-3-319-32582-8_11

19. Khamespanah, E., Mechitov, K., Sirjani, M., Agha, G.A.: Modeling and analyzing real-time wireless sensor and actuator networks using actors and model checking. In: Software Tools for Technology Transfer (2017). http://rebeca.cs.ru. is/files/Papers/2016/Modeling-and-Analyzing-Real-Time-Wireless-Sensor-and-Actuator-Networks-Using-Actors-and-Model-Checking.pdf

20. Khamespanah, E., Sirjani, M., Sabahi-Kaviani, Z., Khosravi, R., Izadi, M.: Timed Rebeca schedulability and deadlock freedom analysis using bounded floating time transition system. Sci. Comput. Program. **98**, 184–204 (2015)

21. Manna, Z., Pnueli, A.: On the faithfulness of formal models. In: Tarlecki, A. (ed.) MFCS 1991. LNCS, vol. 520, pp. 28–42. Springer, Heidelberg (1991). https://doi. org/10.1007/3-540-54345-7_46

22. Polastre, J., Hill, J.L., Culler, D.E.: Versatile low power media access for wireless sensor networks. In: Proceedings of the 2nd International Conference on Embedded Networked Sensor Systems, SenSys 2004, pp. 95–107 (2004). https://doi.org/10. 1145/1031495.1031508

23. Ptolemaeus, C. (ed.): System Design, Modeling, and Simulation using Ptolemy II. Ptolemy.org (2014). http://ptolemy.org/books/Systems

24. Razavi, N., Behjati, R., Sabouri, H., Khamespanah, E., Shali, A., Sirjani, M.: Sysfier: actor-based formal verification of SystemC. ACM Trans. Embed. Comput. Syst. **10**(2), 19:1–19:35 (2011). https://doi.org/10.1145/1880050.1880055

25. Reynisson, A.H., Sirjani, M., Aceto, L., Cimini, M., Jafari, A., Ingólfsdóttir, A., Sigurdarson, S.H.: Modelling and simulation of asynchronous real-time systems using Timed Rebeca. Sci. Comput. Program. **89**, 41–68 (2014). https://doi.org/ 10.1016/j.scico.2014.01.008

26. Sharifi, Z., Mosaffa, M., Mohammadi, S., Sirjani, M.: Functional and performance analysis of network-on-chips using actor-based modeling and formal verification. In: ECEASST, AVoCS 2013 Proceedings, vol. 66 (2013)

27. Sharifi, Z., Mosaffa, M., Mohammadi, S., Sirjani, M.: Performance analysis of gals NoC using actor models. Draft (2017)

28. Sharifi, Z., Mohammadi, S., Sirjani, M.: Comparison of NoC routing algorithms using formal methods. In: Proceedings of PDPTA 2013, pp. 474–482 (2013)

29. Sheibanyrad, A., Greiner, A., Panades, I.M.: Multisynchronous and fully asynchronous NoCs for GALS architectures. IEEE Des. Test Comput. **25**(6), 572–580 (2008). https://doi.org/10.1109/MDT.2008.167

30. Sirjani, M., Movaghar, A., Shali, A., de Boer, F.: Modeling and verification of reactive systems using Rebeca. Fundam. Inform. **63**(4), 385–410 (2004)

31. Sirjani, M.: Rebeca: theory, applications, and tools. In: de Boer, F.S., Bonsangue, M.M., Graf, S., de Roever, W.-P. (eds.) FMCO 2006. LNCS, vol. 4709, pp. 102–126. Springer, Heidelberg (2007). https://doi.org/10.1007/978-3-540-74792-5_5

32. Sirjani, M., Jaghoori, M.M.: Ten years of analyzing actors: Rebeca experience. In: Agha, G., Danvy, O., Meseguer, J. (eds.) Formal Modeling: Actors, Open Systems, Biological Systems. LNCS, vol. 7000, pp. 20–56. Springer, Heidelberg (2011). https://doi.org/10.1007/978-3-642-24933-4_3

33. Sirjani, M., Khamespanah, E.: On time actors. In: Ábrahám, E., Bonsangue, M., Johnsen, E.B. (eds.) Theory and Practice of Formal Methods. LNCS, vol. 9660, pp. 373–392. Springer, Cham (2016). https://doi.org/10.1007/978-3-319-30734-3_25

34. TinyOS: TinyOS community forum: an open-source OS for the networked sensor regime. http://www.tinyos.net
35. Yousefi, B., Ghassemi, F.: An efficient loop-free version of AODVv2. CoRR (2017). arXiv:abs/1709.01786v2
36. Yousefi, B., Ghassemi, F., Khosravi, R.: Modeling and efficient verification of broadcasting actors. In: Dastani, M., Sirjani, M. (eds.) FSEN 2015. LNCS, vol. 9392, pp. 69–83. Springer, Cham (2015). https://doi.org/10.1007/978-3-319-24644-4_5
37. Yousefi, B., Ghassemi, F., Khosravi, R.: Modeling and efficient verification of wireless ad-hoc networks. Formal Aspects Comput. **29**(6), 1051–1086 (2017)

Modular Code Generation
from Synchronous Block Diagrams:
Interfaces, Abstraction, Compositionality

Stavros Tripakis[1]([⊠]) and Roberto Lublinerman[2]

[1] Aalto University, Espoo, Finland
stavros.tripakis@gmail.com
[2] Google, Mountain View, USA
rluble@gmail.com

Abstract. We study abstract, compositional and executable representations of synchronous models in general and hierarchical synchronous block diagrams in particular. Our work is motivated by the problem of modular code generation, where sequential code (in, say, C or Java) must be generated for a given block independently of its context, that is, independently of the diagrams in which this block may be embedded.

We propose non-monolithic interfaces called *profiles* as a representation of blocks. A profile contains a set of interface functions that implement the semantics of the block, and a set of dependencies between these functions. Profiles are executable through the implementation of their interface functions. Profiles are compositional in the sense that a diagram of profiles can be represented as a single profile without loss of important information, such as input-output dependencies. This is contrary to traditional methods which use monolithic interfaces that contain a fixed number of interface functions, usually just one or two. Monolithic interfaces generally result in loss of input-output dependency information and are non-compositional. Profiles are abstract in the sense that they hide most of the internal details of a diagram (e.g., functionality).

We provide methods for profile synthesis and modular code generation: to automatically produce profiles and profile implementations of composite blocks, given profiles of their sub-blocks. Our work reveals fundamental trade-offs between the size and reusability of a profile, as well as between characteristics of the generated code and complexity of the synthesis algorithms. We discuss various algorithms that explore these trade-offs, among which algorithms that achieve maximal reusability with optimal profile size.

This paper unifies and extends the work presented in [30–32]. We gratefully acknowledge the contributions of our co-author Christian Szegedy. Roberto Lublinerman contributed to this work while he was at Cadence Design Systems; he is now at Google. We also thank the anonymous Reviewers of earlier versions of this work. This work was partially supported by the National Science Foundation (awards #1329759 and #1139138), and by the Academy of Finland. We gratefully acknowledge the support of Edward Lee, without whom this work would not have been possible.

M. Lohstroh et al. (Eds.): Lee Festschrift, LNCS 10760, pp. 449–477, 2018.
https://doi.org/10.1007/978-3-319-95246-8_26

1   Introduction

What is the parallel composition of two Mealy machines, or even two stateless functions? Consider, for instance, the block diagram shown to the left of Fig. 1. Blocks A and B represent two stateless functions (over some input and output domains). Block P is a *composite* block formed by encapsulating A and B: P represents the parallel composition of A and B. It is tempting to view P as a new stateless function whose input and output domains are the cartesian products of the input and output domains of A and B, respectively. This is problematic, however, as we then lose the information that the output of A does not depend on the input of B, and vice versa. Such information turns out to be critical when using P in certain contexts. For instance, if we connect P in a feedback configuration, as shown in the middle of Fig. 1, we obtain a diagram with a cyclic dependency: the input of P depends on its output. Although some methods exist to deal with such dependencies, they are expensive or even undecidable in general (see discussion below). Moreover, using such methods is sometimes an overkill. In our example, for instance, the situation is really simple: there is no real dependency cycle in the feedback configuration, as revealed by flattening P (right of Fig. 1).

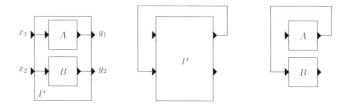

Fig. 1. A hierarchical block diagram (left), a possible way to connect macro block P (middle) and the same connection after flattening P (right).

The problem really lies in the fact that representing the parallel composition of functions A and B as a new function P loses the dependency information between inputs and outputs. In this paper we present a systematic method to represent, maintain and efficiently compute such information. Before further discussing our method and its benefits over alternatives, let us place our work in context.

This work is motivated by the need to develop reliable and efficient methods for the design and implementation of *embedded systems* [25]. Current practice can be qualified as being mostly about *low-level design*: build a prototype system, test it, discover problems, fix them and repeat the process. This is costly both in terms of money and time, and also offers few guarantees of producing reliable systems. So-called *model-based design* (MBD) has been proposed as an alternative. The MBD paradigm is based on the premise of using models for *high-level* design. Models can be analyzed in more exhaustive and less costly ways than prototype systems. MBD relies on powerful implementation techniques to derive executable systems from models. These techniques need to be as automatic as possible, in order to produce implementations efficiently. They also need to preserve as many of the properties of the high-level model as possible. This allows to produce implementations that are, as much as possible, *correct by construction*, which reduces the effort of testing at the implementation level.

In the field of embedded systems, like in many other fields, specialized (sometimes called "domain-specific") languages are used. These languages include features such as *concurrency*, *time* and *system dynamics*, which are integral parts of embedded system design. In this paper, we are particularly interested in *synchronous models*, whose execution proceeds by an infinite sequence of synchronous *rounds*. The synchronous model of computation (MoC) is a fundamental one, especially relevant in the context of embedded systems, since it is prevalent in many application domains, from control software to synchronous hardware.

Examples of synchronous models coming from the academia are the so-called *synchronous languages* [3], such as Lustre [14], Esterel [6,34] or Signal [20,27], or the *synchronous-reactive* domain of Ptolemy [19]. Simulink from The MathWorks[1] and SCADE from Esterel Technologies[2] are two commercial products, especially widespread in the automotive and avionics domains. SCADE has its foundations on Lustre and uses a purely synchronous MoC. Simulink contains both a continuous-time and a discrete-time part: the latter follows essentially the synchronous MoC.

The tools associated with languages such as the above include graphical model editors, simulators and code generators.[3] Automatic generation of code that implements the semantics of a model is useful in different contexts: the code can be used for simulation; but it can also be embedded in a real-time digital control system (*X-by-wire*). In fact, uses of the latter type are increasingly being adopted by the industry. Thus, these tools can be seen as programming languages, debuggers and compilers for the embedded system domain.

In this paper, we use *synchronous block diagrams* (SBDs) [19,32] as a formal model that captures the synchronous MoC. A fundamental concept in our version of SBDs, directly inspired by Simulink, SCADE and Ptolemy, is *hierarchy*: a set of blocks can be connected to form a diagram, which may be encapsulated in a *composite*, or *macro*, block. The latter can be itself further connected and encapsulated. Hierarchies of arbitrary depth can be formed in this way. Hierarchy is essential in graphical formalisms since it allows to master complexity by building designs in a modular manner. Hierarchy facilitates the reuse of high-level components, both during model construction and code generation.

Our work has been motivated by the problem of *modular code generation* from synchronous models such as SBDs. We already explained the importance

---

[1] See http://www.mathworks.com/products/simulink/.

[2] See http://www.esterel-technologies.com/products/scade-suite/.

[3] Primarily software code generators, since software is becoming predominant in embedded systems, but also hardware code generators in some cases.

of code generation in the discussion above. Modular code generation consists in generating code from pieces of a model independently from other pieces. In the context of SBDs, modular code generation consists in generating code from a given block P independently from its context, that is, independently from the diagrams that P is or will be connected to. Just as separate compilation of different files of a large piece of software written in C++ or Java is essential, so is modular code generation from hierarchical models such as SBDs. It allows incremental compilation and scalability of the code generation process. It also allows building reusable model libraries. Finally, it allows to treat blocks as "black boxes" as much as possible. This is important in an industrial context, where intellectual property (IP) of models is a primary concern.

Most existing approaches to code generation from synchronous models are *monolithic*: they consist in generating, for a given block, a single `step` function that computes all block outputs given all its inputs. This is problematic because it loses input-output dependency information, as illustrated above. If the block has state, often two functions are generated, an `output` function to compute the outputs from the inputs and current state, and an `update` function to update the state, as in a Mealy machine. This does not solve the problem either, however, since inputs and outputs are still treated in a monolithic way in the `output` function.

One way to deal with this problem is to follow the approach proposed in [5, 19, 33] and used in Ptolemy [29]. This approach consists in generating two functions per block, an `output` and an `update` function as above (in Ptolemy these are called `fire` and `postfire`, respectively) but with the addition that these functions can operate over a special *unknown* value, corresponding to the bottom element of a complete partial order. At run-time, at every synchronous round, the `output` functions of all blocks are executed repeatedly until a fixpoint is computed. The fixpoint may contain unknown values, in which case the diagram is not well-defined and execution stops. Otherwise, execution proceeds to the next round where a new fixpoint is computed.

One problem with this approach is that it cannot guarantee *statically* (i.e., at compile-time) that no unknown values will be produced at run-time. Therefore, the approach is mostly suited for simulation, and cannot be used to produce code for safety-critical applications. One way to guarantee statically that the diagram is well-defined is to prove that the model is *constructive* in the sense of Berry [5]. Unfortunately, proving constructiveness is generally undecidable for models with infinite domains, and is expensive even for models with finite domains. Moreover, this approach requires semantic knowledge about each block, namely, what is the function that the block computes. Having such semantic knowledge is contrary to the goal of treating blocks as black boxes, that we pursue in this paper.

Our approach allows to make static guarantees. The key idea is to generate for a given block a *non-monolithic* interface, also called *profile*. The latter consists of a *not a-priori fixed* number of interface functions, plus a set of dependencies between these functions. Each function computes some outputs from some inputs. The dependencies capture the IO dependencies of the block. As an

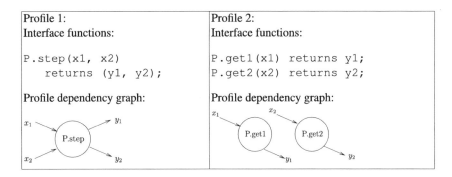

Fig. 2. Two possible profiles for block P of Fig. 1: the left one is monolithic; the right one is not.

example, two possible profiles for block P of Fig. 1 are shown in Fig. 2. The left-most profile is monolithic, and corresponds to the standard approach of treating P as simply a new function from both inputs to both outputs. The rightmost profile is non-monolithic, and corresponds to what one of our methods automatically generates.

The profile can be seen as an abstraction of the information contained in the block (i.e., in its internal hierarchy, which is not exposed in the profile). We present *profile synthesis* methods that allow to generate profiles automatically, and moreover, to explore different trade-offs during the generation of such profiles. In particular, trade-offs between the size of the generated profile and its accuracy. The smaller the size the better, for scalability and IP reasons. On the other hand, a profile that is too small may lose IO dependency information. This in turn results in a profile that is less *reusable*, that is, that cannot be used in some contexts. Apart from profile size vs. reusability trade-offs, we also study other trade-offs, such as between the quality of the resulting code and the complexity of computing the profile.

Contributions: This paper unifies and extends the work presented in [30–32]. This work provides a general and automatic solution to the problem of modular code generation from synchronous models, with static guarantees. Compared to the fixpoint-based approaches discussed above, ours can handle a smaller class of models, namely, those that exhibit no dependency cycles once the hierarchy is flattened (dependency cycles are allowed at higher levels, however, as in the example of Fig. 1). On the other hand, our approach can provide static (compile-time) guarantees, which cannot be generally provided by fixpoint-based approaches, as discussed above. With our method, diagrams (and the corresponding generated code) are guaranteed to have well-defined semantics (no unknown values) at compile-time. Moreover, interface functions are called at most once per round, in a statically determined order. Compared to fixpoint-based methods, where more than one iterations may be required to reach a fixpoint, static execution order has the benefits of smaller run-time overhead, better performance, and better predictability of the execution time of the generated code. All are crucial properties in an embedded system setting.

Organization: The rest of this paper is organized as follows. In Sect. 2 we discuss other related work. In Sect. 3 we explain the syntax and semantics of hierarchical SBDs. In Sect. 4 we present profiles. In Sect. 5 we describe our method for automatically synthesizing profiles and generating code that implements those profiles. Section 6 concludes this paper.

2   Other Related Work

Compositionality of synchronous models, and in particular the problem of cyclic dependencies, has been the topic of extensive study, and a variety of solutions have been proposed (e.g., see [3,15] for overviews). The most general is probably the one used in Esterel [5], however, it is often infeasible as discussed above. Simulink and Lustre compilers both rely of statically detecting cyclic dependencies and rejecting the model if one is found. In order to do this they flatten the model, however, which is not modular. SCADE does not flatten the model, but requires absence of cyclic dependencies at *every* level of the hierarchy, which is quite restrictive.

Equipping models with input-output dependency information has been proposed in [2] and also in [48]. These works use such information mainly for analysis (e.g., distinguish between true and false dependencies). Our goals are also synthesis and code generation. We also study trade-offs such as between profile size vs. reusability, which are not studied in these works.

Code generation for synchronous models and languages has been extensively studied, however, modular code generation has received less attention: in 2003, [3] stated that "a unified treatment [of this problem] remains a research topic". In fact, separate compilation (essentially the same problem) for synchronous languages has been identified as synonymous with monolithic compilation, and as such deemed to be generally infeasible [23,35]. Our non-monolithic framework provides the unified treatment that has been missing.

Although not identified explicitly as such, non-monolithic approaches have been described previously, for instance, in [4,21,24,38]. These works are, however, focusing on different problems, such as static scheduling and code distribution, and as such provide incomplete solutions to the modular code generation problem. In particular, they do not deal with hierarchies of arbitrary depth, they do not identify code generation trade-offs and they do not address the problems of optimizing metrics such as profile size or reusability.

[47] study partial evaluation in Esterel: generating code that computes outputs even in the presence of unknown inputs. Modular compilation for Quartz (a variant of Esterel) is studied in [10,39]. Their work focuses more on problems such as so-called *schizophrenia* which are specific to imperative synchronous languages like Esterel, and less on causality problems which is our main focus. Causality problems are also outside the focus of work on composable code generation from languages like Giotto where by definition all outputs are produced

with a unit delay [26]. The focus there is on compositionality of timing and scheduling, as is the case with work on compositional real-time scheduling [40].

Profiles are rich interfaces. Interfaces are a key mechanism for abstraction, modularity, compositionality, and many other important properties of software and systems. Interfaces have appeared in the literature in many different settings and communities, such as software engineering and programming languages (e.g., *Typestate* [41]), or formal methods (e.g., *interface automata* [1], *relational interfaces* [45], and *timed actor interfaces* [22]). Particularly close to our work here is the theory of relational interfaces which have synchronous semantics similar to SBDs [45]. This work has since been extended into a powerful compositional framework called *refinement calculus of reactive systems* (RCRS) [37]. RCRS includes methods and tools to translate hierarchical SBDs into a formal algebra of contracts which can be manipulated formally (e.g., using a theorem prover) and symbolically [18]. RCRS also includes a formal notion of *refinement* which allows to specify a system at different levels of abstraction, and also to speak formally about *substitutability* (when can a component replace another one) [45].

Interfaces are key for simulation environments like Ptolemy. Most modern simulators are built in a modular fashion, where the simulation engine is separated from the simulated models. This allows the same engine to be used for a large variety of models, and also allows the addition of new models, model components, model libraries, etc. To achieve this modularity in the implementation, a clear API (application program interface) is used. This API is typically implemented by the model components (e.g., "blocks" in Simulink, "actors" in Ptolemy) and called by the simulation engine (although call-backs are also sometimes used, e.g., the `fireAt` method in Ptolemy). A formalization of (part of) Ptolemy's actor interface is provided in [46], as part of an attempt to give formal semantics to the language.

Different simulators typically use different APIs, which hinders the sharing and exchange of models, if these models are written in different languages. The FMI standard [7,8] aims to remedy this by providing standard APIs for model exchange and co-simulation. The development of FMI has received great attention recently as it raises several interesting questions, such as what properties should a "good" co-simulation algorithm have [11,12,16], how to bridge the semantic gap between heterogeneous modeling formalisms and the standard API [9,43], how to integrate FMI in existing simulation tools [17], etc.

The ideas presented in this paper are not limited to models with synchronous semantics. They have indeed inspired us to explore modular code generation and compositionality in other contexts, such as dataflow [28]. Our study revealed that hierarchical SDF graphs used in tools such as Ptolemy are non-compositional in the sense that a composite SDF actor cannot always be replaced by an atomic one [42], a problem reminiscent of the limitations of monolithic interfaces in the case of SBDs. A compositional alternative inspired from the concept of non-monolithic interfaces is proposed in [28].

A broader discussion about the role of compositionality in the science of system design can be found in [44].

3   Synchronous Block Diagrams

3.1   Hierarchical Block Diagrams

We consider a notation based on a set of *blocks* that can be connected to form *diagrams* (see Fig. 3). Each block has a number of *input ports* (possibly zero) and a number of *output ports* (possibly zero). Diagrams are formed by connecting some output port of a block A to some input port of a block B (B can be the same as A). We assume that a port can only be connected to a single other port: *fan-out* can be explicitly modeled using blocks that replicate their input to their outputs. We also assume that every output port in a diagram is connected: again, this is without loss of generality, since outputs can be connected to "dummy" blocks that do nothing. Each port has a given *data type* (integer, boolean, ...) and connections can only be done among ports with compatible data types, as in a standard typed programming language. We will not worry about data types in this paper as these can be handled using standard type-theoretic methods.

Blocks are either *atomic* or *macro*. A macro (i.e., composite) block encapsulates a block diagram into a block. The blocks forming the diagram are called the *internal* blocks of the macro block, or (synonymously) its *sub-blocks*. In the example shown to the left of Fig. 3, block Q is a macro block and A, B, C are its sub-blocks. The connections between blocks ("wires") are called *signals*. Upon encapsulation, each input port of the macro block is connected to one or more inputs of its internal blocks, or to an output port of the macro block; and each output port of the macro block is connected to exactly one port, either an output port of an internal block, or an input of the macro block. Signals inherit the data types of their source ports.

In the context of a modular and hierarchical notation such as the block diagrams we consider in this paper, it is useful to distinguish between block *types* and block *instances*. Indeed, a block, whether atomic or composite, can be used in a given diagram multiple times. For example, a block of type *Adder*, that computes the arithmetic sum of its inputs, can be used multiple times in a given diagram. In this case, we say that the block of type *Adder* is *instantiated* multiple times. Each "copy" of the block is called an *instance*. In the rest of the paper, we omit to distinguish between type and instance when the distinction is clear from context.

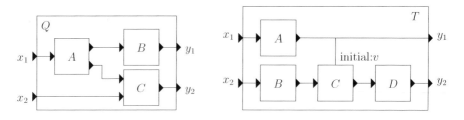

Fig. 3. Left: a hierarchical block diagram consisting of macro block Q with sub-blocks A, B, C. Right: a diagram with a triggered block C.

3.2   Triggers

In a diagram, any (atomic or macro) block may be *triggered* by a Boolean signal
x: the intention is that the triggered block is to "fire" only when x is true. If
x is false, then the outputs of the triggered block retain their value (i.e., the
value that they had in the previous synchronous round). The signal x is called
the *trigger* of the triggered block. A block can have at most one trigger. The
diagram shown to the left of Fig. 3 has no triggers. An example of a diagram
with triggers is shown to the right of Fig. 3: block A produces a (Boolean) signal
that triggers block C.

When a block is triggered, the user specifies initial values for each output
of that block. These determine the values of the outputs during the initial time
interval (possibly empty) until the block is triggered for the first time. We call
such a value a *trigger-initial value*. In the example shown to the right of Fig. 3,
a trigger-initial value v is specified for the (single) output of triggered block C.
Note that if a block has many outputs, a potentially different trigger-initial value
can be specified for each output.[4]

[31] show that triggers do not add to the expressiveness of synchronous block
diagrams and can be eliminated by a structural transformation, which essentially
transforms triggers into inputs. This transformation is not modular, however,
because it propagates in a top-down manner throughout the entire hierarchy, all
the way to the atomic blocks. This contradicts our requirement that blocks be
seen as "black boxes". To achieve modularity, we provide methods that handle
triggers directly, without eliminating them.

Our motivation for studying triggers is to capture Simulink's *triggered subsystems*. Triggers are a simpler and more restricted concept than the concept of *clocks*, used in synchronous languages and more generally in synchronous dataflow [13]. Indeed, signals in a synchronous block diagram are always
"present", that is, they have a well-defined value at every synchronous round.
This includes signals that are outputs of triggered blocks. For this reason, a
sophisticated type-checking mechanism such as a *clock calculus* [13] is not needed
in our case.

3.3   Combinational, Sequential, and Moore Blocks

Blocks (more precisely, block types) can be either *combinational* (i.e., *stateless*)
or *sequential* (i.e., *stateful*, that is, having internal state). Atomic blocks are pre-
classified as either combinational or sequential. A macro block is combinational

---

[4] A Reviewer of an earlier version of this article correctly pointed out that there may
be potential problems with the specification of trigger-initial values. In particular,
complications may arise if downstream models are only valid for certain inputs: what
happens if a trigger-initial value is not a legal input for the downstream model?
While we agree that this is a problem, we feel that it is not confined to the use of
triggers. The same problem might arise in a diagram without triggers. In general,
the problem arises from *non-input-receptive* components. For a thorough study of
such components, we refer the reader to [36,45].

iff all its sub-blocks are combinational; otherwise it is sequential. Some sequential blocks are *Moore* (from Moore machines). All outputs of a Moore block only depend on the current state of the block, but not on the inputs. See also Sect. 3.4.

3.4 Semantics

As we shall see in Sect. 4, each block in our framework is represented by a set of interface functions and a directed acyclic graph whose nodes are these functions. Let f be such an interface function with inputs $x_1, \ldots, x_n$ and outputs $y_1, \ldots, y_m$, where $m, n \in \mathbb{N}$ and $\mathbb{N} = \{0, 1, 2, 3, \ldots\}$. Implicitly, f is also associated with a state variable s (possibly a vector). Denote by D_v the domain of variable v. Then, semantically f is a function

$$f : D_{x_1} \times \cdots \times D_{x_n} \times D_s \to D_{y_1} \times \cdots \times D_{y_m} \times D_s \tag{1}$$

Such a function f then defines the behavior of a SBD as a dynamical system in time. In particular, each signal x is interpreted semantically as a total function $x : \mathbb{N} \to D_x$, where $x(k)$ denotes the value of x at synchronous round k. Suppose, for the moment, that f belongs to a non-triggered block in the diagram (the case of triggered blocks is examined below). Then, if x is an input to f then $x(k)$ is determined by the environment (which can be another function in the diagram), otherwise it is determined by f as follows:

$$\big(y_1(k), \ldots, y_m(k), s(k+1)\big) = f\big(x_1(k), \ldots, x_n(k), s(k)\big) \tag{2}$$

That is, f takes as input the current values of all its input ports and the current value of the state, and produces as output the current values of all its output ports and the next value of the state.

For example, if f_+ is the (unique) interface function for an *Adder* block that has two inputs x_1, x_2, one output y, and no internal state, then semantically f_+ is defined by

$$f_+(v_{x_1}, v_{x_2}, v_s) = (v_{x_1} + v_{x_2}, v_s) \tag{3}$$

which defines the dynamical system

$$y(k) = x_1(k) + x_2(k) \tag{4}$$

As can be seen in this example, stateless blocks can be formalized as blocks with a single, "dummy" state v_s that never changes.

As another example, consider the *unit-delay* block, also denoted $\frac{1}{z}$. This is a stateful block with a single input port x and a single output port y. As we shall see in Sect. 4 the profile of $\frac{1}{z}$ contains two interface functions, one that computes the output from the current state and one that updates the state based on the input. Both are semantically the identity function, and define the dynamical system

$$\big(y(k), s(k+1)\big) = \big(s(k), x(k)\big) \tag{5}$$

The behavior of the unit-delay block is illustrated in Fig. 4. The value of the input signal x at round k is $x(k)$. The value of the state at round 0, i.e., $s(0)$, is denoted s_{init}.

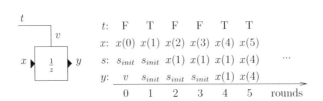

$$
\begin{array}{ll}
x: & x(0)\ x(1)\ x(2)\ x(3)\ x(4)\ x(5) \\
s: & s_{init}\ x(0)\ x(1)\ x(2)\ x(3)\ x(4) \quad\cdots \\
y: & s_{init}\ x(0)\ x(1)\ x(2)\ x(3)\ x(4) \\
& \ 0\quad 1\quad 2\quad 3\quad 4\quad 5 \qquad \text{rounds}
\end{array}
$$

Fig. 4. A unit-delay block (left) and its semantics (right).

We now turn to the case of triggered blocks. Suppose f is an interface function of some block A which is triggered, in the diagram in question, by some signal t. Notice that the semantics of f remain the same, since f is defined independently from context. However, the semantics of the output signals of f change, because of the fact that A is triggered. In particular, let $y \in \{y_1, \dots, y_m\}$ be an output of f. Then, Eq. (2) generalizes to

$$
y(k) = \begin{cases}
f_y(x_1(k), \dots, x_n(k), s(k)), & \text{if } t(k) = \textit{true} \\
y(k-1), & \text{if } t(k) = \textit{false} \text{ and } k > 0 \\
v_y, & \text{if } t(k) = \textit{false} \text{ and } k = 0
\end{cases}
\tag{6}
$$

$$
s(k+1) = \begin{cases}
f_s(x_1(k), \dots, x_n(k), s(k)), & \text{if } t(k) = \textit{true} \\
s(k), & \text{if } t(k) = \textit{false}
\end{cases}
\tag{7}
$$

where f_y, f_s are projections of f to variables y and s, respectively, and v_y is the trigger-initial value specified in the diagram for y.

An example that illustrates the semantics of triggered blocks is given in Fig. 5: t is the triggering signal, "T" and "F" denote true and false, respectively, and v is the trigger-initial value for y.

$$
\begin{array}{ll}
t: & \text{F}\quad \text{T}\quad \text{F}\quad \text{F}\quad \text{T}\quad \text{T} \\
x: & x(0)\ x(1)\ x(2)\ x(3)\ x(4)\ x(5) \\
s: & s_{init}\ s_{init}\ x(1)\ x(1)\ x(1)\ x(4) \quad\cdots \\
y: & v\quad s_{init}\ s_{init}\ s_{init}\ x(1)\ x(4) \\
& \ 0\quad 1\quad 2\quad 3\quad 4\quad 5 \qquad \text{rounds}
\end{array}
$$

Fig. 5. A triggered unit-delay block (left) and its semantics (right).

Now, consider a given composite block P so that the profiles of all its sub-blocks are known. That is, the interface functions of the sub-blocks of P are semantically defined. The internal diagram of P defines a set of dependencies between these interface functions, corresponding to the *scheduling dependency*

graph, described in Sect. 5.1. If this graph contains a cycle, then the semantics of
P is undefined. Otherwise, the semantics is defined in terms of a new function f_P
of the same form as in (1). f_P is obtained by function composition of the interface
functions of the sub-blocks of P. Acyclicity of the scheduling dependency graph
guarantees that the composition is well-defined.

4   Profiles: An Abstract, Compositional and Executable Representation of Synchronous Block Diagrams

4.1   Profiles

A *profile* can be seen as an *interface* or a *summary* of a block type. All blocks,
atomic or composite, have profiles. A block may have multiple profiles, each
suited for different purposes. This will become clear when we discuss tradeoffs
in Sect. 4.3.

The profile of a block contains:

– A list of *interface functions* and their *signatures*. Each such function takes as
  input a set of values corresponding to some of the input ports of the block,
  and returns as output a set of values corresponding to some of the output
  ports of the block. The signature specifies which ports the arguments of the
  function correspond to, their data types, and so on.[5]
– A *profile dependency graph* (PDG). The PDG is a directed, acyclic graph
  (DAG), the nodes of which are the interface functions listed in the profile.
  The PDG specifies the correct order in which these functions are to be called
  at every synchronous round. If $f \rightarrow g$ is an edge in the PDG, then function
  f must be called before function g.

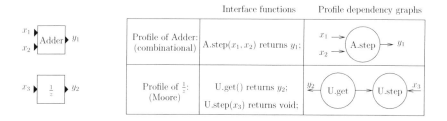

Fig. 6. Profiles for Adder and Unit-Delay blocks.

For example, Fig. 6 shows the profiles of an Adder block and a Unit-Delay
block. Data types are omitted from the signatures of the profiles. The inputs and

---

[5] For sequential blocks (i.e., blocks with internal state) profiles contain a special `init`
function that initializes the state. In our framework, `init` functions of macro blocks
are synthesized from `init` functions of their sub-blocks. This is a simple procedure
whose details are omitted.

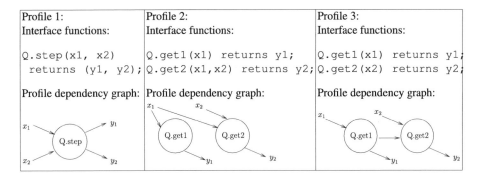

Fig. 7. Three possible profiles for block Q of Fig. 3.

outputs of the interface functions are also shown on the nodes of the PDG: note that this information can be derived from the signatures of the interface functions. Figure 2 shows two possible profiles for macro block P of Fig. 1. Figure 7 shows three possible profiles for macro block Q of Fig. 3. As these examples illustrate, a given block can have more than one profile. Indeed, different profiles realize different trade-offs and thus are more or less suited in different situations, as discussed in Sect. 4.3. Also note that different blocks can have identical profiles, as illustrated by Figs. 2 and 7.

Profiles that contain a single interface function are called *monolithic*. The profile of the Adder in Fig. 6 is monolithic, whereas the profile of $\frac{1}{z}$ is not. Profile 1 in Figs. 2 and 7 is monolithic, whereas the other profiles shown in these figures are non-monolithic.

Let P be a macro block and consider a profile of P. The PDG of the profile induces a set of dependencies between inputs and outputs of the block. In particular, output y depends on input x if the PDG has a directed path from x to y. On the other hand, the internal diagram of P, together with the profiles of all sub-blocks of P, also induce a set of dependencies between inputs and outputs. These dependencies are captured in the *scheduling dependency graph*, formalized in Sect. 5.1. Here we discuss them informally, through examples. For instance, from the internal diagram of block P of Fig. 1 we can deduce that y_1 does not depend on x_2. Now, y_1 may or may not depend on x_1, depending on the profile of A. If A has a monolithic profile, then its output depends on its input, thus, y_1 depends on x_1. If A has a profile like the one of the Moore block $\frac{1}{z}$ then y_1 does not depend on x_1.

We require that all input-output dependencies that are induced by the internal graph of a block P and the profiles of its sub-blocks are also induced by the PDG of the profile of P. We then say that the profile of P is *sound*. The profile synthesis methods presented in Sect. 5 guarantee that the generated profiles are sound.

Note that the profile of a block is independent of whether the block is triggered or not. Indeed, whether the block is triggered is not a property of the block, it is a property of its context: the same block (type) may be triggered in some diagrams and not triggered in other diagrams. The same profile for this block can be used in both cases. Triggering *will* affect how the profile is used, however, as explained in Sect. 5.

4.2   Profile Implementations

The profile contains a list of interface functions. These functions are implemented in a given programming language, e.g., C++ or Java. The implementations of these functions are part of the *profile implementation*. The latter also includes state and other internal variables, encapsulated in some form, depending on the mechanisms that the programming language provides (e.g., a C++ or Java class).

For example, the profile implementations of the Adder and Unit-Delay blocks (Fig. 6) are given below in object-oriented pseudo-code:

```
class Adder {                  class UnitDelay {
  Adder.step( x1, x2 )           private state;
      returns y1
  {                              UnitDelay.init() { state := ... }
    return (x1 + x2);
  }                              UnitDelay.get() returns y2 {
}                                  return state;
                                 }

                                 UnitDelay.step( x3 ) {
                                   state := x3;
                                 }
                               }
```

The implementations of the two profiles of P shown in Fig. 2 are as follows:

```
Monolithic profile:              Non-monolithic profile:

P.step(x1, x2) returns (y1, y2)  P.get1(x1) returns y1 {
{                                  return A.step(x1);
  return (A.step(x1), B.step(x2)); }
}
                                 P.get2(x2) returns y2 {
                                   return B.step(x2);
                                 }
```

In the above example we have assumed monolithic profiles for sub-blocks A and B of P, with functions A.step and B.step, respectively. Unless otherwise stated, we assume monolithic profiles for sub-blocks in all examples that follow.

The implementation of Profile 3 of block Q, shown in Fig. 7, is as follows:

```
Q.get1(x1) returns y1 {          Q.get2(x2) returns y2 {
  (z1,z2) := A.step(x1);           y2 := C.step(z2,x2);
  y1 := B.step(z1);                return y2;
  return y1;                     }
}
```

More examples of profile implementations are given in the sequel.

4.3 Trade-Offs

As can be seen from the examples above, the same block can have multiple different profiles. These accomplish different trade-offs, some of which are discussed below.

Modularity vs. Reusability. This is probably the most important tradeoff. We define reusability in terms of the set of contexts (i.e., diagrams) that the profile can be used in: the larger this set, the more reusable the profile is (note that this is a partial order). It follows that monolithic profiles are no more reusable than non-monolithic ones. Often they are strictly less reusable (e.g., examples of Figs. 2 and 7). Reusability is directly related to the set of IO dependencies defined by the PDG of a profile. The larger the set of IO dependencies, the less reusable the profile. A monolithic profile is the least reusable, as it contains all possible IO dependencies. A profile is *maximally reusable* if it contains exactly those IO dependencies contained in the internal diagram of the corresponding macro block. (A profile cannot contain less dependencies, otherwise it would not be sound.) The non-monolithic profiles of Figs. 2 and 7 are both maximally reusable.

Modularity, in our framework, is a *quantitative* notion: it is measured in terms of the size of the profile, for instance, the number of interface functions, or the size of the PDG. The *smaller* the profile, the more modular it is. In that sense, the most modular profile is the monolithic profile. This definition is justified by a number of considerations. First, *scalability*: the complexity of profile synthesis algorithms is a direct function of the size of the profiles, thus, the smaller the profiles, the better the algorithms scale. A second consideration has to do with IP concerns: the smaller the profile, the less details it reveals about the internals of the block, therefore, the more the block appears as a "black box" to its user.

From the above definitions, it follows that modularity and reusability are in conflict. To optimize modularity we are led towards monolithic profiles, but we may have to pay a price in terms of reusability. Both examples in Figs. 2 and 7 illustrate this trade-off.

Modularity vs. Code Size and Other Metrics. An interesting set of trade-offs arise between modularity and various metrics of the profile implementation,

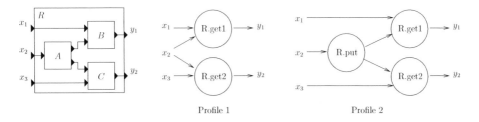

Profile 1   Profile 2

Fig. 8. A macro block R (left) and two possible profiles for R (middle and right).

such as size of the code that implements the interface functions, run-time performance (e.g., worst-case execution time), and so on. We illustrate such trade-offs
here through an example. More details can be found in [30].

Figure 8 shows a macro block R and two maximally-reusable profiles for R.
Profile 1 is smaller, since it contains only 2 functions, whereas Profile 2 contains
3. The implementation of Profile 1 is as follows:

```
R.get1(x1,x2) returns y1 {        R.get2(x2,x3) returns y2 {
  if ( c = 0 ) {                    if ( c = 0 ) {
    (z1, z2) := A.step(x2);          (z1, z2) := A.step(x2);
  }                                  }
  c := (c + 1) modulo 2;            c := (c + 1) modulo 2;
  return B.step( x1, z1 );          return C.step( z2, x3 );
}                                  }
```

It can be seen that the first three lines of code in P.get1 and P.get2 are
identical. These lines serve to guard execution of A.step, which should only be
called once per synchronous round. Since the order of calling P.get1 and P.get2
depends on the context of R, it is not known at compile-time which function will
first call A.step, and the choice is made at run-time.

The implementation of Profile 2 of Fig. 8 is as follows:

```
R.put(x2) {          R.get1(x2) returns y1 {   R.get2(x3) returns y2 {
  (z1,z2) :=           return B.step(x1,z1);     return C.step(z2,x3);
    A.step(x2);      }                         }
}
```

This implementation has better characteristics than the previous one: it contains no conditionals and no code replication. Thus, the code is both smaller in
size and also executes faster. Such differences may seem small in this example,
but they can be critical in the context of a real embedded application, where
memory and execution time are often scarce resources.

Algorithmic Complexity Trade-Offs. Another set of trade-offs concerns the
complexity, in theory or in practice, of the algorithms involved in profile synthesis, against other metrics such as modularity, reusability, or code characteristics.
For example, producing a monolithic profile is trivial and inexpensive. Synthesizing non-monolithic profiles involves more sophisticated algorithms such as
clustering. Many of these algorithms have polynomial worst-case complexity,
but may result in profiles that are non-optimal in terms of modularity, or that
cannot be implemented without conditional code, as with Profile 2 of Fig. 7, or
Profile 1 of Fig. 8. These issues are discussed in more detail in Sect. 5.

4.4   Abstraction, Compositionality and Executability

In summary, profiles in general, and non-monolithic profiles in particular, form
a modular, compositional and executable representation of hierarchical SBDs.

They are executable in the sense that every interface function comes with a piece of executable code: by calling these functions in an order that respects the dependencies prescribed in the PDG, we have an implementation of the semantics of the model. This is in contrast, for instance, to non-executable representations that simply maintain input-output dependencies, as in the works of [2,48]. Profiles are compositional in the sense that a diagram of profiles can be abstracted into a single profile without any loss of information, that is, preserving exactly the same set of input-output dependencies. Finally, profiles are abstract in the sense that they allow many of the internal details of composite blocks to be omitted (e.g., as in Fig. 7) which results in a more compact and thus less costly representation.

5   Profile Synthesis and Code Generation

In this section we describe how profiles and their implementations can be generated automatically. In summary, our method takes as inputs:

1. a macro block M with its internal block diagram;
2. a profile for each type of sub-block of M; and
3. a set of user constraints or goals;

and automatically generates as outputs:

1. a profile for M (this part of the process is called *profile synthesis*);
2. the implementation of the profile in a certain programming language such as C++ or Java.

User constraints and goals include any sort of information that the user may provide to influence the profile and code that is generated. This includes modularity vs. reusability preferences, desired code characteristics, and so on. In practice, this type of information is given as options and inputs to the algorithms involved in the different steps of the process, discussed below.

It is worth noting that although the profiles of the sub-blocks of M are required in the profile synthesis and code generation process, the implementation of the interface functions of these profiles is not required. The implementation of the sub-blocks of M is only required for model execution. This is another aspect of modularity in our approach, and a desirable feature especially for IP reasons, or treating blocks as "black boxes". In particular, only executable code (e.g., object files) need to be made available to the user, and not source code.

Profile synthesis can be applied to SBDs of arbitrary hierarchy depths, in a bottom-up manner. Starting with macro blocks that contain only atomic blocks, synthesizing a profile for the former, and then moving up the hierarchy. Profiles of atomic blocks are inputs to this process. They can be produced "manually", or automatically, for instance, by some method that automatically extracts summaries from the implementation of blocks. How to do this is beyond the scope of this paper. Note that once a profile has been synthesized for a macro block, the latter can be viewed as an atomic block, since no information about its internals (e.g., its internal diagram) is any longer necessary. Thus, apart from the information contained in the profile, the block is a "black box".

5.1   Profile Synthesis

Profile synthesis consists in synthesizing a profile for a macro block M given the internal diagram of M and profiles for all sub-blocks of M. Profile synthesis involves a number of sub-steps, described below:

Building the Scheduling Dependency Graph (SDG). The SDG is a directed graph obtained by connecting the PDGs of the profiles of all sub-blocks of M. The connections are made according to the internal diagram of M, that is, by inserting an edge $f \to g$ if an output of function f is connected in the diagram to an input of function g.

Consider the example of Fig. 9. At the top left of the figure is shown a macro block M and its internal diagram. At the top right of the figure are shown the profiles of all sub-blocks of M. Sub-blocks A and C have a single interface function each, which takes the input and returns the output of these blocks. Block U has two interface functions: U.step and U.get. U.get takes no input and returns the output of U. U.step takes the input of U and returns no output. U is a Moore-sequential block: its get method returns the outputs and its step method updates the state, given the inputs. The PDG of U shown in the figure states that U.get must be called before U.step, at every synchronous round.

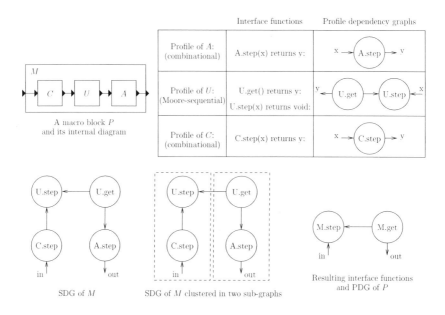

Fig. 9. Example of profile synthesis.

The SDG of block M is shown at the bottom left of Fig. 9. The SDG of M has been produced by connecting the PDGs of sub-blocks C, U and A. For instance, the output port of C is connected to the input port of U. This results in adding

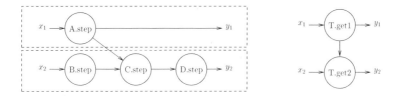

Fig. 10. Left: clustered SDG of macro block T of Fig. 3. Right: profile for T.

a directed edge from `C.step` (which produces the output of C) to `U.step` (which consumes the input of U) to the SDG of M. Similarly with the rest of the edges added to the SDG of M.

When the internal diagram of M contains triggers, these are handled by adding directed edges from the interface function that produces the trigger to all interface functions of the triggered sub-block of M. For example, the SDG of macro block T of Fig. 3 is shown in Fig. 10.

Dependency Analysis. Once the SDG of M is built, it is checked to see whether it contains a directed cycle. If it does, then this implies a cyclic dependency that cannot be resolved, either because the original diagram has a true such dependency, or because the profiles of the sub-blocks of M are too coarse (i.e., not reusable in the context of M). A cycle in the SDG results in rejecting the diagram and stopping the profile synthesis process. If the SDG is acyclic, we proceed to the *clustering* step.

Clustering. Clustering consists in grouping the nodes of the SDG G of M into a set of *clusters*. Every node of G must be included in at least one cluster, however, the clusters need not be *disjoint*, i.e., some nodes may belong to more than one clusters. Each cluster can also be seen as a *sub-graph* of G that contains all the nodes in the cluster along with all dependencies between any two such nodes. For purposes of clustering, input and output ports of M are also considered to be nodes of the SDG, called *input* and *output nodes*, respectively. For example, x_1, x_2 are input nodes in the SDG of T shown in Fig. 10 and y_1, y_2 are output nodes. Nodes that have no outputs (and therefore no outgoing edges either) are called *terminal* nodes. For example, node `U.step` in the SDG of M shown in Fig. 9 is a terminal node.

Once clustering is fixed, each cluster is mapped into an interface function for M. Therefore, the number of clusters is equal to the number of interface functions contained in the synthesized profile of M.

Dependencies between nodes of G that belong to different clusters induce dependencies between those clusters. In the case of disjoint clusters, these dependencies are defined as follows. Let C_1, C_2 be two clusters and let f_1, f_2 be two nodes of G such that $f_1 \in C_1$ and $f_2 \in C_2$. (Notice that, since clustering is assumed to be disjoint, $f_1 \notin C_2$ and $f_2 \notin C_1$.) A dependency $f_1 \rightarrow f_2$ in G induces a dependency $C_1 \rightarrow C_2$ between the two clusters. In the case of *overlapping* (i.e., non-disjoint) clusters, how the dependencies between clusters are defined generally depends on the clustering algorithm. An example is the O^2C algorithm, explained in Sect. 5.1 below.

Once the dependencies between clusters are fixed, they define a directed graph G_M whose nodes are clusters. Since every cluster corresponds to an interface function for M, G_M is also a graph whose nodes are interface functions of M. Therefore, G_M is the PDG of M. G_M needs to be acyclic, therefore, care must be taken so that clustering results in no cyclic dependencies between clusters. The clustering algorithms that we discuss below all have this property. Moreover, the profile of M must be sound, which means that all input-output dependencies included in G, the SDG of M, must also be included in G_M, the PDG of M. This always holds in the case of disjoint clusterings, as follows from the definition of G_M given above. For overlapping algorithms, care must be taken so that the definition of inter-cluster dependencies results in a PDG that is sound. In Sect. 5.1 we show that this is the case for the O^2C algorithm.

From the above discussion, it follows that clustering completely determines the profile of M. This is why clustering is the most important step in profile synthesis. It is also a step where different choices can be made, that lead to different trade-offs. For instance, a coarse-grain clustering results in a more modular profile than a fine-grain clustering. In particular, grouping all nodes of the SDG into a single cluster results in a monolithic profile. A clustering that introduces false input-output dependencies, that is, input-output dependencies not existing in the SDG, results in a non-maximally-reusable profile. A clustering with *disjoint* clusters (i.e., clusters that do not share nodes) results in code without conditionals or replication. Let us illustrate these points through examples.

In Fig. 9, the SDG of M is clustered in two sub-graphs, resulting in a two-function profile for M, shown to the bottom-right of the figure. Observe that the profile of M is identical to the profile of the unit-delay block $\frac{1}{z}$ (Fig. 6). This is not a coincidence, since this is a maximally-reusable and optimal in terms of modularity profile for all Moore blocks. The example of Fig. 9 also illustrates a simple case of reduction in size, where a macro block with three sub-blocks has the same profile as one of its sub-blocks.

Other examples of clustering are the following:

– The non-monolithic profile of P shown in Fig. 2 is produced by grouping all nodes in the PDG of A in one cluster (corresponding to P.get1) and all nodes in the PDG of B in a second cluster (corresponding to P.get2).
– The non-monolithic profile of Q shown in the middle of Fig. 7 is produced by grouping nodes of A and B in one cluster (corresponding to Q.get1) and nodes of A and C in a second cluster (corresponding to Q.get2). In this case the clusters overlap (i.e., are not disjoint). A similar clustering produces the profile shown in the middle of Fig. 8.
– The non-monolithic profile of Q shown to the right of Fig. 7 is produced by grouping nodes of A and B in one cluster (corresponding to Q.get1) and nodes of C in a second cluster (corresponding to Q.get2). In this case the clusters are disjoint.

– The profile of R shown to the right of Fig. 8 is produced by grouping nodes of A in one cluster (corresponding to R.put), nodes of B in a second cluster (corresponding to R.get1), and nodes of C in a third cluster (corresponding to R.get2).

We now briefly describe some clustering algorithms.

Step-Get Clustering (SGC). The SGC algorithm, proposed in [32], generates at most two interface functions for a given macro block M. In particular, if M is Moore, then SGC generates two interface functions for M: an M.get function that computes the outputs of M and an M.step function that updates the state of M. This is an optimal, in terms of modularity, and maximally-reusable profile for all Moore blocks. If M is not Moore, then SGC generates a single interface function for M, that is, a monolithic profile. In this case the profile is not maximally reusable, in general.

The SGC algorithm is simple. It starts by analyzing the SDG of M, checking whether there exists some output of M that depends on some input. If this is the case, then M is not Moore, and SGC produces a single cluster containing all nodes in the SDG. Otherwise, the SDG can be partitioned into two sub-graphs, a "right" sub-graph that contains all nodes that have a path to some output, and a "left" sub-graph that contains all the remaining nodes. The "right" and "left" sub-graphs correspond to M.get and M.step, respectively. SGC has polynomial worst-case complexity.

The SGC algorithm produces the clustering of Fig. 9 where block M is Moore. For all other examples given in the paper, SGC produces a monolithic profile.

Optimal Overlapping Clustering (O^2C). The O^2C algorithm is an improved variant of the *dynamic clustering* algorithm proposed in [32]. O^2C achieves maximal reusability and optimal modularity, that is, a minimal number of clusters (subject to the maximal reusability constraint). Moreover, O^2C is guaranteed to generate no more than $n+1$ clusters in the worst case, where n is the number of outputs of macro block M, and no more than n clusters if M is combinational. O^2C has polynomial worst-case complexity. The only drawback of O^2C is that it may result in overlapping clusters, therefore, in profile implementations that require conditionals.

O^2C executes the following procedure:

```
for each output node or terminal node f do {
  create a cluster C := { f };
  while there exist nodes g in C and h not in C s.t. h -> g do
    add h to C;
}
merge clusters containing exactly the same sets of input nodes;
for each terminal cluster C do
  if there exists cluster C' s.t. inputs(C) is a subset of
    inputs(C') then merge C with C';
merge all remaining terminal clusters (if any) into a single
      cluster;
```

where a *terminal cluster* is a cluster containing a terminal node, and *inputs(C)* denotes the set of input nodes contained in cluster C.

O^2C starts by creating a cluster for every output node and every terminal node in the SDG of M. Then the *backward closure* of each of these clusters is computed, by adding all *predecessor* nodes, i.e., all nodes that have a directed edge to some node already in the cluster, until no new nodes can be added. If at this point two clusters C_1 and C_2 contain the same sets of input nodes, i.e., $inputs(C_1) = inputs(C_2)$, then these clusters are *merged* into a single cluster $C_1 \cup C_2$, and this is repeated until no more clusters can be merged in this way. Then, for each terminal cluster C for which there exists cluster C' such that $inputs(C) \subseteq inputs(C')$, C and C' are merged into $C \cup C'$, and again the process is repeated until no terminal clusters can be merged in this way. Finally, all remaining terminal clusters (if any) are merged into a single cluster named M.step. The rest of the clusters are named M.get1, M.get2, and so on.

The inter-cluster dependencies defined by O^2C are as follows: all clusters of type M.get$i$ are independent from each other; if there is a cluster M.step, then there is a dependency M.get$i$ → M.step, for every cluster of type M.get$i$. In other words, interface function M.step must be called after all interface functions M.get$i$ are called, and the latter can be called in any order.

Examples of profiles produced by O^2C are: Profile 2 of block P in Fig. 2; Profile 2 of block Q in Fig. 7; Profile 1 of block R in Fig. 8; and the profile of block M in Fig. 9.

O^2C has the following properties:

First, if M has n output ports, and therefore the SDG of M has n output nodes, O^2C will generate at most $n + 1$ clusters. This is because there can be at most one cluster per output node, plus at most one terminal cluster, M.step, when O^2C terminates. It can be also shown that for combinational blocks, i.e., blocks without internal state, there can be at most n clusters.

Second, O^2C produces a sound and acyclic PDG. Acyclicity follows from the fact that the only edges in the PDG of M are from some node M.get$i$ to M.step, if it exists, and the latter has no outgoing edge. To see why the PDG is also sound, consider a path $x \to f_1 \to \cdots \to f_n \to y$ in the SDG of M, from some input node x to some output node y. Let C be the cluster that contains y. C is closed by predecessors, therefore, all nodes in the above path from x to y are contained in C. Thus, the dependency $x \to y$ is maintained in the PDG of M.

Third, O^2C achieves maximal reusability, that is, every IO dependency $x \to y$ in the PDG of M is a true IO dependency. Consider such a dependency. By definition of the PDG, there exists a cluster C such that both x and y are in C. Since y is in C, C cannot be a terminal cluster. C is generally the result of merging clusters $C_1, \ldots, C_k$ produced in the first for each loop of O^2C, for $k \geq 1$. By definition, the set $inputs(C_i)$ is the same for all $i = 1, \ldots, k$. Therefore, there exists C_i such that both x and y are in C_i, and C_i was obtained by computing the backward closure of y. Thus, there is a path from x to y in the SDG of M, and $x \to y$ is a true dependency.

Fourth, O^2C is optimal, that is, there exists no clustering with fewer clusters that achieves maximal reusability. Suppose such a clustering $\mathcal{C}^*$ exists. $\mathcal{C}^*$ must merge in one cluster at least two nodes f_1, f_2 that the clustering $\mathcal{C}$ produced by O^2C separates in two different clusters, $f_1 \in C_1$ and $f_2 \in C_2$. Suppose, first, that both C_1, C_2 are of type M.get$i$. Then $inputs(C_1) \neq inputs(C_2)$, otherwise C_1 and C_2 would have been merged by O^2C. Let, without loss of generality, $x \in inputs(C_2) \setminus inputs(C_1)$. Let y be an output node in C_1 (C_1 is not terminal, so it must contain at least one output node). Then merging f_1 and f_2 introduces false IO dependency $x \to y$, thus, $\mathcal{C}^*$ cannot be maximally reusable. Now suppose C_1 is of type M.get$i$ and C_2 is M.step. Then $inputs(C_2) \not\subseteq inputs(C_1)$, otherwise terminal cluster C_2 would have been merged with C_1. Thus, we can find again $x \in inputs(C_2) \setminus inputs(C_1)$ and $y \in C_1$ and repeat the last argument.

Note that O^2C may unnecessarily produce an overlapping clustering. This means that there exists a disjoint clustering with the same number of clusters that is also maximally reusable. For example, for the SDG shown in Fig. 10, O^2C would produce an overlapping clustering where A.step is shared between two clusters, whereas a disjoint clustering of two clusters exists, as shown in the figure.

Optimal Disjoint Clustering (ODC). The ODC algorithm, proposed in [30], guarantees, like O^2C, maximal reusability. Unlike O^2C, ODC always produces disjoint clusters. Finally, ODC generates a minimal number of clusters, subject to the maximal reusability and disjointness constraints. Unfortunately, the problem of partitioning a DAG into a minimal number of disjoint clusters without introducing false input-output dependencies is NP-complete [30]. Thus, the worst-case complexity of ODC is exponential. Nevertheless, ODC uses powerful SAT solvers and performs well in practice, as the experimental results reported in [30] show.

We will only sketch the main ideas behind ODC, and refer the reader to [30] for the details, which are involved. ODC executes the following procedure:

```
partition output nodes according to input dependencies;
let k be the number of output partitions;
i := k;
repeat
   build a boolean formula stating that a solution
      with i clusters exists;
   call a SAT solver to check whether the formula is satisfiable;
   if formula is satisfiable then solution found
   else i := i+1;
until solution found;
```

The first step consists in partitioning the outputs of M into a set of disjoint partitions such that in every partition, all output nodes depend on exactly the same set of input nodes. If k partitions are found then there can be no less than k clusters required to achieve maximal reusability. Indeed, it can be seen that O^2C produces at least k clusters in this case, and since O^2C is optimal, at least k disjoint clusters are needed to achieve maximal reusability. Therefore, we start the iteration by setting i to k. For each i, we build a boolean formula that encodes the existence of a solution with i clusters. A "solution" means a disjoint clustering that introduces no false input-output dependencies. A SAT solver is used to check satisfiability of the formula (and also produce a solution). If the formula is satisfiable we have found a solution, otherwise, no solution with i clusters exists, and we increment i. The procedure is guaranteed to terminate when i reaches the number of nodes in the SDG of M: indeed, clustering every node separately is obviously a valid disjoint clustering.

Examples of profiles produced by ODC are: Profile 3 of block Q in Fig. 7; Profile 2 of block R in Fig. 8; and the profile of block T in Fig. 10.

Disjoint Clustering Heuristics. A number of heuristics can be used to produce disjoint clusterings that are maximally-reusable, albeit not always optimal in terms of modularity. A simple heuristic is to use O^2C and check whether the clustering it produces is disjoint: if it is we are done, otherwise, we turn it into a disjoint clustering by somehow separating shared nodes (a trivial method is to cluster every such node separately). Other, more sophisticated heuristics, are proposed in [42]. More experimental work is needed to evaluate how these algorithms compare in practice, both in terms of execution time, as well as in terms of the optimality of results produced. Such experiments are beyond the scope of this paper.

Non-Maximally-Reusable Clusterings. All algorithms discussed above, with the exception of SGC, are guaranteed to introduce no false input-output dependencies, thus producing maximally-reusable profiles. In SGC, on the other hand, the user has no way of "controlling" the reusability of the produced profile. In some cases, it may be desirable to relax the requirement on maximal reusability, for instance, in order to gain in modularity. This may be the case, for example, if it is known that a given block will never be connected in a context with feedback. Then, a monolithic profile suffices. More generally, it may be known that, even though a certain output y of the block does not depend on a certain input x, it is "safe" to introduce a false dependency $x \rightarrow y$. That is, such a false dependency is known not to result in serious restrictions in the set of contexts that the block can be used in. The above algorithms can be modified so as to allow the user to provide this type of information, thus being able to control the reusability of the produced profile. For instance, in ODC, the encoding of the formula can be modified so that it selectively allows some false IO dependencies, whereas it forbids the rest.

5.2   Code Generation

Profile synthesis determines the profile of macro block M given as input. In the code generation step, code that implements each interface function in the profile of M is generated in a language such as C++ or Java. Any internal state variables, or other persistent variables needed to communicate data between different calls of the interface functions are generated as well. Together with an init function, these functions and data can be encapsulated in a class or other object-oriented mechanism that the target language may provide. In Java, for instance, the code is encapsulated in a Java class, the interface functions become public methods of this class, and the variables become private variables of the class.

The principle of generating code implementing the interface functions is the following. Every interface function f_i corresponds to a sub-graph G_i of the SDG, produced in the clustering step. To generate code for f_i, the nodes of G_i are ordered in a total order that respects the dependencies of G_i: the SDG of M is acyclic, therefore G_i is also acyclic and such a total order always exists. Now, every node of G_i corresponds to an interface function of some sub-block of M. The code of f_i then consists in calling these functions in the order specified above.

Interface functions generally need to communicate data to one another. This arises when an output y of a sub-block A of M is connected to an input x of another sub-block B, and the interface functions producing y and consuming x belong to different clusters. If f and g are two such functions, then a persistent variable z is created, to store the value of y. z is persistent in the sense that it maintains its value across calls to f and g. It can be implemented, for instance, as a private variable in the class generated for M.[6] Whenever f is called, it writes to z and whenever g is called, it can read from z.

Following the above principles, we can generate code for all interface functions without conditionals given in our examples so far. For the additional example of block M of Fig. 9, the implementation of the interface functions is shown below:

```
M.get( ) returns out {           M.step( in ) {
    return A.step( U.get() );         U.step( C.step(in) );
}                                }
```

Slight complications arise in two cases: first, in the case of overlapping clusters; second, in the case of diagrams with triggers. Both cases require code with conditionals.

In the case of overlapping clusters, the objective is to generate code that ensures that, despite overlapping, every interface function of every sub-block of M is called only once at every synchronous round. Notice that calling an interface function more than once is generally *incorrect*, since the function may modify some state variables. Even when a function does not update state variables, calling it more than once in a round is wasteful, thus we want to avoid it.

To do this, we use a counting scheme that keeps track of how many times a function has been called so far in the synchronous round. In particular, for each interface function f of a sub-block of M, let N_f be the number of clusters that f is included in. If $N_f > 1$ (i.e., f is shared among multiple clusters) then we create a modulo-N_f counter for f, denoted c_f: the counter is initialized to 0 and "wraps" again to 0 when its value reaches N_f. Each such counter is part of the persistent internal variables of the class of M. Counter c_f indicates whether f has already been called in the current round: *f has been called iff $c_f > 0$*. Every

---
[6] If f and g belong to the same cluster, a local variable in the corresponding interface function of M can be used to store the value of y.

call to a function f that has $N_f > 1$ is guarded by the condition $c_f = 0$. The counter is incremented by 1, independently of whether the condition is true or false. An example of using this technique is the implementation of the profile shown in the middle of Fig. 8.

We now turn to the case of diagrams with triggers. First, we identify all sub-blocks of M that are triggered. To do this, we use the internal diagram of M.[7] Let A be a triggered sub-block of M. For every output port y of A, a persistent variable z_y is generated in the profile implementation of M. This variable is initialized to the trigger-initial value for y specified in the diagram. It is updated every time A is triggered, and maintains its previous value in other rounds. Let f be an interface function of A. Let t be the signal that triggers A: t is either an input of M, or is produced by some other sub-block of M.[8] When generating code for M, every call to f is embedded in a conditional, guarded by t: if t is true then f is called, otherwise it is not.

For example, consider macro block T of Fig. 3 and suppose its SDG is clustered in two clusters, as shown in Fig. 10. The synthesized profile for T is then as shown to the right of Fig. 10 and the implementation of the two interface functions is as follows:

```
T.get1( x1 ) returns y1 {        T.get2( x2 ) returns y2 {
   z1 := A.step(x1);                local tmp := B.step(x2);
   return z1;                       if (z1) {
}                                       z2 := C.step(tmp);
                                     }
                                     return D.step(z2);
                                 }
```

Persistent variables $z1$ and $z2$ have been added for communication between the two interface functions and for the output of triggered sub-block C, respectively. Note that, even when $z1$ is false, $z2$ has a well-defined value because it is initialized to the trigger-initial value specified for C.

6   Conclusions and Perspectives

We have proposed non-monolithic profiles as an abstract, compositional and executable representation of hierarchical synchronous block diagrams. Our work offers the unified treatment of the problem of modular code generation from synchronous models which has been lacking so far. A prototype implementation of our methods exists and experimental results reported in [30] encourage us to believe that the approach is also feasible and relevant in practice.

A number of issues remain open. Clustering is of course a topic in itself, as mentioned above. Apart from devising new or evaluating new and existing

---

[7] Note that information about triggers is lost in the SDG of M: indeed, in the SDG, dependencies arising due to triggers and those arising due to port connections are indistinguishable.

[8] t cannot be produced by A, as this would result in a cycle in the SDG of M.

clustering algorithms, another aspect of particular interest is integrating user controls in the algorithms. For example, the user could specify which input-output dependencies can be relaxed, i.e., which false input-output dependencies can be admitted in order to obtain better clusterings.

Enriching profiles with additional information is another interesting direction. It has been partly explored in [31] in the case of *timed* diagrams, a subclass of triggered diagrams where triggers are known at compile time (e.g., they are periodic). In that paper, it is shown how profiles can be enriched with finite-state automata representing the set of rounds when a given block is triggered. This allows to avoid redundant function calls in the generated code, and also to identify false IO dependencies during profile synthesis.

References

1. de Alfaro, L., Henzinger, T.: Interface automata. In: Foundations of Software Engineering (FSE). ACM Press (2001)
2. Alur, R., Henzinger, T.: Reactive modules. Formal Methods Syst. Des. **15**, 7–48 (1999)
3. Benveniste, A., Caspi, P., Edwards, S., Halbwachs, N., Le Guernic, P., de Simone, R.: The synchronous languages 12 years later. Proc. IEEE **91**(1), 64–83 (2003)
4. Benveniste, A., Le Guernic, P., Aubry, P.: Compositionality in dataflow synchronous languages: specification & code generation. Technical report 3310, Irisa - Inria (1997)
5. Berry, G.: The Constructive Semantics of Pure Esterel (1999). http://www-sop. inria.fr/members/Gerard.Berry/Papers/EsterelConstructiveBook.pdf
6. Berry, G., Gonthier, G.: The Esterel synchronous programming language: design, semantics, implementation. Sci. Comput. Program. **19**(2), 87–152 (1992)
7. Blochwitz, T., Otter, M., et al.: The functional mockup interface for tool independent exchange of simulation models. In: Proceedings of the 8th International Modelica Conference. Linkoping University Electronic Press (2011). http://www. ep.liu.se/ecp/063/013/ecp11063013.pdf
8. Blochwitz, T., Otter, M., et al.: Functional mock-up interface 2.0: the standard for tool independent exchange of simulation models. In: Proceedings of the 9th International Modelica Conference. Linkoping University Electronic Press (2012). http://www.ep.liu.se/ecp/076/017/ecp12076017.pdf
9. Bogomolov, S., Greitschus, M., Jensen, P.G., Larsen, K.G., Mikucionis, M., Strump, T., Tripakis, S.: Co-simulation of hybrid systems with SpaceEx and Uppaal. In: Proceedings of the 11th International Modelica Conference. Linkoping University Electronic Press (2015). http://www.ep.liu.se/ecp_article/index.en. aspx?issue=118;article=017
10. Brandt, J., Schneider, K.: Separate compilation for synchronous programs. In: SCOPES 2009: 12th International Workshop on Software and Compilers for Embedded Systems, pp. 1–10 (2009)
11. Broman, D., Brooks, C., Greenberg, L., Lee, E.A., Tripakis, S., Wetter, M., Masin, M.: Determinate composition of FMUs for co-simulation. In: Proceedings of the 13th ACM and IEEE International Conference on Embedded Software (EMSOFT 2013), pp. 2:1–2:12. IEEE (2013)
12. Broman, D., Greenberg, L., Lee, E.A., Masin, M., Tripakis, S., Wetter, M.: Requirements for hybrid cosimulation standards. In: Hybrid Systems: Computation and Control (HSCC 2015) (2015)

13. Caspi, P.: Clocks in dataflow languages. Theor. Comput. Sci. **94**, 125–140 (1992)
14. Caspi, P., Pilaud, D., Halbwachs, N., Plaice, J.: LUSTRE: a declarative language for programming synchronous systems. In: 14th ACM Symposium POPL. ACM (1987)
15. Caspi, P., Raymond, P., Tripakis, S.: Synchronous programming. In: Lee, I., Leung, J., Son, S. (eds.) Handbook of Real-Time and Embedded Systems, pp. 14-1–14-21. Chapman & Hall, London (2007)
16. Cremona, F., Lohstroh, M., Broman, D., Natale, M.D., Lee, E.A., Tripakis, S.: Step revision in hybrid co-simulation with FMI. In: 14th ACM-IEEE International Conference on Formal Methods and Models for System Design (MEMOCODE) (2016)
17. Cremona, F., Lohstroh, M., Tripakis, S., Brooks, C., Lee, E.: FIDE - an FMI integrated development environment. In: 31st ACM/SIGAPP Symposium on Applied Computing, Embedded Systems Track (SAC), pp. 1759–1766. ACM (2016)
18. Dragomir, I., Preoteasa, V., Tripakis, S.: Compositional semantics and analysis of hierarchical block diagrams. In: Bošnački, D., Wijs, A. (eds.) SPIN 2016. LNCS, vol. 9641, pp. 38–56. Springer, Cham (2016). https://doi.org/10.1007/978-3-319-32582-8_3
19. Edwards, S., Lee, E.: The semantics and execution of a synchronous block-diagram language. Sci. Comput. Program. **48**, 21–42 (2003)
20. Gamatié, A.: Designing Embedded Systems with the SIGNAL Programming Language. Springer, New York (2009). https://doi.org/10.1007/978-1-4419-0941-1
21. Gautier, T., Le Guernic, P.: Code generation in the SACRES project. In: Redmill, F., Anderson, T. (eds.) SSS 1999, pp. 127–149. Springer, London (1999). https://doi.org/10.1007/978-1-4471-0823-8_9
22. Geilen, M., Tripakis, S., Wiggers, M.: The earlier the better: a theory of timed actor interfaces. In: 14th International Conference Hybrid Systems: Computation and Control (HSCC 2011). ACM (2011)
23. Girault, A.: A survey of automatic distribution method for synchronous programs. In: International Workshop on Synchronous Languages, Applications and Programs, SLAP 2005. ENTCS, Elsevier, Edinburgh, April 2005. ftp://ftp.inrialpes.fr/pub/bip/pub/girault/Publications/Slap05/main.pdf
24. Hainque, O., Pautet, L., Le Biannic, Y., Nassor, É.: Cronos: a separate compilation tool set for modular esterel applications. In: Wing, J.M., Woodcock, J., Davies, J. (eds.) FM 1999. LNCS, vol. 1709, pp. 1836–1853. Springer, Heidelberg (1999). https://doi.org/10.1007/3-540-48118-4_47
25. Henzinger, T., Sifakis, J.: The discipline of embedded systems design. IEEE Comput. **40**(10), 32–40 (2007)
26. Henzinger, T.A., Kirsch, C.M., Matic, S.: Composable code generation for distributed Giotto. In: Proceedings of the 2005 ACM SIGPLAN/SIGBED Conference on Languages, Compilers, and Tools for Embedded Systems, LCTES 2005, pp. 21–30. ACM, New York (2005). https://doi.org/10.1145/1065910.1065914
27. Le Guernic, P., Gautier, T., Borgne, M.L., Lemaire, C.: Programming real-time applications with signal. Proc. IEEE **79**(9), 1321–1336 (1991)
28. Lee, E., Messerschmitt, D.: Synchronous data flow. Proc. IEEE **75**(9), 1235–1245 (1987)
29. Lee, E., Zheng, H.: Leveraging synchronous language principles for heterogeneous modeling and design of embedded systems. In: EMSOFT 2007: Proceedings of 7th ACM and IEEE International Conference on Embedded software, pp. 114–123. ACM (2007)

30. Lublinerman, R., Szegedy, C., Tripakis, S.: Modular code generation from synchronous block diagrams - modularity vs. code size. In: 36th ACM SIGPLAN-SIGACT Symposium on Principles of Programming Languages (POPL 2009), pp. 78–89. ACM, January 2009

31. Lublinerman, R., Tripakis, S.: Modular code generation from triggered and timed block diagrams. In: 14th IEEE Real-Time and Embedded Technology and Applications Symposium (RTAS 2008), pp. 147–158. IEEE CS Press, April 2008

32. Lublinerman, R., Tripakis, S.: Modularity vs. reusability: code generation from synchronous block diagrams. In: Design, Automation, and Test in Europe (DATE 2008), pp. 1504–1509. ACM, March 2008

33. Malik, S.: Analysis of cyclic combinational circuits. IEEE Trans. Comput.-Aided Des. **13**(7), 950–956 (1994)

34. Potop-Butucaru, D., Edwards, S., Berry, G.: Compiling Esterel. Springer, New York (2007). https://doi.org/10.1007/978-0-387-70628-3

35. Pouzet, M., Raymond, P.: Modular static scheduling of synchronous data-flow networks: an efficient symbolic representation. In: ACM International Conference on Embedded Software (EMSOFT 2009), pp. 215–224, October 2009

36. Preoteasa, V., Dragomir, I., Tripakis, S.: The refinement calculus of reactive systems. CoRR abs/1710.03979 (2017)

37. Preoteasa, V., Tripakis, S.: Refinement calculus of reactive systems. In: Proceedings of the 14th ACM and IEEE International Conference on Embedded Software (EMSOFT 2014), pp. 2:1–2:10. ACM, October 2014

38. Raymond, P.: Compilation séparée de programmes Lustre. Master's thesis, IMAG (1988). (in French)

39. Schneider, K., Brandt, J., Vecchié, E.: Modular compilation of synchronous programs. In: Kleinjohann, B., Kleinjohann, L., Machado, R.J., Pereira, C.E., Thiagarajan, P.S. (eds.) DIPES 2006. IIFIP, vol. 225, pp. 75–84. Springer, Boston (2006). https://doi.org/10.1007/978-0-387-39362-9_9

40. Shin, I., Lee, I.: Compositional real-time scheduling framework with periodic model. ACM Trans. Embed. Comput. Syst. **7**, 30:1–30:39 (2008). https://doi.org/10.1145/1347375.1347383

41. Strom, R.E., Yemini, S.: Typestate: a programming language concept for enhancing software reliability. IEEE Trans. Softw. Eng. **12**(1), 157–171 (1986)

42. Tripakis, S., Bui, D., Geilen, M., Rodiers, B., Lee, E.A.: Compositionality in synchronous data flow: modular code generation from hierarchical SDF graphs. ACM Trans. Embed. Comput. Syst. (TECS) **12**(3), 83:1–83:26 (2013)

43. Tripakis, S.: Bridging the semantic gap between heterogeneous modeling formalisms and FMI. In: International Conference on Embedded Computer Systems: Architectures, Modeling and Simulation - SAMOS XV (2015)

44. Tripakis, S.: Compositionality in the science of system design. Proc. IEEE **104**(5), 960–972 (2016)

45. Tripakis, S., Lickly, B., Henzinger, T.A., Lee, E.A.: A theory of synchronous relational interfaces. ACM Trans. Program. Lang. Syst. (TOPLAS) **33**(4), 14 (2011)

46. Tripakis, S., Stergiou, C., Shaver, C., Lee, E.A.: A modular formal semantics for Ptolemy. Math. Struct. Comput. Sci. **23**, 834–881 (2013)

47. Zeng, J., Edwards, S.A.: Separate compilation for synchronous modules. In: Yang, L.T., et al. (eds.) ICESS 2005. LNCS, vol. 3820, pp. 129–140. Springer, Heidelberg (2005). https://doi.org/10.1007/11599555_15

48. Zhou, Y., Lee, E.: Causality interfaces for actor networks. ACM Trans. Embed. Comput. Syst. **7**(3), 1–35 (2008)

Complexity Challenges in Development of Cyber-Physical Systems

Martin Törngren[(⊠)] and Ulf Sellgren

KTH Royal Institute of Technology, 100 44 Stockholm, Sweden
martin@md.kth.se, ulfse@kth.se

Abstract. In embarking towards Cyber-Physical Systems (CPS) with unprecedented capabilities it becomes essential to improve our understanding of CPS complexity and how we can deal with it. We investigate facets of CPS complexity and the limitations of Collaborating Information Processing Systems (CIPS) in dealing with those facets. By CIPS we refer to teams of humans and computer-aided engineering systems that are used to develop CPS. Furthermore, we specifically analyze characteristic differences among software and physical parts within CPS. The analysis indicates that it will no longer be possible to rely only on architectures and skilled people, or process and model/tool centered approaches. The tight integration of heterogeneous physical, cyber, CPS components, aspects and systems, results in a situation with interfaces and interrelations everywhere, each requiring explicit consideration. The role of model-based and computer aided engineering will become even more essential, and design methodologies will need to deeply consider interwoven systems and software aspects, including the hidden costs of software.

Keywords: Cyber-Physical Systems · Complex systems · Complexity
Complexity management · Systems engineering · Software engineering

1 Introduction

The concept of Cyber-Physical Systems (CPS) was introduced 2006 in the US to represent the *Integration of computation, networking and physical processes where CPS range from minuscule (pace makers) to large-scale (e.g. national power-grid)*, (Cyphers 2013). Many definitions have followed, often emphasizing the large scale nature and CPS as *networks of physical and computational components*, (NIST 2017). The mainstream interpretation of the term "cyber" refers to the use of computers or computer networks, see e.g. (M-W 2017). However, the term actually originates from Norbert Wiener who coined cybernetics from the Greek "kybernetike", meaning "governance", referring to feedback systems. Today, both interpretations are relevant for CPS.

A key aspect of CPS is the potential for integrating information technologies, operational technologies in terms of embedded systems and control systems, and physical systems, to form new or improved functionalities. Common trends for CPS also include increasing levels of automation and integration across the design-operation

© Springer International Publishing AG, part of Springer Nature 2018
M. Lohstroh et al. (Eds.): Lee Festschrift, LNCS 10760, pp. 478–503, 2018.
https://doi.org/10.1007/978-3-319-95246-8_27

time continuum, so called DevOps. This positioning of CPS provides unprecedented opportunities for innovation, within and across existing domains. However, at the same time it is commonly understood that we are already stretching the limits with existing systems in terms of development of cost-efficient and trustworthy systems. Consider, for example, the roadmaps surveyed by the project Platforms4CPS (2017) and thrusts towards new systems and software engineering methods to deal with future CPS, (Jacobson and Lawson 2015). National Academies (2016) states the following: "*today's practice of CPS system design and implementation is often ad hoc, ... and unable to support the level of complexity, scalability, security, safety, interoperability, and flexible design and operation that will be required to meet future needs*".

Since future CPS are likely to be unprecedented in their complexity, it becomes essential to understand what characterizes such systems and how we can best deal with them. The line of argument of this paper is to investigate the nature of complexity of CPS through the following perspectives:

- Cyber-Physical Systems and environment, i.e. including other systems with which the CPS interacts, as well as the organizations developing the CPS.
- Limitations of Collaborating Information Processing Systems (CIPS) in dealing with complexity in developing CPS. We use the term CIPS to refer to humans and Computer Aided Engineering (CAE) systems that develop CPS.
- What current methodologies have to offer and what is lacking.
- Proposing ways forward to meet identified limitations and gaps.

In our work, we draw upon state of the art, discussions with industrial experts and our own experiences. Complexity issues relating to CPS is a daunting topic. During our work, we synthesized a CPS complexity view that brings together the above listed perspectives. We present this view in Sect. 2, since the synthesis serves well to introduce the topic, the concepts and the structure of the paper. The state of the art is assessed in Sect. 3, and Sect. 4 analyzes, in more detail, some of the identified facets of CPS complexity. Finally, in Sect. 5, we discuss our findings and draw conclusions.

Of the many types of CPS, see e.g. (Schätz et al. 2015) and (CPS 2016), we focus mainly on mechatronics and robotics applications, i.e. where the physical systems are synergistic configurations of mechanical, electrical and electronics technologies. We include humans as an integral part of developing CPS but do not, in detail, treat the role of humans as part of an operational CPS.

2   A View of CPS Complexity and Contributions

Our overall approach and view on CPS complexity is illustrated in Fig. 1. CPS are designed and realized by Collaborative Information Processing Systems (CIPS) – i.e. by human developers supported by CAE systems and available information and knowledge. CPS operate within an environment[1] which may include other CPS, humans and other types of systems (nature made, social systems, etc., see Checkland 2000)[2].

In our view, we associate various characteristics – or *complexity facets* - with systems. As illustrated in Fig. 1, "system" may refer to a CPS itself, to the corresponding CIPS, as well as to the environment. The complexity facets have *consequences* (see bottom middle box in Fig. 1) for the abilities of humans and projects to deal with the CPS; that is to say, the facets will closely relate to the limitations of CIPS. To deal with these consequences, we thus need to provide adequate methods, theory and tools that address CPS complexity, aiming to bridge the gap with respect to limitations of CIPS; we refer to these as *bridging measures* (see middle box in Fig. 1).

Accordingly, a first contribution of the paper is to structure the various state of the art perspectives. A second contribution concerns a more detailed analysis of (i) relationships between various parts and aspects of a CPS and with its environment, and (ii) characteristic differences among software and physical systems in order to better understand barriers to their integration and some of the origins of complexity. As a final contribution, we identify key bridging measures. The paper structure as outlined in Sect. 1 relates closely to Fig. 1, with corresponding sections indicated.

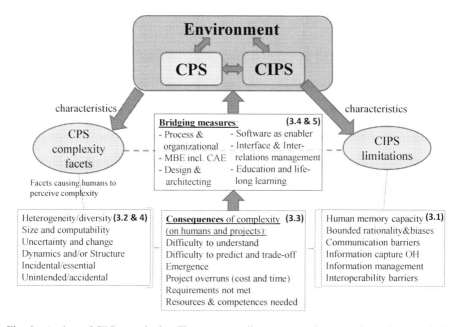

Fig. 1. A view of CPS complexity. The corresponding paper sections are shown in parenthesis.

---

[1] Other terms for "environment" include, for example, "wider system of interest", see e.g. Lawson (2015), or domain specific terms such as operational design domain, J3016 (2016).

[2] The context further includes other organizations and stakeholders, e.g. related to insurances, certification, legislation and standards; this context is only indirectly considered in the paper.

3   Engineering Practices Related to CPS Complexity

Related to Fig. 1, we provide perspectives from state of the art including CIPS limitations (Sect. 3.1), engineering views on complexity (Sect. 3.2), consequences of complexity (Sect. 3.3) and finally CPS engineering approaches to deal with complexity (Sect. 3.4).

3.1   CIPS Limitations in Dealing with Complexity

In this section, we study first humans and teams of humans, and then turn to CAE systems – all through the lens of limitations.

Limitations of CIPS Focusing on Humans: Examples of human limitations in dealing with information and (complex) systems can be found in studies in psychology and economy, see e.g. Simon (1996) and Kahneman (2012):

- *Capacity of the short term memory*; the short term memory is limited to holding and processing in the order of 7–10 "chunks" of information, where a chunk refers to one concept, which may be at different levels of abstraction and may refer to a more elaborate structure held in long term memory.
- *Capacity of the long term memory*; while having impressive storage capability with elaborate association mechanisms, the long term memory takes time to train and is not altogether reliable (see next point). As CPS requires deep knowledge in many areas, and as it takes substantial time for a person to become a deep domain expert, it follows that CPS development will have to involve many people. From our experience we note that it is very rare for a single person to be skilled in physics, logic and spatial concepts, all of which required for a holistic understanding of a CPS.
- *Bounded rationality and biases*; we humans are not as rational as we commonly think. There is, for example, a difference in what we experience and what we remember. Our brains, while mostly operating well, are prone to biases including overconfidence and a tendency to ignore or overemphasize the importance of small risks. Remembering is subject to neglect of duration and the "peak-end" rule, meaning that we give more weight to recent events. Furthermore, we are prone to search for, and to remember, pieces of information that confirm our current belief, which has a significant filtering and thus biasing effect.
- *Span of attention of the "slow" system*; the activation of what Kahneman refers to as the "slow system" of the brain, corresponds to what we could consider as "active thinking efforts". There is a resistance in activating the slow system since it requires considerable energy. Activating the slow system is beneficial when humans have to deal with novel considerations beyond their previous experience, where the "fast system" may not be able to come up with reasonable answers.

Organizations can overcome many of the limitations of a single brain by imposing processes involving, for example, reviews, checklists, detailed system analysis, and by supporting appropriate organizational cultures in the line of continuous improvement and constant quality control, (Kahneman 2012). These measures are closely in line with the best practices of systems engineering (INCOSE 2015).

However, additional challenges arise when dealing with advanced CPS, either in the form of very complex machines, such as a modern car, or in terms of a dynamically forming system of systems (SoS), for example in terms of a swarm of drones that together with infrastructure and other machines perform collaborative tasks.

A key aspect of these challenges refers to how to appropriately arrange communication among people, teams, organizations and CAE-systems, and how to organize them as well as the associated information. The design of an advanced CPS such as an aircraft or a car will require the collaboration of thousands of engineers. Communication among engineers in such settings is often seen as the key system development challenge, see e.g. (Andersson 2017). Organizing development will have to take into account the multitude of aspects and engineering phases of a CPS, while still facilitating proper interactions. Disciplinary experts are moreover schooled into various communities, theories and traditions, which introduces gaps in understanding among the experts, see e.g. Horváth et al. (2017) and Törngren et al. (2014).

For Cyber-Physical Systems of Systems (CPSoS), the challenge further relates to defining goals, policies and mechanisms for interactions among constituent CPS. As a key characteristic, a CPSoS involves CPS developed by multiple organizations where there is no clear responsibility for systems integration, see e.g. CPSoS agenda (2015). The intentions of the interactions within a CPSoS may be incompletely defined, misunderstood or interpreted differently by the involved organizations and experts.

Limitations of CIPS Focusing on CAE Systems: We now turn to limitations of CAE systems as part of CIPS. These include the following:

- *Dealing with tacit and implicit information, including context and meaning of concepts.* CAE systems require explicit formalization of information to be able to reason about CPS. For this time and resources have to be spent - when systems evolve, the information/models also have to be updated and kept consistent In the absence of fully collaborative CAE tools, development engineers use a large number of social communications tools, such as email and messaging. At present, there are very limited possibilities with current CAE tools to record communication interactions and histories into the CAE applications and then associate decision histories (and decisions) with the current design model (s) (Red et al. 2013).
- *Challenges in formalizing, managing and evolving the huge amounts of information and relationships required for CPS engineering.* Information management becomes difficult when considering different versions of components and assumptions and decisions made in developing artefacts such as models. Extra information is required to describe this context, further growing the amount of information. This is a significant challenge in multi-user development, see e.g. Red et al. (2013).
- *Limitations in interoperability and exchange among existing CAE systems.* CAE systems already hold a lot of useful information and models, albeit fragmented into different aspects or parts of a CPS, e.g. into software, electronics, and mechanics. Improved support for interoperability and exchange across CAE systems has the potential to drastically improve CPS management. While there are promising standards available, such as STEP and linked data, overall these have limited adoption so far, see e.g. Törngren et al. (2014), and El-khoury et al. (2016).

For the CAE system, the amount of information is, in itself, not a problem, but that information has to be made explicit. To support humans in development this extends to knowledge management, requiring access to appropriate up-to-date meta-data, clarifying the limitations and validity of the information. Such support will also require efficient interoperability among systems.

3.2 Engineering Views on Facets of Complexity

There are many interpretations and studies of "complexity" encompassing technical systems and humans, extending all the way to socio-political systems. There are also many propositions for metrics, definitions and facets of complexity. However, few metrics appear to be adopted into actual engineering practice. Definitions tend to focus on certain facets (see e.g. Sheard 2015). Frequently discussed facets of complexity include:

- *heterogeneity* of parts and interactions: CPS are strongly characterized by heterogeneity in several dimensions, with artefacts all the way from requirements, functions and technology to stakeholders. CPS represent hybrid, distributed, closed-loop as well as real-time systems, thus requiring developers to deal with a multitude of properties, behaviors and performance targets, see e.g. Derler et al. (2012) and Horváth (2017). As a result of their heterogeneity, CPS will typically be represented using multiple interdependent views, captured with different formalisms and tools, see e.g. Törngren et al. (2014).
- *size and computability related*: Large scale CPS will involve many things in terms of e.g. number of units, connectors, logical interactions, lines-of-code, requirements and stakeholders. Size related facets can also be seen to encompass the amount of information needed to describe an object (Shannon and Weaver 1949), the amount of resources needed to manufacture a product, (Suh 1990), or the computational complexity. The latter refers to the number of operations for solving an algorithm and how they relate to the size of the problem. Several CPS related design topics, such as assignment in space and time, belong to the class of NP-complete problems for which no polynomial time algorithms are known, see e.g. Blondel and Tsitsiklis (2000),
- *uncertainty and change*: Uncertainty can be used to refer to all kinds of unknowns in the context of system development. Uncertainty relates to complexity and risk by increasing the design space and potential for wrong decisions, and by complicating change management, Axelsson (2011). Typical examples include changing and conflicting requirements, unknown properties of technologies and impacts of design decisions. It can also refer to uncertainty of environment perception of a CPS see e.g. ESD (2003) and Sheard (2015),
- *dynamics or structure*: These complexity facets refer to either aspects of behavior that are difficult to predict, e.g. due to highly non-linear and coupled dynamics, or structural aspects such as dependencies among parts and properties. CPS typically represent tightly integrated and coupled systems where the change of one parameter in the design is likely to influence many other parameters. The behaviors and structures may also change dynamically such as in self-learning systems and in CPSoS.

A CPS typically also requires consideration of dynamics and structure at multiple levels or scales, e.g. from unit and subsystem to system level, and with different time horizons, see e.g. Sheard (2015) and Horváth (2017). Parallelism in terms of concurrent cyber and physical parts, and resource sharing in the computer systems further contribute to complexity, see e.g. Derler et al. (2012).

- *incidental vs. essential*: This facet refers to whether complexity arises from a particular way in which a system is designed (for example, due to the use of legacy components), as opposed to being inherent in the problem to be solved, (Brooks 1987). A key example of incidental complexity is that of improper design, or improper design assumptions that leave certain aspects of CPS design undefined, implying that side-effects may occur and/or that behaviors will emerge from the implementation rather than being designed. Examples of this include the lack of time abstractions and practices of hardware design, implying that timing behavior will emerge, see e.g. Lee (2009),

- *unintended and accidental behavior*: These behaviors refer to (known) side-effects or design faults, Qian and Gero (1996). For physical systems, unintended behavior represents a side-effect that may require additional sub-functions for dealing with (e.g. reducing) the undesired side-effect. The side effects are often of the same order of magnitude as the intended behavior and are typically caused by component interactions through their interfaces, e.g., friction-induced thermal effects between surfaces in contact (Whitney 1996). An accidental behavior is an unintended behavior that is caused by an accidental relationship or interaction between product features (e.g., a cable placed too close to a hot engine block). An accidental behavior is likely caused by a design error, Qian and Gero (1996). For cybersystems, an example of a class of accidental behaviors is given by undesirable feature interactions not considered during design, see e.g. Broy (2010).

- *goals and socio-technical context*. This facet refers to the essential complexity of the goals in terms of their feasibility, see e.g. (Suh 1999; Maier 2007), and human/organizational aspects such as competition, conflicts, policies and management (Sheard 2015).

As noted by several authors, various facets of complexity can relate to different types of systems, including the CPS, the environment, and the organizations developing it (compare with Fig. 1), see e.g. Kaushik (2014) and Sheard (2015).

Some of the proposed facets can, at least in principle, be formulated in terms of absolute metrics (e.g. size related). Another type of metric is instead relative, for example in relation to what we try to accomplish or want to know, i.e. as a measure of the uncertainty of fulfilling the specified functional requirements (Suh 1999).

The evolution of CPS, towards more advanced functionality and operation in more open environments has implications for the complexity facets simply by providing "more of everything" including in terms of new or changed risks. As one key aspect, the increasing openness and large scale provide new attack surfaces that need attention to avoid increasing security risks. It will no longer be possible to a priori foresee all scenarios and what might go wrong so dynamic risk management may be necessary (see e.g. Boyes 2013). However, adding more protection mechanisms may further increase system complexity. Uncertainty needs to be considered, for example in sensing, see e.g. Sadigh and Kapoor 2016. While the introduction of AI in terms of machine learning into CPS provides new capabilities, it also increases complexity. The robustness aspects of machine learning systems are currently not well understood, with implications for robustness and safety, see, for example, Wagner and Koopman (2015).

The design space of CPS illustrates several of the complexity facets (including e.g. heterogeneity, size and computability, and uncertainty), with a potentially very large number of design choices and dependencies among desired properties related to design decisions, which, in turn, requires trade-offs to be made (see e.g. Maier and Rechtin 2002). In early development stages, designers have considerable freedom with respect to design decisions, but no full insight into the implications of those decisions. Later in the development process, when they have acquired more knowledge, by experimenting with various models and physical prototypes, they will have less degrees of freedom, because of the decisions made upstream in the process. This dilemma is sometimes referred to as "the cone of uncertainty", e.g. (McConnell 1997) as represented in the right portion of Fig. 2. The cone of uncertainty also emphasizes the view that complexity, as a measure of uncertainty (Suh 1999), is reduced as we learn when we proceed with the development.

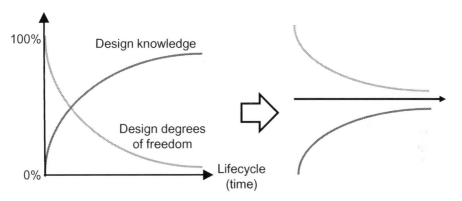

Fig. 2. The cone of uncertainty

We conclude that the interaction and co-existence of the cyber- and physical parts, as well as their development context, give rise to all of the described facets of complexity. This will be further highlighted in Sect. 4.

3.3 Consequences of Complexity

Complexity can be viewed in terms of what Sillitto (2009) referred to as "objective complexity", referring to technical or engineering characteristics, or in terms of "subjective complexity", relating to how humans perceive the systems, see e.g. Sheard (2015). An example of the former would be metrics of the inherent problem size and algorithmic complexity involved in optimizing a CPS. Perceived difficulty of understanding the behavior of a CPS would be an example of the latter. Sheard (2015) makes the interesting observation that while objective complexity is always growing (we build more and more sophisticated systems), the subjective complexity may, in fact, reduce over time once new systems become accepted and better understood.

As depicted in Fig. 1, in this paper we take the approach to try to make these ends meet by contrasting limitations of CIPS (including humans) with various characterizations – facets - of complexity. We believe this is one fruitful way forward since the CIPS will have to deal with the CPS.

Recalling Sect. 3.1, it is not strange that even a moderate CPS poses challenges for humans, who may find even the single facets of CPS complexity difficult to deal with. Combining multiple facets of complexity implies that it becomes non-trivial to predict the behavior of the system, and to understand the impact when making changes in the system. This also implies that trade-offs become more challenging and potentially more subjective.

The concept of emergence is often used when discussing complexity; it is a term that has been given several interpretations. We here use the following one, closely related to the difficulty in predicting system behavior: "The whole is more than the sum of the parts, in the sense that given the properties of the parts and the laws of their interactions, it is not a trivial matter to infer the properties of the whole", (Simon 1996). Emergence stems from difficulties in understanding the effects of interactions among parts and can have positive or negative consequences (recall unintended and accidental behaviors, described in Sect. 3.2).

It is interesting to research the impact of complexity on projects. Sheard (2015) investigated how a number of complexity-related variables (or metrics) contributed to project cost overrun, project schedule delay, and system performance shortfalls. 39 variables in 75 development projects were investigated through a retrospective survey with senior system engineers and project managers. The following three complexity variables were found to correlate positively with problematic outcomes in all three aspects (cost, schedule and performance): (i) number of hard-to-meet, and frequently also conflicting, requirements, (ii) degree of cognitive fog[3], and (iii) stability of stakeholder relationships.

3.4   How is Complexity Dealt with in CPS Engineering

A multitude of approaches, methods and tools have been developed over the years to deal with CPS complexity. In this survey we focus on the following:

(i) *process*, (ii) *model-based and computer aided engineering*, (iii) *design and architecting*, and (iv) *people/organizational*. These approaches are complementary and partly overlapping. There is no silver bullet for dealing with complexity, as phrased by Brooks (1987). Many of them involve ways to divide and conquer a system (in terms of the CPS, the development teams, models etc.) into separate parts to facilitate their management. Despite the importance of so-called front-loaded development, where design decisions and means to improve the management of uncertainty and risk are key

---

[3] With (ii), the question posed was as follows: "The project frequently found itself in a fog of conflicting data and cognitive overload - Do you agree with this statement?".

elements, such practices are still often weak. Integration is generally identified as a (time and cost consuming) challenge, see e.g. INCOSE (2015). Simmons (2005) reports that only a very small amount of the total development efforts is spent on systems architecting, despite the crucial decisions taken in that phase.

Process Approaches: Systems engineering methodologies describe a number of recommended processes, from technical to management, see e.g. INCOSE (2015). Figure 3 illustrates an elaborated V-model for mechatronic systems – focusing on the technical process, where development is divided into stages and into engineering disciplines, VDI 2206 (2004). The decomposition approach is accompanied by providing guidance for risk management (project and product risk), and for step-wise integration of the decomposed entities. The conventional use of rapid prototyping, code generation and various X-in-the loop simulation schemes (e.g. software- and hardware-in the loop) provide examples of this. Software engineering methodologies emphasize agile approaches involving close collaboration within teams, frequent releases and close interactions with stakeholders, see e.g. INCOSE (2015), which helps to reduce development uncertainty and risk. We note that agility is one means to deal with uncertainty (one identified complexity facet) and risk. Nevertheless there are challenges in reconciling agile approaches with safety critical systems development, see e.g. Axelsson et al. (2015). Most disciplinary CPS development today involves frequent iterations and developments in smaller steps, whilst also requiring explicit considerations of the synchronization between software and hardware parts throughout the development and production phases, see e.g. Jacobson and Lawson (2015).

Model-Based and Computer Aided Engineering Approaches (MBE): With MBE we refer to approaches that make systematic use of abstractions and of computer engineering tools, i.e. including CAE, to deal with CPS complexity. Abstractions provide the means to focus work on particular aspects, while neglecting other aspects that have less influence on the issues at hand. To deal with the "Cone of uncertainty" (recall Fig. 2), models and their analysis e.g. through simulation offer ways to increase problem understanding, explore uncertainty and the solution space. Synthesis based on models help to improve efficiency of development by automating certain design steps, thereby removing certain sources of faults, see e.g. Törngren et al. (2008).

Many CPS constitute closed loop systems, implying that MBE approaches are necessary for efficiency; for example, without a model of a controlled system, control development cannot start until the physical system is developed. The closed-loop aspect has also led to a widely accepted use of models in verification; the system behavior arises through the closed loop interactions between the cyber and physical parts. A further key aspect of MBE is that of model verification and validation, ensuring that models are as simple as possible yet adequate for the intended purpose.

The success and increasing use of models has led to a need to emphasize their composition and management. Models become systems in their own right, with assumptions, interfaces, versions and variants relying on modeling environments. Model management is a research area with a surprisingly large number of still open challenges. Efforts in this area stem from a variety of directions including product-life cycle management (mechanical engineering) and application life-cycle management (software engineering), see e.g. Törngren et al. (2008), towards CPS life-cycle management. Correct composition and usage of different types of models can be supported by the use of contracts and explicit dependency models, (see e.g. Westman 2016; Qamar 2013) and references therein, and through uncertainty management, (see e.g. Mohan et al. 2017). Correct composition of simulation models reflecting different types of behaviors and concurrency is essential for CPS (see e.g. Derler et al. 2012). Divide and conquer approaches are also applied to models, through multi-view models and multi-view frameworks. An example of this the CPS architectural framework initiated by NIST, which provides common viewpoints such as functions and interfaces, as well CPS specific aspects such as trustworthiness and timing (NIST 2017).

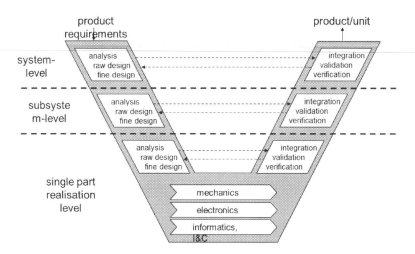

Fig. 3. Design methodology for mechatronic systems development, VDI 2206 (2004).

Design and Architecting Approaches: In this category we include principles, methods, and techniques that aim to reduce the incidental complexity or better manage the inherent complexity of a CPS. Examples of such approaches include (i) the use of deterministic execution platforms to reduce side-effects, facilitating understanding, integration and verification, (Kopetz 2011), and (ii) modularization techniques that use metrics for establishing "low coupling" and well defined interactions at interfaces between modules, see e.g. Börjesson (2014). Lee (2016) recommends the use of deterministic design models as far as possible, since it facilitates the design of complex systems by enabling definitive analysis. It should be noted that deterministic models can efficiently be utilized in probabilistic analyses, e.g. based on Monte-Carlo simulations, to provide knowledge on the effects from known or speculated variations in CPS design, environment and/or operation. An important and complementary approach to reduce incidental complexity is, of course, to reduce some of the essential complexity if that is possible, by relaxing some of the requirements of a system.

Because of the large number of involved stakeholders (including multiple organizations) it is important to realize that it will rarely be possible to optimize a large scale

CPS. Rather it is important to try to find solutions which are satisfactory to the involved stakeholders, (Simon 1996) and (Kahneman 2012).

People and Organizational Approaches: Skills of people and organizational designs are clearly imperative in dealing with CPS complexity. Organizational integration mechanisms including organizational structure, work procedures, training, social systems, and CAE have been shown to be important for improving organizational performance, (Adamsson 2007). Coordination among CAE systems is consequently also essential. Referring to Fig. 3, an organizational structure - such as dividing into mechanical, electronics, software, etc. - will also often imply a division of information and CAE systems along the same structure, leading to potential problems in managing interactions among teams as well as between CAE systems, see e.g. Malvius (2009).

One further important aspect of organizational design is that of "intelligent information filtering", providing people with adequate information that suits their purposes as part of the development whilst avoiding information overflow, (Simon 1996).

4 Analysis of CPS Complexity Facets

In this section we further investigate specific CPS facets of complexity that, to our understanding, are important, but have not received the attention they deserve. These facets include interrelations related to CPS (Sect. 4.1) and characteristic differences among software and physical systems (Sect. 4.2).

4.1 CPS Component Interrelations and Their Implications

We first turn to a CPS component perspective to analyze interrelations. A first relevant question to ask is: what constitutes a CPS component? CPS exist in the small and in the large. Compare, for example, a modern milling machine within a production cell with a manufacturing system that incorporates multiple production cells and their coordination, forming a distributed computer control system. In a CPS that involves humans, e.g. as operators, humans also become "components" within the CPS. The assignment and division of responsibilities among humans and other components is important (although out of the scope of this paper).

Figure 4 illustrates two CPS components of a mechatronics machine: the components are interconnected physically (illustrated in the middle of the figure), and through a communication network (illustrated through the horizontal line labelled "Communication network", connecting the communication subsystem of each component). This illustration would be relevant for vehicles (e.g. cars and airplanes) and production machines, where each component (e.g. brake, engine, transmission, etc.) incorporates mechanical parts and computing. As apparent from Fig. 4, there will be many interactions between the various parts, including between the cyber and physical parts. The direct interfaces between the computer system and the mechanical parts, through sensors and actuators, are of course crucial. However, beyond this, the mechatronic components interact physically with each-other and with the mechanical frame on which they are mounted. The components further interact through information exchange and through the energy subsystem, and they will also have interactions with the environment, e.g. through heat, noise and electromagnetic radiation.

This increasing connectivity enables direct collaboration among machines with external resources such as edge or cloud computing resources. Considering a larger scale CPS, its subsystems and components may thus also include machine external computing and communication resources. We note that such computing and communication resources, while normally considered to be part of the cyber-side of a CPS, indeed also constitute cyber-physical systems in their own right, since they are composed of software, analog and digital electronics, power supplies, cooling and mechanical parts. Design of such CPS will necessarily have to consider and thoroughly manage interactions and integration among these cyber and physical parts.

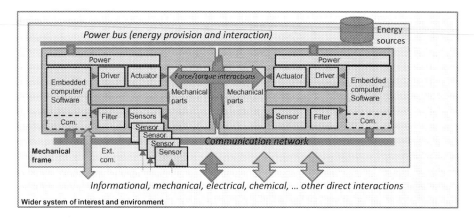

Fig. 4. Illustration of (two) mechatronic components and their various interactions with other components and the environment. Each component may have internal and external sensors. Note that "driver" refers to electronics for the actuators.

Now consider again mechatronic components and the example of interactions between the major components of a car. Figure 5 provides a Design Structure Matrix (DSM) representation of a pre-1970 car (left), vs. an early 21st century car (right).

	Susp	Brake	Steer	Wheel	Diff	Trans	Clutch	Eng	Driver
Susp			X						X
Brake			X						X
Steer			X						X
Wheel	X	X	X		X				
Diff			X			X			
Trans				X			X		
Clutch					X			X	X
Eng						X			
Driver	X	X	X				X		

	Susp	Brake	Steer	Wheel	Diff	Trans	Clutch	Eng	Driver
Susp		P	P	X+P	P	P	P	P	X+P
Brake	P		P	X+P	P	P	P	P	X+P
Steer	P	P		X+P	P	P	P	P	X+P
Wheel	X	X	X+P		X				
Diff	P	P	P	X+P		X+P	P	P	
Trans	P	P	P	P	X+P		X+P	P	P
Clutch	P	P	P			P		X+P	P
Eng	P	P	P	P	P	P	X+P		P
Driver	X+P	X+P	X+P			P	X+P	P	

Fig. 5. DSM representation of a pre-1970 (left) vs. a modern car (right), illustrated through two types of interactions between major car components: X – physical connection and force interaction; P – Programmable relations.

A component-DSM may be used to illustrate different relationships (such as energy, mass, information flow and spatial interactions) between components in a system, e.g. (Steward 1981; Eppinger and Browning 2012). In the left part of Fig. 5, this is illustrated with mainly mechanical interactions, without distinction of the type(s). We note that the DSM-model displays symmetry that is typical for a mechanical system with bidirectional Newtonian interactions. In a modern vehicle, all major components will also have integrated embedded systems, and there is thus an opportunity for information interaction and additional collaboration between components. As an example of this, consider the connections between the steering and the wheels of the car. Apart from a traditional mechanical connection, the steering of a modern car may today also be controlled by a "vehicle stability controller", able to apply individual wheel braking in order to deal with unintended car yaw. This explains the "X" connecting "Steer" with "Brake" in Fig. 5. The control system is able to act much faster than a human driver, and can thus avoid many accidents (subject to key constraints such as the condition of the tires and the road surface condition).

The DSM to the right in Fig. 5 illustrates the large potential in introducing novel functionalities to improve performance. These interactions also clearly illustrate the growing complexity, in terms of heterogeneous components and multiple interactions, with difficulty in predicting and verifying the final behavior. This setting also clearly leads to organizational challenges in setting up clear responsibilities to deal with the interactions/relationships among functions, components, properties, teams and activities. Considering versions of software and variants (e.g. in terms of features in a car due to customer choices or market requirements) further complicates the scene. The car example concerns a tightly coupled dynamical system that strongly incentivizes adding additional cyber-connections (thus increasing complexity). We believe that such interactions will similarly be driven also for less tightly coupled systems as cost-efficiency improves and opportunities for new services arise.

For large scale CPS, e.g. in terms of cloud connected and collaborating vehicles forming a CPSoS, we can clearly envision a DSM representation that expands with more components and interactions.

Beyond direct interactions as so far discussed - for example, between software components, and between sensors and the vehicle environment - a CPS will also importantly feature several types of indirect relations, see Fig. 6.

In particular, most components will be inter-related through assumptions made during design. For example, the software and the algorithms it embodies (e.g. for control and signal processing) are developed based on assumptions of the properties of the mechanical system. Similarly, the software components may incorporate assumptions about the electronics hardware, and the mechanical components may have assumptions w.r.t. the electronics hardware (e.g. size and weight). We note that the case of assumptions is generally valid for both cyber and physical parts, and that these assumptions create dependencies that need to be understood and managed.

To conclude this analysis, we would like to tie the discussion back to Fig. 1, which at the top illustrates relationships between the CPS, the environment and the CIPS. As stated by Simon (1996), a system will be "molded" by purposes related to its environment. In other words, it can be expected that a CPS will have an essential complexity that somehow corresponds to the complexity of the environment with which it interacts.

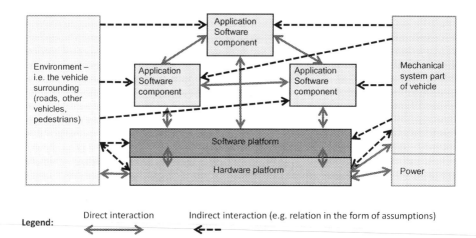

Legend: Direct interaction   Indirect interaction (e.g. relation in the form of assumptions)

Fig. 6. *Direct* and *indirect* relations among CPS parts. Direct information and force interactions take place between parts. Indirect interactions refer to assumptions made in designing a part (the direction of the arrow indicates for which part the assumptions were made).

Consider, for example, the design of a highly automated vehicle (our CPS of concern). To develop this CPS we have to consider its operational context in terms of a multitude of relevant driving scenarios including static and dynamic objects that we may encounter; this emphasizes a number of complexity facets such as heterogeneity, size, dynamics and uncertainty. The complexity of the environment and the required functionality thus requires a lot from the CPS, driving its complexity. Similarly, in designing an organization to develop CPS, the complexity of the CPS will require a lot from the CIPS, thus driving their complexity. The relationships as shown in Fig. 1 are bidirectional in the sense that the systems (CPS, environment, CIPS) are influencing each other.

Finally, for organizations to be effective, investigations have indicated that the DSM product structure should be closely mirrored by corresponding organizational DSMs (i.e. relationships among teams) and processes (relationships among activities/steps)[4], Eppinger and Salminen (2001). In times of technology change it becomes especially important to keep these various "architectures" in sync. CPS embraces a paradigm shift with drastically new functionalities and components continuously being added to the technical architectures, which themselves must evolve. Thus the organizations and the processes need a corresponding evolution.

---

[4] Such DSMs are often referred to as team-based and activity-based, e.g. (Eppinger and Browning 2012).

4.2 Analysis of Distinguishing Characteristics: Physical vs. Software Systems

Dealing with the physical vs. cyber side represents specific challenges, since each side comes with very different traditions and expected properties, for example, from very fast turn-around, open and security aware systems to safety-critical real-time closed systems. We will here focus on software within the cyber-part, since we believe this pinpoints the essential differences. Table 1 summarizes distinguishing characteristics among physical and software systems, elaborated as follows.

Phenomena and Dependencies: A key concern of physical systems is their multitude of aspects encompassing structure, material properties and various types of dynamics in terms of e.g. stresses, heat, motion, vibrations and wear. As discussed in Sect. 3, side effects are often of the same order of magnitude as the intended behavior. Wear, tear and imperfect production imply that parameters will differ from nominal specifications (albeit within tolerances), i.e. they have distributions, and that they will change over time. The natural variation of the physical parameters, such as dimensions and material properties, make the behavior - and thus performance - probabilistic, requiring probabilistic analyses.

In contrast to physical systems, there is an apparent ease with which functions are realized in software systems. This ease relies upon abstraction hierarchies, a multitude of tools and existing software components that enable a direct path from software programs to their execution by microprocessors. Software is an abstraction notion that provides powerful and flexible constructs for describing information, logic and algorithms, without direct physical constraints. This enables us to build systems of unprecedented size, to the point where an incredible state-space complexity is created. This evolution has led to modern cars being fitted with tens of millions of lines of code and large parameter sets, see e.g. Broy et al. (2007).

Table 1. Contrasting characteristics of physical vs. software systems.

	Physical systems	Software
Phenomena & dependencies	Multiple coupled physical phenomena (materials, wear, fatigue, heat, ...) Local direct effect	State space size; bugs; connectivity; variability Local and global direct effects
Dev. Time & iterations	Long (manufacturing)/few iterations	Short/long; large amount of iterations
Abstractions, synthesis, and platforms	Approximations; continuous time and value; No single platform - multiple realization technologies; Behavioral model sim.; Geometry based synthesis (CAD/CAM/); Form as a component or structure property	Digital abstractions; discrete time and value/strong platform foundations; Property preserving model transformations (code synthesis)
Extra-functional (EF) properties including cost	Trade-offs among EF properties; Established cost models	Dependencies create additional relations between EF properties; Difficult to estimate life-cycle cost

A direct consequence of the abstract nature of software is that it only has design faults. Physical systems are, on the other hand, characterized by design faults, random hardware failures and wear-out faults, i.e. faults caused by frequent operations/usage. A consequence of the inherent complexity of software systems, in particular at large scale (see e.g. Brooks 1987), is that design faults are much more predominant in the cyber-side. 10 bugs per 1000 lines of code is commonly estimated for commercial software, with in the order of one bug per 1000 lines for safety critical code, McDermid and Kelly (2006)[5].

Further distinguishing characteristics w.r.t. phenomena and dependencies are that physical systems have strong interactions locally, with weaker remote effects (Simon 1996). These effects can, in many cases, be seen as piece-wise linear. In software and digital systems, potentially any bit-flip or bug may break the system. Cyber-systems are, in this sense, highly non-linear, (Henzinger and Sifakis 2006). Since software systems (executing on hardware) in principle can be provided with very high connectivity, any change or fault or just nominal communication has the potential to have a large impact globally, unless the design explicitly takes this into account. The resulting systems may then come to violate the natural "architecture of complexity" (Simon 1996). Such systems - without barriers, where everything is interrelated - are likely to be brittle and unmanageable.

Development Time and Iterations: In a CPS project of any size, there is a substantial difference in the number of iterations used and time duration for the development of the software, electronics vs. physical parts. As an example, the duration of a project designing a new industrial computer could be in the order of 1-1.5 years. During this period, 2-3 mechanical prototypes, 3 iterations of electronics, and 100 iterations of software might be provided. For mechanical products, design and manufacturing take a considerable amount of time and effort. For electronics, dealing with heat, isolation, ruggedness etc. requires extra consideration and time.

While software does not need the same type of production effort as physical systems, it nevertheless heavily relies on a host of previous developments – a "software infrastructure" - including tools, operating systems, middleware, libraries, and existing application components. This infrastructure is growing over time, and increasingly includes, for example, capabilities to upgrade software and to gather data from running systems. The time to develop software will therefore be strongly dependent on the availability of a proper software infrastructure. There is a tendency that too little emphasis is placed on the software platform (Ericson 2017). According to industrial developers, software development never ends, and is never ready when the product is delivered. The software complexity also gives rise to concerns for effective verification and validation.

Abstractions, Synthesis and Platforms: Digital hardware platforms enable abstractions (programs, code) to be converted into executable/interpretable code. This relies on abstractions of services at different levels, e.g. processor instruction sets and programming instructions to higher-level services that define the basis for even more services. These abstractions of services are often referred to as platforms for digital

---

[5] The number of bugs is only used here to illustrate the complexity; not all bugs are equally important.

systems. This notion is captured by so called Platform-based design (PBD), stemming from the field of Electronics Design Automation. Defining and constraining the set of platforms has the effect of reducing the design space, increasing reuse, and speeding up development, while allowing focus on application development and its mapping (and tailoring) of the platform, see e.g. Sangiovanni-Vincentelli (2002).

The powerful foundation of abstractions and digital platforms have proven very successful for general computing but become a problem for cyber-physical systems, since they do not cover physical effects such as timing and energy consumption, see e.g. Henzinger and Sifakis (2006), and Lee (2009).

For physical systems, we first note that the term platform is used differently, to refer to the "common necessary modules" of a product, Blackenfelt (2001). Compared to software, physical systems have no corresponding general realization platform. Instead, there are multiple candidate technologies, for example for actuation in terms of electrical, hydraulic, or combustion engine technologies. Functional and behavioral descriptions provide goals that will be approximated by the realization technology (good enough) but also leading to side effects as discussed previously.

A second somewhat subtle difference between software and physical systems refers to abstractions and their relationship to synthesis. For software systems, behavior abstractions are synthesized (refined) into executable code. Behavioral models are also common to support physical systems design and analysis, e.g. used for evaluation by simulation. However, synthesis in the form of manufacturing relies on geometry rather than behavior models. Synthesis is thus based on geometrical descriptions (CAD) that can be transferred to computer aided manufacturing systems. It is **not** a given that the geometrical representation adequately represents behavioral models. As an additional aspect of relevance, the geometrical form is an important attribute of physical systems (and thus of CPS). The form may correspond to a structural property or be realized through specific physical components. New manufacturing paradigms, such as additive manufacturing, expand design freedom by removing manufacturing constraints on shape, material combination and product structure imposed by traditional machining operations.

A third difference refers to the view on time and values, with continuous abstractions dominating at the macro-level in the physical world, and with discrete representations in the software (and digital world), leading to quantization and discretization concerns when integrated into CPS.

Extra-Functional (EF) Properties Including Cost: Many physical related EF properties, such as reliability and safety, only become concrete for software when considered in the context of processing hardware together with software. Alternatively properties such as reliability are considered as controversial when applied to software only. The nature of software leads to special considerations for flexibility-related EF properties such as upgradeability and maintainability.

A specific concern for software systems is that they will - for cost and interaction reasons - be sharing various resources such as computing and communication elements as well as data and algorithms. This has the implication that many extra-functional properties will be highly dependent on shared elements and design parameters (e.g. the speed of a network and policies of a server). Unless care is taken in design, the sharing may contribute to complexity by introducing design faults, such as undesirable feature interactions mentioned in Sect. 3.1.

Cost models appear to constitute an industrial challenge especially for software. While hardware costs are relatively well understood, software costs are more difficult to model and predict due to the described characteristics, e.g. accounting for the costs of the software platform, verification, and maintenance. A typical implication of this lack of awareness is that emphasis is often placed on reducing hardware costs, while software costs are disregarded. An example of this would be the introduction of two hardware platforms (of different costs), suited to different customer segments, even though this causes the software complexity (and therefore cost) to increase in order to deal with two variants. Another example relates back to resource sharing, where the drive to reduce hardware costs results in additional engineering effort to ensure that algorithms, computing platforms and available memory together meet the requirements e.g.in terms of accuracy, speed and predictability.

5   Discussion and Concluding Summary of Bridging Measures

5.1   Discussion

Reconsidering Fig. 1, the development of CPS has to consider its physical and cyber parts, the CIPS, and the environment. Facets of complexity appear in each of these "systems" and can moreover be considered for different aspects of these systems, including their behavior, structure, requirements, and relations among those and with external system aspects.

Figure 7 provides a corresponding elaboration of complexity facets applied to different types of systems and aspects of those systems. Fig 7 draws inspiration from Sheard (2015) in the distinction between the top and lower level. The complexity facets (right bottom box in Fig. 7) are the results of the analysis in this paper. The system aspects (left bottom box in Fig. 7) roughly correspond to key systems engineering development steps, see e.g. Oliver et al. (1996).

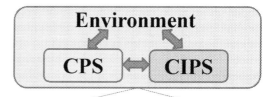

Fig. 7. Complexity facets applied to different types of systems and aspects of those systems.

Our review of the state of the art and our analysis reveals that all aspects of complexity discussed in this paper are relevant for developing future CPS. The analysis, however, reveals that the facets identified in Fig. 7 are of particular importance.

In particular, the tight integration of physical and software parts, and CPS components, results in a situation with interfaces and interrelations everywhere (compare with Figs. 4, 5 and 6). The properties of the complete product appear as a result of the component, software and physical system properties and their interactions. Intricate relationships between components will contribute to a number of properties such as functionality, performance, safety, security, flexibility and interoperability. Changes in some component properties or interrelations may affect multiple properties, in essence leading to tensions that will require these interrelations to be understood and that appropriate trade-offs are made. It thus becomes central to manage both explicit and implicit interrelations, including uncertainty in information. This is of relevance for all the types of systems depicted in Fig. 7, i.e. the CPS, the environment and CIPS.

Development of CPS, moreover, has to face the combined consideration of physical and software facets of complexity, including those described in Table 1. One important aspect of this is the need to enhance a mutual understanding across cyber- and physical (related) disciplines, posing an educational challenge.

The significantly increasing system complexity for CPS, compared to traditional systems, has the effect to increase the uncertainty that remains when a new system is launched to the market as well as the amount of information (models, data, etc.) required to describe the CPS. Recalling the "cone of uncertainty" in Fig. 2, this corresponds to a widening of the cone – see Fig. 8; the more complex a system is, the more uncertainties will remain even after the system has been deployed.

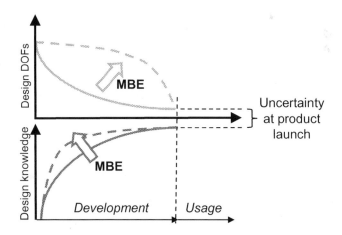

Fig. 8. MBE may enable early knowledge capture and deferred decisions

Such a situation may require development to be extended to the usage life-cycle phase, with diagnosis, condition monitoring and proper management of service and maintenance information to guide a process aimed at refining the CPS with continuous uncertainty reduction.

CPS development provides more options and thus more degrees of freedom (DOF's) in design compared to traditional systems, consequently requiring more knowledge to manage uncertainty and risks. The role of model-based engineering (MBE) is indicated in Fig. 8. MBE has a potential to create design knowledge at a significantly faster pace than design by physical prototyping, and also enables decisions to be delayed, i.e. keeping the design degrees of freedom for a longer time, see e.g. Sellgren 1999. There is consequently a very strong need to systematically implement methodologies that are model-based and where a reduction of the knowledge gap is driven by model-based analysis.

5.2   Bridging Measures Concluded

In the state of the art (Sect. 3.4), we described four approaches for dealing with CPS complexity. We believe that these approaches are very valid but will not be enough for future CPS. Trends towards connectivity, new services, automation, smartness, etc. imply that we are embarking towards both CPS and CPSoS of unprecedented complexity. Such systems will, in turn, be developed by large-scale CIPS. These trends unfortunately place further stress on the described limitations of CIPS. It thus becomes even more important to emphasize bridging measures.

The analysis indicates that it will no longer be possible to rely only on a subset of the approaches covered in Sect. 3.4. That is, approaches that we have encountered in industry for dealing with complexity, for example, placing specific emphasis on architectures and skilled people, or process and model/tool centered approaches, will most likely not suffice for the CPS of tomorrow. Instead, there will be a need for a broader set of tools – "bridging measures" to deal with future complexity. In the following we briefly summarize such bridging measures. These include the four approaches from Sect. 3.4, here grouped into three "reinforced" measures. To these we add measures to deal with software, including its hidden costs and as part of integrated design methodologies for CPS, interrelation management (drawing upon Sect. 4.1), and finally, education, ending up with the following six measures:

- *Processes and organizations for CPS.* Processes and organizations for CPS need to be able to explicitly address synchronization and integration among the diverse aspects and parts of a CPS, and consider integrated life-cycle engineering. The difference in speed of development of software and hardware needs explicit attention (synchronized processes, version and variant management, agile vs. safety practices), supported by architectures, and verification and validation methods. Key aspects for the successful development of CPS include insightful leadership and the use of integration mechanisms among teams for large scale CIPS.
- *MBE including CAE systems and frameworks for data management as design assistants.* Humans and organizations will need much better support for dealing with future CPS. Considering large scale CIPS (and CPS), means to support efficient and effective communication among people/teams will become even more important. Examples of areas with strong potential for dealing with the consequences of complexity (recall Fig. 1) include visualization, augmented/virtual reality, traceability and change management (e.g. managing interrelations), data

analytics, automation, and improved support for large-scale concurrent engineering. Advances in CAE capabilities with respect to semantic and contextual understanding and in dealing with large amounts of data will be necessary. Progress in AI is likely to provide entirely new capabilities to deal with many of those issues, including data analytics, model synthesis, and in providing decision support. Considering DevOps, CAE systems and underlying theories, concepts and strategies need to be developed for information and knowledge management that encompasses the entire life-cycle. A better understanding is also needed for how to balance static analysis, simulation, and physical tests, and how they can complement each-other.

- *Design and architecting.* New architectures and architectural representations are needed to support safety, security and availability, while managing evolution including software upgrades. Principles, interaction protocols, and architectures are also needed to support scalability, robustness and avoidance of side effects among interacting CPS parts of a CPSoS. Further, new methods and models are needed that explicitly manage relationships between extra-functional properties, incorporate uncertainty and concepts of dynamic risk management, attempting to mitigate risk even in the face of the unknown.

- *Software as enabler:* Software comes along with hidden costs and relies on extensive software assets that deserve attention because of their critical impact on end system properties. Better insights and cost models are needed to improve awareness. Software systems form an essential and growing part of CPS. Development methodologies need to incorporate core aspects of both systems and software engineering. The software communities need to embrace and explicitly consider the various direct and indirect physical effects of software.

- *Interfaces and interrelations management.* CPS will have interfaces and interrelations everywhere, across systems, components, data, models, tools and people. System level methodologies need to deal much more explicitly with these, including their design, analysis and management.

- *Education and life-long learning.* There is also an urgent need to address these new challenges with a reshaped undergraduate education, and to implement a system for continuous professional competence training. Foundations and the T-shaping of engineers are becoming more important. Engineers increasingly need to be able to work efficiently in teams and to obtain a broader understanding than what is provided by a traditional disciplinary education (e.g. in computer science or mechanical engineering). Establishing such a broader level of understanding corresponds to the horizontal upper part of the T, see e.g. Törngren et al. (2016). Considering the speed of technology evolution, there are also strong needs to develop and adopt approaches for life-long learning, see e.g. Törngren et al. (2015), i.e. to continuously deepen and broaden the domain expert knowledge.

We emphasize that these bridging measures need to be considered in conjunction. In this sense, individual bridging measures can be seen to provide specific viewpoints for CPS development.

Relating these measures to a number of roadmaps/agendas in the area, see e.g. Platforms4CPS (2017), we find that design and architecting and MBE receive a lot of attention, while the others sometimes are not covered or covered indirectly.

This work has been motivated by the increasing complexity of CPS, and also by the desire to bridge the gap between the cyber and physical dimensions. One direction of future work is to fully expand the role of humans as part of CPS. We hope that this review of various facets of complexity of CPS will contribute to invigorate a multi-disciplinary debate on how to deal with the CPS of tomorrow!

Acknowledgements. Feedback and insights from Erik Herzog (SAAB), Martin Nilsson (RISE) and Tor Ericson (ÅF) are greatly acknowledged. We also acknowledge valuable feedback from the anonymous reviewers. This work has been partially supported by the European Commission H2020 projects Platforms4CPS and CPSE-Labs.

References

Adamsson, N.: Interdisciplinary integration in complex product development: managerial implications of embedding software in manufactured goods. Ph.D. thesis, Department of Machine Design, KTH Royal Institute of Technology, Stockholm, Sweden (2007)

Andersson, H.: Henric Andersson, senior expert, SAAB. CPS summerschool lecture, Halmstad (2017).   https://www.youtube.com/playlist?list=PLRM7eLJHoNde-iM3ET-2-bHsh-KSAWLs3. Accessed Sept 2017

Axelsson, J.: On how to deal with uncertainty when architecting embedded software and systems. In: Crnkovic, I., Gruhn, V., Book, M. (eds.) ECSA 2011. LNCS, vol. 6903, pp. 199–202. Springer, Heidelberg (2011). https://doi.org/10.1007/978-3-642-23798-0_20

Axelsson, J., et al.: Notes on agile and safety-critical development. In: XP2015 ASCS Workshop (2015)

Blackenfelt, M.: Managing complexity by product modularization. Ph.D. thesis, Department of Machine Design, KTH Royal Institute of Technology, Stockholm, Sweden (2001)

Blondel, V.D., Tsitsiklis, J.N.: A survey of computational complexity results in systems and control. Automatica **36**(2000), 1249–1274 (2000)

Boyes, H.A.: Trustworthy cyber-physical systems—a review. In: 8th IET International System Safety Conference Incorporating the Cyber Security Conference (2013)

Brooks, F.P.: No silver bullet: essence and accidents of software engineering. Computer **20**(4), 10–19 (1987)

Broy, M.: Multifunctional software systems: structured modeling and specification of functional requirements. Sci. Comput. Program. **75**(12), 1193–1214 (2010)

Broy, M., et al.: Engineering automotive software. Proc. IEEE **95**(2), 356–373 (2007)

Börjesson, F.: Product platform design – architecting methods and tools. Ph.D. thesis, Department of Machine Design, KTH Royal Institute of Technology, Stockholm (2014)

Checkland, P.: Systems Thinking, Systems Practice. Wiley, New York (2000)

Cengarle, M.V., Bensalem, S., McDermid, J., Passerone, R., Sangiovanni-Vincentelli, A., Törngren, M.: CyPhERS: Characteristics, capabilities, potential applications of Cyber-Physical Systems: a preliminary analysis, Deliverable D2.1 of the CyPhERS FP7 project, November 2013. http://www.cyphers.eu/sites/default/files/D2.1.pdf. Accessed Sept 2017

Derler, P., et al.: Modeling cyber-physical systems. Proc. IEEE Spec. Issue CPS **100**(1), 13–28 (2012)

El-khoury, J., et al.: A model-driven engineering approach to software tool interoperability based on linked data. Int. J. Adv. Softw. **9**(3 & 4), 248–259 (2016)

Engell, S., et al.: CPSoS: D3.2 Policy Proposal "European Research Agenda for Cyber-Physical Systems of Systems and their engineering needs". Report D3.2 from the EU project CPSoS (Towards a European Roadmap on Research and Innovation in Engineering and Management of Cyber-Physical Systems of Systems) (2015)

Ericson: Personnel communication with Tor Ericson, senior manager at ÅF (2017)

Eppinger, S.D., Browning, T.R.: Design Structure Matrix Methods and Applications. MIT Press, London (2012)

Eppinger, S., Salminen, V.: Patterns of Product Development Interactions. Int. Conf. on Engineering Design, ICED 01, Glasgow, August 2001

ESD: ESD symposium committee overview: engineering systems research and practice. Engineering Systems Division MIT (2003). http://esd.mit.edu/ESD_Internal_Symposium_Docs/WPS/ESD-WP-2003-01.20ESD_InternalSymposium.pdf. Accessed Sept 2017

Henzinger, T.A., Sifakis, J.: The embedded systems design challenge. In: Misra, J., Nipkow, T., Sekerinski, E. (eds.) FM 2006. LNCS, vol. 4085, pp. 1–15. Springer, Heidelberg (2006). https://doi.org/10.1007/11813040_1

Horváth, I., et al.: Order beyond chaos: introducing the notion of generation to characterize the continuously evolving implementations of cyber-physical systems. In: Proceedings of the ASME 2017 International Design Engineering Technical Conferences & Computers and Information in Engineering Conference, Cleveland, Ohio, USA, August 2017

INCOSE: Systems Engineering Handbook: A Guide for System Life Cycle Processes and Activities, 4th edn. International Council of Systems Engineering. Wiley (2015)

Jacobson, I., Lawson, H.: Software and systems. In: Jacobson, I., Lawson, H. (eds.) Software Engineering in the Systems Context, Chap. 1. College publications (2015)

J3016: Taxonomy and Definitions for Terms Related to Driving Automation Systems for On-Road Motor Vehicles. SAE Surface Vehicle Recommended Practice, September 2016

Kahneman, D.: Thinking, Fast and Slow. Penguin Books Ltd. (2012). ISBN 9780141033570

Kopetz, H.: Real-Time Systems - Design Principles for Distributed Embedded Applications. Springer, Heidelberg (2011). https://doi.org/10.1007/978-1-4419-8237-7

Kaushik, S.: Structural complexity and its implications for design of cyber-physical systems. Ph. D. thesis. MIT Engineering Systems Division, September 2014

Lawson, H.: Attaining a systems perspective. In: Jacobson, I., Lawson, H. (eds.) Software Engineering in the Systems Context. College publications (2015)

Lee, E.A.: Computing needs time. Commun. ACM **52**(5), 70–79 (2009)

Lee, E.A.: Fundamental limits of cyber-physical systems modeling. ACM Trans. Cyber-Phy. Syst. **1**, 3:1–3:26 (2016). Article no. 3

Maier, M.: Dimensions of complexity other than "complexity". In: Symposium on Complex Systems Engineering. RAND Corporation, Santa Monica, CA, 11–12 January 2007

Maier, M., Rechtin, E.: The Art of Systems Architecting. CRC Press, Boca Raton (2002)

Malvius, D.: Integrated information management in complex product development. Ph.D. thesis, Department of Machine Design, KTH Royal Institute of Technology, Sweden (2009)

McConnell, S.: Software Project Survival Guide (Developer Best Practices). Microsoft Press, Redmond (1997)

McDermid, J., Kelly, T.: Software in safety critical systems: achievement and prediction. Nucl. Future **02**(03) (2006)

Mohan, N., et al.: ATRIUM - architecting under uncertainty: for ISO 26262 compliance. In: IEEE SysCon (2017)

National Academies: A 21st Century Cyber-Physical Systems Education. National Academies of Sciences, Engineering, and Medicine. National Academies Press (2016)

NIST (2017). https://www.nist.gov/el/cyber-physical-systems. Accessed Sept 2017

Oliver, D.W., et al.: Engineering Complex Systems with Models and Objects. McGraw-Hill, New York (1996)

Platforms4CPS (2017). (see Foundations of CPS – Related Work). https://platforum.proj.kth.se/tiki-index.php?page=HomePageExternal. Accessed Sept 2017

Qamar, A.: Model and dependency management in mechatronic design. Ph.D. thesis, KTH Royal Institute of Technology, Stockholm, Sweden (2013). ISBN 978-91-7501-664-1

Qian, L., Gero, J.S.: Function-behavior structure paths and their role in analogy-based design. Artif. Intell. Eng. Des. Anal. Manuf. **10**, 289–312 (1996)

Red, E., Jensen, G., Weerakoon, P., French, D., Benzley, S.: Architectural Limitations in Multi-User Computer-Engineering Applications. Center for e-Design Publications 7 (2013). http://lib.dr.iastate.edu/edesign_pubs/7. Accessed Sept 2017

Sadigh, D., Kapoor, A.: Safe control under uncertainty with probabilistic signal temporal logic. In: Proceedings of Robotics: Science and Systems (RSS), June 2016. https://doi.org/10.15607/RSS.2016.XII.017

Sangiovanni-Vincentelli, A.: Defining platform-based design. EEDesign of EETimes (2002)

Schätz, B., et al.: Research Agenda and Recommendations for Action, Deliverable of the CyPhERS FP7 Project, March 2015

Sellgren, U.: Simulation driven design – motives, means, and opportunities. Ph.D. thesis, Department of Machine Design, KTH, Stockholm, Sweden (1999)

Shannon, C.E., Weaver, W.: The Mathematical Theory of Communication. The University of Illinois Press, Urbana (1949)

Sheard, S.: Complexity, systems and software. In: Jacobson, I., Lawson, H. (eds.) Software Engineering in the Systems Context. College Publications (2015)

Simon, H.: The Sciences of the Artificial, 3rd edn. MIT Press, Cambridge (1996)

Simmons, W., et al.: Architecture generation for moon-mars exploration using an executable meta-language, vol. AIAA-2005-6726. American Institute of Aeronautics and Astronautics (2005)

Sillitto, H.G.: On systems architects and systems architecting: some thoughts. In: Proceedings INCOSE, Singapore (2009)

Song, H., et al.: CPS: Cyber-Physical Systems: Foundations, Principles and Applications. Elsevier, New York, September 2016. ISBN 9780128038017

Steward, D.V.: The design structure system: a method for managing the design of complex systems. IEEE Trans. Eng. Manag. **EM-28** (1981). https://doi.org/10.1109/tem.1981.6448589. Accessed Sept 2017

Suh, N.P.: The Principles of Design. Oxford University Press, New York (1990)

Suh, N.P.: A theory of complexity, periodicity and the design axioms. Res. Eng. Des. **11**(2), 116–132 (1999)

Thomas Telford Journals M-W (2017). Merriam-Webster: https://www.merriam-webster.com/dictionary/cyber. Accessed Sept 2017

Törngren, M., et al.: Model based development of automotive embedded systems. In: Navet, N., Simonot-Lion, F. (eds.) Automotive Embedded Systems Handbook. Taylor and Francis CRC Press Series. Industrial Information Tech (2008)

Törngren, M., et al.: Integrating viewpoints in the development of mechatronic products. J. Mechatron. **24**(7), 745–762 (2014)

Törngren, M., et al.: Education and training challenges in the era of Cyber-Physical Systems: beyond traditional engineering. In: Workshop on Embedded and Cyber-Physical Systems Education (WESE) at ESWEEK 2015, Amsterdam (2015)

Törngren, M., et al.: Strategies and considerations in shaping cyber-physical systems education. ACM SIGBED Rev. – Spec. Issue Embed. Cyber-Phys. Syst. Educ. **14**(1), 53–60 (2016)

VDI: Design methodology for mechatronic systems - VDI 2206. VDI Guidelines, Beuth Berlin (2004)

Wagner, M., Koopman, P.: A philosophy for developing trust in self-driving cars. In: Meyer, G., Beiker, S. (eds.) Road Vehicle Automation 2. LNM, pp. 163–171. Springer, Cham (2015). https://doi.org/10.1007/978-3-319-19078-5_14

Westman, J.: Specifying safety-critical heterogeneous systems using contracts theory. Ph.D. thesis, KTH Royal Institute of Technology (2016)

Whitney, D.E.: Why mechanical design cannot be like VLSI design. Res. Eng. Des. **8**, 125–128 (1996)

Augmenting State Models with Data Flow

Nis Wechselberg[(✉)], Alexander Schulz-Rosengarten, Steven Smyth,
and Reinhard von Hanxleden

Real-Time and Embedded Systems Group, Department of Computer Science,
Kiel University, Olshausenstr. 40, 24118 Kiel, Germany
{nbw,als,ssm,rvh}@informatik.uni-kiel.de

Abstract. Numerous modeling languages have adapted a graphical syntax that emphasizes control flow or state rather than data flow. We here refer to these as *state diagrams*, which include classic control flow diagrams as well as for example Statecharts. State diagrams are usually considered to be fairly easy to comprehend and to facilitate the understanding of the general system behavior. However, finding data dependencies between concurrent activities can be difficult as these dependencies must be deduced by matching textual variable references.

We here investigate how to extract data flow information from state diagrams and how to make that information more accessible to the modeler. A key enabler is automatic layout, which allows to automatically create dynamic, customized views from a given model. To set the stage, we propose a taxonomy of state and data-flow based modeling and viewing approaches. We then compare traditional, static view approaches with dynamic views. We present implementation results based on the open-source Ptolemy and KIELER frameworks and the Eclipse Layout Kernel.

1 Introduction

In model-driven engineering (MDE), instead of directly programming a certain behavior, the developer creates a model, specifying the behavior of the system in a more abstract form. The model is then usually used to generate specific code for the target system or to simulate the behavior beforehand. One feature often found in modeling languages is a graphical *diagram* of the model, be it as the primary input like in Scade[1], Simulink[2], LabView[3], or Ptolemy[4] [20] or generated from a textual model like in SCCharts[5] [12].

The graphical diagrams can be grouped in two major styles, *control flow diagrams*, which include *state diagrams*, and *data flow diagrams*. Both of these styles have their own benefits and drawbacks in practical application.

---

[1] http://www.esterel-technologies.com/products/scade-suite.
[2] https://de.mathworks.com/products/simulink.
[3] https://www.ni.com/labview.
[4] https://ptolemy.eecs.berkeley.edu/ptolemyII.
[5] https://rtsys.informatik.uni-kiel.de/kieler.

© Springer International Publishing AG, part of Springer Nature 2018
M. Lohstroh et al. (Eds.): Lee Festschrift, LNCS 10760, pp. 504–523, 2018.
https://doi.org/10.1007/978-3-319-95246-8_28

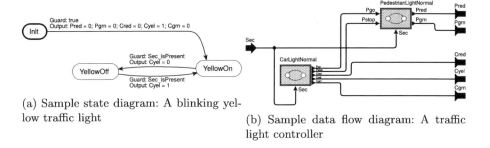

(a) Sample state diagram: A blinking yellow traffic light

(b) Sample data flow diagram: A traffic light controller

Fig. 1. State and data flow diagrams

State diagrams are usually composed of *states* and *transitions*. States are places the execution of the program rests in, while transitions control the change from one state to another. A basic example of a state diagram can be seen in Fig. 1a. The initial state Init is highlighted by a bold outline. The outgoing transition from Init is guarded by the trigger true, meaning it is always taken. As soon as the transition is taken the Output action comes into effect, in this case setting the Cyel output to 1 and other outputs to 0. The control flow then reaches the state YellowOn. From this point on, the control alternates between the states YellowOn and YellowOff each time the input Sec is present. Every time the state is changed, the output Cyel is turned to either 0 or 1.

Most languages expand this basic form of state diagrams by adding more features such as, for example, concurrent control flows or hierarchical composition of state diagrams. One benefit of state diagrams is that the model is usually close to the natural description of the behavior and to the developer's mental model. However, as noted before [2], some model aspects are rather difficult to infer from state diagrams. For example, if the model employs concurrency and shared data, the exact nature of data sharing is not graphically visualized, but requires the modeler to scan the textual transition labels and look for common variable names.

More insight in the usage of shared data is presented in data flow diagrams. The nodes in a data flow diagram represent *actors* that are all executed concurrently [17]. Two actors are connected if they share data. A simple example is shown in Fig. 1b. The input signal Sec is passed to the CarLightNormal and PedestrianLightNormal actors, which communicate through Pgo and Pstop and produce the outputs Pred, Pgrn and so forth.

Motivation. One way to overcome the shortcomings of a specific diagram style (state or data flow) is the combination of the different aspects. This approach is known as *multimodeling*. Here multiple different kinds of diagrams can be combined to form the complete model. This approach has been used in Ptolemy II [20] by embedding *modal models*, which contain some form of extended state machine, into normal data flow models and allowing *refinements* of states in state machines to contain data flow models. Multimodelling is now well understood from a semantic level. However, as we argue here, there is still room for improvement concerning the *pragmatics* of multimodelling [8], that is, how to support the user in applying multimodeling in a productive manner. Specifically, the traditional modeling approach of having the modeler produce the one and only static view of a model, which we here refer to as a *static view*, limits productivity and hampers human model analysis and understanding.

Contributions/Outline. We first propose a taxonomy of modeling and viewing alternatives, see Sect. 2. In Sect. 3, we survey traditional approaches based on static views in more detail. The main contribution follows in Sect. 4, where we present how to automatically derive hybrid state/data *dynamic views* from state models. We also investigate how dynamic views can help model analysis, in particular concerning schedulability and synthesizability. Related work is discussed in Sect. 5. We conclude in Sect. 6.

2 State and Data—A Taxonomy of Models and Views

In the domain of software engineering, the distinction of models, views and controllers is common place, not the least because of the MVC pattern [21], the perhaps most widely employed software design pattern [9]. However, in the MDE community this distinction seems less common, even though it can (and as we argue should) be employed there as well.

2.1 Models vs. Views

State and data diagrams adhere to some concrete, visual syntax, which, for example, entails that edges (representing for example state transitions) must have some source and sink nodes (representing a states). We say that such a diagram is a *view* of some underlying *model*, which comes with a certain semantics. The work flow of today's modeling tools typically prescribes that the model developer directly works on such graphical views, as shown in Fig. 1, using some WYSIWYG graphical editor. This is so common that modelers typically regard the view they draw as "the model," even though the modeling tool first has to translate that view into a model. However, as argued elsewhere, this unification of view and model has some drawbacks [8]. To just name a few, modelers often spend an inordinate amount of time with drawing activities [16]; comparison and version management of visual models is difficult; there is just one and only view for a model. In particular this last issue is central to the work presented in this paper, as we wish to argue that especially when working on applications that have both a state and a data aspect, one would like to have flexible, dynamic views available.

As a general remark, in our experience this unfortunate unification of models and views in MDE is mainly due to two factors: (1) the automatic synthesis of a view from a model requires automatic graph drawing capabilities, which most tools lack, (2) users want to keep control of the views and are skeptical that an automatic drawing algorithm can do a good job, just as the first high-level language compilers at the day were not necessarily welcomed by experienced assembler programmers. However, our experience also indicates that when (1) users get to work with a modeling tool that makes high-quality, state-of-the-art automatic graph drawing a priority, and (2) users employ automatic view synthesis from the beginning instead of first drawing model views manually, they do appreciate the ability of focusing on a model and getting automatically created, well-readable, customizable views for free. We thus in the following build on the premise that models and views can and should be treated separately.

In the remainder of this section we present an overview classification of different modeling and view options. The subsequent sections will explore these in more detail.

2.2   Modeling Options

We first consider the different options of what is modeled explicitly by a human developer. This is not always clear cut, but we identify broadly the following categories:

State Model (M1). This is the traditional state-based modeling approach, using implicit data flow through signal scopes and name matching. This modeling style is supported by various Statecharts tools.

Data-Flow Model (M2). This uses only data flow diagrams. This is typically used for models that do not really have a notion of state. This is provided, for example, by Simulink (without Stateflow).

Multimodel (M3). This uses state diagrams as well as data flow diagrams, explicitly modeled by the user. This is supported, e. g., by Ptolemy, SCADE, or Simulink with Stateflow.

Again, this classification concerns *what* is modeled, not *how* it is modeled. Concerning the latter, this could be either done the traditional way, using some WYSIWYG graphical editor, or it could also be done for example by providing a textual description of the model.

2.3   Viewing Options

As mentioned in the introduction, we distinguish between *static views*, which are directly created by a human modeler (with a varying degree of layout support from the modeling tool) and from which a model is derived, and *dynamic views*, which are synthesized automatically from a model. Orthogonal to the static/dynamic distinction, we here propose the following classification:

State View (V1). This is the traditional view for state-based modeling languages, showing only the state diagram without visual indication of shared data or data flow. Statechart tools traditionally offer static state views, an example is shown in Sect. 3.1.

Data-Flow View (V2). Analogously, this consists of data flow diagrams only, as in a typical Simulink diagram.

Multimodel View (V3). This shows data flow as well as state diagrams, using separate diagrams for each purpose. This is what is provided by Ptolemy (see Sect. 3.3), SCADE, or Simulink with Stateflow.

Hybrid View (V4). This uses a single diagram for data flow as well as state, combining the different layers of hierarchy. Static V4 is offered by SCADE (see Sect. 3.4), dynamic V4 is provided by the Ptolemy Browser (Sect. 4.1) and the KIELER SCCharts tool (Sect. 4.4).

Data Overlay View (V5). This is an enriched version of V1, with added indication for access to shared data. This is also offered by the KIELER SCCharts tool (Sect. 4.3).

Naturally, both V1 and V2 can be seen as special cases of V3, V4 and V5. Thus, tools that support V3–V5 also support V1 and V2.

3   Static Views

As explained before, the traditional modeling approach entails that the modeler creates one static view of the model. In this section we review the different options that have emerged so far, following the model/view taxonomy presented in Sect. 2. We also introduce a canonical example, a simple traffic light controller, that we will use throughout the paper.

3.1   State Modeling (M1) and Viewing (V1)

Figure 2 shows the traffic light controller modeled with a state diagram. The example has been presented in previous work on multimodeling [2] as a SyncCharts model [1] and has subsequently adapted to different modeling languages. The diagram in Fig. 2 is SCChart [12], which can be viewed as a conservative extension of SyncCharts, which in turn can be viewed as a synchronous version of Harel's Statecharts [13]. However, for the purpose of this paper, the specifics of SCCharts are not relevant. We can thus see SCCharts as a generic place holder for a state-oriented modeling language. Furthermore, the diagram in Fig. 2 happens to be automatically synthesized from a textual model that the modeler has written in the SCCharts Textual (SCT) language[6], and is thus is, technically, a dynamic view. However, the same type of diagram is also used for static, user-created diagrams in traditional Statechart tools, hence we show it in this section that focusses on existing modeling approaches.

The idea of the traffic light controller is that there is a street with a pedestrian crossing controlled by one traffic light each for the pedestrians and the cars (and any other street traffic). There are three lights for cars, Cgrn, Cyel and Cred, as well as two lights for the pedestrians, Pgrn and Pred. In normal operation, the traffic light should alternate between cars and pedestrians passing, with the green lights active for a few seconds in each cycle. In case of an error, the lights

---

[6] http://www.sccharts.com.

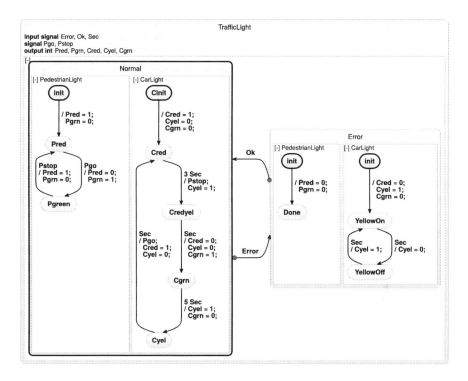

Fig. 2. Simple traffic light controller created as state model (M1), shown in state view (V1)

for pedestrians should be turned off completely and the cars should be alerted by a blinking yellow light.

The model has a main state TrafficLight which consists of two hierarchical states. The state on the left, Normal, manages the normal operation of the traffic light, while the state on the right is activated in the case of an error. The Normal state is marked as initial, shown by the thicker outline. There are signals, Error and Ok, generated by the environment, that guard the transitions between the two states. If Error is signaled, the normal operation is aborted and the control changes from Normal to Error. If OK is signaled, the control switches back, leaves the Error state and restarts normal operation.

Both states in the main module are hierarchical and employ two concurrent regions each. In both states, the left region controls the lights for the pedestrians and the right region controls lights for the cars.

This state model/view nicely expresses the behavior of the application, however, the data handling is not obvious, in particular concerning the potential interactions between concurrent regions, as detailed next.

3.2   Data Flow Questions

There exist many semantic variations of data flow languages [14]. A prominent example are Kahn process networks (KPNs) [15], where concurrent actors communicate by producing and consuming *tokens*, and data flow edges represent unbounded FIFO queues. In the data-flow examples we present here, as far as it matters for the subject of this paper, we assume a *synchronous* setting with a clocking regime [3], and communication through shared variables.

One typical question, regarding the semantical validity of a model, is whether there is any *feedback*, that is, a mutual inter-dependence of concurrent regions (region A writes some x that concurrent region B reads, and B writes some y that A reads). Some modeling languages (including Ptolemy, or SCADE with "black-box scheduling") forbid such feedback outright, unless delays (registers) break the cycle, while others (such as SCCharts, or SCADE with "white-box scheduling") only allow it under certain circumstances [12].

Another typical question is whether there may be *conflicting writes* (concurrent regions A and B both write x). Again, some modeling languages always forbid it (Ptolemy, SCADE), others allow it under certain circumstances. For example, some synchronous languages, including SyncCharts and SCCharts, have the notion of *combination functions*, which can be used to combine concurrent writes in a deterministic manner, similar to resolution functions used in hardware design for signals that have multiple drivers. For example, a commutative, associative function such as addition is a valid combination function, and for a shared integer x, two concurrent writes x += 2 and x += 3, if executed atomically, do not impose a race condition; no matter how they are scheduled, their effect will be x += 5. More generally, a valid combination function f on x, y must fulfill that for all $x, y_1, y_2, f(f(x, y_1), y_2) = f(f(x, y_2), y_1)$ holds. For example, "minus" is a valid combination function, even though it is not commutative.

In SCCharts, we say that assignments of the form $x = f(x, e)$ are *relative writes*, provided that f is a valid combination function and e is an expression that does not depend on x and whose evaluation does not have side effects. To clearly delineate relative writes for the compiler (and the modeler), we use the convention that relative writes must be written as *compound assignments*, such as x += 2 instead of x = x + 2. All relative writes of the same type are *confluent*, meaning they can be scheduled in any order. *Absolute writes* are those that are not relative, meaning they do not use a combination function, and absolute writes may also be confluent if they write the same value and do not have side effects. All told, the SCCharts scheduling regime permits concurrent writes to some variable x as long as, within a reaction (logical tick), all absolute writes to x are confluent and are scheduled before all relative writes to x, and all relative writes are of the same type [12]. Furthermore, writes must precede reads, which corresponds to the KPN scheduling constraint that tokens must be produced before they can be consumed.

Again, these questions are rather difficult to answer with the state view, more helpful here are Data-Flow modeling/viewing (M2/V2), or the multimodeling approach (M3/V3) described next.

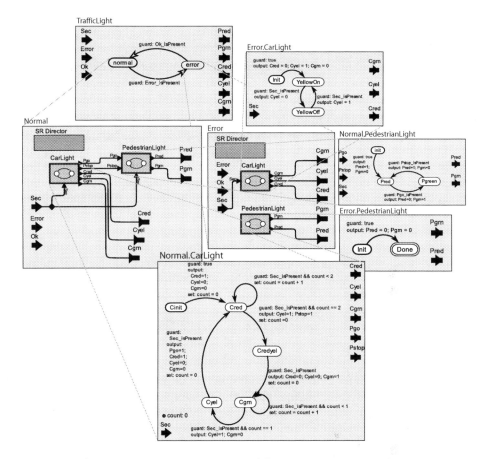

Fig. 3. Traffic light controller in Ptolemy II [2], illustrating multimodeling (M3) and multimodel view (V3) (Color figure online)

3.3 Multimodeling (M3) and Multimodel View (V3)

In multimodeling tools, like Ptolemy II, the developer is not restricted to a single type of model. Instead the model can be composed of different types of actors. In Ptolemy II, main building blocks are *Modal Models*, which are used to define finite state machines [7], and *Composite Actors*, which can model different kinds of data flow models. Each of these types can be used in different levels of hierarchy.

Figure 3 shows the traffic light controller introduced in Sect. 3.1, modeled as a hierarchical model with separate data flow and state machines [2]. Each of the boxes shows one part of the hierarchy, gray lines show the relation between actors and the contained model.

The highest level of hierarchy is the state diagram TrafficLight in the top-left corner. It is equivalent to the first hierarchy level of the model described in

Sect. 3.1. The two states are marked green to indicate the presence of a *refinement*, a child hierarchy, inside the state. The refinement of the normal state is shown at the center left. This refinement is the data flow model already shown in Fig. 1b. Unlike in the state view shown in Fig. 2, the connection via Pgo and Pstop between the two controlling regions and the absence of feedback is immediately visible.

Note that to be precise, Fig. 3 is an enhanced version of what the modeler usually sees and works with. The different state/data flow diagrams are arranged carefully not to hide any information, and gray lines are added manually to show the inter-relationships. In practice, when working with a modeling tool, the modeler will have OS-managed windows for each data flow or state diagram. When exploring a complex model, this routinely requires re-organization of the windows on the screen. It may also pose a mental burden on the modeler to remember which part of the model is where on the screen, as some parts may become completely hidden behind other parts.

One approach that avoids the problem of overlapping parts of the view is presented next.

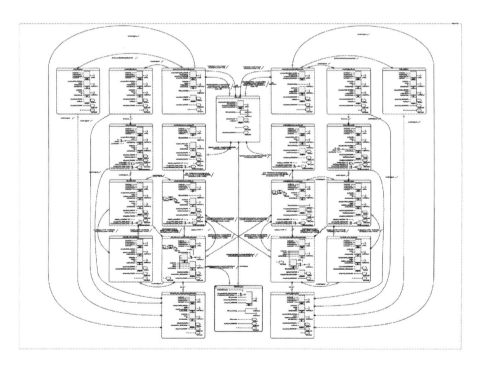

Fig. 4. Railway model in SCADE, illustrating multimodeling (M3) and static hybrid view (V4) and the fact that this can become rather unwieldy (from [24])

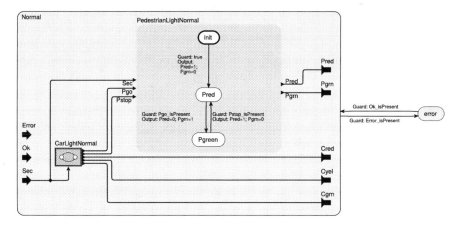

Fig. 5. Partial Ptolemy model, shown in KIELER Ptolemy Browser [25], illustrating multimodeling (M3) and dynamic hybrid view (V4)

3.4 Multimodeling (M3) and Static Hybrid View (V4)

Some modeling tools allow to mix data flow and state in the same diagram. Figure 4 shows a railway controller modeled with SCADE. At the top level, there is a state machine, each state is refined with a data flow sub-model. This view exposes the whole model in one diagram, thus there are no overlap issues as in the multimodel view (V3). However, as this example illustrates, there are two issues with this: (1) a high manual effort in producing the drawing (this example has consumed 50+ hours of mere drawing time), (2) details are not legible when viewed as a whole, as is the case in this paper with Fig. 4, unless the viewing area is very large, e. g., if the paper happens to be printed on A0.

4 Dynamic Views

To avoid the burden of manually creating a view while modeling, dynamic views provide automatic representations of the model. Consequently, additional or derived information can be displayed to the user without interfering in the actual creation of the model.

4.1 Multimodeling (M3) and Dynamic Hybrid View (V4)

Figure 5 shows a partial view of the same model as Fig. 3. The view has been generated, based on the original Ptolemy model, by the KIELER Ptolemy Browser, using automated view synthesis as well as automated layout algorithms, in this case provided by the Eclipse Layout Kernel (ELK)[7].

The view allows the user to expand or collapse any hierarchical actor as needed by clicking on it. In Fig. 5 the error state and the embedded modal model

---

[7] https://www.eclipse.org/elk.

CarLightNormal are collapsed, while PedestrianLightNormal has been expanded. The hierarchy depth is visualized by a background gradient getting darker on deeper levels.

The Ptolemy Browser also supports different ways to filter diagram elements. In Fig. 5 port labels are only shown for PedestrianLightNormal. Additionally the directors, visible in Fig. 3, are currently hidden.

4.2   Inferring Data Flow

Before showing the enriched viewing options V5 and V4 for state models (M1), we briefly describe the way the data flow is extracted from the source model. This approach is not specific to a certain modeling language but should be adaptable to any state-based language using concurrent regions.

The data flow analysis is performed in a postfix depth-first traversal order of the model hierarchy. This allows us to first analyze the usage of data in all child states of a region and to immediately use the data to visualize the data flow.

For each state, multiple sets of *valued objects*, meaning variables, signals or other kinds of data used in the model, are gathered. The objects are placed in different sets, to separate objects used locally in the state from objects used in a nested hierarchy and to separate read objects from written objects.

For each region, the sets corresponding to the child states are collected and combined with the objects used on the transitions inside the region. These aggregated data then contain all the valued objects, used in the region directly or in some nested hierarchy within the region.

To compute the resulting data flow, the sets of each region are compared to the concurrent regions in the state. Any valued object read in one region and written in a different region results in data flow. Additionally, reading valued objects that are marked as model inputs, or writing valued objects marked as outputs, should be regarded as data flow. These set intersections are used to create the inferred data flow visualizations presented in Sects. 4.3 and 4.4.

When the data flow between the regions is found, the sets of the regions are combined and propagated upwards to the parent state. This analysis can gather all data flow information in a single pass over the model.

4.3   State Modeling (M1) and Data Overlay Viewing (V5)

Using the information gathered in the data flow analysis, we can show the data flow as an overlay on the original state diagram as shown in Fig. 6. Every data flow between concurrent regions is shown as a direct connection from the writer to the reader of the data.

In the example, we can see dependencies in the Normal state, from the write accesses to Pgo and Pstop in the CarLight region to the read accesses in the PedestrianLight region. These are the connections that have been manually modeled in the Ptolemy model. One benefit of this approach is the *stability* of the diagram. The original diagram of the model is not changed, but only enhanced with new

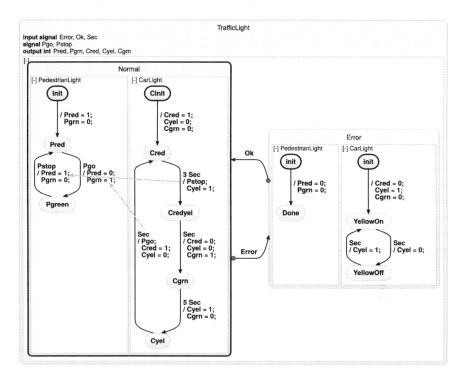

Fig. 6. SCCharts traffic light controller with dependency overlay (green dashed arrows), illustrating state modeling (M1) and data overlay viewing (V5) (Color figure online)

information. The *mental map* of the developer is preserved [19]. However, compared to the Ptolemy model, this view lacks information about the inputs and outputs of the model regions. In particular, potential conflicting writes to the same output are not directly visible.

The overlay shows the connections between concurrent regions in as much detail as possible. Every relevant connection is individually drawn. In more complex diagrams, this may be more information than can reasonably be displayed visually, as illustrated in Fig. 7, which is part of another railway controller model. The data flow indications overlap each other and create a diagram that is rather unreadable. This problem can partially be addressed through proper filtering, i.e. only showing the dependencies for a selected element. Still, for models of this complexity, the data overlay viewing seems inappropriate to answer, e. g., the questions concerning possible feedback and write conflicts formulated before.

Looking at diagrams as the one in Fig. 7, one may wonder whether visual representations are appropriate for models of this complexity in the first place. In fact, past experience of working with complex models in a tool that offers textual modeling suggests that users are quick to dismiss the automatic graphical views altogether and just stick to the textual models. However, with dynamic, customizable views, graphics may become usable and valuable again. For example,

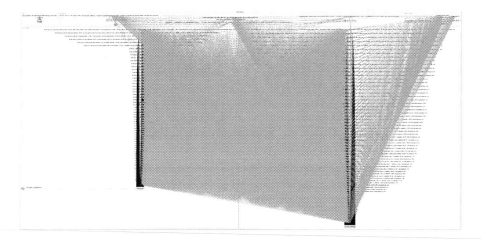

Fig. 7. Railway model, illustrating the limits of data overlay viewing (V5)

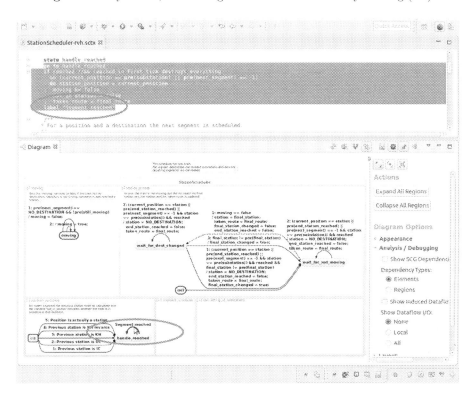

Fig. 8. Screen shot of the railway model with selective region expansion and selected transition label in the KIELER SCCharts tool (Color figure online)

consider Fig. 8 for an the alternative view of the same railway model. The two regions that due to their size caused trouble in Fig. 7 are collapsed, and the remaining three regions are small enough to be viewed at once.

Figure 8 also illustrates another feature of view management, namely the use of an abstract, summary graphical representation together with a detailed textual representation. The top part of the screen shot contains the textual SCChart description as written by the user. The lower part contains a state view of the model, where some transitions are labeled with a more compact summarizing text instead of the concrete trigger and action. One such transition is labelled Segment reached (see added green oval); when clicking on the transition, the part of the textual source that describes the details of the transition trigger/action is automatically scrolled to and highlighted. Finally, the screen shot also illustrates how comments (the "post-it" notes) can be shown in the dynamic view, constructed from semantic comments in the textual model.

4.4   State Modeling (M1) and Dynamic Hybrid View (V4)

An alternative view, that aims to avoid the potential cluttering issues of the data overlay view (V5) that was illustrated in Fig. 7, is the dynamic hybrid view (V4) again. In Sect. 4.1, the dynamic V4 was synthesized from a multimodel, which already had explicitly modeled the data flow. We now synthesize dynamic V4 from a state model.

The main idea behind this visualization is to use the previously "unused" hierarchy layer between regions to show the data flow. In normal Statecharts there are no connecting edges between regions and the placement of the regions next to each other usually carries no semantic meaning except concurrency. To enrich the diagram, we leverage this hierarchy level and add the data flow between the regions.

The Traffic Light Example. Figure 9 shows the inferred data flow with *local* inputs and outputs, automatically created from the very same SCCharts model from which the state view of Fig. 2 was synthesized. Local inputs and outputs are the valued objects that are used on the same hierarchy level as the input or output. Alternatively, all inputs and outputs, including usages in nested hierarchy levels, could be shown, or all input and output nodes could be hidden, leaving only the concurrent data flow between neighboring regions. Inside every hierarchical state, each shared valued object is represented by one (hyper)edge. All writers of the valued objects are sources of the edge and all readers are sinks.

On the top hierarchy level, input nodes for Error and Ok are added because these signals govern the transition between the two top-level states. Inside the Normal state, the local data flow between CarLight and PedestrianLight, the reading of the Sec input, as well as the written outputs have been added. In terms of visualized information, the resulting diagram is similar to the corresponding Ptolemy diagram in Fig. 5. One deviation occurs in Normal.PedestrianLight, which in the manually specified data flow part of the Ptolemy model defines

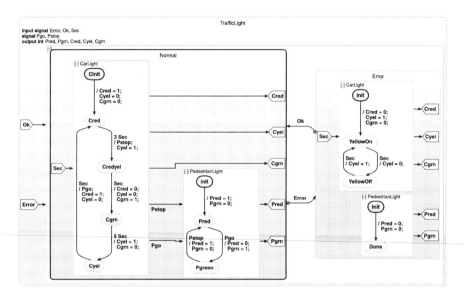

Fig. 9. SCCharts traffic light controller with inferred data flow, illustrating state modeling (M1) with a dynamic hybrid view (V4)

Sec as an input, even though Sec is actually not read in PedestrianLight. This "modeling glitch," manifested also in Normal, is probably not on purpose, as for example the Sec input is (correctly) omitted for Error.PedestrianLight. This glitch in such a small, well-studied example indicates that dynamically created data flow visualizations not only offer the convenience of not having to explicitly re-model information that is already present in the state part; dynamic, automatically inferred views also help to keep state and data flow consistent, in particular as models become more complex.

Another noteworthy detail is the order of the regions CarLight and PedestrianLight inside the Normal state. Compared to the original diagram in Fig. 2, these two regions switched their place in the diagram. This is done by the automatic layout algorithm, to always draw the data flow edges from left to right if possible. If the data flow edges create a cycle, one of the edges has to be reversed and will be drawn as a feedback edge from right to left, thus making potential feedback obvious to the modeler.

Compared to the overlay presented in Sect. 4.3, the precision of this approach is a bit reduced. The usages of the objects are not indicated directly, but only on a per-region granularity. On the other hand, this approach always produces a clean diagram without edges potentially overlapping relevant parts of the diagram. Additionally, this approach can show the data flow between regions, even when the regions itself are collapsed and the child states are not currently visible.

The Railway Example. Dynamic hybrid views also let us draw the railway example, shown before in the rather inaccessible Fig. 7, in a cleaner and more readable way. By collapsing all regions and configuring some label management we can create the diagram shown in Fig. 10.

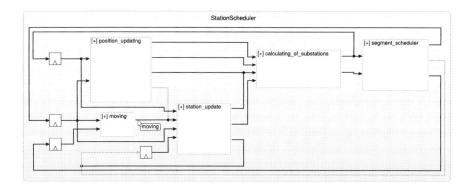

Fig. 10. Railway model with data flow, illustrating multimodeling (M3) and dynamic hybrid view (V4) for a complex model, with absolute/relative writes (black/green edges) and mouse-over annotation of data flow edges. (Color figure online)

The view exhibits feedback, visible in the edges routed around the outside of the diagram. In this case, all feedback edges end in a register. These registers are automatically created, both in the code synthesis and in the inferred data flow view, if the value is not used directly but instead read in a **pre** operator. In SCCharts, as in other synchronous languages, the **pre** operator accesses the value a variable had at the end of the previous reaction. This is similar to a *delay* actor in Ptolemy.

As can be seen in Fig. 10, the automatic layout of the SCCharts editor tends to place registers at the left of the diagram. Specifically, when the layout algorithm encounters a cycle in the graph that makes it impossible to draw all edges in the same direction, it tries to break the cycle by reversing edges that enter a register. This is another convention that helps the modeler to quickly grasp whether feedback is broken by a register or not.

Another feature in Fig. 10 can be seen on the hyperedge from two writers, **moving** and **position_updating**, to the reader **station_update**. As explained in Sect. 3.2, multiple writers may indicate a problem in a model. However, the write performed by **position_updating** is a relative write (see again Sect. 3.2), indicated by a green edge segment. A closer inspection of Fig. 8, where the textual SCCharts description shows the relative write access **moving &= false**, confirms that this is a relative write of type conjunction. Thus, it can be safely combined with the absolute write (black) from **station_update**. A similar situation is present in the model with an absolute write from **station_update** and the relative write from **segment_scheduler**. These two writes are combined and fed back to the corresponding register. There is another concurrent write, where **position_updating** and **station_update** perform absolute writes to the same value, but these happen to be confluent because they write the same value. As a possible extension to the current tooling, this fact could be fed back visually in the diagram as well, e. g., by showing some kind of error marker in case there are non-confluent absolute writes.

As a last detail, for compactness the dynamic view from Fig. 10 has been configured to not show any data flow labels. However, a mouse-over on an edge, such as the aforementioned hyperedge, shows the shared variable in question, in this case moving.

5   Related Work

Beyond the work on multimodeling mentioned in the introduction [2], there are several proposals on combining different model types [4, 10, 26]. However, there appears to be little comparable work that focusses on modeling pragmatics the way we do here, compared to the large body of work on semantic and synthesis issues. There are some works, such as by Petre [18], which compare the utility of graphical and textual views.

Human-centered software engineering aims to improve usability in software development, but not with a focus on modeling [22]. Another related community focuses on software visualization [6]. Smyth et al. have presented an approach to extract SCCharts from legacy C code [23]. Together with the work presented here, this now allows a data flow view of C programs.

The synthesis of diagrams advocated here builds on automatic layout, for which the graph drawing community has developed a large variety of approaches, as for example surveyed by Di Battista et al. [5].

6   Conclusions and Outlook

We have illustrated that data flow views do not necessarily have to be created manually by a modeller, as is long-standing tradition, but can be inferred automatically, in our case from state models. More generally speaking, we made the argument that views can and should be separated from models. Designers should be able to concentrate on creating and maintaining models, in whatever formalism is most convenient, and a modeling tool should infer different, customizable views according to the task at hand. This not only saves valuable developer time, but can also help to avoid model inconsistencies.

Even though we did not question the difference between state models and data flow models here, the fact that a data flow view can be just synthesized from a state model begs the question of how fundamental that difference really is. For example, going in the other direction, ongoing work indicates that it is not too difficult to synthesize fairly concise SCCharts from Lustre [11], which is generally viewed as a data flow language.

There are numerous directions to go from here. For example, we have focussed on showing data flow relations between concurrent regions/actors, implying that this is what the modeler is most interested in. However, data flow languages are also used to express sequential computations, and one might extend the work here to infer data flow for sequential computations as well. For example, referring back to the existing work on the model extraction from legacy C code [23], it might be interesting to infer the data flow from a C program that performs some complex signal processing using various components. Conceptually, these components can be seen as actors and could be visualized as such, even if the actors may not be concurrent anymore but typically are already sequentialized in the C program.

Another, largely open question is how to give good visual feedback on more complex causality questions. As briefly alluded to, feedback may be permitted in some cases, such as when back-and-forth scheduling between concurrent actors is permitted within a reaction. This is a powerful language feature, but may lead to models that are hard to debug in case they are not schedulable.

Finally, as the concept of dynamic views hinges on the capability to automatically draw well-readable diagrams, the area of automatic graph drawing is called upon. We believe that auto-layout is already good enough to be usable in practice, with open source libraries that make state-of-the-art algorithms freely available and have stable interfaces. Thus auto-layout should become a standard feature in today's modeling tools, as is, for example, already the case in Ptolemy (which uses ELK). However, further improvements are still possible. One detail is the handling of hyper edges, which sometimes is still unsatisfactory. A broader issue is that of "interactive" layout, where the modeler can influence the model drawing without having to fall back to manual layout.

Acknowledgements. We thank the participants of the 2008 and 2017 editions of the model railway project conducted at Kiel University for the SCADE and SCCharts models they contributed. We also thank the contributors to the open source projects such as Ptolemy, as well as KIELER, ELK, Xtext and numerous other Eclipse projects, that made this work possible.

This work has been supported in part by the German Science Foundation, as part of the Precision-Timed Synchronous Reactive Processing (PRETSY2, DFG HA 4407/6-2) and Compact Graph Drawing with Port Constraints (ComDraPor, DFG HA 4407/8-1) projects.

References

1. André, C.: Computing SyncCharts reactions. Electr. Notes Theor. Comput. Sci **88**, 3–19 (2004)
2. Brooks, C., Cheng, C.H.P., Feng, T.H., Lee, E.A., von Hanxleden, R.: Model engineering using multimodeling. In: Proceedings of the 1st International Workshop on Model Co-Evolution and Consistency Management (MCCM 2008), a Workshop at MODELS 2008, September 2008
3. Caspi, P., Pouzet, M.: Synchronous Kahn networks. In: Proceedings of the first ACM SIGPLAN International Conference on Functional Programming ICFP 1996, pp. 226–238 (1996)
4. Combemale, B., DeAntoni, J., Baudry, B., France, R.B., Jézéquel, J., Gray, J.: Globalizing modeling languages. Computer **47**(6), 68–71 (2014)
5. Di Battista, G., Eades, P., Tamassia, R., Tollis, I.G.: Graph Drawing: Algorithms for the Visualization of Graphs. Prentice Hall, Upper Saddle River (1999)

6. Diehl, S.: Software Visualization: Visualizing the Structure, Behavior and Evolution of Software. Springer, Heidelberg (2007). https://doi.org/10.1007/978-3-540-46505-8

7. Feng, T.H., Lee, E.A., Liu, X., Motika, C., von Hanxleden, R., Zheng, H.: Finite state machines. In: Ptolemaeus, C. (ed.) System Design, Modeling, and Simulation using Ptolemy II. Ptolemy.org (2014)

8. Fuhrmann, H., von Hanxleden, R.: On the pragmatics of model-based design. In: Choppy, C., Sokolsky, O. (eds.) Monterey Workshop 2008. LNCS, vol. 6028, pp. 116–140. Springer, Heidelberg (2010). https://doi.org/10.1007/978-3-642-12566-9_7

9. Gamma, E., Helm, R., Johnson, R., Vlissides, J.M.: Design Patterns: Elements of Reusable Object-Oriented Software. Addison-Wesley, Boston (1995)

10. Grundy, J.C., Hosking, J., Huh, J., Li, K.N.L.: Marama: An Eclipse meta-toolset for generating multi-view environments. In: Proceedings of the 30th International Conference on Software Engineering (ICSE 2008), pp. 819–822. ACM (2008)

11. Halbwachs, N., Caspi, P., Raymond, P., Pilaud, D.: The synchronous data-flow programming language LUSTRE. Proc. IEEE **79**(9), 1305–1320 (1991)

12. von Hanxleden, R., Duderstadt, B., Motika, C., Smyth, S., Mendler, M., Aguado, J., Mercer, S., O'Brien, O.: SCCharts: sequentially constructive statecharts for safety-critical applications. In: Proceedings of ACM SIGPLAN Conference on Programming Language Design and Implementation (PLDI 2014). ACM, June 2014

13. Harel, D.: Statecharts: a visual formalism for complex systems. Sci. Comput. Program. **8**(3), 231–274 (1987)

14. Johnston, W.M., Hanna, J.R.P., Millar, R.J.: Advances in dataflow programming languages. ACM Comput. Surv. (CSUR) **36**(1), 1–34 (2004)

15. Kahn, G.: The semantics of a simple language for parallel programming. In: Rosenfeld, J.L. (ed.) Information Processing 74: Proceedings of the IFIP Congress 74, pp. 471–475. IFIP, North-Holland Publishing Co., August 1974

16. Klauske, L.K., Dziobek, C.: Improving modeling usability: automated layout generation for Simulink. In: Proceedings of the MathWorks Automotive Conference (MAC 2010) (2010)

17. Lee, E.A., Neuendorffer, S., Wirthlin, M.J.: Actor-oriented design of embedded hardware and software systems. J. Circ. Syst. Comput. **12**(3), 231–260 (2003)

18. Petre, M.: Why looking isn't always seeing: readership skills and graphical programming. Commun. ACM **38**(6), 33–44 (1995)

19. von Pilgrim, J.: Mental map and model driven development. In: Layout of (Software) Engineering Diagrams 2007. Electronic Communications of the EASST, vol. 7 (2007)

20. Ptolemaeus, C. (ed.): System Design, Modeling, and Simulation Using Ptolemy II. Ptolemy.org (2014). http://ptolemy.org/books/Systems

21. Reenskaug, T.: Models - Views - Controllers. Xerox PARC technical note, November 1979

22. Seffah, A., Gulliksen, J., Desmarais, M.C.: An introduction to human-centered software engineering. In: Seffah, A., Gulliksen, J., Desmarais, M.C. (eds.) An Introduction to Human-Centered Software Engineering-Integrating Usability in the Software Development Lifecycle. HCI, vol. 8, pp. 3–14. Springer, Netherlands (2005). https://doi.org/10.1007/1-4020-4113-6_1

23. Smyth, S., Lenga, S., von Hanxleden, R.: Model extraction for legacy C programs with SCCharts. Poster presented at the 7th International Symposium on Leveraging Applications of Formal Methods, Verification and Validation (ISoLA 2016), Corfu, Greece, October 2016

24. Smyth, S., Motika, C., Schulz-Rosengarten, A., Wechselberg, N.B., Sprung, C., von Hanxleden, R.: SCCharts: the railway project report. Technical report 1510, Department of Computer Science, Christian-Albrechts-Universität zu Kiel, August 2015

25. Spönemann, M., Fuhrmann, H., von Hanxleden, R.: Automatic layout of data flow diagrams in KIELER and Ptolemy II. Technical report 0914, Department of Computer Science, Christian-Albrechts-Universität zu Kiel, July 2009

26. Sztipanovits, J., Bapty, T., Neema, S., Howard, L., Jackson, E.: OpenMETA: a model- and component-based design tool chain for cyber-physical systems. In: Bensalem, S., Lakhneck, Y., Legay, A. (eds.) ETAPS 2014. LNCS, vol. 8415, pp. 235–248. Springer, Heidelberg (2014). https://doi.org/10.1007/978-3-642-54848-2_16

On the Road to Conviction:
An Email Exchange with Edward Lee

Reinhard Wilhelm[✉]

Saarland University, Saarland Informatics Campus, Saarbrücken, Germany
`wilhelm@cs.uni-saarland.de`

Abstract. This is a somewhat unusual contribution to a Festschrift. I had a long email conversation with Edward, and when the invitation to contribute to his Festschrift reached me I proposed to the editors to include this email exchange. They reacted positively, and also Edward felt that this was a nice idea.

An email conversation is seldom sequential. The possibility to include answers in the text of a received message disturbs the sequential flow and instead introduces some hierarchy in the text. I have therefore carefully selected excerpts from our e-mail exchange and serialized them so that the discussion is easier to follow. I only deleted unnecessary text, corrected spelling, and added references to the articles we discussed.

Our conversation centers around three different topics. The first topic is real-time computing. In Sect. 1 we discuss the extent to which timing properties can be predicted or verified, whether or not predictable timing necessarily comes at the cost of performance overhead, and how timing is affected by threads and interrupts. The second topic, discussed in Sect. 2, is the semantics of time in distributed systems. Finally, in Sect. 3, we exchange thoughts about the principles behind modeling and abstraction that underpin the ideas discussed in Sects. 1 and 2.

1 Precision Timed (PRET) Machines

Our discussion started after Edward sent Jan Reineke and me a draft of a planned submission titled *What is Real Time Computing* [8]. One of Edward's claims was that traditional use of interrupts rendered timing verification impossible.

1.1 Timing Verification

Reinhard: I don't share your view of interrupt handling in real-time systems: Temporarily disabling interrupts and using delayed preemption allows timing verification [10].

Edward: (...) I think I can defend better my view on interrupt handling in real-time systems. Disabling interrupts for a block of code helps some, in that it prevents disruption of the assumptions on machine state that are used in

© Springer International Publishing AG, part of Springer Nature 2018
M. Lohstroh et al. (Eds.): Lee Festschrift, LNCS 10760, pp. 524–537, 2018.
https://doi.org/10.1007/978-3-319-95246-8_29

worst-case execution time (WCET) analysis. But it doesn't help enough. Consider a block of code that must be executed by some deadline. Suppose this block of code disables interrupts. Consider now that an interrupt may be asserted just before or just after we disable interrupts. Suppose that in the first case, the pause time of the interrupt makes it impossible to meet the deadline, and in the second case, the deadline is met. Then in this case, no matter how good our WCET analysis, we cannot guarantee that the deadline will be met.

And in any case, timing is nondeterministic, because we can't control when the interrupt will be asserted. It could be asserted before or after interrupts get disabled. And presumably, we don't disable interrupts until we know that we need to execute some critical code, but then it might be too late, because an interrupt may have already been asserted.

Reinhard: This block of code, having an associated deadline, would usually be considered a task or job and would be subject to a conventional WCET analysis. Your situation, potential interrupt before or after the execution of this task/job, would be subject to a schedulability analysis, which may indeed produce the answer "No." The delayed preemption I proposed would be used for preemptions *within* tasks to keep the WCET-analysis problem feasible.

1.2   Performance Overhead

Edward: In FlexPRET [12], an interrupt has exactly zero (zero!) effect on hard-real-time threads. Moreover, it has a bounded effect on soft-real-time threads (it imposes a percentage slowdown rather than an unbounded pause time). This really is fundamentally different, because we can have interrupts enabled all the time (guaranteeing low-latency responses) and still guarantee deterministic timing for tasks that are running when the interrupt is asserted. Here, determinism is as good as the logic determinism of programs (i.e., up to hardware failure and soft errors).

Consider for example a scenario where two devices can assert interrupts at arbitrary times, and in response to each interrupt, we have to compute some reaction within, say, $50\,\mu s$. In FlexPRET, we can guarantee these responses with timing jitter as low as one clock cycle, regardless of how the actual interrupt assertions align. That is not possible with a conventional processor. And we can make this guarantee up to the point where the pipeline and memory system are fully utilized, where every clock cycle is busy. No headroom is needed.

Reinhard: I don't buy your argument that there is no loss of performance; you statically reduce performance by reserving resources, i.e. cores/threads, for interrupt handling. These resources could have been used for other hard real-time threads, whereby the system would have exhibited a higher performance. In the extreme, i.e., when no interrupts occur, these cores/threads are idle.

Edward: Your reading of FlexPRET is not correct. Interrupts consume zero resources when not active. Interrupts are handled in soft-real-time threads, which are scheduled opportunistically in cycles not being used by hard-real-time threads.

You are right that if the hard-real-time threads require 100% of the cycles, then interrupts (and all other soft-real-time tasks) cannot be handled without violating real-time constraints. But isn't this true of any processor? FlexPRET cannot perform magic. If your hard-real-time tasks require 100% of the machine, then nothing else can be done without violating their constraints.

On the first point, delayed preemption (and in fact any scheduling decision) cannot be performed without a preemption occurring. The OS scheduler is a task like any other. No scheduling decision can be made without executing this task. My basic points in this analysis and the example are twofold:

1. FlexPRET can deliver precise timing with jitter as low as a clock cycle, repeatably and predictability. No conventional interrupt-driven mechanism can do that. This is about *determinism* and *repeatability*. It delivers timing determinism at the same level as the logic determinism of a processor.
2. For WCET analysis to be valid, extreme care is required if interrupts are used at all. First, as we agree, interrupts must be disabled during execution of any code for which we depend on the WCET analysis. This introduces timing jitter at the granularity of task sizes, much larger than a clock cycle. Second, the decision to execute a code block on whose WCET we rely must be made *atomically* w.r.t. interrupts, or else the WCET analysis is invalid. This is very difficult to do. It requires that all interrupt service routines that may result in a scheduling decision immediately and atomically disable interrupts, something that only a few processors do (and it must be done in hardware, in theory). And then it requires extremely careful coding. I suspect most RTOSs don't get it right...

The way to prove these points is to use an example like the one I tried to illustrate in the last part, where there are two independent external events that require a response within a fixed latency. With FlexPRET, if the real-time constraints are feasible, then they can be handled, and the jitter in handling them is less than a clock cycle. The deadlines are feasible if and only if both events can be handled simultaneously within their deadlines at $\leq 100\%$ utilization. I've attached a picture of a sketch of this proof (see Fig. 1).

Admittedly, my proof makes some approximations. Specifically, I assume that a hard-real-time thread can be scheduled so that it uses any real-valued percentage of the processor between 0 and 100%. In practice, these percentages will be quantized. But in principle, we can make the quantization as fine as we like, at the cost of hardware.

Try the same example with conventional interrupts. Even with the most careful possible coding, the timing jitter will be at least equal to the execution time of the tasks, so the WCET estimate for task 1 is invalid: You must add to it the WCET estimate of task 2 to get a real deadline. Specifically, $WCET_1$ is *not* a bound on the response time to event 1. The only bound you can give is $WCET_1 + WCET_2$, which will be $\geq$ the bound given by FlexPRET (since in FlexPRET, the two tasks execute simultaneously). However, FlexPRET delivers the results with deterministic timing (up to a clock cycle). Conventional interrupts do not.

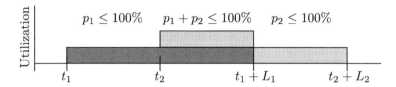

Fig. 1. Assume there are two hard-real-time tasks, where t_1 is the start time of the first task and t_2 the start time of the second. Without loss of generality, assume that $t_1 \leq t_2$. Let L_1 and L_2 denote the maximum latency of the respective tasks, and p_1, p_2 denote the percentage of CPU utilization required to meet the deadlines $t_1 + L_1$ and $t_2 + L_2$. Observe that the schedule is infeasible if at any given time the sum of required CPU time is greater than 100%. When utilization is less than 100% there are cycles available for soft-real-time threads, which, among other things, can handle interrupts.

1.3   Interrupts and Threads

Reinhard: Aren't you changing the semantics of interrupts? In my intuition they have higher priority than the tasks they should interrupt. In FlexPRET they have lower priority than all hard real-time tasks and may encounter (predictably) long delays. Which kind of interrupts are you thinking of? Are they all insensitive against such delays?

Edward: Actually, in FlexPRET, interrupt service routines begin executing immediately (within four clock cycles in our latest FlexPRET) regardless of what the hard-real-time tasks are doing. So actually, they have higher priority in FlexPRET than in a conventional approach, where the hard-real-time code has to disable interrupts, thereby introducing uncontrollable delays to handling interrupts.

FlexPRET uses hyperthreading, where there are several register sets, and for each register set there is one hardware thread. Some of the threads are hard-real-time threads. Those are scheduled in the pipeline according to a fixed deterministic schedule (determined by a memory-mapped register). Assuming that those don't use 100% of the cycles (a necessary assumption for feasibility even in a conventional processor), then the remaining cycles are used for soft-real-time threads.

In FlexPRET, if there are, say, three hard-real-time threads and one soft-real-time thread, then the soft-real-time thread (typically) gets at least one of every four clock cycles to launch an instruction. The exact pattern depends on what is written in the memory-mapped register, but a typical pattern would make such a guarantee. The soft-real-time thread may get more than one cycle of every four because whenever a hard-real-time thread stalls (its work is done for now), its cycles are made available to the soft-real-time threads. Hence the maximum four cycle latency to start executing an ISR the soft-real-time thread.

In principle, one could mess up this strategy by scheduling too many cycles to the hard-real-time threads. But this is not a good idea regardless of whether there are interrupts or soft-real-time tasks because it introduces pipeline bubbles and variable memory latency, making WCET analysis much more difficult. Hence, a typical hard-real-time thread will use no more than one cycle of every four, and by this mechanism, it achieves rock-solid, perfectly deterministic timing.

Again, I emphasize that the primary goal is determinism...

A side effect of this approach is that if there is enough concurrency (enough threads with work to do), then aggregate performance is *better* than a conventional processor because there are no pipeline bubbles and no stalls due to DRAM accesses. Every clock cycle does useful work... Moreover, the nondeterministic timing that soft-real-time threads experience is because they opportunistically use cycles that become available. Hence, exact WCET bounds are also achievable for the soft-real-time threads, but unlike the hard-real-time threads, they may do *better* than these bounds. For the hard-real-time threads, the only timing variability is due to paths through program (data-dependent programs), never due to interactions with other threads or interrupts.

As you can see, I feel pretty strongly that we have solved the real-time problem at the microarchitecture level. The challenge is convincing people, and then building the software stack that can make use of it. This is why I really don't want to write a paper that does not talk about PRET. It wouldn't be telling the world what I know.

Reinhard: Hyperthreading indeed changes the scheduling setting. I didn't see that before. I was assuming traditional scheduling. However, you still reserve HW resources, namely at least a register set for soft real-time tasks, right? There are a limited number of register sets, and you could use this register set for another HW thread.

I am still looking for the magic or the shortcomings in PRET. My long life has told me that miracles are rare.

Edward: It's not a miracle, it's a paradigm shift. To accept the paradigm shift, you have to believe in the value of determinism. Most people are only very weakly committed to determinism, if at all...

A register set is cheap in hardware. It's a tiny fraction of the chip area. The reason that register sets aren't bigger than they are (more registers) is not because of the cost of the register set memory. It's because of the number of bits required in an instruction to address a register.

And anyway, we expect that just about every application will have need for at least one soft-real-time thread (e.g., for a UI, a network stack, or an OS). That thread can always be used to handle interrupts. You don't need another register set for just interrupts.

Reinhard: Well, let me tell you how I see the traditional approach and the PRET approach: In the traditional approach, one is able to safely exploit the capacity of a given architecture up to the limits of the WCET bounds and the schedulability algorithms, which, however, use (safe, but possibly crude) approximations. In the PRET approach, one is inherently limited by architectural parameters, e.g. the maximum number of threads that can be executed in an interleaved fashion. Although register sets are cheap, there will be fixed number of them in a PRET architecture.

Actually, my PROMPT [11] approach, where architecture would follow applications, which I never really worked out, was much more radical and would require a different system-development process: First design, analyze, and implement your set of applications and then design the architecture. This would free you from the limitations due to architectural parameters mentioned above.

Edward: If the number of hardware threads is a limitation, then it's a more serious limitation with a conventional processor, which has only one. In Flex-PRET, you can set the control registers to use only one register set, and then you have a conventional RISC-V.

Maybe one point that isn't clear is that a soft-real-time thread in PRET is an ordinary instruction stream. It can run an OS kernel supporting interrupts, multithreading, and a file system, for example. The fact that it shares hardware resources with hard-real-time threads does not change any of this. You can think of the hard-real-time threads as stealing cycles from a conventional machine. And the cost of providing this capability is very modest... Michael Zimmer's design shows that its effect on the hardware complexity is negligible.

By the way, I don't think PRET solves all problems. It in fact creates many new problems (very interesting ones) at the software level. There is no point in solving these problems, however, if we don't have the hardware.

So the real statement is that I believe PRET solves the real-time problem at the microarchitecture level. And it makes WCET analysis much easier. And it makes disabling interrupts obsolete.

Reinhard: My question is whether the paper will report success or failure. You will probably say, failure for commercial off-the-shelf (COTS) architectures and success for PRET.

We had a talk from another group here yesterday who declared success by exploiting the concept of single-core equivalence. The holes in the approach were visible.

Edward: (...) at best this makes the multicore problem no worse than the single core problem. But the single core problem is still unsolvable.

Reinhard: I thought we had pretty much solved it [5].

Edward: The root of the problem: COTS approaches fail to separate the map from the territory.

Reinhard: I don't understand this metaphor. Do you mean that a WCET tool has to be newly instantiated for every new processor? In this respect I agree with you.

Edward: Consider an analogy. Suppose that the x86 instruction set did not define the number of bits in each register. Then every program would have to be verified for each and every particular implementation of x86.

This is what we do with timing properties of architectures.

PRET solves that problem (...) not in exactly the same way as the x86 analogy, which wouldn't work very well... That is, it does not define the actual execution time of each instruction. What it does is that it parameterizes the implementation so that the execution time is easily determined, and MTFD instructions can be included to guarantee timing properties (...) see this paper for MTFD [2] (...) (that paper is about an earlier version of PRET, which has a fixed number of hardware threads). MTFD works fine with FlexPRET as well, where the number of hardware threads can vary from just one (conventional pipelined processor) to some fixed number N.

So yes, COTS has failed and will continue to fail. We have to separate the map from the territory.

Reinhard: I am still puzzled.

Edward: The metaphor is explained in this paper [7].

1.4   Conclusions (Part 1)

There is a competition between more or less traditional architectures, made more predictable by means proposed (partly by us) in the literature [1], in combination with sound and precise, but sophisticated WCET-analysis techniques and with state-of-the-art preemptive scheduling methods including methods to determine preemption costs on the one side, and PRET architectures using thread-scheduling and simple, but precise WCET-analysis techniques, and software based on Edward's concept of determinism and maybe repeatability on the other side.

At this point in the conversation I had not yet seen a proof of the no-loss-of-performance claim, but our exchange lead to a paper [9] that provides a formal proof. I still think that a comparison with preemptive scheduling needs to be done. I have my doubts about an easy match between requirements of a set of applications to a given PRET architecture due to limitations resulting from its fixed hardware parameters. Then, thread scheduling reduces program locality, which will have an effect on the performance at the interface to memory. Therefore, our discussion still leaves me somewhat mystified.

2   A Programming Model for Distributed Real-Time Embedded Systems (PTIDES)

We then started a discussion about the possibility of having a global time. The reader will notice quite a bit of confusion; about physical time, about time stamping as an approximation to a global physical time, about synchronization protocols and their error margins, and what faithfulness to physical time meant. My point was that causality should be preserved under all circumstances. Edward's notion of determinism was not always clear to me: Did it mean semantical determinism or timing determinism? Edward would argue that the former should include the latter.

Reinhard: I went through the paper [8] and am puzzled. My view of the world was that relativity effects in distributed systems prevented one from having a global time, and that only a partial order on events was possible, and that Lamport's vector time was the basis for ensuring the preservation of causality, and that GALS (globally asynchronous, locally synchronous) [6] were the way to go, at least my friends in ARTIST and ARTIST DESIGN had convinced me of that.

Now, you confront me with tons of new developments that seem to make global time again a viable concept. I still don't get the full picture. However, I have the following bad feeling: You can make the time error/deviation as small as you can afford, but there is still the possibility that two causally related events happen within the remaining error interval such that causality is lost. True? In that case you would have sacrificed semantics determinism an the altar of time determinism.

Edward: I'm guessing you are referring now to PTIDES [4] rather than PRET.

I think you are confusing the map with the territory. Time stamps are numbers. What PTIDES does is to ensure events are processed in time-stamp order. If this assumption is met, then the model is deterministic.

EVERY deterministic model of computation makes assumptions that, when violated, lead to nondeterminism. A single-threaded imperative program will not behave correctly if the chip is melting. A synchronous circuit will not behave correctly if it is clocked too fast.

Processing events in time-stamp order is clearly physically possible. It has been done since the 1970s in distributed discrete-event simulation. Nothing about relativity makes this impossible.

The only remaining question is whether it can be made efficient and robust to failures. PTIDES does both of these by leveraging synchronized clocks. Clocks are never perfectly synchronized. Not even in a synchronous circuit on a chip nor in a synchronous program. You just have to assume bounded margins of error. Lamport used synchronized clocks way back in the 1980s to achieve fault tolerance.

PTIDES goes a step further and associates time stamps with real-time clocks at sensors and actuators. And we show that not only can we make the distributed execution deterministic (events are processed in time-stamp order), but under certain assumptions (including bounded execution time), we can ensure that events are delivered to actuators on time.

PTIDES makes explicit the assumptions. If you can bound the communication latency, the clock synchronization error, and the execution time, then you get deterministic execution and on-time delivery of events to actuators in a distributed real-time system.

Are these too many assumptions? Only if they are costly to realize. But they aren't. Synchronizing clocks has become easy (to precisions of nanoseconds with IEEE 1588 and 802.1AS). Bounding communication latency is routine in real-time networks (TTEthernet, FlexRay, and forthcoming TSN networks). And PRET makes bounding execution time practical.

Your skepticism, unfortunately, is extremely common. I really must be doing something wrong in writing about these results because the reality is that nobody believes me. Maybe it's something about my writing style... I should switch careers and start writing fiction. :-)

Processing events in time-stamp order is clearly physically possible. It has been done since the 1970s in distributed discrete-event simulation. Nothing about relativity makes this impossible.

Reinhard: I remember a dissertation at INRIA proving that relativistic effects prevented one from having a global time, but can't find the reference. Doesn't a global time-stamping system need a global time? You need all components of the distributed system.

Edward: The *physical* idea of global time is a Newtonian fiction, yes. But this doesn't mean you can't have a *semantic* notion of global time. Time stamps are numbers in a number system that is totally ordered. Hence, the mathematics of a total order gives us a global temporal semantics.

I think what bothers you is perhaps related to how time stamps are assigned. In PTIDES, when a sensor takes a measurement, we use the local clock to assign a time stamp to that measurement. That measurement can then be sent out on a network (together with its time stamp). When another processor receives the message, it's job is to merge that message into its own local notion of time. It needs to respect the remotely assigned time stamp and process all messages, wherever they originated, in time-stamp order.

One way to achieve this is an old technique called the Chandy and Misra approach. This approach assumes that messages are sent in streams with reliable delivery that preserves order. That is, the order in which messages are received is the same as the order in which they are sent. This is achievable with TCP/IP. In the Chandy and Misra approach, a processor waits until it has received a message from every remote source of messages. It can then safely process the one with the lowest time stamp, preserving the global semantics of time. No problems with relativity.

The Chandy and Misra approach, however, has two key drawbacks. First, if a source of messages fails, everything stops. Second, every source of messages needs to keep sending messages even if it has nothing to say. Chandy and Misra called these "null messages".

PTIDES solves these two problems by assuming synchronized clocks and bounded communication latencies. Under these two assumptions, if a processor has NOT received a message by a certain time (per the local clock), the processor can locally calculate a lower bound on the time stamp of all future messages. That's all it needs to proceed with processing time-stamped events. I.e., because clocks are synchronized, the LACK of a message conveys information.

An interesting thing about this model is that when you simulate a system, you need multiple time lines that progress at different rates. We call this "multiform time". Ptolemy II supports multiform time and can simulate PTIDES models with arbitrarily good or bad clock synchronization. You can even simulate relativistic effects using this mechanism... The resulting models can be very confusing because we don't have natural language constructs that talk about multiple time lines simultaneously.

Reinhard: Now, having a semantic notion of global time means that all events in the system happen at some point in this time. In order to work with this semantic notion of global time one needs an implementation, and this implementation is the time-stamping mechanism. This implementation mechanism should be truthful to the semantics. That's where my troubles are! Synchronization does not deliver a truthful implementation of semantical global time. It is not perfect. If event A happens very briefly before event B then synchronization may produce both sequences AB and BA after time stamping, right? This may induce non-determinism in the interaction with the environment, I think.

I know how Lamport's vector time merges the state of local clocks upon communication. I don't actually see how this merging happens in Ptides.

Edward: If you have two sensors making measurements, and sensor A reports a reading of 9.1 while sensor B reports a reading of 8.9, but in actuality in the physical world, the phenomenon being read by B is larger than that being read by A, then does this mean that your program that operates on these sensor readings is nondeterministic?

If so, then you are right. PTIDES is nondeterministic. So is EVERY possible reaction to any physical phenomenon. The mere fact of having inputs from the physical world makes the system nondeterministic. E.g., if a synchronous program takes inputs from the outside world, it too is nondeterministic, because an event that it reacts to could be seen in tick n or in tick n+1. There is no physics that can prevent this ambiguity.

Determinism is a sufficiently contentious concept that you could defensively take this position. But I believe that a more useful notion of determinism separates inputs from reactions. In my definition, if there is exactly one reaction allowed to a given set of inputs (in a given state), then the system is deterministic.

In your definition, a system is deterministic only if there is exactly one react to a PHYSICAL REALITY (vs. inputs).

This latter definition is unfortunate. Physical reality cannot be measured perfectly and isn't even well understood. This latter definition simply eliminates determinism as a tool for engineers.

I don't feel that we are converging. The conversation has convinced me more than ever that both PRET and PTIDES are paradigm shifts, in the sense of Kuhn. Kuhn cites Max Planck in saying that paradigm shifts don't get accepted through convincing people. They get accepted when a new generation starts using them. I am convinced that will happen. But probably not by you or me.

Reinhard: You (and Jan) have convinced me more than you seem to feel. Still, it is hard to fully switch to your view of the world.

Thanks for your patience!

3   Models and Abstraction

After reading a new draft of Edward's planned submission *What is Real Time Computing?* I commented this draft. Issues were what a model is, because this notion played a major role in the draft, how abstraction relates to determinism, and what it means that a model is faithful to a system.

Reinhard: A few philosophical remarks and some minor quibblings:

Your introduction of *model* by way of many examples in the first paragraph of Sect. D suffers from the 7 examples admitting at least 8 different notions of what a model is. I complain about this because the notion of *model* is central in this paper, and your notion is very fuzzy. Sometimes, e.g. in the case of physics, *model* means abstraction. You have the world and you are looking for the laws. Sometimes, e.g. in the case of digital circuits, you look for implementations. And two other examples, ISAs and program, match neither of these two notions.

Patrick Cousot has developed a beautiful theory of abstraction [3]. He has an abstraction operator and a concretization operator, and in some cases both are related by a Galois connection. A local correctness condition describes what you probably mean as being faithful. You essentially have a commuting diagram. This way he can prove the correctness of an abstraction. In this theory, one may abstract a program to the set of its traces, you may say executions. Unfortunately for your argumentation, his abstractions often *introduce* non-determinism in order to go from undecidable or complex systems to decidable or efficiently decidable abstractions. What should concern you is that the analyzability of models—which you require—is obtained this way.

Your is–faithful–to relation sometimes goes one way, sometimes the other. I wonder whether it really is symmetric. Also sometimes it smells like a bisimulation. But overall it remains fuzzy. For instance, when you require that a computer program should be faithful to the behavior of a modern silicon microprocessor chip, the reader has to invest a lot of time in defining *behavior* to accept this statement. The relation between a program and the behavior of a modern silicon microprocessor chip too complex to be easily subsumed under Faithfulness. Think of compiled and interpreting implementations, of in-order and out-of-order pipelines.

As for timing (second page of Sect. D):

You completely conceal the existence of timing *requirements* and where they come from. Even traditional approaches start with timing requirements. Admittedly, timing verification is based on timing properties for a particular implementation. However, assuming that several PRET architectures are possible, wouldn't you in the end have to verify that the selected one fulfills the assumptions made for the real-time software?

In Sect. C, first page: Is it really physically impossible for these actions to be simultaneous, or is it impossible to decide whether they are simultaneous?

Further down you say, "Note that this requirement is independent of timing precision".

Whose timing precision do you refer to? Do the events A and B and the observer necessarily have the same timing precision?

I find the definition of sporadic stream rather loose.

Hope my comments help!

Edward: Thanks very much! These are very helpful comments.

Cousot's notion of abstraction is actually a relation between *models*.

Reinhard: Yes, in your sense.

Edward: What I'm talking about is more the relationship between a model and Kant's das Ding an sich. I don't think Cousot's view can really say anything at all about that relationship...

Reinhard: That raises an interesting point. The Ding an sich is an intellectual construct. The philosophical question is whether you can think about it without words or terms. As soon as you have the necessary terms and if they have a semantics then you could use Cousot's abstraction. However, you would claim that one has constructed a model using these terms.

So, I should probably declare defeat.

Edward: I will work on trying to refine the ideas, and I will acknowledge you (thanks!).

3.1   Conclusions (Part 2)

The comments above will leave the reader puzzled because he lacks the context if he is not familiar with this paper. However, the final version of Edward's paper shows at least some impact of my comments, not as much as I had hoped, though.

As I said in one of my contributions, the European embedded-systems community, led by the synchronous-languages colleagues, has arrived at globally asynchronous, locally synchronous systems as the most promising metaphor. It is supposed to combine the success of synchronous languages for non-distributed systems with the asynchronous behavior of distributed systems. It would be interesting to see how this metaphor fares in comparison with Edward's globally timed, deterministic systems concept.

What would be my overall conclusion? It definitely was an interesting discussion. Edward can argue very convincingly. He definitely caught me on the wrong foot several times.

Acknowledgements. My thanks go to Jan Reineke, who explained many details about Edward's approach to me, Marjan Sirjani for asking the right questions and giving good comments, to the reviewers for the comments and suggestions, and last but not least to Edward for patiently discussing so many issues in our email exchange.

References

1. Axer, P., Ernst, R., Falk, H., Girault, A., Grund, D., Guan, N., Jonsson, B., Marwedel, P., Reineke, J., Rochange, C., Sebastian, M., von Hanxleden, R., Wilhelm, R., Yi, W.: Building timing predictable embedded systems. ACM Trans. Embed. Comput. Syst. **13**(4), 82:1–82:37 (2014)
2. Bui, D., Lee, E.A., Liu, I., Patel, H., Reineke, J.: Temporal isolation on multiprocessing architectures. In: Design Automation Conference (DAC), pp. 274–279, June 2011. http://chess.eecs.berkeley.edu/pubs/839.html
3. Cousot, P., Cousot, R.: Abstract interpretation: a unified lattice model for static analysis of programs by construction or approximation of fixpoints. In: Graham, R.M., Harrison, M.A., Sethi, R. (eds.) Conference Record of the Fourth ACM Symposium on Principles of Programming Languages, Los Angeles, California, USA, January 1977, pp. 238–252. ACM (1977). https://doi.org/10.1145/512950.512973
4. Derler, P., Lee, E.A., Matic, S.: Simulation and implementation of the PTIDES programming model. In: Roberts, D.J., El-Saddik, A., Ferscha, A. (eds.) 12th IEEE/ACM International Symposium on Distributed Simulation and Real-Time Applications, Proceedings, 27–29 October 2008, Vancouver, BC, Canada, pp. 330–333. IEEE Computer Society (2008)
5. Ferdinand, C., Heckmann, R., Langenbach, M., Martin, F., Schmidt, M., Theiling, H., Thesing, S., Wilhelm, R.: Reliable and precise WCET determination for a real-life processor. In: Henzinger, T.A., Kirsch, C.M. (eds.) EMSOFT 2001. LNCS, vol. 2211, pp. 469–485. Springer, Heidelberg (2001). https://doi.org/10.1007/3-540-45449-7_32
6. Gao, B.: A globally asynchronous locally synchronous configurable array architecture for algorithm embeddings. Ph.D. thesis, University of Edinburgh, UK (1996)
7. Lee, E.A.: The past, present and future of cyber-physical systems: a focus on models. Sensors **15**(3), 4837–4869 (2015)
8. Lee, E.A.: What is real-time computing? A personal view. IEEE Des. Test **35**, 64–72 (2018)
9. Lee, E.A., Reineke, J., Zimmer, M.: Abstract PRET machines. In: RTSS, December 2017

10. Markovic, F., Carlson, J., Dobrin, R.: Tightening the bounds on cache-related preemption delay in fixed preemption point scheduling. In: Reineke, J. (ed.) 17th International Workshop on Worst-Case Execution Time Analysis, WCET 2017, 27 June 2017, Dubrovnik, Croatia. OASICS, vol. 57, pp. 4:1–4:11, Schloss Dagstuhl - Leibniz-Zentrum fuer Informatik, Wadern (2017)
11. Wilhelm, R.: The PROMPT design principles for predictable multi-core architectures. In: Proceedings of the 12th International Workshop on Software and Compilers for Embedded Systems, pp. 31–32. ACM (2009)
12. Zimmer, M., Broman, D., Shaver, C., Lee, E.A.: FlexPRET: a processor platform for mixed-criticality systems. In: 20th IEEE Real-Time and Embedded Technology and Applications Symposium, RTAS 2014, Berlin, Germany, 15–17 April 2014, pp. 101–110. IEEE Computer Society (2014)

Author Index